FOLK ART

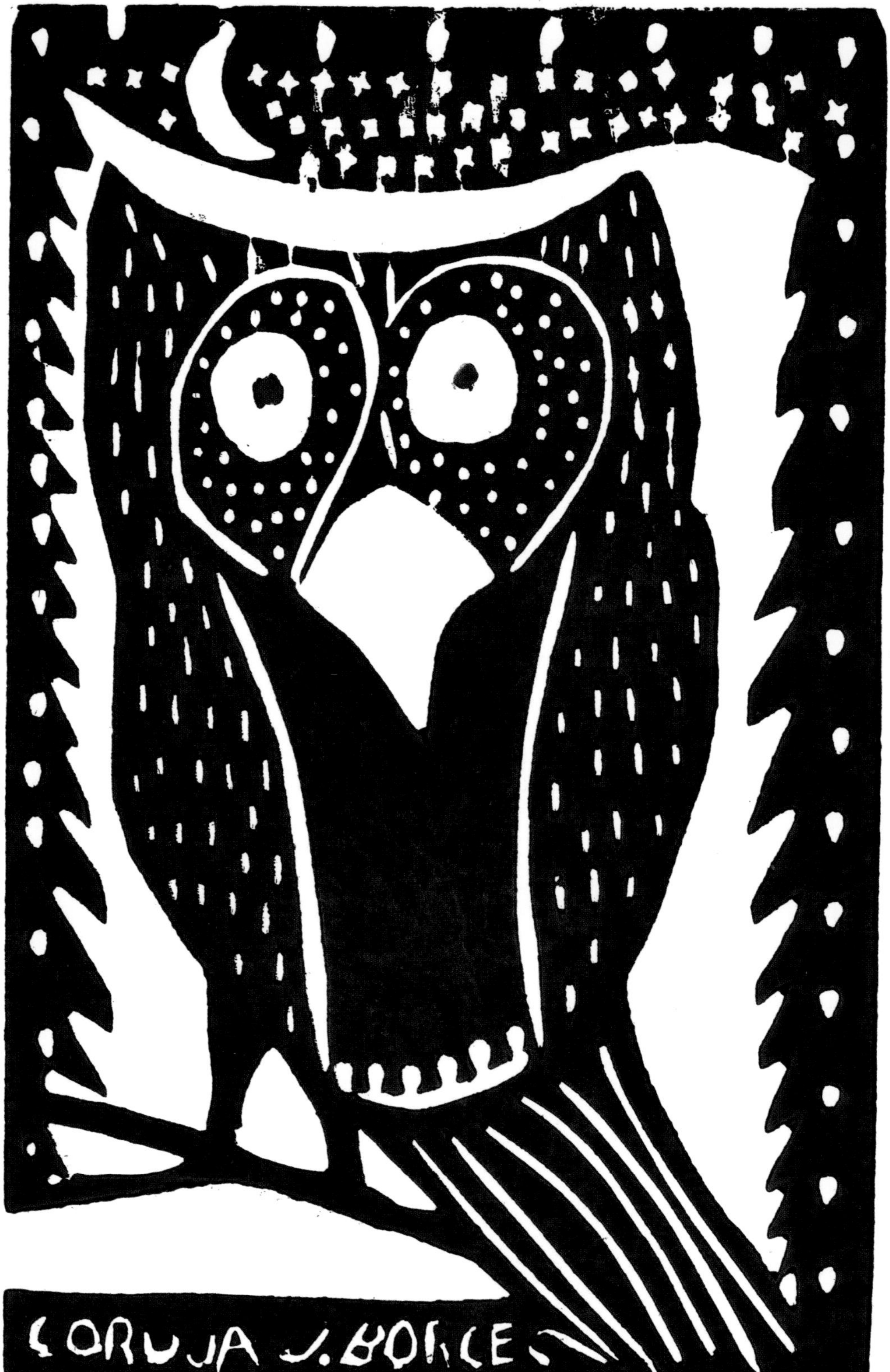
CORUJA J. BORGES

FOLK ART

Continuity, Creativity, and the Brazilian Quotidian

HENRY GLASSIE *and* **PRAVINA SHUKLA**

Photographs by the Authors

INDIANA UNIVERSITY PRESS

This book is a publication of

Indiana University Press
Office of Scholarly Publishing
Herman B Wells Library 350
1320 East 10th Street
Bloomington, Indiana 47405 USA

iupress.indiana.edu

This book is printed on acid-free paper.

Manufactured in China

First printing 2023

Cataloging information is available from the Library of Congress.

ISBN 978-0-253-06721-0 (cloth)
ISBN 978-0-253-06722-7 (e-book)

Frontispiece: Owl, woodblock print by J. Borges, Bezerros, Pernambuco, Brazil, 2015

CONTENTS

For the artists
of the Brazilian Northeast

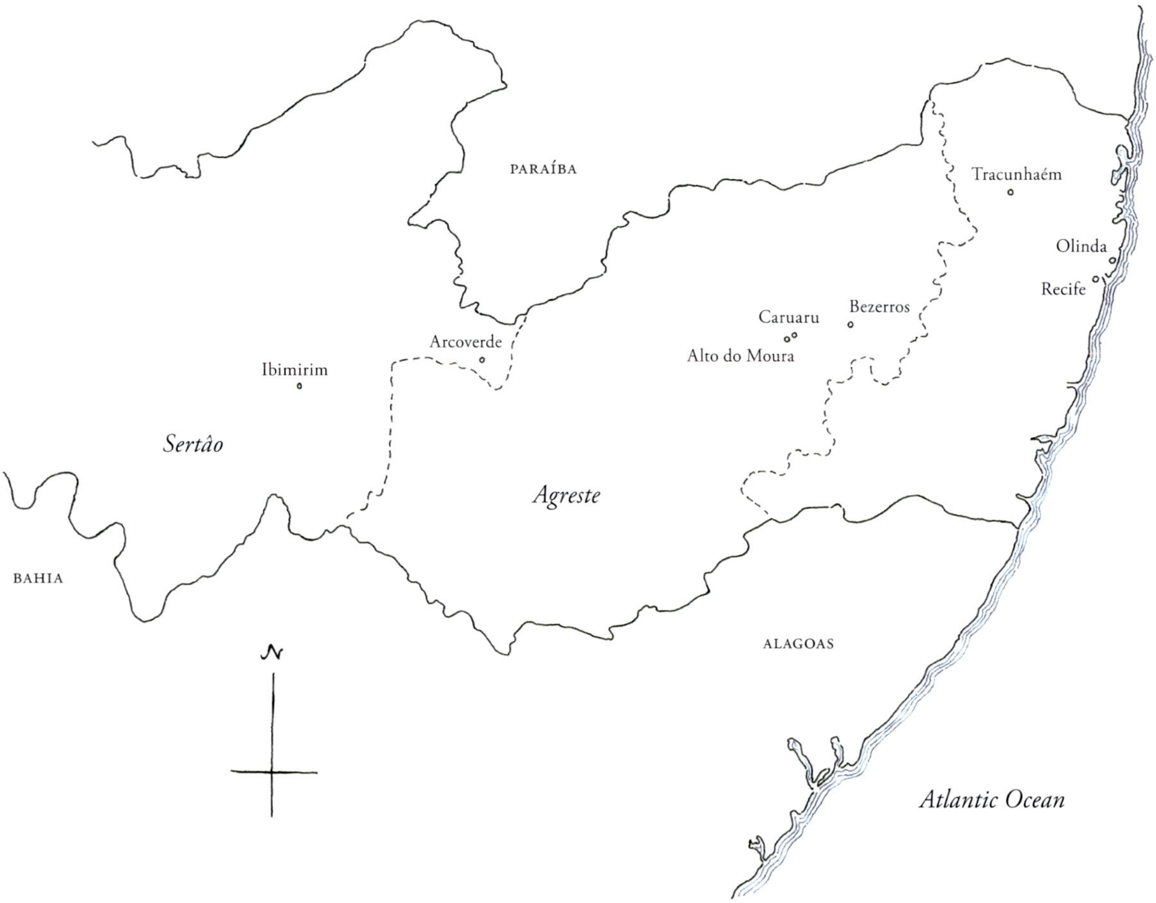

Eastern Pernambuco,
this book's central territory

Introduction

The Agreste of Pernambuco

The Agreste of Pernambuco

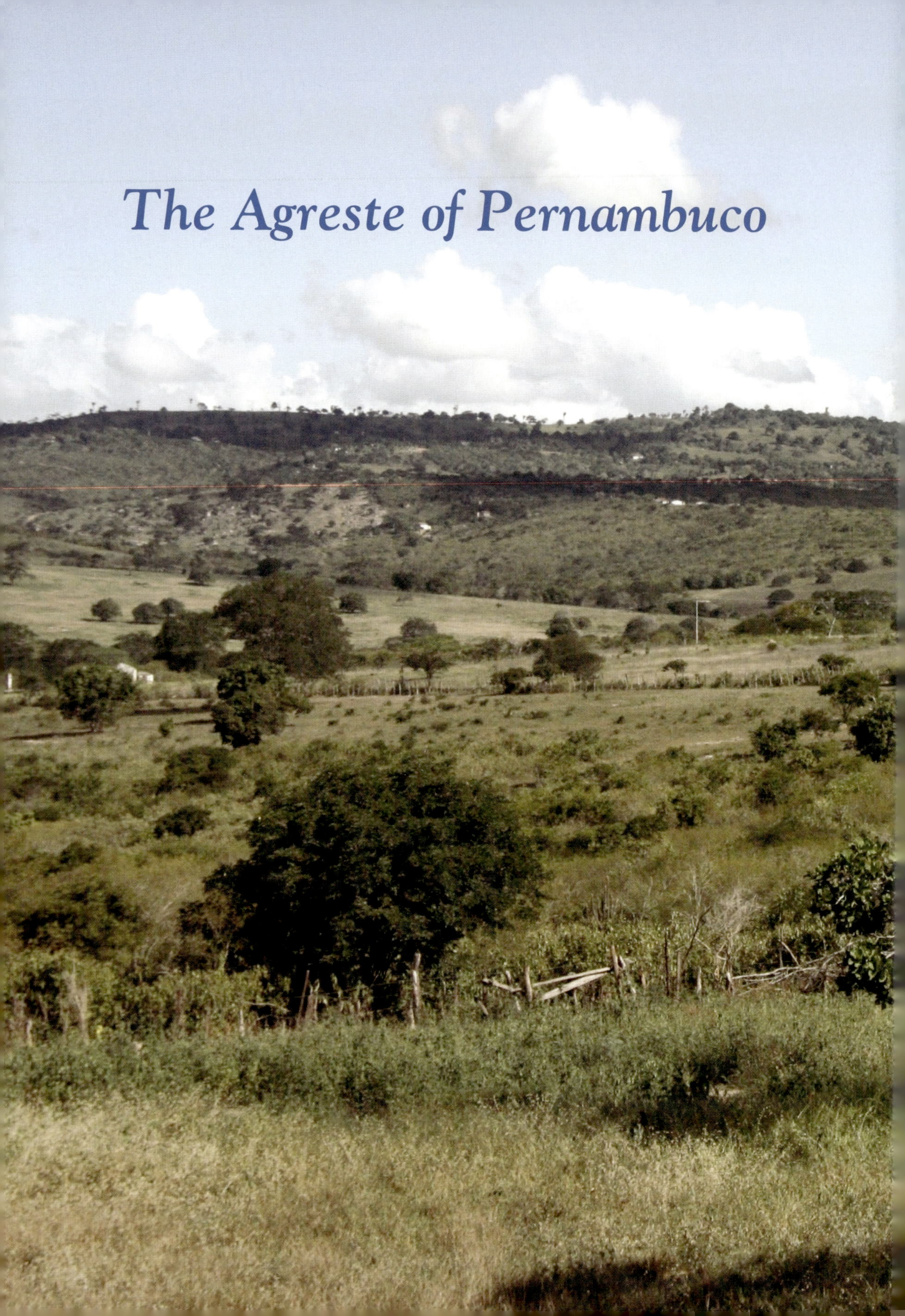

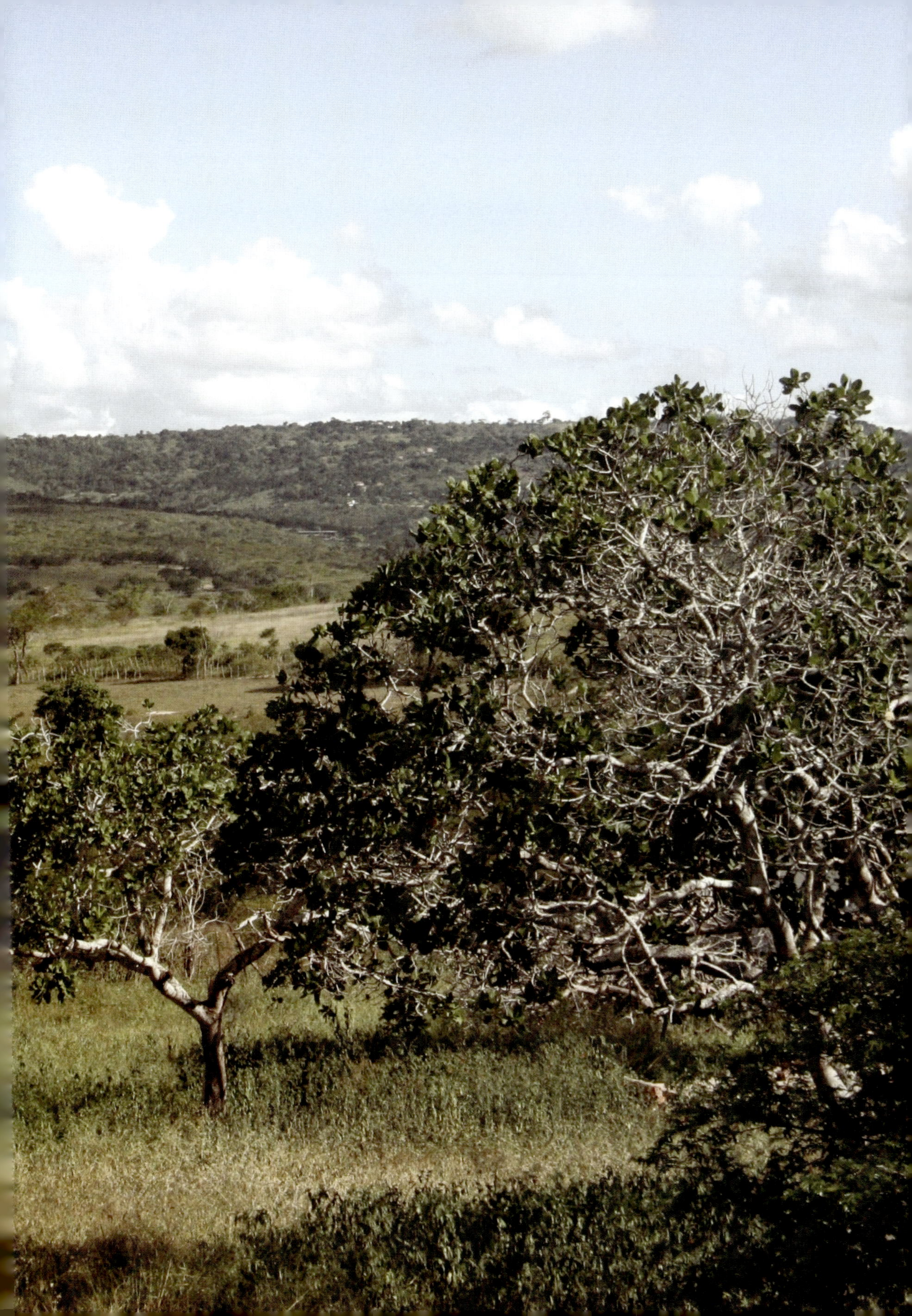

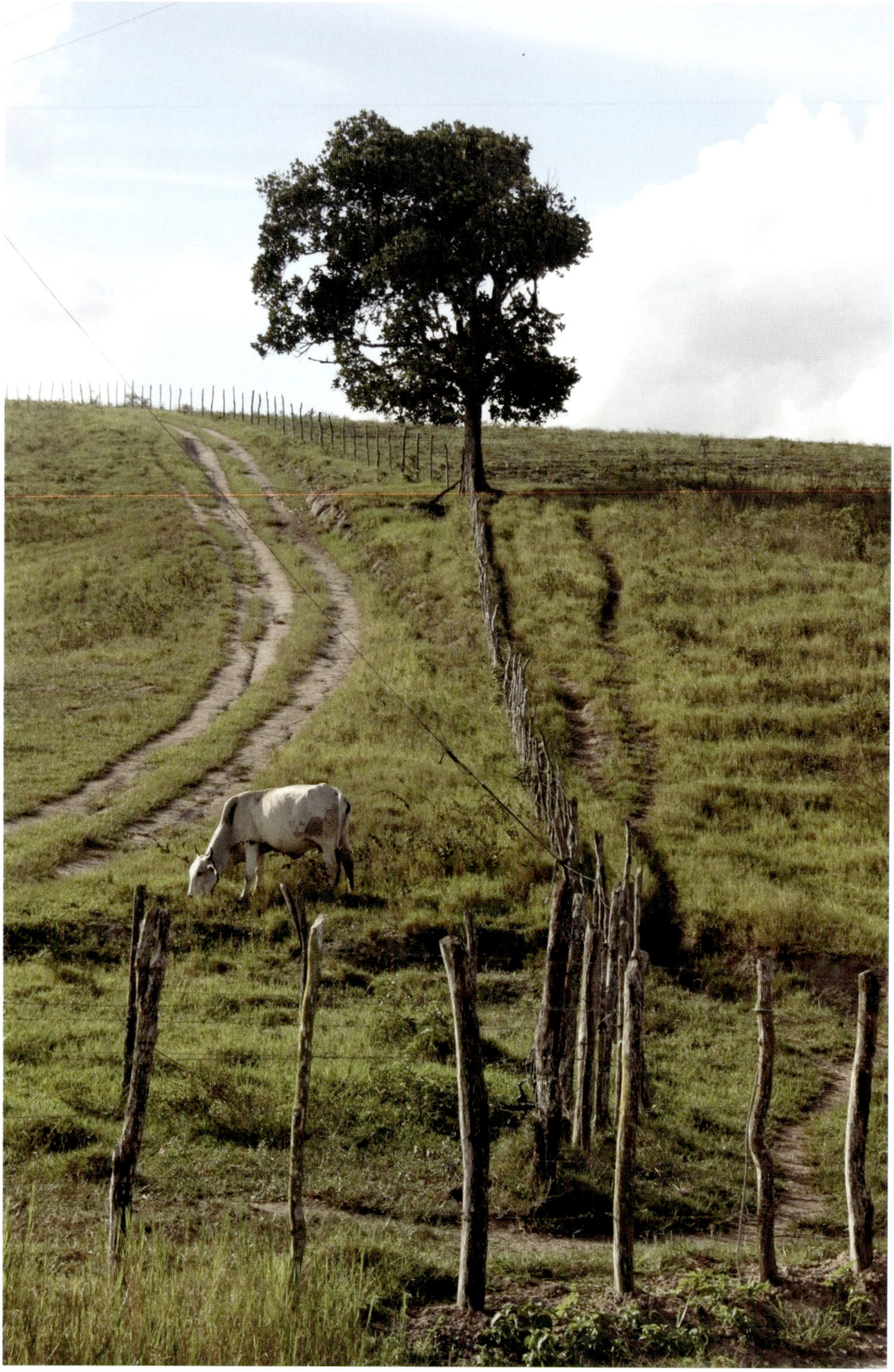

Agreste, 2019

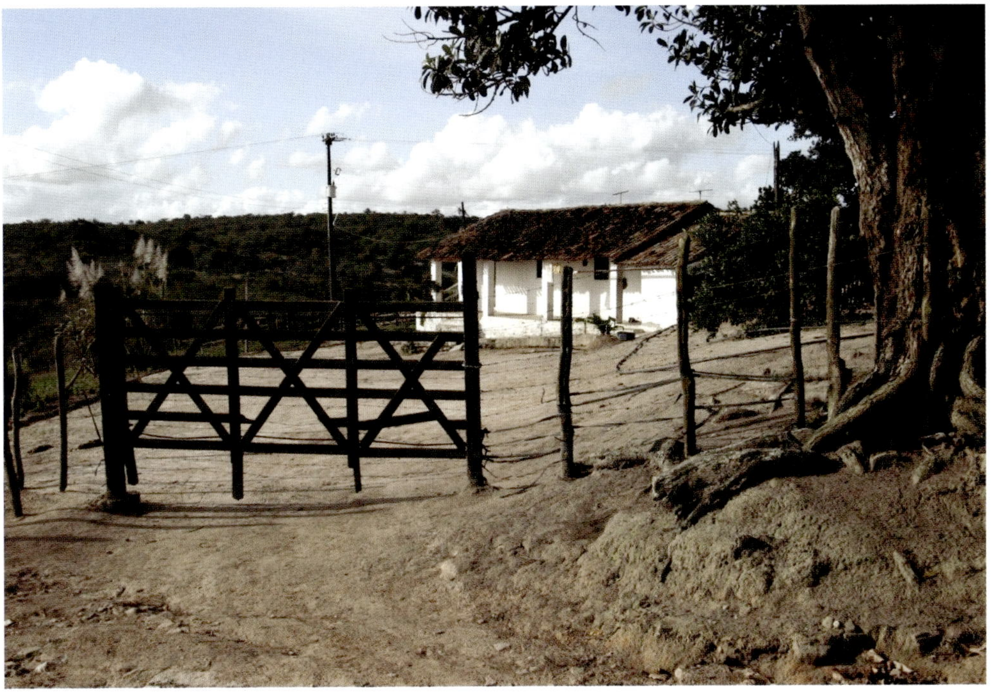

Farmstead in the Agreste, 2019

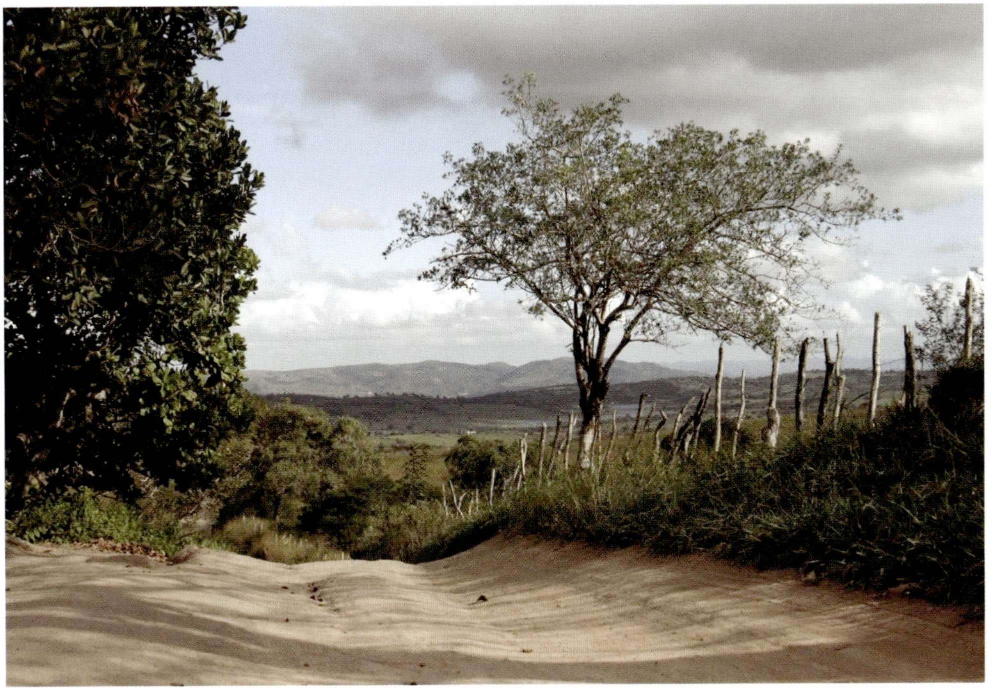

Road through the Agreste, 2019

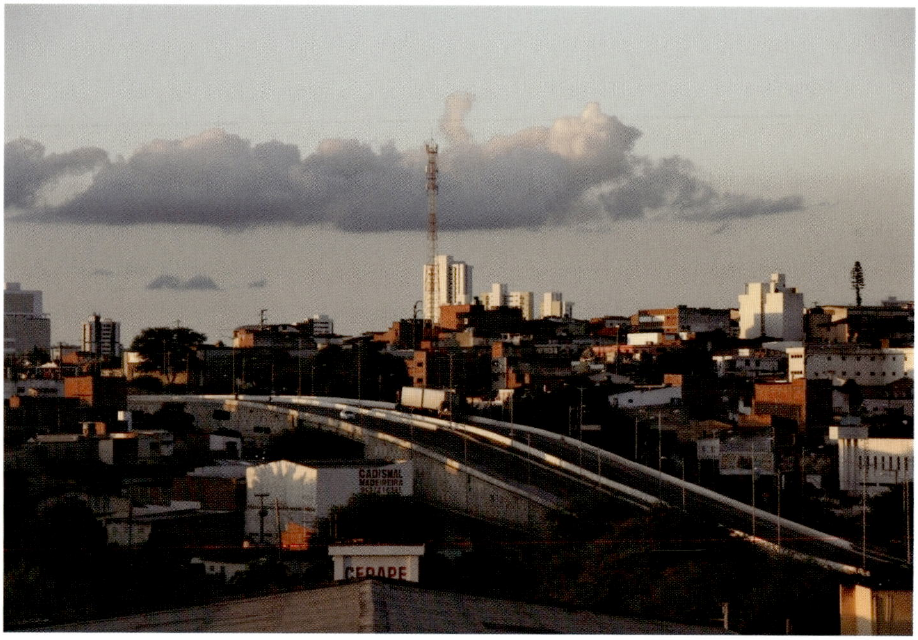

Caruaru, 2019

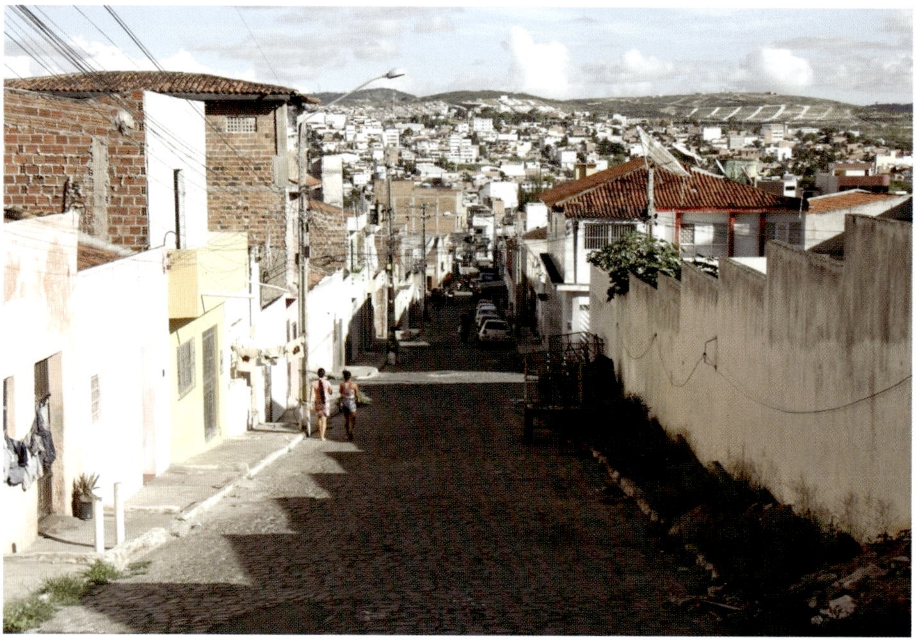

Caruaru, 2019

I

Caruaru

This book is about the reach from need to excellence, a variety of creative action universal among humankind. Let us, to begin, call it folk art and settle into a place where it thrives. In the hilly interior of the Brazilian Northeast, in the vicinity of Caruaru, there are so many dedicated artists busily at work that we are not obliged to make much out of little, relying on speculative interpretations of antique artifacts or contriving abstract arguments out of weary theories. We can proceed empirically, talking with people, watching them work, and letting them lead. Our aim is not to study them, but to stand with them in mutual appreciation of their creations.

First, we will introduce the artists and listen to them. Then after patterns have shaped toward principles, we will be able to make comparisons with the results of fieldwork in many other locations, concluding that, despite all the historical differences, what might be called folk art is a central revelation of our common humanity.

That is the goal, but in the meantime we digress, trusting that a sketch of this book's origin will prove useful. We are a married couple, professional folklorists, trained in anthropology and committed to the foundational importance of ethnographic work in the field. With individual projects behind us in the United States, in Ireland, England, Sweden, Turkey, India, Bangladesh, Japan, and Nigeria, we went together to Brazil in 2007. We met Edival and Izaura Rosas in Salvador da Bahia. We met Severino Vitalino and Manuel Eudócio in Alto do Moura. Attracted by the unworried warmth of the people and the quality of their art, having experienced the pleasure and efficiency of collaborative work in the field, we returned in 2009, and then with a major project in mind, we returned for longer stretches in 2014 and 2015.

There are petty annoyances, sure, and serious troubles with health, but this is how time passes in the field. Every night we write a narrative of the day's doings. Every morning we plan the day's adventure, a plan quickly and happily abandoned to circumstance. The tasks divide. Henry looks, noticing details, drawing maps, taking the photographs. Pravina listens. Raised in Brazil, her first language was Portuguese, and she speaks it like a native of São Paulo. She conducts the interviews, transcribes them in Portuguese, then translates them literally into English, her third language. At the end we have an abundance of oral texts — not squashed into black blocks, nor falsified as conventional prose, but rendered to capture the cadences of speech — texts that honorably represent their speakers while providing the evidence that will accumulate toward sharable understandings.

We had a single book in mind, and to make the project manageable we limited ourselves to the large Northeastern states of Bahia and Pernambuco, but once we had reviewed the masses of pictures and transcripts, once we had gotten a grip on what we had done, we divided the data — just as Brazilian artists divide their repertories — into the sacred and the quotidian. Then with sacred art as the focus we returned in 2016, and when our book *Sacred Art: Catholic Saints and Candomblé Gods in Modern Brazil,* was published, we returned in 2018, with overweight suitcases crammed with books, to give copies to all the artists in it.

In 2019, we returned to concentrate on the quotidian, a lengthy, pleasant, and productive visit. Our plan was to go back in 2020 to get the last facts and photos. Then the pandemic hit. Inept despots in the United States and Brazil precipitated deadly disasters in both countries, and time trapped us in a dilemma. We wanted to wait until it was safe before returning to get the final details that would enable us to hold to our ethnographic standards. We wanted to rush the book into publication so we could get it into the hands of its people. Two of the artists to whom we gave copies of *Sacred Art* in 2018 have since passed. Iraquitan Gomes da Sá was delighted to see his portrait and photos of his works in the book, and he said he was now immortal; he would live forever in the book. He died within a year. His friend Sergio Perboni, who painted the portrait that appears on the back flap of the dust jacket, received his copy and was swept to death by Covid a year later.

A change in leadership brought quick relief in the United States. Conditions improved more slowly in Brazil. During the summer of 2021, we were resolved to rush into print without risking a last visit, but in the autumn the number of vaccinated people in Brazil began to rise past the number in the United States. The artists wrote us that everyone was well and life had become endurable, so we risked it, and dashed back, masked, in November of 2021, visiting with dear friends, meeting our scholarly goals, and completing the book you have in your hands. Through it, the year 2019 runs the line of the present tense, but later data from 2021, and earlier, reaching back to 2007, expand the story.

Fieldwork is, like all human endeavors, conditioned by uncontrollable forces. Time is one. With the luxury of an empty year, you can settle into a place and adjust to the local calendar's rhythms. If time throbs with obligations and swirls with problems, you can gather fragments in sequence and move to the beat of historical time. This project, of necessity, was spread over fifteen years, yielding understandings of change while holding to its spatial center in Caruaru.

Called the capital of the Agreste, Caruaru is the prime city of the Pernambucan interior. East of Caruaru, Pernambuco runs to the Atlantic coast near the point closest to Africa. On the coast, Pernambuco's capital, Recife, soars with slick white towers, just south of the lovely old city of Olinda. West of Caruaru, Pernambuco spreads through the Sertão, a wide, dry region of beautiful skies and long melancholy horizons.

The Agreste is the transitional zone between the damp coast and the dry Sertão. Within the Agreste, the town of Bezerros lies thirty-four kilometers east of Caruaru, and the small town of Alto do Moura stands immediately to the west. These are the artists' places, joined by representational repertory, divided by medium. In Bezerros, they make woodblock prints. In Alto do Moura, they shape clay into images. Both towns have an acknowledged progenitor of tradition — J. Borges in Bezerros, Mestre Vitalino in Alto do Moura — and in both locations familial lineages contain numerous productive creators, working to meet the desires of a wide, indeed nation-wide, popular market.

Here is the land. The Rio Ipojuca rises near Arcoverde in the Sertão then flows eastward on a meandering course across the floor of a wide valley. The river runs just south of Alto do Moura, passes through Caruaru and Bezerros, and then swings to find the ocean south of Recife. From Recife the main highway, BR 232, breaks through the coastal wall and carries traffic westward, skimming just south of Bezerros, Caruaru, and Alto do Moura on its way into the Sertão.

The river and road run through the middle, and on each side, away to the north and away to the south, low mountains form long horizons. From afar, the high horizons seem to be continuous, uninhabited ridges, but go up there and you will find a turbulent expanse of rounded hills, spattered with cactus and gnarled, stunted trees. Narrow dirt roads, fit to motion on motorcycles or horseback, twist and dip and lift, lacing together a place of steep slopes and separate steadings. Were you to travel those roads along the upland from Bezerros to Alto do Moura, you would wind through a pastoral landscape where small farmhouses stand far apart, shouldering alone into the hillsides, and white cattle graze across the high pastures.

This is the landscape that abides in the mind, a highland stretch of the Agreste that resembles the Sertão and forms the backdrop for the creators of art in Bezerros and Alto do Moura.

We will settle down first in Alto do Moura.

Part One

Alto do Moura

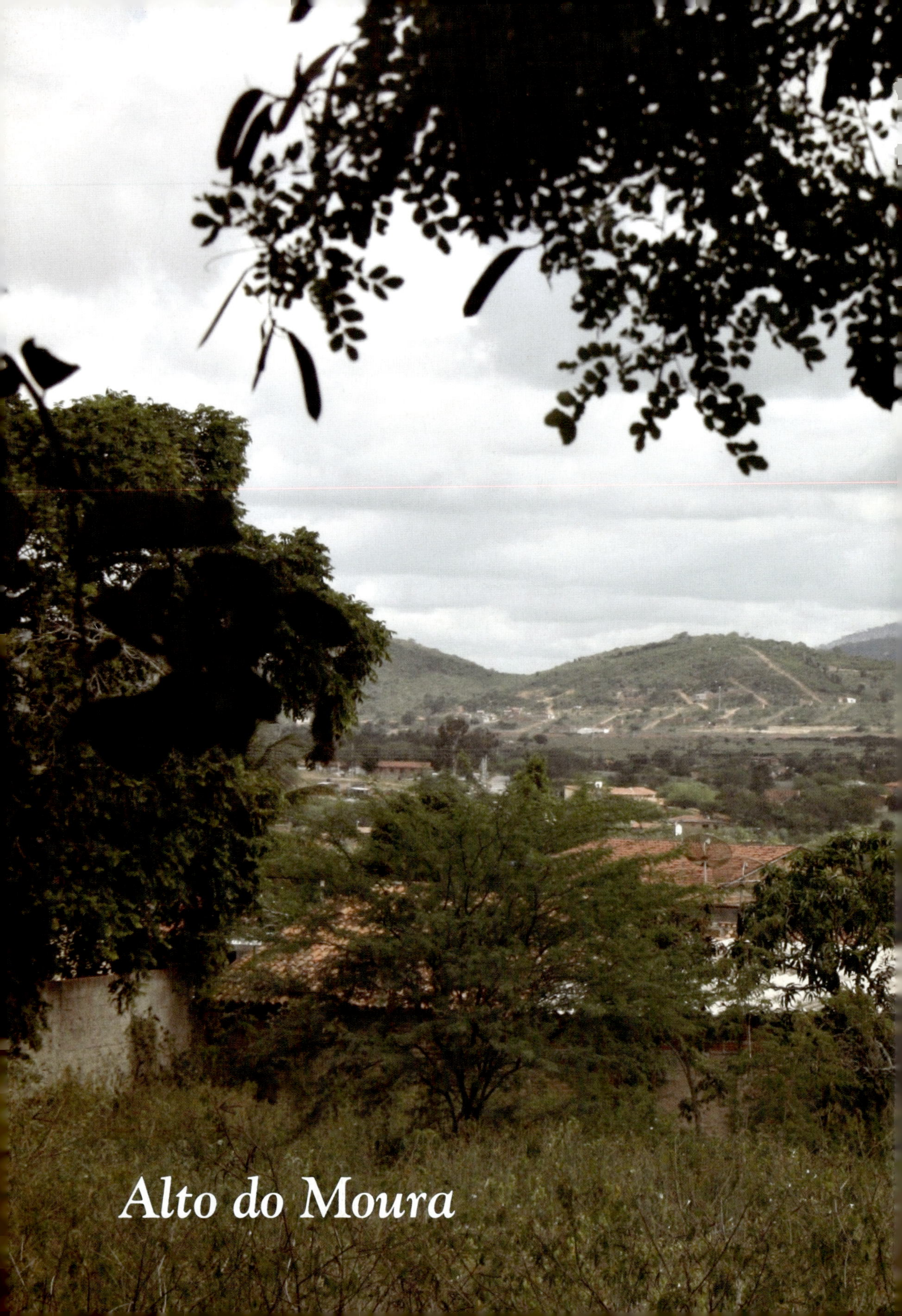

Alto do Moura

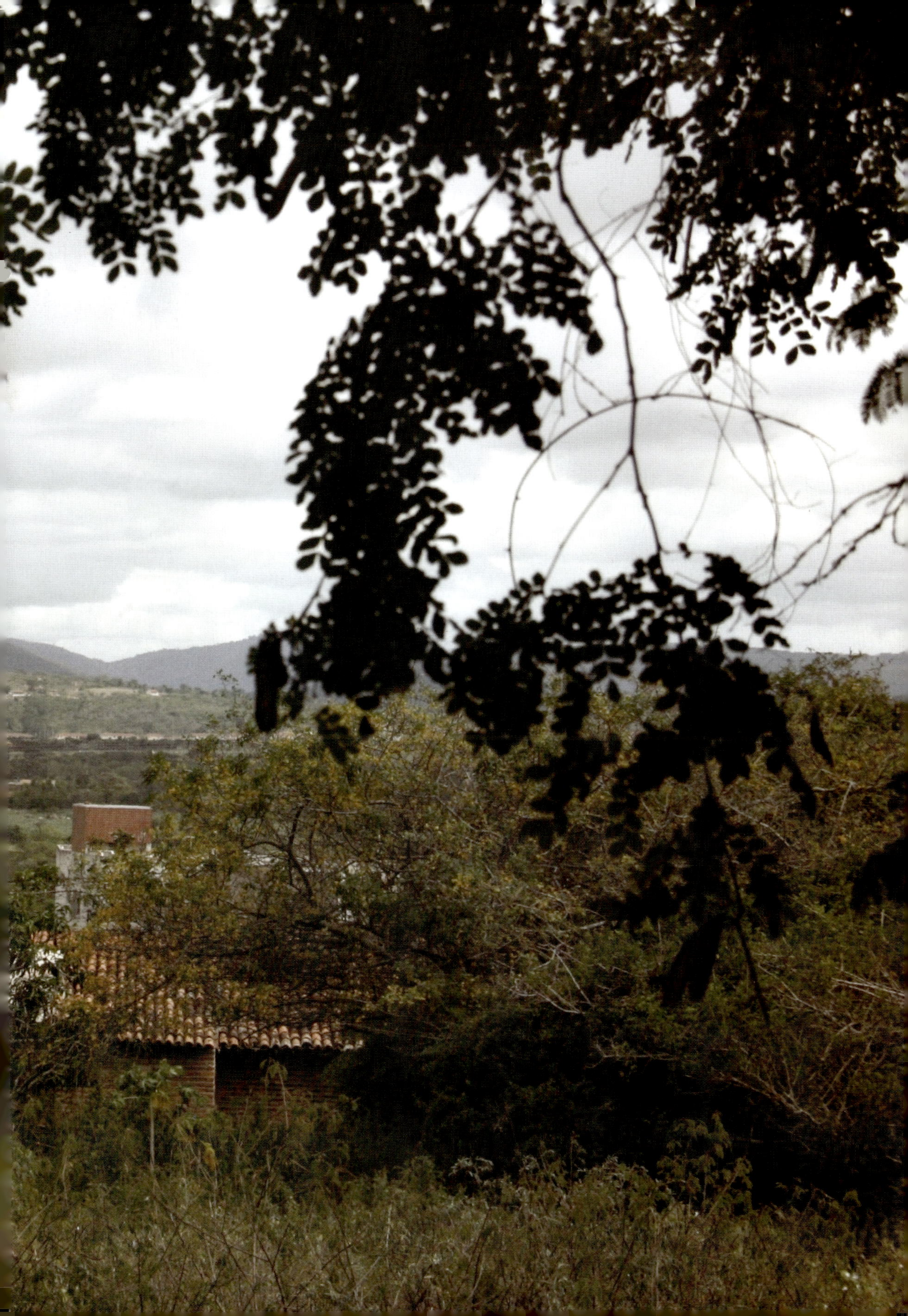

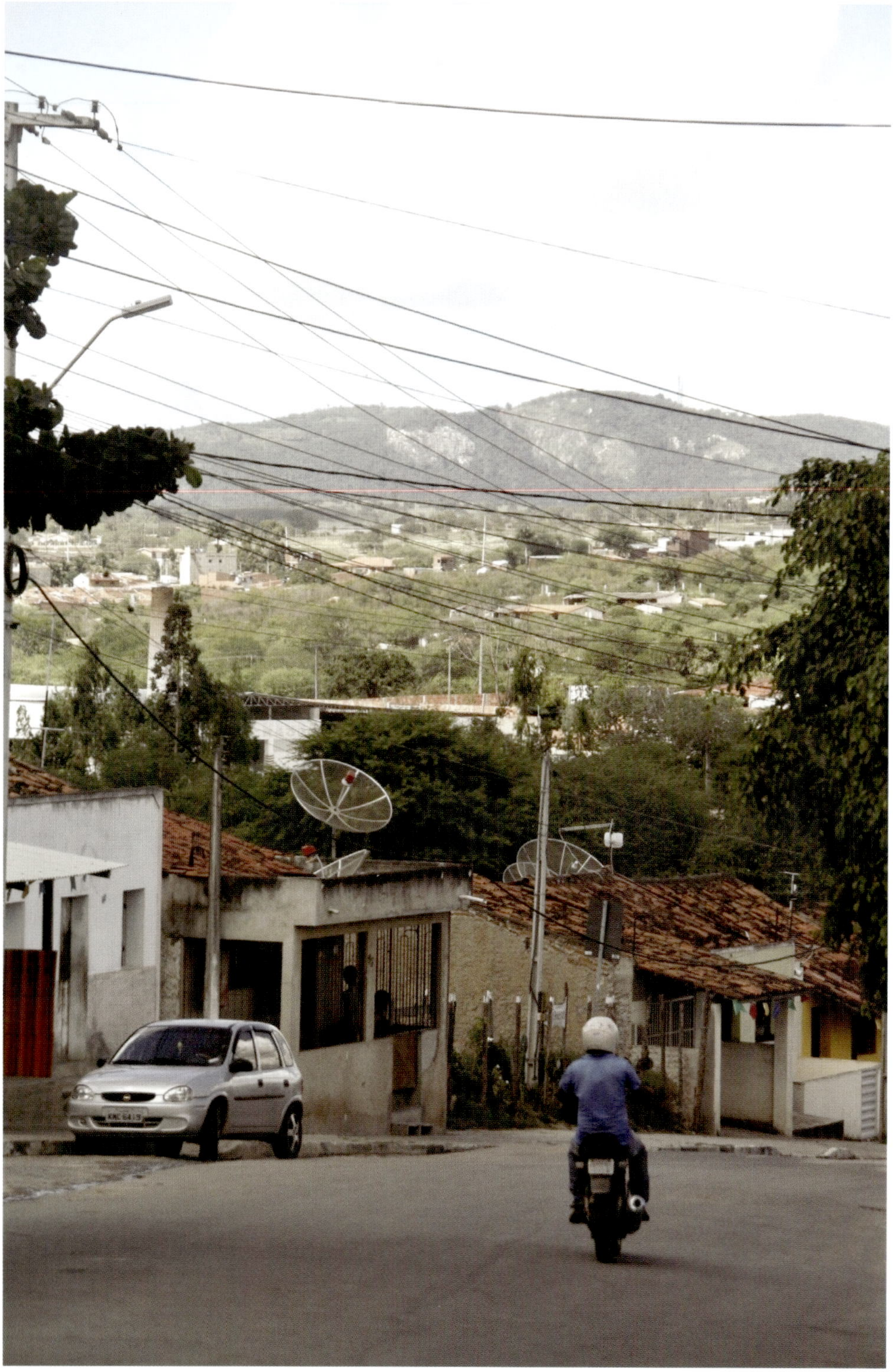

Alto do Moura: Rua Mestre Vitalino, the street of the artists, 2019

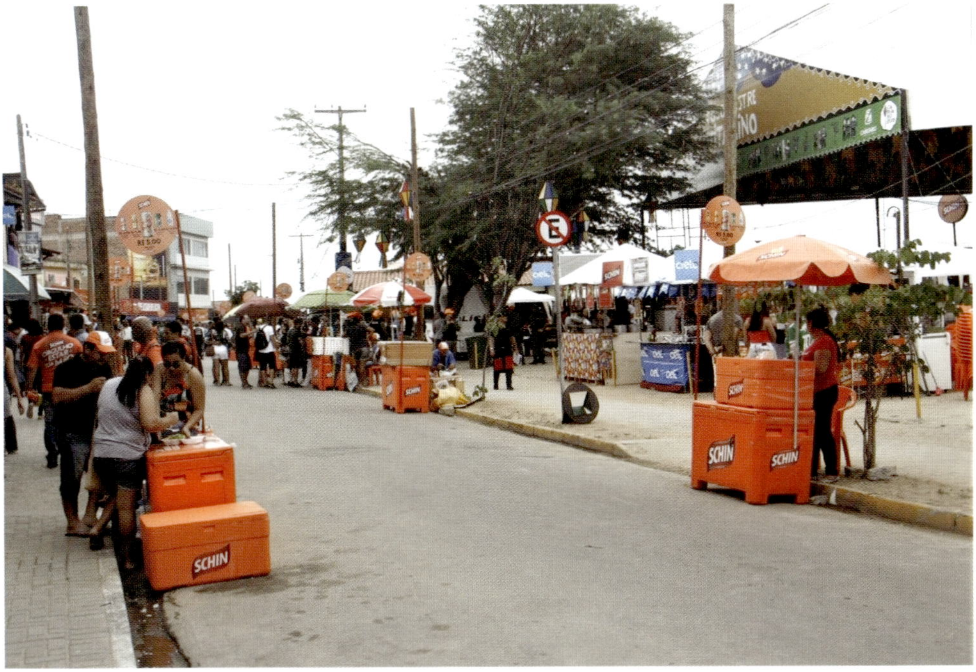

Alto do Moura: Rua Mestre Vitalino, the main street during the June Festival, 2019

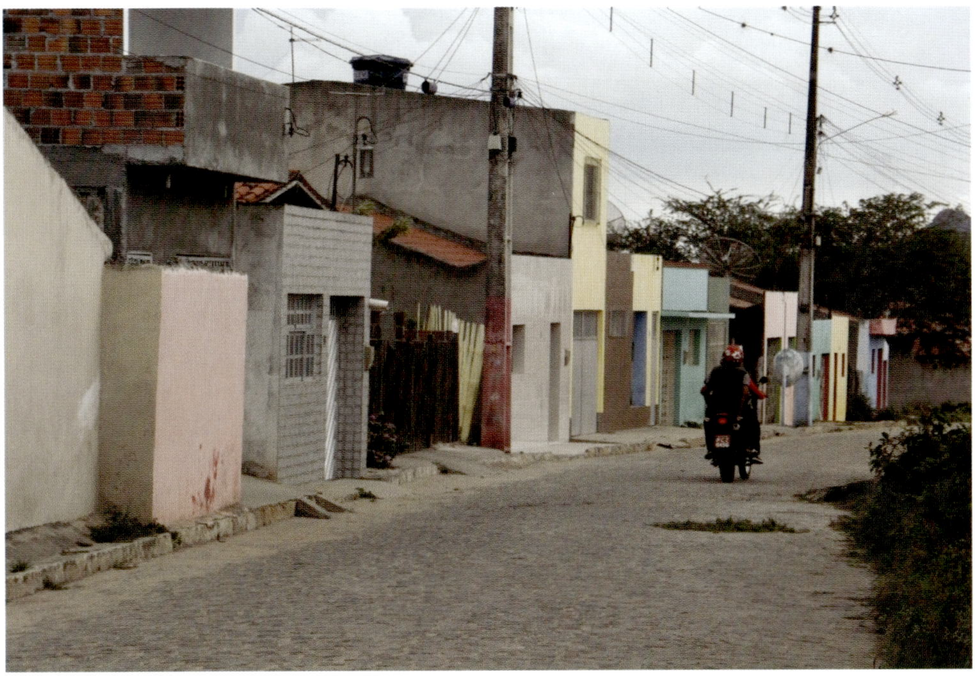

Alto do Moura: back street, 2015

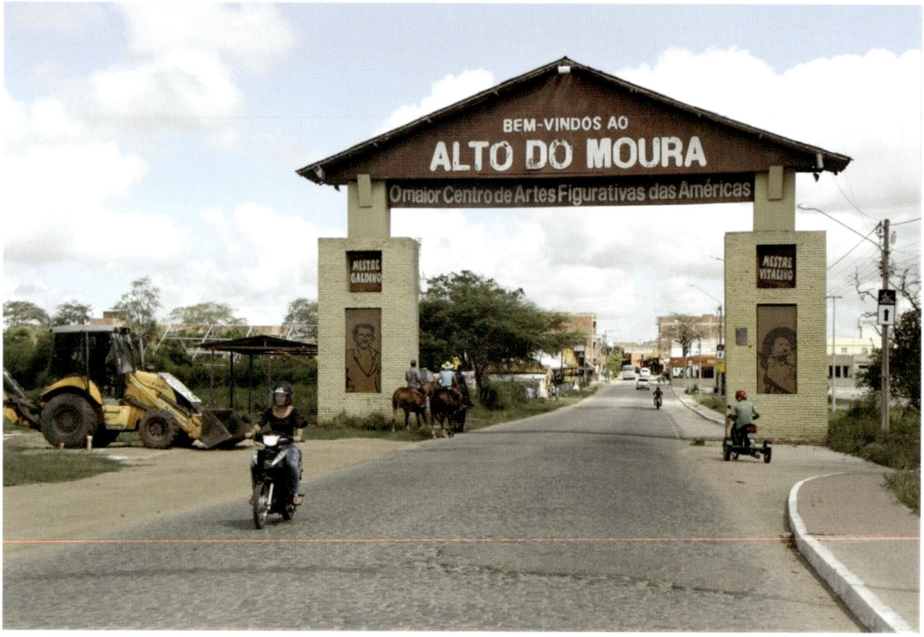

The road into Alto do Moura, 2019

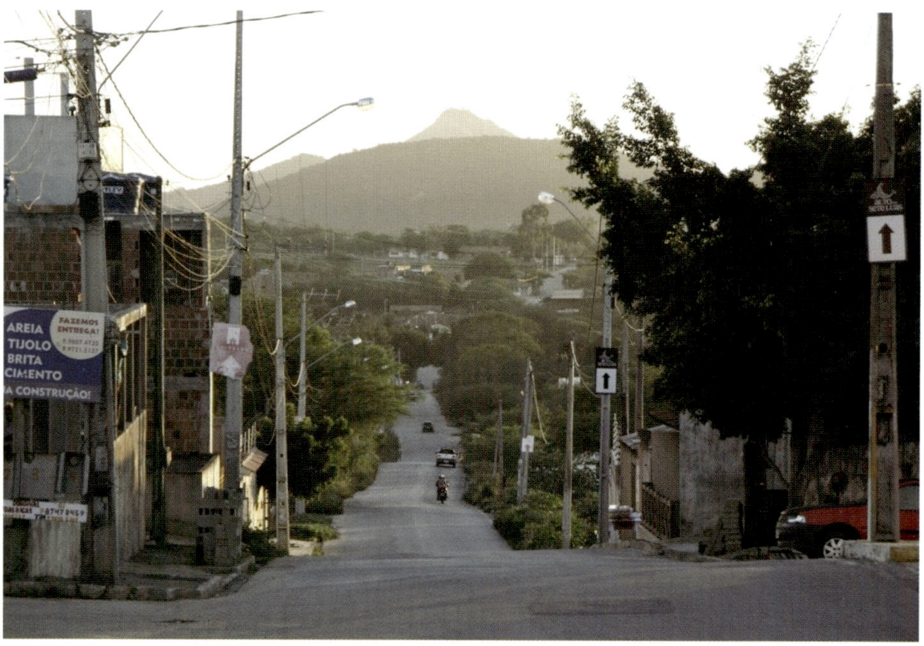

The road out of Alto do Moura, west to the Sertão, 2019

2

The Vitalino Family

The road into town runs to the west. Along it eighteen shops, most of them on the northern side of the street, offer handmade statues in clay, most of them bright in color, affordable in price, and portable in size. They wouldn't be here, neither the shops nor their stock, were it not for Mestre Vitalino. An illiterate, inventive country man, Vitalino once lived here, making the ceramic images of Northeastern rural life that brought him public honors and invitations to travel down to the big cities, Rio and São Paulo, far away to the south. The street is named for him, and it continues on its westerly course into the country toward the Sertão.

Before the street leaves, near the western edge of town, it crosses through an intersection. The street on the left, also named for him — the Rua Mestre Vitalino — slopes southward, passing in its gentle descent the places where the families of Vitalino's followers live, make, and sell. First on the right, the west, comes Luiz Antônio's family, and on the east the family of Zé Caboclo. Farther down, the family of Manuel Eudócio spans the street. Still farther down on the east Vitalino's family remains, first his son Severino, then Severino's son Elias, and, at the bottom, the street stops at the street named for Saint Sebastian, the town's patron saint.

Just there, where Vitalino meets Sebastião, a workshop has been converted into a museum dedicated to Mestre Galdino, the progenitor of a distinctly different tradition of ceramic sculpture. Then Sebastian's street heads west, along the line of the Rio Ipojuca, arriving at the point where the river's bank supplies the clay used by all the artists of Alto do Moura.

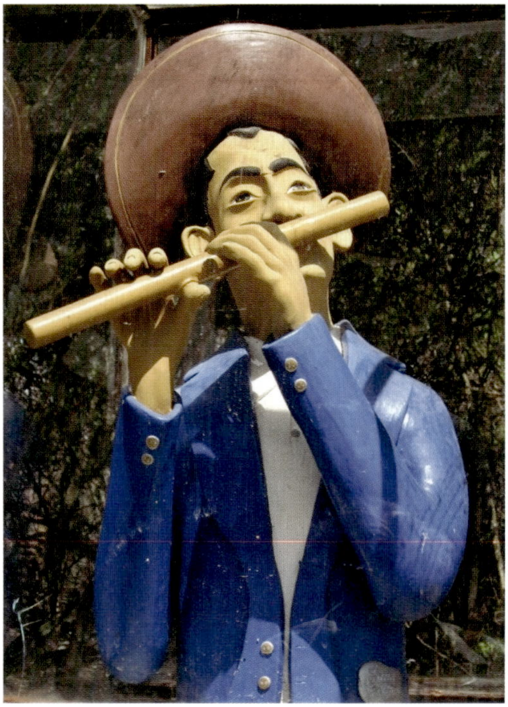

Vitalino with the *pífano* by Luiz Galdino

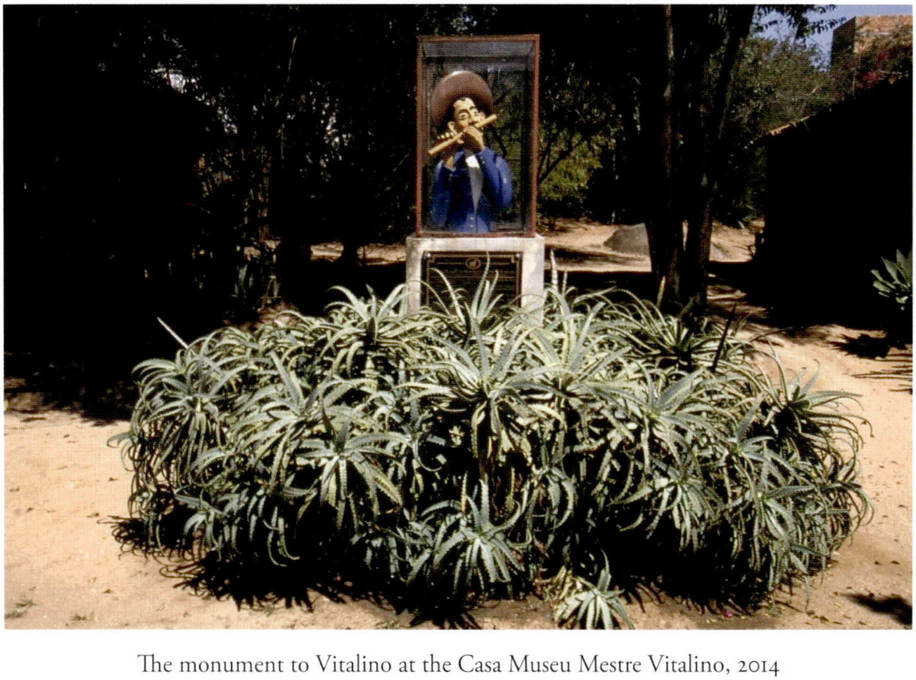

The monument to Vitalino at the Casa Museu Mestre Vitalino, 2014

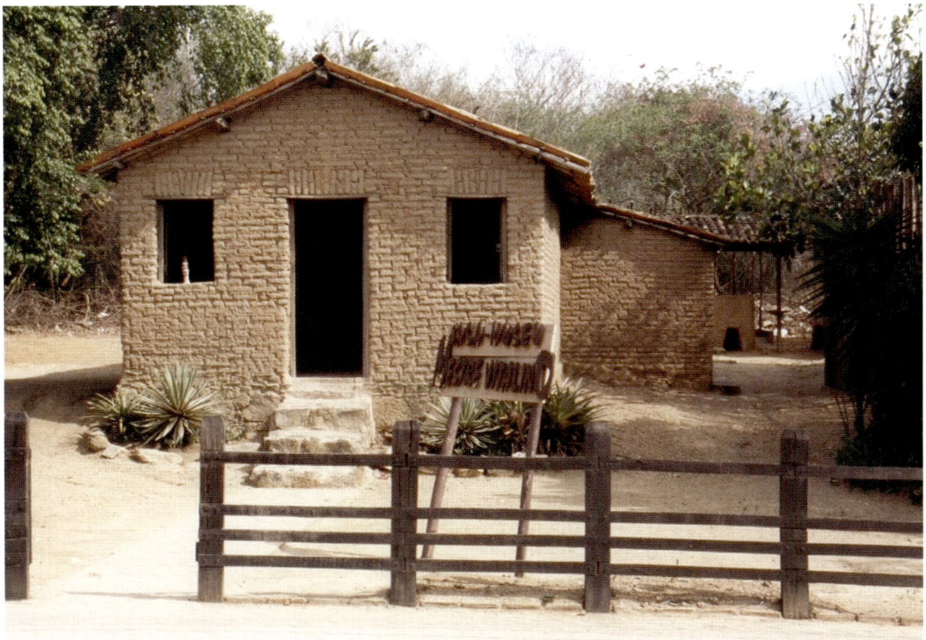

The Casa Museu Mestre Vitalino, Alto do Moura, 2007

Back uphill, on the southern side of the main street, a bit east of the corner of Vitalino and Vitalino, the master's house museum — the Casa Museu Mestre Vitalino — welcomes occasional Brazilian tourists and seasonal streams of school groups, happy on fieldtrips in orderly, noisy lines.

The house is a modest instance of the usual houses of its region: one story, a door in the gable end, walls of handmade brick, a tiled roof supported on purlins. In the dusty yard to the left, a trim cement slab lifts and bends to support a glass case enclosing a painted clay portrait in the local style, showing Mestre Vitalino playing the *pífano*, a rural instrument from the flute and fife family. The portrait was made in the nineteen-nineties by Luiz Galdino, Mestre Galdino's nephew. Luiz's shop stands across the street. Behind it in a roofed courtyard, there are other statues of Vitalino by Luiz, one of him at work, another with the *pífano*. When the artists of the next generation, and the next, depict Vitalino in clay, he appears most often as tall and lanky, a hat on his head, the *pífano* to his lips.

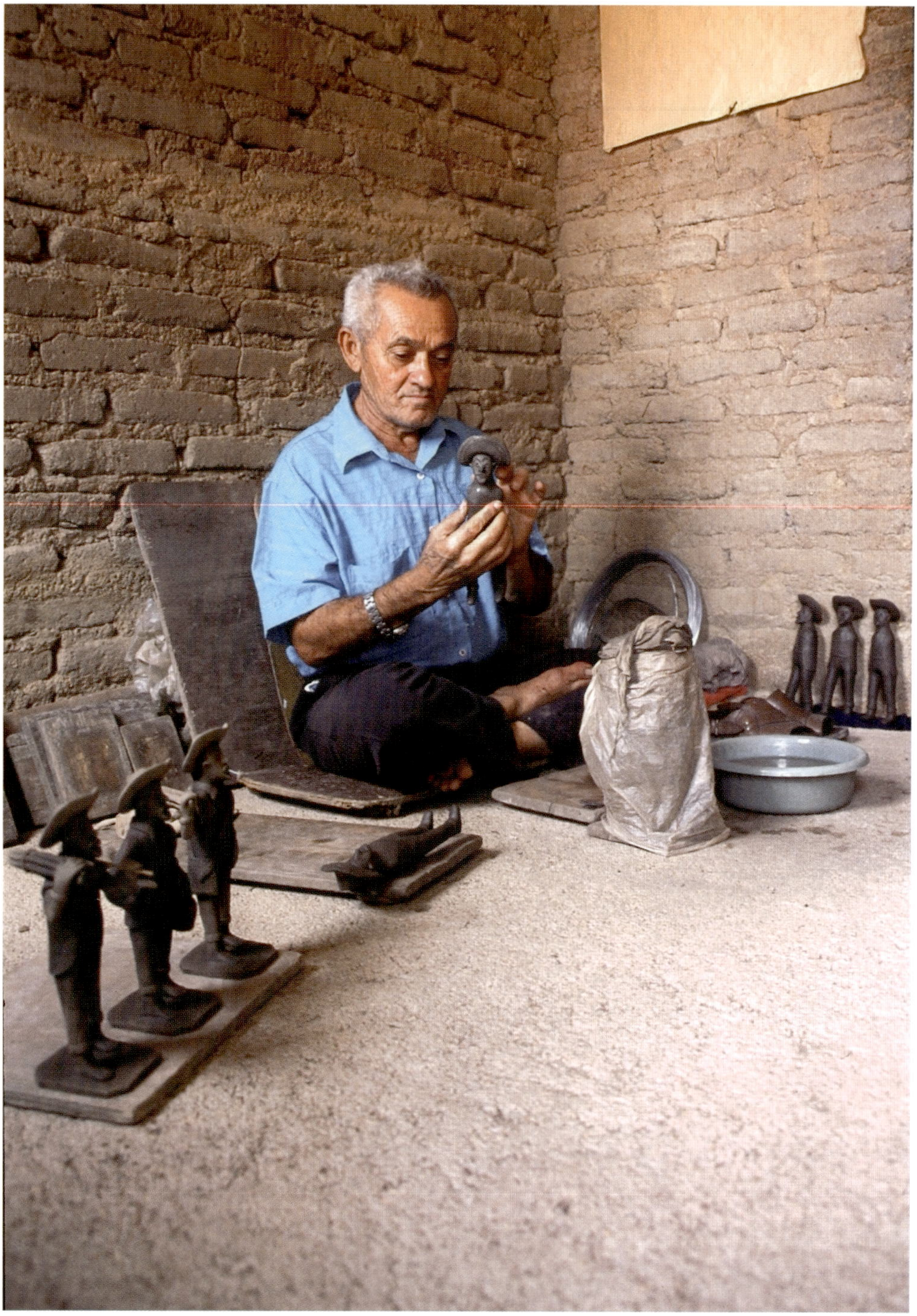

Severino Vitalino at work in the Casa Museu Mestre Vitalino, 2007

Severino Vitalino

On the twenty-third of January in 2007, when we step through the front door for the first time, Severino Vitalino, the master's fourth child and third son, is sitting cross-legged in the corner of the museum's wide front room, modeling clay into small statues of farm workers. His position matches his father's pose in the more naturalistic sculptural portrait of Vitalino that will be installed in the yard to the right of the house two years later.

Severino Pereira dos Santos took the first name of his father, Vitalino Pereira dos Santos, for his last name, and he signs his works, in proud cursive, Severino Vitalino. He tells us that his father was born in 1909, in Sítio Campos, two kilometers from Alto do Moura. There Vitalino worked, walking eight kilometers to the *feira*, the big market in Caruaru, to sell his pieces. In 1948, he moved to Alto do Moura, living first up the hill behind us, then moving several times until, in 1959, he made the brick and built this house. It had no electricity, no running water, but it was his. He had a home of his own.

When Mestre Vitalino, by then a famous man, died in 1963, the mayor of Caruaru moved his widow and children into a house nextdoor and had their old home restored. It opened officially as a museum in 1971. Maria José, Vitalino's youngest daughter, was put in charge, then when she tired of the task, Severino took over on March 14, 1990. He said:

"So, I greet tourists, then I go home to sleep at night. Now I have more time here than in my house.

"I used to work at home, but I can work well here. Not in every period is this house full. I always work here. Here I can make my pieces well.

"I receive people here, college students, all the people, tourists who come to learn the history of Mestre Vitalino. I am available to all the people — TV, newspaper, whatever it might be — I am always here.

"It's very good. I like it."

Severino works the clay here, then carries the figures down the long street to fire them in the kilns behind his home. Some finished pieces will return, standing for sale on shelves in the museum's front room where they took shape. In that room, generously accommodating us as interested foreign tourists, Severino sketched his craft in words and allied it with his father's. That was enough, for at the time we only wanted to learn a little, feeding our shared and general interest in traditional art. In retrospect, it was an open probe of the sort essential at the origin point of a serious project. Once we had imagined a

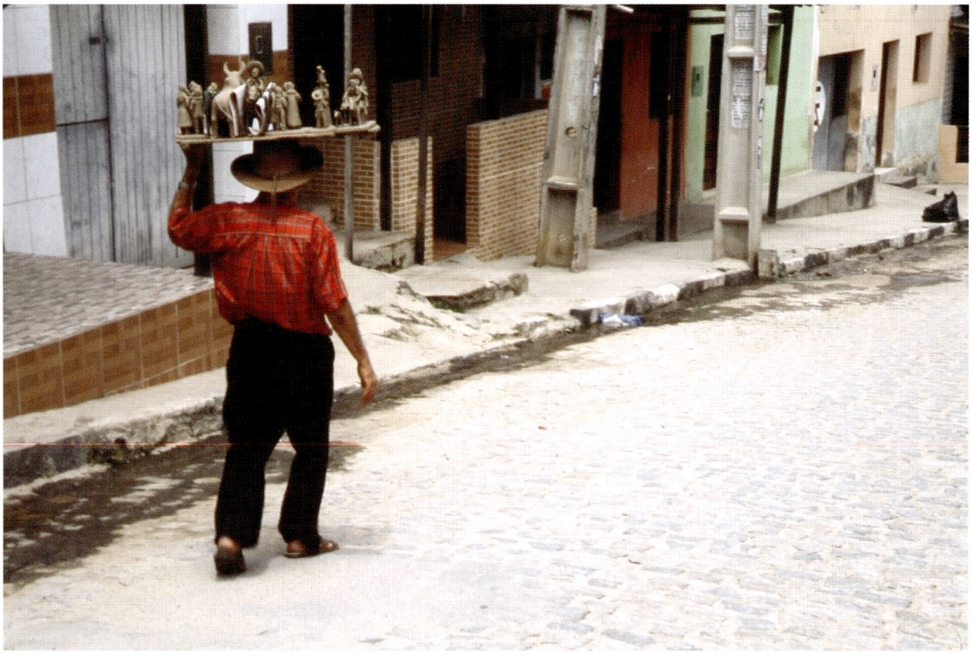

Severino Vitalino carrying works home for firing, 2014

worthwhile field project, ripe with fruitful possibilities, and envisioned a book to report it, we returned in the autumn of 2014 and the spring of 2015, intending to stay longer, determined to understand.

After we got back, Severino invited us to dinner at his home, which perfectly exemplifies the houses of Alto do Moura's artists. Low on the street that rolls down toward the Ipojuca, Severino's place occupies a narrow and deep double plot, a workshop on the left, the house to the right, not more than a wall between them. In the shop, Severino's finished pieces gather in the front, and there his wife, Dona Nina, directs the work done by a team of their older children; they have, all together, thirteen of them. Their house is a tidy, fine version of the dominant vernacular house type of northeastern Brazil. Vitalino built a humble version of the same architectural form. Out on the farms, amid the fields, such houses stand alone, shady verandas on the front and flanks. In town, as here, dwellings of the kind line side by side, terraced tightly along the streets.

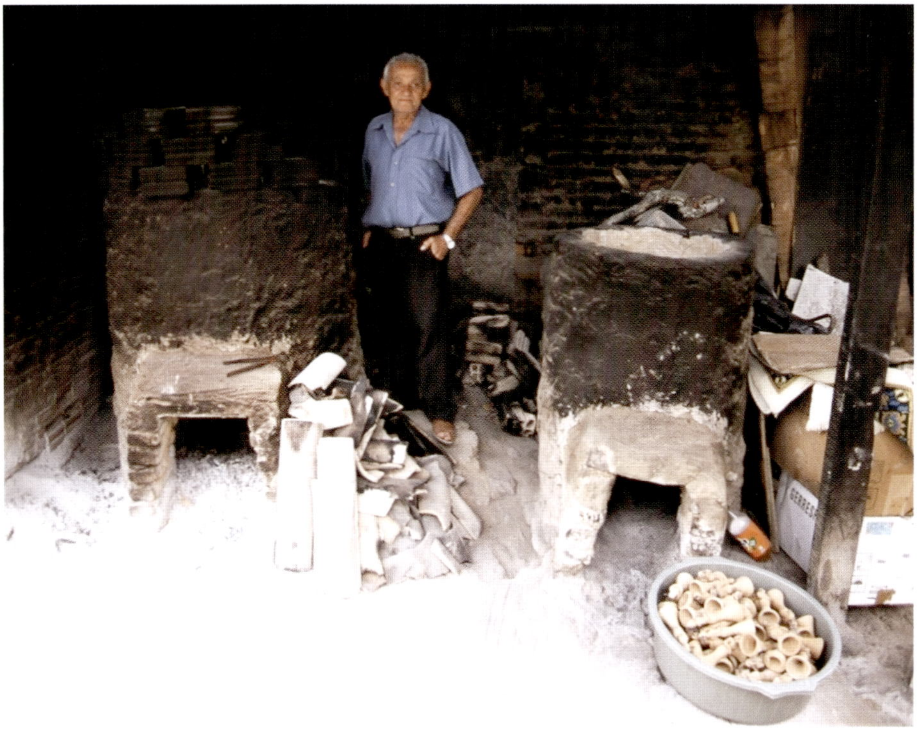

Severino with the kilns behind his home, 2014

Severino's front door gives directly into the front room, just as the door does in Vitalino's museum. There is a television to the right, a statue of Vitalino playing the *pífano* on the left. The walls carry pictures of Vitalino, of Our Lady of Grace and the Sacred Heart of Jesus. A doorway in the back wall funnels motion into a corridor that passes a closed bedroom and ends at the kitchen. There, at a big table beneath a picture of the Last Supper (not Leonardo's though), we enjoy a bountiful, delicious meal of rice, beans, and peas. Bless the hands of Dona Nina.

The back doors of the kitchen and workshop open onto a spacious, lush garden, with a trim flowerbed to one side and a flourishing abundance of olives, onions, and pomegranates, *acerola* and *maracujá* in the back. Severino says that he wishes he were prosperous enough to own a small ranch in the country, since gardening is a profound pleasure for him. Then he takes us to a shed on the right and shows us his pair of small kilns. They are cylindrical, wood-fired, and updraft, like all the kilns in Alto do Moura, like all the kilns we have seen in rural Brazil.

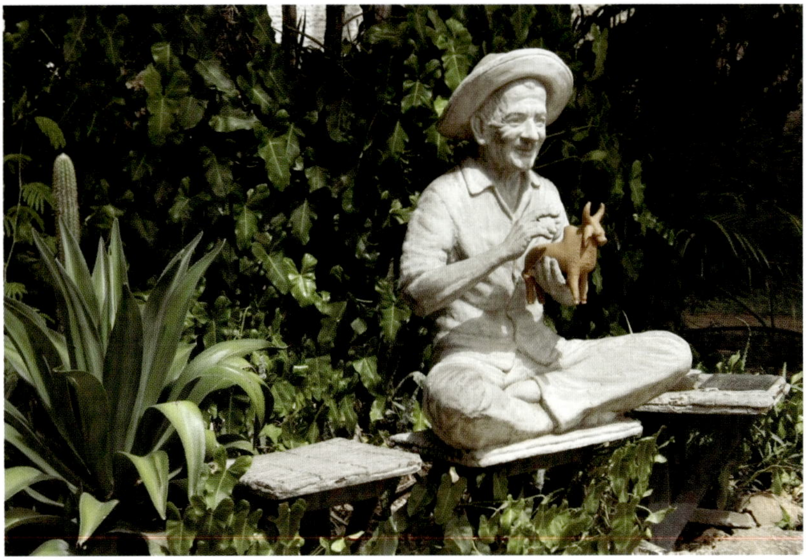

Vitalino with his bull, the newer of the statues at the Casa Museu Mestre Vitalino, 2014

The time has come for long interviews. We know something now about the tradition, friendships with several of the artists are maturing, and our collaborative field procedure is smoothly in motion.

Sitting with Severino Vitalino, we ask him first to tell us about his father. There are two books about the master. René Ribeiro's slim *Vitalino: Um Ceramista Popular do Nordeste* brings the story into the nineteen-fifties. Paulino Cabral de Mello's thick *Vitalino, Sem Barro: O Homen* carries the story past his death into the nineties. They contain the basic biographical facts, but we are less interested in the man who walked around and died than we are in the man who lives in the mind, the man of memory who continues to influence the creations of the artists we know. They are the ones we seek to understand. The recorder is running and Severino Vitalino, speaking on the record, says:

"Mestre Vitalino is the inventor of figurative art in Brazil, right?

"So, he was born in one thousand, nine hundred and nine. At six years of age is when he commenced to make these first works of figurative art.

"Because my grandmother was a potter, making domestic pottery, the pottery of the house — pots, pans, these were the kinds of things she made. She made them and sold them."

Severino's word for potter is *louceira*, indicating that she built her pots by hand, as women in her day generally did, in contrast with the *oleiro*, who throws pots on the wheel, usually a job for men.

"At six years," Severino continues, "my father would take the leftover scraps of clay my grandmother was working with. He would make a little ball of clay

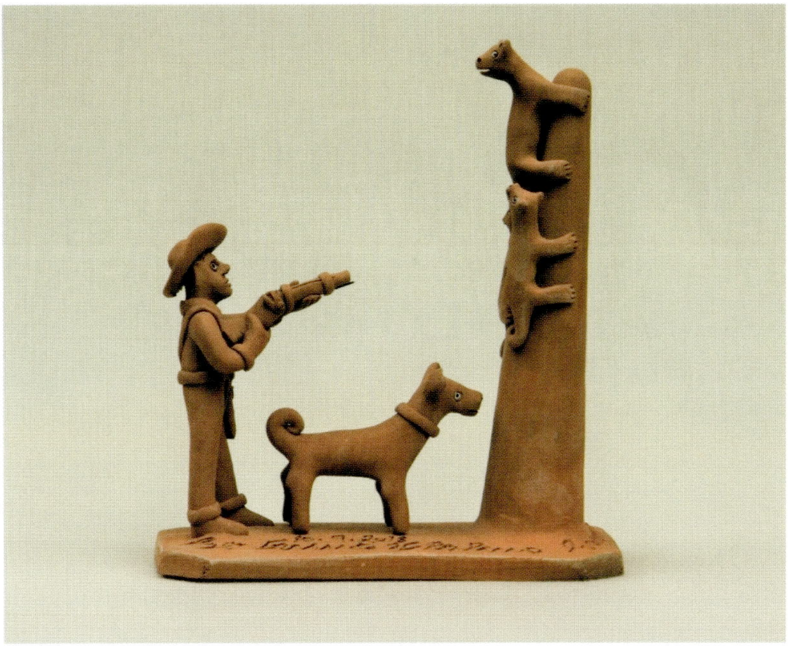

O Caçador de Maracajá, by Severino Vitalino (21 cm tall), dated 2013

and make a little bull for him to play with, because he was very humble, didn't have money to buy the toys of the city.

"Then he commenced from there.

"And my grandfather was a farm laborer, worked in the fields. He was really poor, humble, and he really liked to hunt with a dog and such.

"So, my grandfather was a hunter. So my father would depict whatever he saw, in the life of the people, and he made a piece, made a tree, put the cat up high, and the dog, the man shooting.

"The first piece he made — when he was actually six years of age — is called *O Caçador de Maracajá*."

This piece, The Hunter of the Margay, shows a man with a gun whose dog has treed three wildcats. It is a prime piece in Vitalino's repertory, and he later reversed it into comedy by putting the cat below and the hunter up the tree. Severino continues to recreate the original, an homage to the master, and he sets one of his own in an open front window at the museum to announce without words the place of Vitalino. The bull that was his father's plaything in childhood is also a signal piece. In the newer of the statues out in the yard, Vitalino is making a bull — a burly brahma, humped to be yoked for traction — that Severino and his colleagues make as well, calling it *Boi de Vitalino*. Severino goes on:

"When he got older, he married and he was the father of six children. I am one of the six children of Mestre Vitalino. And today I am continuing, making the quotidian work, what you see day-to-day here in Brazil."

Working-class artists, our friends in the interior of Brazil, divide the repertory of creation into contrastive halves: the quotidian (*arte do cotidiano*) and the sacred (*arte sacra*), a category centered on images of the saints.

"So," Severino continues, "he was the one who passed it on to me. I started at seven years of age, more or less.

"So, I am here, working today at seventy-four years of age, still in this activity.

"In one thousand, nine hundred and sixty-three, he died. God took him away. So, he left six children who are always giving continuity to the work, right? And demonstrating this work for the people of the world.

"He was the inventor, because he had never seen work like this. He thought about it and made it.

"He did not see a work of clay except the pots made by my grandmother. But for figurative work, he received a *dom* and made it.

"He had a *dom*."

That is a key word in the vocabulary of Pernambuco's artists. *Dom* is a gift from God. More than the gift of innate talent, it is a gift to the will that draws people into creation, making them want to learn and to keep learning as they strive for an unattainable perfection, then to keep working through hard times when the body falters, the market slumps, and nobody seems to care. *Dom* matches the "inner necessity" that the great Kandinsky — the first and most sane of abstract painters — used to define art. Art is not in the eye of the beholder or the pocket of the patron. It is in the will of the creator, issuing from the passion within to take sensate form as a sign of the self.

With the *dom*, Severino has brought his introductory statement to a close, saying what he wanted to say while shaping a frame for specific questions. He stressed transfer and continuity, so we ask directly about teaching and learning. His answer harmonizes with all we have seen or heard from others: artists learn little from instruction, much by watching and working.

"It was like this," Severino says. "We were always at the side of our parents. So, when I was seven years of age, he didn't want us to go and work on a farm, because that was a life of suffering.

"He would say, Come here, and the four children, the males, we would stay around him. He worked, and we would take the clay and commence to make something, a bull, a horse.

"So, sometimes he would say, No, not that way.

"So, first God, and then, in the second place, my father's hands, and so we have gotten here. We learned the same style of his, how to work.

"He was always teaching. We were always working. Then there was another thing. We *wanted* to learn.

"Because it was not like a lesson plan, the teacher standing there.

"Art is different.

"You can get explanations, but you also need a *dom* and a desire to make that thing there.

"So, I got there. Not all of the other brothers had the *dom*. Some didn't have all the qualities, and they didn't get there. Because some of my brothers stopped too soon, some of them.

"But I, no, I got there. Since my seven years of age, thank God, I only stop when I have medical problems, or when I am traveling."

Vitalino's first son, Amaro, never married, never quite mastered the craft. He tried, but he was bedeviled by drink and his eyesight failed. Antônio, the fourth son, also didn't marry. He left behind some works of quality when he was murdered in 1977. So, Manuel, the second son, and Severino, the third, were the ones who married, had children, and carried it on. Summing things up, Severino says, "We today, inside our family, have a base of fifty people. So, combining the sons, grandchildren, and great-grandchildren, we have a base of fifty people. We have our little houses, with our children, all working. So, everyone is here."

Learning happens naturally inside the little houses when families work together, as on a farm, the young learning beside the old during joint labor. But learning here is not confined in familial lines. The little houses stand close. People meet constantly in the shops and churches. They see the pieces made by others, they talk together, trade tricks, and useful information flows down the street they share, gathering all into a community of creation. The work they do — Severino estimated their numbers at eight hundred — provides the economic foundation for the town of Alto do Moura.

We ask when Vitalino's art spread beyond the family and Severino replies, "My father began in one thousand, nine hundred and fifteen. He became famous, and other artists started imitating him, following him from forty-eight to now, the families of Manuel Eudócio and Zé Caboclo. So, there is the history."

The year Severino mentioned, 1948, is the most important year in the tradition's history, the major turning point. In that year, when Severino was eight,

Vitalino moved to Alto do Moura and met Manuel Eudócio and Zé Caboclo, contemporaries of the master's oldest children and brothers-in-law; Zé Caboclo married Manuel Eudócio's sister. They learned from Vitalino and — claims conflict — it seems that he also learned from them. From the evidence that survives in old pieces, it feels right to say that in collaborative exchange, all of them working together, they made the changes that have become general traits of today's artistic production.

Figures slimmed and lengthened. Rubbery arms and legs gained elbows and knees. Women's bodies gained modest curves. The hole Vitalino poked to make an eye was filled with a tiny ball of clay to get a more natural look. Vitalino joined parts with soft clay, melding the margins, but now snips of thin wire pinned parts together, sharpening lines between the hat and the head, the hand and the tool, the feet and the base. And the finish, painted or not, was part of the change.

Severino tells us that before 1948 Vitalino painted all his pieces, though old works suggest he painted many but left some "natural," the word also used by Brazilian artists who carve wooden saints, or forge iron images of the Yoruba gods, then leave them unpainted. After the great moment of change, though, Vitalino no longer painted and Severino, who was learning at the time, followed him. Severino says:

"When my father commenced as a child, and from one thousand, nine hundred and fifteen to one thousand, nine hundred and forty-eight, all his work was painted.

"Then in the years from forty-seven to forty-eight, there came some people from Rio. They said, Vitalino, I want this work. Don't put paint on it. Make it and just leave it there, natural.

"So, by one thousand, nine hundred and fifty, my father was painting nothing anymore.

"So, this is what happened. My father made his works during the week, went to the market" — in Caruaru — "to sell, and to see if he was able to get some money to buy food for the family.

"So, he would take pieces to the market unpainted. So, until today I maintain this tradition. I don't paint."

As a result, artists today have two options — to leave the work natural or to paint it with fastidious precision. Some generally work one way, some the other, and some alternate.

Their repertories, shifting constantly, slowly growing, all different, share a foundation in Vitalino's work. Severino tells us that his father began with

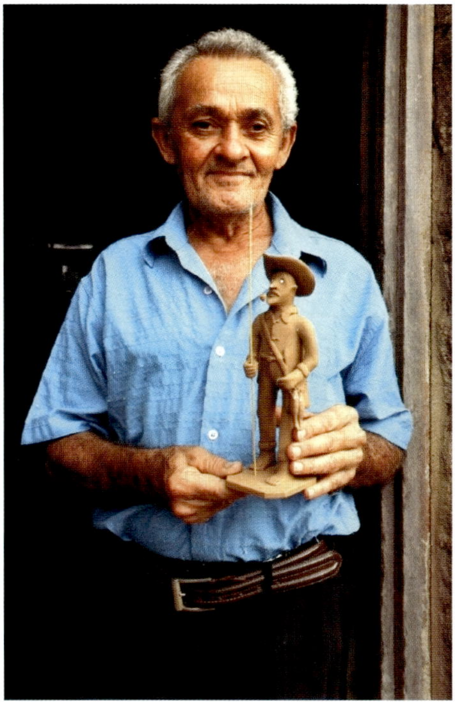

Severino Vitalino with his fisherman, 2007

the bull, then made the hunter of wildcats, and as his fame widened and he gained a name, his repertory reached 118 pieces — that is, distinct types that varied with each realization while holding to an abstract, conceptual form. The number, 118, comes from information René Ribeiro gathered in the fifties and reported in his book *Vitalino*. Some people today doubt its accuracy, thinking it too low, but the number has drifted into oral tradition and it gets repeated to express, with particularity, a general notion of Vitalino's imaginative breadth.

Severino says his work differs from his father's "because my father — since he was the first, the inventor of this art — his work is rustic, and I give a finish that is finer, more special. So, the difference is this.

"But I am one of his imitators. I continue to make replicas of the work of Mestre Vitalino. Sometimes, from time to time, I even create a new piece, but it is difficult because I always want to work within my father's repertory."

He has narrowed away from his father's fantastic extremes and concentrated on three themes. The first is rural life. Severino calls it the quotidian and defines it as "the life that is lived here in our Brazil, in Pernambuco, right?" Then he goes on to say:

"It was poor, our Agreste of Pernambuco. We had no industry here, we had nothing. So, who had art, lived on art. Others lived by working the farm. Others live in the sugarcane regions and live by the cutting of the cane.

"Quotidian means the classical life that is lived, that we represent, right?

"It is The Oxcart, The Return from the Field, The Fisherman, these things that represent this quotidian that is lived.

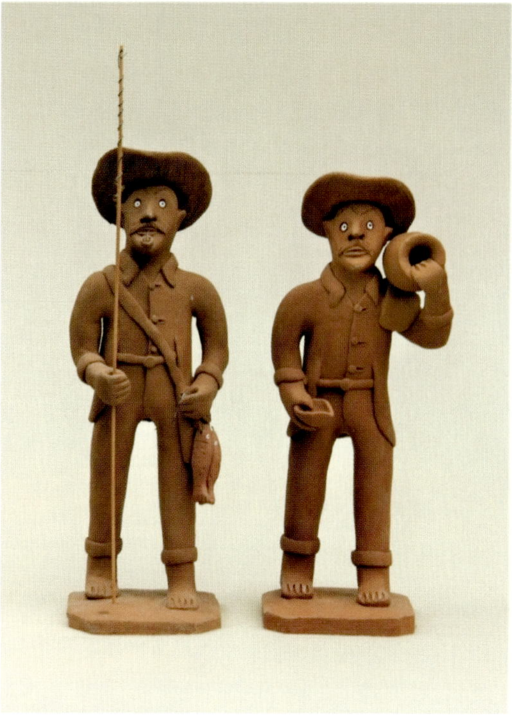

Rural workers by Severino. Left: fisherman (24 cm tall), 2007. Right: farmer searching for water (23 cm tall), 2015

"It is the one who goes to the farm, the one who goes to fish, the one who goes to market, right?

"This is what my father saw. God gave him a *dom*, so he created. He made *Os Retirantes*. That was something we had here in the Agreste of Pernambuco, in the Sertão really.

"So, people would escape the drought. They would get a cat, a chicken, a dog, and travel. So, this is what he represented, depicted, right?"

Os Retirantes, also called *A Família de Retirantes*, is the masterwork of the rural theme. Invented by Vitalino, made by Severino and all the leading artists of Alto do Moura, it assembles the members of a family into a composition that rises in profile then smoothly descends. From piece to piece the form holds, details vary. The family moves forward in a tight line. Mounted and smoking a pipe, the grandmother comes first, then the father with a parrot on one shoulder, a rifle, axe, or hoe on the other. The mother is next, a bundle on her head, a baby in her arms; the father might be carrying a baby too. Their children follow, first the oldest daughter with a bundle on her head or the oldest son with a dog in his arms, then a younger daughter carrying a hen, and the smallest boy comes last. Walking beside them, on one side, there is a dog or two and a goat.

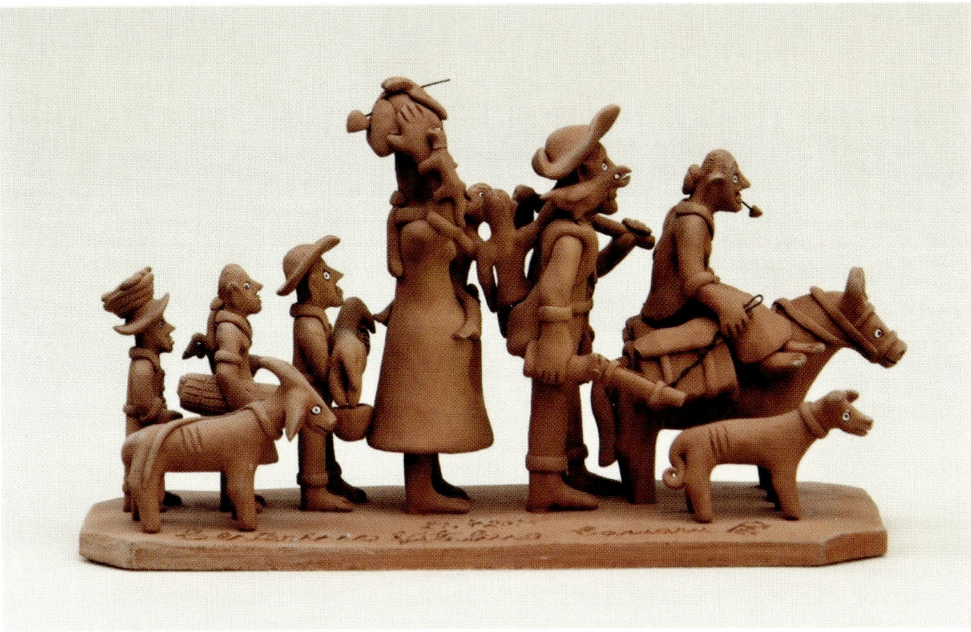

Os Retirantes, by Severino Vitalino (35 cm long), dated 2014

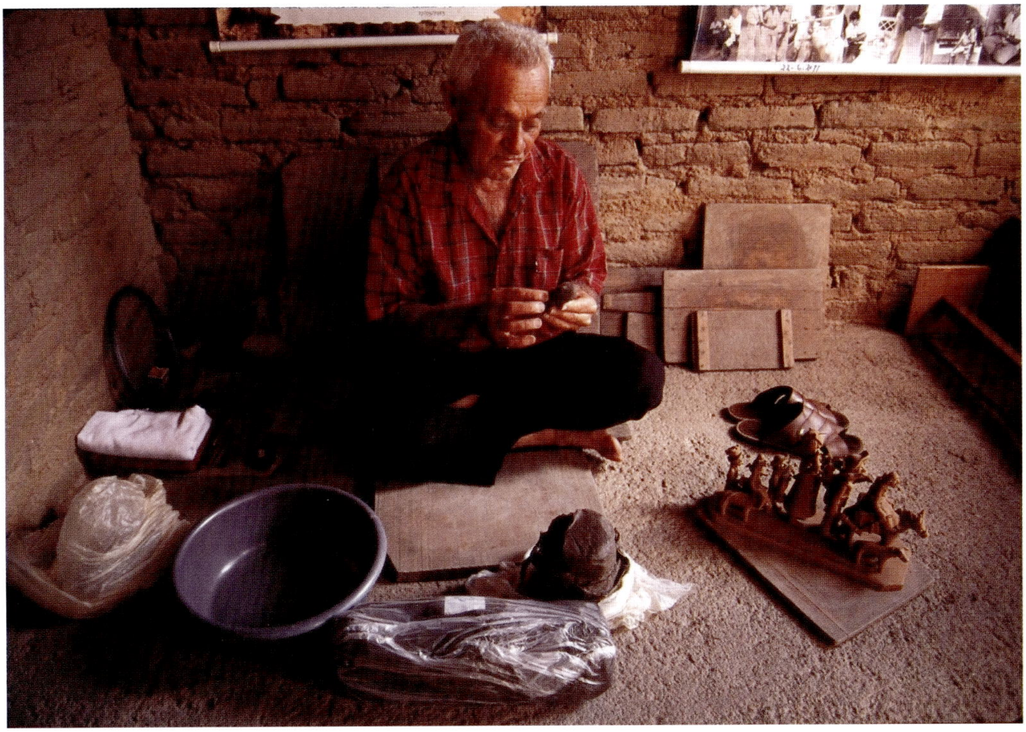

Severino Vitalino making *Os Retirantes*, 2014

These folks are fleeing from one of the droughts that swept death across the desert-like Sertão. They seek life on greener farmland or in the cities to the east and south where they will find bad jobs as agricultural laborers or domestic servants. Exiles like them have established connections, along lines of longing, between Pernambuco and the vast industrial city of São Paulo, much as rural migrants in the United States once connected Mississippi and Chicago, Appalachia and Detroit.

With its images of workers and work, rural life is one of the themes, the one containing the most pieces. Music is another. Severino tells us that, in addition to being an artist, his father was a musician who played the *pífano* in bands like those that still perform around Caruaru so, naturally enough, he depicted musicians in clay and others followed along.

The theme of rural life enfolds two main images of groups: *Os Retirantes*, which might be rendered in English as The Exiles or Escape from the Sertão; and *A Volta da Roça*, The Return from the Field. And comparably, there are two in the musical theme: *O Trio Nordestino*, the Northeastern trio, showing a man with an accordion, flanked by a drummer and a man-jangling a triangle; and *A Banda de Pífano*, a band with two men playing the *pífano*, others with drums, one with a triangle.

Sounds made by the *pífano* and accordion are as emblematic of the Brazilian Northeast as the clay figures made by the artists of Alto do Moura. It is no surprise, then, that within the third theme of their collective repertory — the theme of the heroes — the artists craft portraits of musicians: Vitalino with the

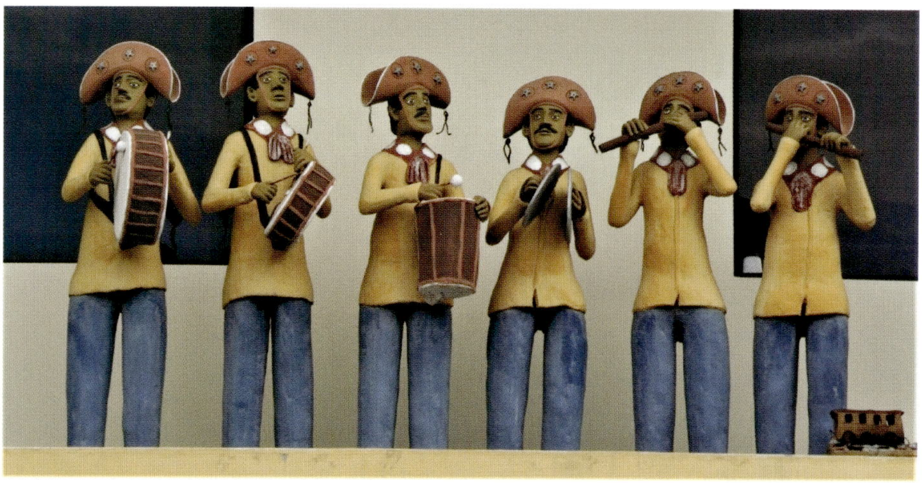

A Banda de Pífano, above the entry to Luiz Antônio's shop, 2014

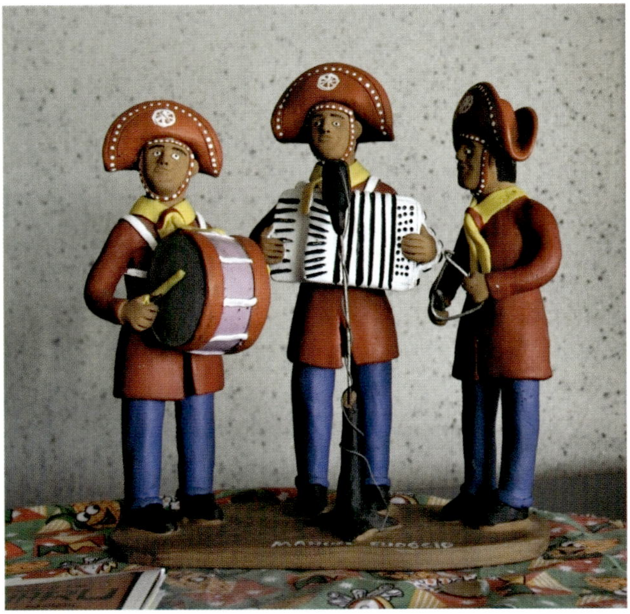

O Trio Nordestino, by Manuel Eudócio, displayed in the lobby of a hotel in Caruaru, 2015

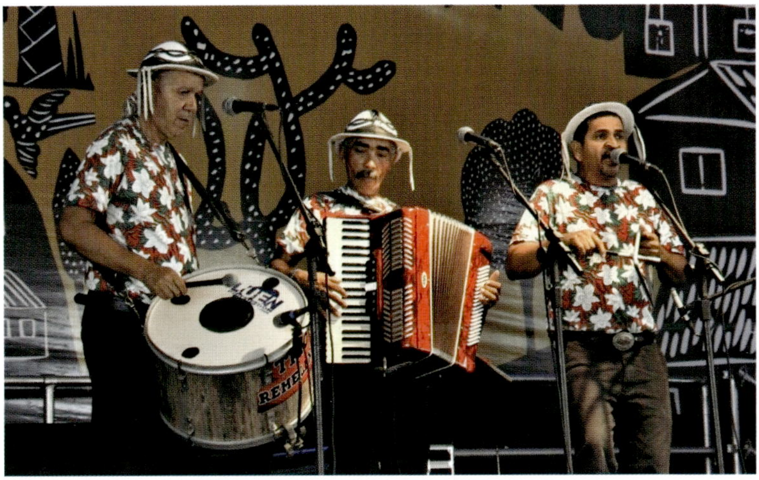

The Northeastern trio performing during the June Festival, Alto do Moura, 2019

pífano and Gonzaga with the accordion. Luiz Gonzaga extended the Northeastern trio while developing his region's most popular music. Luiz Gonzaga is the father of *forró* as Bill Monroe is the father of bluegrass — not an idle conjunction, since *forró* and bluegrass are both innovative brands of country music favored by exiled country folks — and Gonzaga's songs movingly capture the moods of his people and the symbols of their place: the white-winged birds of the Sertão and the rural figures Vitalino shaped in clay and sold in the urban market of Caruaru.

"Luiz Gonzaga," Severino says, "was a person who made our Pernambuco known. My father depicted it, and Gonzaga sang the story that is Pernambuco. The state that is his, and the state that is my father's, Pernambuco.

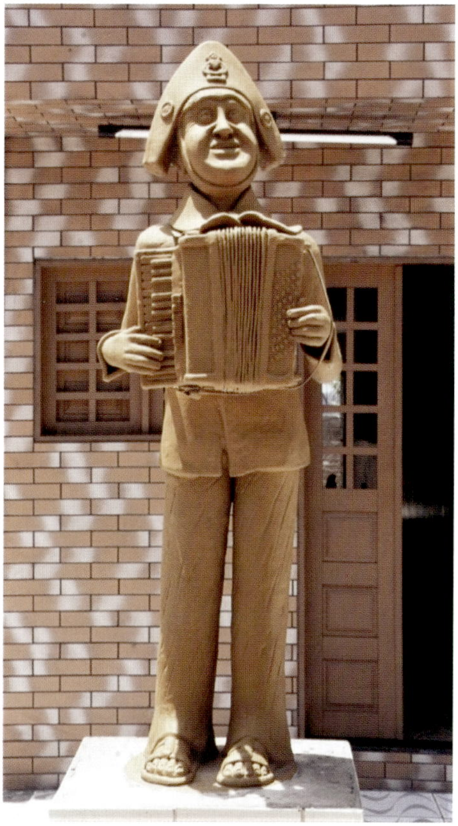

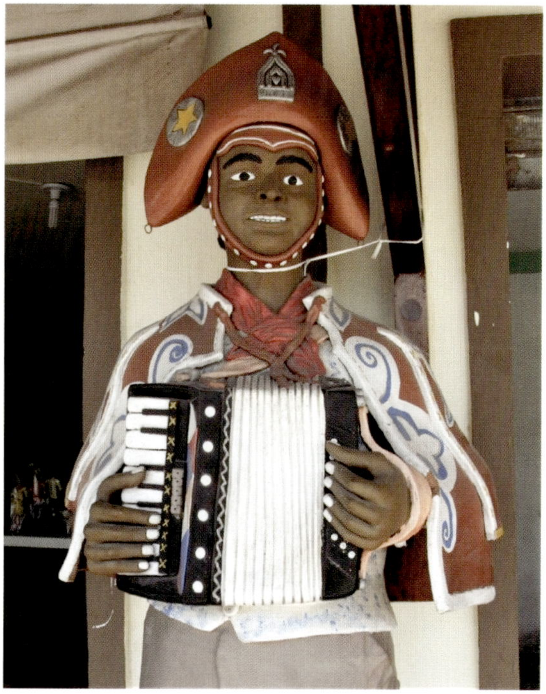

Life-size statue of Luiz Gonzaga, by Gilliard Gonçalves Simões, standing outside Gilliard's shop, 2019

Life-sized statue of Luiz Gonzaga, by Manuel Bernardo, standing outside Leonildo Nascimento Silva's shop, 2007

"Gonzaga is beloved here, very, very, very much. I met him. I got to meet him in person in one thousand, nine hundred and seventy-eight.

"My father met him earlier. In the years fifty to fifty-eight, Gonzaga would come to Caruaru. It was a very small city then. He would come by car to do a show. It was only three people then, which is the real *forró*. It was Gonzaga with the accordion, a drum, and the triangle only.

"In the year seventy-eight I met him and he had a band, already with a big band, special, beautiful."

Alto do Moura's repertory features images of Vitalino and Gonzaga. In public, there are two statues of Vitalino at the Casa Museu Vitalino, and six life-size statues of Gonzaga stand along the town's streets. But, by far, the hero most abundantly portrayed is Lampião.

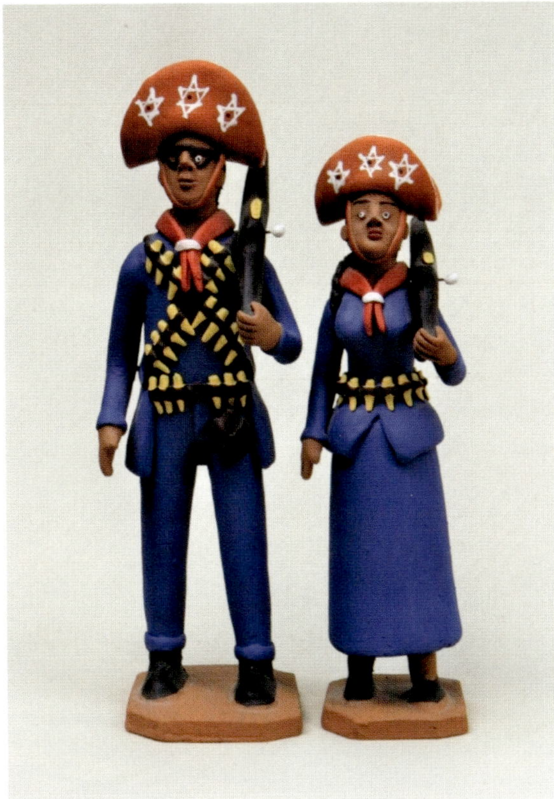

Lampião and Maria Bonita in blue, by Zé Caboclo's son Paulo, 2007

Severino tells us that, after the bull, his father most often made images of Lampião, and today "everyone makes the story of Lampião, everyone in their own way. They paint it. My father didn't paint, but the image painted with that uniform, a beautiful blue, it calls attention to itself."

Lampião, as most frequently rendered, stands with his comrade and lover Maria Bonita, both in uniform, both armed. Lampião wears glasses, one eye missing, and he wears the characteristic upturned hat of the Northeast that Gonzaga and Vitaliano also wear, that Maria Bonita sometimes wears too. Lampião and Maria Bonita pose in formal frontality like saints.

Born Virgulino Ferreira da Silva in Pernambuco, Lampião raised a small army in the back country of the Northeast and, with Maria Bonita at his side, waged war against authority until they were betrayed, killed, and beheaded in 1938. Our friends in Brazil disagree. We are told that Lampião was driven to violence by his father's murder, that with virtuous egalitarian intent, he took from the rich and gave to the poor. We are told that Lampião was an unhinged maniacal killer.

Much, very much, has been written about him; there's even an excellent book in English, *The Bandit King* by Billy Jaynes Chandler. But as it was when we asked about his father, when we ask Severino about Lampião, we aren't after accurate facts (the books have them); we want the artist's understanding that conditions creation. Severino says:

"I, personally, consider Lampião a hero. He was an important person for the people in that period.

"In that period, the colonels — the colonels were the ones who had a farm. They had a piece of land, a ranch. So, they would take what belonged to the poor.

"There is the population. They are all suffering the crises of hunger, let's suppose. Of hunger.

"So, the richer ones on these ranches, they had plenty. Lampião would go there, take what they had and donate it to these people in poverty.

"So, these colonels — there would be a fight. They would try to keep it, what they had.

"For this reason the history of Lampião is important, and it is important for people to preserve this history in clay, because there have been so many years since he passed, right?

"It is like the history of my father. Because my father, he was the inventor of this art. So, my father was inspired to make the history of Lampião because he had that affection, that love for him.

"So the story of Lampião increased. That is the story of Lampião that we know.

"He was a person, a hero, a person who gave so much. He even gave a bad taste to some families. But he gave to so many people who survived through what he did for the people.

"He was a character who represented a beautiful thing. He represented culture. The image of Lampião creates a feeling in the people. He represents a special side of our culture."

With Severino as our guide, we have sketched the repertory, from the bull to Lampião. Questions remain; first: what's missing? "I don't make saints," Severino says. "Here almost nobody makes saints." He remembers a man, Elias Francisco dos Santos, who "used to make religious imagery. So, if people wanted a saint, a Saint Francis, a Crucifix, he would make it. He was the only one who liked to make saints. Mister Elias, he has passed, and now no saints are made."

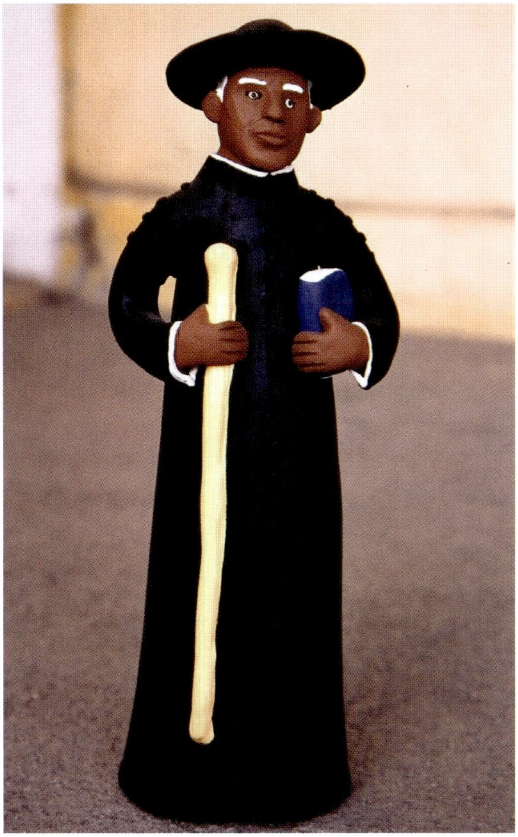

Padre Cícero, by Manuel Eudócio, 2014

In explaining the absence, Severino says that many of the artists are Evangelical, opposed to the creation and worship of saints, but even among Catholics, he says, the making of saints is rare. Luiz Antônio, he tells us, is a devout Catholic and he does make images of processions, of people carrying the statue of a saint through the street, a common scene in the day-to-day life of modern Brazil. Manuel Eudócio, one of his father's close friends and followers, sometimes makes saints, Severino says, and, indeed, Manuel Eudócio portrays both Saint Francis and Saint Anthony, Franciscans and colleagues, who are the male saints most frequently imaged by Brazilian *santeiros*.

Manuel Eudócio also shapes portraits in clay of Padre Cícero, a priest from Ceará, the state north of Pernambuco, and, like Lampião, one of the popular heroes of the Northeast. Severino tells us that his father revered him, regularly traveling to Juazeiro do Norte in Ceará to attend the Mass in October for Padre Cícero. Vitalino had in his home two plaster statuettes of the man Severino calls "the saint of the Northeast," but his father made no images of Padre Cícero, just as he made no images of saints.

"I don't know why others don't," Severino says. "Now, my father, I do know why.

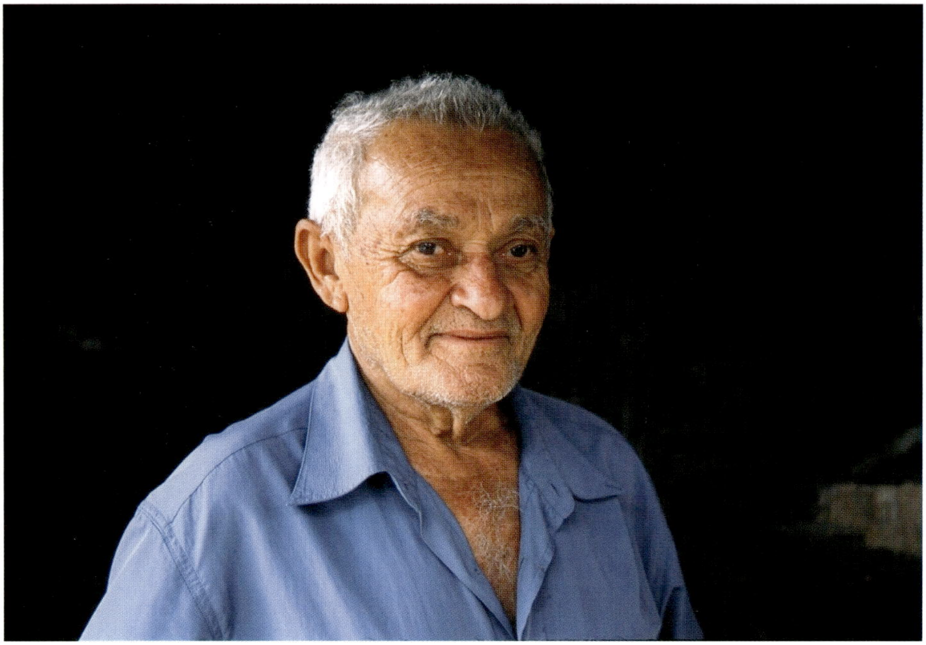

Severino Vitalino, Alto do Moura, 2014

"My father was Catholic, very Catholic. He would say that to make a living off the clay, to use the clay to make an image, he had to burn it to make a living. He did not make Jesus or a saint because he thought that burning them is a sin.

"He was very devout. To make the image, a resemblance to Jesus or any saint, he was very devout, and he found it very difficult. And to burn it. He did not do that.

"He did not take it to the kiln and burn it. So, I have stayed the same. I got used to the repertory that my father passed on to us, and I don't make saints."

The collective repertory has expanded and contracted, but Vitalino's repertory remains at the root, and he made no saints. Quotidian imagery is the town's prime sign and the reason why people come from afar and travel the narrow dusty road to Alto do Moura. Almost all are Brazilians; some are tourists, some are collectors, and some are merchants whose purchases will fill the galleries in the cities and the shops in the airports. It's working commercially — why disrupt it? — and the repertory is sufficiently spacious for men, and increasingly for women, to work within it, making what they want to make in the way they want to make it, just as the region's musical repertory offers variety enough for musicians to find within it the songs and melodies they want to perform. An artist, that is, performs a statue by Vitalino with pleasure and sincerity, just as a singer — let's say his follower Dominguinhos — performs a song by Luiz Gonzaga.

When we request Severino to list the most important towns where art is currently created in Pernambuco, he starts, as he certainly should, with Alto do Moura, doesn't mention Ibimirim to the west in the Sertão where many artists carve wood into saints, but he does name Tracunhaém to the east, northwest of Recife. There, as in Alto do Moura, work in clay shifted from the utilitarian to the figurative, though Tracunhaém's figures, generally larger than Alto do Moura's, many life-sized, depict the saints. It is still the case that more people make, and more people buy, religious images, but Alto do Moura has no serious competition; it's your place for the quotidian.

Saints are peripheral to the repertory that brought fame to Alto do Moura. But that repertory, which we have treated so far, within which Severino works, does not contain all the things of clay that bring money to Alto do Moura. When we ask the next question — what else? — Severino sharply splits the town's production into two lines.

The first line of production, the one we've been following, yields objects called *arte* (art) or *artesanato* (a term, combining Latin and Arabic words for art, that names fine craft). Their makers are called *mestre* (master), *artista* (artist), or *artesão* (artisan). These are the ones who shape the form and sign the piece, though frequently other members of the family paint it.

The second line of production yields decorative objects, sometimes also called *artesanato*, but generally called *bonecas*. The dictionary prompts translation of *boneco* as doll, but for working artists, in Portugal as well as Brazil, the *boneco* is a statue of any size; the monumental clay saint of Tracunhaém is a *boneco*. With the diminutive suffix, *bonequinho*, it is a small statue. With the feminine ending, *boneca*, it is a statue of a woman. The artistic repertory of the first line contains many quotidian images of women, now, in fact, more images of working women than working men, but the *boneca* of the second line differs from them in several ways.

For one, the *boneca* is quick to make. The body is thrown on the wheel, the face is molded. In the artistic first line, though, no wheel, no mold, the image is shaped slowly and carefully, entirely by hand. For another, the parts of the *boneca* can be made by different people, even in different shops. Then the *bonecas* are assembled and painted by a team. No individual can claim the finished piece; it is not signed.

Severino's family illustrates the difference. He makes the art alone. Meanwhile, his wife and children, working together in the shop beside the house, make the *bonecas*. Thus the work done by few divides from the work done by many, and people separate art from craft, not lethargically by materials, but knowledgeably by process and commitment.

Differences of method match differences in history. Alto do Moura's artistic line began in 1915 when Vitalino created the hunter of wildcats, then broadened in 1948 when Zé Caboclo and Manuel Eudócio joined him. That tradition, created right here, carries images that incarnate local culture, local history. The *bonecas* come from elsewhere. It is generally thought that they were invented in Minas Gerais, beyond Bahia to the south, and they were introduced to Alto do Moura around the turn of the century, not so long ago, by a businessman who thought that the town's people, skilled in the clay, could supply attractive commodities for a wide market. *Bonecas* are not burdened with complex local significance. They are just pretty women, pretty Brazilian women with slim waists, ample hips, and sweet faces. They come in a variety of types. In the beginning, most were black with twisted wire for hair, but most of them now, like the people who make them, are attractively mixed in race.

Severino spreads the difference into history, saying, "Things have changed because people got away from the history of my father.

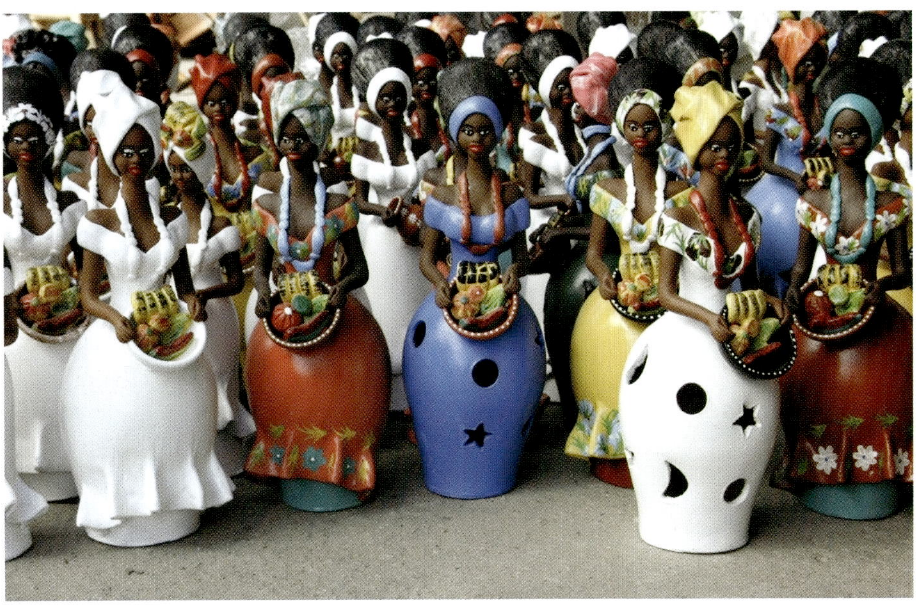

Bonecas in progress, Alto do Moura, 2019

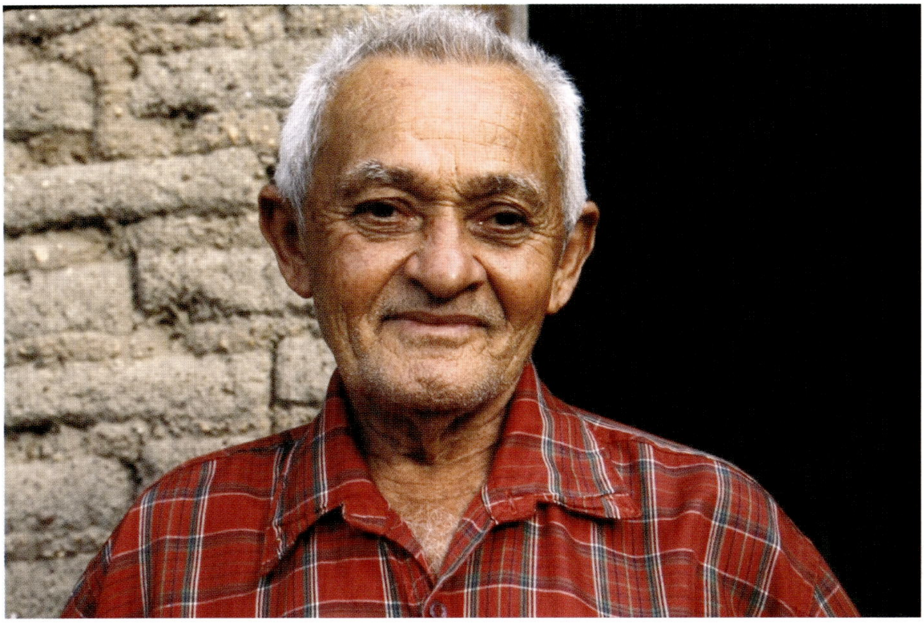

Severino Vitalino, 2014

"So, we have in Alto do Moura many *bonecas*, many things, like, for decoration, many things that my father did not make.

"So, they created that, a very different thing. To decorate the house, they made *bonecas* of various types, with wire hair.

"So, that was something that got away from the art of my father. And it is what we have the most of today in Alto do Moura. And the art like my father made, few people are working in it."

In the spirit of a restrained jeremiad, Severino overstates the case to register his complaint about the trend. Certainly today there are more people making *bonecas* than there are making art in his father's tradition — just as, in the not so distant past, more people were making useful pots than were shaping clay into images.

The people who learned directly from Vitalino, the people of the second generation, Severino's generation, have died, stopped working, or they are elderly. But in the third generation, the generation now in the lead, there are many more artists than there were in the second, and — the creators of the tradition's finest works — they will all take their turns later in this book. It is true that interest seems to have declined among the young people of the fourth generation, though many of them have learned, some are at work, and it would be nearly as easy to imagine a robust revival as an end to it all.

But Severino's worry is deep and it leads him to shift from the topic of difference in production to the topic of continuity that runs a thread of connection through all four of our interviews, the last on May 6, 2015, ten days before Alto do Moura celebrated a century of Vitalino's work. Severino says:

"Me, my son Elias, the family of Zé Caboclo, we are the ones that give continuity.

"There is Manuel Eudócio who works, imitating the work of my father. There is Luiz Antônio who also gives this continuity.

"I always live by the art of clay to give continuity. Look, I passed it to my son. He is the grandson of Mestre Vitalino, and my son Elias has his atelier right next to my house."

Severino Vitalino passed it on, knowing that others would adjust it to suit themselves. Then he was gone.

3

Elias Vitalino

It is May 29, 2019. We are sitting in his workshop with Elias and he tells us that his father passed away in January. His mother died in 2017, but his father was still hard at work when he was struck down by a heart attack. Severino, Elias says, was admitted to the Hospital Mestre Vitalino in Caruaru on the twenty-third of October in 2018. He remained in the hospital for a long time, then the doctors operated, and after many days in intensive care, Severino Vitalino died on the seventh of January in 2019.

Elias Rodrigues dos Santos followed his father when he took his grandfather's given name for his artistic surname. The line runs straight; Elias Vitalino says:

"The work that my father inherited from my grandfather, he passed it on to all the children, right? And we intend, for many years, to make the small statues" — the *bonequinhos* — "of Vitalino.

"I am the first grandchild of Vitalino, the first son of Severino. I don't remember my grandfather. He died when I was only two years and six months old. I was born in one thousand, nine hundred and sixty, on the twentieth of July.

"I don't remember him, but according to my mother, he liked his grandchildren, and she said that he would play much with me. He would also play the *pífano*.

"But I don't remember my grandfather, unfortunately. I learned from my father.

"I learned with him by watching — *watching* my father making. I would always stay by him, observing, especially at night. I used to sleep in a hammock that was attached to the wall, and I would stay awake, observing.

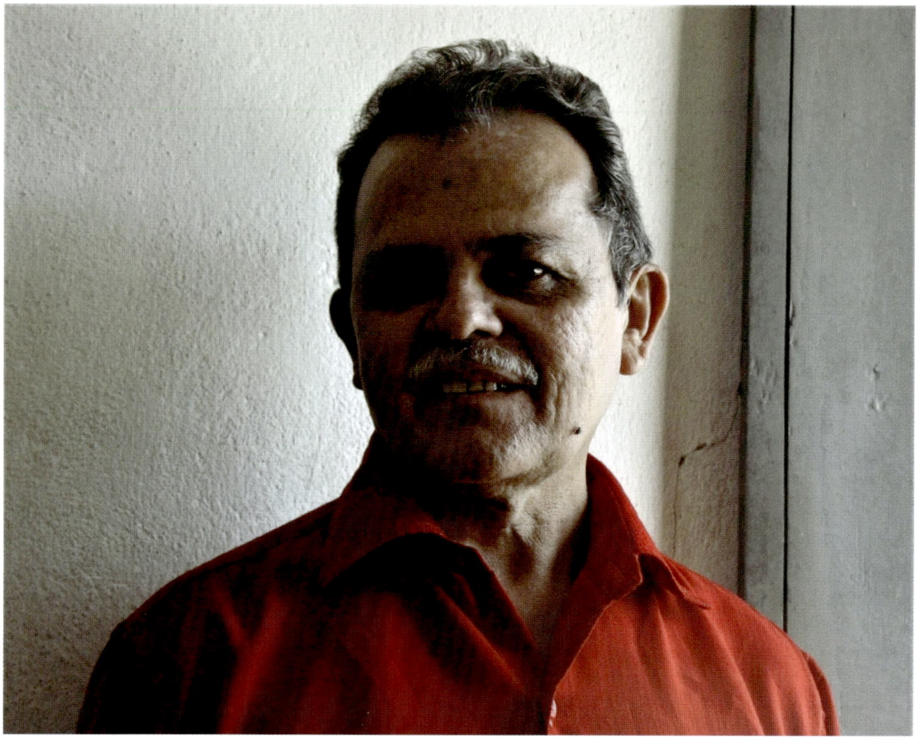

Elias Vitalino, 2019

"I became curious to make too, so I started. At around six years of age, I started to make small statues, actually little horses and bulls, like my grandfather. Later came the human figures."

Severino learned by watching and trying. So did Elias and so did Elias's three children:

"All of them make, but I did not teach them. They were just observing. They were always by my side and they started to make. They grew up watching me. They acquired a taste and then started.

"I gave them some orientations, right? Look, do it like this, right? Handle the clay in this way. You have to roll the clay on the board to make the shape of an arm, to make an arm.

"But they already had a notion, because they were always *seeing* me making a piece."

From hand to eye, with slight verbal direction, the tradition passes in a way that permits open reception and personal adaptation. At once, artists please themselves and maintain continuity.

Unlike his father and grandfather who would make no saints, Elias says, "I make saints, no problem. Not frequently, but I make them when someone commissions them. Saint Francis and Saint Anthony, there are always commissions for these images. I also make Nativity scenes; I always make Nativities and processions."

But the images that Vitalino invented and Severino continued to make — these are the ones that center Elias's repertory. He says:

"I seek to preserve the tradition, right? The quotidian, our day-to-day, right? Many pieces that I make, actually, are still pieces that he" — Vitalino — "created. Some are my creations, but the majority, for sure, are pieces created by my grandfather.

"This art was passed to us, and we passed it to our children. Its significance is great. The cultural value is very important, not only for Caruaru, but for the Northeast, and for Brazil. Even for the world, really."

Like his father and like his grandfather at the end, Elias generally leaves his pieces unpainted. Occasionally, though, and on request, he will paint them, but he doesn't enjoy painting. His pleasure is shaping the images passed to him, down the familial line, but his works depart radically in scale:

"I make everything traditional in the style of my grandfather, and I make it in his way. But with the difference that my work is miniatures, for sure. I always make miniatures.

"Because that is how I like it. When I started, it was much smaller than the usual work. The ones I make now are seven or eight centimeters, and they used to be four or five centimeters."

Elias's version of *Os Retirantes* has the same number of figures that his father's and grandfather's did, but it is half the size. Severino's version reaches twenty centimeters in height and thirty-five centimeters in length, while Elias's is nine centimeters tall and seventeen centimeters long. He makes the other leading piece of the rural theme, *A Volta da Roça*, Return from the Field, at the same scale, and, like others before him, he sometimes decreases the number of farm laborers coming home from the fields to two or even one. All are tiny, and a delicacy of touch at a reduced size is the key to Elias's personal style.

His miniatures invest small subjects with fatherly affection. He makes tiny quotidian images of children playing the games of childhood, little girls skipping rope, little boys shooting marbles. In a painted miniature from 2005, titled *Papai Noel Nordestino*, Elias depicts Santa Claus distributing gifts to the poor kids of the Northeast.

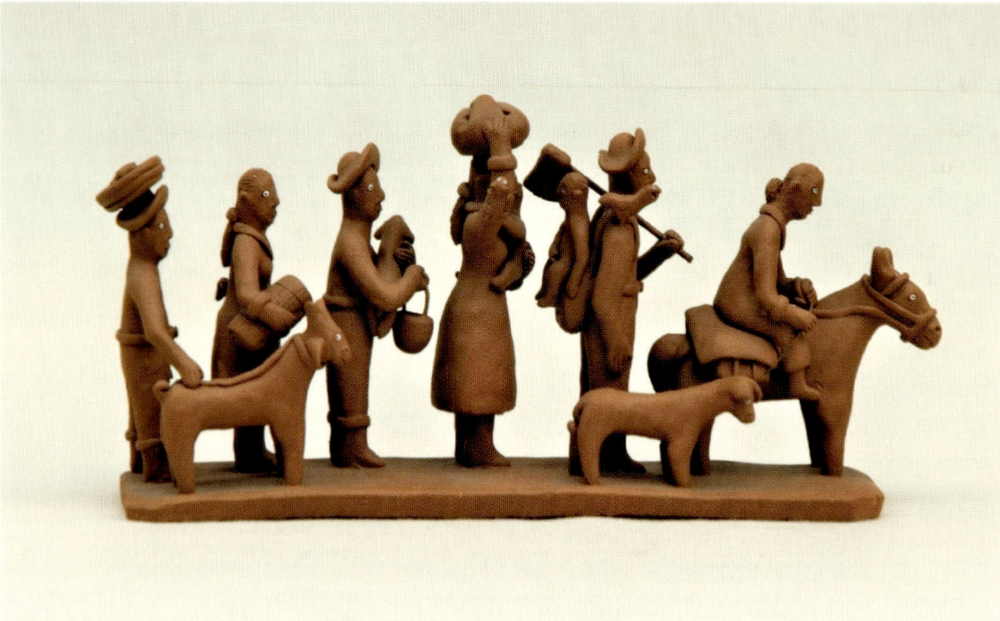

Os Retirantes, by Elias Vitalino (17 cm long), 2019

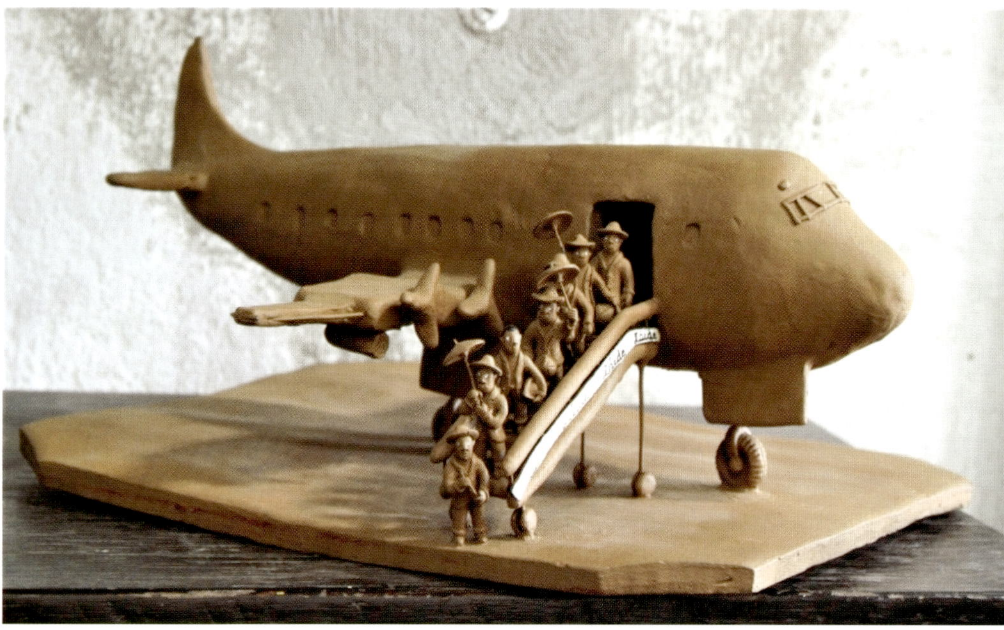

Arrival in Rio, by Elias Vitalino, 2009

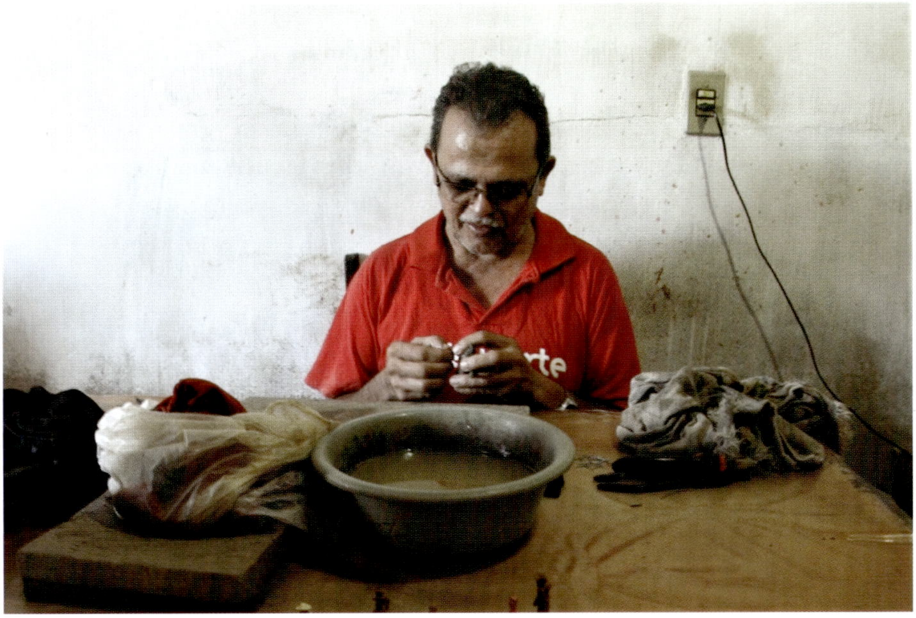

Elias at work, Alto do Moura, 2019

Miniaturization brings large subjects into control. In 2009, Elias created *Mestre Vitalino Chegando no Rio com a Banda de Pífano*, which shows Vitalino leading his *pífano* band out of an airplane on their arrival in Rio de Janeiro in October of 1960, a great event in the master's life. In another composition, he arranged a ring of tiny admirers at the base of the gigantic statue of Luiz Gonzaga that stands in a plaza in Caruaru. These are among the special miniatures that remain, not for sale, in Elias's private collection.

A dedicated artist like his father, Elias shares his father's complaint and concern. When — knowing that Elias is one of thirteen children — we ask about the others in the family, he says:

"Some of my siblings also make, but the majority don't work with the traditional pieces of my grandfather. They majority work with *bonecas*.

"They know how to make, but they produce these *bonecas*, these *dondocas*, right?"

A *dondoca* is a pampered, pretty woman; the word is an alternative for *boneca*. Elias continues:

"These are the things you see here in Alto do Moura, actually, these *bonecas*. I have also made them, but what I most like to make are the traditional pieces, right?

"These *bonecas* were not created inside of Alto do Moura. This is something that came from outside. Someone saw it there and brought it to Alto do Moura, understand?

"And it spread because of the ease of production and the accessible price point. So then the business people — the owners of shops — sell these things that are cheaper, for sure.

"It's a question of commerce."

Elias pauses and returns to our question about the family:

"Now, my children, they make a bit, but I have four grandchildren, and they have nothing to do with the clay. They don't deal with it. Some try to paint, but they are making nothing.

"So, I see a future that — I don't know — seems a bit frightening. For sure, the name Vitalino will never die, right? But traditional art? I am not so sure."

4

Emanuela and Emanuel

One answer to the question of the future is now to be found in the Casa Museu Mestre Vitalino, where we began a dozen years earlier. When Severino was hospitalized, he put the museum in the hands of his youngest daughter, Emanuela, and his youngest son, Emanuel — Elias's youngest siblings. Severino was thinking strategically about the future.

We met Emanuela first and gave her photographs of her father that we had taken. She received them with a sweet, sad smile and said they would make her cry. Years before, we sent photos we had taken to Severino, and he arranged them within a proud, personal montage on the museum's wall.

In the corner of the museum's front room, where his father sat to work, Emanuel has positioned a table where he makes pieces like his father's. A couple of weeks later, after some friendly chats, we ask Emanuel to describe his work, and he drives straight into the *bonecas*:

"So, it is like this. I learned from the beginning by working with my father and with my mother, right? With my father Severino Vitalino, making the traditional small statues. But a tendency has arisen in the last twenty-five years that is the *bonecas*, right?

"It is made of clay, but it is a different kind of *artesanato*. It is not the *artesanato* that my grandfather created that depicts the scenes of the Northeastern quotidian. He is famous today in the entire world, my grandfather, Mestre Vitalino.

"But to tell the truth, due to financial difficulties, I started making these *bonecas*.

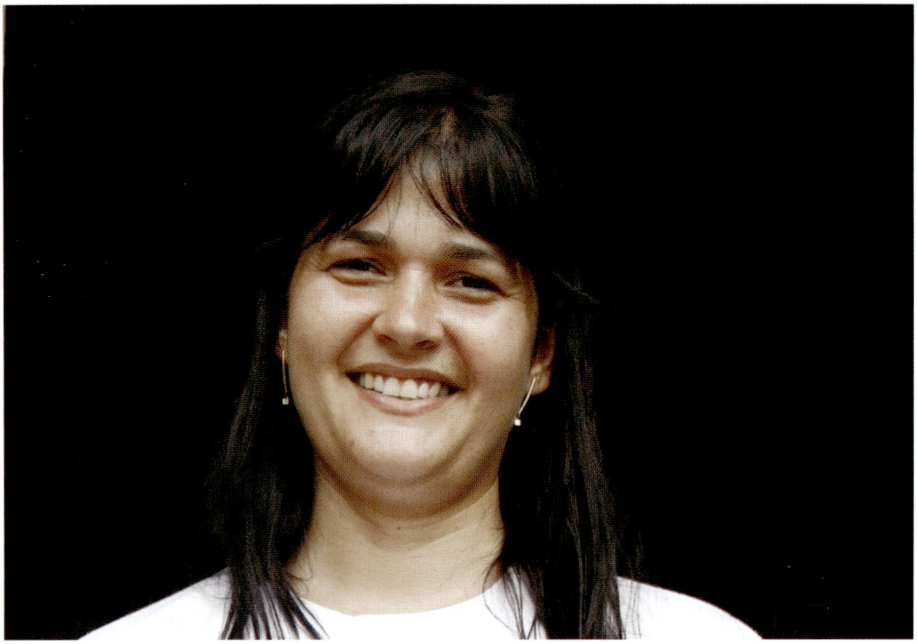

Emanuela, 2019

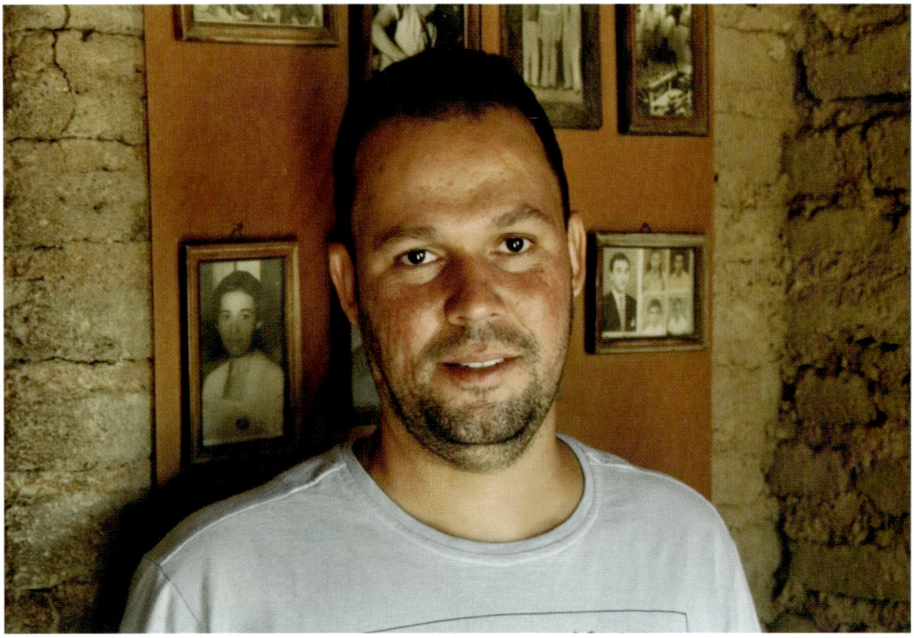

Emanuel, 2019

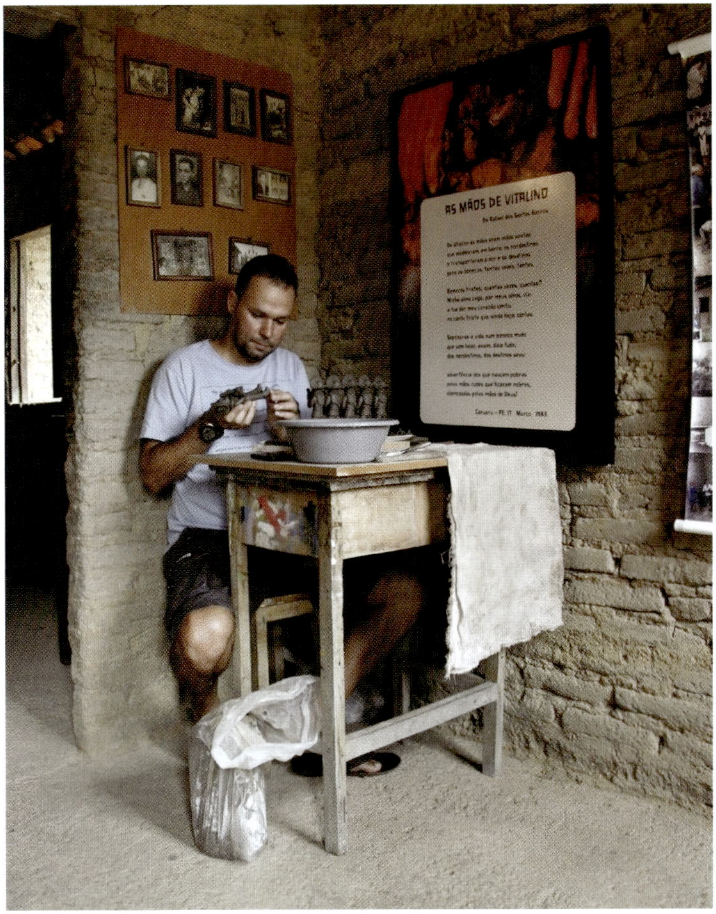

Emanuel working in the Casa Museu Mestre Vitalino, 2019

"But, before my father's passing, when he was still in the hospital, he chose me to assume his position in the Casa Museu Mestre Vitalino.

"So, now, I have returned to the traditional, and I am giving continuity to the art that my grandfather created.

"Now, I make the traditional small statues, those my grandfather used to make, and to keep this art alive for many and many years, right?

"But it is very well known, unfortunately, that to live from the art my grandfather created — the traditional art we call it — is very difficult.

"People like it very much, admire it very much, but the sales compared to this other kind of *artesanato* that is the *bonecas* are totally different.

"That is how it is.

"It is very hard, nowadays, to live by the traditional art, to tell the truth. But we must keep this art alive. We must be strong in the fight. Day to day, God willing, this art that my grandfather created, it will never die."

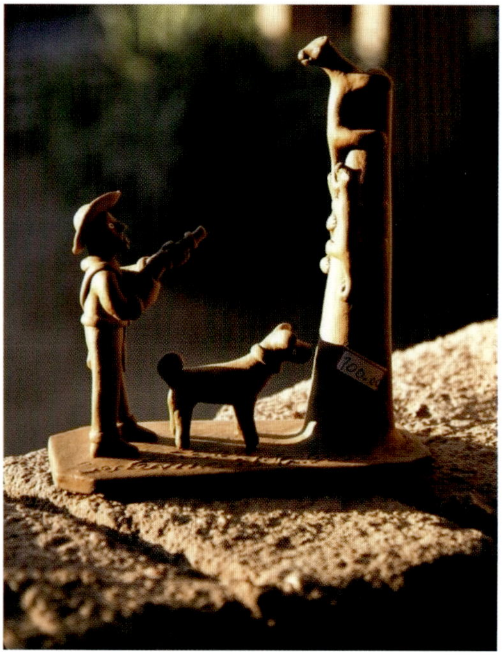
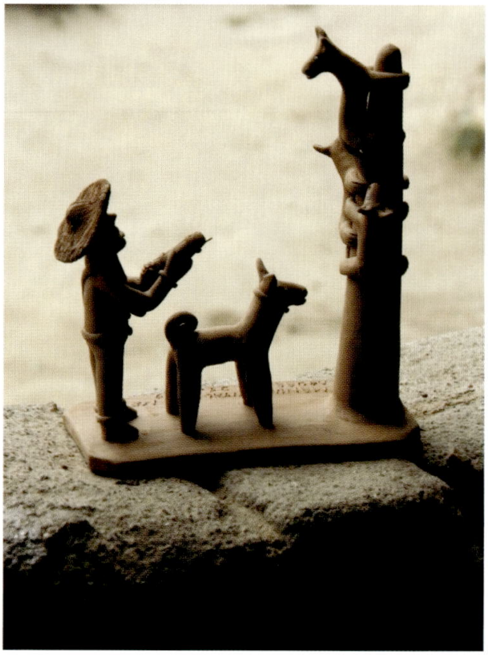

Hunters of Wildcats in the museum's window. Left: by Severino, 2015. Right: by Emanuel, 2019

By watching his father and trying his hand at small figures, then working beside his mother and crafting *bonecas*, Emanuel developed the skills that enabled him to return gracefully to traditional art. He is doing what he wants to do, and others might do the same. Times will change as they always have, and in the unlikely event of an upturn in the Brazilian economy, others whose skills were preserved by making the *bonecas* might join him in a general revival. Perhaps, as Emanuel hopes, the art will never die. You never know.

In the museum's front window where Severino's version of his father's first major piece, the hunter of wildcats, stood when we were first here, there is now a fine version of the same piece made by Emanuel. And other of Vitalino's classics, made by Emanuel, stand for sale on the shelves in the museum where Severino's once stood. Emanuel Rodrigues dos Santos signs his work Emanuel Vitalino Neto, Emanuel Vitalino's Grandson.

Impressed by the quality of his work, we ask Emanuel to expand on his learning, and he says:

"I was already making by childhood, right? I commenced with six, seven years of age, making little oxcarts, little donkeys, and such, small pieces.

"Then when my father went to the hospital, he chose me to stay here. Then I had to do what?

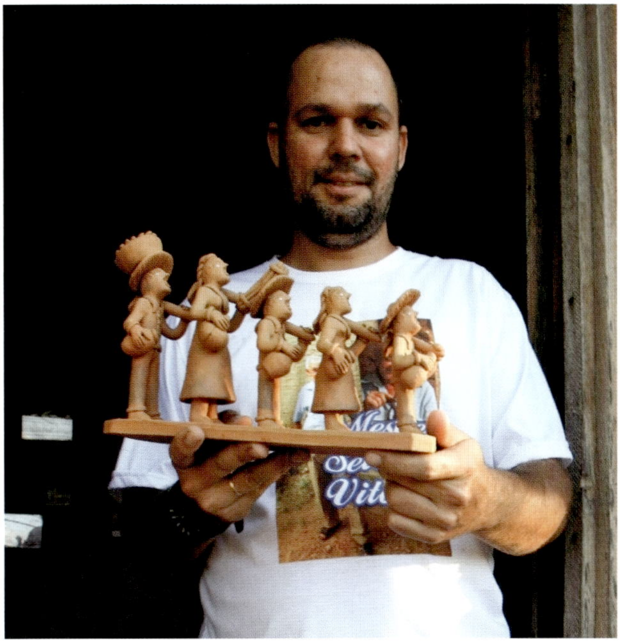

Emanuel with his version of *A Volta da Roça*,
Casa Museu Mestre Vitalino, 2021

"To give continuity to this art, right? I had to make small statues. It is like riding a bicycle, right? You learn, then you spend ten, twenty, thirty years without riding. Then you return to do it the same way as before. You are making again.

"And in this case, I am now giving sequence to the art. I try to make it in the way my father used to make.

"My father's importance is *very great*, right? My grandfather had six children, but the last one giving continuity to the art of my grandfather was my father, Severino Vitalino.

"My father was the last one giving sequence to the art, continuing the legacy of my grandfather. With much humility, the way he was, my father was affectionate with the visitors, with everyone, and during his entire career he worked on the trajectory of my grandfather's art, giving this continuity.

"So, since my father played this key role in continuity, it is what I am trying to do, making pieces in the way he used to make them, in the same style and size, unpainted.

"So, my work is similar to his, but each person has his own way of making, his own techniques. That is the case, right? At the maximum, we can come close to what he used to make, right? That is what I am trying to do.

"God willing, I will succeed."

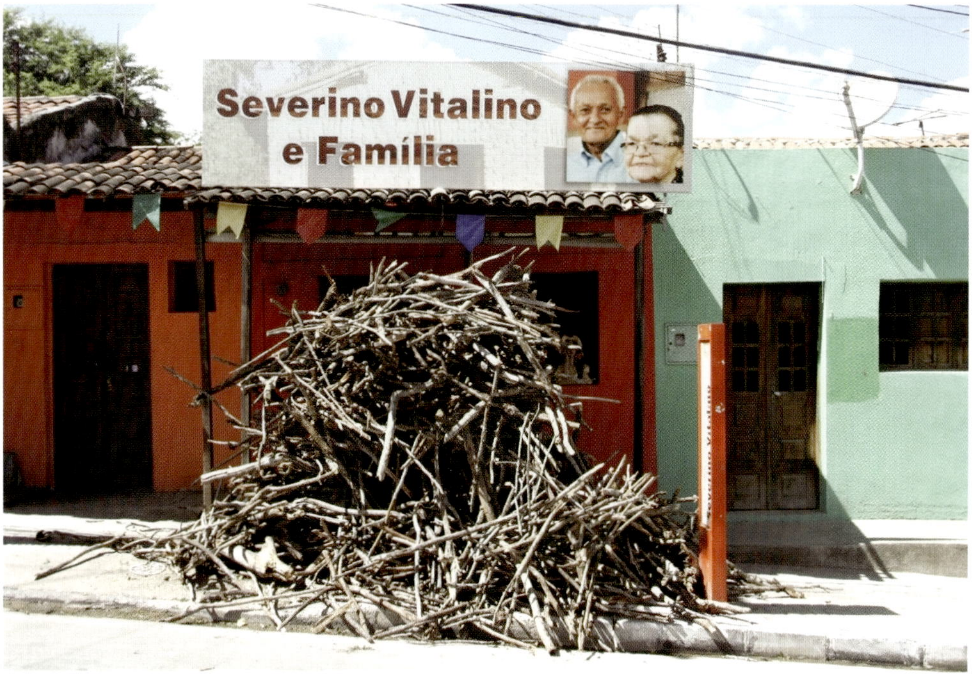

Severino Vitalino's old home and shop, 2019

As he spoke, Emanuel swung from himself to his father. Severino remains in the mind. During the month of May in 2019, when we got to know Elias, Emanuel, and Emanuela, when Severino's death was a constant topic among the artists and a picture of Severino and Dona Nina hung in front of their old home, the town of Alto do Moura was preparing for the *Festa Junina*, the June Festival.

June embraces the feast days for Saint Anthony, Saint Peter, and Saint John. They appear on a trio of colorful banners, sold in the market to hang in the home. Saint John's is the longest day, the festive high point, and the *Festa Junina* is usually and simply called *São João*. The month of June provides a time to celebrate the country culture of the Northeast. Alto do Moura is, like Caruaru, a center of the festivity. Visitors arrive in great numbers to drink, dance, and browse in the shops for handmade clay souvenirs, though they rarely venture down the long street of the artists where the work goes on as usual. The happy action happens up on the main street.

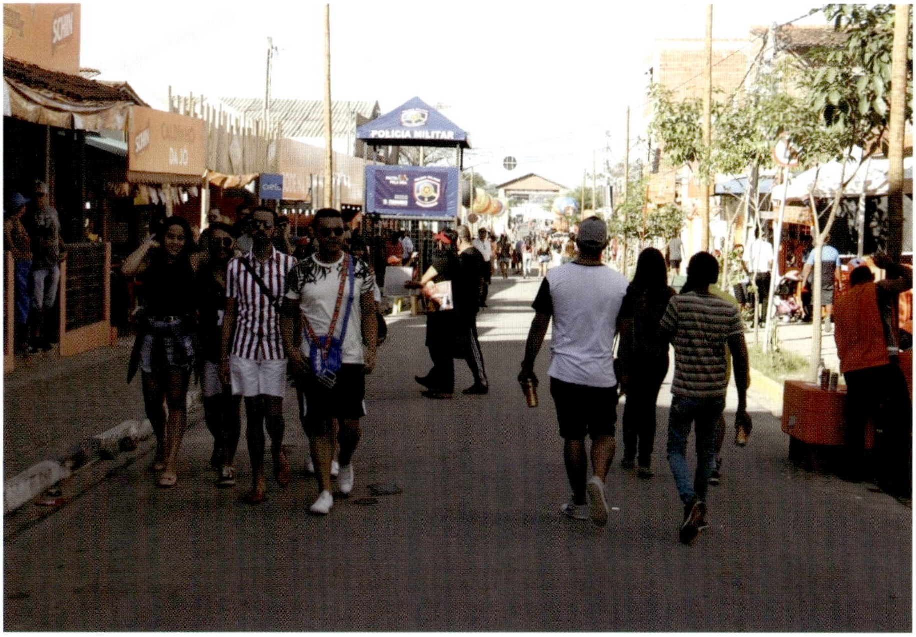

Alto do Moura's main street during the June Festival, 2019

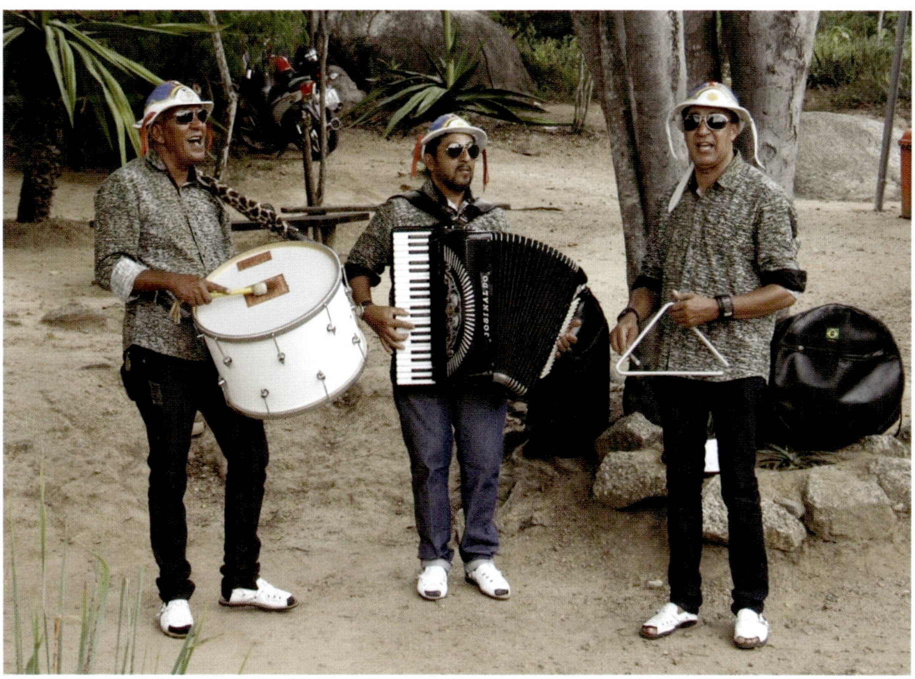

Northeastern trio (Trio Pé de Serra Gavião) performing at the
Casa Museu Mestre Vitalino, June 2019

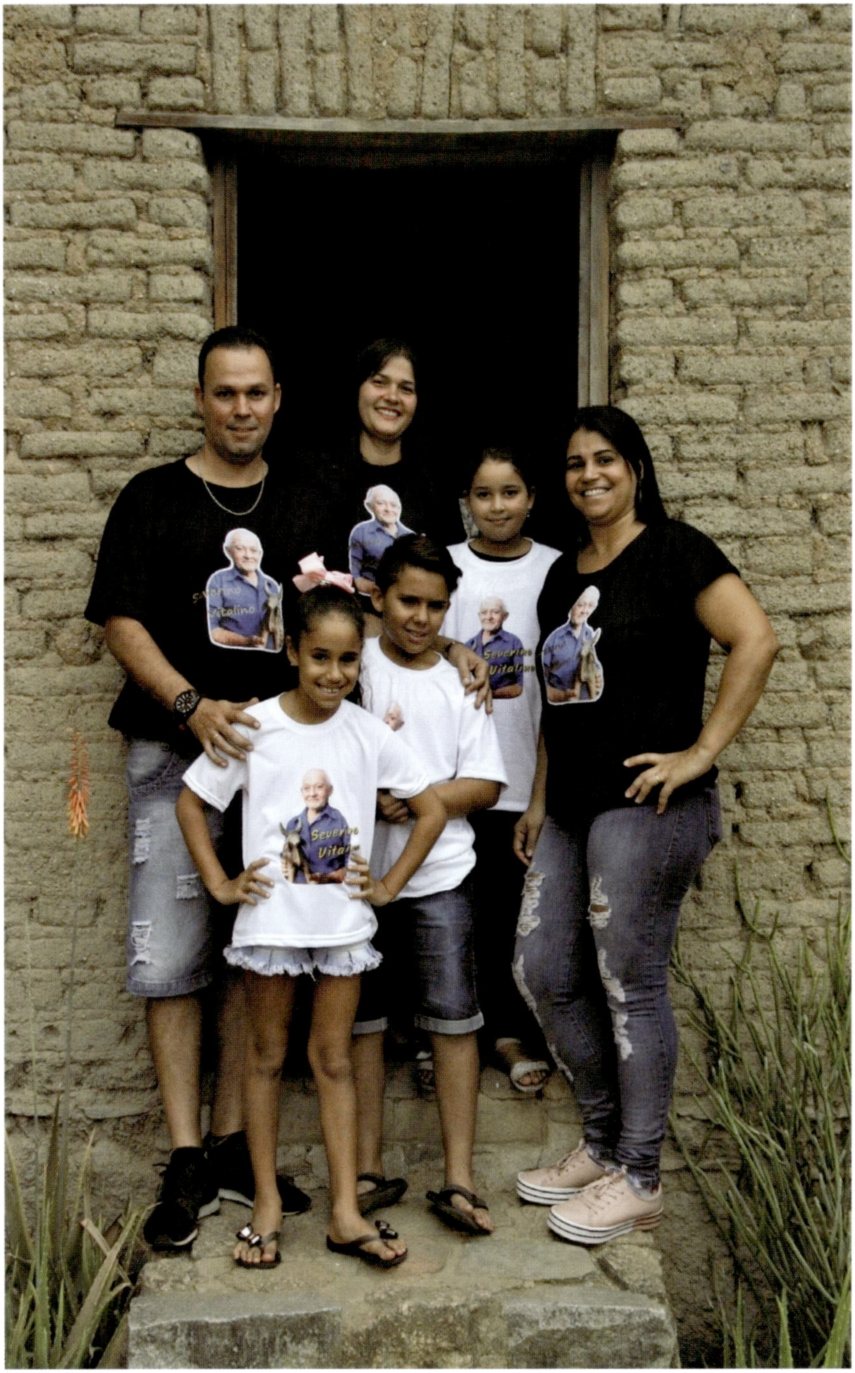

Emanuel and Emanuela, along with Emanuel's wife, Juciene, his daughter, Stephanie, his niece, Isabela, and nephew, Daniel — all wearing shirts printed with a portrait of Severino Vitalino during the June Festival in Alto do Moura, 2019.

On the opening day, the first of June, Northeastern trios — like those in clay: accordion, triangle, and drum — are performing Luiz Gonzaga's songs on a big stage to the east, on a street clogged with dancers to the west, in a shady bar, and on the dusty grounds around the Casa Museu Mestre Vitalino. There, Emanuel and Emanuela await visitors, wearing commemorative T-shirts with their father's portrait on the front. Alto do Moura's political leaders have dedicated this year's June Festival to the memory of Severino Vitalino.

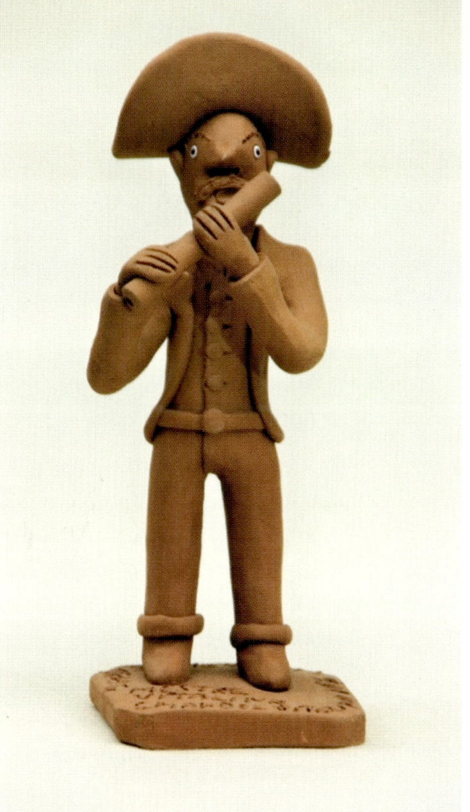

Mestre Vitalino, by Emanuel (20 cm tall), 2021

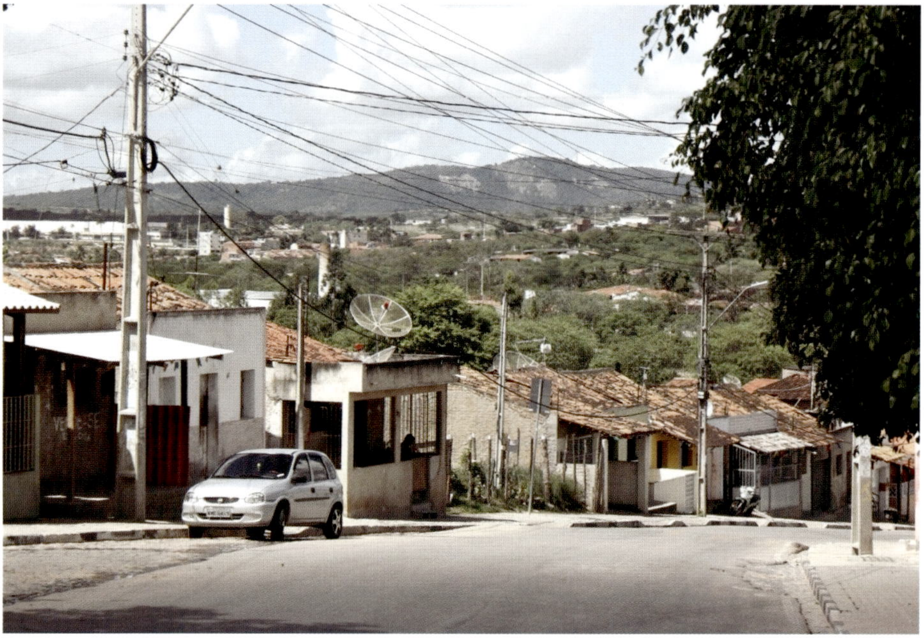

Alto do Moura's long street of the artists, looking southward, 2019

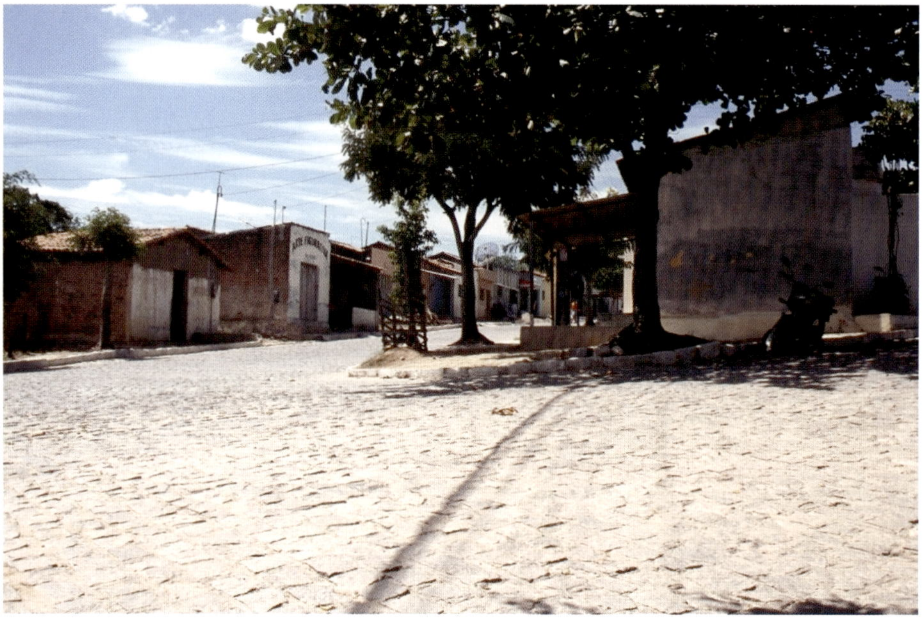

Alto do Moura's long street of the artists, looking northward, 2007

5

Vitalino Neto

On the street where the artists live, a handy convenience store meets the immediate needs of the people coming up or going down. Named for Mestre Vitalino, the shop is managed by Vitalino Pereira dos Santos Neto, called Vitalino Neto, and his wife Maria da Silva Santos. We are sitting in the shop's back room, the recorder is running, and Vitalino Neto, one of the master's grandsons, introduces himself, saying:

"I am the son of Manuel Vitalino, the second son of my grandfather Mestre Vitalino. I learned like the majority of people here, during my childhood, by observing the work of my parents.

"In my case it was *my mother*, because my father, in this period, was working in publicity, disseminating the name of Vitalino, and the *artesanato* of Alto do Moura, in the grand centers of the country. Which is very important work.

"During that period, he would go to Rio de Janeiro, and many other grand centers: São Paulo, Brasília, Belo Horizonte. And with all of this, who was working here every day, during my phase of learning, was my mother, Maria Santina.

"So, it was with her that I learned.

"It was like this. When you go back, when you travel to the generations long ago, then artists like us didn't exist.

"They were potters" — *louceiras* — "who made utilitarian ware. Who existed then were agricultural laborers and potters. It was not until my grandfather that the figurative *artesanato* came in.

"Her parents did not get to be artisans because when my grandfather commenced, they were adults. They took care of the fields and things like that. But

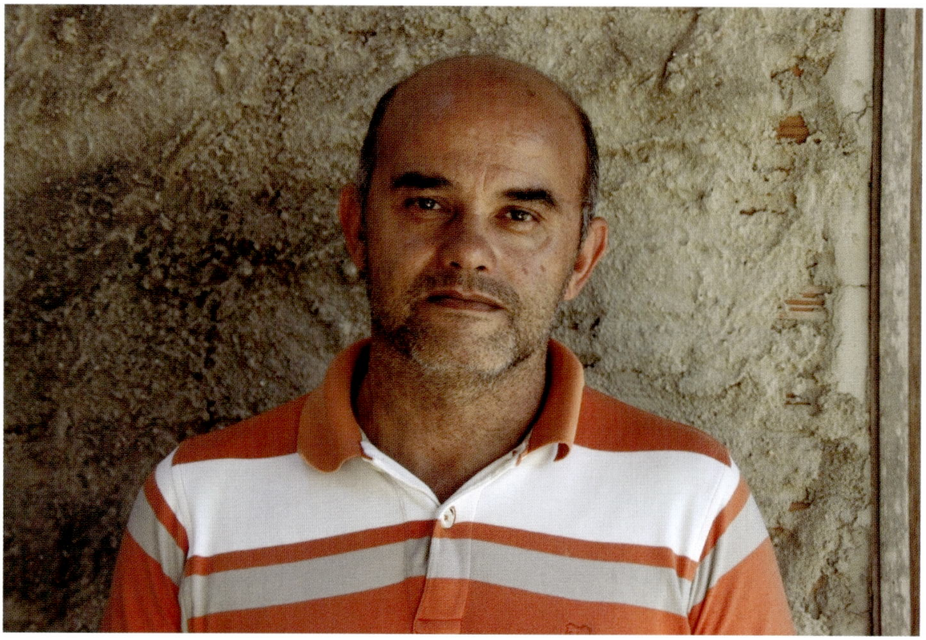

Vitalino Neto, 2019

since my mother was almost the same age as my father, she got to learn just as he did.

"So, she started; she was the first in her family and she was the one I learned from.

"And since my father traveled much, he would take my childhood works to Rio de Janeiro. He would sell them there and my mother's as well. That is what happened."

Mestre Vitalino was a wonder of creative originality, but he might have died in local obscurity had word of him not spread. Vitalino Neto speaks of the benefit provided by René Ribeiro's *Vitalino*, which was printed for the second time in 1972, a year after his birth, and he repeats that, during his childhood, his father, Manuel, traveled to open commercial channels between Alto do Moura and Brazil's big cities. As a young man, Vitalino Neto followed him:

"I spent twenty years on the road, right? I spent twenty years going to all the big cities, like my father did in the past.

"I worked in publicity for *artesanato*, participating in events, participating in fairs, participating in exhibitions, making connections with places to send merchandise."

When Vitalino Neto settled down and opened this shop, his idea was to sell his own work along with the art of others. One plan was to assemble matched sets of Vitalino's classics made by the artists of the second generation, Severino Vitalino and Manuel Eudócio.

"Right now," he says, "you are in my establishment that was for *artesanato*. This space had shelves with boxes of *artesanato* in stock, with works on display here.

"Sales were not good. Today I have to sell — it is only a convenience store, and we have to fight to have a little neighborhood market. Why? Is this a choice?

"No, it is not. It is a necessity. Because, as a result of different factors, the real *artesanato* does not bring us a living."

Learning beside his mother, Vitalino Neto mastered the style of his father and grandfather, but economic conditions have forced him to make lesser things:

"Look, today we have to attend to the demands of the market. I know how to make everything, but now I make what the store owners want, what they commission. I make what dovetails with certain market demands.

"Today we follow the market, precisely to be able to survive. To be an artisan in Brazil today is an adventure. To make a living from the traditional culture is an adventure.

"We had a great period when the culture was valorized. The things of the classical culture would sell easily because of the media, because it was supported by previous politicians, the politicians of two decades ago.

"It has always been an adventure. So, we always live by seeking niches in the market. What is the demand?

"So, I am making simple little pieces, small pieces really different from what my grandfather made. Because that is what people want.

"So, we ground ourselves in this today to have a base for our work. Now they are small things, the majority are miniatures. So this is what we do."

Market demands have forced Vitalino Neto to work in a third line of production that runs between the line of traditional art above and the line of the *bonecas* below. He makes miniatures, but he carefully distinguishes them from the miniatures made by his cousin Elias and those made by Zé Caboclo's fourth daughter, Marliete, who is today the most famous and successful artist in Alto do Moura. Their excellent miniatures are made, one by one, with patience and astonishing skill.

The miniatures of the third line borrow topics from traditional art, but they are swiftly made in big batches, maybe a hundred at a time, to fill a merchant's order, all exactly the same in size, all exactly the same in form. Unlike the creations of Elias and Marliete, they lack any sign of an individual's hand, eye, or mind. They are not, that is, art. Though handmade of clay, they might as well have been made by a machine, but they do bring some cash to skilled people in need, and, not void of regional reference, they are sold in shops as souvenirs at very low prices.

Vitalino Neto carries a local reputation as a critic, and he says his father was a critic before him. Communities of creators seem always to have a critic within who faults others for straying from tradition or for holding too tightly to tradition. Vitalino Neto is critical of the work he must do, but before he has finished describing it, he turns, with vim and venom, to the *bonecas*:

"Now in Alto do Moura there are trucks of *bonecas* — an area I will not enter. So, for me to continue making, publicizing, and fighting for the school of Vitalino, there is little left for me to do.

"The demand is very great for these *bonecas*. You can see various artisans, from day to night, wasting their lives in the production of these *bonecas* — I would say the factory-fabrication of these *bonecas*.

"Which is half necessary, half absurd.

"They are not genuine *artesanato*, but, finally, there is a great demand. The state of Bahia embraced the *bonecas*, and they say the *bonecas* are theirs.

"So, there are eight or ten trucks buying *bonecas* here to take there. So there is a great demand.

"Salvador" — the capital of Bahia, the vast state to the south — "is bigger than our capital here, so there is a big market there for the things made anonymously by people here.

"Look, the story here is that some people associated with interior design, with architecture, started sending images to one or two artisans here and they started commissioning copies: Look, make something like this. It was a thing for interior decoration.

"So, it opened a panorama in the minds of people here who were also inspired by what already existed here.

"So, they make a bust of the *namoradeira*" — the girlfriend, a half figure smiling in a window — "and the *namoradeira*, that one is from Minas Gerais. So, it already existed there. It is adapted here and it takes off, you know.

"The fashion is the *boneca!* The fashion is the *boneca!*

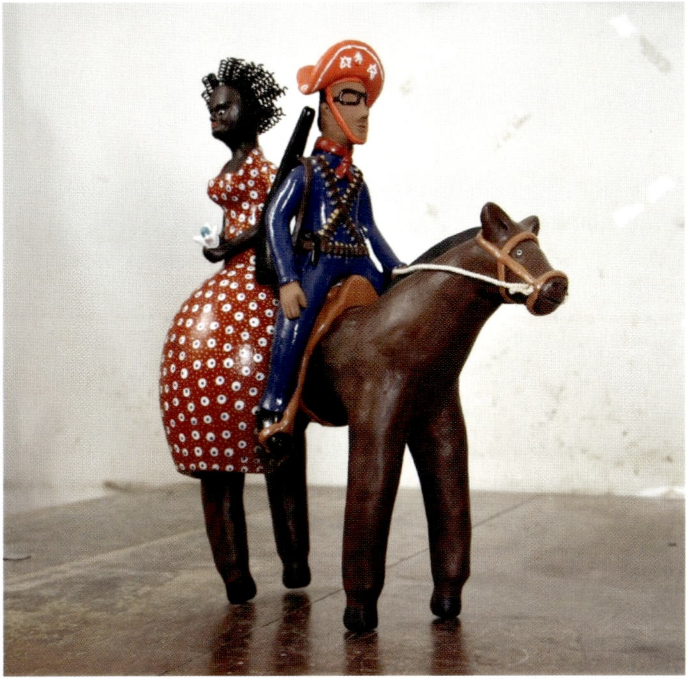

Adultério, by Vitalino Neto, 2019

"Then different types were being created. So, now here today, we make *bonecas* that portray the *artesanato* of Minas Gerais.

"Then many types of *bonecas* came. One is the *negra maluca*" — the wacky black lady with wire hair — "that mixes Bahia with Africa, so it is a miscegenation within the art of Alto do Moura.

"And it has *nothing* to do with the history of Vitalino. It is a school apart that doesn't have much history.

"The worst thing I think is this: it does not have much history.

"With these *bonecas* there is no identity. You go to Salvador and ask, Who made this? They say they did. But, no, it is from Pernambuco.

"The *bonecas* have no identity. They have no claim, they have no roots.

"They have no history."

Vitalino Neto shaped his critical opinion into a work of art that gained local fame. He only made it once, and it was so emphatically his that others have made no copies. He began with an unusual, though not rare, image of Lampião and Maria Bonita on horseback. The horse he shaped precisely in Vitalino's style, an insistent memory of the master. Then he replaced Maria Bonita with a *boneca*, the *negra maluca*, and titled it *Adultério*, Adultery, because Lampião has ridden away, abandoning Maria for another, just as the artisans of Alto do Moura have abandoned traditional art for *bonecas*.

Mestre Vitalino's direct descendants are the ones most concerned about continuity, most vexed by the *bonecas*. Continuity is a familial obligation; cash is a grim necessity. Severino, the last of the master's sons at work, narrowed the repertory to shape the classic pieces and improve their finish, while his wife and children were crafting *bonecas*. His oldest son and his youngest son, committed now to continuity, have also made *bonecas*, and his talented nephew is stuck in the production of cheap souvenirs.

When we ask, in 2019, how the tradition fares, Vitalino Neto answers:

"It is threatened I think, and it is going to decrease even more because access is restricted to the *artesanato* of quality. Who buys it are collectors, prosperous admirers, but the *artesanato* produced in mass, it has no identity, no history, and people buy it like they buy an industrial toy imported from China.

"So, I think it is threatened, it will decrease even more. It will not be swallowed up on one day. It will not be erased, but decrease, yes, it will decrease even more."

Then he turns to his family, telling us that Mestre Vitalino's first son, Amaro, is alive but impoverished and living in a public shelter. The second son, his father Manuel, is also alive but no longer making. Severino, the third son, has passed away and the fourth son, Antônio, has been dead for more than forty years. Of the sons, he says, Severino's work was close, but Manuel's work was even closer to his father's, so close that today it can't be visually distinguished from Vitalino's. It is well known that many works that bear Vitalino's stamp were, in fact, made by his sons. They all worked together.

That generation is gone, Vitalino Neto says, so it is fortunate that Mestre Vitalino was a generous man who taught artists beyond the family:

"Mestre Vitalino is totally incomparable in terms of publicity and influence on the ceramic art that exists.

"There are various masters today — Master One, Master Two, Master Three, but Mestre Vitalino is the only one. He is the top of the pyramid.

"The majority of those who are masters today, they learned directly from my grandfather.

"My grandfather would clear a little corner of his table, his stand at the market in Caruaru. Put your statues here, he would say.

"He would say, This here is a real artisan; he is just starting. Or, This is my friend, or It is my relative.

"So, they have a history. These guys have a history. We have respect for them. They have their own value.

"But Mestre Vitalino is incomparable. No one can go where he went.

"This is Mestre Vitalino. You see the name he has today, which he totally deserves.

"He was generous, with a generosity that, if it harmed him, he would still do it. But he never changed. He was always like that.

"I did not get to know him. I was born ten years after his death, but we have reports, we have stories, we have writing. Today is it very easy to have good information."

Mestre Vitalino, all agree, was as generous as he was creative, and when he moved to Alto do Moura in 1948, he befriended Manuel Eudócio and Zé Caboclo. They learned, his work changed, and Vitalino Neto provides the conclusion:

"The production in our family today is little. Uncle Severino was the last.

"In our family, many migrated to the *bonecas* because it was more financially beneficial. But Uncle Severino never made a *boneca* in his life. Today there is my cousin Elias, but in the Manuel Eudócio family there are more who make the traditional art.

"It is also like that with the family of Zé Caboclo. They are a group of people that the majority stayed with the tradition, with the school of Vitalino.

"The same thing happens with the family of Luiz Antônio. Some make *bonecas*, but Luiz Antônio is still there making the traditional *artesanato* he learned from my grandfather."

When the interview is over and the shop is silent, we ask, as we usually do, if there is something else he would like to say.

"I feel like I have already said too much," says Vitalino Neto.

Here at the end of one family's story, attending to the words and works of the creators, we have respectfully located our center for study in the most highly valued of a range of options for production. It is called *arte* more often than *artesanato* and qualified as traditional, more often than popular. It is topically more quotidian than sacred. It is culturally significant, not merely decorative, and more regionally significant than nationally significant. It is historically local, intensely local. It appears in distinct representational forms that are carefully and entirely made by hand, that are claimed by individuals with signatures. It is learned directly from acknowledged individual creators, more by observation than instruction, in an open process that simultaneously enables personal choice, social continuity, and collective identity.

Manuel Eudócio's family follows.

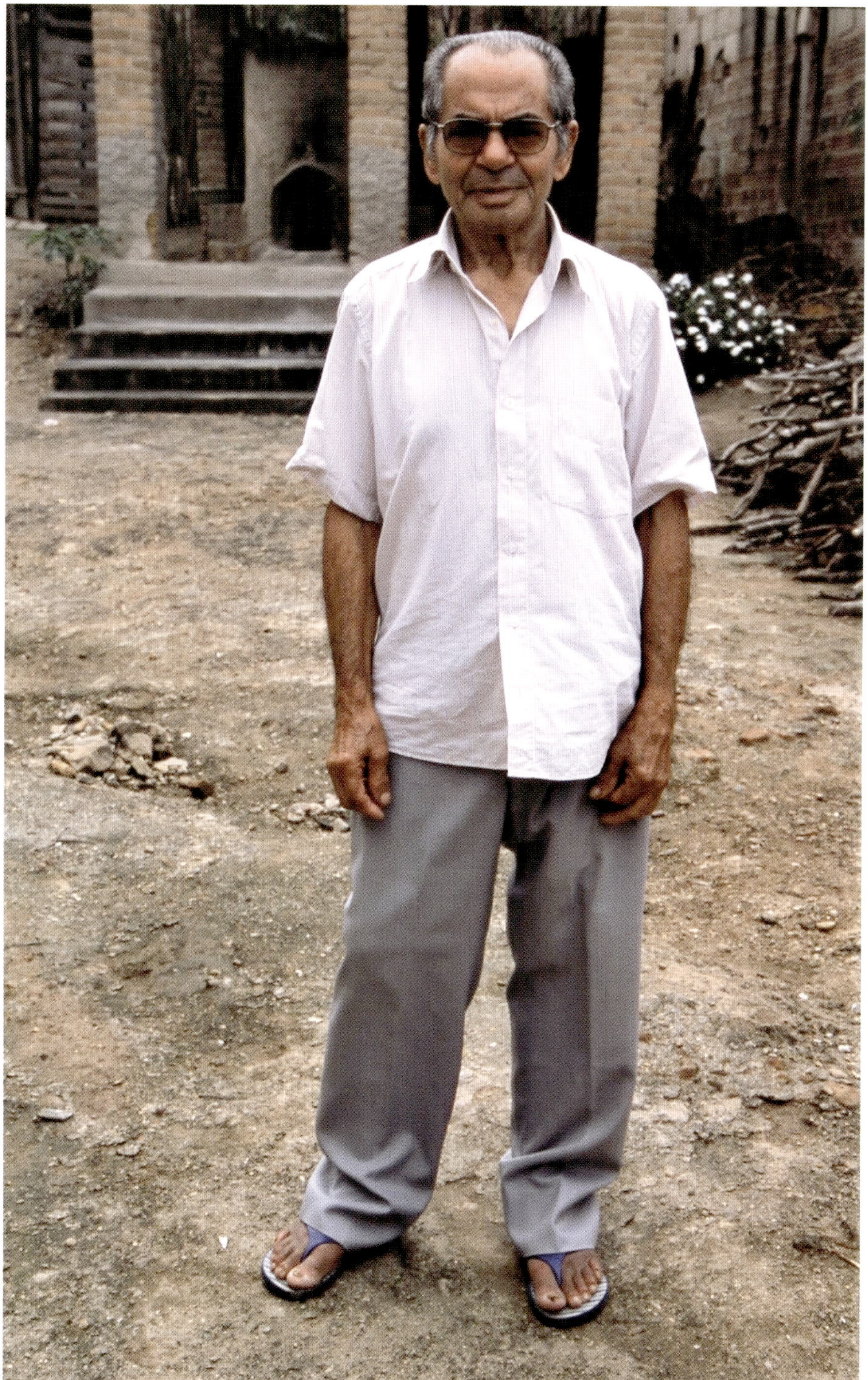

Manuel Eudócio, behind his shop, in front of his kilns, 2014

6

The Manuel Eudócio Family

Manuel Eudócio, his hands in perpetual motion, works at a table on the right, toward the back of his narrow and deep shop. Shelves along the wall on the left crowd with bright finished pieces. The back door opens on a garden where his kilns stand in a trim shed. The rackety street runs past his front door, descending toward the banks of the Ipojuca, the source of his clay.

His hands remained busy about their job — they love the clay — while he spread his story through long interviews in 2007, 2014, and 2015. The facts are scattered, but the outline is perfectly clear.

Manuel Eudócio Rodrigues was born on January 28, 1931. When he was three years old his mother died, and he was raised by his grandmother, Tereza Maria da Conceição. She was a potter, a *louceira*, who made useful vessels by hand and sold them, along with the painted clay toys she also made, at the big market in Caruaru. Manuel Eudócio, like Vitalino, was raised by a woman who worked in the clay, and, like Vitalino, he had clay in his hands from early childhood. He recalls:

"It was a time of serious poverty, here in Alto do Moura. My grandfather had died. My grandmother was a widow, and she sold the things she made in the market to buy groceries to feed the family.

"She carried the provisions on her head, because there was no transportation from the city to here. In that period there was no transportation.

"She made little animals to sell in the market. In the beginning, I learned from my grandmother to make little horses, little bulls. With eight years of age, I was already making things to sell.

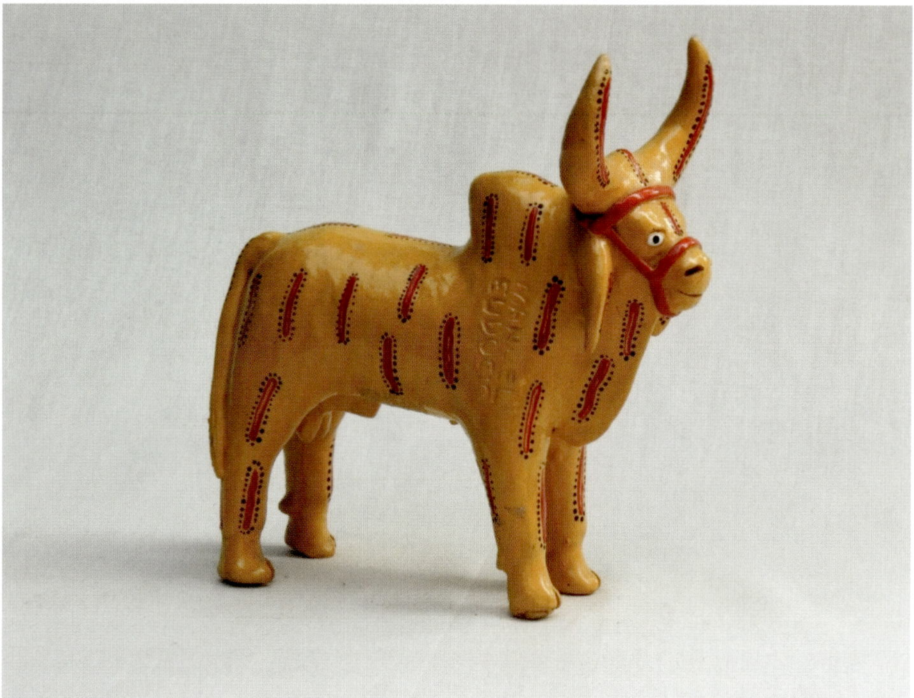

Painted bull by Manuel Eudócio, c. 2005

"I was a child, eight years old. I would go to school, and at noon I would eat lunch, and then sit on the floor because it was my time to work. And I worked until five in the afternoon.

"I would make little horses, little bulls — to sell in the market, to help my father. He was a farmer. He had nothing in this life."

Manuel Eudócio's works are exactingly painted in strong colors. So are those of his sons who live on the street near him, Luiz Carlos and Ademilson. The contrast is clear with the late works of Vitalino, and the works of his son Severino, which were left natural. The families were rooted in the same earth, but they branched differently. Manuel Eudócio says:

"My grandmother painted everything, using all the colors, red, blue, yellow. She prepared the paint herself, melting resin in fire, coal fire. Then she mixed it, put in the powders, and got her colors.

"So, when I was eight years old, I made little horses, little bulls, and I painted them with my finger, using my hand.

"So, I started painting the statues."

The first pieces Manuel Eudócio sold in the market were painted, but four years later — when he was twelve, let's say — he began leaving them natural, and he found that they sold well. Then:

"After a period of only taking natural pieces with no painting whatsoever, Doutor Xavier came to the market. He had a shop in Recife.

"He said, I am going to give you a dozen little cans of paint, one-hundred-gram little cans. He gave me twelve little cans of paint.

"Paint these pieces for me, he said. Enough Doutor, I said. I don't paint anymore. The smell of the paint was very strong. I did not want to paint any more pieces.

"No. You paint these pieces for me. Don't paint for anyone else. So, he was a very good customer. He used to buy much. So, I painted.

"The people, they found it beautiful. So, I have painted until today."

In fact, Manuel Eudócio's wife, Maria Luzinete Rodrigues, painted his works, but she passed in 2006, and, he says, "who paints today is my daughter, Elisoneide.

"She paints all the pieces. I tell her, Look, paint this like this. But the colors, she is the one who does it, who paints it.

"For example, in the wedding couple, I tell her, Paint the bride white, the groom blue, and the horse a tone of brown. The rest she decides.

"She does it. All of it is her. She already knows."

One aspect of Manuel Eudócio's style is set. His pieces are painted. Now his story gathers toward the moment when Manuel Eudócio and his friend Zé Caboclo began working with Mestre Vitalino, the moment when, Vitalino Neto said, Manuel Eudócio and Zé Caboclo introduced little balls of clay to make better eyes for the figures, when the bodies of the figures generally improved, and the formal aspect of Alto do Moura's current artistic style was set. To understand what it was like in that moment of convergence, it is helpful to know that in 1948, Vitalino was not yet forty, Zé Caboclo was twenty-seven, Manuel Eudócio was seventeen, and Severino Vitalino was eight, and it is important to know that before Vitalino moved to Alto do Moura, Manuel Eudócio, with eight years of work in the clay behind him, had already encountered Vitalino's creations at the market in Caruaru:

"With eight years of age I was already making, because my grandmother worked with little toys. And I didn't even know who Vitalino was in that period. That's it.

"Then when I was about sixteen years old, I used to go to the market" — the Feira de Caruaru — "then I saw his statues at the market.

"Then I said to my grandmother, Mother — I called her Mother because she raised me — Mother, when I get home, I'm going to see if I can make one of these statues.

"She responded in this way: Don't make it, my son. This is very difficult. Who makes it is Vitalino.

"But, for the next market, I started to work to see if I could make it.

"I worked *alone*, and I learned in this way. From my own head."

At the time, Vitalino still lived in Sítio Campos, and when Manuel Eudócio took fifteen pieces, inspired by Vitalino's work, to the market in Caruaru, he met Vitalino who was sitting at a table with his works arrayed for sale:

"So, I said to him, Can I put these pieces here, near yours? He said, Put it. Put it, Manuel Eudócio!

"So, I put my pieces there. I left there fifteen pieces. Now, they were small pieces. It was not many things. Farm-related themes.

"I made — I remember that I made — an old farmer with a bundle of sticks on his head. I made a *rendeira*" — a woman making lace — "and I made a priest taking confession from a woman, and a chicken thief, because in this time there was much stealing of chickens.

"I made a thief, a thief stealing chickens. I made another thief being taken away by the police.

"So, these were the first pieces of the kind that I made."

All were lifted from Mestre Vitalino's repertory, and Manuel Eudócio continues, saying:

"So, when I arrived there, Was it you?, he said. It was, Mister Vitalino, it was me who made it. Put it here, he said. Put it here.

"When a gentleman arrived, he said to Vitalino, Vitalino, are these little pieces yours?

"Then he said, No, they are by my disciple" — my apprentice — "Manuel Eudócio.

"Just like that, my disciple.

"So, he says, Was it you, boy, who made these?

"It was. It was I who made it.

"Are these the first ones that you made?

"They are.

"I am going to buy the little statues of his, because he will be a master like you, Vitalino. Teach him.

"Don't worry about it. I will teach him.

"But I never went there. I never went to Vitalino's house to learn. I learned because when God gives you a *dom*, for work, for anything, there is no need to ask anyone for an explanation. You know it from inside."

When Mestre Vitalino moved to Alto do Moura, he lived nearby, but Manuel Eudócio, a teenager then, was reluctant to visit: "I thought I better not go there, because he would say, I don't want any boys around here; it would disrupt my work."

From his grandmother, Manuel Eudócio learned everything about the clay, about its varieties and processing, and he gained all he needed to know about form by looking at Mestre Vitalino's pieces and trusting the *dom* within. His relationship with Vitalino involved learning but no teaching, and it tightened when Manuel Eudócio set his table for sales next to Vitalino's in the market. They had time galore to talk and a deep friendship developed.

Side by side they sat to sell, and Manuel Eudócio recalls the time, early on, when his works, being fine in finish and painted, were a "novelty" and they sold quicker than Mestre Vitalino's:

"There were times when Mister Vitalino would sell nothing in the market.

"He would say, Well, Manuel Eudócio, do you have a bit of money there?

"I do, Mister Vitalino.

"Will you set me up so I can do my shopping, since I didn't sell anything. Look, when some money falls on me, I will pay you back.

"That's not necessary. Take the money.

"Then when he got some money: So here's your money.

"That is how it was."

There were times, too, plenty of them, when no one had any money. Manuel Eudócio says:

"It is my life to work with art, but I also worked with agriculture.

"Sometimes in the winter period, sales for art would get really weak. Then Vitalino, Zé Caboclo, and I would get a little plot to plant corn, beans. We planted manioc — to make flour."

They sold the plot's produce, the yield of their sweat in the soil, to see them through the hungry days. Then, for art, they had their best sales after Christmas in the hot summer month of January. (Alto do Moura lies south of the Equator. It is always hot, but hottest in January, coolest in June.) Manuel Eudócio remembers:

"We sold much, but we only sold our art in the market at Caruaru; it was the only place we sold.

"If customers come to your house — great. If not, then in the market. Back then, no one came to the house to buy.

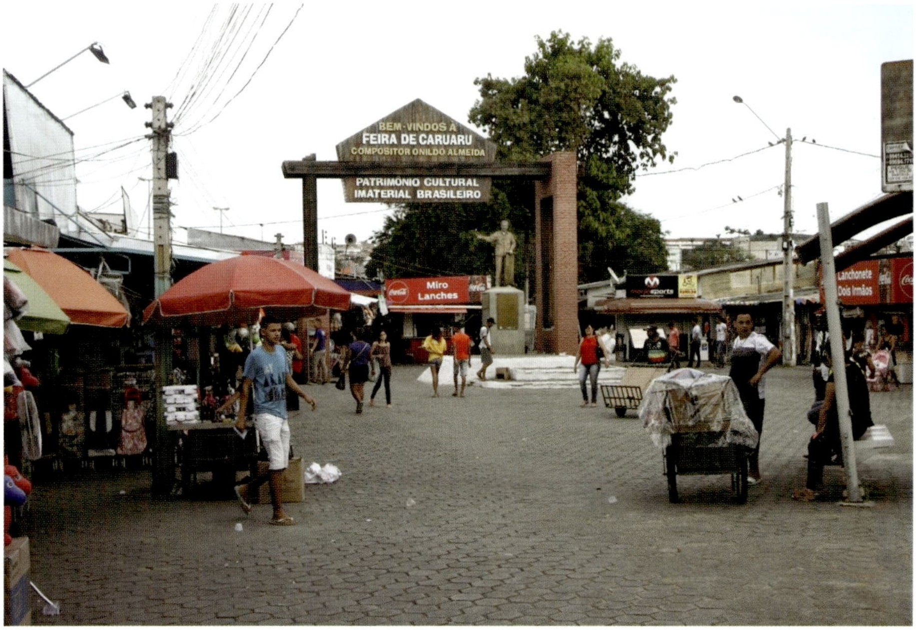

Entrance to the Feira de Caruaru, 2019

"Today, no, it is all at the house. No one goes to the market anymore. Neither the artisans nor the masters sell at the market anymore. Now, it is all sold from the house."

When they sat side by side to sell, the Feira de Caruaru was located by the grand church of Nossa Senhora da Conceição. Then it was shifted within the city to spread in orderly, sheltered rows beside the Ipojuca. No artists sit there at tables to sell, but retailers do offer works in clay made in Alto do Moura, predominately, but not exclusively, from the second and third lines of production. A similar mix is found in the stock of the retail outlets on the main street of Alto do Moura. It is, though, surely the case that today the most splendid pieces are sold out of the workshops attached to the houses of the artists.

With early success, in 1953, Manuel Eudócio bought a house in Caruaru, thinking it would be convenient for trade in the market, but times were changing, his reputation was growing, and customers, intending to buy, traveled to Alto do Moura, only to be told that he had left. He realized that he was "losing, losing" and he was determined to return. His wife was horrified, saying she would rather drink poison than go back to Alto do Moura. Her concern

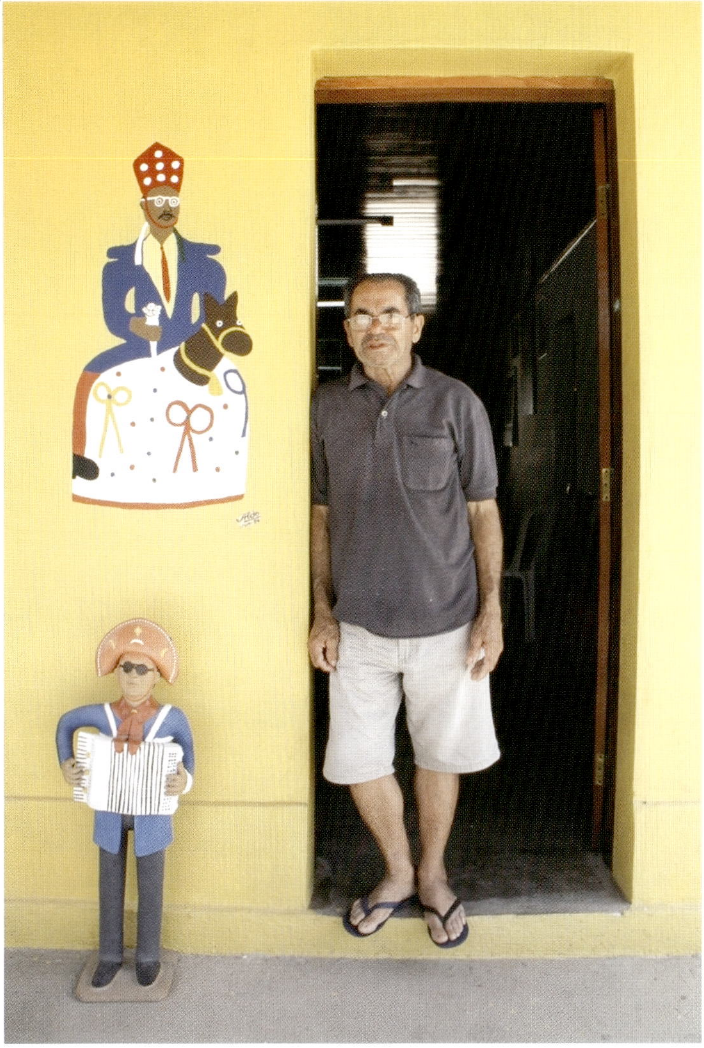

Manuel Eudócio in front of his shop, Alto do Moura, 2007

was her children's education since Alto do Moura had only a primary school. Manuel Eudócio promised that when he returned he would buy a car to take his children to the city, early every morning, so they could attend high school. He did as he promised, and his children are grateful to him for the education they got in the city, which had nothing to do with art, but much to do with managing a profitable business. Artists must be savvy about commerce. So, after seven months in the city, Manuel Eudócio returned, built a kiln, set up a shop next to his house, and prospered. The people who take the trouble to find their way there, always buy. No merchant takes a cut. As Manuel Eudócio said, art is best sold directly from the house.

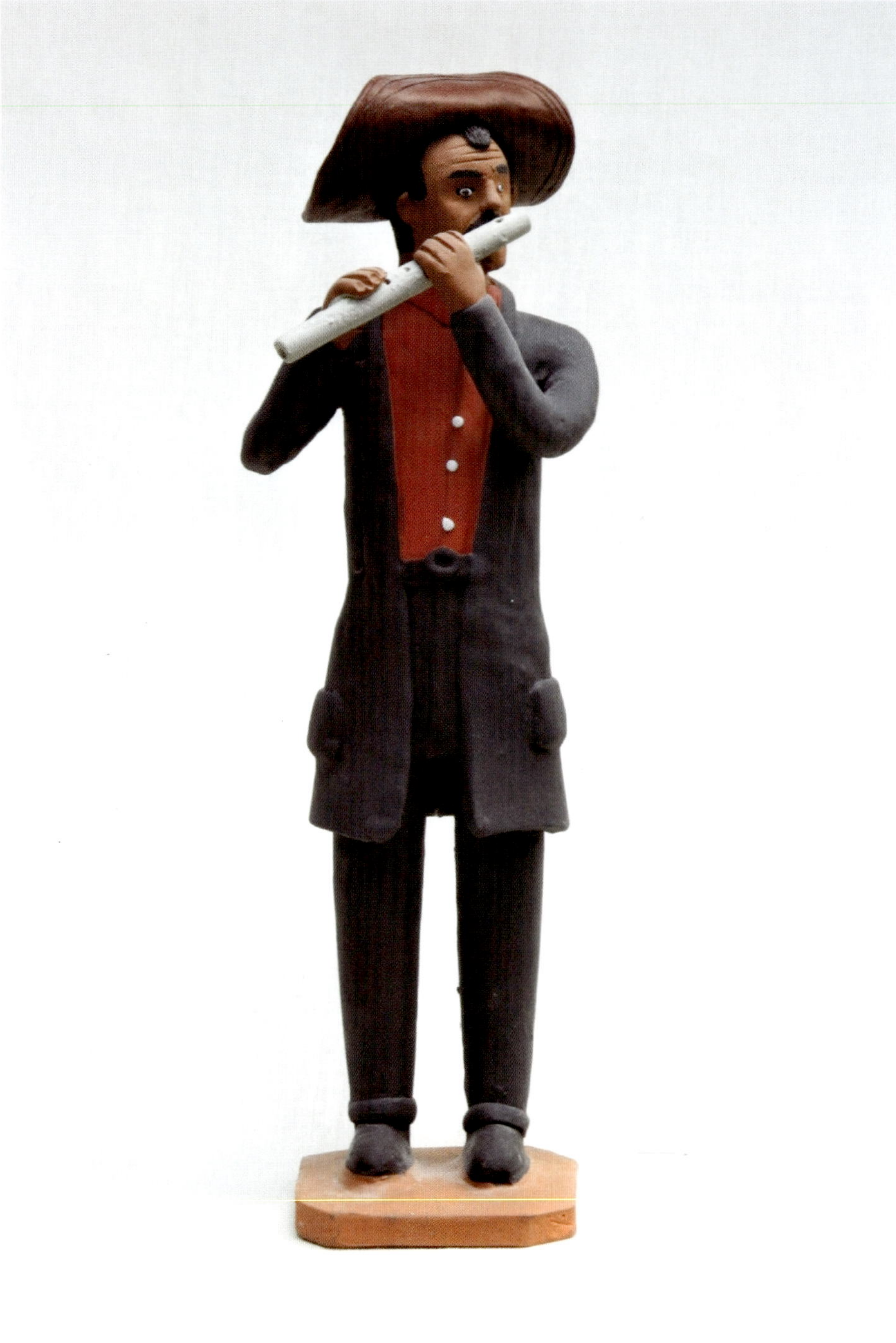

Mestre Vitalino, by Manuel Eudócio (34 cm tall), 2007

Now Manuel Eudócio is set successfully in place and his story settles on his friendship with Mestre Vitalino:

"This is how it was. There was none of this jealousy. Some people are jealous of others. He and I were loyal friends, really friends.

"He was a fine person. And his children, I like all of them. They all like me. It is like that.

"We were really tight friends, he and I. We used to talk much together in the market.

"And we traveled to São Paulo, we traveled to Rio de Janeiro, he and I. We traveled for exhibitions."

They traveled together, sometimes along with Zé Caboclo and Severino Vitalino. Travel was exciting: the flight on the airplane, the reporters, photographers, and crowds on arrival. But they ran slam into troubles too. Honest men from the back country, they were easy marks for tricky urban merchants.

On their first trip to São Paulo, sponsored by a Brazilian airline, the businessman who invited them took custody of all the works they had brought to sell. Then when Mestre Vitalino and Manuel Eudócio were demonstrating their art, he sold all their pieces at shockingly inflated prices, claiming he had bought them in Recife. He gave the artists nothing. It was a scandal. They were left without a *centavo* in their pockets, and were it not for a chance encounter with a kind man who gave them a ride home, Manuel Eudócio says with a laugh, "We would still be standing in the streets of São Paulo."

Commerce was one problem. Another was Mestre Vitalino's taste for *cachaça*, a rough rural rum, close in clarity and flavor to moonshine, the white lightning of the back country in the southern United States.

Despite his great fame, Manuel Eudócio says, Mestre Vitalino suffered, his life was hard, and he escaped his pain in drink and gambling:

"The money he earned, whatever was left after he bought the groceries, he lost it all in gambling. We invited him, and every time he came to our house, he would enter and talk too much, crazy with drink.

"He drank much and gambled much. I thank God that I have all my things in order, because I never drank, gambled, or wasted my money.

"I was just with my children, my wife, my house, organizing everything."

Manuel Eudócio recalls an early trip — "when Vitalino was going to travel, and he wanted his sons to go with him. They did not want to go, not the oldest ones, not Amaro, not Mané. Severino was still small.

"The boys would say, You are going to get drunk. You will embarrass us. We are not going.

"He came to my house and talked with me. Do you want to go with me?

"I will go, Mister Vitalino, if you don't drink.

"I promise you I won't drink.

"Mister Vitalino, we will drink a little glass of *guaraná*" — a soft drink, something like ginger ale — "it is nothing, no alcohol.

"He said, I don't want it. If I drink it in a cup, it will remind me of the little white one" — *cachaça* — "so I won't drink it. I will only drink coffee and water.

"We spent thirty days traveling, and when we got back, he said to my wife, Manuel Eudócio is mine! Where I go, he will come with me.

"He was a fine person. He was."

Without a pause, Manuel Eudócio goes on to the end:

"He died without a doctor. He got sick and spent *thirteen* days in bed, with so much fever.

"Today they call it variola. In that time they called it smallpox.

"It exploded; the smallpox was so strong that they used banana leaves to lie down on, because, with the boils of pus, they could not bear to lie on a bed.

"But he refused to be vaccinated. That is how he was. He never took injections of any kind. I was vaccinated at six years of age, but he did not allow his children to be vaccinated. All of them took the disease, but they lived. He got the disease; it seized him and killed him.

"The smallpox started to leave, but it remained and killed the man.

"Dona Joaninha, his wife, and the children, they were taken to the doctor.

"Dona Joaninha" — the doctor said — "Vitalino is in a desperate situation. He might get better. They gave him tea to drink, but he got worse. They went in search of a doctor.

"And when the doctor came, he would not accept the vaccine, and he was not talking anymore. He was already in a state of coma.

"Frei André, the missionary, he is the one who came. The priests, the ones who should come, did not come, because they were afraid to catch the smallpox.

"So, Frei André came, but he could not talk anymore. He made no confession because he could not talk anymore.

"That is how he died.

"He used to say like this to me: Vitalino is one who knows when he is going to die. You will come, don't worry, and you will go. That's what he used to say.

"And what he said would happen is what happened.

"When he was about to die, José Lyrio Filho, the mayor, raised the money for the funeral, for the coffin and a car to carry the body.

"But it was such a day — it was the twentieth of January — it was such a day of tremendous rain.

"The rain was so heavy that none of his students, as he called them, were able to go, because they couldn't.

"The car took him alone to the cemetery.

"It was on the twentieth of January in sixty-three that he died.

"We had a trip planned to go to New York, to get to know the city there. We were about to get our passports, but then he got sick and died on the twentieth of January.

"So, I didn't go. I was not going to go alone.

"And he died like that."

One biographical arc, from his grandmother's instruction to his mentor's death, is complete. It was, though, only one of our topics for talk.

Manuel Eudócio's Repertory

Manuel Eudócio is a master, his works are art. His repertory, he says, is unified by a quality that he calls creativity and clarifies by contrast with the *bonecas*:

"I don't stay with only one thing. There are people who do only one thing. These *bonecas* with wire hair, they make many of them.

"There are hundreds of people who work only on that *boneca*, here in Alto do Moura. But not me. I never made one. I never wanted to make one. It is not original; it is not from the person's head.

"The store owners have them make the body on the wheel. The face is made with a mold. All you have to do is make the arms and the details of the clothing. It is easy, right?

"But to *create*, it is difficult. To be able to invent and then create with your hands, it is difficult. You really have to be a master."

Creation, that is, involves shaping an idea in the head and then realizing it in the world's materials. The resultant work is "original," not in the sense of new and unique, but because it emerges from within the creator's complete and personal command, then endures as an authentic sign of the self.

Now Manuel Eudócio refines his concept in contrast with the things made in the third line of production, the line of the souvenir, when he says that he will, reluctantly, make two or three similar pieces on commission, but he firmly refuses to make large numbers of pieces, all exactly the same: "I don't like to make duplicate pieces. What I like is to *create*. Creativity is what I like." He makes his pieces one by one, entirely by hand, in intense concentration, so the works arranged for sale on the shelves in his shop are all, every one of them, different. They display his creative scope. He duplicates a piece only after one like it has been sold, so the new one will fill a void in the exhibition of his complete repertory.

Unified by creativity, Manuel Eudócio's repertory is also unified, he says, by representational intent:

"It is something Northeastern. It represents the entire country. The pieces have value because they represent something that is Northeastern, something made by hand, something folkloristic.

"They represent many things about Brazil, about the Northeast. They acquire a value like nothing else."

His repertory divides thematically, and within the theme of rural life Manuel Eudócio estimates that he makes about half the number of particular pieces that Mestre Vitalino made before him. He makes bulls, oxcarts, and flour mills. He makes women nursing babies, making lace, making bread, ironing clothes, feeding chickens, selling produce in the market. He makes men carrying wood, getting a shave, stealing chickens, arrested by the police, snatched by the Devil. He makes couples getting married and newlyweds sitting, standing, and riding a horse together.

He makes both of the masterworks of the rural theme, both with six figures in a tight line: *A Volta da Roça*, Return from the Field, which he sometimes reduces to two figures, husband and wife, and *Os Retirantes*, The Exiles, which he explains like this:

"The *Retirantes* represent the drought here in the Northeast. People would leave, removed to a place where they could live. Because in that time, when there was a drought, people here would die of hunger.

"They would leave, the entire family, and go to a little corner where there was rain, so they could work and earn some money."

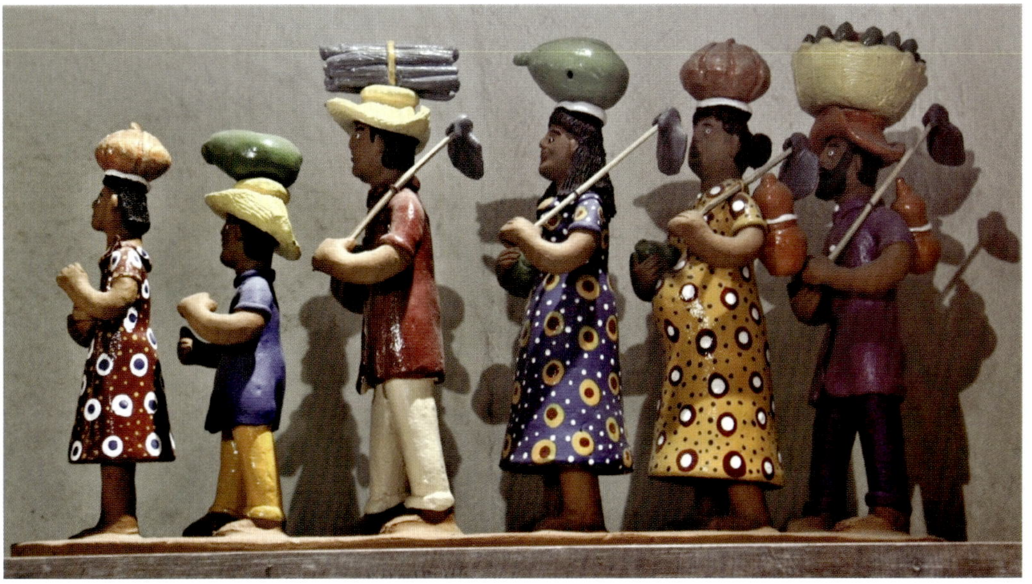

A Volta da Roça, Return from the Field, by Manuel Eudócio, c. 2014

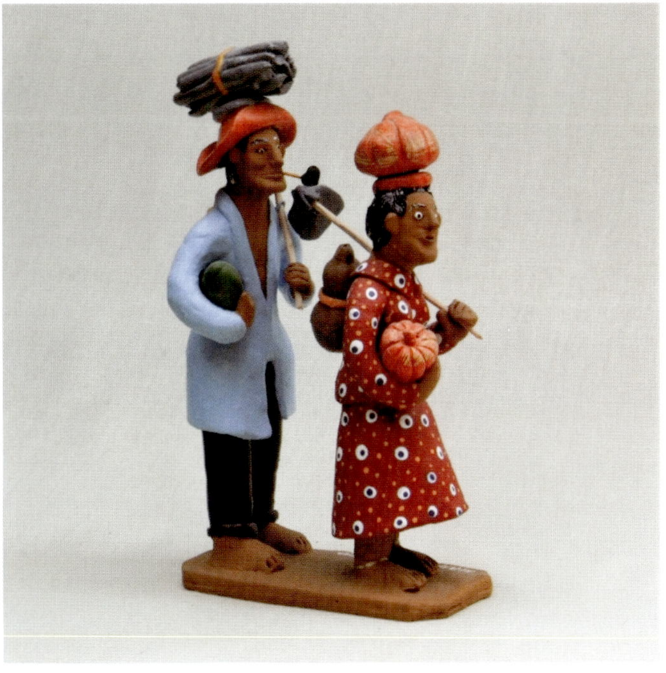

Return from the Field,
by Manuel Eudócio
(23 cm tall), 2015

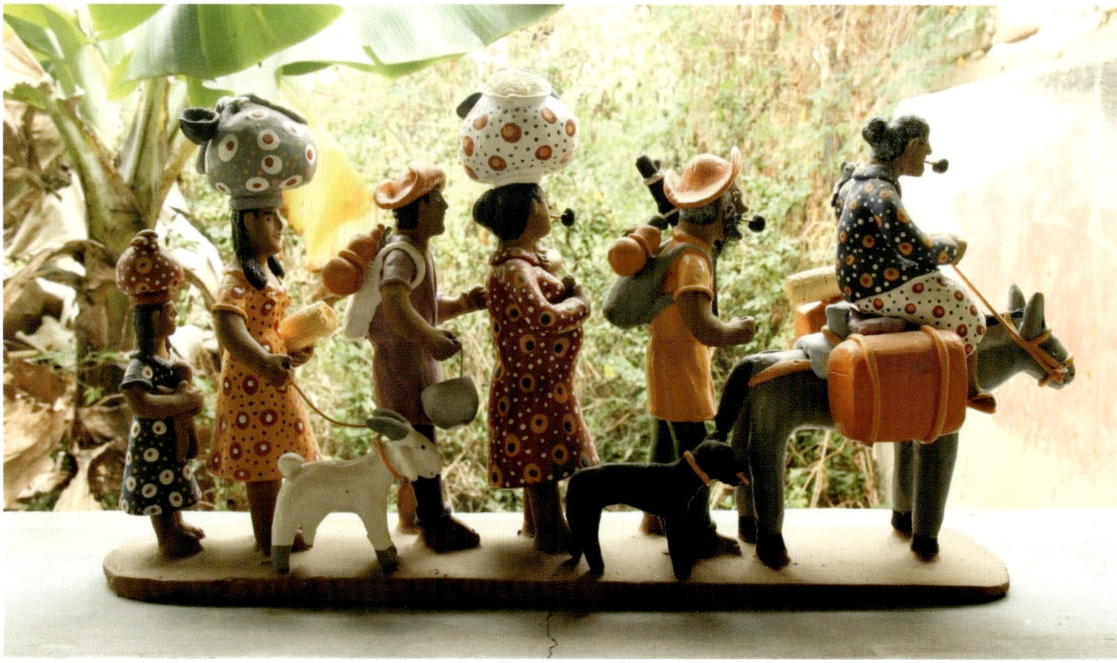

Os Retirantes, by Manuel Eudócio, c. 2014

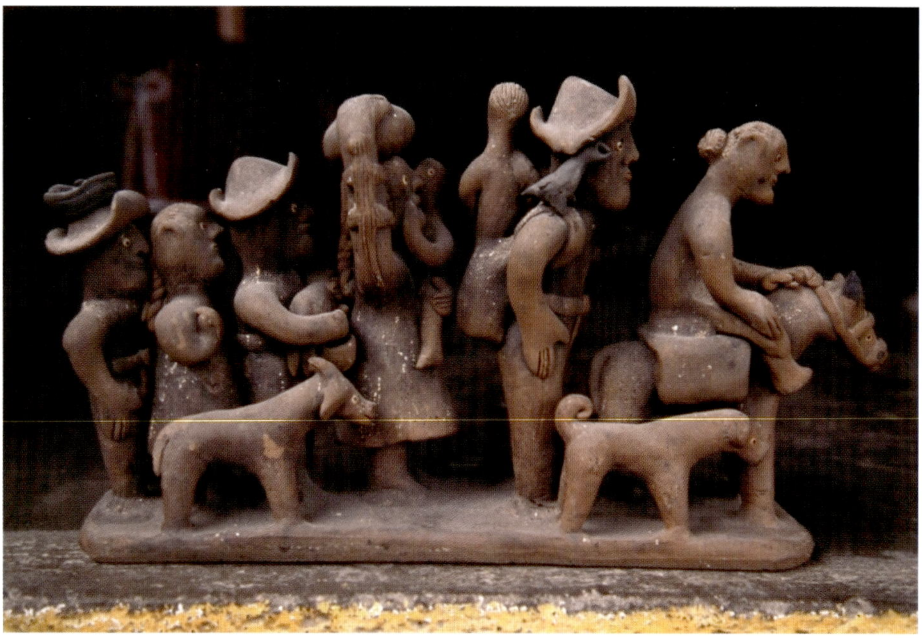

This *Retirantes*, owned by Manuel Eudócio, bears Vitalino's stamp, though he thought it was made by one of Vitalino's sons, probably Antônio, about 1975.

Manuel Eudócio pauses to tell us that *Os Retirantes* is his most expensive piece, and he is proud that when Lula was Brazil's president he commissioned a version of *Os Retirantes* to give as a gift to the Pope.

Here is one point to note. It is a certain indication of the national significance of Alto do Moura's art that the country's president, Luiz Inácio da Silva, called Lula, would commission Manuel Eudócio to make a gift for Pope Benedict XVI. It is further evidence of the wide regard for Pernambuco's traditional art that powerful politicians commissioned Mestre Manoel Cordeiro — a carver in Ibimirim, out in the Sertão — to create statues as gifts for Pope John Paul II and then Pope Benedict XVI. Later, Pope Francis appeared on Brazilian television with Mestre Manoel's statue of Santa Paulina, the first Brazilian to be canonized. In the national view, Pernambuco is the prime source for folk art.

And here's a bit of pertinent background. Our friends, the artists of the Northeast, none of them rich, all of the working class, generally align with the PT — the Partido dos Trabalhadores, the Workers' Party — and they joined with large Northeastern majorities to elect PT presidents, Lula in 2002 and 2006, then his chosen successor Dilma Rousseff in 2010 and 2014. A rightist conspiracy, they believe, unjustly impeached Dilma and imprisoned Lula on a weak corruption charge in 2018. They understand that corruption is a concomitant of political success, not only in Brazil, and, they dismissed the charge, saying "When you feed the baby, you lick the spoon." When Lula was stoically jailed, WANTED posters were stuck by night to walls in Pernambuco, declaring that Lula's crime was lifting millions of Brazilians out of poverty. Ubiquitous banners read *Lula Livre:* Free Lula. Lula's policies greatly benefited the poor, and *Os Retirantes* made an apt symbol of Lula's concern for the poor. Manuel Eudócio goes on to recount the commission:

"When Lula was the president, he commissioned me to make this piece. People came by car to make the commission. He" — Lula — "did not come to my house. He asked for the piece to be commissioned from me, and I made it.

"He gave me eight thousand, four hundred, and seventy *reais* for the piece. They didn't say who it was for. So, it goes to Recife, and then it was shipped to Brasília. And about three months later, I received a photograph of Lula with the piece.

"Why didn't you tell me the commission was for Lula?

"No, then you would have charged too much."

Manuel Eudócio releases a wonderful laugh, tells us that Lula gave his piece to the Pope, and concludes:

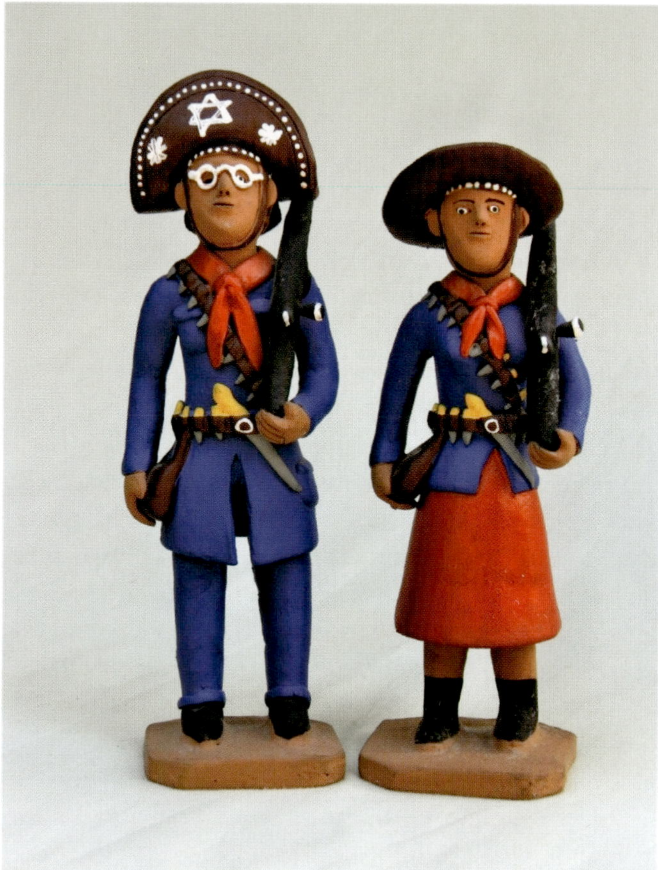

Lampião and Maria Bonita, by Manuel Eudócio (20, 18 cm tall), 2007

"This *Família de Retirantes* is from the period of the poor, because in Brazil then there was no benefit of any kind, no retirement.

"Today there is retirement, there are benefits. You get it when you fall into old age. But in that period; in the period of the forties and fifties, there was nothing."

Manuel Eudócio's rural images reflect influence from Mestre Vitalino and they parallel Severino Vitalino's in topic. Then in the musical theme he also makes *O Trio Nordestino* and *A Banda de Pífano*, and among the heroes he also portrays Lampião and Maria Bonita, Mestre Vitalino, and Luiz Gonzaga, all in various sizes. Some difference begins with the religious imagery. Manuel Eudócio depicts Padre Cícero in three sizes and sells as many as he makes to Padre Severino, a priest in São Paulo. Though Elias, Vitalino's grandson, occasionally depicts on commission the most popular male saints, Francis and Anthony, Manuel Eudócio shapes and paints both of them frequently and in several sizes.

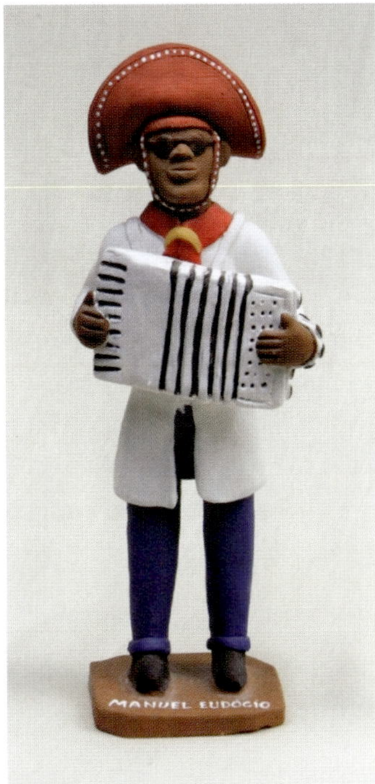

Luiz Gonzaga, by Manuel Eudócio (23 cm tall), 2007

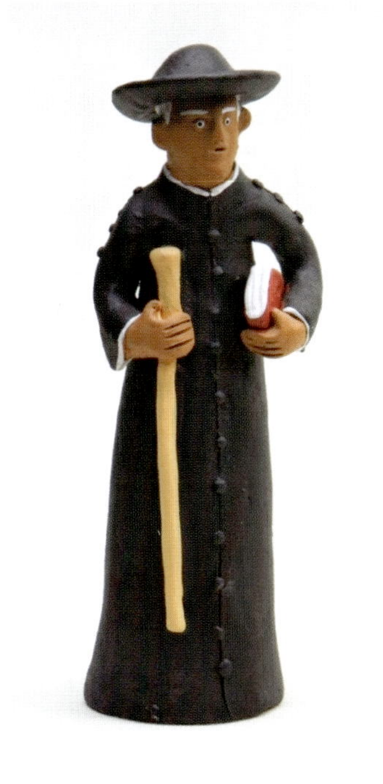

Padre Cícero, by Manuel Eudócio (19 cm tall), 2015

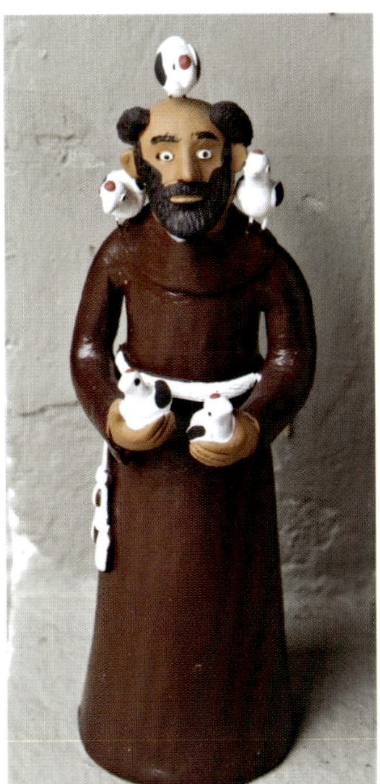

Saint Francis, by Manuel Eudócio (24 cm tall), c. 2005

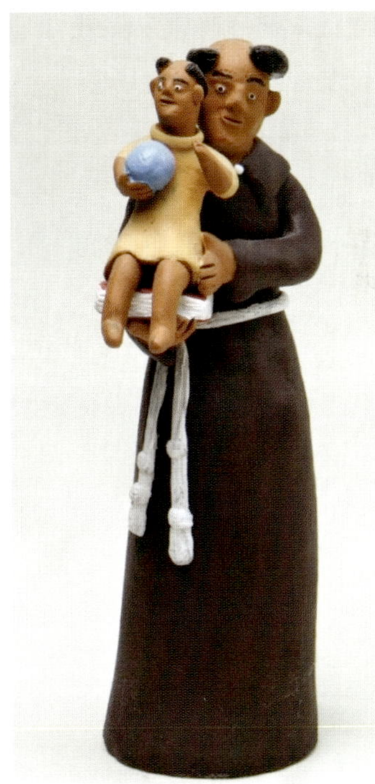

Saint Anthony, by Manuel Eudócio, (24 cm tall), 2015

The artists of the second generation, those who learned directly from Mestre Vitalino, all reduced Vitalino's repertory to suit themselves. But then the artists who were not direct descendants, the ones unhindered by familial loyalties — Manuel Eudócio, Zé Caboclo, and Luiz Antônio — also added a multitude of new pieces to Alto do Moura's repertory, which, without abandoning connections to Vitalino, has continued to expand right to the present.

Manuel Eudócio's great contribution was the *Reisado*. A distinct and coherent repertory within the wider repertory, the *Reisado* offers images for all of the artists to make, and it is a major source for the repetitive miniatures in the third line of production.

Reisado is the local name for a performance usually called *Bumba-Meu-Boi* in Brazil. It belongs to an extended family of rural entertainments that were once known widely in Europe, though they have been best documented as mumming in England and Ireland. Generally the performance includes a house visit, a masked procession with music, and a drama of death and resurrection. In Greece, a bridegroom is killed, then revived by a doctor. In Ireland, a saint is killed, then revived by a doctor. In Brazil, a bull is killed, then revived by a doctor. Performances normally occur in a season centered on a religious holiday, Christmas most often, and the *Reisado* is no exception. It takes its name from Epiphany, the Day of the Kings; *Reisado* means "Of the Kings."

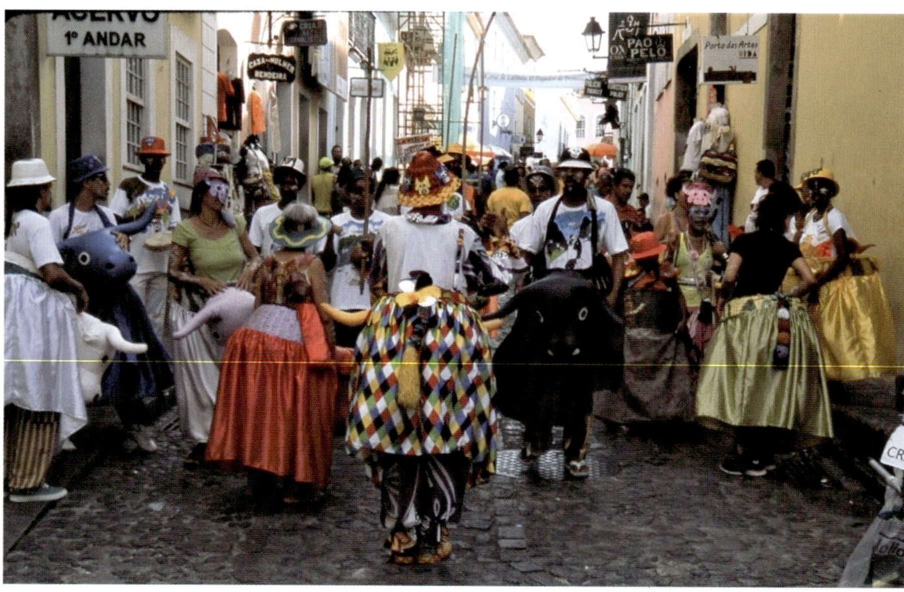

Bumba-Meu-Boi, revived as a frame for musical performance, Salvador da Bahia, 2014

When we ask, Manuel Eudócio affirms that the *Reisado* and *Bumba-Meu-Boi* are the same and he recalls performing in Alto do Moura's *Reisado*:

"When I was an adolescent, sixteen, seventeen years of age, there was the *Reisado*, the one enacted here in Alto do Moura. So, I was the First Gallant, that was my character.

"It was started in one thousand, nine hundred and forty-seven. So, the Captain, he was Cavalo Marinho, he was the one who commanded all the characters.

"The Captain invited us to go and perform on all the farms. And it was a beautiful performance. Twenty-eight people, all from here, all from Alto do Moura. There was nobody from outside, no. It was an uncle, a brother, a brother-in-law. It was a cousin. All from here, all from Alto do Moura.

"Twenty-eight men, all were men. Some in women's clothes. The ladies were adolescent boys, like fifteen or sixteen years old. They were wearing women's clothes.

"It was a man, but nobody could recognize you, because we used to make masks of cardboard. So, we used to make a mask with flour paste, with starch, then we painted it, and that was how we covered our faces.

"Not me. I didn't use it. I performed without a mask. Me and Cavalo Marinho, we had no mask.

"I was seventeen years old. My character was called the First Gallant. There was also a Second Gallant. And there were other characters, Catarina, Mateus, and there were other characters who played instruments for us to dance in the performance."

Over time's long duration, collective rural performances like Alto do Moura's *Reisado* or Ireland's mumming seem to endure through cycles of death and rebirth that echo the dramas they enfold. They depend on mature, community-minded individuals who gather a youthful group for performance and take command, bringing the old tradition to life once again. In 1947, Manuel Inocêncio gathered the actors, took the role of Cavalo Marinho, and directed the action. He was, Manuel Eudócio says, an elderly man, a neighbor of his, and he died in 1950. His death chanced to coincide with Manuel Eudócio's coming of age as an artist, which began with Vitalino's arrival in Alto do Moura in 1948. With the Captain's passing in 1950, the *Reisado* was at an end. Then Manuel Eudócio, at nineteen, took charge of the *Reisado*, not by gathering actors and putting them on the road, but by rendering the characters in clay:

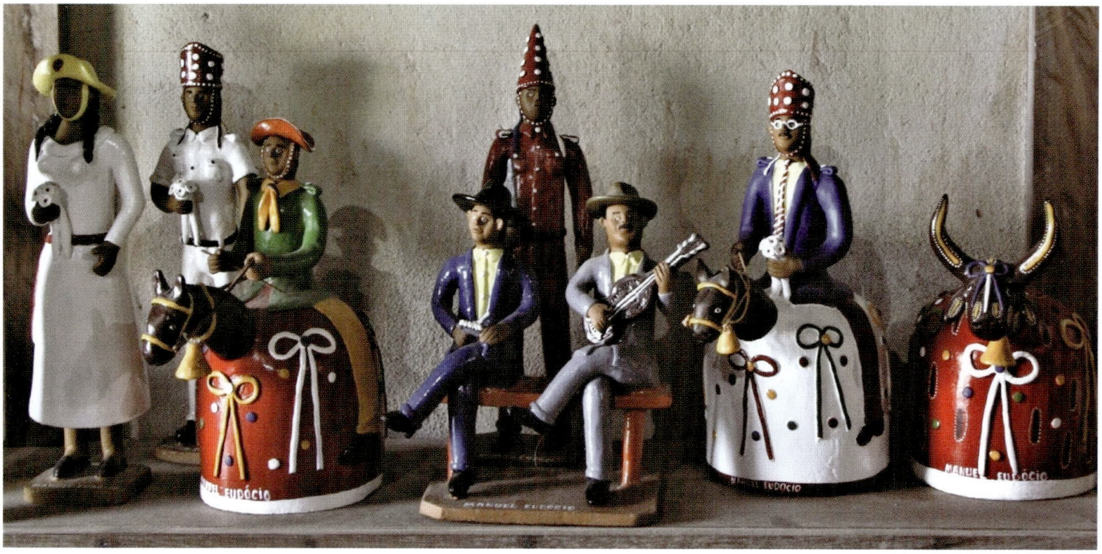

Reisado characters, left to right: Lady, Gallant, Cowboy, Musicians, Tangir, Captain, Bull

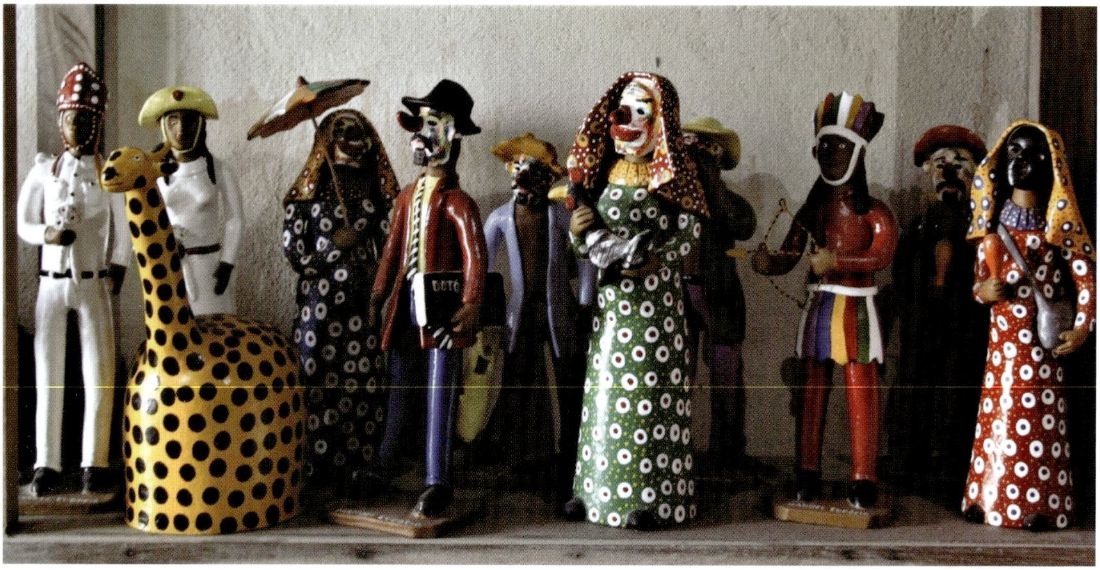

Reisado characters, left to right: Gallant, Lady, Giraffe, Dona Joana, Doutor, Tobias, Old Lady of the Bird, Chorão, Indian, Mateus, Catarina. All of these figures were made by Manuel Eudócio in 2014 and 2015.

"When the Captain died, I started to make it in clay. When we finished, when we stopped, I made it in clay. And until today, it is what I sell the most, a set of twenty-eight pieces. I invented the *Reisado*."

A straight line glides from the *Reisado* to a key feature of Alto do Moura's art. Different numbers of actors showed up for each performance. Sometimes there were fourteen, eighteen, or twenty-two, but twenty-eight made for a full cast, and there were twenty-eight clay figures in a full set, implying — and implying correctly — that images of the *Reisado* don't depict scenes of interaction from the performance. They are, instead, identifiable portraits of the individual characters.

Alto do Moura's compositional options are two: the scene and the icon. In the scene, the figures occupy a setting, within which their lines of sight are confined. The early piece by Vitalino, as repeated by Severino, is a clear instance. The hunter and his dog are looking at the cats in the tree. In the icon, the figures pose frontally to look directly at the viewer. Vitalino's fisherman, as repeated by Severino, is a perfect example. He is not depicted in the act of fishing, as the hunter is in the act of hunting. Rather, he looks straight ahead and displays the attributes of a fisherman: a rod in one hand, a couple of caught fish in the other.

The icon borrows the traits of the saint: the attributes that enable clear identification and the solitary, frontal stance that enables direct contact, eye to eye, with the beholder. The saint stands ready to receive adoration and prayers, and once the saint in the church was the most common, perhaps the only, work of art in the people's experience, simultaneously a container of sacred and aesthetic principles. So, when the artists of the quotidian looked around for subjects, they found fishermen, musicians, and women busy with household chores, and when they turned to creation, to give their ideas palpable presence, they positioned their figures frontally and supplied them with attributes of identification as though they were saints.

Both compositional options, the scenic and the iconic, are available. Lampião and Maria Bonita might be set in a sylvan scene, seated and looking at each other across a campfire, but generally they pose side by side, looking forward and identified by their warlike gear. Among the artists, the iconic option is the most frequently employed, and when Manuel Eudócio decided to render the *Reisado* in clay, he created a new repertory of iconic characters identifiable by specific traits.

His iconic rendering was only one aspect of the ingenuity Manuel Eudócio displayed within the ambit of the *Reisado*. For another, he tells us that he in-

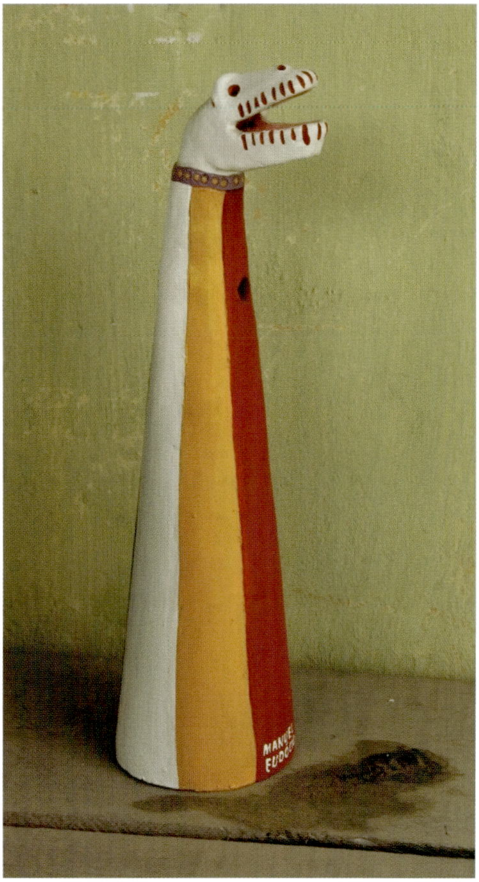

Large *Jaraguá* by Manuel Eudócio, c. 2014

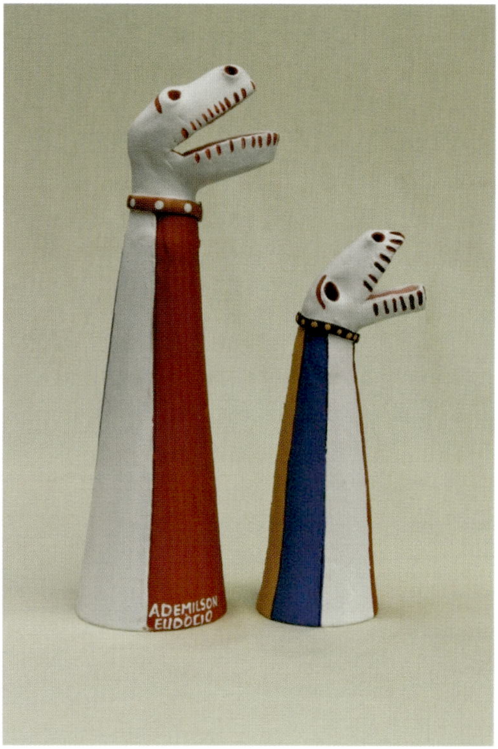

Small *Jaraguás*, made by Manuel Eudócio's sons in 2021. Left: by Ademilson (25 cm tall). Right: by Luiz Carlos (18 cm tall)

troduced a twenty-ninth character to his local *Reisado*, known elsewhere, but new to Alto do Moura. One time when he and his brother were hunting back in the bush, they came upon a rotting body.

"It was under a tree," he says. "It was a bull or a horse. It had been dead for a long time; it was just a skull with these teeth.

"Then me and my brother — he was named Josué. I said, Josué, we are going to make a character for the *Reisado*. So, I invented this character, and I put the name Jaraguá on it.

"It was in the performance, and I make it until today."

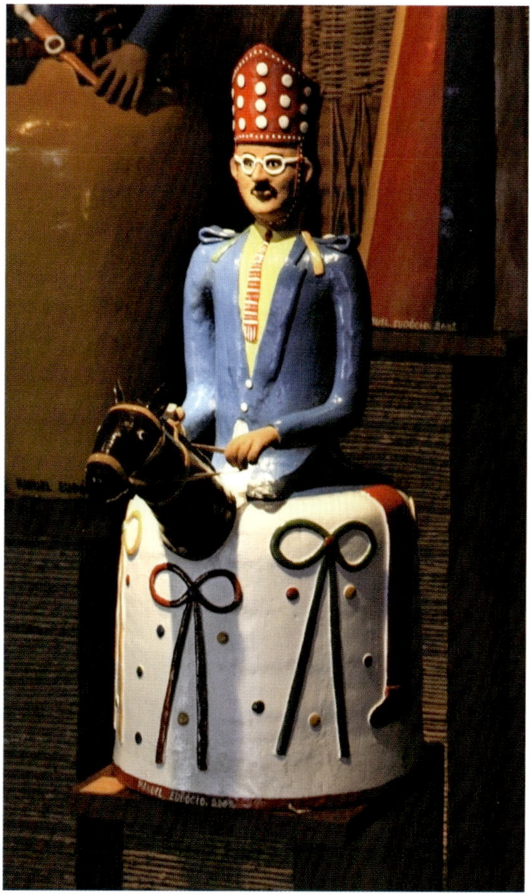

The Captain, by Manuel Eudócio, displayed at the Center for Artesanato, Bezerros, 2015

The Jaraguá is not a jaguar, an elegant animal regularly portrayed in clay by Brazilian artists, and, in fact, there is a jaguar, an *onça*, in the *Reisado's* cast. The name, Jaraguá, seems to derive from a Tupi-Guarani word for an herb from the undergrowth in the bush. The form bears some resemblance to the *carrancas*, the figureheads on the boats that ply the waterways of western Pernambuco. In performance the Jaraguá consists of a tall tube of cloth that hides the man within and carries at the crest a grotesque, toothy skull like that of a horse, cow, or dinosaur — and that's how Manuel Eudócio and his sons render it in clay.

Although Manuel Eudócio does create complete sets of the *Reisado's* cast, he much more often makes and sells depictions of particular characters. The Captain and the Bull are a popular pair. In action, both are versions of the hobby horse, once performed throughout Europe. The Captain moves in an armature that pokes a horse's head out of the front and drapes his body from the waist down. The man in the Bull is wholly hidden, his character signaled by a bull's horned head. In clay, the Captain and the horse's head emerge from one

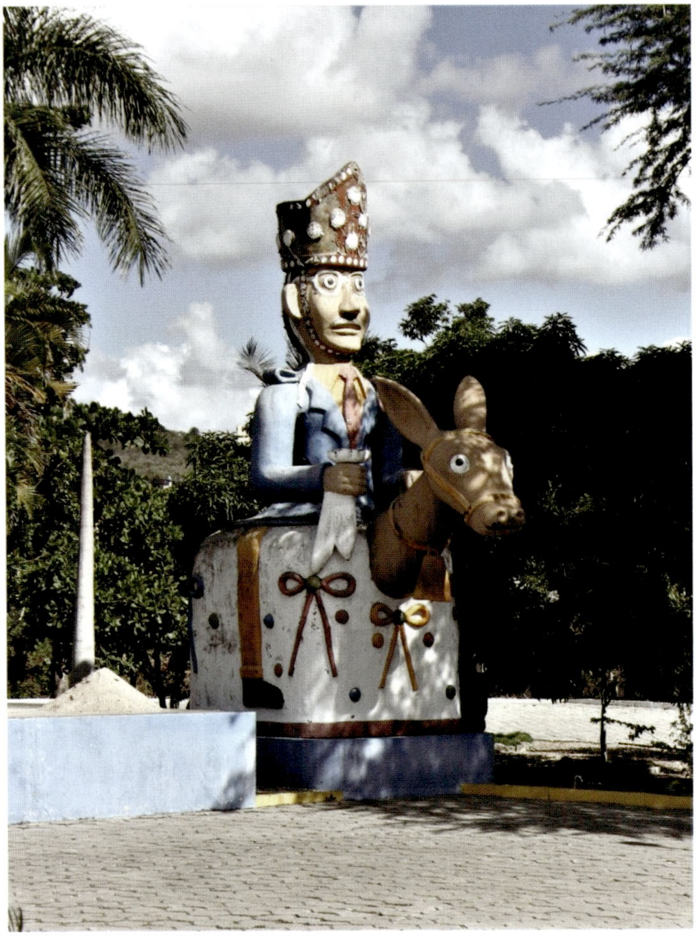

Statue of the Captain, Center for Artesanato, Bezerros, 2015

dome, the Bull's head from another. This recognizable pair, pictured on Manuel Eudócio's business card, is a staple within the flow of inexpensive miniatures in the third line of production, and alone the Captain, Cavalo Marinho, joins Lampião and Mestre Vitalino's humped brahma bull as one of the clear and constant symbols of Alto do Moura's artistic tradition. In the museum for *artesanato* at the edge of the town of Bezerros, the Captain by Manuel Eudócio is featured inside, and outside a gigantic statue of the Captain stands to attract the travelers zipping past on the highway.

When Manuel Eudócio is at his most innovative, though, is during his free play with the figures in the *Reisado's* repertory. We have already encountered such repertorial play in Vitalino Neto's *Adultério*. He began with a conventional piece, made by many and showing a bride and groom on a horse, then he replaced the newly married couple with Lampião and Maria Bonita, and then he replaced Maria with a happy black *boneca*, fusing the figures to enhance the significance.

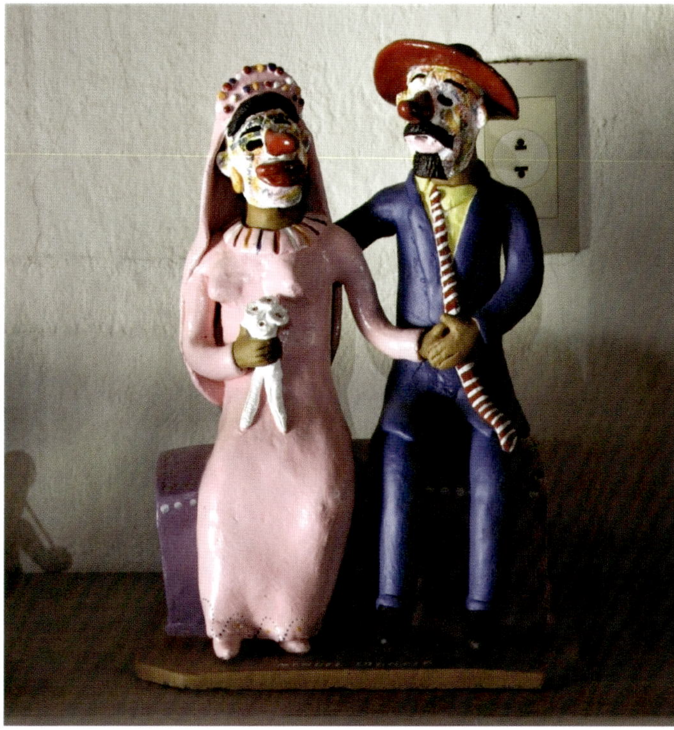

Dona Joana and the Doutor, by Manuel Eudócio, 2014

In his coupling of the Doutor with Dona Joana, Manuel Eudócio clearly reveals his playful process. To begin: the *Reisado* already contains a couple, Catarina and Mateus. Catarina, black and pregnant, wants a bull's tongue for medicinal purposes. Her desire leads to the death and resurrection of the Bull. The Doutor is the angel of that miracle. But in the midst of artistic action, Manuel Eudócio ignores Catarina and Mateus, and he usually relieves the Doutor of medical duties. In Brazil, the one called Doutor might be a doctor or he might be a lawyer, but he is certainly an educated and prosperous gentleman (much as a colonel could be a military man, but he is surely the owner of rural land). Then Manuel Eudócio lifts Dona Joana from the drama's periphery and makes her a proper partner, the right wife for the Doutor.

As the masked central couple of his personal, artistic *Reisado*, the Doutor and Dona Joana can be shifted about and put wherever Manuel Eudócio wants them to be. He portrays them dancing together, fishing together, or sitting affectionately together on a bench. He places them, a new-married pair, on a horse, or on Vitalino's humped bull, or on a motorcycle, or in an oxcart, or in a bright red automobile, and in a freewheeling departure he places them atop the *Reisado's* domical red Bull, where no one in the performance had ever been. That act, an imaginative meshing of three separate characters, a witty disruption of the *Reisado's* logic, is a surefire sign of the master's mind at play.

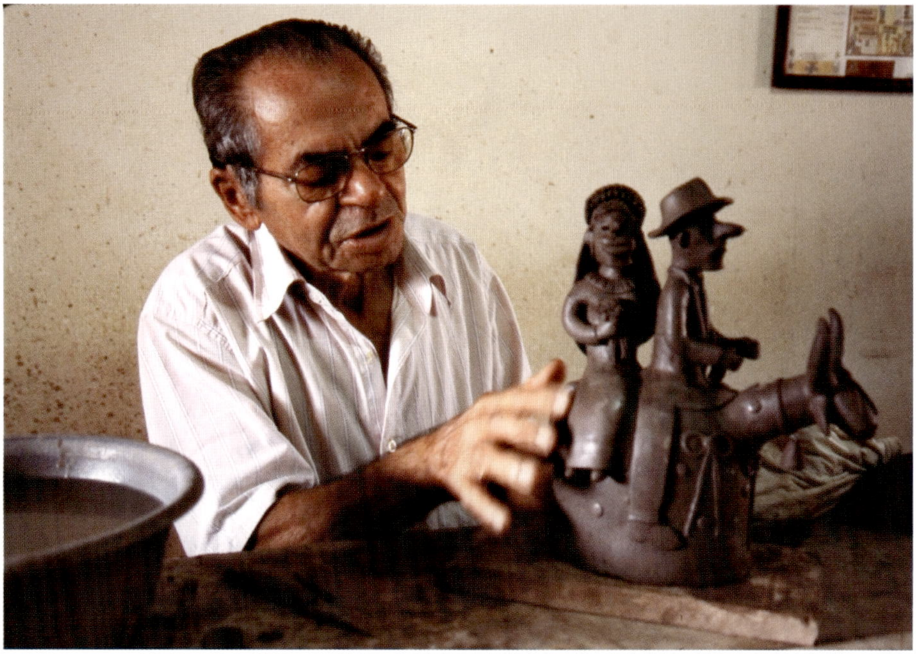

Manuel Eudócio making the Doutor and Dona Joana riding the *Reisado's* bull, 2014

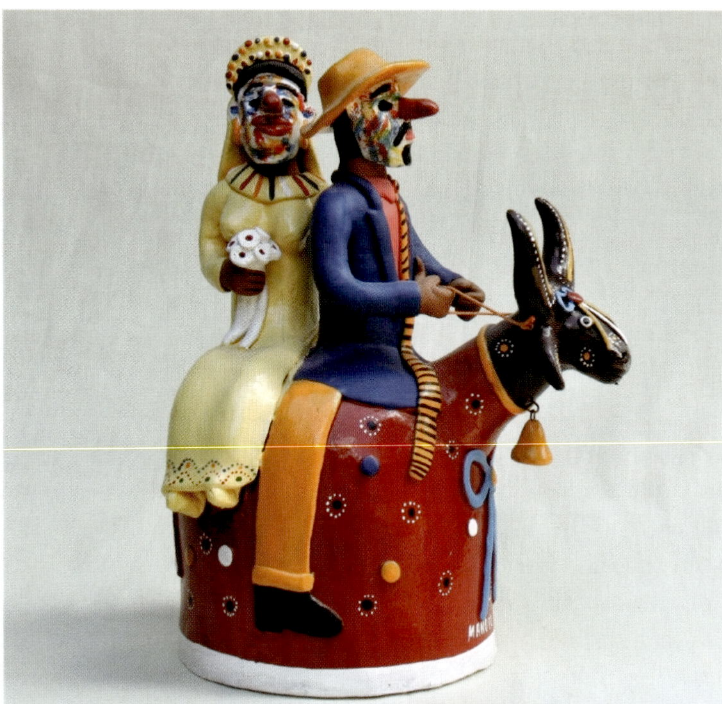

The Doutor and Dona Joana on the Bull,
by Manuel Eudócio (28 cm tall), 2014

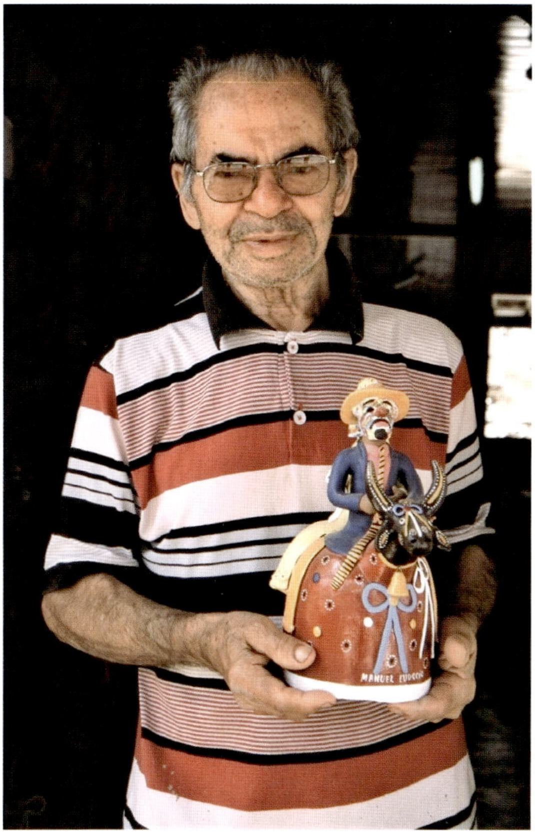

Manuel Eudócio with his couple on the bull, Alto do Moura, 2014

At once a conscientious craftsman and an inventive artist who added a host of new figures to his community's repertory, Manuel Eudócio was a master, and — as a master must — he honored the master before him and he passed it on:

"Vitalino was my master. He didn't teach. None of us were taught. I sat beside him. We learned by watching.

"My children used to watch me work. Look, I would say, I'm going to make a little horse.

"When they were children, they were already making little things that I would put on a little table, next to my stand. And what they made were little horses, little bulls. They would make items of toy furniture — chairs, they made tables. They made refrigerators. They would make many little things.

"I would sell with the oldest, who was Luiz Carlos. Or with Silvano. One time one of them came with me. The other time I took the other.

"They learned to deal with customers. They would price the piece, and they would sell it. They would arrive back and say, Mom, look here what I sold.

"She would keep the money, and at the end of the year she would buy fabric and have the seamstress make them pants and shirts. All their clothes were bought with the money they earned.

"Then later they started, like at fourteen, fifteen years of age, they started to make the statues then.

"Now, there were some who didn't want to make. The youngest one Neide" — Elisoneide — "she paints my pieces. She didn't want to learn. No problem. She paints my pieces. I pay her a percentage, and she is able to survive.

"Now, my sons. Some make a living in other ways, with a shop, in a bank. But Luiz Carlos, Silvano, and Ademilson, they make, and they are living well."

Those words convey the practicality that has sustained Manuel Eudócio, a man who doesn't drink, gamble, or waste his money. At his side, his sons learned to make and they learned to sell, blending artistic and commercial understandings to prepare for comfortable and fulfilling lives as adults. Work brings cash and it brings the daily delight of engagement in a worthwhile task.

Manuel Eudócio loved the clay and he was still at it in the spring of 2015, when he was eighty-four. Still at it, but with an old man's complaint, a rage against the dying of the light:

"I am tired. These days I can't even walk to my house, where I live.

"I'm on a diet. I'm weak, shaking, unable to walk. I lost weight, and I was shaking, so I went to the doctor and he allowed me to eat a few more things.

"I am still working because I am used to it, but my eyes are bad. Sometimes I don't see the little details, and they will have to operate on the cataracts. It is an easy operation. The cataracts really affect my vision.

"My son Ademilson, I said to Ademilson, I have a desire to stop this work.

"You are going to stop and do what? He said, You don't have the patience to cross your arms and sit in the corner doing nothing.

"At home, I can't just stay in bed. One day they will be able to operate on my eyes.

"It has been many years. Many years of work."

By that time, four big books, surveys of Brazil's *arte popular*, had given Manuel Eudócio up to four pages each, and he had given us a tiny book with slight text but excellent photographs. Titled *Manuel Eudócio: Um Cronista do Seu Tempo*, the booklet carries on its cover a photo of the Doutor and Dona Joana mounted on a red humped bull. He had gathered fame and the end was near. We noticed that the managers of some art galleries had removed his works from the shelves and stored them away to await the spike in prices his death would bring. We noticed that the works that remained for sale suddenly bore high prices. In a posh gallery in Salvador da Bahia, a piece like one we had just bought cost twenty times the price we had paid.

Death took him away on February 13, 2016, at the age of eighty-five. Weakened by diabetes, he was unable to recover from a case of mosquito-borne chikungunya.

To commemorate Manuel Eudócio's life in art, an exhibition of one hundred and sixteen pieces, featuring his bright figures from the *Reisado*, was held at Sobrado 7, a fine gallery in Olinda. By chance we were there for the show's opening on July 24, 2016.

In Alto do Moura, Luiz Carlos, the master's oldest son, looked over the abundance of works that were left in the old shop. He selected pieces and arranged them into ten groups that were equal in value, one for each of the children. They drew lots and chose in order. Luiz Carlos made certain that the recent works remaining on the shop's shelves fully and accurately represented his father's creative breadth. On the table where Manuel Eudócio worked, the parts of the piece he was making when he died remain as he left them. The workshop of the master has become a museum.

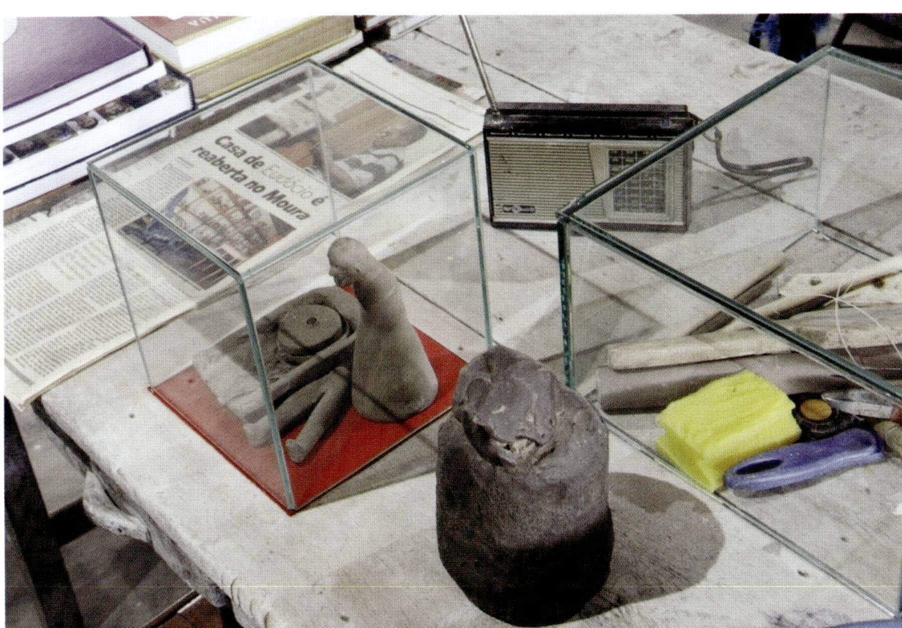

The master's last work remains unfinished on the table in his shop, 2019

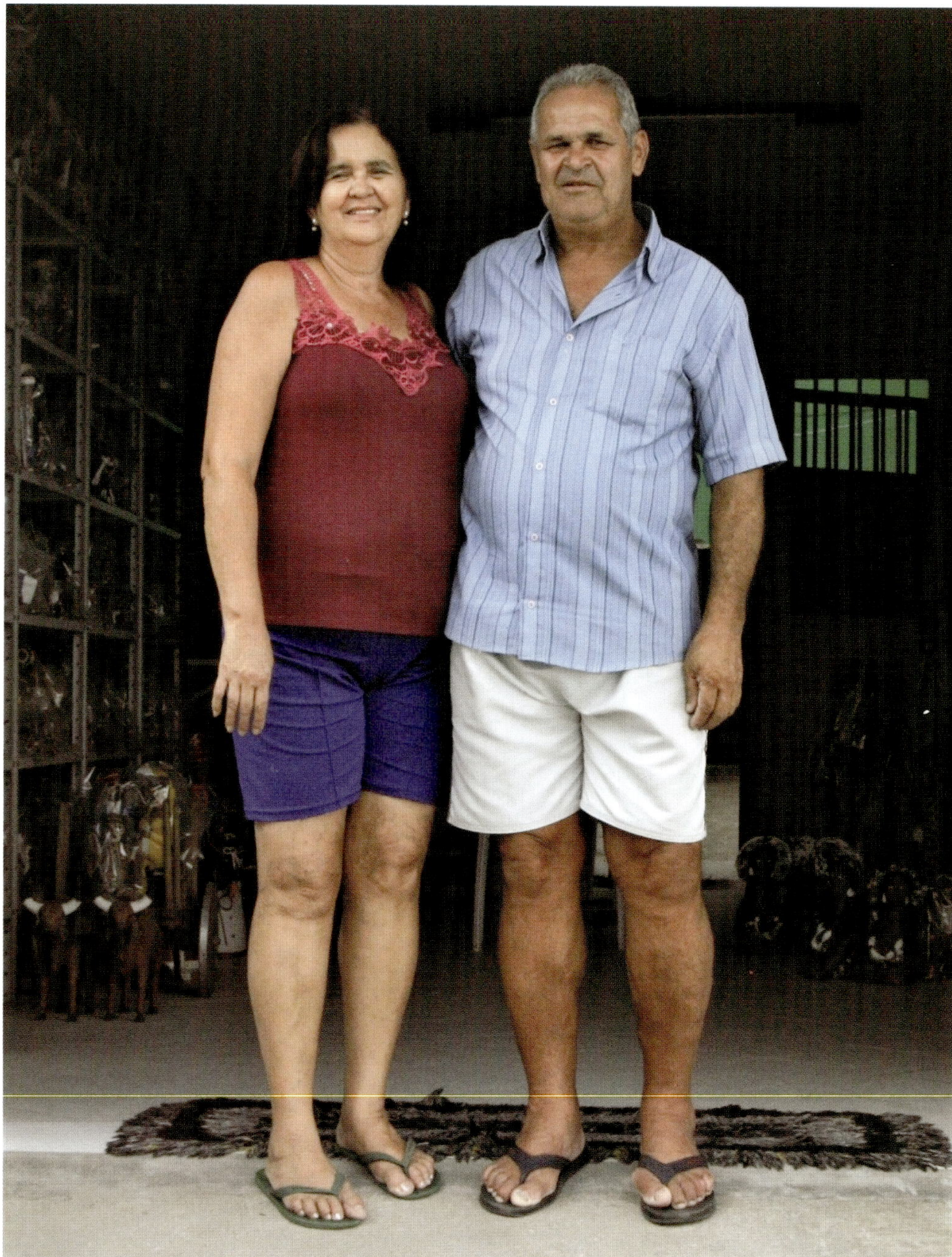

Genilda and Luiz Carlos in front of their shop, 2019

7

Luiz Carlos and Genilda

At a time when his father's health was failing, Luiz Carlos Rodrigues began the first of our interviews in 2014 by saying:

"I started working with my father at six years of age. I was already shaping some pieces. And with the passage of time, receiving some orientations from him, with his explaining ways to improve the work, I kept on perfecting the work. And I started to make bigger pieces, right?

"And until today, I continue with the same art, making the same work, with some innovations as well.

"And I am always working within our culture, the day-to-day.

"I don't work exactly like my father. There is some similarity. My work looks like his because of all the time I worked with him. I picked up some similarities with his work, right?

"Sometimes people say, Your work looks much like the work of your father. And it is true because of the time I worked with him, learning from him, so there is an identifying quality with his work.

"But my finish is finer because I'm a younger person, right? I am younger, right, my vision is better. He is already eighty-three years old. So his finish looks a bit rustic.

"But he continues, the quality of his work continues. He is very creative.

"He has been working since he was a child, seven, eight years old. And really, it is tiring.

"And he — every day, from Monday to Friday, he is working. He doesn't spend a day without working, no.

"He likes it. He loves this work of his. I like it too, but I don't like it as much."

Luiz Carlos smiles, then laughs and concludes:

"Look, at six in the morning, he is already there, working at six in the morning. Every day.

"It's therapy for him. We have said to him, You should stop, take rest.

"Yes, but if I stop working, I will get sick.

"He has found himself alone. My mother has already passed. If he stops, he will be even lonelier. He has to keep making."

And, sure enough, a few hours earlier we had found Manuel Eudócio, just down the street, at work in his shop, happy to chat, happier to be bringing the clay into shape.

With us it goes like this. When the recorder clicks on, the person before us already knows us and knows something about our interests from past conversations and purchases. We buy key pieces to use as material texts, to analyze while the writing proceeds, and to serve as documentary illustrations for publication. And we bought a masterwork from Luiz Carlos in 2007. At an interview's beginning, we ask no questions. Instead, we invite a statement on the artist's life, so the first response is implicitly a question: Is this the sort of information that interests you? It always is, and it always skips through topics that we will pluck out and formulate into requests for elaboration. In this instance, the topics Luiz Carlos raised and we will pursue are: learning, finer finish, larger size, the day-to-day, and the repertory as it follows and departs from his father's.

Our first topic is learning. Luiz Carlos says, as everyone does, that he learned by watching, but we ask specifically about the place of instruction — orientation is the word in Alto do Moura — in the process, and he says:

"Sometimes I would be making a piece, and then he would say, The arm is too thin. It is wrong according to the rest of the body. The arm has to be thicker to fit the form of the body.

"Or the bull. I used to make the bull when I was a boy, and he would tell me about the position of the legs and the horns of the bull.

"And I was always receiving orientations from him, and I would modify the piece. He would give me advice, guiding how it should be."

Finer finish comes next. Luiz Carlos says:

"I never had another profession, other than our work. And I am fifty-six years old.

"I studied a bit, but I have never left this work. I remained making.

"We had a period when it was better, sales were better. But we have continued to create new things. Different painting, right?

"I always seek to give a better finish to my work, to improve the work.

"I don't mind how much time that I put into the piece. I like to improve my work, you know.

"This is important to us, the finish, because it makes the difference in the quality of the work, right?

"In reality, the price might be the same, but the work has a better quality, right?

"So, I seek to make some pieces *new* with the painting that attracts people, right?

"The people who buy, they like to see really bright colors. This I seek to do in my work.

"A few pieces, when they come out of the kiln *perfect*, then I will leave them natural, unpainted. But almost all of them are painted, colorful.

"Color leaves the pieces so beautiful, no? I find the colored pieces very beautiful."

Luiz Carlos is clear about his values. Profit is an aim; an artist has to sell to live. Cash is one reward, but a higher reward comes with the inner satisfaction of taking his time, shaping and painting beautifully while he pushes through improvements toward artistic excellence. (Sounds too idealistic? Reread what he just said.) Then like finer finish, larger size is a challenge. Only a few others in Alto do Moura — one of them is Luiz Antônio's son Leonildo — can capably create at large scale, and Luiz Carlos says:

"The majority of the people in Alto do Moura, they work with small pieces, right?

"Today who is making the majority of the big pieces, in this work of ours, it is me.

"My father is making some big pieces, but not like he used to do before. Because a big piece weighs much, and for him it is difficult to make, right?

"He has stopped making big pieces, but once he made a piece that was a meter and a half in size. He made that.

"I once made a piece that was one meter, ninety" — about six feet and three inches — "tall. It was a Lampião couple, Lampião and Maria Bonita.

"After that, the biggest I have made is that one there."

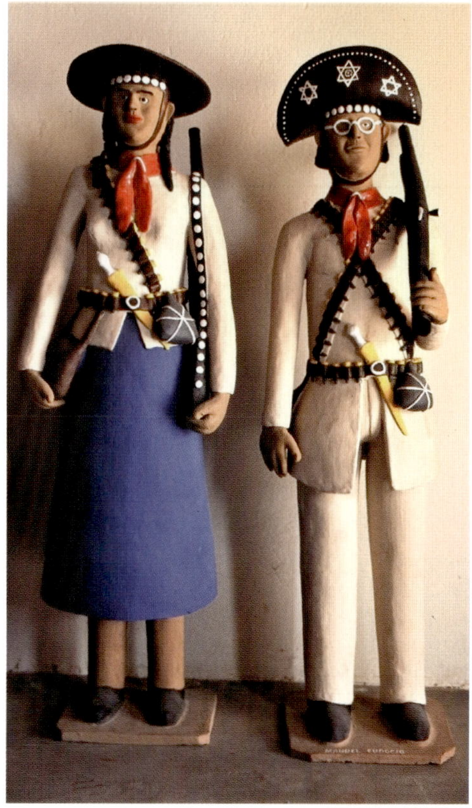

Lampião and Maria Bonita, the tall couple to which Luiz Carlos pointed in 2014

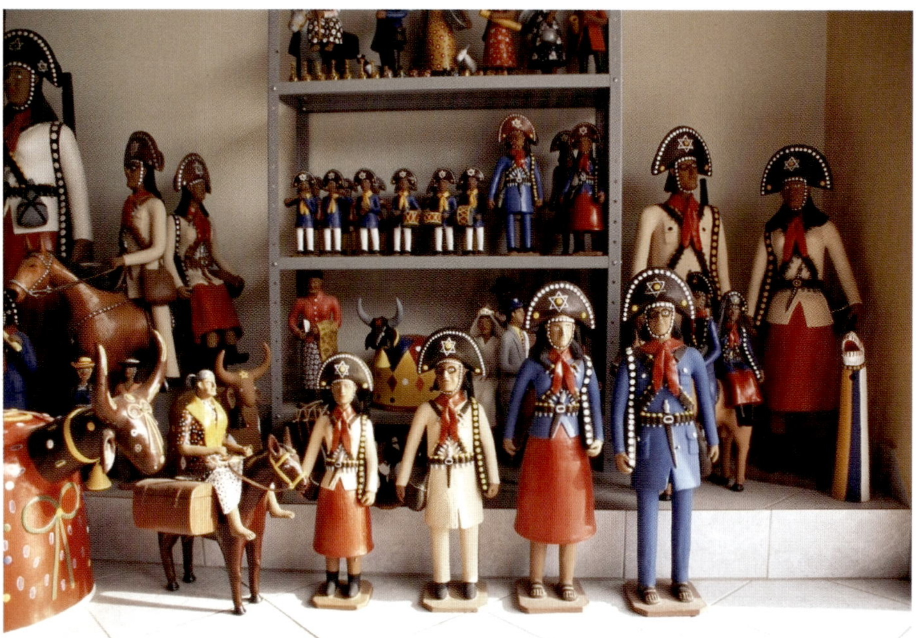

Stock in Luiz Carlos's shop, with Lampião couples in several sizes, 2007

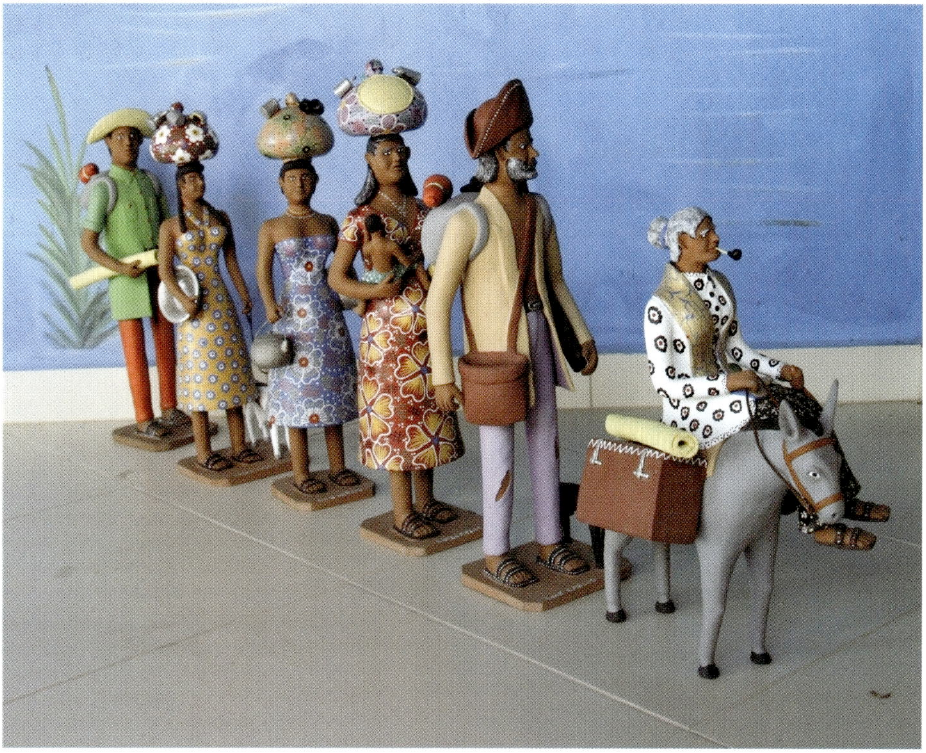

Os Retirantes at a large scale, by Luiz Carlos, 2019

He points to a pair of Lampião and Maria Bonita standing in his shop, well over a meter in height.

"I told my wife, I'm going to leave it here. If someone wants to pay the price, I will sell it. If not, no, because I am not going to make it again.

"Because it is really labor-intensive. Really heavy. I don't want to make such big pieces anymore."

Though he is determined to craft no more such giants, Luiz Carlos remains unusual in his ability to work smoothly from the normal range of Alto do Moura's clay figures — twenty to twenty-eight centimeters in height — right on up to a meter, which is plenty big for ceramic pieces. He makes, for example, *Os Retirantes* in about the same size that Mestre Vitalino and Manuel Eudócio did, but he has also created a set of the exiles in flight from the drought that is fully five times larger. They stand in line, on separate bases, in the open loggia next to the swimming pool in the yard behind his house and shop. At grand scale, too, Luiz Carlos shapes well-observed sculptural portraits of domestic animals from the agricultural landscape.

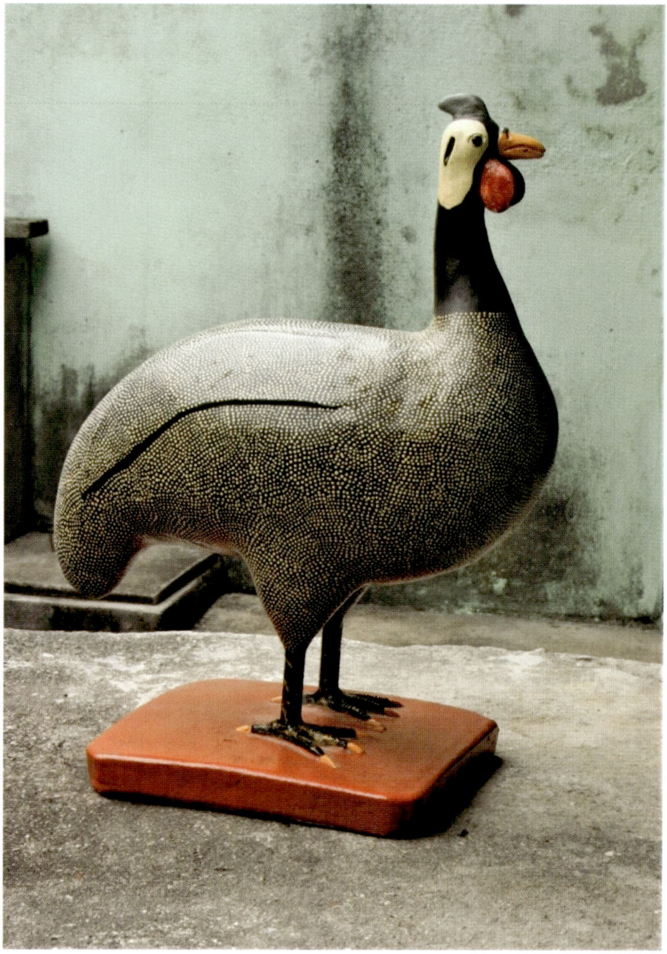

Guinea hen, by Luiz Carlos, 1995

When we ask him to expand on the next topic, the day-to-day, Luiz Carlos provides a key to understanding the character of his own repertory:

"Look, this work of ours, it always depicts our culture, the day-to-day. It is the *pífano* band, the Northeastern trio, the family of the *Retirantes*. It is Lampião and Maria Bonita, the Return from the Field. It also has Cavalo Marinho and the Bull, who are characters from our folklore.

"And it continues like this, always repeating, but sometimes we make innovations as well.

"But we always create within the day-to-day. It is for us to keep the culture alive, the day-to-day, right?

"We always depict the day-to-day, because these are the visible things that we are seeing. So, we see it, we make it, and we create within it."

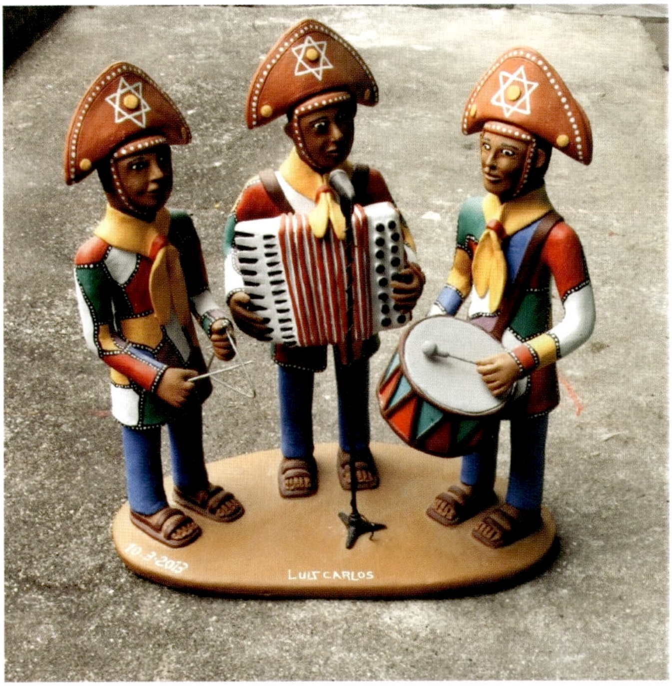

O Trio Nordestino, by Luiz Carlos, 2013

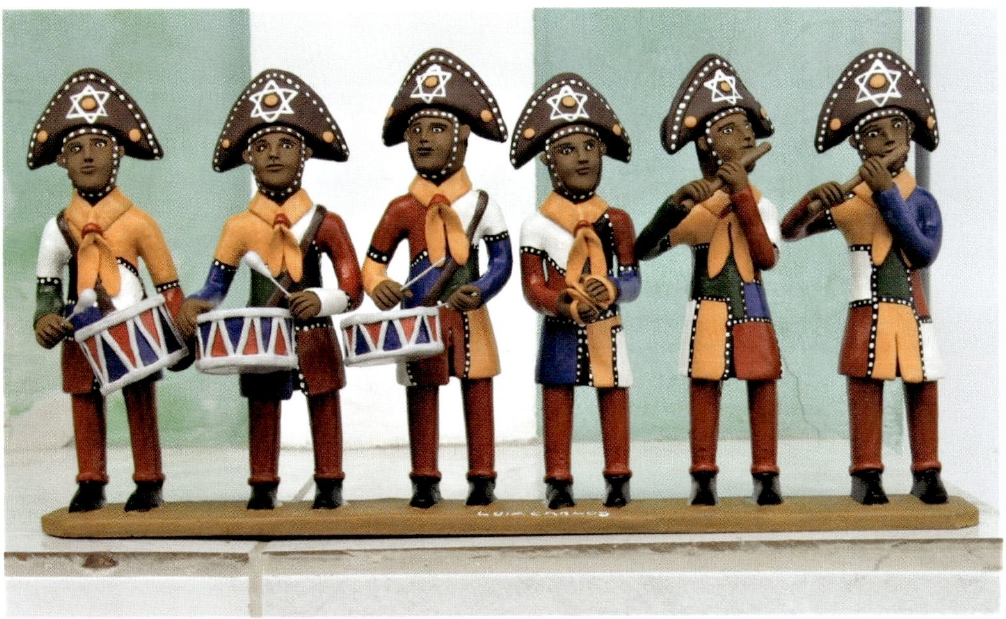

A Banda de Pífano, by Luiz Carlos, 2014

The day-to-day is what we see, and what we see are the traditional images that depict the past (Lampião, *Retirantes*, and the *Reisado*), the images that depict the living present (the *Trio Nordestino*), and the scenes that surround us every day. Luiz Carlos's day-to-day is an inclination within the quotidian. The quotidian repertory, by definition, contains no saints.

"A while back," Luiz Carlos says, "I made some pieces like the *Presépio*" — the Nativity — "that have sacred figures. But later I eliminated them from my work because they are only sought once a year. They are not marketable.

"So, for now, I am not making them anymore. Sacred figures I do not make.

"I do not make them. With me being an Evangelical, I know a bit about the word of the Lord.

"That is not to say that this is something we are not allowed to do. You can make it; there's no problem at all. But I don't have any intention to make any kind of religious art.

"My father does. He makes saints. In Tracunhaém, they make many sacred pieces. But I don't want to make them anymore."

We are moving through his repertory now to understand Luiz Carlos and the implications of the day-to-day. The *Reisado* offers one entry. It was still vital, Luiz Carlos tells us, in his father's day, sixty-five years ago. An effort was made to revive it thirty years ago, but it wasn't successful, and Luiz Carlos has never seen it, knows nothing about the sequence of performance or the drama's plot.

"Look," he says, "the *Reisado*, I know it only by the figures. The story I don't know, but I know the figures, the names of the characters."

That is what remains today. Luiz Carlos created a complete set of the figures, which he keeps in his home, next to the shop. He took us to see it, and later, after his father's death, he assembled a full set of his father's figures on the shelves in the old shop. He took us to see it too, and identified all the characters.

With the recorder running, Luiz Carlos reels off the names in quick confidence: Cavalo Marinho (the Captain), Boi Bandeira (the Bull), Mateus, Catarina (the wife of Mateus), the Doutor, Dona Joana (the Doutor's wife), the Violeiros (two seated men with guitars), the First Gallant, the Second Gallant, the First Lady, the Second Lady, the Soul, the Angel, the Devil (who fights the Angel for the Soul), the Enemy, Tobias (who wears a colorful necktie), Matuto da Goma (a smoking back-country man), Mané do Loló, Tangí, Jaraguá (the

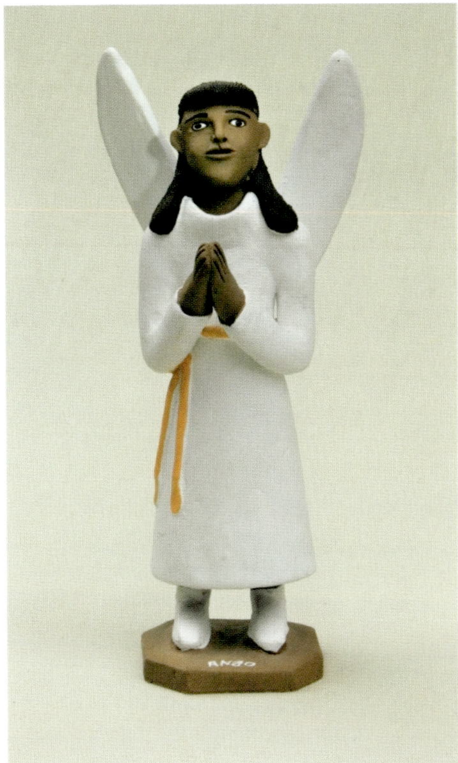

The Angel from the *Reisado*, by Luiz Carlos (21 cm tall), 2021

largest figure), the Giraffe, the Jaguar, the Dog, the Mule, the Old Lady of the Birds, the Indian (with a bow and arrow), the Chorão (the weeping boy), and the Guard.

The repertory of the *Reisado* provides a plenitude of possibilities, but, like his father before him, Luiz Carlos most often chooses to make and sell certain characters, especially two pairs: the Captain and the Bull, the Doutor and Dona Joana.

His father placed the Doutor and Dona Joana on a red bull, but Luiz Carlos removes them from the *Reisado* and locates them in familiar environments. He sits them on a bench, then lets time pass. Manuel Eudócio portrayed them as newlyweds. Luiz Carlos shows them as a comfortably married couple. Dona Joana is making lace; the Doutor is sitting beside her with their son. Or, all still masked, the three of them are sitting together for supper. They are leading a conventional life in a conventional domestic setting. The shift toward the day-to-day is clear: the actions are undramatic and they are contained in a scene. Given their compositional options, Manuel Eudócio inclined to the iconic, Luiz Carlos to the scenic.

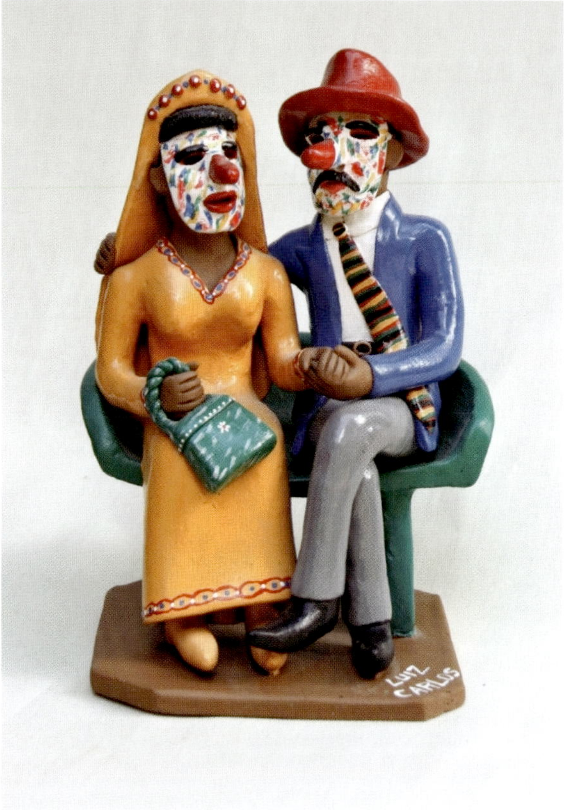

The Doutor and Dona Joana, by
Luiz Carlos (25 cm tall), 2014

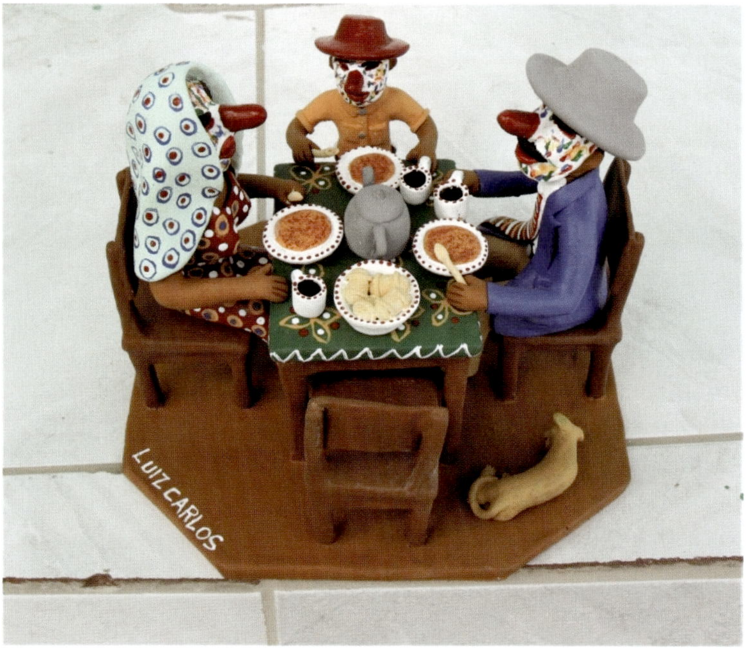

The Doutor, Dona Joana, and their son at supper, by Luiz Carlos, 2019

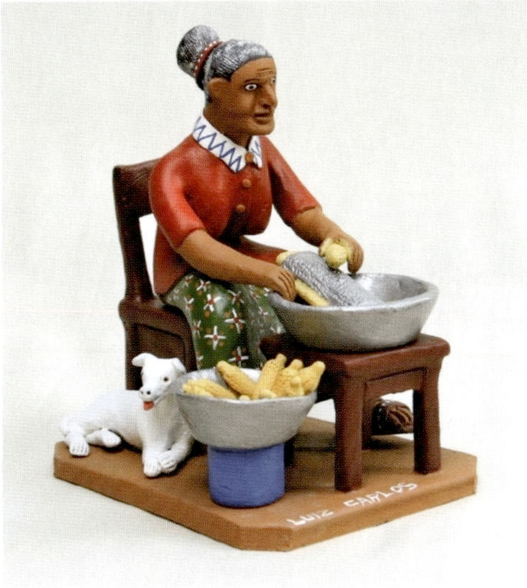

Grating corn, by Luiz Carlos, 2019

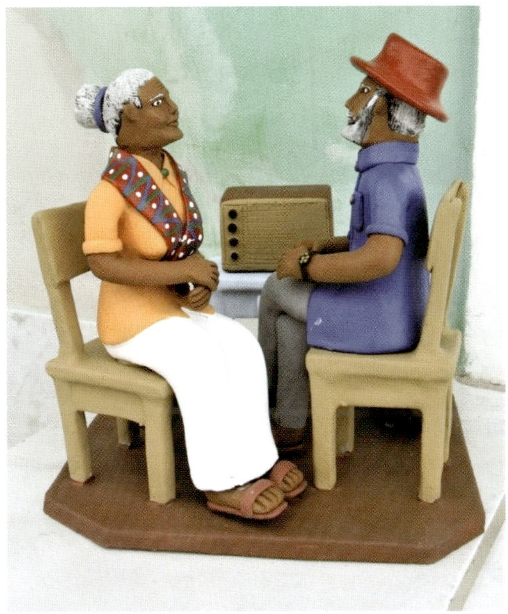

Listening to the radio, by Luiz Carlos, 2019

Common acts in common scenes thread a line of connection through Luiz Carlos's repertory. Within the theme of daily life, pulled to the rural by others, Luiz Carlos portrays an elderly couple sitting together and listening to the radio. He repeats a piece of his father's, showing an old woman removing a splinter from an old man's foot. He depicts women making pots, grating corn, grinding corn, and cooking. The works are excellent, intricately detailed and finely finished, but the subjects are ones you might expect, and where his personal taste becomes remarkable is among the heroes who are usually represented in iconic frontality like saints.

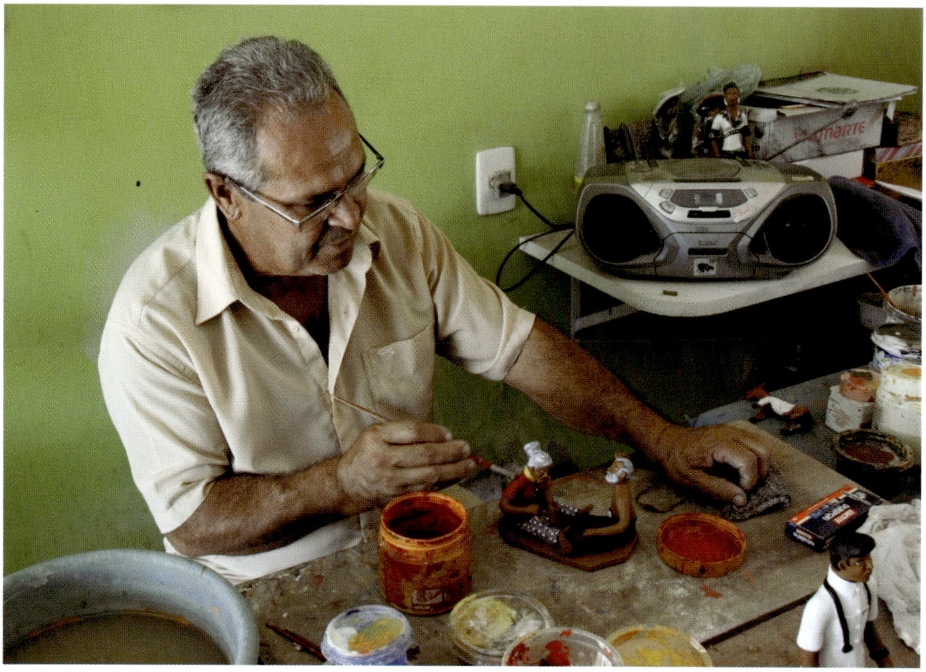

Luiz Carlos painting the splinter's removal, 2019

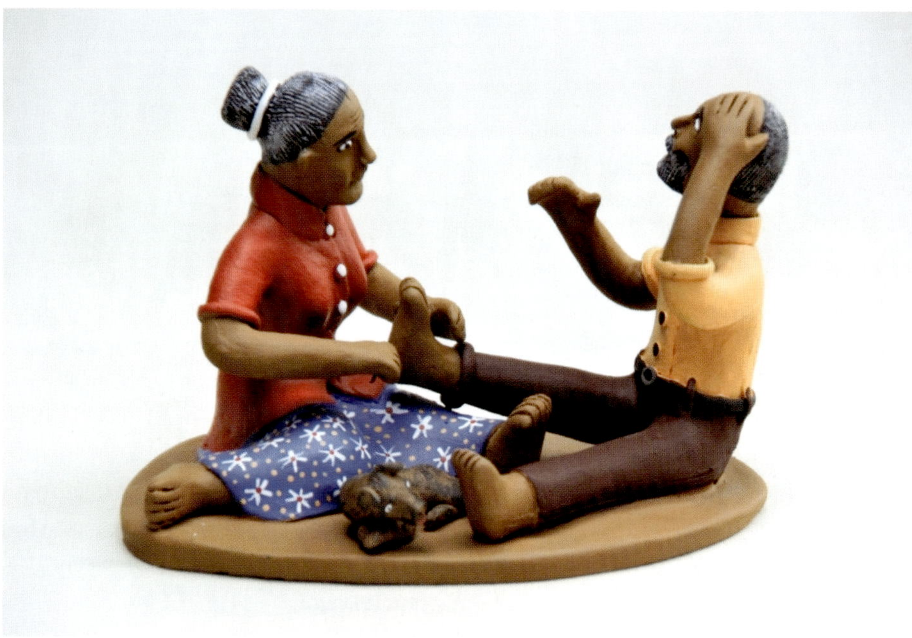

The removal of the splinter, by Luiz Carlos (18 cm wide), 2019

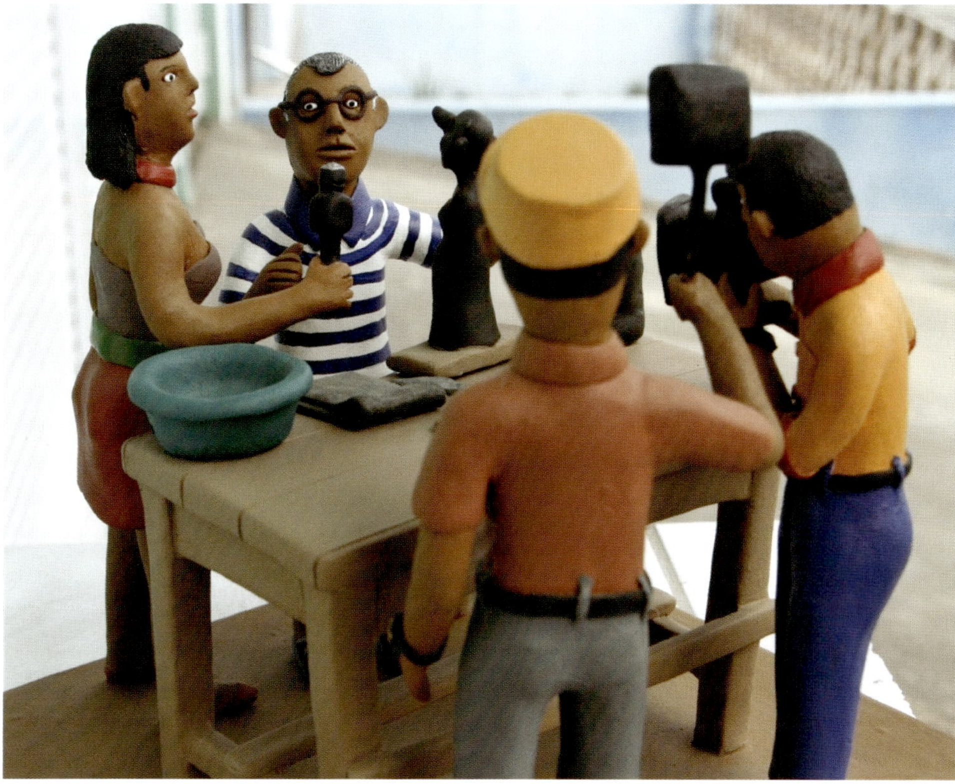

Manuel Eudócio and the media, by Luiz Carlos, 2019

One hero for Luiz Carlos, and for others as well, is his father. Manuel Eudócio made self-portraits in clay, showing himself at work. His sons, Luiz Carlos and Ademilson, also make images of their father, and one by Luiz Carlos exhibits his personal style. He takes you right into the scene. His father is modeling a figure on the table in his shop while the minions of the media crowd around him, recording his words and snapping his photo. Manuel Eudócio, you see, was famous, a newsworthy Patrimônio Vivo de Pernambuco, a Living Patrimony of the state.

Luiz Carlos, like his father and like most of the artists, portrays Mestre Vitalino standing and playing the *pífano*. In a charming departure we saw for sale in Recife, he also showed Vitalino standing, though lacking the *pífano*, he had instead a furled umbrella hooked on one arm. Then, in an unusual move fit to his own style, Luiz Carlos places Vitalino in a scene, playing along with the other three members of his own *pífano* band.

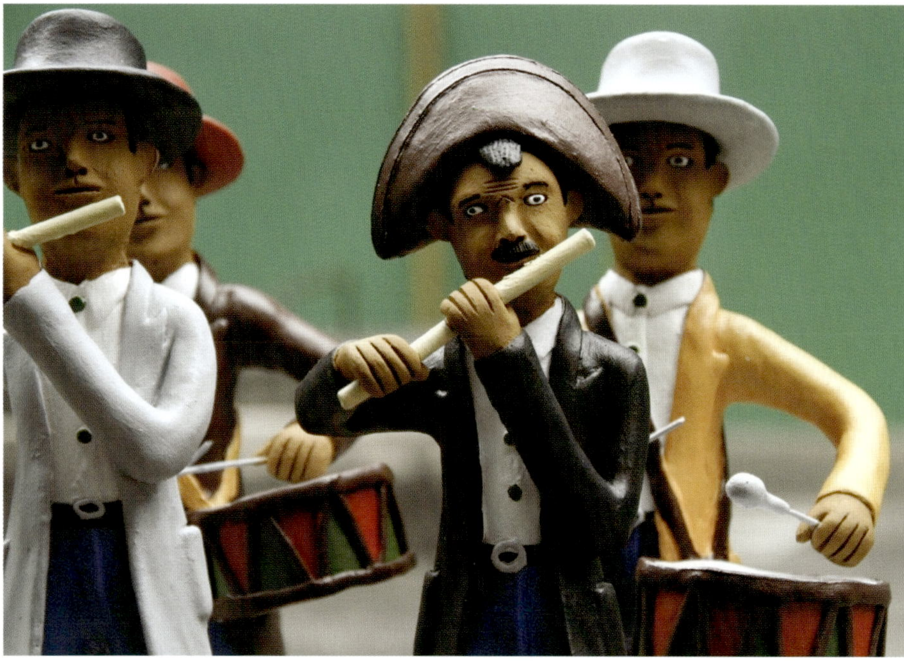

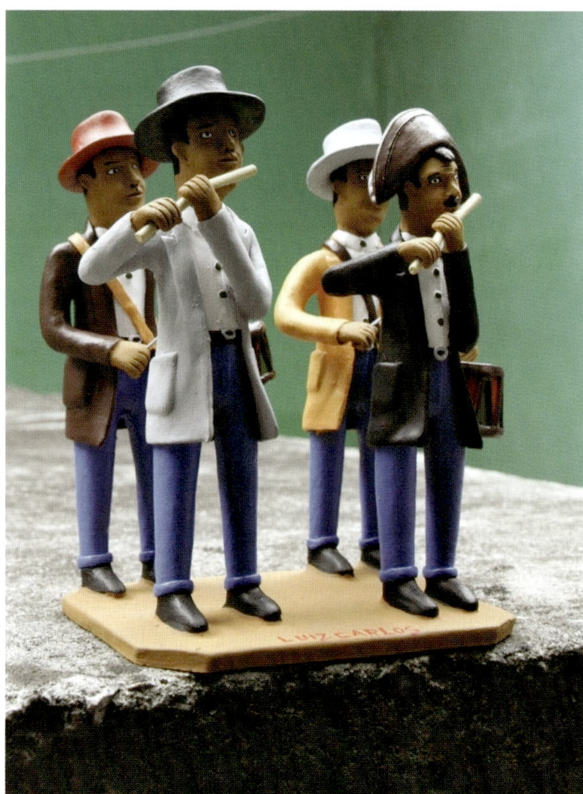

Mestre Vitalino performing with his *pífano* band, by Luiz Carlos, 2019

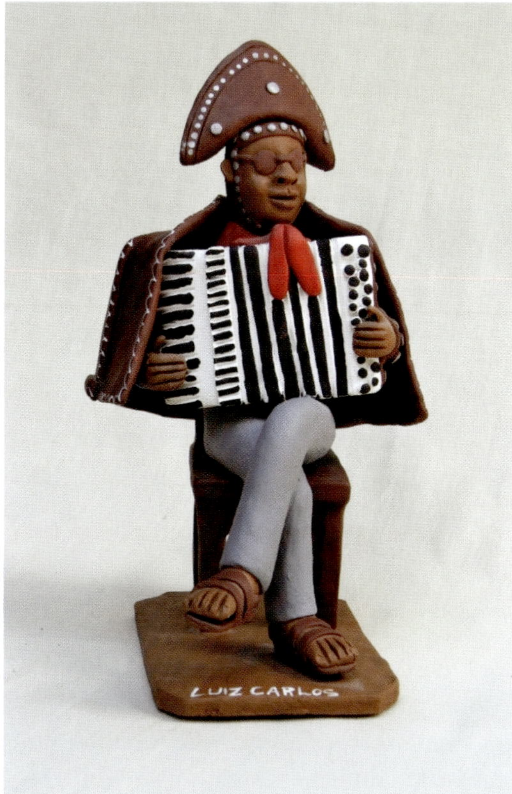

Luiz Gonzaga, by Luiz Carlos (27 cm tall), 2014

Vitalino, then Gonzaga:

"Luiz Gonzaga," Luiz Carlos says, "is a man who sang and charmed the Northeast. He sang the life of the Sertão through his music. He showed everything about the Sertão through the melodies he used to sing — to the entire country of Brazil.

"He was a well-known person, and the Northeast suffered a great loss when he died. Almost everyone loved the music of Luiz Gonzaga because it recounts our history. Each of his songs have something that represents our reality."

Gonzaga's songs, that is, are like Vitalino's images, and Manuel Eudócio told us that once when he was young and sitting beside Mestre Vitalino at the market in Caruaru, a pleasant fellow walked up and bought a statue of Gonzaga playing the accordion. It was Luiz Gonzaga himself. In Gonzaga's famous song, "A Feira de Caruaru," the wonders of the world for sale in the market include the "*bonecos de Vitalino.*"

Luiz Gonzaga standing and playing the accordion is one of Alto do Moura's signal images. Manuel Eudócio portrayed him like that and so does Luiz Carlos, both of them in several sizes. But Luiz Carlos also depicts Gonzaga sitting, and, in his own way, sets him in scenes. In one, Gonzaga is sitting in

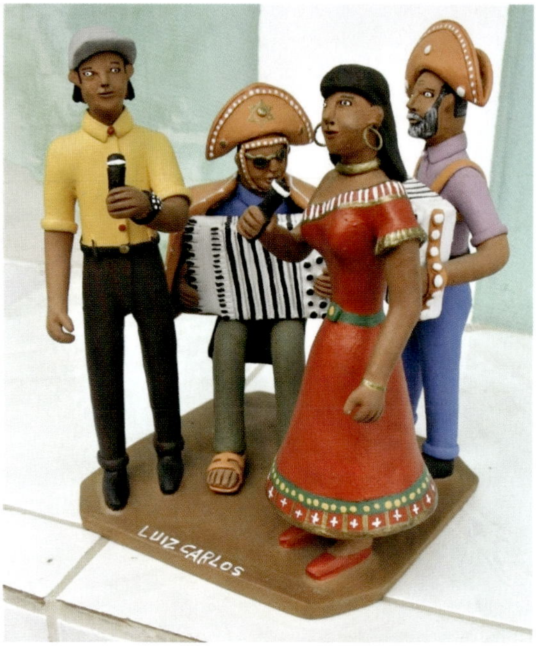

Gonzaga's band in performance, by Luiz Carlos, 2019

conversation with Onildo Almeida, the composer of several of his songs, including "A Feira de Caruaru." In another, as he did with Vitalino, Luiz Carlos places Luiz Gonzaga in the midst of performance with his band.

Lampião and Maria Bonita are the historical personages imaged most often, and Luiz Carlos works within the general tradition and follows his father when he stands them side by side and paints their uniforms blue or khaki. But he also places them in a back-country scene, sitting across from each other and cooking at a campfire, a calm, day-to-day moment in their turbulent, violent lives. Luiz Carlos says:

"Lampião is a piece we make, and it is a particularly beautiful piece, right? Because of the things we add to it, like the rifle, the canteen, it becomes a well-decorated piece, an attractive piece. And people like it because it deals with the Sertão, the scrubland.

"It is really a Northeastern piece. For this reason, it is a piece that is very sought after, Lampião.

"His story, for many people, is not so pleasant, right? Because he was a *cangaceiro*" — a bandit — "along with the people who accompanied him.

"And, in reality, there are people who feel that Lampião was a person of justice. And there are people who don't value Lampião too much. But there are others who admire him because, in reality, he acted within his rights. Because there were crimes against the people. And he reacted. For many people he is a hero.

"For many, he is a hero, right? Now, for others, he is not a hero in any way.

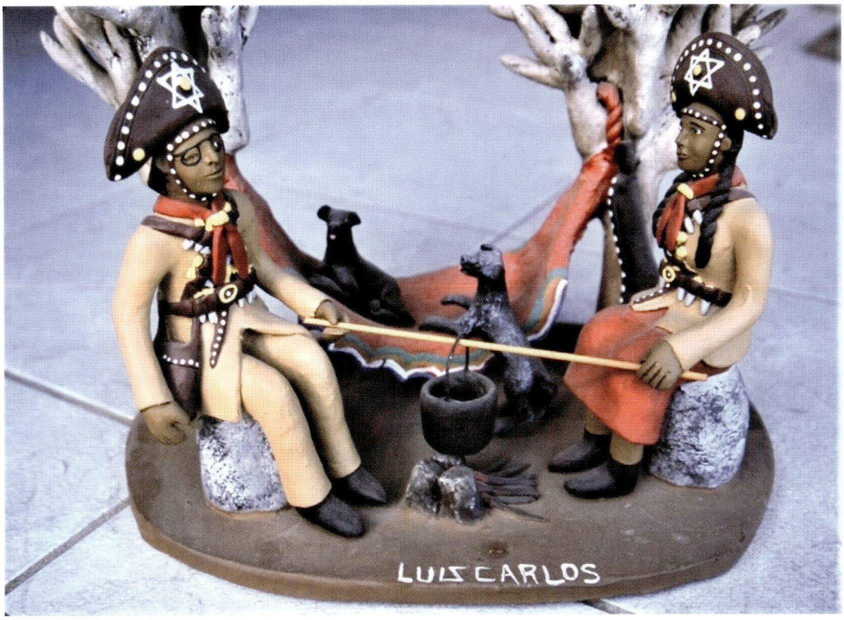

A campfire scene, with Lampião and Maria Bonita making supper, by Luiz Carlos, 2015

"From what I know about the story of Lampião, which someone told me, he was a person who acted within his rights. They murdered his parents, and he took justice into his own hands.

"So, he gathered a gang. It was not just him alone, right? Others accompanied him.

"And there are people who are still alive, who are in their eighties and nineties. They know the story better because they are of an age, and they know a better story to tell because they have experience of it."

Luiz Carlos has a photograph of himself with a *cangaceiro's* daughter. Genilda, Luiz Carlos's wife, who works at a table beside his, was listening, and when he ended, she said:

"Lampião, it is like this. For us, he brings commercial benefit. Because we make in clay Lampião and Maria Bonita. And they have become well known through our work.

"Gonzaga also. Luiz Gonzaga, for us he is a very important person. We make statues of him, and the people really like it. And so, for us, it is good. He was a beloved person.

"But for Lampião, there are two sides to him. A good side, and a side that people find *bad*, right?

"He was not of our era; he died in thirty-eight. He is a legend for us. We only know what other people say."

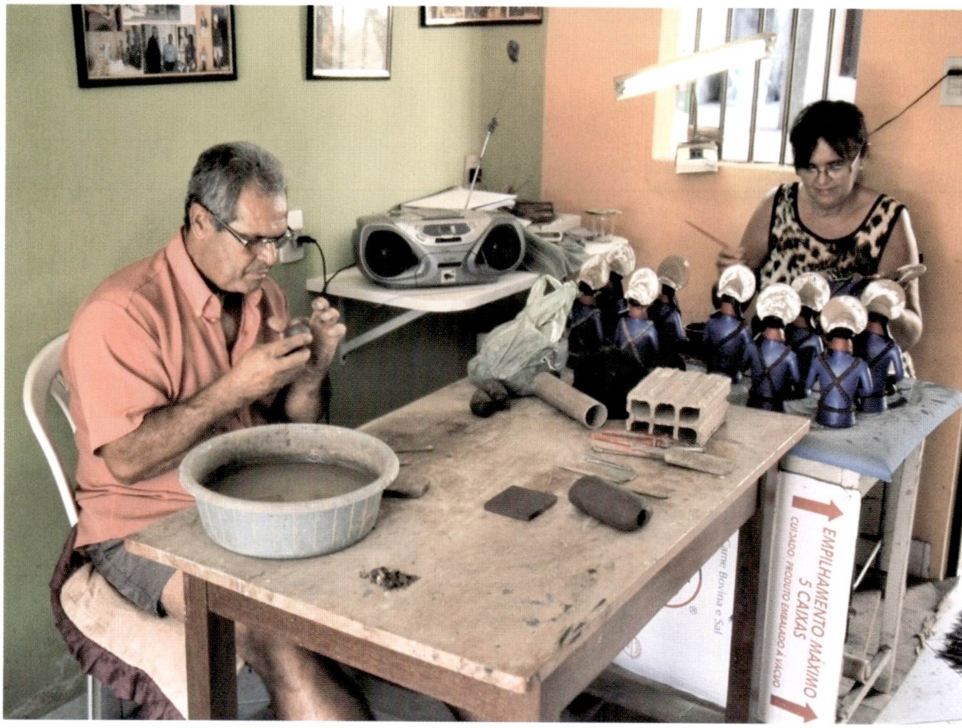

Luiz Carlos and Genilda at work in their shop, 2015

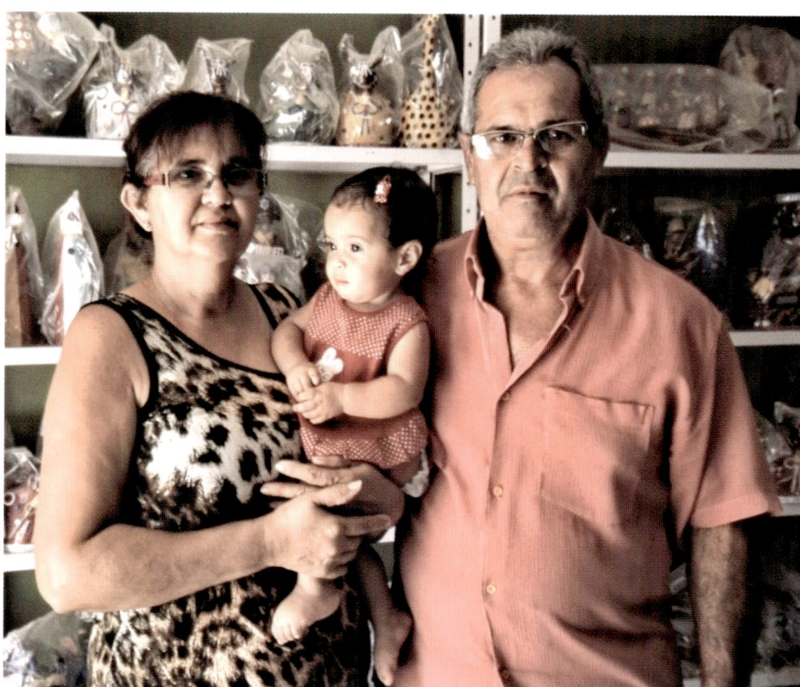

Genilda and Luiz Carlos with their granddaughter, Clarice Esther, 2015

The Process of Creation

Over the years, we have become particularly close to Luiz Carlos and Genilda. The front of their shop is open to the street. On the shelves along the sides, their works are wrapped in plastic to protect them against the dust. By the light of a window in the back wall, Genilda works at one table, Luiz Carlos at another. We stop by to visit frequently. Recorded interviews are rare, but they like to chat while they work, and our talk drifts in every direction.

We have watched Clarice Esther, their delightful granddaughter, grow. We have watched them work. Genilda is normally busy with a swarm of identical pieces — little Lampiãos, Northeastern trios, maybe pairs of the Captain and the Bull — small in size, large in number. Luiz Carlos works on a wide variety of larger pieces, one by one, usually completing one in a long day. His process is a fine, patient version of the procedure shared by all the leading artists of Alto do Moura, and the time has come to describe it. When you watch, it seems logically to be the only way to work in the clay with figurative intent, but it is not.

It is done quite differently in Tracunhaém, a pottery town to the east in Pernambuco, where work in the clay has shifted, as it has in Alto do Moura, from the utilitarian to the figurative. Differences in repertory — quotidian imagery in Alto do Moura, sacred in Tracunhaém — are not the cause of the difference in process. They stem from the personal practices that were developed in the beginning by the towns' predominant progenitors — Vitalino for Alto do Moura, Zezinho for Tracunhaém — who then passed them on to their sons and associates.

Antônio Pimpo, an artist in Tracunhaém, demonstrates his town's process. He begins with a rough hollow cone of clay. It could be thrown on the wheel, though Antônio Pimpo, like the other artists, chooses to shape it by hand. Then using an *espalda*, a slim, sharpened, chisel-like stick, he works in the manner of a carver of wood, cutting in, slicing away, and sculpting the form. Edival Rosas, the great sculptor of sacred images in Salvador da Bahia, says work in the clay is easier than the subtractive carving he does in wood, or others do in stone, because mistakes can be corrected by patches of clay added during action. In fact, Edival adds as well as subtracts; the hands of Saint Anthony and the wings of Saint Michael are added. During creation, Antônio Pimpo's process is something like that of the sculptor Edival Rosas. It is primarily subtractive. He removes sections from a block to reveal the form and adds scraps of clay while he shapes and smooths his saint, carving fine details with his handy *espalda*.

Work is subtractive in Tracunhaém, additive in Alto do Moura, but one act is the same. While they work, artists in both places pierce the piece, poking a multitude of tiny holes in the clay to eliminate the air bubbles that could detonate diminutive explosions in the kiln, and then they erase them, smearing the surface smooth.

Some general traits characterize Alto do Moura's process. Tools like Antônio Pimpo's *espalda* are uncommon and peripheral. Fingers do the foundational work, pinching and squeezing, patting and tapping constantly, like the smith's hammer on the anvil, urging the clay to accept its new form, just as clay thrown on the wheel does while it spins. Memories in the fingertips enable the artists to handle small details that are hard to see by shaping them nearly completely by touch and feel before sharpening them with the point of a knife. Few tools and few measurements. From long experience, artists like Luiz Carlos have developed a deep sense of proportion, so small parts made separately combine efficiently into larger wholes without resort to devices of measurement. Hands and eyes are basic.

The main trait of Alto do Moura's process is the additive sequence, generally: body, head, arms, ornaments. Here's a simple instance.

Luiz Carlos is going to make a half figure, from the waist up, of Lampião. He paddles a broad, flat band of clay, attaches the ends into a hollow cylinder, flattens the cylinder from round to ovoid in section, and closes the top, establishing the torso. He pokes one hole in the center of the top and another high on each side. Then he makes the head, then the hat, and loops threads of clay to make eyeglasses for the head and decorative stars for the hat. He pins the hat to the head with clips of fine wire, then sticks the head's long neck through the hole at the top of the torso. Next he rolls ropes of clay for arms of the same length and inserts them into the holes on the torso's sides, leaving them spread wide. He flattens narrow strips and crosses them on the chest, models a rifle and rests it on the left shoulder, bends the left arm around to support the rifle, and bends the right arm across the chest — all the while patting and smoothing, smoothing and patting the clay.

Now here is a finer, more complex example. In 2019, Luiz Carlos was commissioned to make a small version in clay of the newer of the two statues in the yard at the Casa Museu Mestre Vitalino, the one showing Mestre Vitalino sitting tailor-style with his famous bull.

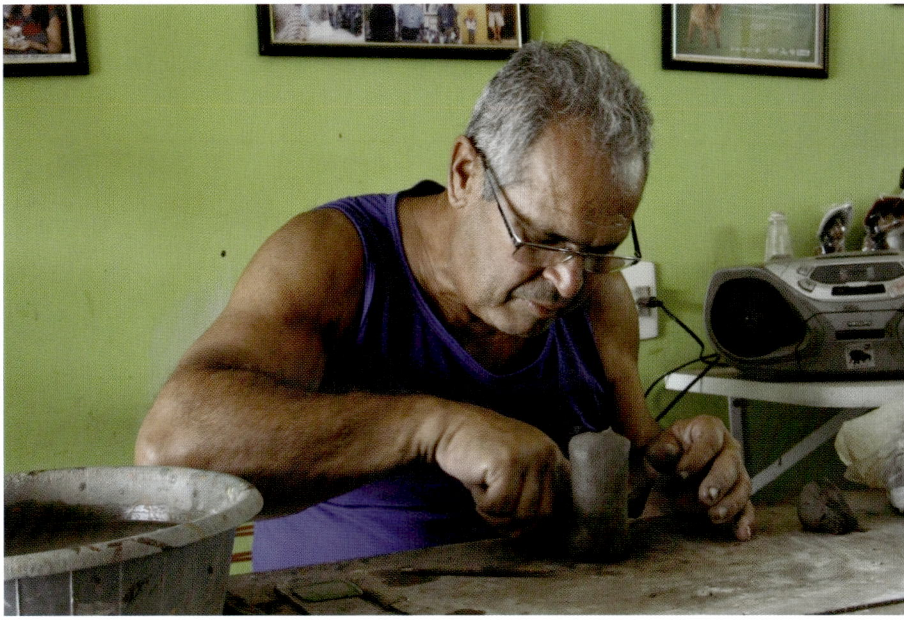

Luiz Carlos begins with a hollowed, forked tube of clay, 2019

To begin, Luiz Carlos rolls a long, thick cylinder of clay which he constantly strokes and pulls down, smoothing and unifying the clay as a potter does when making the handle for a jug. Then he shoves a pointed wooden rod, a *brunidor*, halfway down the cylinder, hollowing and stretching the top section that will become the torso. Next he splits the lower section into halves that will become the legs. The size of this hollowed and forked cylinder will set the proportions for the whole piece.

He shapes feet at the bottom of the legs, then stands the figure. Balanced verticality is a sign of sculptural competence. Were this to become a standing figure, a fisherman, say, or Luiz Gonzaga, it would be tested during the process for its ability to stand erect on small feet. At the end it would be pinned to a wide base for stability, but it must be able to stand properly without a base. This figure, though, will sit, so having evaluated it for anatomical accuracy by standing it upright, Luiz Carlos bends the legs and makes sure it looks right sitting.

Continuing to stroke the torso, Luiz Carlos closes the top, pokes a hole through it with his finger, then sets the figure, now bent at the waist, aside.

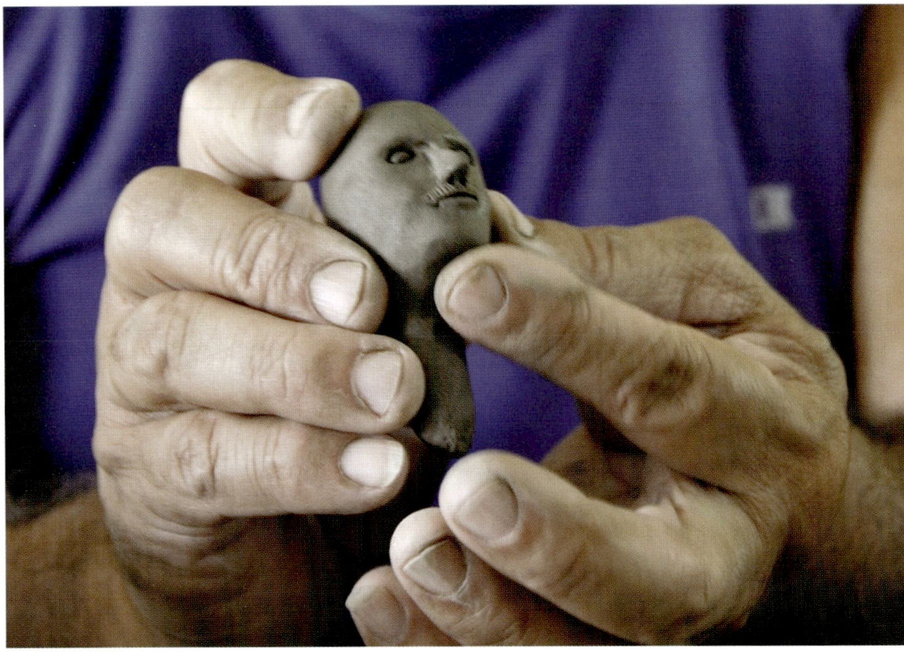

Luiz Carlos shaping the head

The head is his job now. He lifts a bit of clay, rounds a dome at the top, pulls a long neck down, and knowing what Vitalino looked like, he shapes a straight nose and a strong jaw with his fingers, then sharpens the features with a plastic knife. Luiz Carlos pricks holes for the eyes with a pointed *palito* then rolls and inserts tiny balls of clay, much as a sculptor of wooden saints digs holes in the face and fills them with glass eyeballs. Then with quick slices of a knife point he gives Vitalino a moustache. With curls of clay he gives him ears. With a patch of clay and a little plastic comb Luiz Carlos gives Vitalino the lock of hair that the balding master combed vainly forward.

Next he slides the neck into the torso's hole and adds clay around it to fuse the parts together. The hat is now his task. Luiz Carlos flattens a circle of clay for the hat's wide brim, and rolls it like a wheel on the table to perfect its circularity. Then he sticks a rounded lump of clay atop the head and places the circular brim over the lump so it bumps up to shape the hat's low, domical crown. He pins the hat to the head, and bends the brim up in front and back to create the characteristic hat of the Northeast. That's how it developed historically. A broad-brimmed hat was bent up on three sides to make the foppish, eighteenth-century tricorn, and it was bent up on the front and rear by Napoleon, Lampião, Gonzaga, and Vitalino.

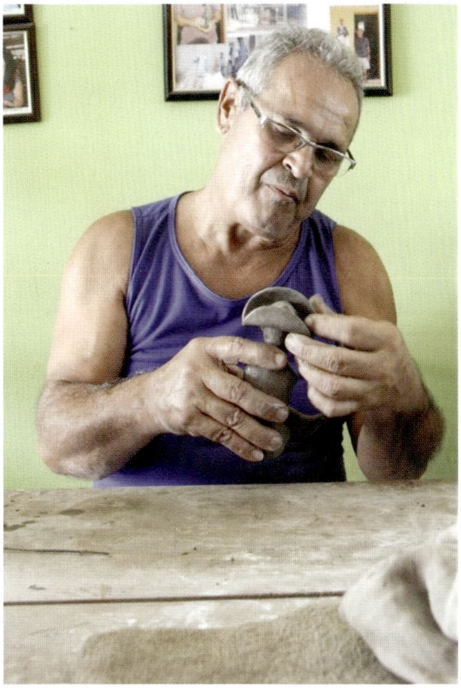

Luiz Carlos attaching the head to the body

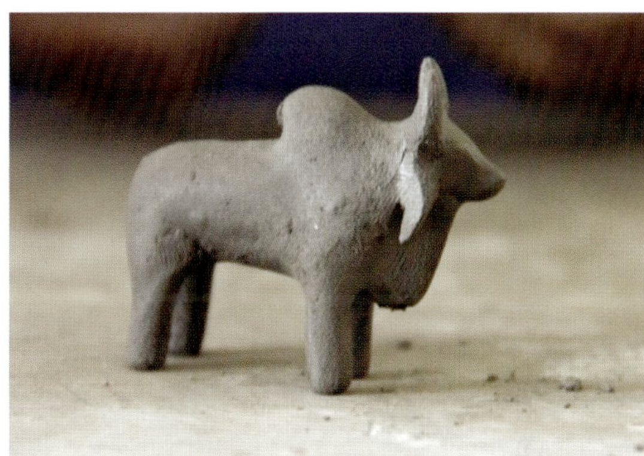

The bull

Now Luiz Carlos uses his knife to open holes in the torso for the arms. He rolls a rope of clay, flattens it, and places it to thicken the torso. He rolls and flattens another to make cuffs at the ends of the trousers on the legs. He sits back, looking and thinking, then bends the torso forward and adds a small roll of clay on the bottom of the back. During this slight pause for pondering, Luiz Carlos pierces a flurry of holes through the clay, then pats and smooths the entire surface before adding a slender strip of clay for Vitalino's belt and then wee strips for the belt loops, a fine touch.

Luiz Carlos turns now to the miniature bull, using his fingers to shape the body, then the horns, and last the legs. He stands his little bull on the table, checking for balance.

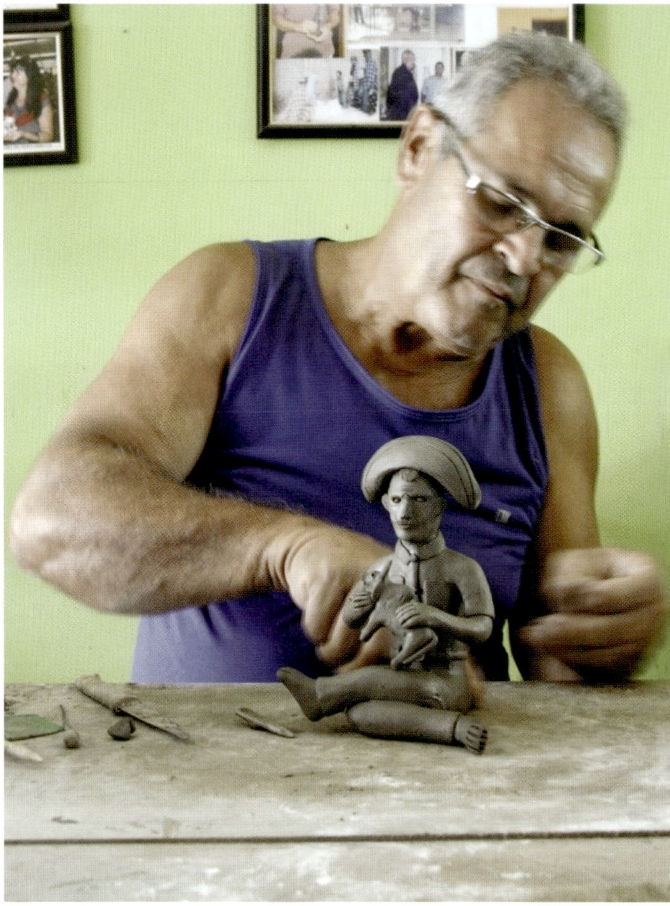

Luiz Carlos adds the arms

Things, at last, are ready for the arms. Luiz Carlos rolls two ropes and shapes their ends into the beginnings of hands, now like mittens with the thumbs expressed. He smooths them, checks their lengths, inserts the left arm, then the right, and leaves them sticking straight out. Now he flattens bits to shape the collar, pockets, and cuffs for Vitalino's shirt. He sharpens the little bull's details with a knife, then bends the left arm in to hold the bull, slices fingers into the hand, bends the right arm to the bull, slices the fingers, and there is Vitalino, sitting before him, the bull in his hands.

Luiz Carlos sends his hands out to rove over the whole form, smoothing and smoothing more. The figure is done. The process is clear. By working from large to small, proportions are preserved. By working from the inside to the outside, the sequence of assembly advances without a flaw.

Now Luiz Carlos flattens a base, places the figure on it to be sure the size is right. It is, and he flips the base over to stamp it.

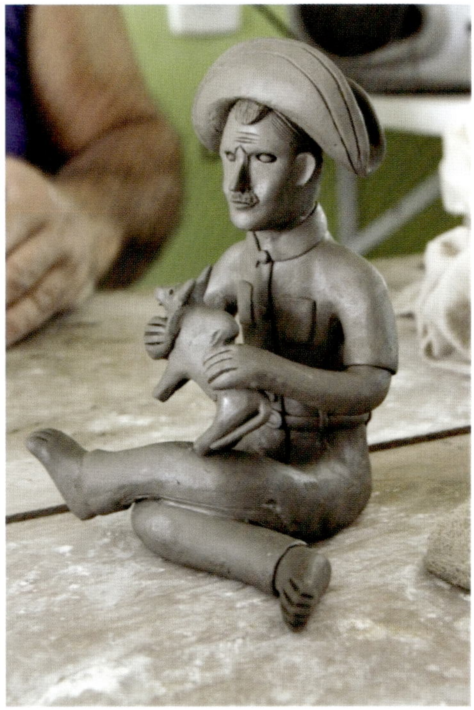

Vitalino with the bull, nearing completion

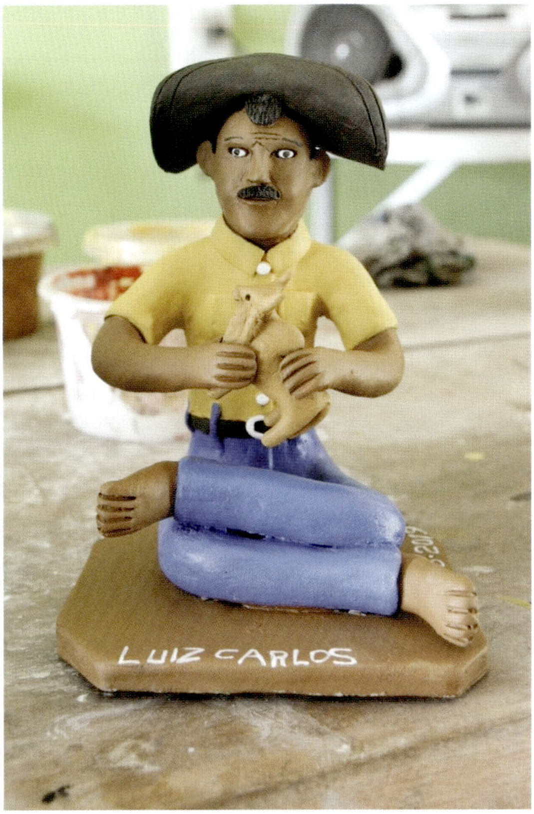

Mestre Vitalino with the bull, fired and painted by Luiz Carlos, 2019

Manuel Eudócio told us that, once at the market in Caruaru, a lady professor told Vitalino he should sign his works. Since he was illiterate, unable to sign his own name, Manuel Eudócio and Zé Caboclo made a stamp for him to use. It was wrong because they didn't realize that the letters had to run in reverse to achieve a correct impression. So they made another for Vitalino, made stamps for themselves as well, and Luiz Carlos says that, though he will paint his name on the base, as his father did, the stamp on the bottom is the guarantee of authenticity.

The bottom of the base is stamped, its corners have been clipped into the octagonal shape normal for sacred figures as well. The figure, pinned to its base, is complete, and Luiz Carlos will paint it as soon as it comes from the kiln.

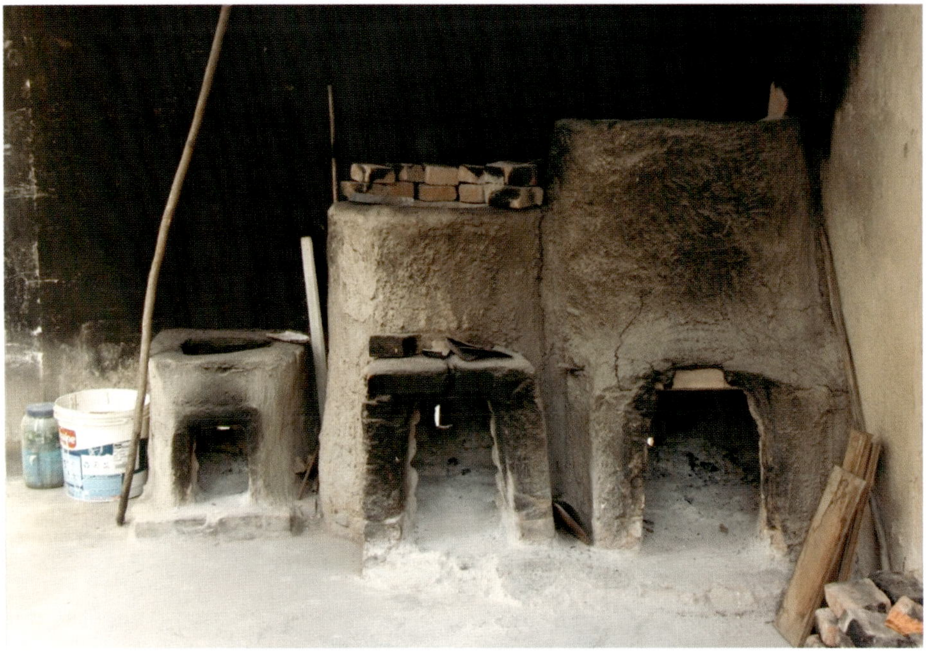

The kilns behind Ademilson's shop where Ademilson and Luiz Carlos fire their pieces, 2021

Firing is next in the process. The kilns of Alto do Moura are all of one basic type, cylindrical, wood-fired, and updraft. Kilns of the same kind are used in Tracunhaém and in Maragojipinho, a pottery town far to the south in Bahia. The kiln is loaded through its open top. The pieces, dried for a few days, are piled, jumbled and crowded, on the iron grate above the firing chamber at the bottom, which has an entry for fuel on the side. Luiz Carlos has used his father's kilns for firing big pieces, but he fires now in the small kilns behind Ademilson's shop, across the street.

The procedure is simpler than the long, complicated sequence required for firing stoneware at high heat. This is earthenware. It is done in a day, not a full week, and Luiz Carlos estimates that the heat only reaches five hundred degrees centigrade (less than half the peak heat of stoneware). But they don't use pyrometers in Alto do Moura; they gauge the heat by eye.

For four or five hours, thick sticks are stoked and the temperature rises slowly. Then when the smoke shimmers and the fire glitters, stoking speeds up, the pieces blacken and tongues of flame flicker through the gaps between the sheets of iron that cover the kiln's open top. Then after forty or fifty minutes, stoking stops. If the peak heat were held longer, the pieces would buckle and warp out of shape. Luiz Carlos rakes through the ashes to be sure that all flames have been snuffed, then he lets the kiln cool over night and removes the pieces the next day, ready for painting.

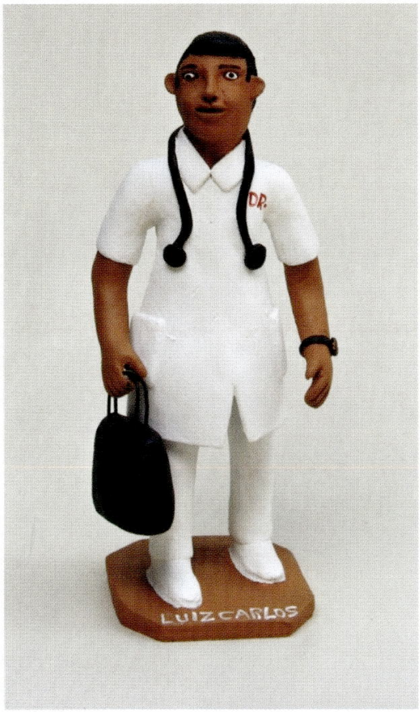

Doctor by Luiz Carlos (22 cm tall), 2019. This figure did not begin as a doctor, but during the process began to look like a doctor and so became one.

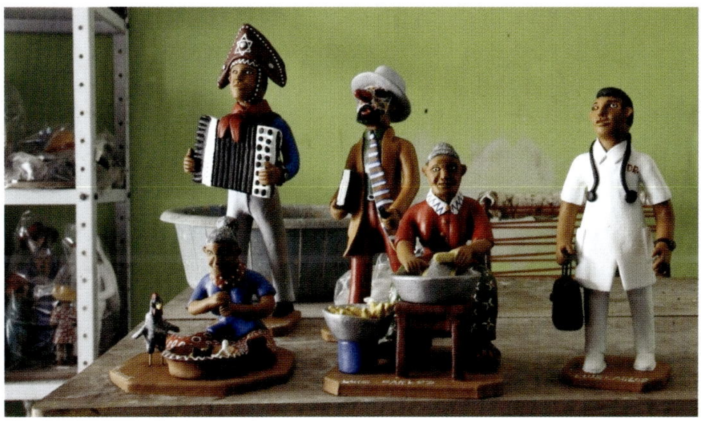

The yield of one week of shaping, firing, and painting by Luiz Carlos, 2019

Luiz Carlos usually fires once a week, so he has a week's worth of work, say five or six pieces, fired and ready when he sits down to paint. That he does is unusual since most artists pass their pieces to others for painting. Men have wives, sisters, and daughters. Women have daughters or nieces. But Luiz Carlos enjoys the break in the rhythm of work that painting provides, and he paints as carefully as he makes. In the past, Genilda painted the pieces that Luiz Carlos made. She still does occasionally, but recently, while Luiz Carlos paints his own works, Genilda has concentrated on painting the miniatures that she shapes herself, and shapes excellently, within the third line of serial production.

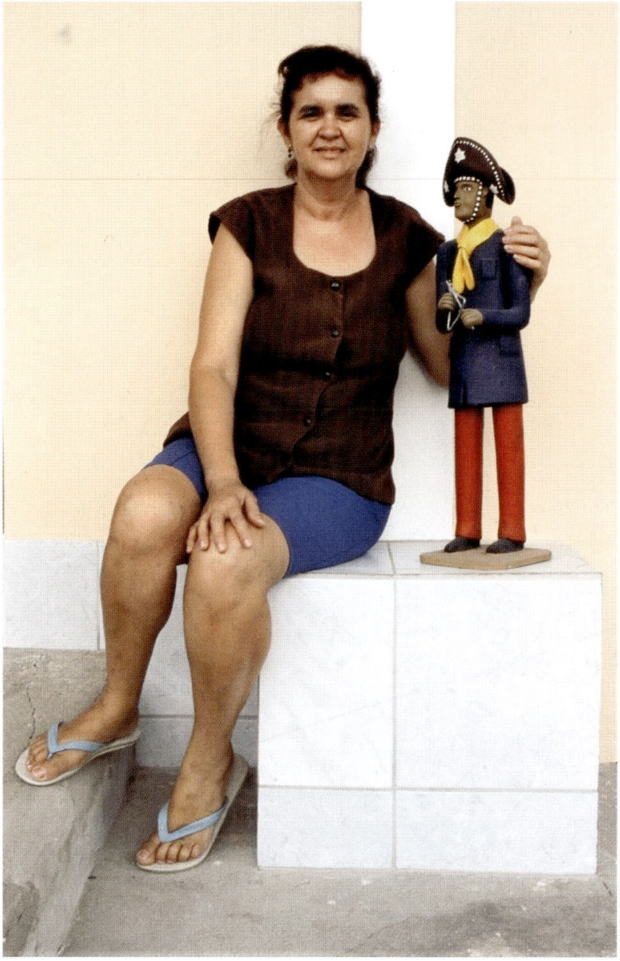

Genilda in front of the shop, 2007

Painting concludes the creative process. In 2015, we interviewed Genilda as a particularly knowledgeable and accomplished painter who generally uses the conventional strong, primary colors but has also experimented with soft, subtle mixed hues. Genilda da Silva Rodrigues begins with her own story:

"I was born in Caruaru, and came to Alto do Moura. Since childhood, my mother brought me up this way; she worked in the clay, with the clay. She made and she painted too.

"I would also make together with my father. They would make. Then it would go into the kiln and it was burned.

"So, I started to learn to make, and to paint. She would teach me how to make and paint. I think I was about eight years old, more or less, when I started to make my own pieces.

“I started to make little things in clay. I would make a little horse. I would make a dog. I would make a cow. I always made these.

“Later I started to make decorations in the clay. I would take the clay and form a flower. I used to make a flower, a rose petal, and glue it on a vase.

“My father made vases on the wheel, and we made the decorations for these vases. But these vases weren’t painted.

“And later I made the statue” — the *boneco* —“that is called *o boneco de Vitalino*. And I started to make little tables, little chairs, sofas, stoves. I used to make these things in clay.

“Later my father would burn it in the kiln. He would burn it, then I would paint it, and it was sold in the market in Caruaru. I was already living here in Alto do Moura. I am now fifty-three years of age, and Alto do Moura has always been my home.”

She pauses briefly in thought, then continues:

“And later I met Luiz, then we got married. The year we married” — 1979 —“I was eighteen years old. And when I got married, then I started to make another style, more detailed, better made.

“He started teaching me, and I started to make other types of pieces. Very different.

“I started to make better, and he would teach me how to make it, how to get the details.

“And I learned to make miniatures, really small. I learned to make the Northeastern trio, the *pífano* band, to make Dona Joana and the Doutor, the couple that Luiz made and you bought, sitting on a sofa. Then I started to make Cavalo Marinho and the Bull, all in miniature.

“I learned. Then I would make it. It was burned, and I myself would do the painting, the decoration, and I would sign my name. Just my name, Genilda. It would be there, and I would sell it.”

Genilda has reached an end, and we ask her to tell us about painting. When she married, she says, painting was her task. She painted for Luiz Carlos and for Manuel Eudócio as well. Then, “I stopped because the paint at the time, it was a glossy paint, and it has a very strong smell. And it started to harm me. So, I had to stop. The paint now is a different paint.”

The paint then was an oil-based enamel. It gave a fine shine, but it smelled terrible — Manuel Eudócio also complained about its odor — and it made Genilda ill; the doctor forbade her to use it again. The paint now is a water-based acrylic, far easier to use. It dries quickly and, put in the sun to dry, it gives gloss enough. We ask her to describe the process of painting, and Genilda says:

"The process of painting. We have to first prepare the paint, right?

"It has a process. We can't just open the paint and start painting. We can't. We have to prepare the paint. For our work, it does not come prepared.

"It is paint for the walls. We work with it. We prepare it in our way.

"We buy two cans. One is white. The other has a color. And we mix it to get the tone. When we use the blue, the blue can't be the one that comes from the can. We mix the blue with the white to get our blue.

"All the paints are like that. We have to mix them to prepare them.

"And the important thing is the white glue that is used in schools. We put half the container of glue into more or less the same amount of water, and we mix it really soft.

"And we put that inside each color as well. We mix it with the paint so it will stick to the piece."

She tells us that broken pieces can be repaired with epoxy, that cracks can be filled with spackle, that one coat of paint is usually enough, though patchy surfaces will get a second coat. Then we ask her about the choice of colors, and Genilda says:

"The colors we must have, that can't be missing, are blue, yellow, green, black, and white, and red. These colors can't be missing.

"And most important, actually, is the color of clay, the color of the *skin* of the statue. This color has to be present."

A fine feature of Alto do Moura's art is that the local clay, when fired and left unpainted on faces and hands, ranges from mellow tan to rich brown, accurately matching the skin tones of the people of the Northeast. Genilda continues:

"So, from these colors, we start to mix other colors. We start making the lilac, we make the light green, the dark green. From the green paint, we can get up to three colors in addition to the original.

"For the clothing I am the one who chooses the colors of the piece, what it will be. I painted a *Retirantes* last week. I can look and already see the right colors it will have."

The colors are at once decorative and informational. By painting the dresses of rural women with bright colors in small-figured overall patterns — notably in *Os Retirantes* and *A Volta da Roça* — Genilda separates them from urban

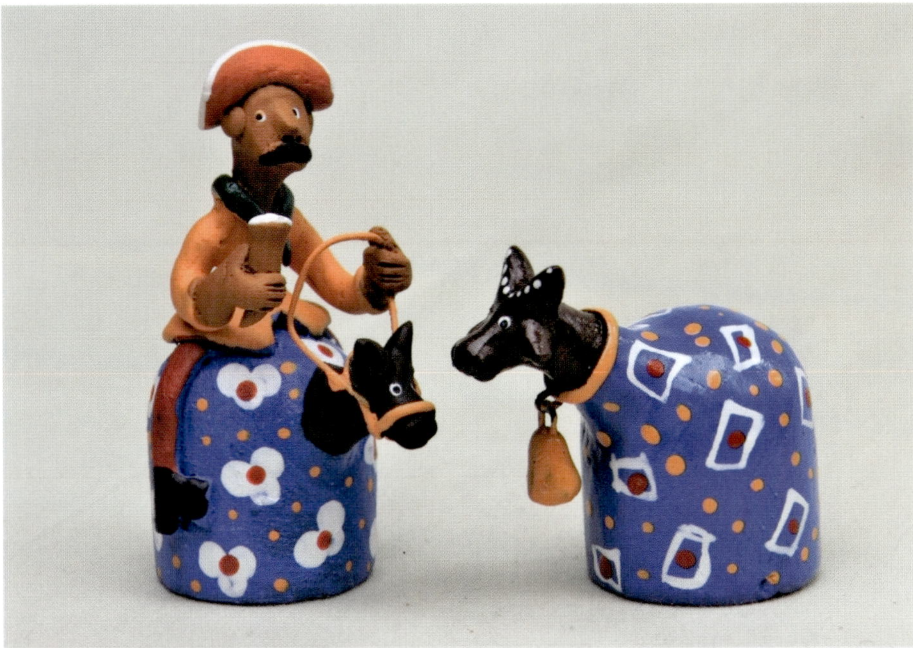

The Captain and the Bull, miniatures by Genilda (5.5, 4 cm tall), 2019

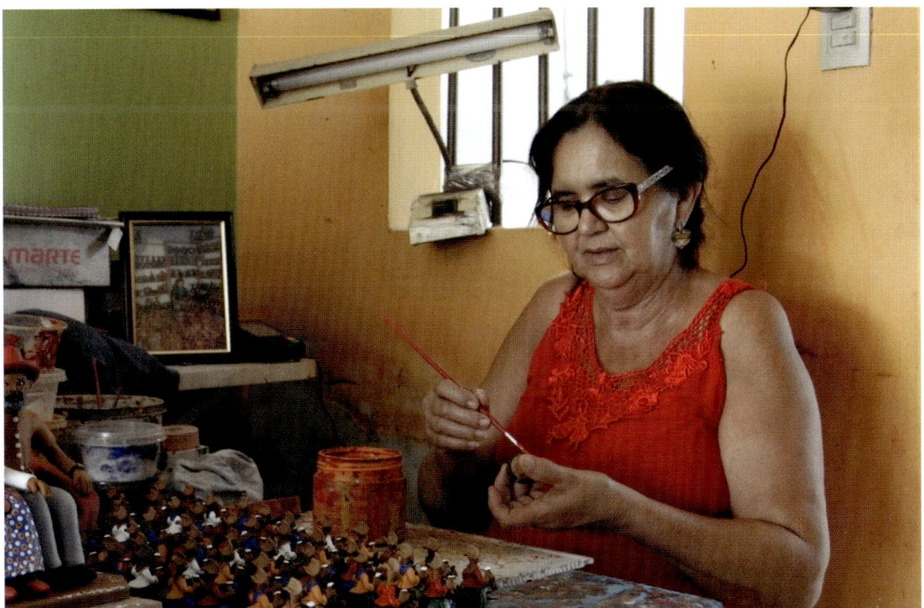

Genilda painting miniatures, 2014

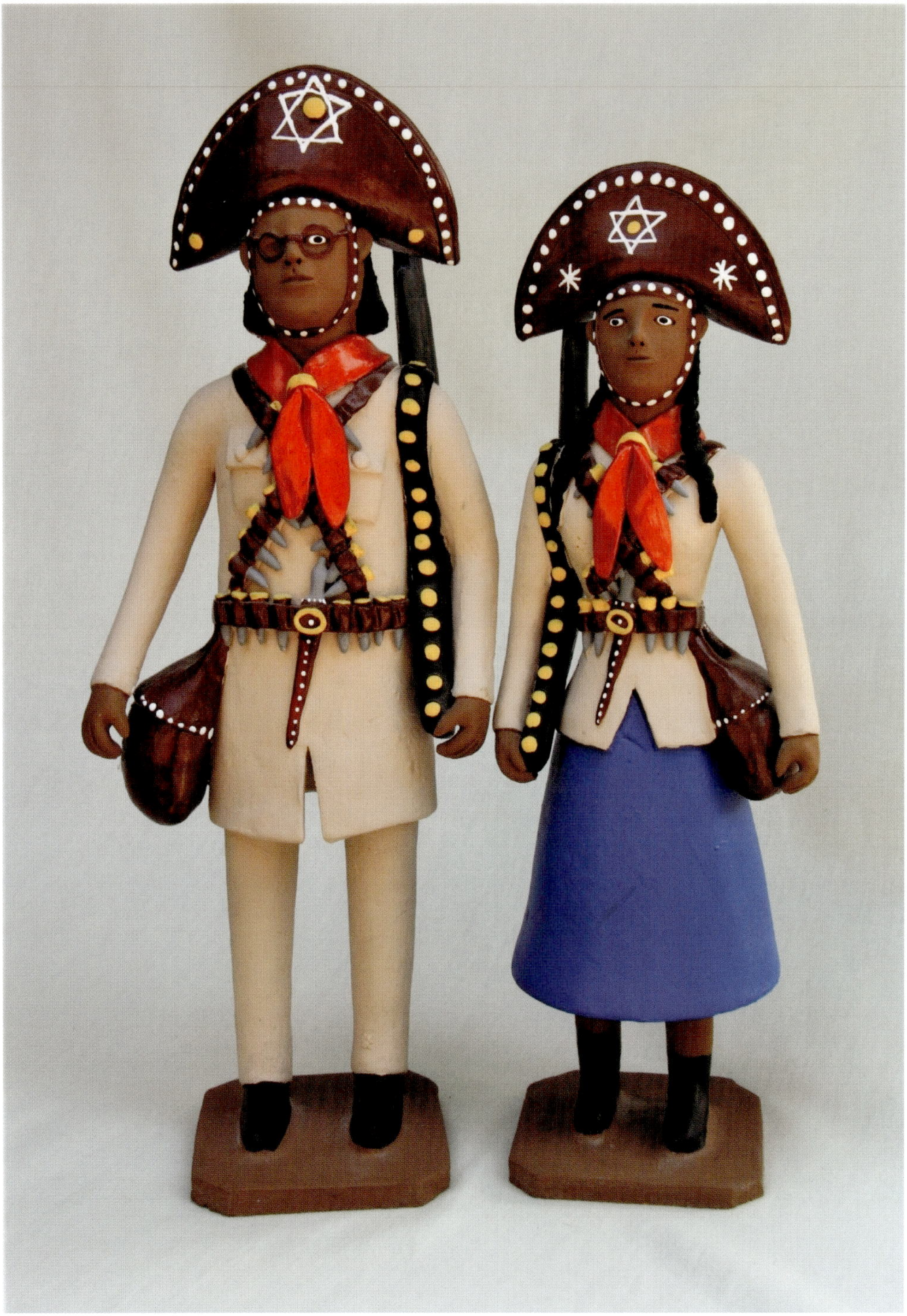

Lampião and Maria Bonita, shaped by Luiz Carlos, painted by Genilda (39, 35 cm tall), 2007

women and locates them on the farm. With colors in mind, Genilda turns to Lampião.

"For him," she says, "we use different colors. He used to wear khaki; he used to wear it inside the scrubland to be disguised.

"He used to wear it to disguise himself" — like camouflage — "in the scrubland, which is called the *caatinga*. He would be more disguised. You could not see him very well.

"And the blue, the blue clothes he used to wear, they say it was more for when he was at parties, he would wear it. It was called *brim grosso*" — thick denim —"like the fabric of jeans.

"It was *blue*, real strong. Real strong. So that was what he used to wear for parties."

Luiz Carlos, listening while he works, says, "Usually for the color of the clothes of Lampião we use two colors. Some people like the tan, some the blue. We use two so people can choose the color they like." Genilda agrees and turns to Maria Bonita:

"For Maria Bonita, we can change the colors. We can put a khaki blouse and a red skirt. We can put the khaki with a blue skirt.

"She always used to wear something that matched the clothing of Lampião. There has to be something that is also in the clothing of Lampião.

"Lampião and Maria Bonita, they have to be beautiful. The painting is part of the beauty of the piece."

Her last comment could stand as an apt conclusion, but without a pause Genilda continues:

"There was a time in the beginning when I started to learn to paint, I used to paint with my grandmother. I think of her as my grandmother. She was married to my grandfather, and I think of her as my grandmother.

"And she taught me to paint.

"The process of that paint, it was a very *difficult* process. It was a different process from the one I use now, and it was different from the shiny one I used when I was just married.

"It was a *different* process."

But it was like the process Manuel Eudócio's grandmother used when he was a boy. Genilda goes on:

"We used to buy paint in powder form. We had a fire and we would melt resin in kerosene. The resin melted and got soft.

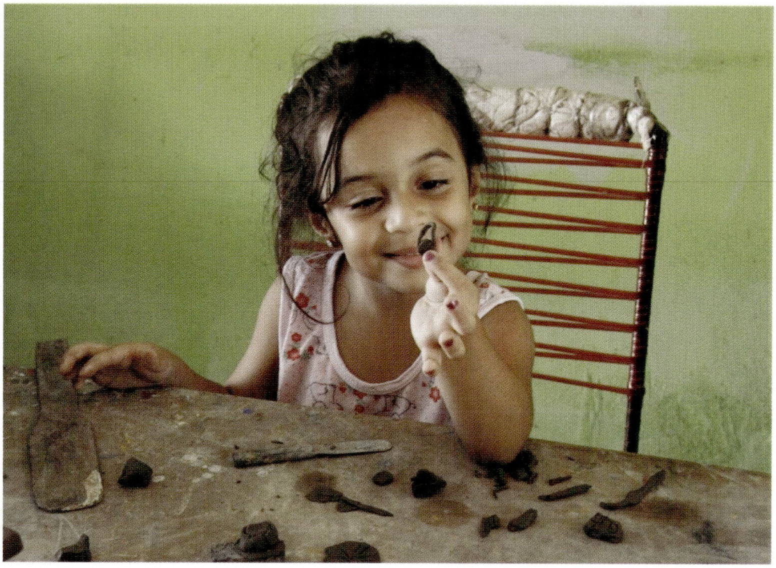

Clarice Esther playing, 2019

"Then we dampened the powder with water. When the resin got soft, we would throw the powder in and keep mixing until it got to the point of paint. The paint was thicker. Because of the resin, the paint was thicker.

"When it got cold, we would transfer it to a container, and then use it to paint, not with a paintbrush, but with our hands."

Manuel Eudócio remembered painting little horses, little bulls with his finger. Genilda remembers:

"The paint would get under your nails. It would enter the skin and cover your arms, up to the elbows. And we would take the piece, with our hands, and pass the paint until it was all painted, all with our hands.

"We would paint it and leave it there. And it was a process that took a long time to dry. And it was shiny, and it would be beautiful.

"And it would be beautiful.

"But the process started advancing. With time, we started looking for something easier, and we had gotten to the process we have now.

"But that was the first process of my painting that I learned from her. That I learned with my grandmother."

Time runs in lines of development: the process of painting has gotten progressively easier. And time rolls in repetitive cycles. Manuel Eudócio learned beside his grandmother. His daughter-in-law, Genilda, learned beside her grandmother. Now, Clarice Esther is learning beside her grandmother, Genilda. Clarice's parents leave early for work, and since she attends her school's afternoon session, she spends the mornings in her grandparents' workshop, playing around and watching what is going on, getting used to the centrality of serious creation in everyday life.

A month earlier when Luiz Carlos was gone, Clarice sat in his chair and played with the bits of clay left on his table, just as Vitalino once played with the leftover scraps of his mother's clay. Now, in June of 2019, Clarice is sitting and painting, learning beside Genilda. Her grandmother, intense in concentration, is painting the miniatures assembled on the table before her. Clarice has her own little table next to Genilda's, and she is also painting the miniatures her grandmother made.

While she watches the point of the brush pull color over the clay, Clarice doesn't lift her eyes when her grandmother gives her a rare, brief, but firm piece of orientating advice. Clarice keeps painting, rapt in effort, doing her best, getting better, and we have been given a glimpse of the very beginning of art.

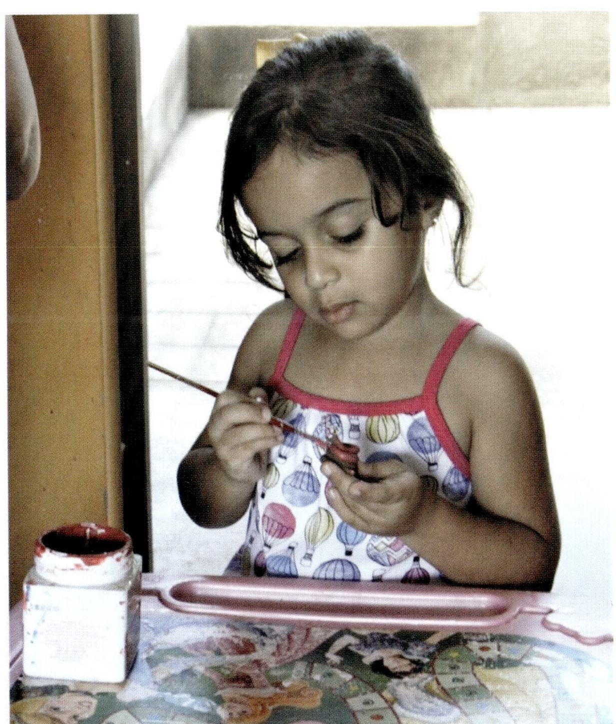

Clarice Esther painting, 2019

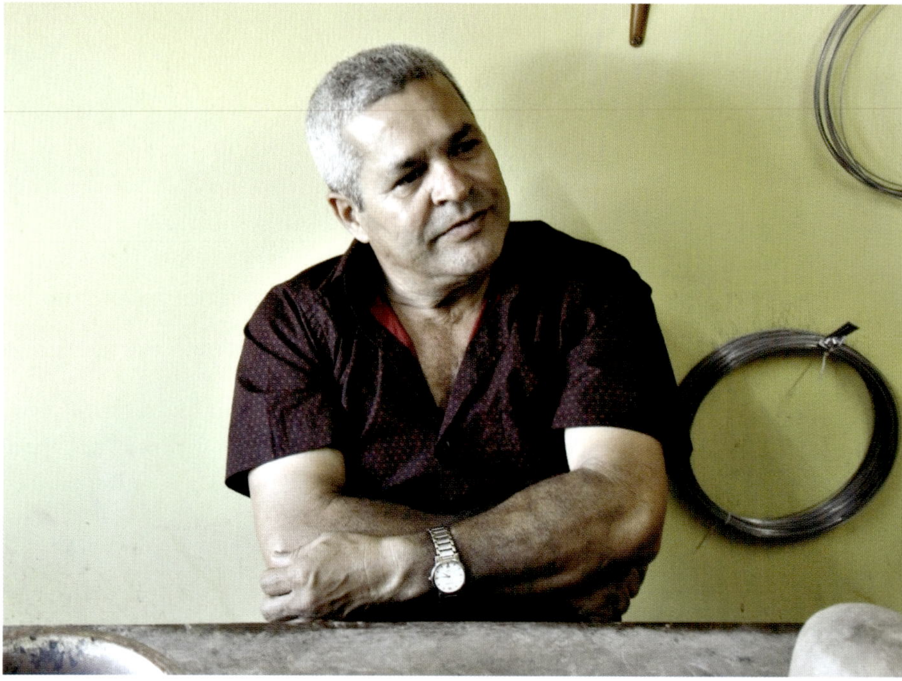

Ademilson, 2019

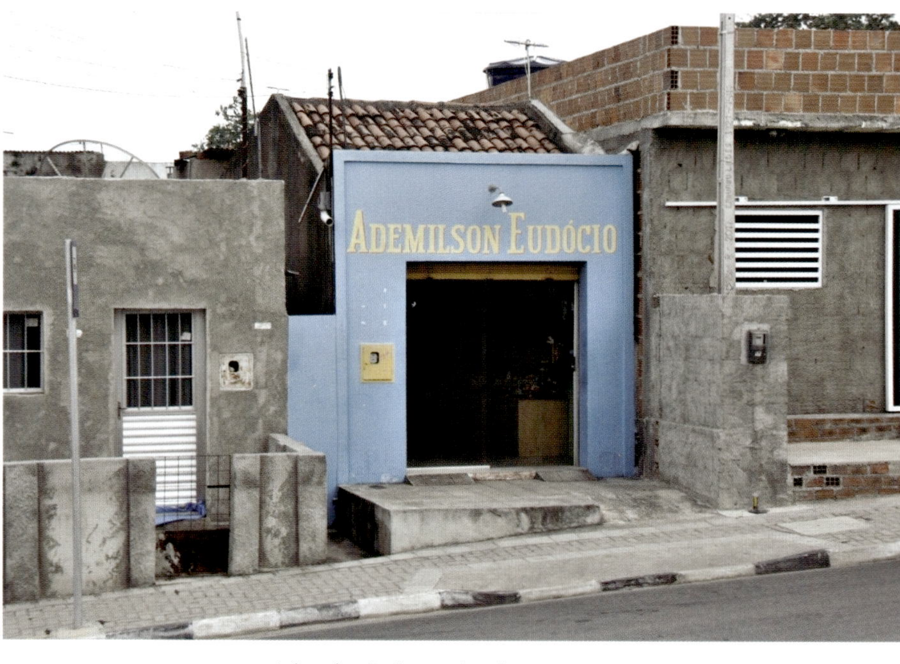

Ademilson's shop, Alto do Moura, 2019

8

Ademilson and Elisoneide

Ademilson, Manuel Eudócio's son, Luiz Carlos's younger brother, remembers the beginning:

"Our life in art commenced at a very young age. We picked up the clay to play, to make toys.

"And this playmaking improves, improves, improves. We are always watching Daddy working.

"And then it happens. The first pieces, they are taken to the market and sold. And then it stops being playmaking, and it starts being a profession.

"I was still very young, a child, ten, twelve years of age, already working, and the product was already being sold in the Feira de Caruaru.

"And then you continue. All the children from here, they continued working.

"And you become an artisan, you become an artist. In this way, without any pressure, without any pressure from your father.

"Daddy never put us to work, no. We were freely at ease. We would take some clay to play with, or he would give us some clay to play with, sometimes next to his own table, with us sitting on the floor.

"And you learn.

"And time passes, time passes, and you need money. And these little pieces that you would make — little horses, little bulls, these are the first pieces — they would sell. Then the interest in working, the interest in money comes.

"That is how it happens."

It happened by practice, not formal instruction: "Daddy gave advice. But it was not like teaching, no. Not: I'm going to teach this boy so he can become

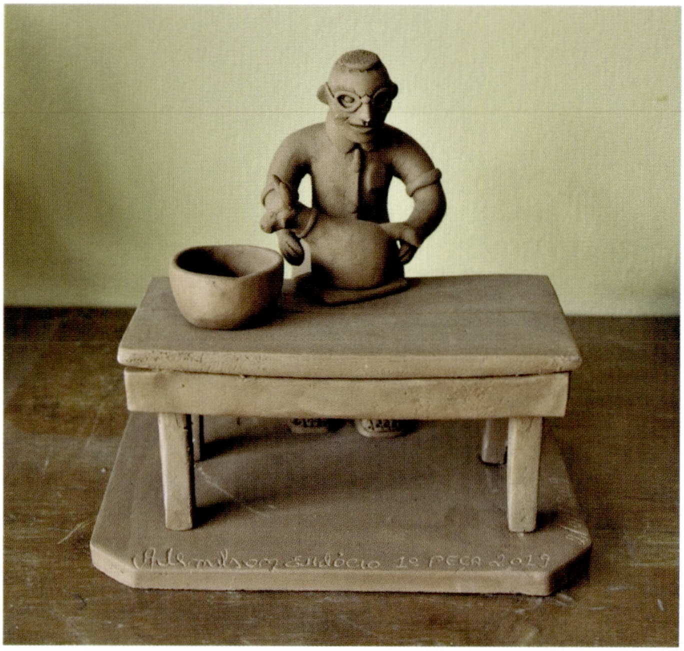

Manuel Eudócio, a portrait in clay by Ademilson, 2019

a good artist. No. He would give advice. When he saw us make something wrong, he would say, This is not like this. It is like this.

"But for him to sit down and orient us like a teacher — no, never.

"He did that with none of his children. It was spontaneous, spontaneous. And we learned."

Ademilson Rodrigues has taken his father's middle name for his artistic last name. Above the door of his shop and on his business cards, the name is Ademilson Eudócio. For commercial reasons, certainly, but more out of affection and admiration, he wants to preserve this interlaced connection. During two long conversations in 2019, Ademilson told us about Manuel Eudócio. The second ended like this:

"Daddy was an innovator in art, in the art of Vitalino.

"Just look. Vitalino's work was more rustic, revolving around the life of the country person, the person of the Northeast. Then Daddy arrives with Zé Caboclo and they are already putting details that Vitalino would never put on the pieces, right?

"Daddy innovated, and he was inspired to create. It was, I believe, a divine thing with him. He would create. Every week he had new pieces in his atelier. New things, understand. He created.

"I mean, if you were to go to Severino Vitalino's atelier, when he was still working, he would be maintaining that *same* tradition as Vitalino. He made a point of fulfilling the art of his father, Severino Vitalino. He died preserving it.

"But Daddy, being one of the first, he did not confine himself. He *expanded*, he innovated in our art. So, he had, with Zé Caboclo, a *very* important role in this art. A very important role.

"And today, almost all of the museums have his pieces. They have Vitalino, they have Zé Caboclo, and they have his pieces. He is very well known.

"I am very grateful to God for having had him for my father.

"And I am grateful that he had the opportunity that he had as a folk artist" — an *artista popular* —"as an artisan, because in our Brazil, especially in the Northeast, the folk artists, they have a very difficult life, right?

"For them, the money was not good. They were not recognized. Folk artists in Brazil, especially in the Northeast, many of them died in pitiful circumstances, only to be recognized after death.

"So, I think that does no good for the family, or the person who died. It is important to be recognized in life. And this recognition Daddy had in his life.

"Thank God, he had a very favorable trajectory in his life. He had no difficulties in any moment in this art.

"He sustained his household of ten children by himself, through his work, understand?

"He always owned a car, and he died with a car in his garage.

"I mean to say, he had a fortunate life. He was recognized by the authorities, the governor of Pernambuco, the mayor of Caruaru. He had support, he had recognition. Many honors.

"And I am *very* grateful to God for this recognition, for all that he received, for the life that he had.

"Daddy lived the life that he wanted to live.

"In reality, he was humble. Very humble. He had no vanity about him. He was modest, humble.

"He had a car to take him to the market, to accomplish his errands. When a house came up for sale, here in the community, he would buy it. He would buy a house and give it to one of his children.

"He had merit. He had intelligence. He knew how to manage that which came into his hands. He knew how to teach.

"I mean to say, he had a life as a folk artist that few have. Few have had this privilege.

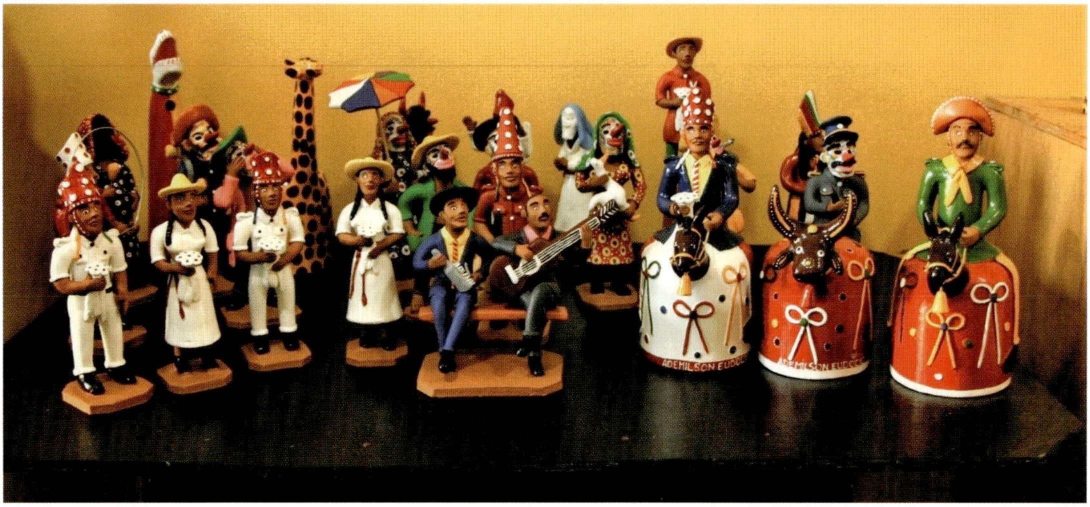

A full set of the *Reisado* by Ademilson, 2021. Gallants and Ladies to the left, the Jaraguá and Giraffe behind them, musicians in the middle, Captain, Bull, and Cowboy to the right.

"When he passed, thank God, he left all his children established, secure. Nothing was lacking for anyone. There is a reason to thank God for this.

"He was recognized in this life of art.

"He died happy."

Our conversations are untied by a swirling nebular pattern. As he did when he characterized his father's life and work, Ademilson swings every major topic on an arc away from a steady, single center: his father's innovative spirit. When we raise the topic of his own repertory, Ademilson begins with Manuel Eudócio's creative contribution of the *Reisado*, for which Ademilson also uses the more common Brazilian name, *Bumba-Meu-Boi*:

"*Bumba-Meu-Boi* is a piece that Daddy invented. He found much to make inside it.

"The *Bumba-Meu-Boi*, it has twenty-eight characters, right? Twenty-eight characters. The *Bumba-Meu-Boi* is composed of these pieces, and each piece has its own role in the play.

"And Daddy performed in the *Reisado* when he was young. There was a *Reisado* here in Alto do Moura, and he was the Gallant. Then he passed it into clay. He created it in clay.

"In the year seventy-eight, he recreated the *Reisado* here in Alto do Moura with a cousin of his, Zé Amácio. They recreated the *Reisado*.

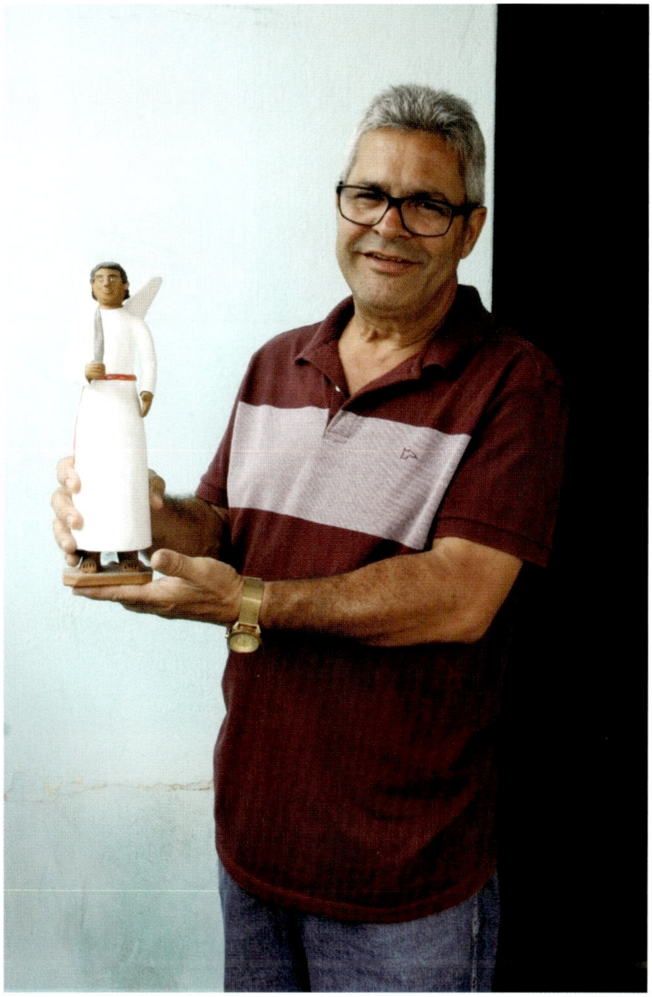

Ademilson with his father's rendition of the Angel, the role Ademilson played in the brief revival, 2021

"And in this *Reisado* I participated. I was one of the characters. I was the Angel. I played the role of the Angel.

"I was an adolescent, and Daddy said, You will be good to play the role of the Angel. Play the Angel. When I was an adolescent, right?

"But that *Reisado* lasted just a little while. Only one year, more or less, one year and a bit. Then it also ended."

With personal experience behind him and his father's works in his mind, Ademilson says, "The pieces of *Bumba-Meu-Boi*, they are the ones I most like to make. I have dedicated myself to this line." He has made all of the characters, but a few of them stand out and get created most often:

"Within the *Bumba-Meu-Boi*, the Bull, Cavalo Marinho, Jaraguá, these are characters that stand out. But the Doutor and Dona Joana stand out with more intensity.

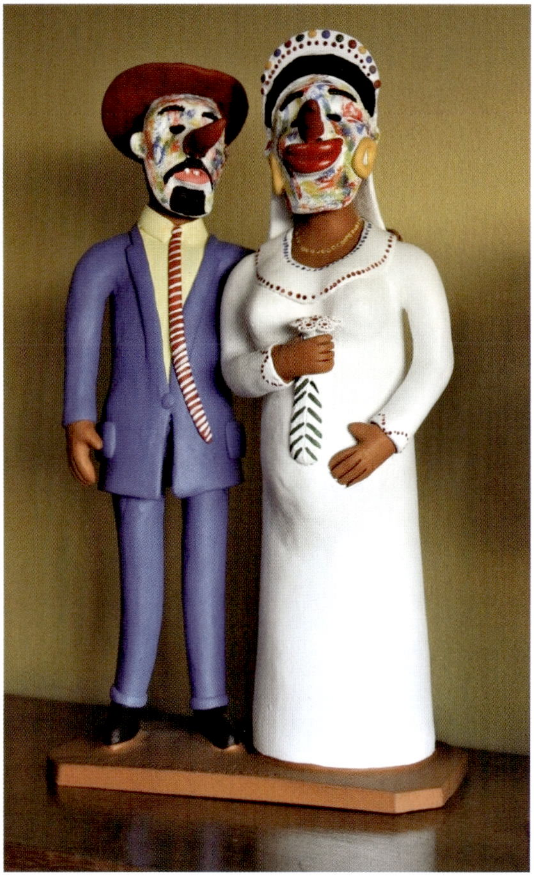

The Doutor and Dona Joana, by Ademilson, 2019

"Daddy created the marriage of the two, of the Doutor and Dona Joana, that has nothing to do with the play. The piece of the marriage is not in the play, understand?

"He simply had the idea. The characters were already known, but he married them, and from there he started to make other scenes: the Doutor and Dona Joana riding bicycles, the Doutor and Dona Joana in a car, the Doutor and Dona Joana with their son. I created them getting divorced.

"He focused on that, and it is, in reality, the best-known piece from the *Bumba-Meu-Boi*.

"In the play they were not married. The play has only men, men dressed as women, playing the roles of women. Just men.

"There was Dona Joana with a big belly, pregnant. And there was Catarina, also pregnant. There was the Old Woman of the Bird, also pregnant. Just men. There were no women.

"The marriage was only in Daddy's imagination."

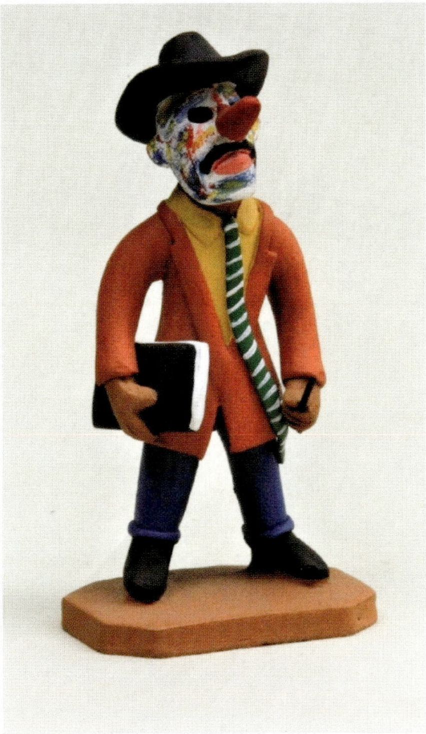

The Doutor, by Ademilson (14 cm tall), 2016

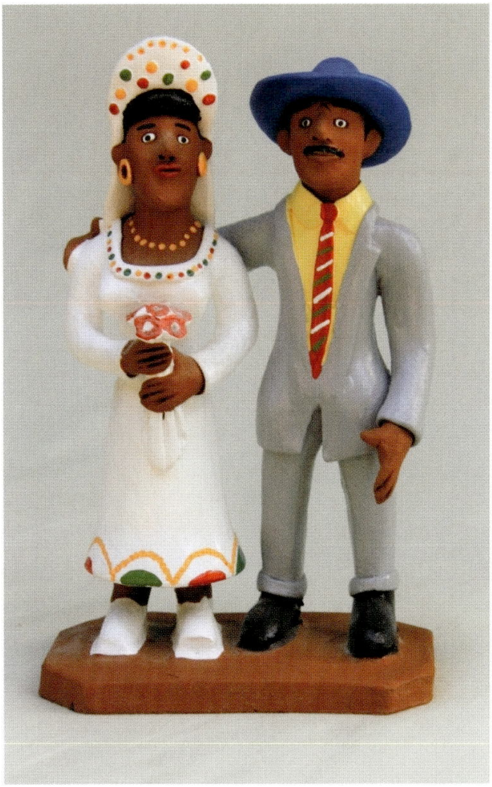

Wedding couple, by Ademilson (16 cm tall), 2018

The *Reisado* occupies the center, but his repertory, Ademilson says, contains "a great variety of pieces" and, citing the familiar total of Vitalino's works, 118, he says that, though he has never counted, he believes — and we agree — that his repertory is larger, and so was his father's. Set in his repertory, the *Reisado* fits within the master category Ademilson calls "the quotidian of the Northeast."

When he names his Northeastern pieces, Ademilson begins with *Os Retirantes* and *A Volta da Roça*, *A Banda de Pífano* and *O Trio Nordestino*. Then he mentions scenes of marriage and baptism, scenes of grocery stores and barber shops. He portrays Mestre Vitalino with the *pífano*, and while he doesn't make saints, he does portray Padre Cícero because "it is a piece of our region; it pertains to our culture. It is part of the culture of the Northeast." And, of course, he makes many and various images of Lampião and Maria Bonita. One afternoon, thirty-eight works stood for sale on shelves in his shop. Fourteen came from the *Reisado*, nine depicted Lampião and Maria Bonita.

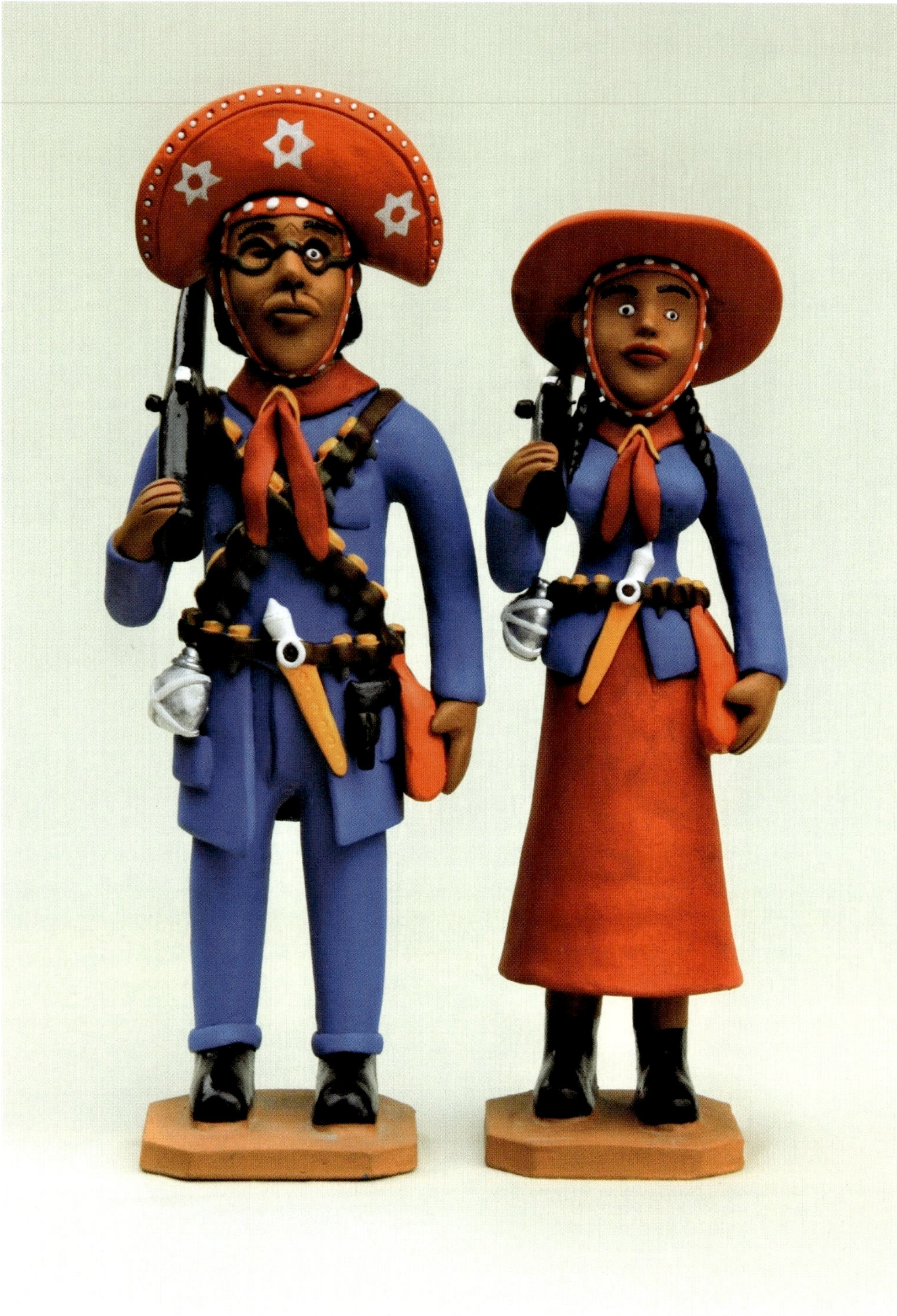

Lampião and Maria Bonita, by Ademilson (32, 29 cm tall), 2021

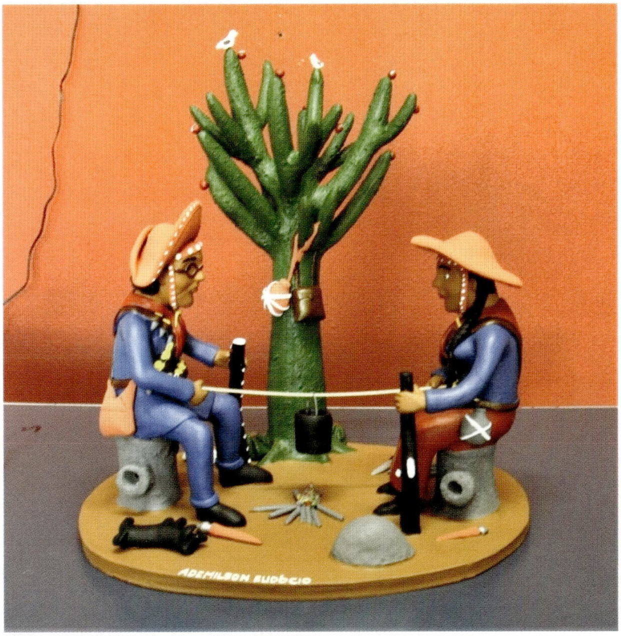

Campfire scene of Lampião and Maria Bonita
making supper, by Ademilson, 2019

"Lampião was a very violent person," Ademilson says. "But Lampião is part of this Northeastern culture, right? Lampião's gang, the *cangaço*, was distinguished for its violence, unfortunately.

"Some will say that Lampião was seeking justice. Others will say he was a bandit. According to history, we understand that Lampião entered the world of crime to seek justice with his proper hands. But history also says that many people, many innocent people, paid with their lives for the justice he sought.

"I recuse myself from this debate. But I find the culture interesting, this disposition he had: an eye for an eye, a tooth for a tooth. This is what attracts me.

"And in particular, I find the Lampião couple a very interesting piece. We make many scenes of Lampião: Lampião on horseback, Lampião preparing supper, even Lampião courting. I have even made Lampião with Maria Bonita on horseback.

"And so, he enriches our culture, our art. He is a very interesting person. And the piece sells well. It sells well."

Wonderfully diverse in subject, ranging from a barbershop with four men to the portrait of a solitary chicken, Ademilson's creations are unified by a distinct personal style. Ademilson and Luiz Carlos, both grounded in their father's work, share basic traits: an inclination to the scenic, fine finish, sharp details, careful modeling and painting. But in his handling of the clay and in his palette, Ademilson differs, displaying an impulse to elaboration and exaggeration that can head for humor. For example: in one of his renditions of the common image of a bride and groom on horseback, which Vitalino Neto altered into critique, Ademilson turned the piece to comedy by making the bride very tall and the groom so short that he had to carry a ladder along so he could climb it to get a kiss.

Humor is a latent possibility, but the general look of the work flows from a tendency to exaggerate for identification, which can be called caricature if the word is stripped of trivializing implications. Long ago, when the search for distinctive national traits was a fashion in anthropology, Gilberto Freyre, Pernambuco's great historian, argued that caricature is the prime trait of Brazilian creativity. He saw it in the eighteenth-century sculpture of Aleijadinho, Brazil's most famous artist, and he saw it in the twentieth-century novels of Jorge Amado, Brazil's most famous writer. For Freyre, Aleijadinho and Amado were both caricaturists, and it could reasonably be argued that Alto do Moura's artists are all caricaturists, with Ademilson in the lead.

If you were to place a version of *Os Retirantes* by Ademilson next to one by another artist — both the same size with the same number of figures — you would find Ademilson's inclination to exaggeration revealed in the amount of baggage on the grandmother's donkey, the size of the bundles on the heads of the wife and oldest daughter, the number of animals trailing along, and the variety of bright colors.

Bright colors join with an expansive repertory to divide Vitalino's followers: Manuel Eudócio and his sons to this side, Severino Vitalino and his sons to that. When we ask Ademilson about his colors, he replies:

"I make a piece, then I burn the piece, and when it comes out of the kiln, I *imagine* the colors that will go well on the piece.

"Then I say, Elisoneide, paint it like this. The suit of the Doutor paint blue, paint black, yellow.

"The piece needs to match the scene also. When it is a marriage scene, I want more blue. When it is a baptism, I want more yellow, red. It is like that. The colors come from the imagination. There are no rules.

"People say, You have an assembly of colors that is very beautiful on your pieces. Elisoneide does it well."

Elisoneide, Ademilson's sister, lives just down the street, across from Manuel Eudócio's shop. When we get the recorder going and ask about painting, Elisoneide Rodrigues da Silva says:

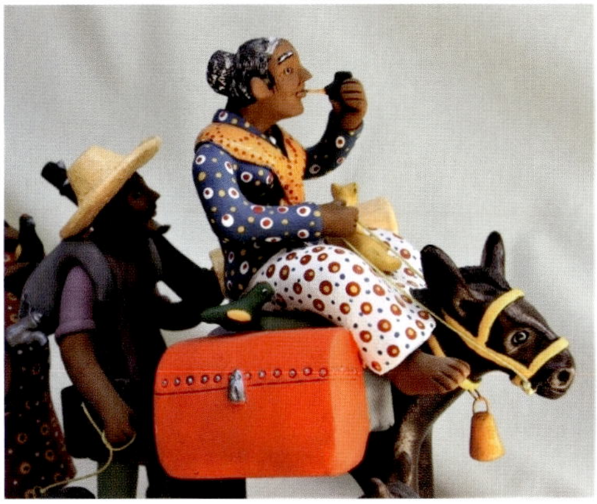

Grandmother

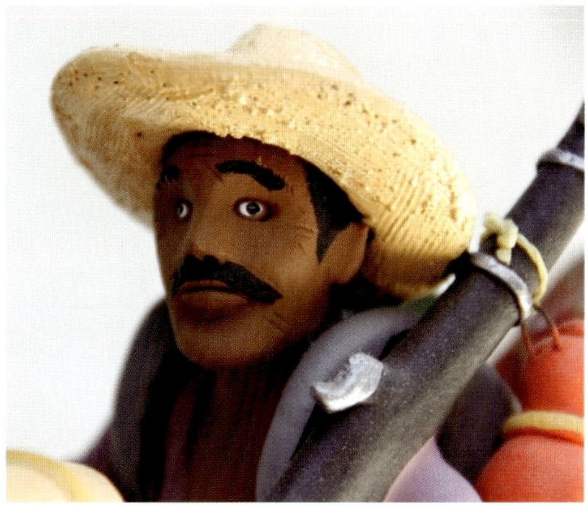

Father

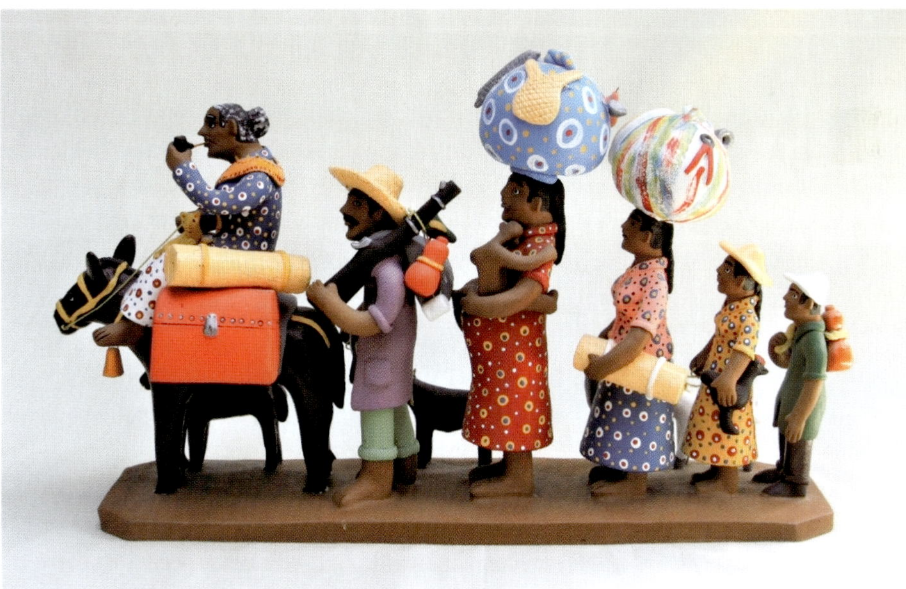

Os Retirantes, shaped by Ademilson, painted by Elisoneide (40 cm long), 2019

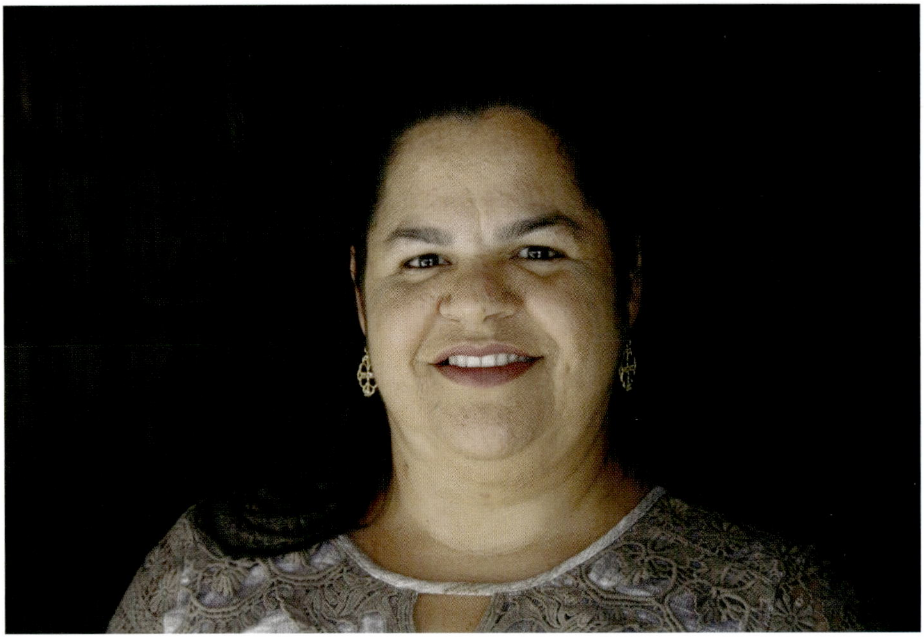

Elisoneide, 2019

"I never worked with the clay. I never had, like, the opportunity to make. So, I only do the painting.

"I was seeing people working, and I picked up a little statue, and started painting. I started to learn.

"So, I started painting my brother's pieces. Adenildo, he has passed away. Then I started painting his pieces, Daddy's. I started working with Daddy.

"He would say, Look, this one here, you paint it in this color. They were the colors that matched.

"So, generally, it was him who gave the opinion. Some pieces that I would paint, it was based on my opinion. But it was more often that he would say what color it should be painted, and I would paint it.

"Later, he was not seeing so well, and he was not making the pieces with perfection like he used to. So, when I went to paint, it was to take away some of the defects that they had. So, I was giving more finish to the piece.

"And now I work for Ademilson. I paint all of his pieces."

We ask about changes over time, and Elisoneide tells us:

"Today the pieces are more colorful. Because in the period of Vitalino, he would not work with paint, right?

"Vitalino's pieces were natural. It was the color of clay, the color that the piece had when it left the kiln. That was the color it remained in. He would not paint.

"So, afterward Daddy started painting the pieces. He was the one who started it. My mother also would paint.

"And there were other people also, some neighbors who would work with him. But he was the first. Then the painting started here. That's it.

"And now the colors are brighter, more vivid."

When we ask Ademilson about change over time, he returns to 1948, establishes the trace element for progress in his father's particular excellence, and proceeds to his own mission:

"Inside our culture, our art was created by Manuel Eudócio, Zé Caboclo, and Mestre Vitalino. Then this is what happened.

"In the new generation, the *second* generation, which is us, we sought to give more details, more finish."

We think of Ademilson's generation as the third, the second being composed of those who learned directly from Vitalino, and the third including those who learned from them, but Ademilson bundles those before him — Vitalino, Zé Caboclo, and his father — into one generation, and calls his the second. He goes on:

"You have seen the work of Mestre Vitalino. It is more rustic, more rough. Zé Caboclo's also. But Daddy's was more refined, with a finer finish from the start. When Daddy was young, he already had a good finish on his pieces.

"You take an old piece of Daddy's, and you see that the finish is better than that of Zé Caboclo's, better than Vitalino's, right?

"With age: no. After many years, his vision deteriorated, and he didn't have such a good finish.

"So, you notice that the children of the second generation are all following more or less in his line. The children of Zé Caboclo, they have more details and more finish. Me also. I continue with Daddy's fine finish. Luiz Carlos also.

"And that's how it went from family to family. The finish of the Vitalino family, the children of Vitalino, it is also excellent. The finish is exceptional; the finish of their pieces is very good. But they maintained the tradition of Mestre Vitalino. They did not create new things.

"But we of the second generation, we are also seeking to create other things, new things. To make what is distinct from what many artisans are making around here, right?

"You walk around Alto do Moura, and you notice that there is an enormous quantity of work, but not all are works of art. Much is *artesanato* that is made in serial production.

"It brings some money to people in need, and that is a good thing. But that type of work, I don't like. I like to make one piece a day, or two, to be able to create, to follow in the line Daddy left us.

"I think that makes all the difference in art. It is a matter of awakening us to new, better possibilities, to further enrich our art."

Ademilson stops, looks out the front window, across the street toward Luiz Carlos's shop. His first take on change was brief and positive like the interviews he gives to journalists on the move. We are in no hurry. He thinks, returns to the topic of change, and begins a longer answer, at once more personal and general:

"What has changed in my art is the following.

"In the past, during the epoch of my adolescence, children would work only for play. But as adolescents we started to become interested in gaining money. In my period there wasn't an option other than art.

"To say it like this: it was hard in Alto do Moura, even to study was hard.

"So, if your parents weren't artisans, the majority of the children would migrate to São Paulo, and look for work in the city, usually São Paulo. And they would live there.

"But when the parents are artisans, and arrange a life out of art, the children would follow on that same path. They wouldn't think of leaving home, and they would dedicate themselves to art.

"Here in our community, in Alto do Moura during that period, there were only primary schools, and most people could not study; they didn't have the means to study. It was difficult.

"But I had the opportunity to study in the city. Daddy had a car so he would take us. My brothers and I did study, but the majority did not get that chance. So, this became the only option for survival: art.

"And it was possible to live, possible to live.

"At twenty years old, I started to build my own house. I married and I thought I could make my living from art. My wife, since her young days, was also an artisan. I was an artisan. And I was certain that it was possible to live well, with no worries.

"But with the changes in technology, with the financial difficulties in my country, my main commercial target became the collector.

"It is the collector. I don't work in series or sell in quantity. No, it is the collector. A very constricted group.

"But nowadays, the collectors are very few. The group is small. And this makes survival difficult. It makes survival difficult.

"Those who work in serial production" — what we have been calling the third line — "they work hard, and they are able to get a little money. Still, it is hard. It is hard.

"And in our case, in my case, in the case of Luiz Carlos and the other artists of Alto do Moura, it is hard because our principal target is the collector. And the collector, he is almost extinct. He is older, and when the collector dies, the family takes his pieces and sells them cheap.

"There are many examples of the children of the collector unloading his pieces here in Alto do Moura. They want to know if anyone will buy: My father died, and I don't want to look at this thing anymore.

"So, this makes it hard to make a living from art."

From remote Alto do Moura, Ademilson is witness to a wrenching international change. Fashionable technology takes command, tastes shift. Young minds are lost in cyberspace. The market for art shrinks. The prices of antiques decline. Bookshops close. In the audience at the avant-garde theater, the heads are gray. Ademilson continues:

"And the children, who are the third generation, they don't want to work with art anymore. The grandchildren of the traditional families, few are working.

"Some of Vitalino's grandchildren and great-grandchildren, they are working in the art. They still continue.

"I have three children. None of the three follow this option. They never wanted to, and I never forced them.

"My daughter is a teacher. She knows how to make some things, but my sons, no, they weren't interested.

"In the other families, the majority have migrated to other things, seeking employment. Here in Caruaru there is an industrial district that offers work to the youth.

"It is not possible anymore to live from art. If it is not possible, then seek something else. And I believe our art is not going to last. It's not going to last.

"You see, Vitalino died, Zé Caboclo died, and Daddy is dead. Severino Vitalino died recently. And what will happen in the future?

"In the future, there will not be an artist in Alto do Moura who will be able to survive in art.

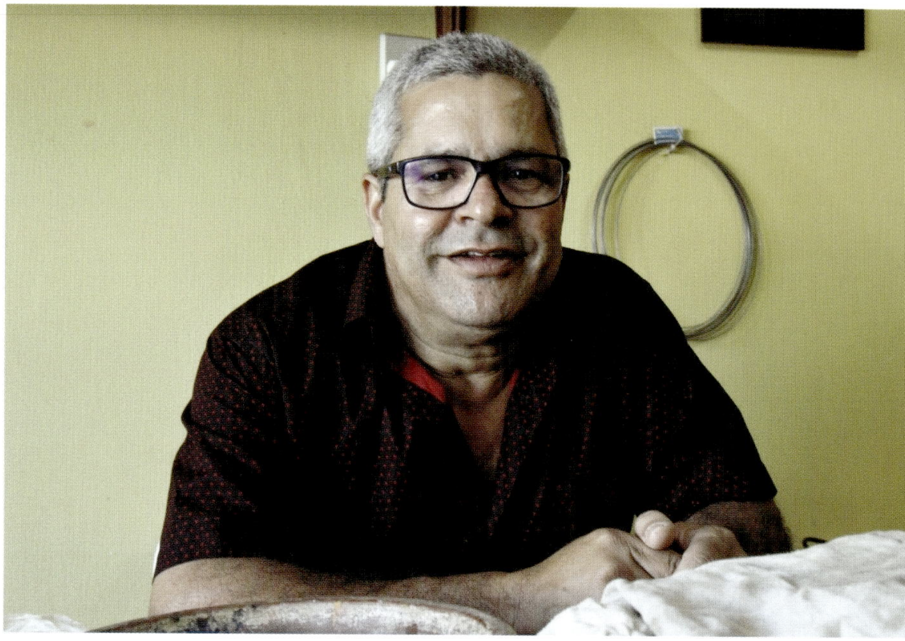

Ademilson, 2019

"I see it like that.

"The government gives some support, not like it should, but it is not a lack of support. It is not a lack of incentive. It is a lack of buyers.

"That is what makes survival difficult."

Within this difficulty, the choices are few. One is to leave. The *boneca* is another. *Bonecas* aren't art, but that worries Ademilson less than it does others. Among Alto do Moura's workers in the clay, there have always been many who made things that weren't art. His concern is that the makers receive little money and the profit for the merchant is slight, what with the costs of materials, pay, wrapping, and shipping, and he feels the demand is already diminishing. "It is no longer possible to maintain yourself by making these *bonecas*."

Ademilson's solution for his family was a second source of income. In 1997, when "there was a crisis in our art," he bought a store to sell the things artists need, paint and brushes, wire and wrapping. He kept working in the clay, he always will, but for a hectic while he was also managing the store. The stock expanded, the store succeeded, and he put his oldest son in charge. "Today the little shop is well established, and it allows my son to support himself; he is married. And it provides a salary for my younger son too."

A buoyant, energetic man, Ademilson is always racing around, helping his boys, but he delights in moments of calm with the clay in his hands. He puts it directly, passionately:

"I do not want a business anymore. It is very stressful. The clay is better, so I remain in the clay.

"With the clay, since I am now of an age — I was born in one thousand, nine hundred and sixty-four — my expenses have declined. When you are old there is no vanity. There is not that much travel.

"I manage myself here, and I am happy. This life, the life of an artist, of an artisan, simply put, is a life full of pleasure.

"It is a life in which you are your own boss. You don't have anyone *ordering* you around. Your mind is your workshop. Your mind is your boss.

"Sometimes we arrive at the place of work, without inspiration, without motivation. You are dispirited, but when you start to *handle* the clay, knead it, ideas emerge, new pieces emerge. Something new emerges.

"And this is the *moment*. This is the moment.

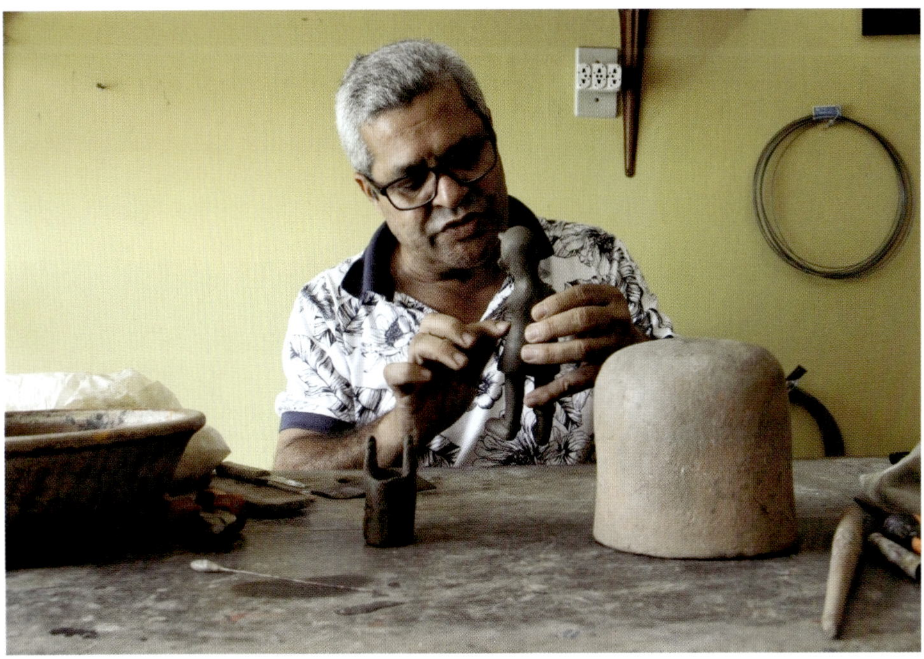

Ademilson at work, 2019

"This is the moment in our day-to-day, in the quotidian. This moment is everything. This is the moment when life passes into art.

"And art is life.

"Art, it transmits life to the one who is making it, and *life* to the one who appreciates it, and to the one who *likes* it, who buys it and has it in the house.

"I think that art is life. It transmits a very positive energy. It could be in clay, it could be in wood.

"*Art.* Art is life itself.

"For me, the best thing that there is comes when I finish a work of art, when it is done and standing there. I look at it and sometimes I can't believe that I was the one who made that piece.

"That happens, understand?

"And you sell it, because it is a means for survival, but the desire is *not* to sell it.

"So, when you make it with love, make it with affection, you don't think about money. You think about art.

"I work thinking about art.

"After it is finished, then I think about monetary value. Then I price it, because I admire it and see that it has monetary value, it has a price. And the one who buys it also understands.

"That's it. Art for me is this.

"Art is life."

9

Helton

Helton da Silva Rodrigues — Manuel Eudócio's grandson, Luiz Carlos's son, Clarice Esther's father — speaks for the next generation:

"The young people today, they want to have a good cellphone. They want to have money in their pockets. They want to go to the movies. They want to go to the shopping center. And to live off the traditional art, this would be impossible.

"They are not able to live among their friends by making this type of thing. It is very complicated."

Helton's parents have saved a piece he made of clay when he was young, depicting a *futebol* player. Soccer, a national passion, is surely a part of the contemporary quotidian. At night, the television in Caruaru streams an endless sequence of high-quality regional matches.

"I learned this art," Helton says. "I am thirty-eight years old, but I learned when I was twelve years old.

"I learned by watching my father. He learned from my grandfather. It was passed from generation to generation.

"I passed hours and hours there in my grandfather's shop, watching him. He was still creating at eighty-five years of age. That was impressive.

"So, I would sit there to talk, to listen to the history. He would pass to us all his knowledge, telling us about the difficulties he encountered when he was a child, a youth.

"Then there came a time in his life when he was able to help *all* of his children. He was able to do *much* for each one.

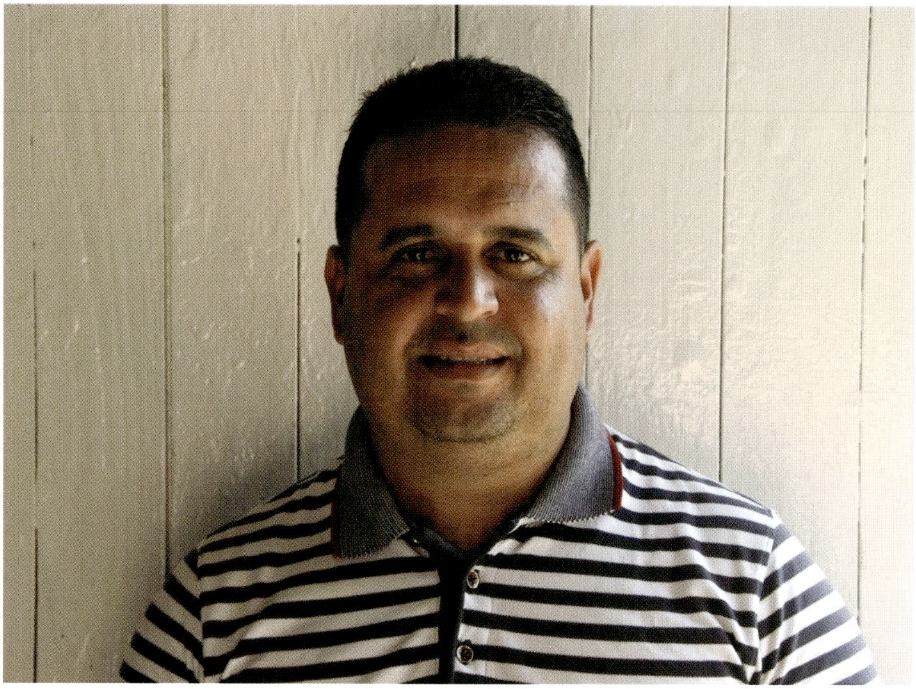

Helton, 2019

"With ceramic art, with his hands, God blessed him and allowed him to succeed and help his family."

He learned, but Helton makes his living by managing a store on the main street where *artesanato* made by others is sold. Across the street, Silvano, Luiz Carlos's younger brother, Ademilson's older brother, owns a comparable shop. Silvano has moved away from town, and, though he can create capably in Manuel Eudócio's tradition, he fills his shop with a mixed stock, including *bonecas* aplenty. Helton tells us that his uncle, José Silvano Rodrigues, was one of the first to make *bonecas*.

Helton holds a staff position in ABIMA, the Association of the Clay Artisans and Residents of Alto do Moura. Founded by artisans in 1938, the Association's mission, Helton says, "is to fight for the rights of the artisans, in the town, in the state. To hold exhibitions and fairs and workshops.

"That is very important. The day-to-day benefit is important.

"We are always here, making sure that the visitors, when they arrive, they don't depart with a bad taste because of the poor conditions in the town. We want them to gain from their visit."

Visitors find the Association's headquarters — once distinguished by large images of the Lampião couple, now painted bright yellow — west of the Casa Museu Mestre Vitalino, on the main street. In his office there, we interviewed Helton, whose position supplies him with accurate general information.

Alto do Moura's population, he says, approaches six thousand. The Association has nearly four hundred members, though perhaps twice that number gain their livelihood from work in the clay. Today few people are making utilitarian ware; the *oleiros* who work on the wheel, Helton says, number only from ten to fifteen, and most of them are old. There are still artists who make the "difficult, traditional, quotidian" pieces, but by far the most are crafting "decorative things that are not traditional, these *bonecas*."

Helton estimates that there are about one hundred places for work in the town, but only a few full ateliers, like his father's, with a house and a separate workshop from which pieces are sold directly to customers. Most people work in a room in their homes, and they must share the profit with a merchant who makes the final sale.

With the statistically prevalent *bonecas* and the culturally preeminent traditional works in mind, Helton moves toward a summarizing conclusion:

"The *bonecas* came from outside ten or so years ago. Store owners came to see if the local artisans could make them. And artisans here started to make them and copy the pieces that were selling.

"The *bonecas* are a good thing, not a bad thing. People can make some money and they can have a dignified life. They are able to give a better life to their children. Many have gained from that.

"But today, because of the great quantity produced, there is a diminished number of sales. Because everybody already has it, so the demand diminished. And it goes on diminishing.

"And what remains, in reality, are the traditional works of art. But the artists, like my father, like my grandfather, their numbers are also diminishing.

"What has diminished is the demand. The demand is diminishing due to the economic crisis in our country.

"So, that is our concern. We are concerned about the tradition, about the history.

"We have to fight so that our art, really, does not die, right?

"The line left by Vitalino, the line others gave continuity to — like my grandfather who was a Living Patrimony of the state — we can't let it die.

"It has to live, to continue, for all of us here in Alto do Moura, the largest center for figurative art in the Americas."

With Helton, we have finished our story of Manuel Eudócio's family, prepared to generalize about the artist's life, just as we generalized about the art, after Vitalino Neto at the end of our story about Vitalino's family.

The artist lives a life of connections, connections backward through a lineage of learning toward history, connections outward through understandings of other familial lines toward community. It is a life of dedicated work, centered on a daily practice that is complex, diverse, and mutable enough to engage the full person, hand and eye, mind, body, and soul. Though conditioned by economic variables that roll beyond control, threatened by declining demand, the work is freely conducted without external direction. There is no boss to make demands and intrude ignorantly — an absence profoundly appreciated in Brazil, where industrial labor is the alternative today and agricultural labor was the alternative when the colonels' plantations outlived the abolition of slavery late in the nineteenth century. The artist's work is satisfying and satisfactory. It doesn't eventuate in wealth, but it yields sufficient comfort: a small, clean house with a decorated front room, an efficient kitchen, and reliable electricity; a well-lit space to work; a used car, handy for getting away to the country for a few days of fishing with your pals.

Zé Caboclo's family comes next.

10

The Zé Caboclo Family

José Antônio da Silva was called, as his father had been before him, Zé Caboclo. Zé is short for José, as Joe is for Joseph. Caboclo carries a tight tangle of meanings. It can mean a descendant of the Indigenous people of Brazil. More commonly it names the person of mixed Indigenous and Portuguese descent. Or it can mean a person from the back country, the wide, dry interior of the Northeast.

Zé Caboclo died in 1973. Less has been published about him than about his comrades and collaborators, Mestre Vitalino and Manuel Eudócio, but that presents us no problem. We want pertinent biographical information and we get it from the people we know. We want to see and understand works from the past so we can gauge changes from generation to generation, and that need is met by an excellent museum in Caruaru.

Outside stand big statues of Vitalino's bull and of Lampião and Maria Bonita, apparently inspired by Manuel Eudócio's work. Inside the two great traditions of the Brazilian Northeast are celebrated. The ground floor is given to the Museu do Forró: Luiz Gonzaga. There photographs and memorabilia introduce Gonzaga, whose monumental statue stands in the adjacent plaza. On the upper floor, the Museu do Barro, the Museum of the Clay, dedicated to Zé Caboclo, has three permanent galleries. One holds works from Tracunhaém, including many large statues of saints, assembled by the renowned collector Abelardo Rodrigues of Recife. A second, of importance for us, fills with work of Mestre Vitalino and his sons. The third exhibits works by other artists in Alto do Moura: Manuel Eudócio and Luiz Carlos, Mestre Galdino and Luiz Galdino, Luiz Antônio, Zé Caboclo and his children.

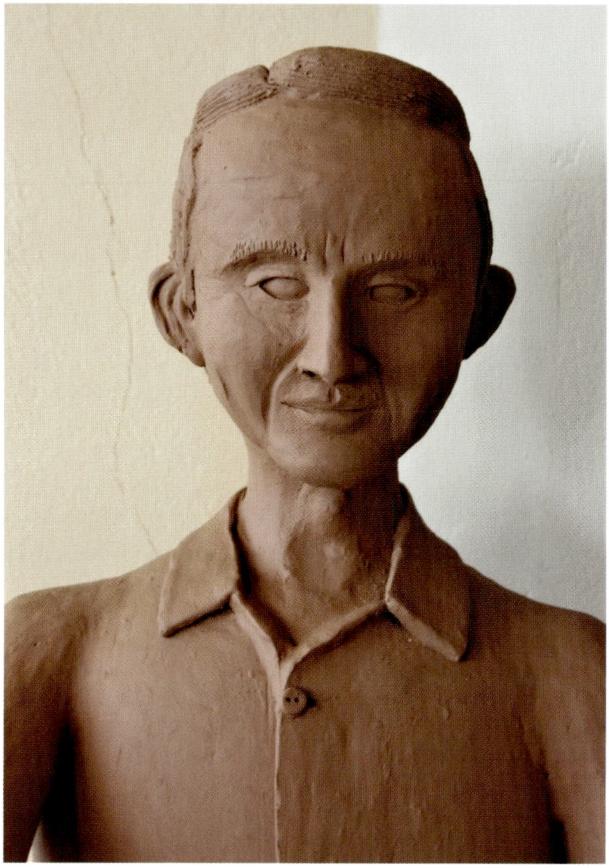

Zé Caboclo, a portrait in clay by his son Horácio, 2019

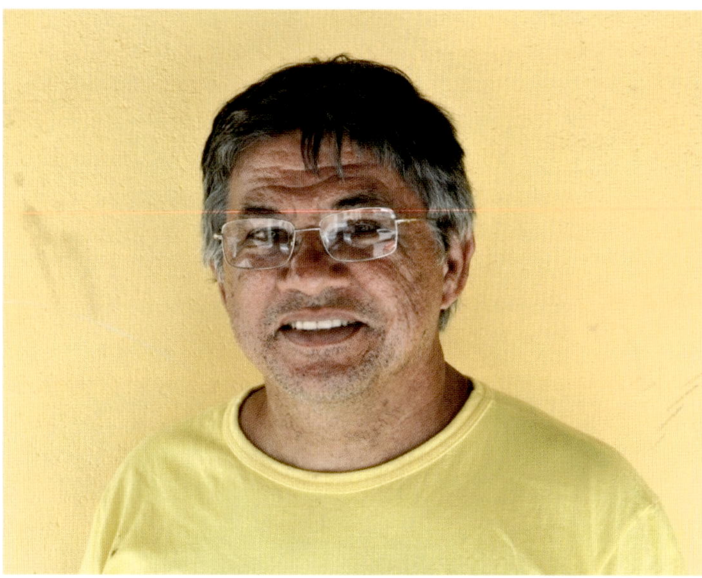

Horácio, 2021

In that gallery, beginning first on your left, four cases crowd with Zé Caboclo's pieces: large and small, sacred and secular, familiar figures like Lampião and Padre Cícero, and full sets of the *Reisado* and *Maracatu*. Farther in, four cases display the works of his children, featuring, in particular, Zé Caboclo's daughters Socorro and Marliete.

Today six of Zé Caboblo's eight children are among the artistic leaders in Alto do Moura: his sons Paulo, Antônio, and Horácio, and his daughters Socorro, Carmélia, and Marliete.

Marliete, his youngest daughter, has traveled widely, gathering a bundle of prizes for her work. When the Olympic games were held in Rio de Janeiro in 2016, Marliete was one of those chosen to carry the Olympic torch for a stretch. A friend of ours in Bezerros calls her "that famous lady in Alto do Moura." Her older sisters call her *nossa professora* — our teacher. She is the one who knows the history, the right one to introduce Zé Caboclo and his tradition.

Just down the street from the shop where her brothers Paulo and Antônio work, Marliete lives in a lovely house. A door opens directly into the front room where she works and where she patiently explained things to us during two long interviews.

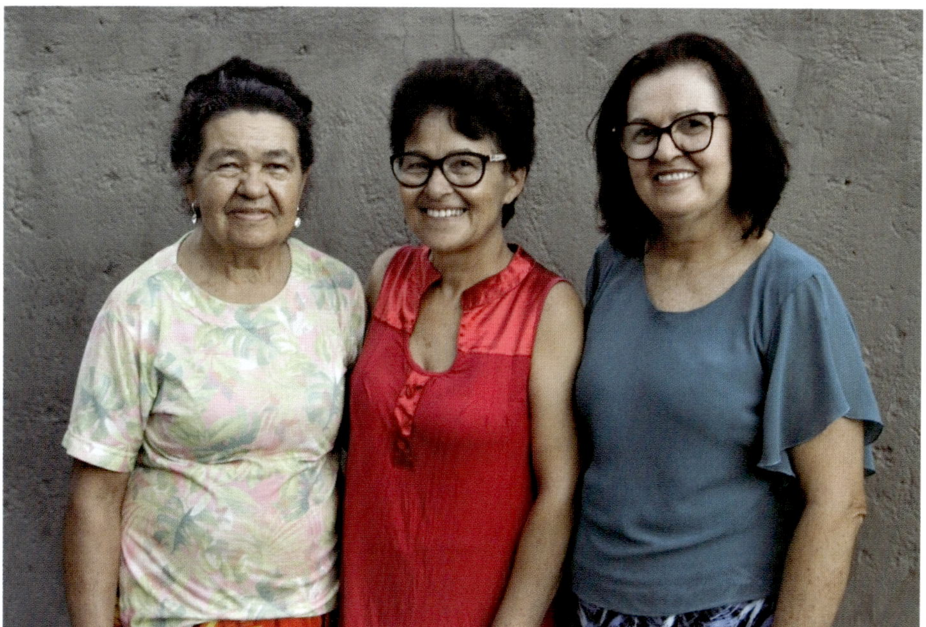

Three of Zé Caboclo's daughters: Helena, Soccoro, and Marliete, 2019

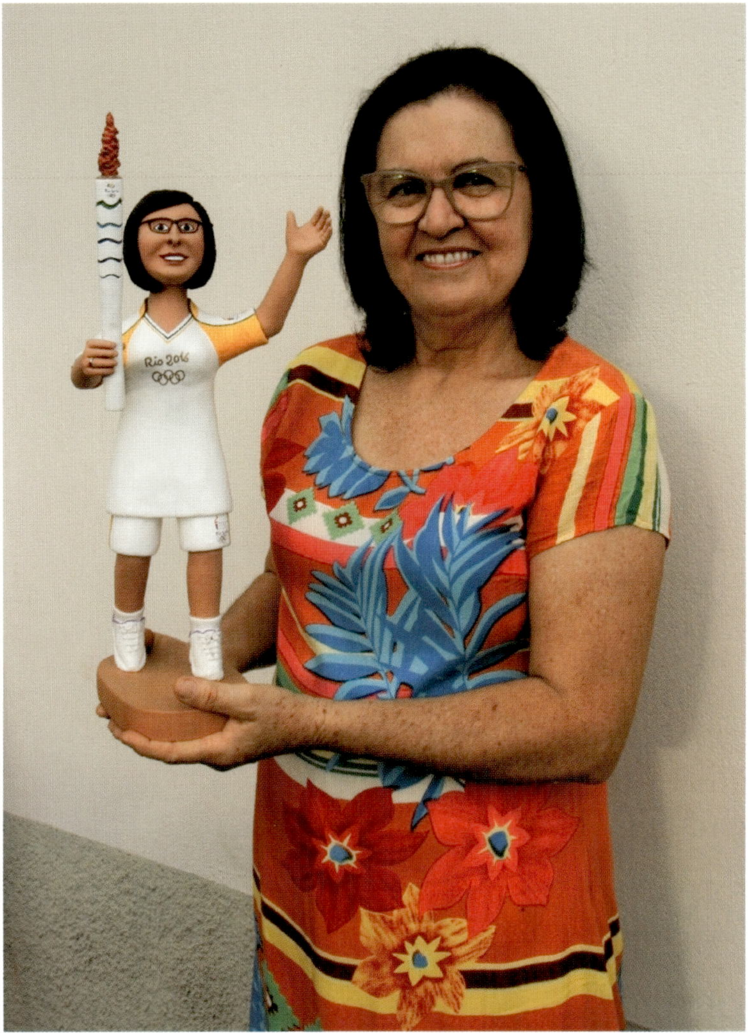

Marliete with her portrait of herself, carrying the Olympic torch, 2021. Looking at photos and the shirt and shoes she was given, she spent ten days making this statue in 2016.

Marliete

Marliete Rodrigues da Silva tells us about her father:

"My Daddy was Zé Caboclo. He was one of the first disciples of Mestre Vitalino. And there was a *very strong* friendship between them.

"They would talk much about art. And they would discuss their creations, their discoveries. And my Daddy would always speak of Mestre Vitalino as a great friend. He had a great affection for him and he had a great affection for Daddy, right?

"It was a beautiful thing. There was no jealousy. They worked together, one in one style, the other in another, and Daddy was inspired by Mestre Vitalino's work.

"Daddy had already worked with clay since he was a child, making little toys. Because his mother was an artisan, working with utilitarian works.

"So, when Mestre Vitalino created figurative art, Daddy got involved and commenced to make. And they began that great friendship, always discovering things together.

"It was very beautiful, right?

"And there was so much care that one had for the other, with them always being together in the Feira de Caruaru, selling side by side, right?

"And this beautiful friendship remained between our families. Even today we have a beautiful friendship with the family of Mestre Vitalino."

The talk drifts for a few minutes, then Marliete brings us back to friendship, saying that Zé Caboclo and Manuel Eudócio had been friends since childhood and that her mother, Celestina, was Manuel Eudócio's sister. They were born in Alto do Moura, but her father was born in Sítio Campos, "where Mestre Vitalino was born, which is very near to here, to Alto do Moura.

"And when Daddy was one year old, my grandparents came here, to Alto do Moura.

"And they commenced their friendship in childhood. Daddy with Mom and Daddy with Manuel Eudócio.

"They worked together when they were young, making little toys. And they would go to the city, to Caruaru, to the Feira de Caruaru, together to sell in the market.

"And when Mom got older — she was seven years younger than Daddy — when they got older, when they became a young woman and a young man, they started to court, and they got married.

"Daddy was the first boyfriend of my mother. Mom was the first girlfriend of Daddy. They lived very happily. They spent twenty-six years married, right? It was a very happy life. And we always remember that beautiful union that existed between them.

"They had eleven children and raised eight. Three died young. But they had a lovely life, a beautiful union between them.

"And we had a beautiful connection with the family of Manuel Eudócio. He was my godfather at baptism. And I was the godmother of his oldest daughter, Elizabete.

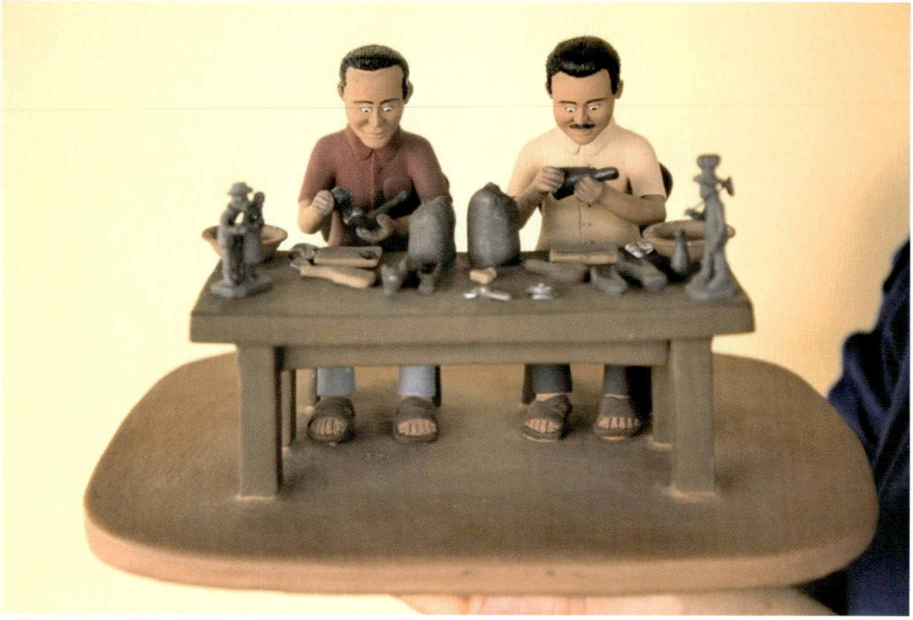

Zé Caboclo and Manuel Eudócio working together, by Marliete, 2005

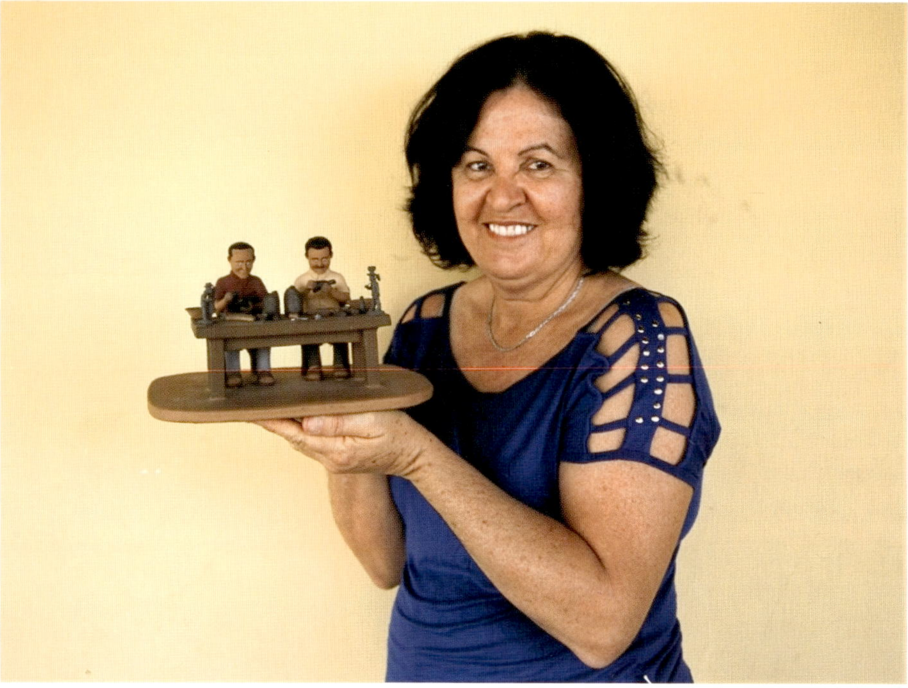

Marliete with her clay image of her father and uncle working together, 2015

"And so, Manuel Eudócio was my uncle, my godfather, and my *compadre*.

"I loved him very much, as if he were *my father*, right? I would always go to talk with him, to seek advice about life, about work. We would talk much, about everything."

History begins to complicate and clarify. When the three of them began working together, in 1948, Vitalino was a master, but Zé Caboclo and Manuel Eudócio were not raw apprentices. They had years of experience in the clay behind them. They were already working and selling together, and Marliete has created a fine piece showing her father and uncle working side by side at a table.

Alto do Moura's art has continued to advance — the works have gotten finer, the repertory has expanded — but it is true that Vitalino, Zé Caboclo, and Manuel Eudócio, working in quick collaboration, made the changes that remain foundational. Marliete points to two key changes and credits them to her father, which seems reasonable since Vitalino had been working for more than thirty years and would be unlikely to welcome radical changes in his practice, and Zé Caboclo was ten years older than Manuel Eudócio. Marliete says:

"Daddy started making the little balls of clay, he did. After they talked, he had this idea of making the little balls of clay.

"The first works of Mestre Vitalino, they have holes pierced for the eyes. The first works.

"Then after them talking, it was Daddy who made the discovery of putting little balls of clay for the eyes.

"And it was also his idea to use wire to attach some details; we use wires in our work. And it was Daddy who had the idea of using the wire.

"Daddy was observing things very much, and he was always seeking to learn, to make something different. I think I have inherited much from Daddy, always seeking to make, to create, to look at a work and improve.

"He was always seeking, seeking to learn, to discover. He gave much expression to his work."

With Vitalino's repertory at the base, with the additions of Zé Caboclo's technical innovations and Manuel Eudócio's fine painting, the origin of Alto do Moura's art can be located in the collaboration of 1948, or it can be dropped back to 1915 when Vitalino crafted the hunter of wildcats. But Marliete objects, saying the history runs more deeply into time, and it has been distorted because women have been left out of the record. Hers is a virtuous and accurate, general complaint about conventional historical practice. Marliete's success will make the omission of women impossible in future books, but her concern is with the women of an earlier generation.

The famed masters all first learned with women. Vitalino began with his mother, Zé Caboclo with his mother, Manuel Eudócio with his grandmother. Those women were *louceiras* who made useful pots by hand. But they also made toys, and at their direction the boys began their figurative work in the clay by shaping little animals, not fantastical wild beasts, but familiar domesticated animals — little bulls, little horses — and domesticated animals, quotidian farm stock, remain common in the collective repertory.

Marliete centers her revisionist account on her great-grandmother, Manuel Eudócio's grandmother, Tereza Maria da Conceição. One of Marliete's exquisite miniatures depicts her great-grandmother selling pots in the market. Three children sit beside her; one is Marliete's uncle Manuel Eudócio, another is her mother, Celestina. Marliete says:

"My great-grandmother, my mother's grandmother, taught my mother. Her name was Tereza; she was known as Tetê. She was a person who took much care with the quality of the work.

"My mother said that when she was a little girl, seven years of age, she started with her grandmother. And she worked for seventy-eight years in this work. She made pots and toys.

"She was enamored of this work. And she said that her grandmother, who was my great-grandmother, used to orient her, telling her to take care, to have quality in the work to be able to sell it at a better price.

"So, she learned this very early, these orientations. The quality of the piece makes all the difference, to be able to sell at a better price.

"So, then, this idea of quality comes from my family, from my mother's side and from my father's side, from my grandmother, who was my father's mother, who was also an artisan.

"She made clay pieces, but it was utilitarian ware, jars, pots, utilitarian. She also passed things to us. My father learned from her to make little toys when he was a child.

"So, our history comes from very far back.

"So, this history, I find this history very beautiful, because from our great-grandmother we get this care, this love for the work that they had.

"And it was a struggle for survival through the clay. For everyone here in Alto do Moura.

"Mestre Vitalino, he was very recognized because he created figurative art, depicting the history of our day-to-day, our folklore. My father created many pieces, so did my uncle, so did various other artisans.

"But in the middle, there were women.

"Ernestina, she was the first artisan who worked, following in the line of Mestre Vitalino. She has passed away. And before her there were many women in Alto do Moura who were working with the clay in the town's first families.

"In the period of my great-grandmother, there were many women who worked with the clay, making pots to prepare food in, jars to keep water in.

"There were many who worked in this utilitarian line of work. And the majority were women. Some of them worked with utilitarian ware, like my grandmother, and some worked with toys, like my great-grandmother, Tetê, and my mother who continued in her line.

"So, Mother would tell us the story of the women, of the friends she had here in Alto do Moura.

"When she was a child, she knew the old people who were working with toys or making pots and selling them at the Feira de Caruaru.

"She would tell me the names of these women. Many women. There were many women who are not in the history of books. They did not enter the history of books, but they remain in the history of being remembered.

"They have been remembered. They have been honored."

In her historical account, Marliete takes a stand against simplistic reduction, conspicuously against the reduction of history to male activities, and more consistently against the reduction of art to representation. Ceramic work of high quality might yield representational figures, but it always entails care and a reach for excellence. In some great ceramic traditions — notably in China and Japan, in southwestern England and the southeastern United States — pots utilitarian in shape rise to art through dedicated attention to form and finish. And in Marliete's view, women in the Brazilian past comparably created fine utilitarian ware.

When the men, the artists of the second and third generations after Vitalino — Severino, Elias, Manuel Eudócio, Luiz Carlos, Ademilson — speak of progress, they always stress fineness of finish. They don't credit the women of an earlier generation for directing them toward improvement. But Marliete does. Men, for her, are the source of the figurative aspect of her work, but women are the prime source of the care and quality of her work, the base of her distinction. She owes her fame to her father and uncle, to her grandmother and great-grandmother who made useful pots excellently, but most of all she owes it to her inner drive for improvement.

At six, Marliete was watching her father and mother while they worked, and she was making toys with her brother José and her sisters Socorro and Carmélia. When she was eight, her father began selling her pieces, along with his own and those of her siblings, at the Feira de Caruaru:

"So, I started in this way, with eight years of age, helping with the expenses of the household. The family was big. Daddy had difficulties. So all of us started working, started helping with the expenses.

"And I got very interested in the work. I very *much* liked to handle the clay. I became *much* enamored.

"I would go to study, and when I returned from school, I was already thinking about the work.

"And, after the toys, I moved to making figures, imitating the work of my father. And the work of Mestre Vitalino, and of my uncle Manuel Eudócio.

"And I spent a good amount of time copying their work."

At an early point, hoping to help with the household expenses, Marliete worked swiftly with quantity as her goal: "I would make much every day, little horses, little toys. And then I started to have a problem with sales. Because if it was not well made, it would not sell well."

Her grandfather, her mother's father, Eudócio Rodrigues, sternly told Marliete that her work had to improve. "And I was sad because I wanted to sell, to help with the household. But he gave me this advice: You need to take more care, to improve.

"It was the first lesson, and a very good one, which I received at the beginning of my work; it was this orientation from my grandfather: Improve your work and you will sell more.

"Then I began to work with care, to improve, and make the work better.

"My father also gave me this advice: Your pieces are plentiful. Your production is too much, and it makes the pieces hard to sell. He could see that.

"So, I also started with these orientations from him: to take more care, to make better work so it would sell better."

Zé Caboclo died in 1973 when Marliete was sixteen. By that time she was making large figurative pieces, up to a meter in height, and, oriented by her father and grandfather, by her mother, grandmother, and great-grandmother, she was working with care and steadily improving.

Blessed with a *dom*, Marliete says, "My great pleasure is to be always learning, seeking. I know that I can improve. I can improve. I can make things better. Which is a delight. This is what delights me: to be always learning, always improving."

Marliete's quest for excellence has led her to focus on three aspects of quality: size, form, and color. Of these, size is most basic, and she says:

"After Daddy died, I had a phase of making big things. I made many big saints. I would send big statues of Saint Francis to São Paulo.

"And then later I started to get tired of big ones, and I began making smaller ones. My sister Socorro helped me, and when I started to decrease the size, I got more interested in the work.

"So, then I really started to create. To create things, like, in my own style.

"Before that I would copy what Daddy made, what Mestre Vitalino made, what Uncle Manuel Eudócio made. That is what we would see, right?

"And later when I started to decrease the size, I really started to sell. That is what I found. Let's say it like this: This is mine. Then I started to develop, creating something different within my own style.

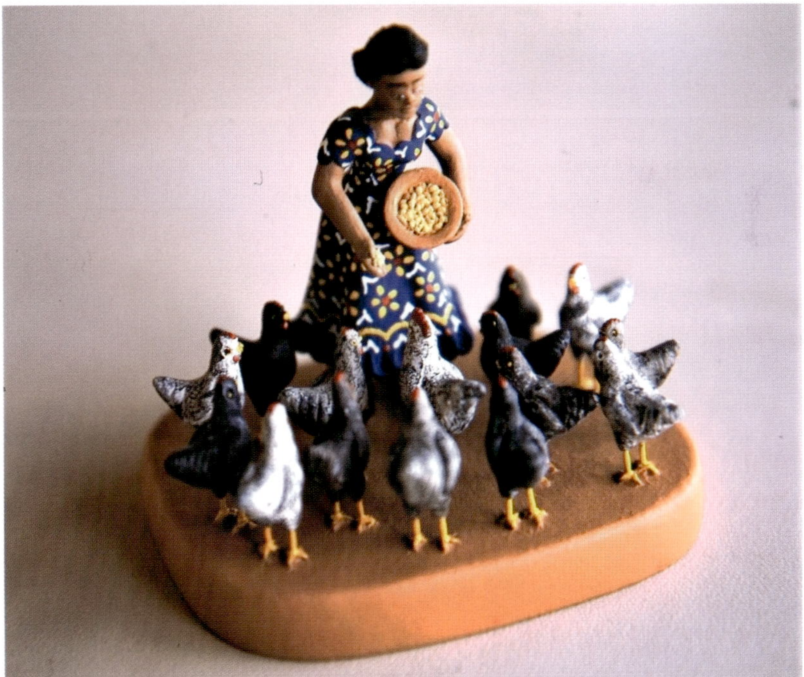

Feeding the chickens, a miniature by Marliete (6.5 cm tall), 2015

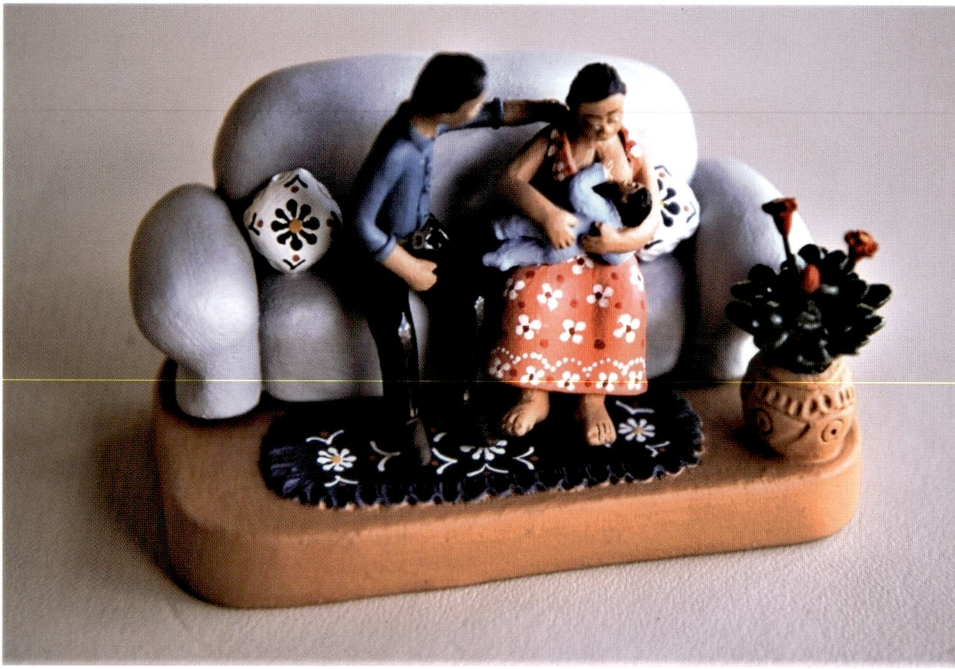

Nursing the baby, a miniature by Marliete (6 cm tall), 2015

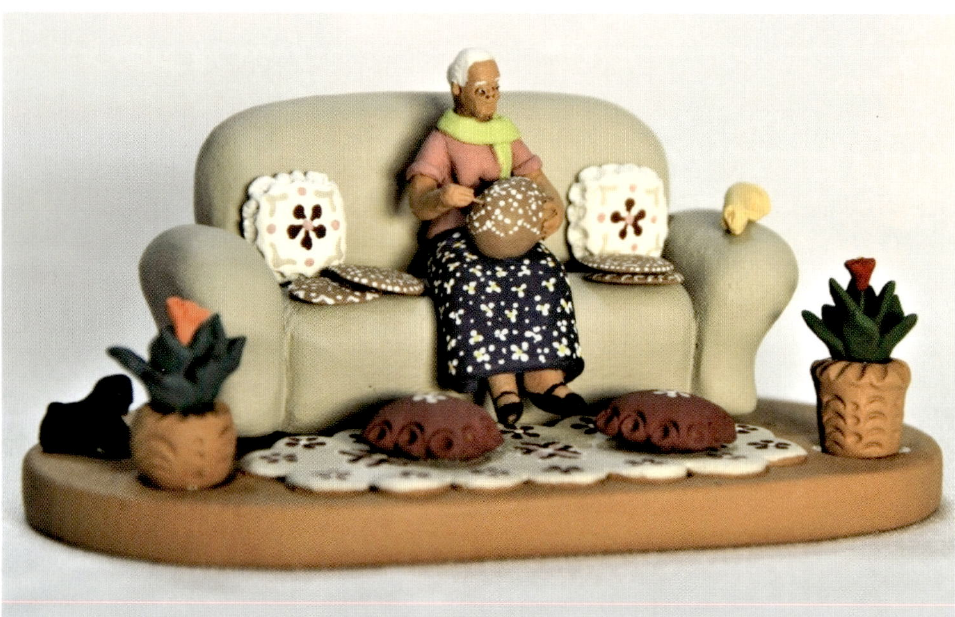

Grandmother making lace (5 cm tall), 2019

"When I started to change, the pieces got smaller, smaller, smaller. I was making even at two centimeters, figures two centimeters in height. But the pieces I make most are four, five centimeters. That is what I make most.

"I have the liberty to work in various sizes, but I am most delighted by the miniatures. I love to make the smaller things.

"I like it very much, though it demands much *concentration*. It is more work. It is more demanding, but it is something I like very much.

"I like the challenge of seeking the difficult, the difficult to make."

The miniature tests the hand and eye, logically concluding a quest directed by care toward perfection. Though her work remains diverse in topic and scale, Marliete's repertory centers on miniatures of children at play and women in domestic settings — telling stories to their grandchildren, feeding chickens, watering flowers — and her fastidious miniatures are the base of her fame and financial success. Tiny size matters most, but Marliete also strives to improve her renditions of the human form:

"Each day I am seeking to learn. I am preoccupied with *proportion*, always trying to make the parts the right size so the body, the arms, the face all match.

"I don't like to make figures that all have the same face. I am always searching for different faces.

"I am always observing, curious to observe people and their ways, the differences that exist in our country, with much mixing of the races, right?

"I observe much. I really like to be inspired by the faces of people, and then turn to the clay, trying to remember the differences. I find it good to make different faces. One younger, one older. Children. I spent a long time without being able to perfect the faces of children, because they are different.

"So, I am always seeking to observe and discover new things. That is what is good about this work."

Painting ends the process. Marliete's narrative of change accords with Genilda's. The first paint was prepared at home by making a fire and mixing resin and powder in heated kerosene. Then Zé Caboclo and Manuel Eudócio switched to purchased paints that gave a wider variety of hues, first oil-based enamel, then water-based latex, and finally water-based, quick-drying acrylics. "So we are always learning." Marliete says at the end, "always discovering new things so our art can continue. And it grows, it continues, this history of ours."

Of her own painting, Marliete says, "I take a long time to make and a long time to paint. With the painting of my work, I am very demanding. I paint with much care.

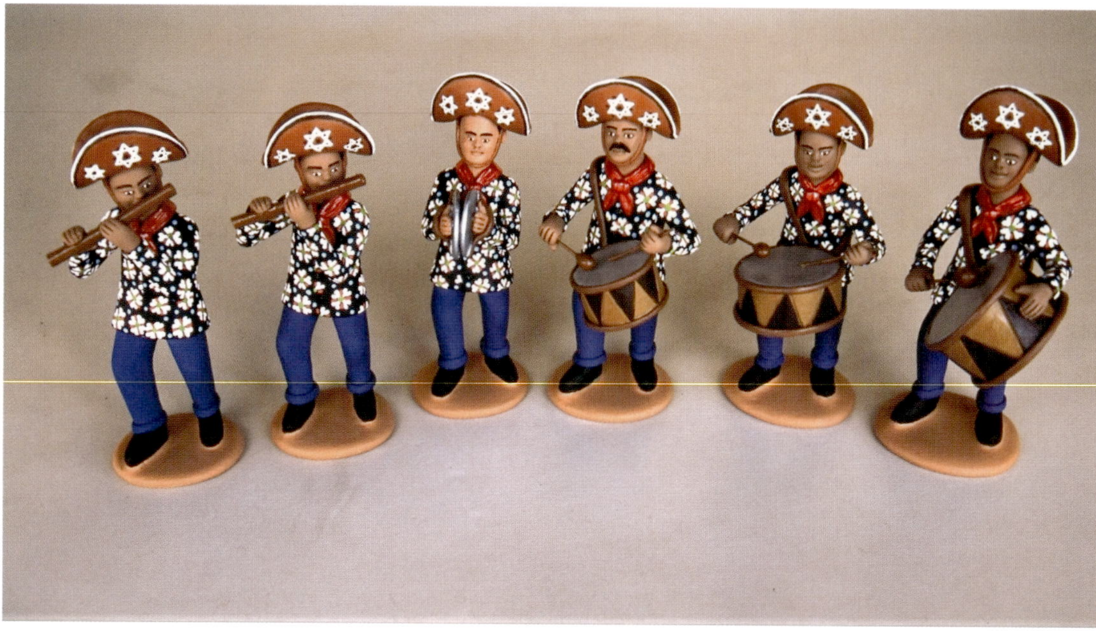

A Banda de Pífano, miniatures by Marliete (6 cm tall), 2015

"I am always researching, seeking types of paint that the clay will accept, right? Paint of good quality. And I am always mixing the colors to get all the tonalities.

"When I am painting, I always look at the combination of colors. This is important. It gives more beauty to the work.

"My painting, it comes from the history of care."

Care at a small scale, care with anatomical accuracy, care in mixing and applying color: care unifies Marliete's repertory. The miniatures that "record our family's story" — depictions of her father and uncle at work, of her grandmother telling stories — occupy her repertory's emotional core, but she aligns with her colleagues in Alto do Moura when her repertory expands to contain the usual images of the Northeast:

"When I am showing my work outside of Brazil, the people find it very important that we are showing the history of our place. The day-to-day of our region.

"And if we take a different piece, people are not so interested. But when you say, Here is *A Banda de Pífano* of Caruaru, then it is successful.

"They perform in the folkloristic festivals of Saint John in the month of June. But they also perform in other periods. They perform and take happy music to the whole world.

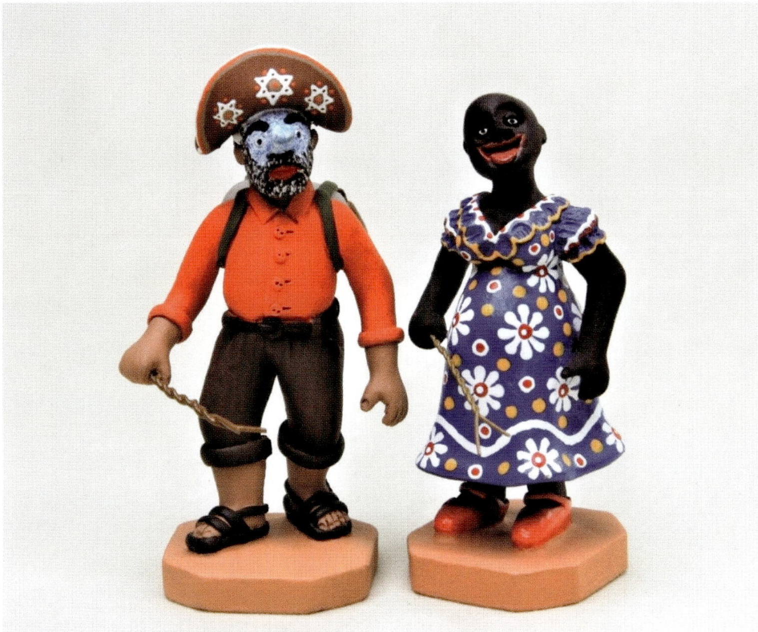

Mateus and Catarina from the *Reisado*, by Marliete (10, 9 cm tall), 2015

"The people are very interested. I am making a portrait of the *pífano* band that enlivens the life of the people, right? They make people happy, and they are appreciated.

"Music is so important.

"The story of Lampião, this is a story that is a well-known story in the whole world. So, I also take Lampião and Maria Bonita to other places. They fought. They were unjustly treated and they rebelled. They sought justice with their own hands.

"So, we have their history. And what is really important is this. It is to portray our history.

"It is our life, our past, our present. It is the history of Brazil, but mostly of the Northeast.

"Like the dances of *frevo* from Recife. And the *forró* of Caruaru, the people dancing, the trio playing; the *Trio Nordestino* makes the music of *forró*.

"So, we look, we observe, and portray what is most interesting."

Marliete's interest intensifies at the intersection of her family's history with Alto do Moura's artistic tradition, at the point where major contributions were made to the town's collective repertory by her uncle's gift of the *Reisado* and her father's gift of *Maracatu*. Zé Caboclo and Manuel Eudócio, being friends from

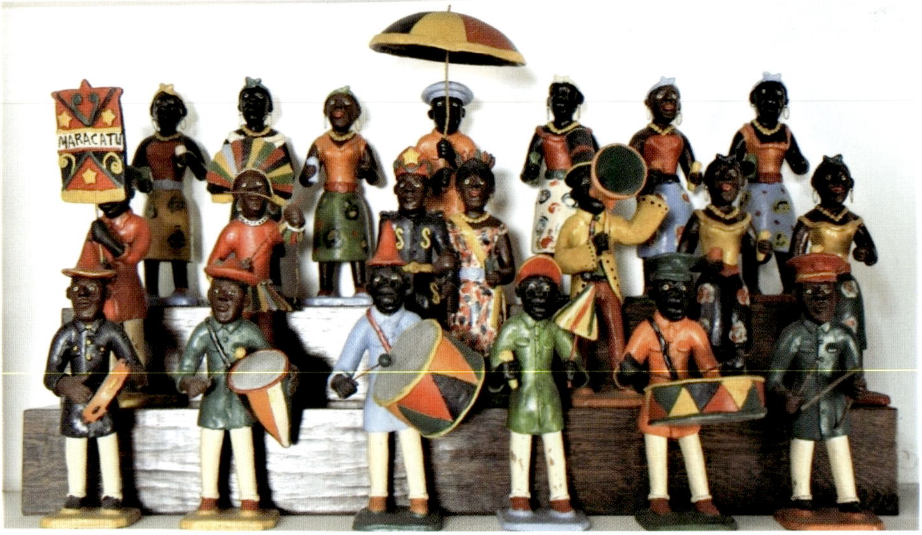

Full *Maracatu* set by Zé Caboclo, c. 1970, on display at Sobrado 7, Olinda, 2019

childhood, performed together in Alto do Moura's *Reisado*, and Marliete crafts images from the *Reisado*, the Captain and the Bull, Mateus and Catarina. She says her father helped when her uncle was inventing the *Reisado* in clay, and "Daddy invented *Maracatu*."

The origin story of the *Maracatu* in clay, Marliete says, goes like this. Zé Caboclo's sister, Maria José, found employment in the big city of Recife. On a visit home, she told him that during Carnaval in Recife, "she saw a lovely *Maracatu*. Then she went on to tell him about the women dancing and the men playing music.

"And Daddy began thinking about what she was describing. Then he said, It will turn out very beautiful for me to make little statues of the *Maracatu* that you are telling me about.

"Then she said, Oh, make it and it will turn out very beautiful, because it has these beautiful *morenas*" — brown-skinned women — "who wear necklaces and earrings.

"Everything that she was saying, he was memorizing. And she kept saying, Make it, make it, and it will turn out beautiful.

"Then he started to make it, inspired by the story she told.

"And his *Maracatu* has twenty-two pieces. I make the *Maracatu*. I spent a good amount of time making it, and I made it in the same style as Daddy's, that same way.

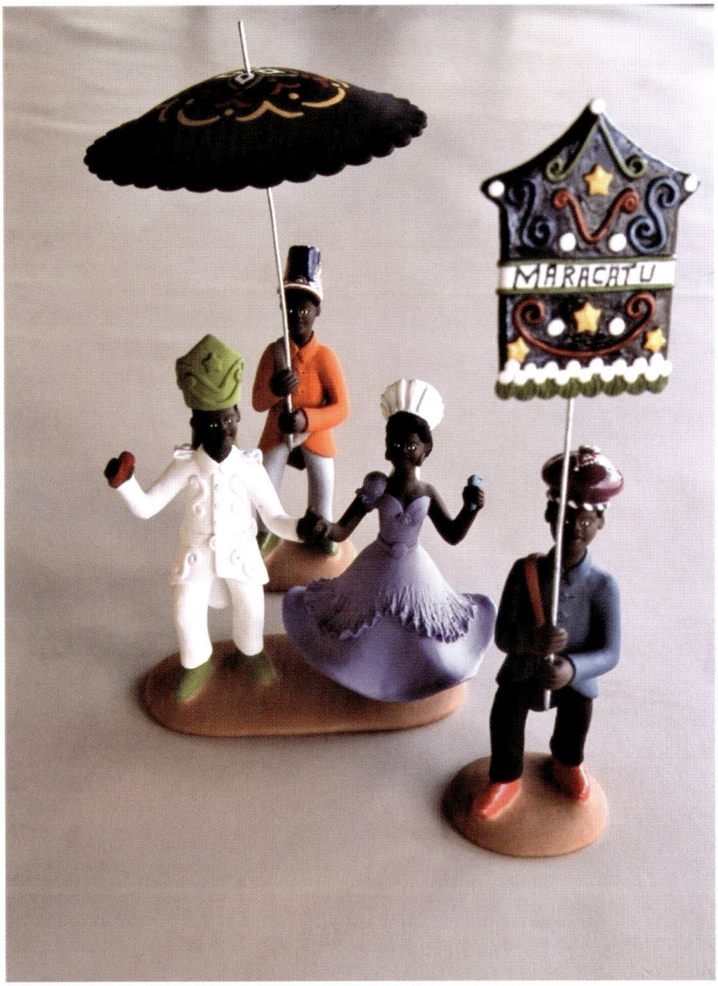

Maracatu miniatures by Marliete, 2015

"But later I commenced to invent, like, to give a different expression to the *Maracatu*, in the clothes of the women and the movement of the body in dance.

"There are many different details that I started to make, creating the *Maracatu* in my own style."

Both are big sets. The *Reisado* has twenty-eight pieces, *Maracatu* has twenty-two. Zé Caboclo and Manuel Eudócio both made both of them, but full sets take time, and they are rarely made. Instead the sets supply — the *Reisado* much more than *Maracatu* — single pieces and pairs for Alto do Moura's artists to shape and paint.

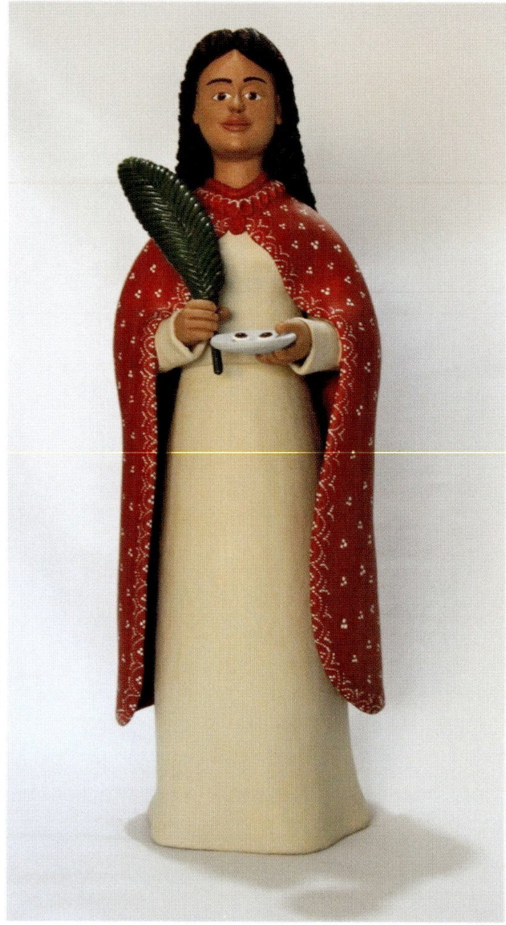

Santa Lucia, by Marliete, 2019

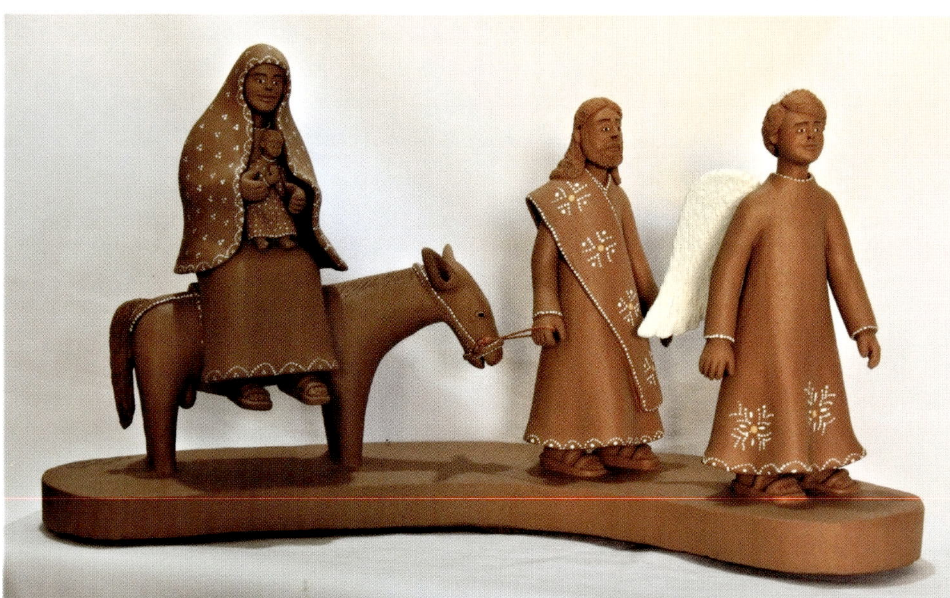

The Flight into Egypt, by Marliete, 2019

Our sketch of Marliete's repertory ends with religious imagery. Few of Alto do Moura's artists make saints today, she says, but her father did and she follows him, specializing in sacred scenes:

"I always made scenes that represent the scenes from the Bible, like the Baptism of Christ. I make the Angel Expelling Adam and Eve from Paradise. I make the Flight into Egypt. Saints, I make many images of saints, female saints especially. I like very much to make these also.

"Daddy made the *Presépio*, the whole scene of the Nativity. We also made it; me and my siblings, we continue to make Nativities. We are always seeking our own way.

"We take inspiration from what they made in the past. We are connected to that style of theirs, making our art to enhance what they left to us.

"It is important not to escape, to seek things that have little to do with our roots, right?

"This is an interest of mine. I talk with my siblings and with the artisans of Alto do Moura. I have a great friendship with everybody.

"So, I always say to them, We have to take much care to maintain our *beautiful* history so that it never dies.

"We must enhance our work more and more, seeking quality and a variety of creativity, right? To be always creating within our roots, in our own style."

At once directly and eloquently, Marliete has articulated the ideals of the folk artist. She aims for improvement and authentic self-expression, while holding to a received and shared historical tradition. She is a distinct and fully realized individual who is committed to community:

"I have much gratitude. I am always remembering the good things that the people before left to us. We continue, always following.

"And that is very important for people who didn't get much education. Neither Mestre Vitalino nor my father got a chance to study. Daddy wanted very much for us to study, but we didn't get a chance to study. But even with little study, we inherited the richness he left, this beautiful example of a union with other artisans.

"It is very beautiful for us to have this union with other artisans that continues today. To be able to help people who need help to improve their work.

"There are many problems in the work, sometimes with the clay or something that is not working so well. So, we help people improve their situation, helping with the difficulties they are having with the work that sometimes cause them harm.

"We are very united, always helping others so there can be a union of artisans. We are always talking together to solve the problems of the community.

"There are always problems. There are some people who complicate things. But if you look at the whole, this is a very positive place. There is more good than bad.

"Thank God we are able to have this union."

As a member of her community, Marliete is deeply worried about the future of Alto do Moura's art. The *bonecas*, though, are not her concern. When they emerged more than a decade ago, she says, they were a "novelty" and people bought them for decoration. "They found them pretty, these pretty women with really colorful clothes.

"But many people did not approve, because the *bonecas* were escaping the style, the tradition of Mestre Vitalino, of our father and uncle.

"But there was much demand, and people started making them to improve their financial situation. At that time, the economy in our country was very bad.

"Not everyone is able to work with the traditional art, because it is a kind of work that demands much work, much knowledge. It is much work; it is difficult.

"So, when they started making these *bonecas*, they discovered it was much easier. Many people who did not know how to make, they started and, all of a sudden, a few days after starting, they had something ready to sell.

"Many people had financial difficulties, and they were able to improve their lives. So there was a good side. The *bonecas* helped many people.

"But now, in the last few years, the demand has fallen.

"But the traditional style never leaves, right? The tradition that Mestre Vitalino created, and that Daddy and Uncle Manuel Eudócio and the others continued. It always continues.

"The demand continues. There are always people with good eyes who see that this art has a history. It was created. So they are always searching.

"But there are always phases that make it difficult to sell. And in this moment, it is hard in our country."

In this moment when neither the artists nor their patrons have much money, what worries Marliete is less the decline in demand, which worries Ademilson, than the decline in the workforce. Marliete gathers women around her, most of them relatives, most of them young, and teaches them her style. But most of the young people, as Elias and Ademilson said, are not interested.

They don't want to learn beside their elders in a workshop. What they want, Helton said, is money. Here is how Marliete put it:

"We are worried about the future because many young people, many young people are leaving the art and seeking jobs that guarantee stable employment.

"So, many young people need to study. There are many young people who are students. In my period we hardly studied. We did not have the financial means, and it was hard to get to the city. Today it is easy for everyone to study, both here and in the city of Caruaru.

"And today many people have the opportunity to study and find a profession. They are seeking security and employment, a job with better benefits and better money. And our art can't offer this security.

"My family, we are still maintaining the tradition, to encourage others, to give continuity to the art. But, in general, I am worried about Alto do Moura.

"We remain in the fight. And actually the art is more valorized today than it was in the period of my father and Mestre Vitalino. Without a doubt.

"But we have to work with much care, so that it continues. This art already has one hundred years of history, right? It is important for us to work with care, so it will continue."

Marliete's generous, general worry is focused on her community's need to attract young people into the art. In her family, in her generation, six successful artists are at work. In the next generation, there are two: Carmélia's son Emerson and Antônio's daughter Amanda. From her personal experience, Marliete draws the solution: If people work with care, as she does, the art will continue. She shares her community's concerns, but, as an individual, she has no worry about continuity:

"Right now" — in 2019 — "in this moment, we are in a phase that is difficult. But, *for me*, I never stop getting commissions. People seek me out to see the pieces I make.

"Many customers come, seeking me. My *customers*, the majority of them are collectors who buy to keep a collection at home. They have collections, and I continue to sell. My production is small, and I am always working."

Commissions keep coming, her work is fine, and she is always behind. Marliete is the only artist who never has ready pieces on her shelves to sell to random visitors. Her collectors, who probably have more money than space for display, are thrilled by her miniatures and happy to pay her price, knowing her reputation.

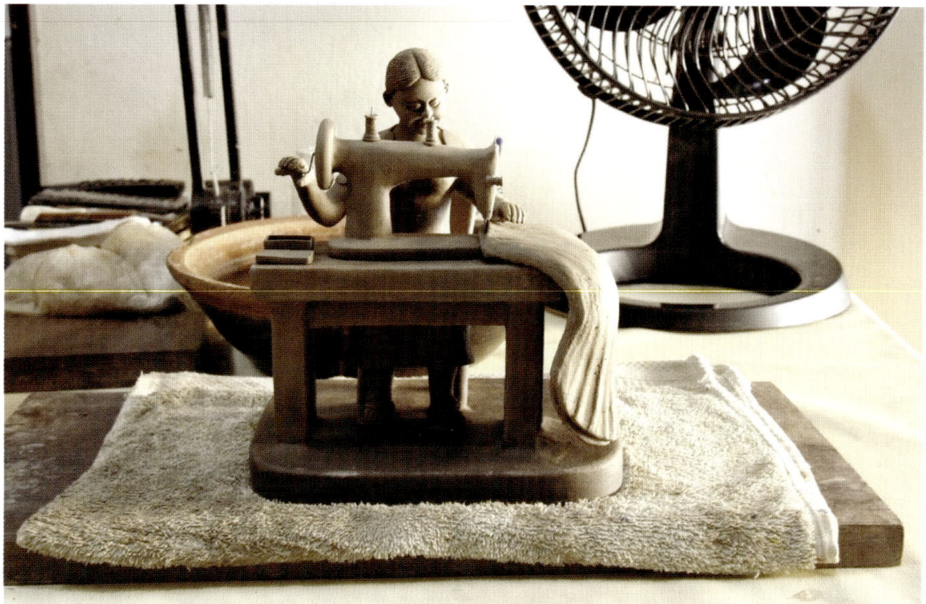

The table in Marliete's studio, 2019

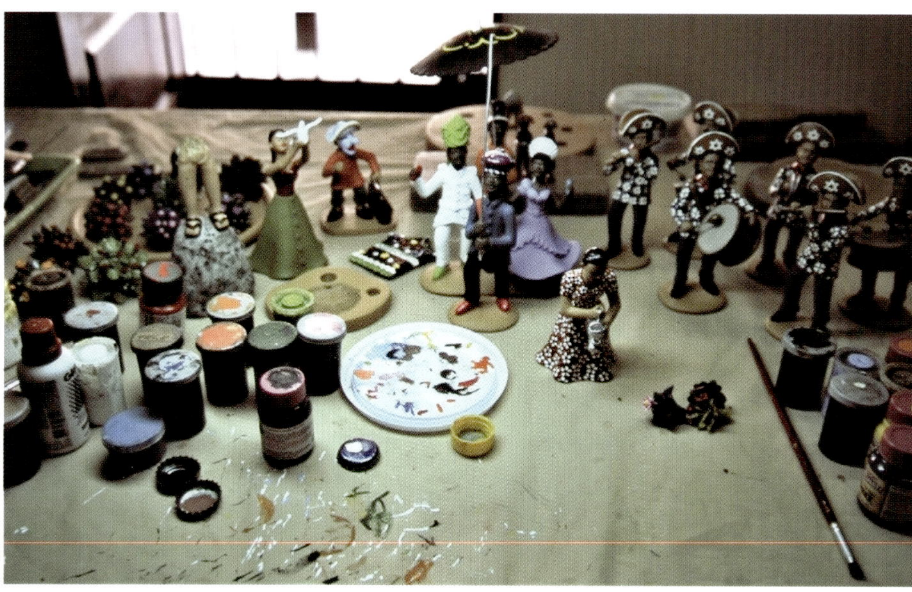

The table in Marliete's studio, 2015

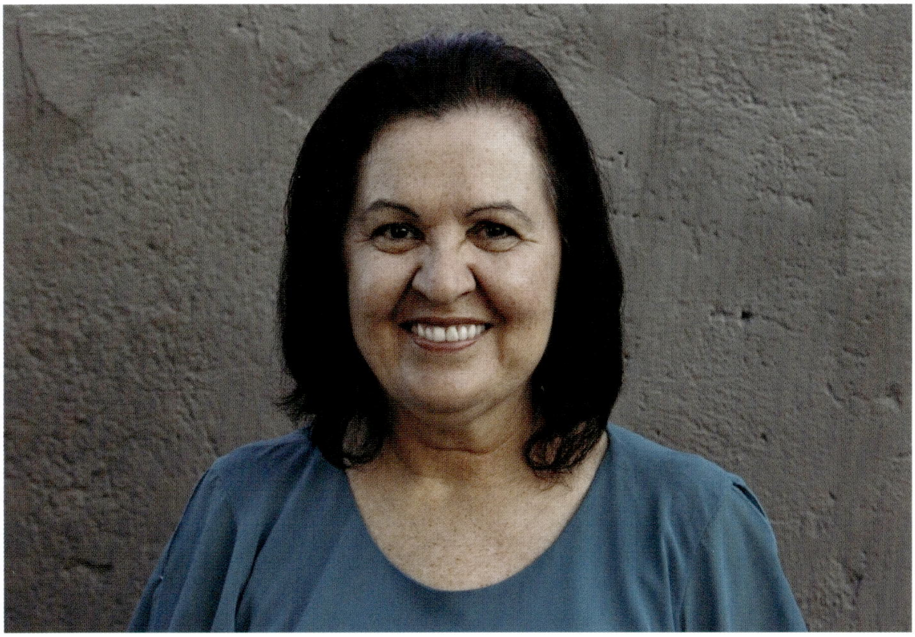

Marliete, 2019

Marliete has traveled to exhibit her work throughout Brazil, to Rio and São Paulo, to Maranhão, Brasília, and Minas Gerais. She has been, by invitation, three times to France and twice to Portugal. Back home in Pernambuco, she is a regular star of the show at Fenearte.

Fenearte — the Feira Nacional de Negócios de Artesanato — bills itself as the largest craft fair in all of Latin America. Since 2000, it has been held every July in the beautiful coastal city of Olinda, drawing thousands of visitors and pulsing production for the artists. In Alto do Moura, in Ibimirim and Tracunhaém, artists work toward the show during May and June, creating new pieces and building their stock with an eye to sales and prizes. At Fenearte, Marliete says, "we do good business, the whole family. We sell there at the *feira*, and we get commissions that we can keep making for the whole year.

"At Fenearte, we see our customers who come from the South, from Rio and São Paulo, and we stay in touch with people who make commissions.

"We show our pieces, and we show photos of different pieces because it is not possible to take all the things we make. We show the photos, and some people say they want a new piece that we can also create.

"And there is a Salão de Arte" — a Salon of Art — "where we participate with new works to receive prizes. And the piece in the Salão de Arte is for sale too. Whoever wants to buy it can buy it. So, this helps much."

In Olinda's convention center, the exhibition space divides. One of the thirty rows of booths is given to Pernambuco's acknowledged masters, all expenses paid. Marliete is one of them and she comes with as many as twenty members of her family. The booths in the other rows are rented for display of merchandise. Marliete is here, as many artists are, more for commissions than direct sales, but the prizes that confirm her status and excellence excite her the most.

Marliete tells us that the Salão de Arte Popular, which she usually calls the Salão de Arte, was established at the beginning within Fenearte, and it works like this: Artists from all over Brazil submit photographs of their work to the Salão. A committee selects pieces to exhibit, and then awards prizes, one for work in clay, one for work in wood, and another for art in a different medium. In addition, there is a public prize, determined by a vote of all in attendance. The works on display can be purchased, but Marliete says, "The piece that receives a prize, that one you cannot sell. That is a prize piece. The artist receives money, and the piece remains in the collection of the government, a collection they have of the Salão de Arte of Fenearte.

"So, I won in two thousand and four; I won the prize of the public with my piece of my grandmother telling stories. It is my beloved grandmother, the mother of my father. It was sold because at that time the one that won the prize of the public, it could be sold.

"And then in two thousand and five, I won another prize of the public with *A Noite de Núpcias*" — the Wedding Night.

"And in two thousand and eleven, I won another prize, of the public also, for a scene of confession. It shows Frei Damião, a priest who did very beautiful work here in Brazil, in the Church. So, I made that scene. It shows people in line, waiting for confession.

"And then in two thousand and eight, I won the first prize for *A Foto de Família*, which shows a big family in front of a house with a photographer taking their photograph. I won a prize, first place. And this one went into the collection of the government.

"I have made copies for customers, for collectors who asked for it. But the original one is in the government's collection.

"I was very happy with these prizes. I have also won other prizes in other competitions.

"And what is important is the encouragement that it gives us. We become more interested in the work, we believe more in the work. The work becomes more valorized, right?

"And we concern ourselves more with creativity. Our work improves. It continues, it continues.

"Our art must continue."

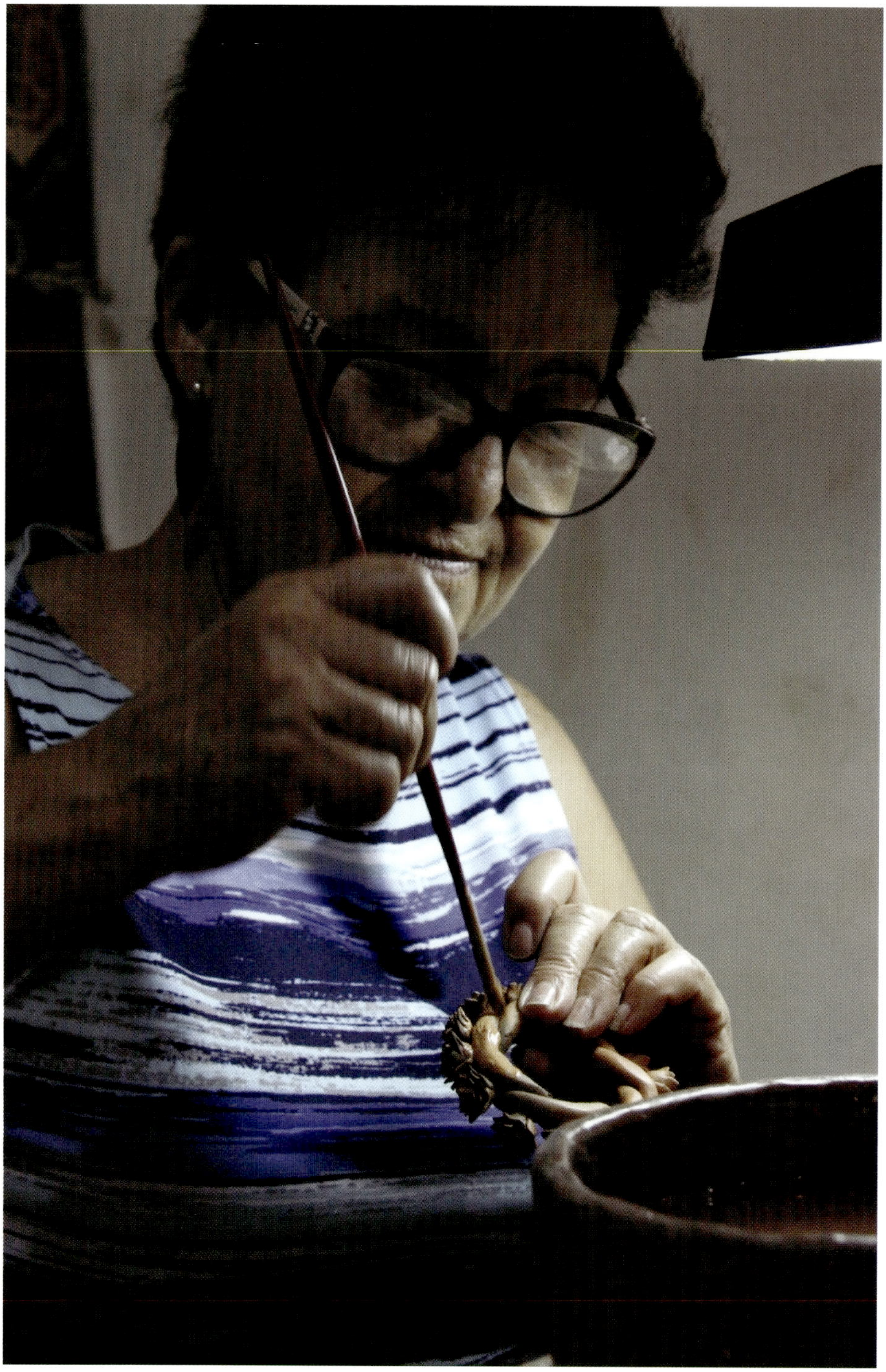

Socorro painting in her shop, Alto do Moura, 2019

11

Socorro and Carmélia

Learning in the home of a renowned master, developing a personal style within the widening collective repertory, finding a way forward in a time of decline — these topics link into a frame for the words of the generation now in the lead. Ademilson and Marliete expanded on all of these themes. So did Marliete's older sisters Socorro and Carmélia.

Socorro, Zé Caboclo's fifth child and second daughter, and Carmélia, his sixth child and third daughter, tell the tale of learning much as Marliete did. Socorro Rodrigues da Silva put it like this:

"I learned by watching my parents work. My father Zé Caboclo and my mother Celestina Rodrigues, who worked until she was eighty-five years of age."

Celestina's brother, Manuel Eudócio, also worked until he was eighty-five; they came from a hardy line. Socorro continues:

"When we were children, six or seven years of age, we liked to handle the clay, interested to make something, even our own toys, little horses and little bulls. And later we actually made things to sell. When we were children we made things to sell, to be able to buy some sweets on Sunday.

"And from there we went on to acquire a taste, right? Always watching. My father always made larger pieces, but as a child, eight or ten years old, I started to make small ones, replicas of my father's work: the Family of *Retirantes*, the Return from the Field, *Bumba-Meu-Boi*, *Maracatu*, the folkloristic dance sets.

"As a child I started to make them small, miniature. It was more work, but I *liked* it. And today I make miniatures."

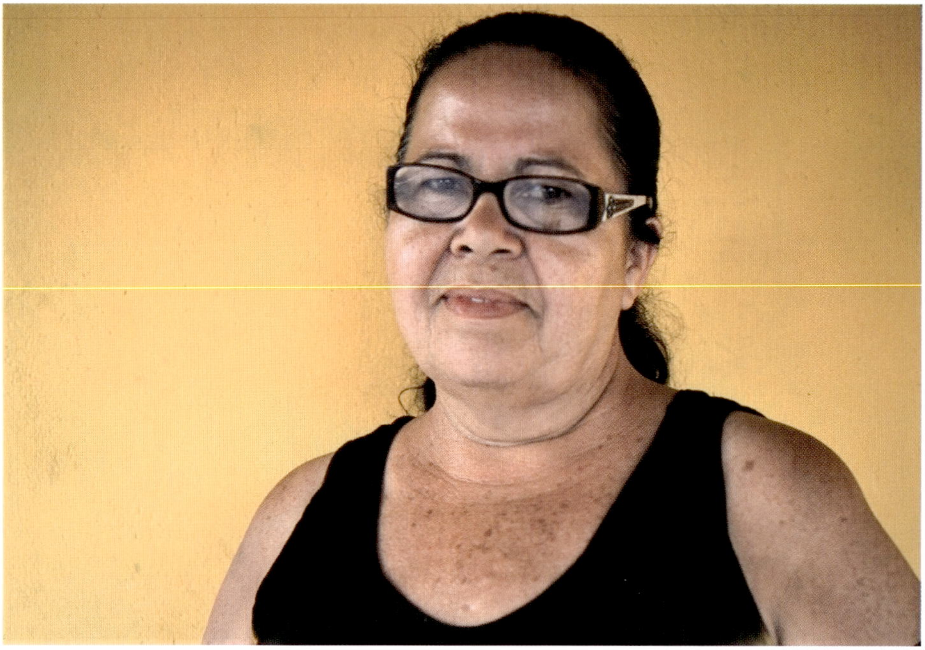

Carmélia, 2015

Carmélia Rodrigues da Silva provided a comparable account of learning and then she added to our understanding of her parents:

"We watched our father working. We were always around him, since he was a father who was very loving. He played with us very much. My father was very playful. He was a happy person, always laughing. He was a person everyone liked, and we were always at his side.

"He loved his work, and we were always watching.

"And my mother would be making pots and pans of clay. I very much liked to help her. When she would work, like, in the afternoon, I would be at her side helping.

"We have many beautiful memories of our father and mother; we have *saudades* for them."

Saudade is a key word in the Northeast; scattered through the lyrics of Luiz Gonzaga's songs, it evokes a lonesome mood of wistful longing. Carmélia continues:

"We keep remembering the time when we were children. Because we grow up and things change.

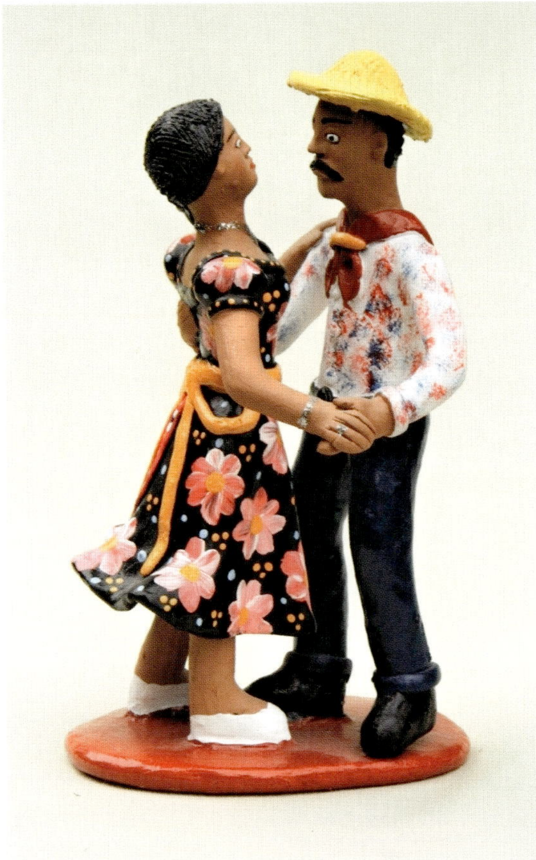

Forró dancers by Carmélia (22 cm tall), 2015

"My mother lived to be eighty-five, thank God. But my father died very young, with fifty-two years of age. I was seventeen years old when he passed. I felt it very much. He was a very good father. He left many memories.

"He died of schistosomiasis" — a tropical disease caused by freshwater parasites. "He went to take a bath in the river. And he died young, my father.

"What a pity. He died young and left a family, a large family."

While they were still learning at home, both of them had found the route toward their mature repertories. Socorro was working with her youngest sister, Marliete, helping her with the miniatures, and Socorro's repertory today, like Marliete's, centers on miniatures, featuring, in particular, children at play, girls jumping rope and boys shooting marbles and spinning tops. Meanwhile, Carmélia was working with her older brother Antônio, making figures from her father's repertory. She makes miniatures and statues half a meter in height, but she concentrates in the usual middle range of size. And, though she makes the usual pieces — Lampião and Maria Bonita, she says, sell best — Carmélia has developed a distinct inclination within the traditional repertory and added new pieces that are adamantly her own.

Carmélia most enjoys making images of dancers, finding it a delight to get the colorful clothing and the bodily movements just right. Her repertory fills with dancers of different kinds, and among them her *forró* dancers can make a set with the musicians who play *forró*, the *Trio Nordestino*, also a favorite image of hers. The trio of accordion, drum, and triangle provides the sound for the June Festival, and the trio gave Carmélia the idea for her most admired creation, a festive meshing of three musicians and three saints. The feast days of Saint Anthony, Saint Peter, and Saint John, you will recall, all fall in the month of June, and the festival is customarily named for the last of them, São João. Carmélia describes her creation:

"I thought of making a piece with a São João theme. So, how should I make it? And I got a good idea. I thought, São João is very much about parties and pleasure, right?

"I am going to make Saint John with an accordion. Then Saint Peter — people say he is the keeper of the key to the sky — I am going to make him with a drum. And Saint Anthony, I will give him the triangle.

"The first one I made, it has only three. I made Saint Peter, Saint John, and Saint Anthony. Then later I thought, You know who would also be good, Saint Francis. I put the little birds, and I made him playing the *pífano*. Then it became a quartet.

"I have made many, many. People commission the piece. I like it very much. It is very beautiful, it is. My business card has a picture of the quartet."

Carmélia's creation has become an accepted symbol of the June Festival, itself a symbol of the Northeast. A large version of her work stands in the exhibit about the festival in the Museu do Forró: Luiz Gonzaga in Caruaru. When she decided to include Saint Francis, Carmélia welcomed the most popular male saint of the region where the Rio São Francisco flows between Pernambuco and Bahia. Immediately identifiable in images by the birds in his hands or on his shoulders or on his head, Saint Francis is the Father of Ecology, the protector of animals, the saint for farm folks whose fortunes ride on their livestock. When Carmélia gave him the *pífano* to play, she brought him to Alto do Moura, subtly fusing him with Mestre Vitalino, a good Catholic, usually portrayed playing the *pífano*, and something of a regional symbol himself.

Carmélia and Socorro are both noted and successful artists who are worried about decline. Socorro has two children, neither of them interested in the work, though her daughter-in-law, Patrícia Maria da Silva, is a skilled and clever artist who has already had a piece accepted for the Salão de Arte at Fenearte.

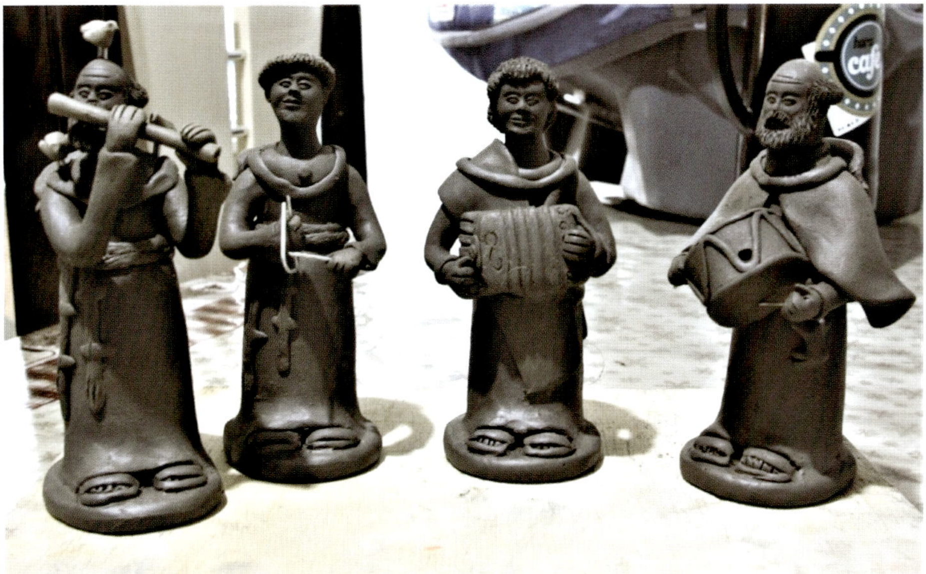

The quartet in progress on Carmélia's table, 2019

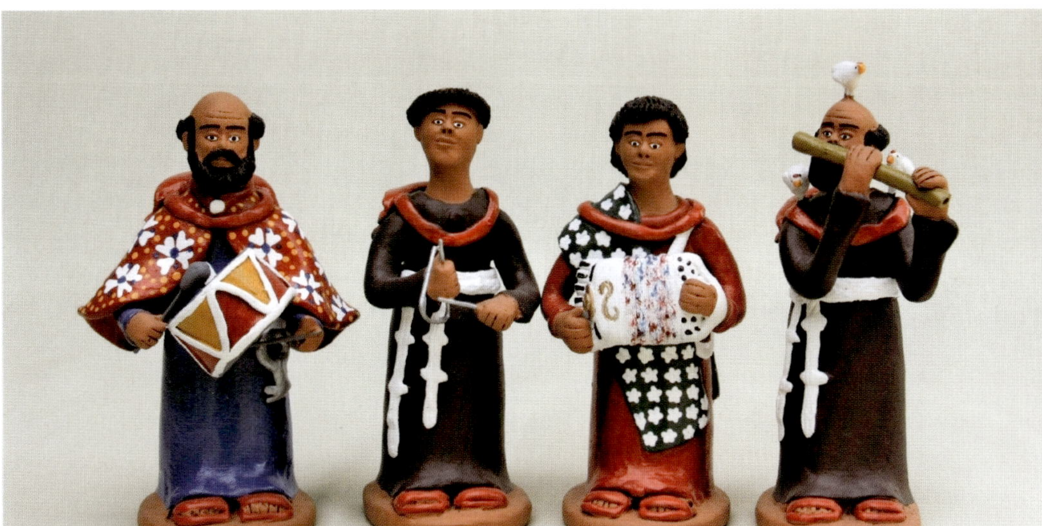

Carmélia's quartet — Saints Peter, Anthony, John, and Francis — fired and painted, 2019

Socorro, wearing the shirt that advertises the shop named for her mother, Alto do Moura, 2019

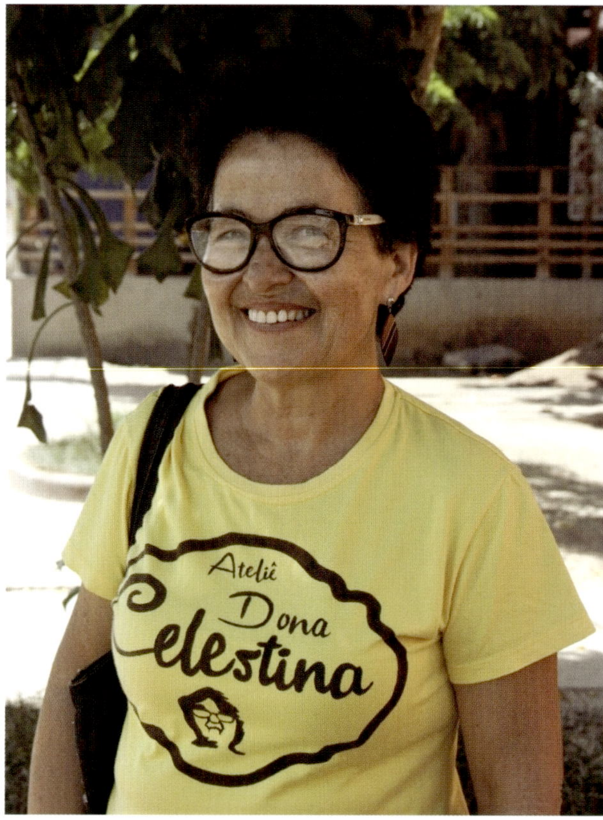

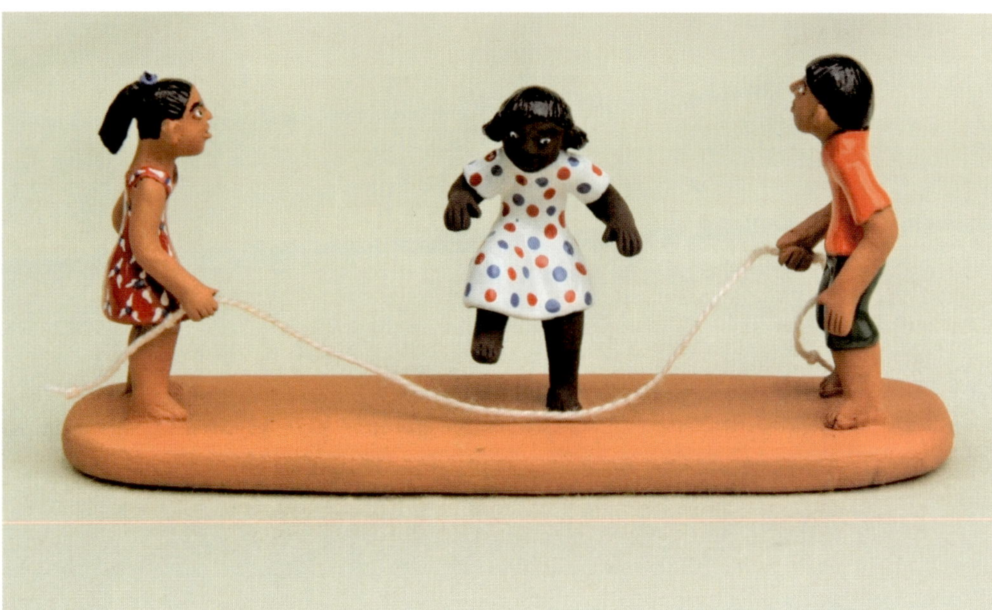

Skipping rope, a miniature by Socorro (4 cm tall), 2021

Carmélia has four children. Her daughter Olga paints her pieces and her son Emerson works with his uncles in the family shop. In this moment, thinking about the future, Socorro and Carmélia are working in different ways to ensure continuity.

Socorro tells us that at a time in the past when sales of traditional art were weak, Lula's beneficent government established a program that provided educational opportunities of a kind that had not been available to the poor before. Young people from Alto do Moura went off to college and after graduation they found secure employment, leaving the clay behind. Those unable to study turned to the quick and easy *bonecas*, gaining money enough to live. But now, Socorro says, *boneca* sales are slack and she believes the traditional art will endure, sustained by exhibitions where works are sold, exhibitions that will also, she hopes, bring the next generation into the community of creation:

"I am always working so I can participate in the shows. We participate in the Salão de Arte at Fenearte. We always participate.

"It is a good thing for us, for the artisans, because we are always creating new pieces. It is an honor to get prizes, to be chosen for the museum of the Salão de Arte at Fenearte.

"To this day, I am passionate about my art.

"And in two thousand and fourteen, we decided to create a group. We started this group of women, Flor do Barro" — Flower of the Clay — "with the intention of encouraging people, young women especially, and offering workshops. We are holding many workshops in the high schools.

"We are hoping that the high school groups will come to us, to encourage the artists and give continuity to the art.

"Because we are worried about the future."

To encourage the artists and stimulate general interest, Socorro arranged a public exhibition of works by the members of Flor do Barro for the June Festival in 2019. To provide an economic base for her family, Socorro has opened a shop at the eastern end of the line along Alto do Moura's main street. Named for her mother, Dona Celestina, the shop supplies a studio for Socorro. For visitors it offers a mixed selection of souvenirs in clay and — in a glass case — excellent pieces by Socorro, her daughter-in-law Patrícia, and her niece Amanda.

Carmélia locates her hopes for cash and continuity in the big city markets of Recife. In her father's day, she says, artists sold in the Feira de Caruaru, but no longer. Now the stores in Alto do Moura fill with small, repetitive things, and some artists, with Luiz Carlos as her example, have shops for display and sales attached to their homes. Carmélia doesn't, so once a week she packages her pieces and heads for Recife.

Carmélia lives in a house of the usual local type. You enter directly from the long street where the artists live, pass along a corridor on the side and come to the spacious kitchen in the back where Carmélia works at a cleared space on the table to the left. An energetic, upbeat person. Carmélia has hands that fly with rapid confidence. Around her gather crowds of dancers and musicians, drying and awaiting their trial by fire. She works so swiftly, with such enthusiasm, that she might have two kilns burning at once.

Three kilns stand out the back door, in a shed behind her house, and a few paces along the slope the five kilns shared by Zé Caboclo's descendants assemble in a tight cluster. She, of course, can use those too, and here is how Carmélia describes the firing:

"To do the firing we must have patience, heating with much calm. My pieces are small, so I burn for four or five hours, six hours.

"You have to burn depending on the type of the piece, with much care.

"First I make a little fire, and it is only smoke. Then later it starts to heat, it starts to heat.

"And then it goes, and we must be very careful, using only the coals left by the wood when it starts to heat, because if it makes a loud pop, the pieces will be broken, and they will be a great loss.

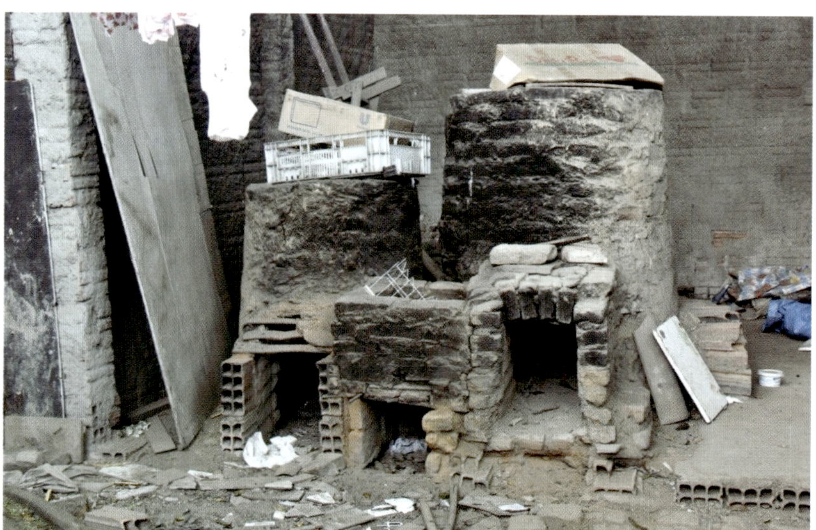

Carmélia's kilns, 2019

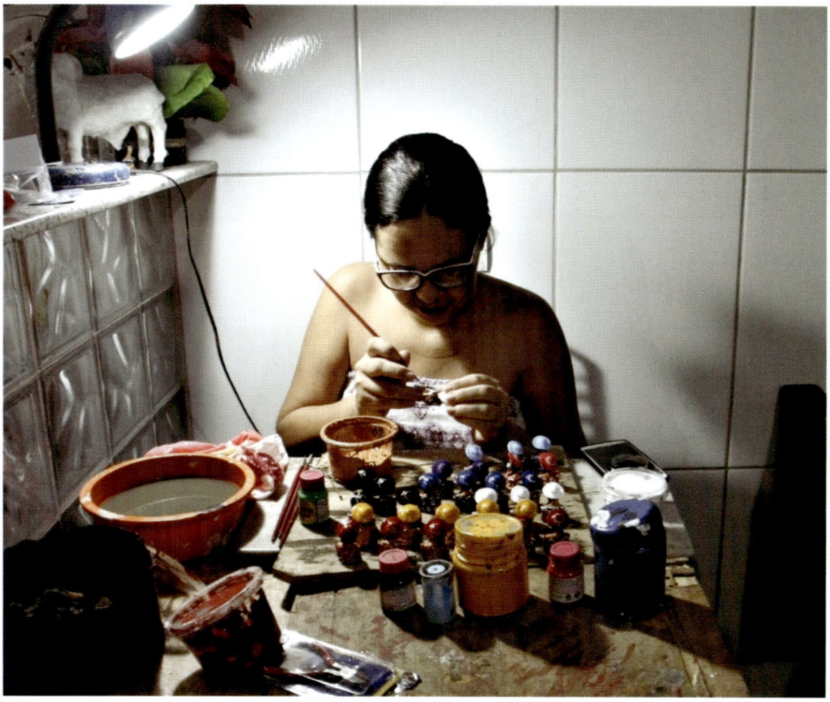

Olga painting Carmélia's pieces, 2019

"When it heats, the pieces start to change. They get black. They turn black.

"The warmth, we know, increases, increases, increases. Then the fire goes *vowooo*. It is a beautiful thing. Then later the pieces turn red, really red. Then you let it cool.

"After two hours, three hours, we open the kiln. Then two, three hours later, the warmth starts to diminish, depending on the size of the kiln, and soon we can take the pieces out.

"If it is a small kiln, we put the little pieces in a can" — like a saggar — "then we put the can in the kiln, and it is easy to take out. Big pieces don't need the can, but the small things, if we don't put them in a can, they will break and get lost."

After firing, Carmélia's pieces are painted by her daughter, Olga Nogueira da Silva, who works in a space where the corridor widens before the door into the big room where Carmélia shapes the clay and packs the finished works into boxes for their trip to Recife. She tells us about her day in the city:

"I work here in my house. Then every Friday I go to Recife to make deliveries. We always go.

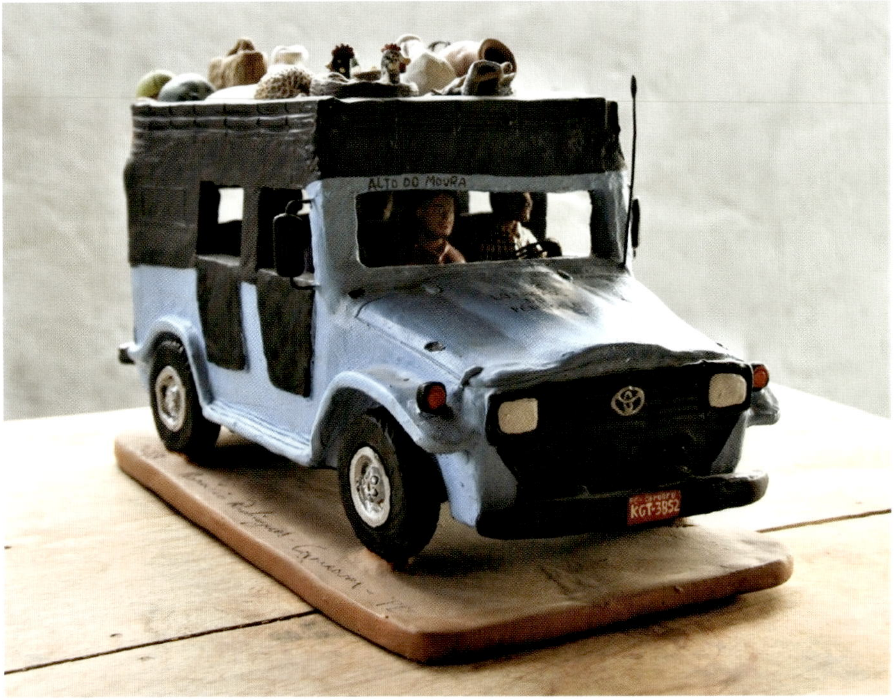

Toyota in clay, by Carmélia's brother Horácio, 2021

"On Thursday we have to prepare, to wrap. We leave at dawn, we leave here at two or two-thirty in the morning to get there really early.

"We go in a Toyota" — a stretched jeep — "and every Friday three Toyotas leave from here. About ten artisans go.

"We get there really early and form a line at the Casa da Cultura. We start forming a long line to enter. At six o'clock they open the gate and then the cars start entering.

"Then we go, open the boxes and put our pieces on little stands, under a mango tree. It is very beautiful.

"The people who own stores, they go there to buy, and I sell at resale prices. I find it entertaining. I like to talk to the customers. I like it. I have met many people there already.

"And I really feel good. I really like it, but it is tiring."

The Casa da Cultura is a repurposed old prison. Its cells have been converted into small shops, many with Alto do Moura's clay figures for sale. The weekly market, held outside on the grounds, is not open to the public. Merchants with stores in the region buy there, and Carmélia's Friday has begun.

"Then when it is about eleven o'clock," she says, "I take a taxi to the airport, and take the merchandise to this store, Arca."

At Recife's Gilberto Freyre Airport, a woman named Vaselique manages Arca, a store with works from Tracunhaém as well as Alto do Moura, commissioned directly from the artists. "It is like this," Carmélia says. "She tells us, Look, I want these pieces. Then I make the pieces she wants and the amount she wants. And I sell at a resale price. She puts them in the store. She has already bought it, paid me, and I deliver it."

If unsold pieces remain in her hands, Carmélia has two more options in Recife. She can try at the Mercado de São José, a covered market for fish and vegetables that also has stalls selling decorative objects for modest homes. That market, caught in a web of narrow, crowded streets, stands halfway between the Casa da Cultura and the Centro de Artesanato de Pernambuco. The Center for Pernambucan traditional art, set in a plaza by the waterfront, is customarily named for its location, Marco Zero. Attractively spacious, orderly, and bright — tough competition for the Casa da Cultura — the Center displays fine works, conscientiously labeled with the names of the artists, including Luiz Carlos and Ademilson. Carmélia can leave pieces there on consignment:

"When we put a piece at Marco Zero, it will get sold. Then at the beginning of the month, they tell me how much I sold in the month before. They do accounting. They put it on our account.

"And it is very good for us, because they are always selling, all the time. And sometimes our sales are weak. It is good for us in times of financial crisis."

Quite early one sunny Friday morning, the seventh of June in 2019, we met up with Carmélia on the shady grounds around the Casa da Cultura in Recife. Paths divide the stalls of the vendors into four main sections. Artisans have come from many places, eleven from Alto do Moura, and they sell to merchants who look through the stock, assemble groups, and buy in quantity.

Carmélia has a booth in a good position, with cardboard boxes piled behind her, filled with stock, and spread on the table before her she has samples of the works in the boxes. The ones she shaped and Olga painted, all in the smaller sizes fit to commerce, are these: Lampião and Maria Bonita, Luiz Gonzaga, the São João quartet, the *pífano* band, the *Trio Nordestino*, dancers, and a sweet piece that brings the trio and the dancers together.

She also has on display works from her family. From the husband of her daughter Simone, she has *bonecas*. Her older brother Antônio, with whom she

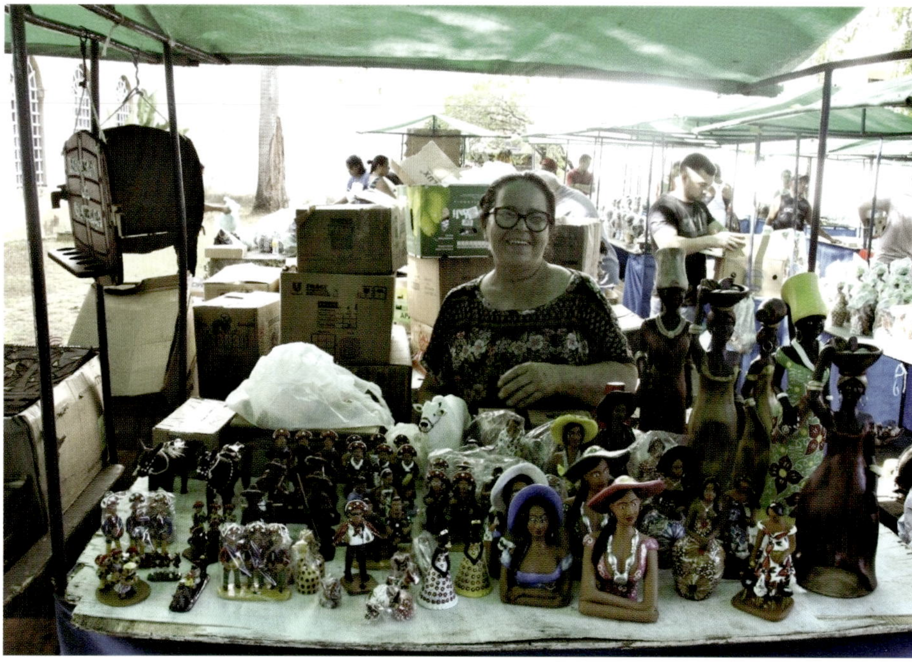

Carmélia at her booth, Casa da Cultura, Recife, 2019

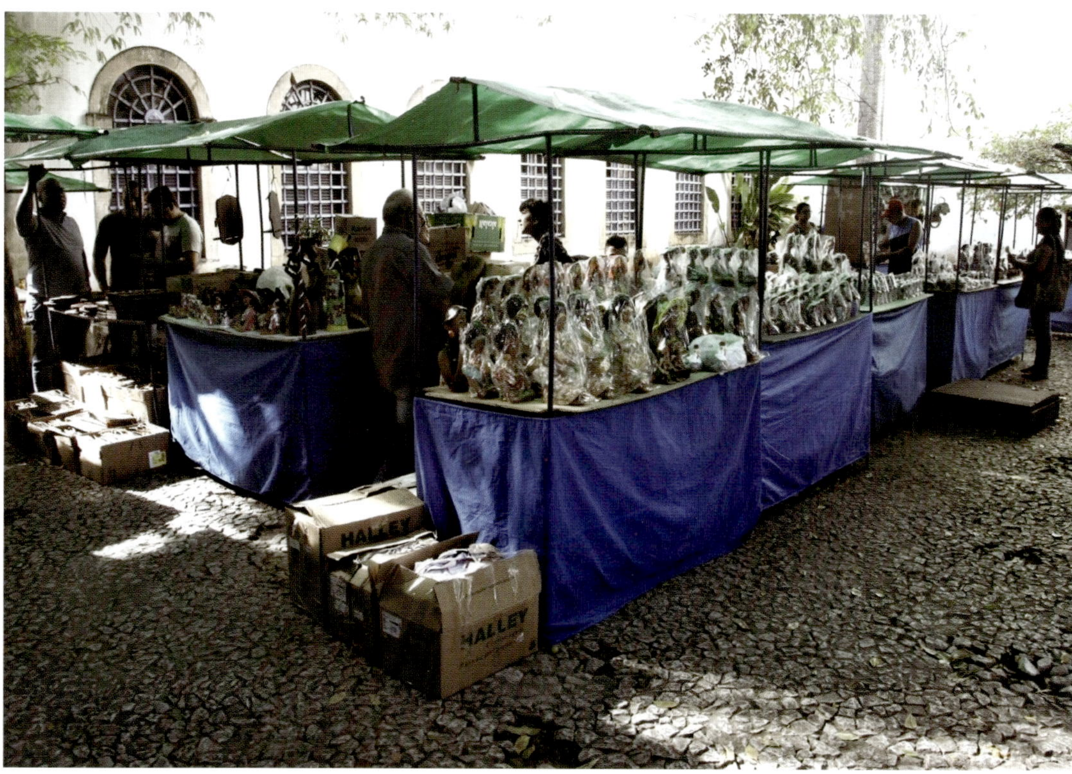

Friday morning sales at the Casa da Cultura, Recife, 2019

worked as a child, only sends commissioned pieces, none this time, but from her oldest brother Paulo, she has unpainted farmers and fishermen in Vitalino's style, and from Paulo's wife she has a mass of tiny saints. The customers today often ask for saints, and Carmélia tells us she ought to make more images of Saint Francis.

During the chat in the gaps between buyers, Carmélia frankly explained the situation. She, Socorro, and Marliete were all married. Though she was Zé Caboclo's sixth child, Carmélia was the first to marry. She was nineteen and her son Emerson, born the next year, was Zé Caboclo's first grandchild. Carmélia's husband left her, Socorro's husband left her, Marliete's husband left her, Olga's husband left her. Art is how they survive.

Marliete, she says, is the youngest of the sisters, but she is the family's teacher, the source of the best new ideas. Marliete travels often to demonstrate and sell, so she and Socorro are wise to concentrate on easily transportable miniatures. Carmélia once went to Brasília to do as Marliete does, but she didn't enjoy it, and by traveling overland to sell in Recife she can make the pieces — larger than miniatures — that bring her pleasure in creation and sell well enough to sustain herself, Olga, and Olga's two children, one of them still a baby.

It is necessary. Artists must make to sell and sell to live. Ebullient Carmélia is fortunate that she enjoys both making and selling. She looks around us at the artists selling and the merchants buying. The sun is shining, the mood is fine, and she says, "I like it here. I love my work."

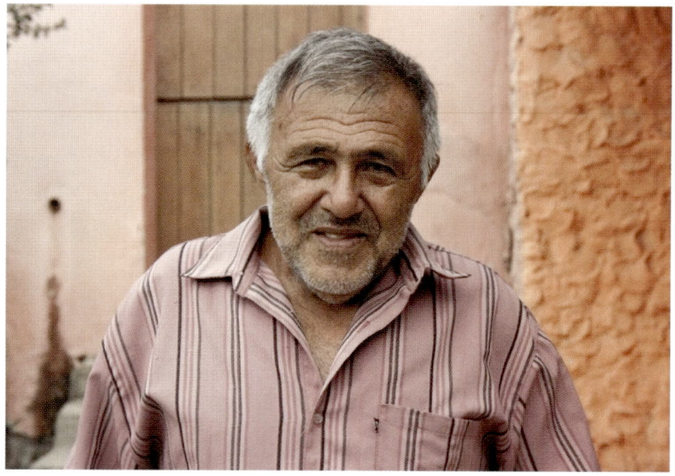

Paulo, 2019

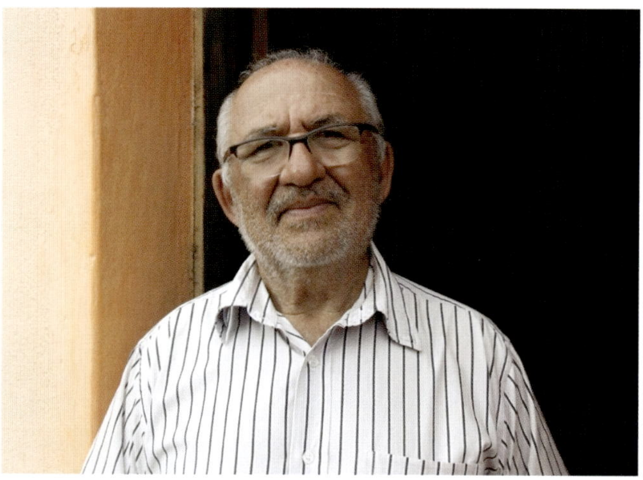

Antônio, 2019

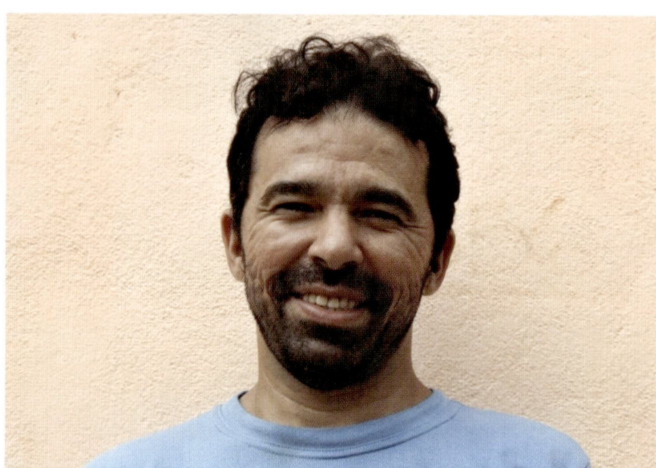

Emerson, 2019

12

Paulo, Antônio, and Emerson

Downhill from Carmélia's home, uphill from Marliete's, the family shop opens two doors to the long street named for Vitalino. The door on the right leads into a space for storage where finished pieces wait to be sold. The door on the left leads into the place of making. Paulo Rodrigues da Silva, Zé Caboclo's second child and first son, works at a table shoved to the back wall on the left. Antônio Rodrigues da Silva, the master's third child and second son, works at the next table on the left along the wall. Emerson Nogueira da Silva, Carmélia's son and Zé Caboclo's first grandchild, works beside his uncle Antônio at the next table on the left. The last table on the left and the first to the right in the back are normally vacant.

During a couple of weeks in the spring of 2019, these artists in this shop completed our understanding of Alto do Moura's process of production. Our work, like theirs, depends on cooperation. The texts that animate our writing spin out of collaborative exchange. While the recorder runs and long interviews unfold, the artists arrange their thoughts into words saying what they choose to say and giving us the information we need when it comes time to write. In return they receive the human gift of complete, unhurried and undistracted, attention. For everyone it is a blessing to be taken seriously. Antônio commented that our conversations were encouraging, helping them to carry on, and the resulting book, he said, will be doubly beneficial. The artists and their history will become part of the permanent record, available in libraries, and that record will help in unpredictable ways, serving as a vehicle of publicity that might spark wide interest and bring new customers. In many years of fieldwork, we have found most people to be grateful and a few who became

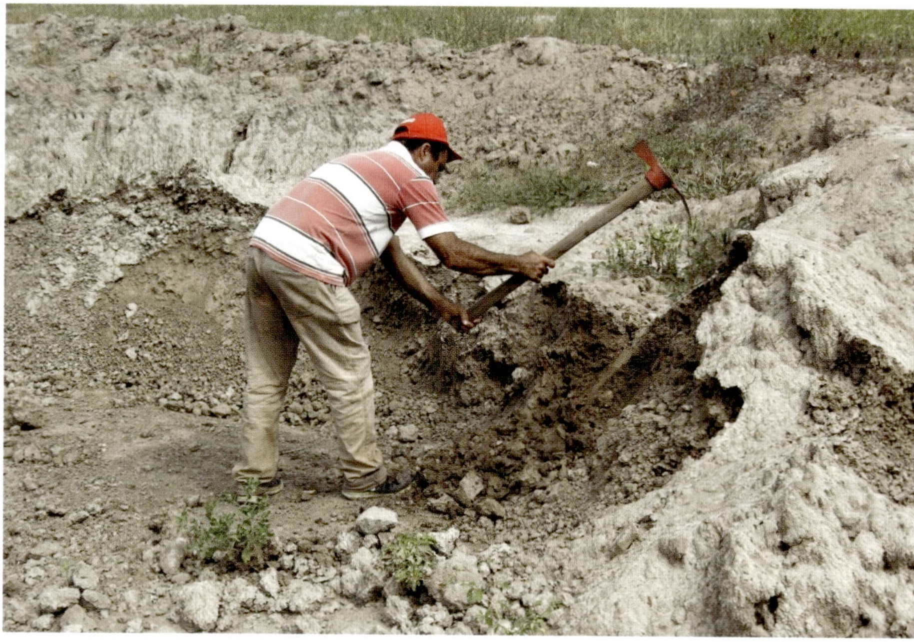

José digging clay by the Ipojuca, 2019

so interested in our project that they took on the role of voluntary colleague. Luiz Carlos and Genilda helped in many ways, and, from this shop, so did Emerson.

We went with Emerson and his friend José Fernando de Freitas to witness the beginning of the process. The town owns a clay bank to the west, about twenty meters from the Rio Ipojuca and fifty meters from the road back into town. Only members of the Association of the Clay Artisans and Residents of Alto do Moura are allowed to dig here. Swinging his mattock, José digs clay enough to fill the bed of his pickup truck. Every time he digs, José pays the Association twenty *reais*, about five dollars, and for the load of clay, the artists will pay José sixty *reais* and give another twenty to the Association.

Before it gets to the artists, the clay will be processed, low on the street where they live, at the home of Genário Lopes da Silva and Marli Maria Lopes da Silva. Their granddaughter, Maria Cecília, six years of age, is already creating her own wee creatures of clay. In front of the house, the clay is spread to dry, its chunky lumps broken up and trampled down. The clay — *barro* — is generally called *massapê*, meaning kneaded with the feet, though now, if it is to be used for shaping figures, it will also be milled as fine as flour in a shop behind the house, dampened, wrapped in plastic, and delivered to the artists.

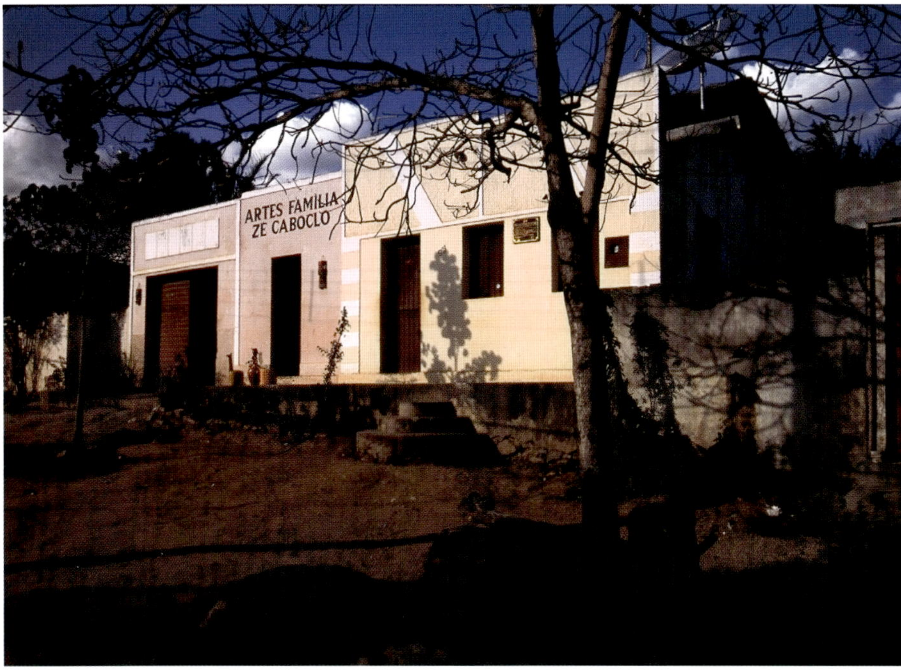

The Zé Caboclo family shop, 2015

The clay to shape has arrived, and for a brief spell in the spring, all three of Alto do Moura's lines of production are running simultaneously through the workshop of Zé Caboclo's family.

In the middle, Antônio works independently at his own steady pace, creating a masterwork in the first line of artistic production. Antônio always goes to Fenearte with Marliete. "At Fenearte," he says, "there is a Salão de Arte. It gives us an opportunity to create new things to show at the *feira*, to show and participate in competitions for prizes, and to show our work for commercial benefit." Antônio had just completed two new works for Fenearte. One is an updated version of *Os Retirantes*, a big bus crowded with people and carrying bundles and luggage on the top. Titled *Estamos Indo Embora*, We Are Leaving, it represents, he says, "a quest for better things. Everything is already on top of the truck, and they are leaving, searching for a better place."

Antônio has finished his work for Fenearte and turned to a commission for an unusually large and fine version of the traditional image of an oxcart. While the others are bent to their tasks, Antônio shapes the parts, assembles them, and, once it is finished, he paints his masterpiece to give it the look of polished wood.

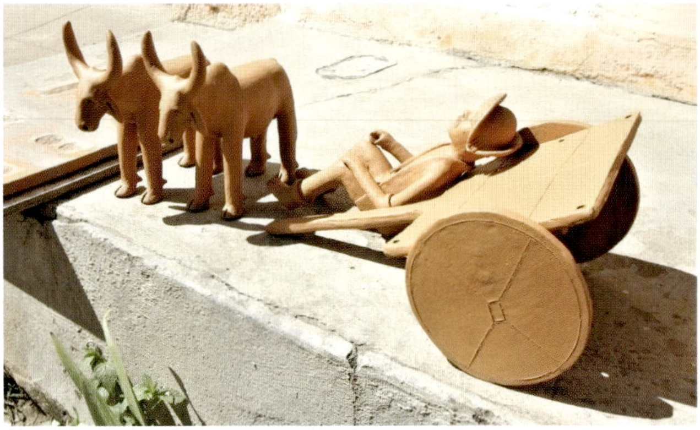

Oxcart parts, drying in the sun

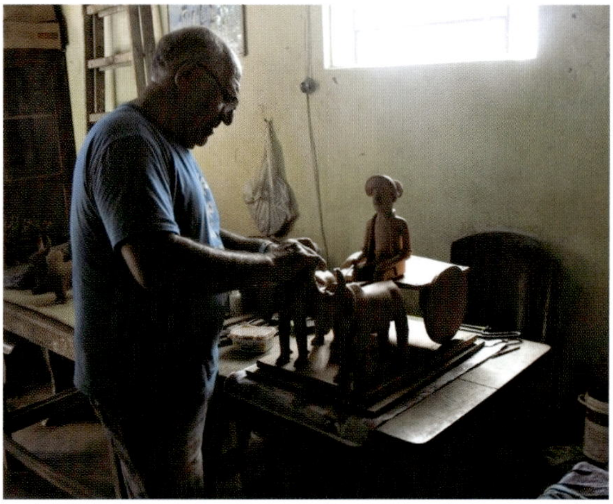

Antônio finishing his oxcart

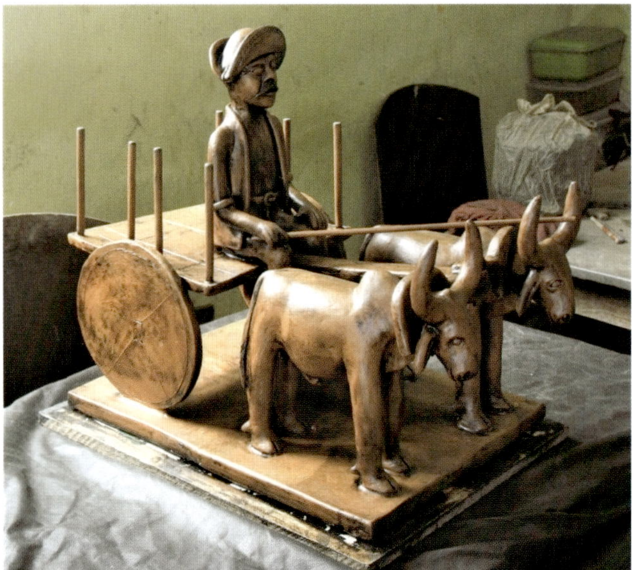

Antônio's oxcart complete, 2019

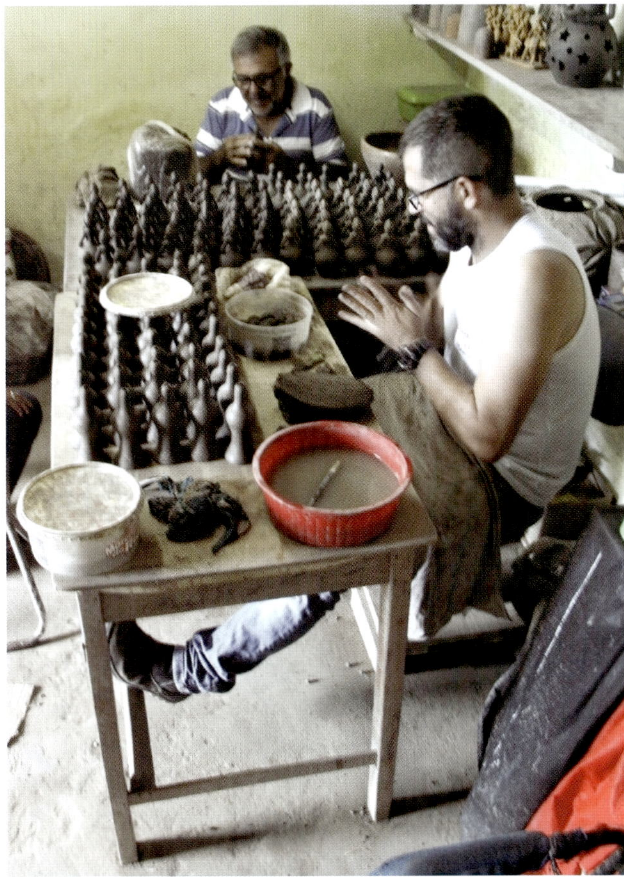

Evandro and Paulo making *bonecas*, 2019

Meanwhile in the back of the shop, the *bonecas* of the second line are taking shape. The process begins when a potter is paid to throw a plenitude of identical forms on the wheel. Made by an *oleiro*, they come in boxes in two sequential batches of a hundred. Evandro, Antônio's son, sits at the table on the right with lines of turned forms before him, first forms that sweep up and swell out like Korean vases, then forms that swell out and sweep up like bowling pins. Both get treated in the same way. Evandro has secured employment far from the clay, but, raised in Antônio's house, he knows enough to be helpful in his spare time. He lifts each piece, reams the interior to thin the walls, smooths the base, pokes a hole in the top, and passes it to Paulo.

Behind his table in the corner, Paulo manages the more difficult and skilled part of the job. He sticks a head in the hole at the top, rolls a pair of arms and puts them in place, then he uses a plaster mold to give the head a face. After the *bonecas* are fired, Paulo's daughter will be paid to paint them.

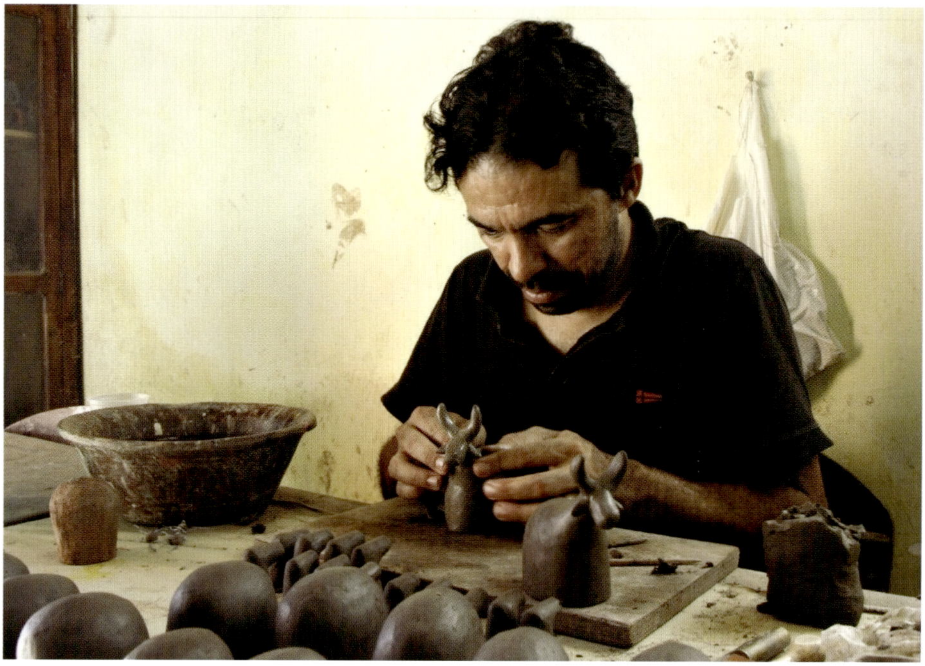

Emerson shaping little bulls, 2019

At the same time, Emerson is working in the third line of serial production, making a herd of small versions of the Bull from the *Reisado*. He has an ovoid, domical form of fired clay. Around it he wraps a flattened band of clay, joining it at the back and over the top. Then he scratches the clay high on the front, just as a potter does when preparing to add a handle to a jug. Using his fingers, Emerson models a bull's horned head. He frees the damp clay from the dry form, and attaches the head to the scratched patch on the front. Emerson's Bull now resembles the larger ones made by Luiz Carlos and the smaller ones made by Genilda, and he finishes his piece by poking three or four holes in the top to make a holder for pens on a desk, or he digs a wide opening to make a planter for cactus.

Antônio has finished his splendid oxcart. He sits at the table next to Emerson's, and it is not beneath him to help with the little bulls. The work is repetitive, but the process remains within one creator's command, engaging enough for the mind and hands. It is better, Antônio says, than making *bonecas,* for they break the process into uninteresting segments and bring slight compensation to those who make and those who sell.

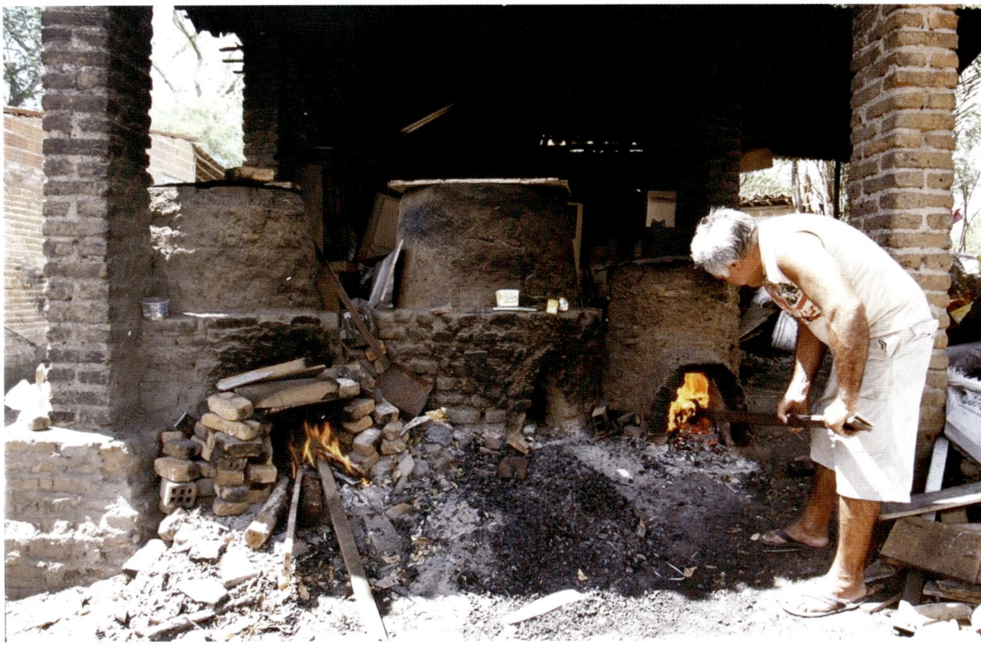

Paulo firing the family kilns, 2015

"So many *bonecas* arrive at the store," Antônio says, "that the store fills up, and they stop selling. The price is cheap, and competition between the store owners keeps driving the prices down. For the store owner the investment is high and the profit is very low.

"But the people who work in this traditional art, they are able to sustain themselves. The demand, it is always changing, but the traditional art, it maintains itself. It maintains itself. The price of the traditional art, it never falls."

Despite differences of process, profit, and pleasure, significance and quality, all the products flowing from this shop — and from the others in Alto do Moura — are made by hand out of local clay and fired with wood, general markers of traditional ceramic craft. They all pass through the cylindrical, updraft kilns that cluster up the slope next to the shop, where we have often gone with Paulo and Emerson.

Emerson divides the firing into three phases. The pieces, dried for three or four days in the shade, are loaded through the open top of the kiln and the top is closed with an iron lid that can be moved to monitor progress by color. During the first phase, the *queimar*, sticks are slowly stoked and after two hours the heat has risen to about two hundred and fifty degrees centigrade. Then the stoking picks up, and the second phase, the *esquentar*, ends in three or four hours when the smoke shimmers, spit sizzles on the iron lid, and the pieces turn black. The temperature has reached five or six hundred degrees, and the kiln is ready for the third phase, the *cadear*. The firing chamber is stuffed with two quick stokings. In thirty or forty minutes, the pieces turn red, the color of terracotta, and stoking suddenly stops. If it continued, or if flames remained among the ashes, the pieces could distort or explode. Now the kiln is left to cool, though cooling can be hastened by removing the lid or even splashing water from above. Tomorrow the pieces will be ready for painting, but this shop's artists, Paulo, Antônio, and Emerson, though they do paint, are more likely to leave their fine figures the color of burned clay, natural.

Speaking of his own work, Paulo says, "Everyone has his own style. My work doesn't resemble so much the work of my father. I make the same figures but with different details. The details are different. The shape of the face is more rounded, right? The physiognomy is a bit different.

"My brother, Antônio Rodrigues, his works are very similar to our father's. My brother's works resemble our father's."

Antônio says, "I make almost everything. Beside the quotidian figures my father made, I have also created a few new types.

"It is important for us to tell the story of the people, of the people of the Northeast. Our Pernambuco is a state really rich in folklore, right? In its customs, its culture.

"It started with Mestre Vitalino telling the story of the quotidian, of folklore. And we continue today because our work tells our history and people like it.

"People come from the South, from other states, and they admire it, right? Our work. And it is known internationally. In the entire world."

Antônio stands proud against outsiders who view the Northeast negatively; from print we quote one of them who characterizes Antônio's region as a place of "misery, hunger, and disease, social despair and early death." For Antônio, his place, poor in money, is rich in culture — rich in culture but once so poor in money that the *Retirantes* gathered their humble belongings and left, searching for a better place. It is all a part of the history they reveal through the clay.

When, at our request, Antônio lists the pieces that he and Paulo make most frequently, they are the ones that you, reading along, would predict: *Os Retirantes* and *A Volta da Roça*, *O Trio Nordestino* and *A Banda de Pífano*, Lampião and Luiz Gonzaga, figures from *Bumba-Meu-Boi* and *Maracatu*.

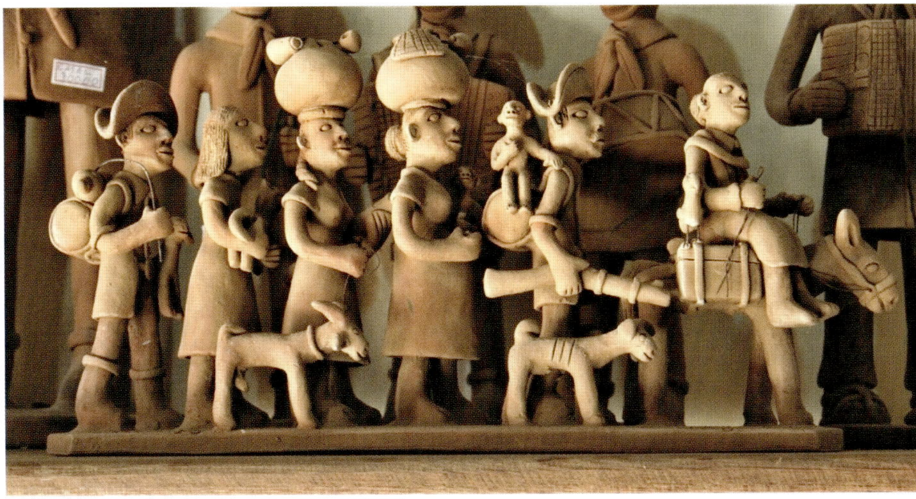

Os Retirantes, by Antônio, 2019

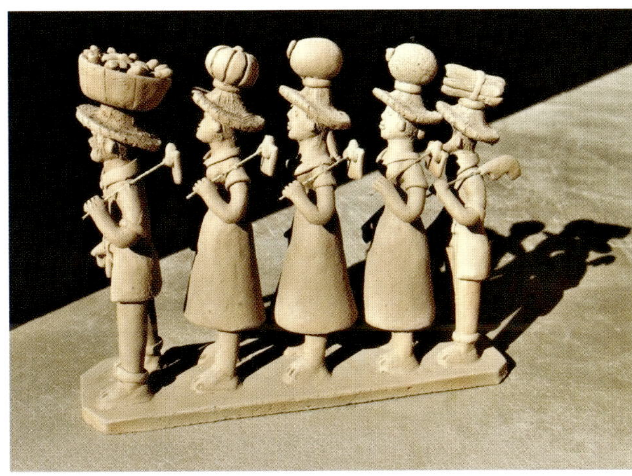

A Volta da Roça,
by Paulo, 2019

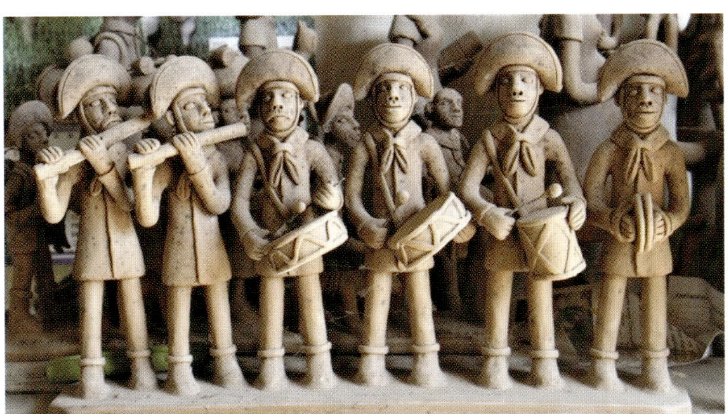

A Banda de Pífano, by Antonio, 2019

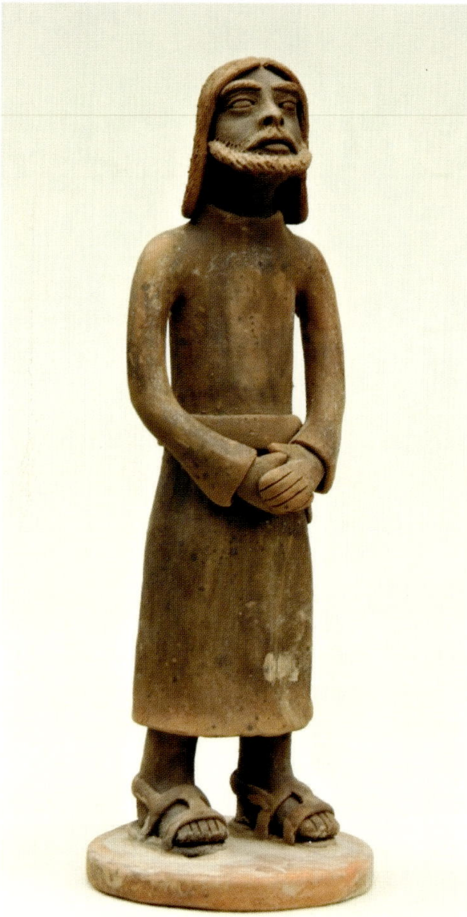

Daniel, by Antônio (35 cm tall), 2019

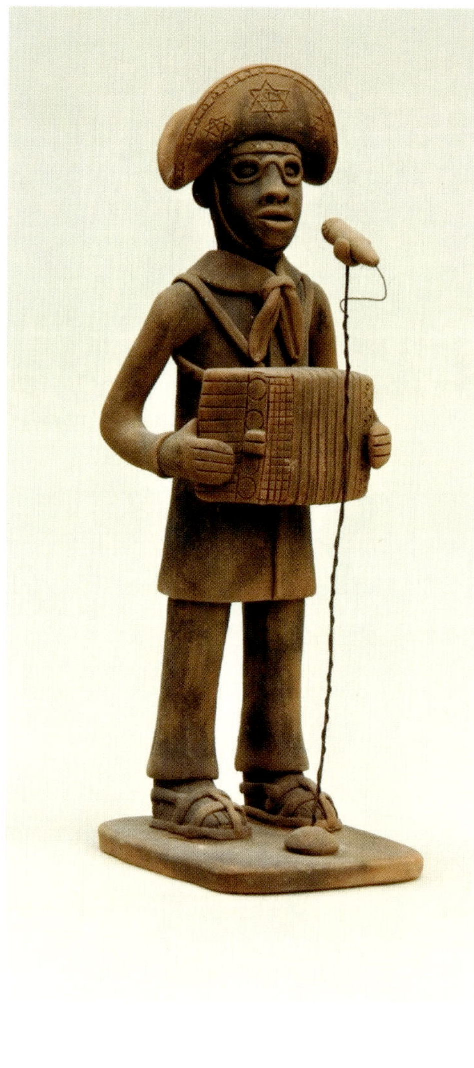

Luiz Gonzaga, by Antônio (33 cm tall), 2019

Antônio follows the trace blazed by Vitalino, his father, and his uncle, but he insists, and insists correctly, that he is constantly creating new pieces. Zé Caboclo, he says, made saints and though he doesn't, one of his original works was drawn from the Bible's tale of Daniel in the lion's den. Antônio tends to work at a larger than usual scale, and he began by making a large Daniel. It turned out to be too big for the scene he imagined, so he stood the statue on a shelf (where we found it) and made a smaller Daniel, surrounded by six docile lions, within a circular arcade, evocative of the Colosseum.

Emerson, the first in the next generation of Zé Caboclo's family, makes many of the classic pieces his uncles make, and he has also explored new territory. Emerson says:

"We always depict the quotidian, the quotidian life of the people of the Sertão, pieces like the fisherman, the oxcart, Cavalo Marinho, Lampião and Maria Bonita. Pieces like that, showing the folkloristic side of our culture, right?

"I have already made sculptures one meter tall, a meter and a half, different characters. I make *O Trio Nordestino*, *A Banda de Pífano*. Also the Jaraguá and the Bull of the *Reisado*. Everything that revolves around the tradition, the culture here, we are making, we are creating, we are making.

"We are always maintaining. And today we make more pieces in a modern area. People now want a computer, an airplane, a *futebol* player, pieces like that. So, we are always renewing the art, always making different things."

Married and the father of a teenage daughter, Emerson works with his uncles, helps his mother, and for fifteen years he has been conducting workshops on ceramics, first in Recife, now in the schools of Caruaru. "I am invited by the teacher," he says. "We agree on a little honorarium to cover the costs. I discover talent. The children, the teenagers are making works in clay, and I love it. I like to teach even more than I like to make."

When we met Emerson in 2015, he had just made a "traditional" image of Lampião and a "modern" image of a soccer team. He works within both categories, more in the traditional than the modern, and he also pursues a personal specialization in commissioned "caricatures," using photographs to portray individuals in clay. He made one for a golfer in the United States, another of a little boy for his parents. With photos before him of all the members of a family, he made statues of each one and arranged them on an oxcart. From photographs he made an image of his grandfather selling in the Feira de Caruaru, now on display in the Museu do Barro. He made one of Julius Caesar

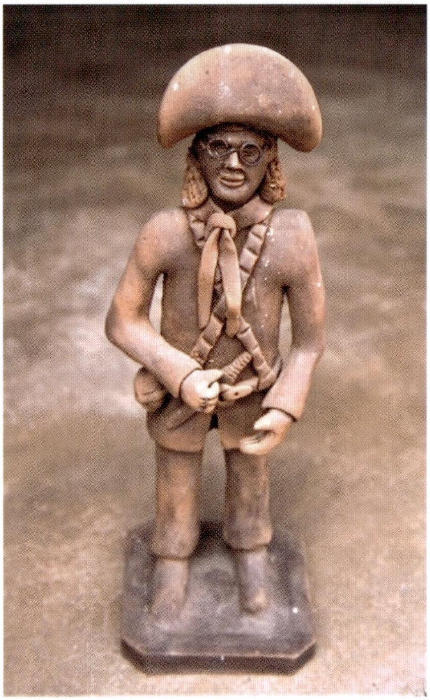

Lampião, by Emerson (24 cm tall), 2015

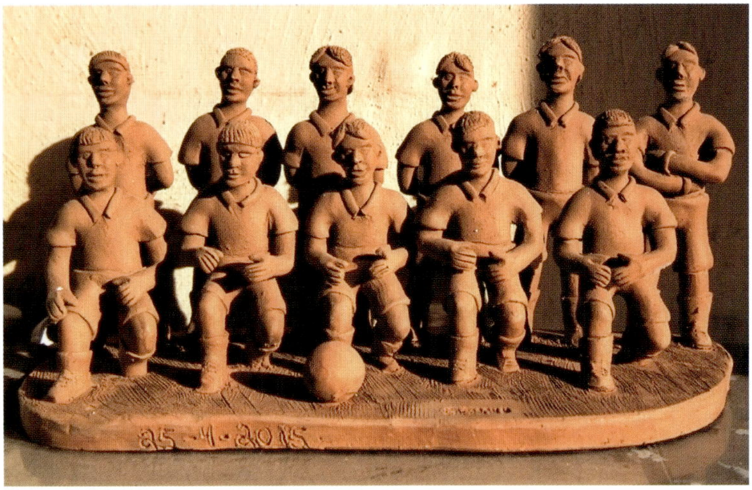

Futebol team, by Emerson, 2015

for himself, and he was commissioned to depict a famous chef, Lucas Corazza, who was trained in France, lives in São Paulo, and appears on television. Once when we were there, a jovial, burly policeman from Rio followed the answers to his inquiries through the streets and found Emerson in the shop. He wanted a small clay statue of himself.

In 2019, when the officer placed his order, we were watching while Emerson shaped and fired a fine version of Vitalino's bull, a prime symbol, like Lampião, of Alto do Moura's collective artistic tradition.

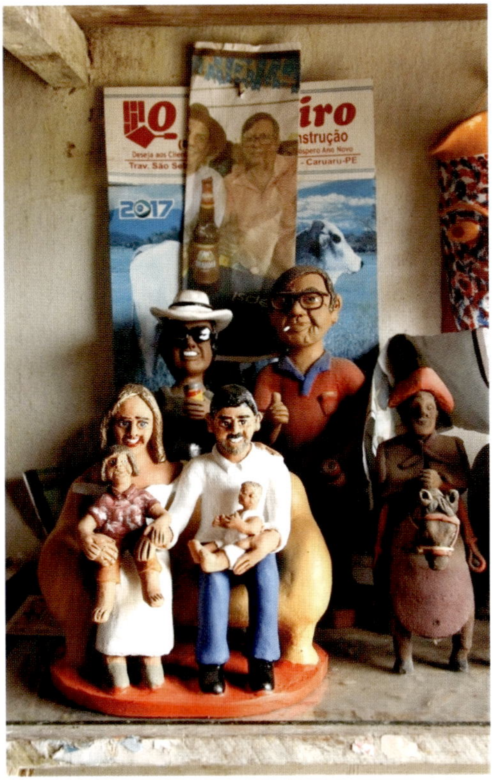

Emerson's caricature display in the shop, 2021

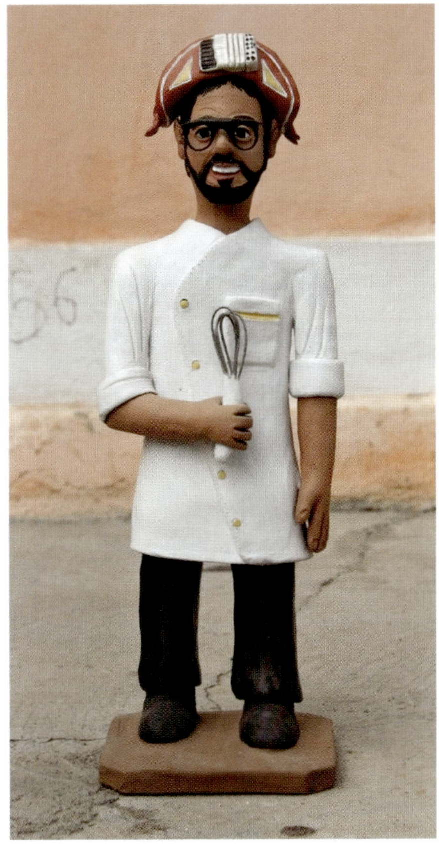

Lucas Corazza, by Emerson, 2019

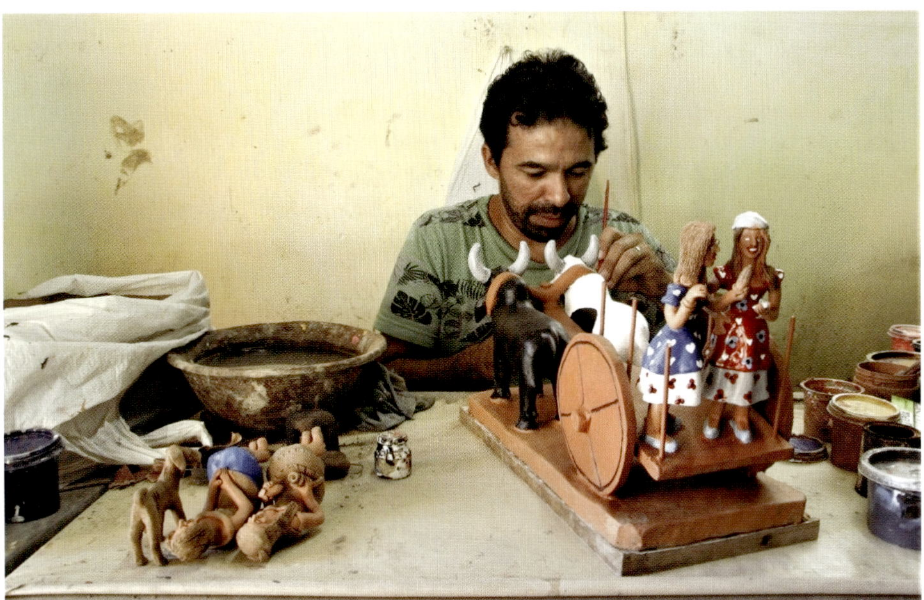

Emerson's commissioned oxcart in progress, 2019

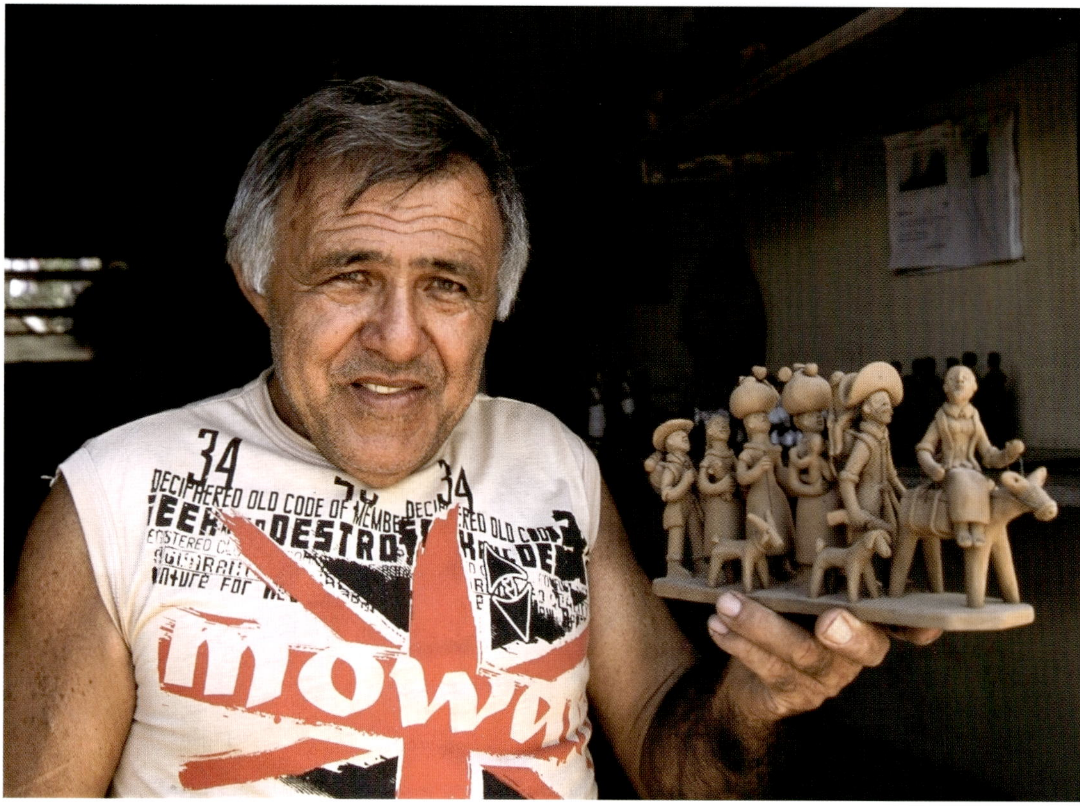

Paulo with his *Retirantes*, 2015

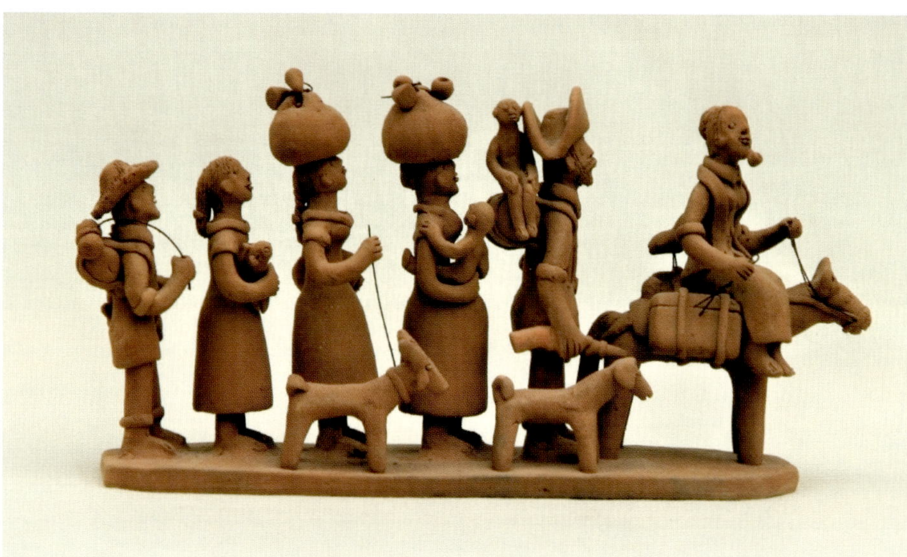

Os Retirantes, by Paulo (28 cm long), 2015

Amid all this diversity of production, lineages of learning have yielded a culture of creation, centered in personal commitment and reaching toward social coherence. Here is what these artists said on different days during one-on-one interviews:

Paulo said, "My father started working with Mestre Vitalino. And it was a great inheritance that he left to us.

"I commenced with sixteen years of age. I was watching my father work, and I started to make little toy horses to sell to children, right?

"And from there I continued, watching my father make statues. Then I started to learn. After eighteen years of age, I was already selling the statues too.

"In that period, the market was very weak, right? There were few artists. My father wanted us to study, to find some other line of work. Because he thought there would be no future in it, but we liked art, and we continued. We continue until today, and we remain in this art."

Antônio said, "I commenced when I was a youngster, more or less ten years of age. I got interested by painting some of my father's pieces and making children's toys, little horses, little cooking pots for girls. Things for children.

"Starting at fifteen years of age, I already started to make small statues, copying my father, seeing him work.

"We learned by watching him work, and we went on, learning how to handle the clay, how to make a piece. He did not teach us, and he did not encourage us. He wanted us to find another line of work; he wanted us to study. But we ended up with no other option. And we acquired a taste for this art, and we continue."

Antônio also said, "My father was a very influential person in this art. He worked beside Mestre Vitalino, beside Manuel Eudócio. They worked together and they went on learning together, one from the other.

"My father passed in seventy-three. I was born in fifty-one, so I remember him very well, and I actually remember Mestre Vitalino. When Vitalino passed, I was twelve years old.

"On the days of the market, he would come back from Caruaru, and me and my siblings and some friends, we would go to see him play the *pífano*. He was a musician. We liked it very much.

"There was a bench, and we would sit there and listen to him play the *pífano*. He told us stories. He was a loving person, a humble person.

"I have many memories of Mestre Vitalino. He passed in sixty-three. At one point some people told him he should *register* his work, claiming it for himself.

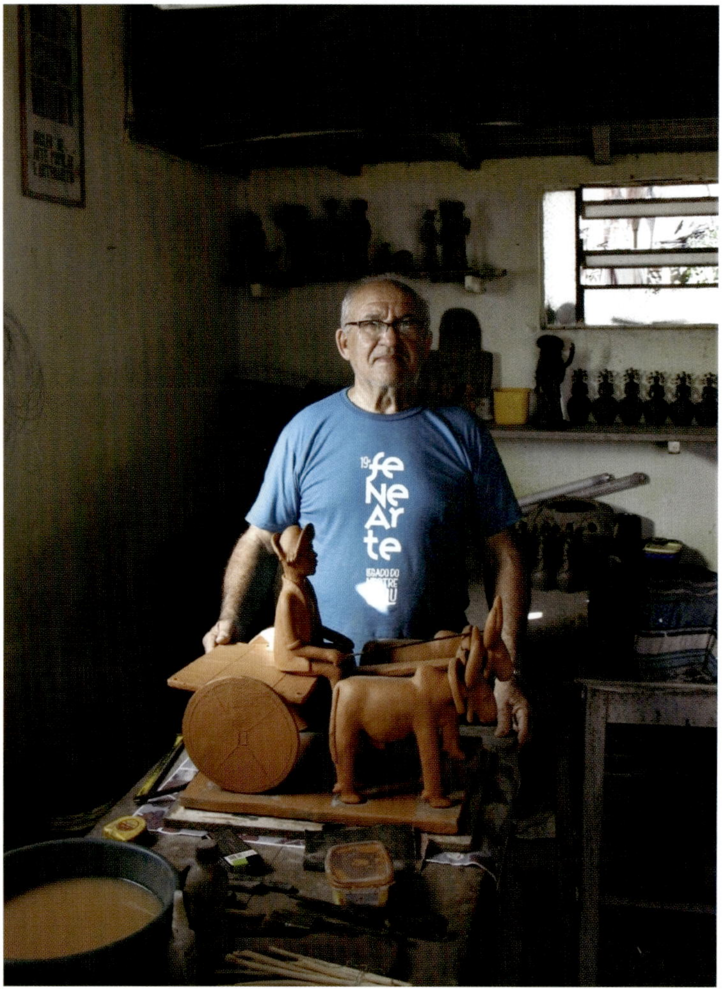

Antônio with his grand oxcart, 2019

"He said, No, this art is for everyone. Leave it for everyone to be able to make a living from it.

"He left it free for everyone to work, to learn. Yes, and everyone has learned it. He was humble. He had no ambition, no jealousy. A very humble man, very gentle, very friendly.

"He left this art for all of us."

Emerson said, "I commenced when I was a child, playing with the clay, making little cows, like a normal child, just playing, right?

"I was encouraged by my mother and aunt. They worked, with me watching them. I would play with the little statues, and I would make little pieces. I would see my mother making some pieces and I wanted to imitate them. And in this way I went on growing.

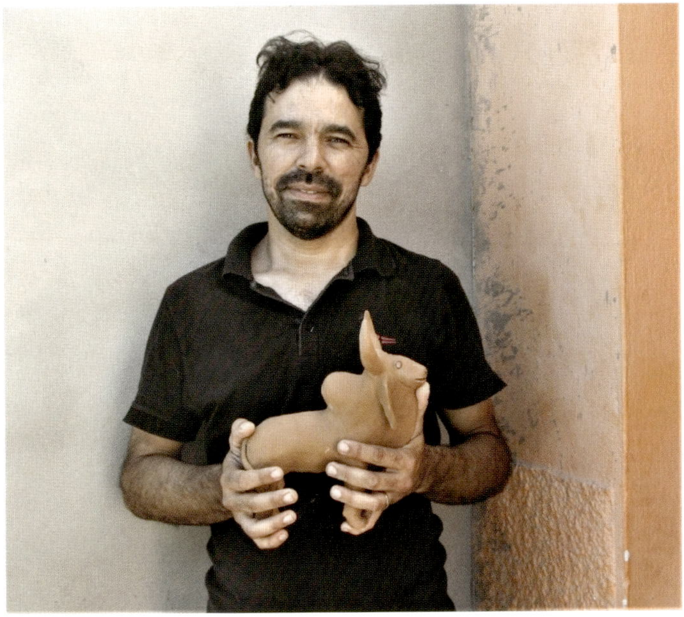

Emerson with his bull, 2019

Emerson's bull at the kiln before firing, 2019

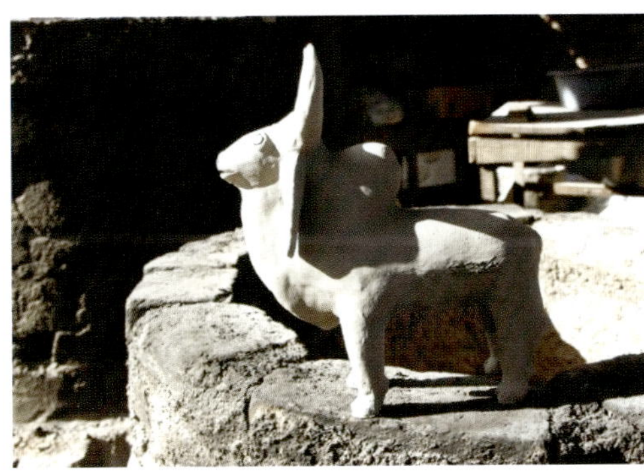

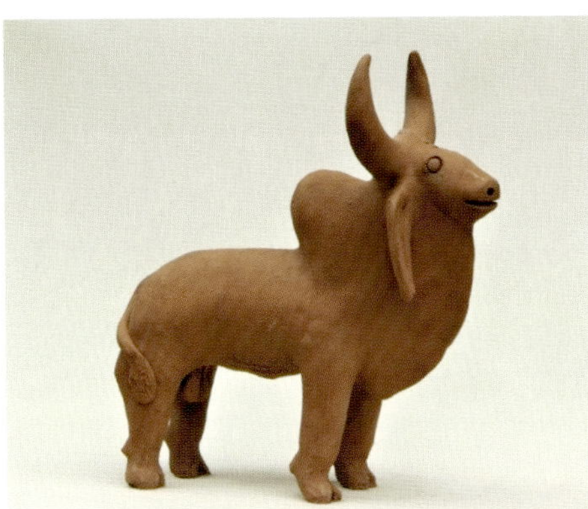

Emerson's bull, fired and finished (26 cm tall), 2019

"With twelve years of age, thirteen years of age, I was making little cows, and my mother would take them to the *feira* to sell. And I was super happy.

"So, I was always watching. I am curious, always observing, always fighting to improve. It became a *pleasure* to work in the clay. I mean, I started to work alone, observing, and I kept making. And later as an adult, I was making my own work. I have a *profession*.

"And I feel happy in this art.

"And I have traveled to different states to exhibit my work and sell it, in São Paulo, in Rio, in various states.

"I like it. I take much pleasure in it."

Emerson also said, "My grandfather was one of the first artists, one of the first followers of Mestre Vitalino.

"Vitalino was ten years older than my grandfather. When he came to Alto do Moura, he made statues of clay. One of the first he encouraged was my grandfather, Zé Caboclo.

"My grandfather was young in that period, not married. He learned with Vitalino, and we can still see the great humility of Mestre Vitalino. He said, Everyone can make a living from art. I want the work to spread, and everyone can make it.

"I find this an infinite greatness. A wonderful greatness. He was a humble person, a modest person.

"He encouraged all of the people to work. And I think it has to be like that.

"This work, this exchange between artists, it is an exchange of ideas. And all of us are burning together. We have a kiln there, a kiln of the family. Everyone burns together.

"So, this is very beautiful. It is a unity of work, a unity of art, here in our place."

13

AMANDA

WHEN ANTÔNIO LOOKS TO the future his worry, like Marliete's, is the shrinking workforce. "The masters are going away," he says, "the old ones. And we are seeing that the next generation is not interested like in the old days, right?

"There are very few who have an interest in creativity, in the art actually.

"It is because, before, there was a period of difficulties. Sales got weak. And there were new opportunities. The youth were studying, seeking other ways of life. They studied and found employment, thinking there are many things better than art. So, because of this the interest is very low.

"Today we see that it is not like it was in our period. Our children and the grandchildren, we see that they don't have much desire to follow in this art.

"I have four children. Evandro, he works in a company. He can make these little *bonecas*, but he did not acquire a taste to make as I make, everything traditional. There is another one who used to make, but he found a job and he is not making anymore.

"Who works in the clay, only one works. Three do not. I have only one daughter who is making the traditional like I make: Amanda."

Antônio is justifiably proud of Amanda. Her life is hard, but her work is excellent, and Antônio arranged a meeting in the shop so we could talk. Born in 1982, Amanda Paes Rodrigues Pereira is six years younger than Emerson, but she began as he did, working beside his mother, her aunt Carmélia:

"I learned beside my aunt. I learned by helping her. So, I started helping her by shaping parts of her works. I would shape a little table, or an arm.

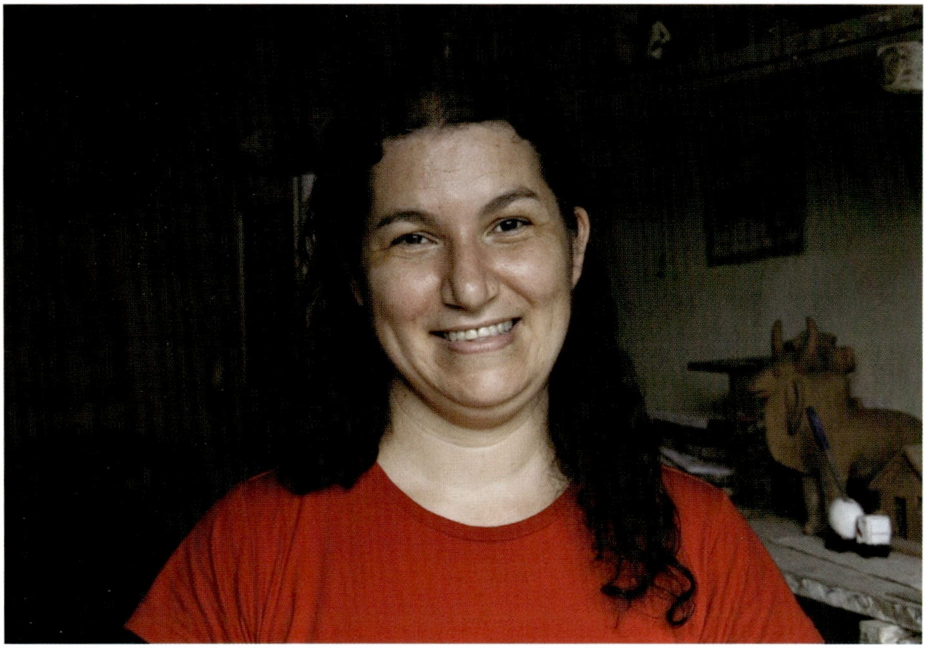

Amanda, 2019

"Then later when I was watching her, working with her, then I was able to make by myself. When I was around fourteen, fifteen years of age, I started to make by myself, already making my own pieces.

"I made them, I painted them, already my own pieces. And today I am still working, thank God."

Early on, Amanda made some of the classics — Lampião and Maria Bonita are her example — but quite quickly she found her own themes:

"Look, what I most like to make are the scenes of women at work. Working women, like I am, working women. At work on domestic chores.

"Also many themes, the themes of daily life. Many scenes: *A Mãe Amamentando*" — The Nursing Mother — "The Dancing Couple, Watering the Plants, Giving a Bath to the Child, Making Lace, The Washerwoman.

"Also I make the street vendors, like, selling. Selling roasted corn on the street. I really like to make the itinerant vendors on the street, understand? Like selling *cachorro quente*" — hot dogs — "selling many things. I really like to make these scenes.

"But I most like to make scenes of working women. Because I am a woman who works, who *likes* to work. And I find it interesting. I think it is very important, the work of women, right? In our society, in the whole world, right?

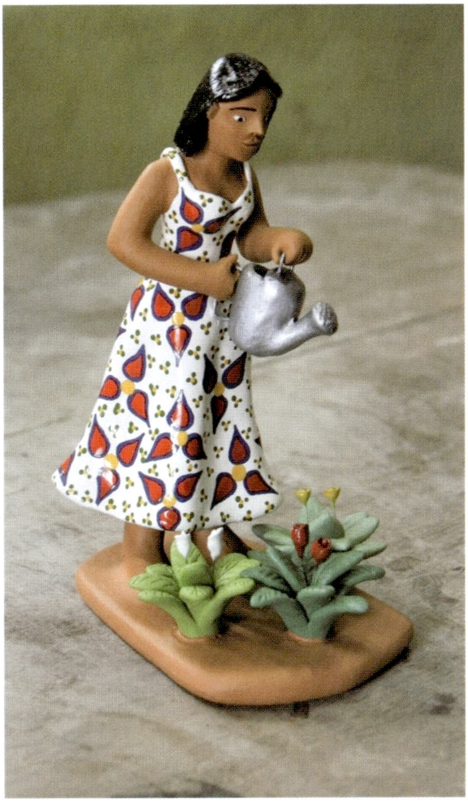

Watering the plants, by Amanda, 2019

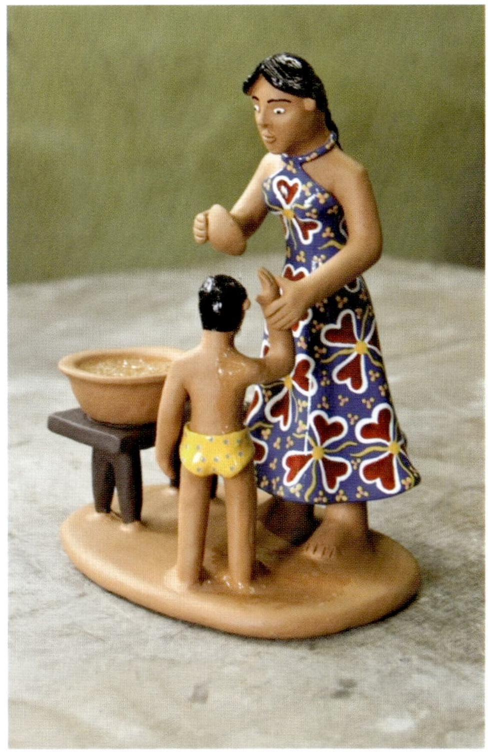

Giving a bath to the child,
by Amanda, 2019

"Even though my time for work is very short for work. I have two daughters, one with twelve years of age, one with four years of age who has Down Syndrome.

"So, there are her therapy sessions, and my time is very rushed, with the housework and taking care of her.

"So, there is little time left for me to work. But still, I never stop working.

"In every little bit of time that remains I am working. In the daytime, at night, and when she is at school, since she has started to study.

"So, whenever there is a little time left, I run to the table to work."

Amanda's work, carefully crafted, always carefully painted, brings her pleasure and deep satisfaction. Time is her problem. She continues in the line of her grandfather, and if she had time, she says:

"I would create many new things. I also have a desire to make the traditional ones, *Retirantes*, *Maracatu*, *Bumba-Meu-Boi*. I have much desire to make them. I never have. I never have, but I have a desire to reproduce them also.

"But it is like this. I really like to make new scenes that are not — how do I say it? — not so traditional.

"So, I find these new scenes, scenes of working women, scenes of street vendors, very interesting, and I am always trying to make them.

"The tradition is always changing, right? Every day it changes a bit more.

"Right now we see the lack of interest among the youth. They don't want to continue, right? For example, my daughter says, Oh, I don't want to learn to make.

"She has learned, she is painting. But she paints like this: without much desire. She does not have that interest to *learn*, right? She does not have it.

"We don't see this interest in the youth of today."

Like her father Antônio, Amanda considers the failure of interest among the young to be the chief change of the moment. Then shifting to the topic of the market, she says:

"When it comes to the tourists, these visitors, sales have fallen, they have diminished much. Each time it goes down. Only those who really know the art, they are always seeking it. But the majority who come to visit, they stay up on the street, drinking in the bars.

"Sales for the *artesanato* have diminished much. There was a period when the *dondocas*, these *bonecas* were selling. It devalued our work. But with time the demand went down, went down.

"But nowadays, thank God, the really *traditional* work — those who really know our art, they *value* it. The collectors, they are always seeking it, always."

With Antônio, Amanda acknowledges decline, but, like her father and Marliete, she believes demand is sufficient and the traditional art will endure. Her optimism is founded on Fenearte:

"I have participated I think, if I am not mistaken, since two thousand and seven. Every year I participate. I submit my work to the Salão de Arte. Only on two years it was not selected.

"But always, every year, I make for Fenearte.

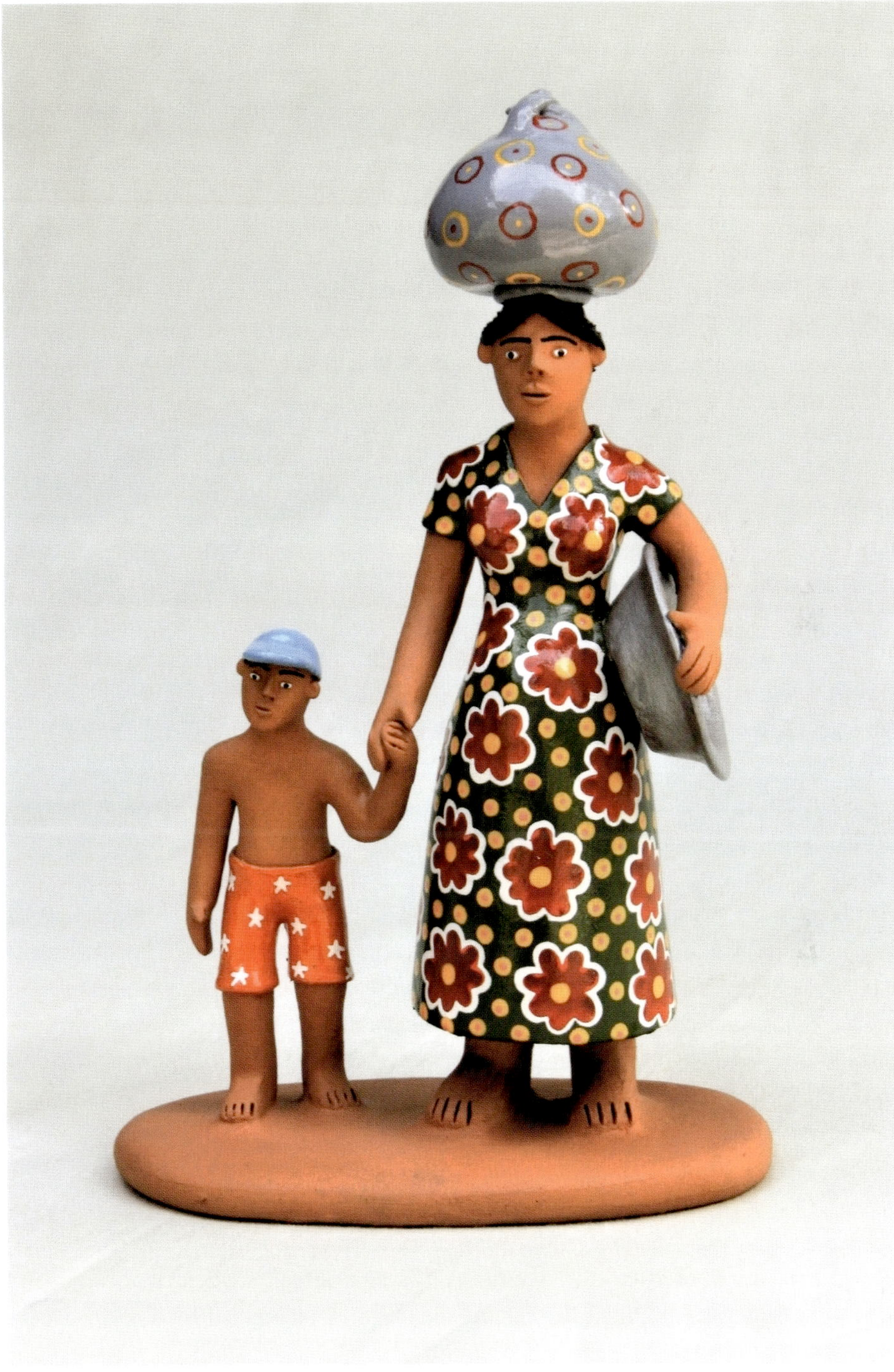

The Washerwoman, by Amanda (20 cm tall), 2019. Pregnant and leading her son, she carries another woman's laundry on her head.

"The first piece I made, it showed the barbecue that they sell on the streets, the cart of the barbecue that we call *churrasquinho de gato*" — barbecue of cats, cooked cats.

She laughs and continues, "And I made a scene of many people collecting nuts around a cashew tree.

"I also made *Laça Garrafa*" — Hoop the Bottle. "There was always this in the amusement park, right? There are many bottles, and you throw to hoop a bottle and win. There were various drinks. So, the bottle you hoop, you take it home with you, the drink.

"Last year, I participated with a piece I created, *Ave Maria Sertaneja*, which is a scene based on a song by Luiz Gonzaga. I created this scene."

Gonzaga's song, unusually slow and sad in performance, offers this scene: a Sertanejo, a man of the Sertão, down on his knees in prayer, asking the Immaculate Virgin to heal the infirm and give us the strength and courage to carry the cross we must bear.

Amanda's works assemble into a local view of the day-to-day: the constant, competent work in the home, the light delight of entertainment in the street, the supportive touch of the divine.

Her father, Amanda says, feels it is wrong to portray the saints, since he is Evangelical, but she is a Catholic, drawn to sacred imagery.

Marliete told us that the Salão de Arte Popular was established at the beginning of Fenearte, but a second salon was added recently, a Salão de Arte Religiosa, doubling the chances for selection, sales, and prizes. This year, 2019, Marliete and Carmélia are making works to submit to the Salon of Religious Art, and so is Amanda. She is creating a scene of Jesus surrounded by little children. Even if they win no prizes, works selected among the seventy exhibited will surely sell. Amanda can't spare the time to attend, but she sends her pieces with Marliete and Antônio, and sales at Fenearte bring an annual surge in her earrings, enough to keep her going.

Amanda bears her cross with strength and grace. Her husband is unemployed. Her youngest daughter needs attention. But she runs to her table whenever she can. Art is her solace, her victory over conditions.

With Amanda, we have ended our story about the third of the three families at the center of Alto do Moura's traditional art. At the end of Vitalino's family, we generalized about the art. At the end of Manuel Eudócio's family, we generalized about the life. Here at the end of Zé Caboclo's family, we will join art and life to generalize about the sequence of existence.

You were born into a place with good clay by the river and wood for firing in the hills; born into a town where pots have been made since time out of mind, where Vitalino's gift of art was refined by his friends Zé Caboclo and Manuel Eudócio; born into a house with clay all around you. At six you were playing. At eight the toys you made were being sold. At fifteen you were making statues like the ones your parents made. At twenty, as Ademilson and Antônio said, you had only one option. You didn't complain. You worked, acquiring a taste and finding it interesting to do the work you had to do. Then, as Marliete said, you learn to take care, to dedicate yourself to perpetual improvement, certain that the work in your hands is the best you can do, that the next will be better. That is the foundation: a reach for perfection, materialized in the moment.

For you to survive, this thing must be sold. In the past, back at the beginning, the pieces were sold along with agricultural produce — all of it the yield of the land — in the Feira de Caruaru. Then Vitalino, Zé Caboclo, and Manuel Eudócio traveled to the richer markets in the cities far to the south. Vitalino died before seeing New York, but travel in the next generation became international. Marliete went to Portugal and France. Severino went to Portugal. Antônio went to France. Now, you arrange a place to sell in or near your home, or, like Socorro, you open a shop up on the main street. You package pieces to ship to Rio, São Paulo, or Brasília. You travel regularly to markets in Recife, to Fenearte in Olinda. People write about you, your reputation grows, but, at last, it all depends on taking time, taking care, and creating works of art that please you and will, with luck, please someone else as well.

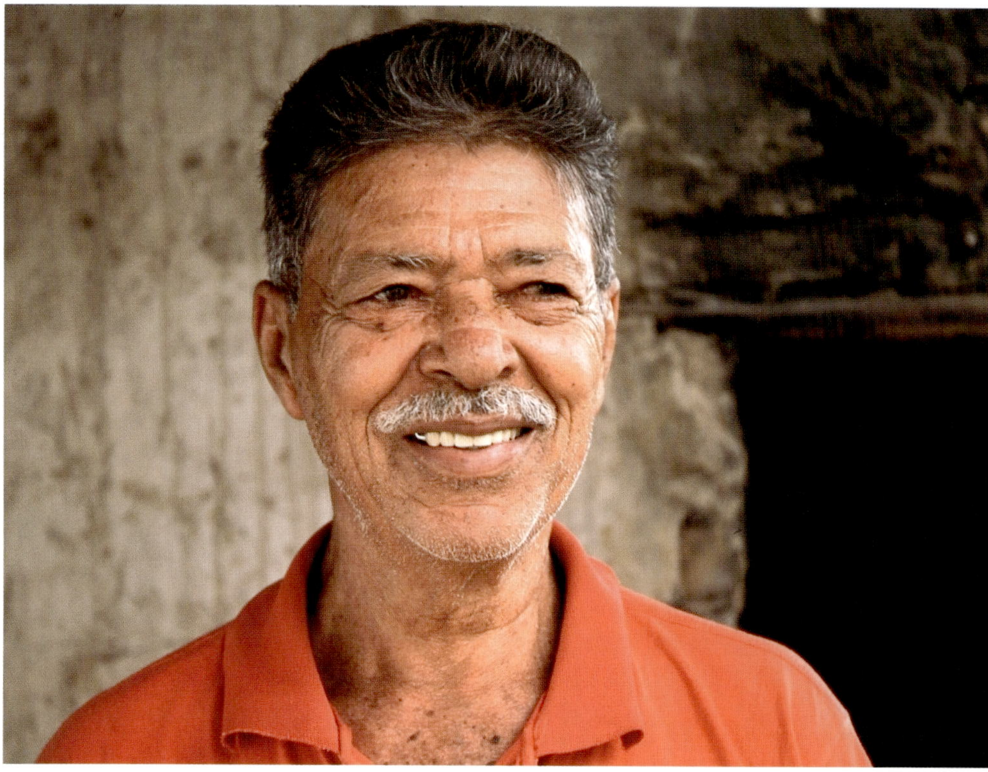

Luiz Antônio, 2014

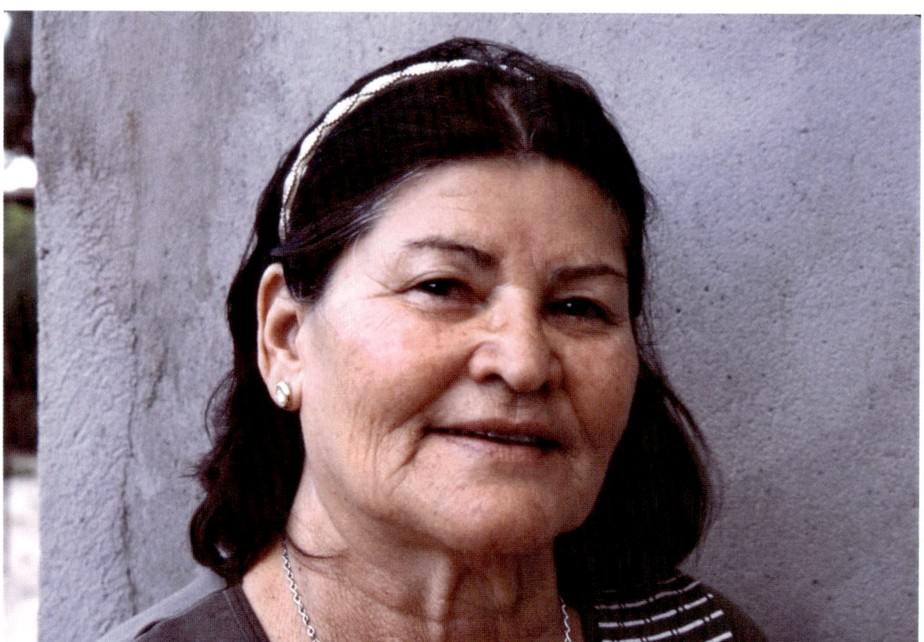

Odete, 2015

14

Luiz Antônio and Odete

In 1962, Luiz Antônio approached Mestre Vitalino at the Feira de Caruaru and asked if he could put his pieces on a box next to Vitalino's stand. Vitalino welcomed him warmly, saying, "Art is for everybody." The next week, Luiz Antônio placed his stand next to Vitalino's, and during the conversations that followed, week after week, Vitalino gave him generous advice about making and selling quotidian figures. Vitalino died the next year, Zé Caboclo died ten years later, Manuel Eudócio died in 2016, and when Severino died in 2019, Luiz Antônio was crossing the street to share his grief with Marliete when he was stopped, struck in the middle of the street by the fact that, at eighty-four, he was the last one at work who had benefited from direct contact with Mestre Vitalino.

Luiz Antônio da Silva began our first recorded interview in 2014 by introducing himself and claiming a connection to Mestre Vitalino:

"I am a son of Alto do Moura. When I was born, there was already a tradition of art in Alto do Moura. My parents would make toys of clay for children. The women would make pans and jars. So, seeing my parents doing this work, I already started to make works with them, right?

"Then later, Vitalino emerged in the community. Mestre Vitalino began to advance the art that was made for children and move it toward decorative work, right?

"Vitalino did not teach, because there was already a tradition of art in Alto do Moura. Then Vitalino comes with these new works that he made, and we could see them, right?

"Then Vitalino said, I want everyone to be able to live off art. And it opened a path.

"Then I started to work with Vitalino. Then he died. So then who remained in the art were the disciples of Vitalino. And I was one of those who sought to create, to do everything so this art would not fail.

"I have created various works that are mine, to preserve our culture through creativity.

"And I have passed the entire time making the art of Mestre Vitalino in our community. And we have the responsibility of making works in his line, in the style of Vitalino, right?

"I raised ten children; there are twenty-six grandchildren. And I work for the love of art."

Luiz Antônio has endured many interviews. In his practiced opening statement, designed to meet the needs of a journalist on the move, he made two quotable points: there was a tradition of ceramic art in Alto do Moura before Vitalino's arrival, and Luiz Antônio is one of the artists committed to carrying Vitalino's line onward. In passing, he mentioned works of his own. The recorder kept going, the talk did not stop, we remained attentive, and after a sketch of his success, Luiz Antônio returned to his own work, saying:

"My work is creative. I don't like to make what others make. If another makes a new piece, I will *not* make what he made. I only make what I make, right?

"Not every artisan seeks the love of creation. Art is a *dom*, given by God. We have to work for love. If God does not like it, we will not get there.

"I have gotten there. Today, thanks to God, I have the name of *mestre*. To be a *mestre* is to work with love and to make work that the public likes, to become known, and to be popular.

"This title of *mestre*, it is not proper for any artisan to say that he is a *mestre*. Who will say that a person is a *mestre*, it is the public — after all the time you have worked and become known as a creative person.

"To become known in the newspaper, on television, then you are called an artist. Today the technology is very advanced, everything is easier, and it is possible for us to be known as individuals.

"So, this is what it is to be a *mestre*. You make things that exist. You make sculptural works that bring you pleasure.

"Art is a divine secret."

In quick succession, Luiz Antônio declared that he is dedicated to working with others to continue Vitalino's line, and that he only creates works that bring him personal pleasure and fame. Any apparent contradiction of collective and individual goals finds resolution in the local concept of tradition, and we will stay for a while with Luiz Antônio to consider Alto do Moura's tradition. When acts or objects are qualified as traditional — *tradicional* in Portuguese — ideas of creation and continuity are entailed, and thought is clarified by contrast with the *bonecas*, which are consistently characterized as not traditional. The *boneca's* defense is that it provides a bit of cash to people in need. The *boneca's* failing, for Luiz Antônio, is that it does no more:

"Those *bonecas* have spread much, too much. Grab a truck in Bahia, come here and fill it. Grab another truck and take it to Rio.

"Then in some shopping center, in some store there, people buy it and put it in the house. If they sell, if there's profit, then the store owners ask for more.

"And if they put it in the store and it doesn't move, they remove it and forget it. It's about money, nothing else."

Bonecas are made to sell. Traditional art is also made to be sold; its creators are professionals, not hobbyists. But the *bonecas* bring only money, while traditional art brings benefits of greater value. In his opening statements, Luiz Antônio caught those benefits with specific words. His work, he says, "preserves our culture." Gathering out of a collective past, it stands as the historical manifestation of a culture — local, regional, Brazilian — that draws the artists into union and connects them to others who share, or appreciate, their culture. Through inherent cultural significance, works of traditional art encourage social association, and it was precisely the absence of cultural significance that provided the basis for Vitalino Neto's case against the *bonecas*.

Culture is one, love and pleasure are the other words that Luiz Antônio gave us at the beginning. In his view, traditional art is created out of love, a love that flows from the *dom*, and God is pleased that the gift has been accepted and honored through a lifetime of dedicated striving for perfection. The artist's blessing is the deep pleasure found in daily work.

In the midst of the "divine secret," the artist at once meets the social responsibility of continuity and experiences the personal pleasure of creation. Continuity and creativity blend in traditional action. That blending is achieved differently when the clay is shaped into distinct forms and when subjects are selected during the building of a distinct repertory. We'll take shaping first.

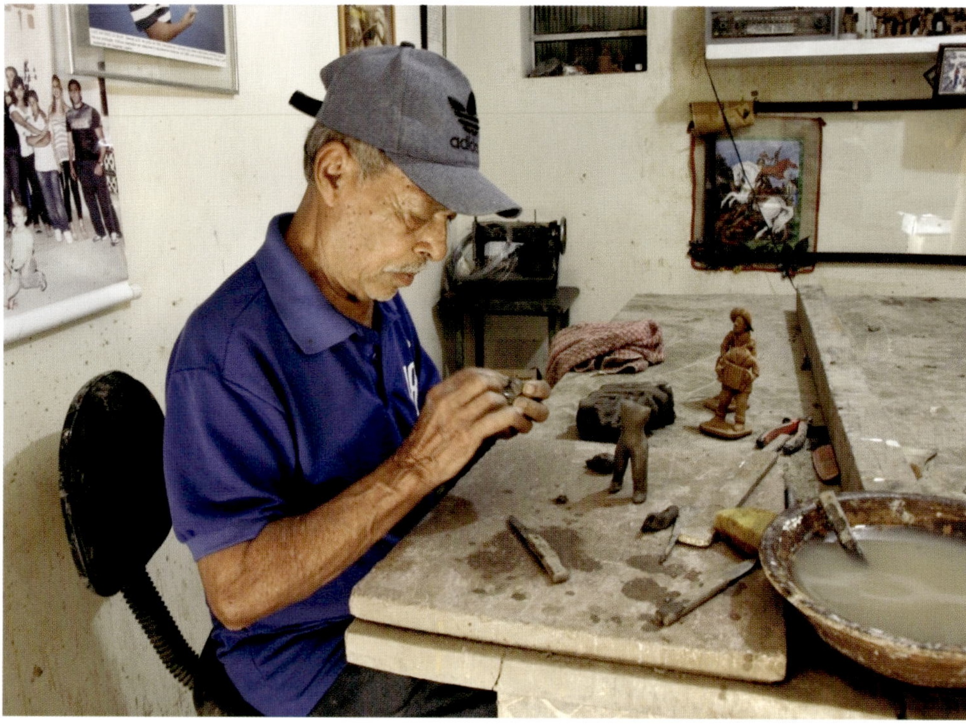

Luiz Antônio at work in his shop, 2019

Dug, milled, and trucked up the street, local clay enters the most important phase in the process when it is shaped by hand. "Everything has to be made by hand," Luiz Antônio says. "We work by hand and don't use molds. So, if you go into a store and look, you will say, I know who made this statue. I know who made this piece. You already know; you see the hand in the piece."

Luiz Antônio's point is that the open method at the center of the traditional procedure answers the artist's desire for self-expression and it eventuates in objects immediately recognizable as the creations of specific individuals. (Works of traditional art are anonymous only to the ignorant outsider.) The *boneca* again provides the contrast. Easy to make, Luiz Antônio says, thrown, molded, and assembled by a team, the *boneca* can't be attributed to a nameable maker. Though, in fact, made by hand, the *boneca* is like an industrial commodity; if there is art, it lies in design, not production. But traditional art, Luiz Antônio argues, is difficult, and therefore it is interesting, engrossing, a source of pleasure. Design and production occur in fused simultaneity. The fingers, free and unmediated, busy in the clay, shape figures that the initiated can assign at a glance to a particular creator.

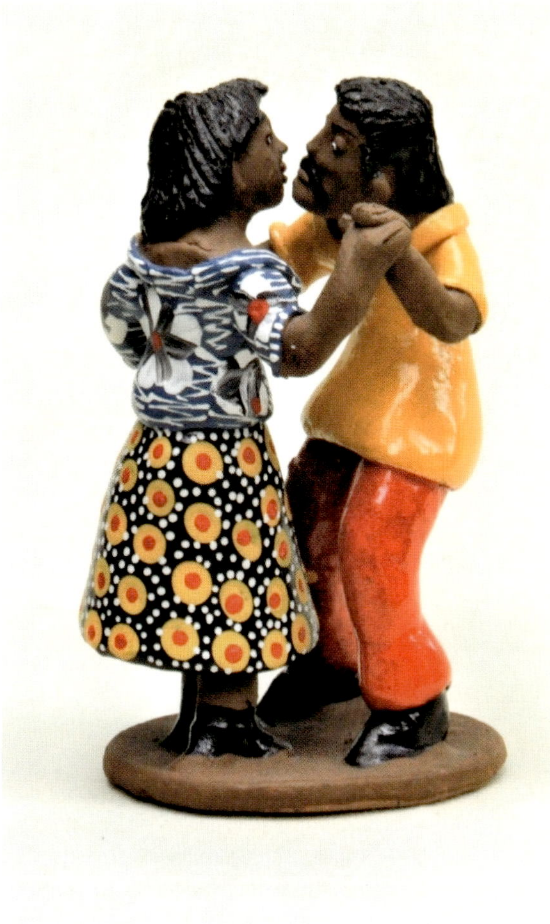

Forró dancers, by Luiz Antônio (16 cm tall), 2014

When Paulo said that all of the artists have distinctly different styles, he located the key to his own style in the shape of the figure's face. Finish, details, everything in the piece signals its author — and Luiz Antônio's surfaces are quick and energetic — but anatomical proportions offer a ready guide to style. Brazilian creators of sacred images work today within three proportional patterns. In the neoclassical style, the body, from sole to shoulder, is five heads in height. In the baroque style, the body is four heads tall. In work influenced by African precedents, the body might be two heads tall. Made visually, without measurements, Alto do Moura's figures generally take shape in the baroque range and stand erect like saints. In relation to that norm, the figures that come from Luiz Antônio's hands have slightly enlarged heads — a feature exaggerated in smaller pieces but lost in the elongated largest ones — and they are apt to adopt more hunched, wrenched, and lifelike postures. They are his.

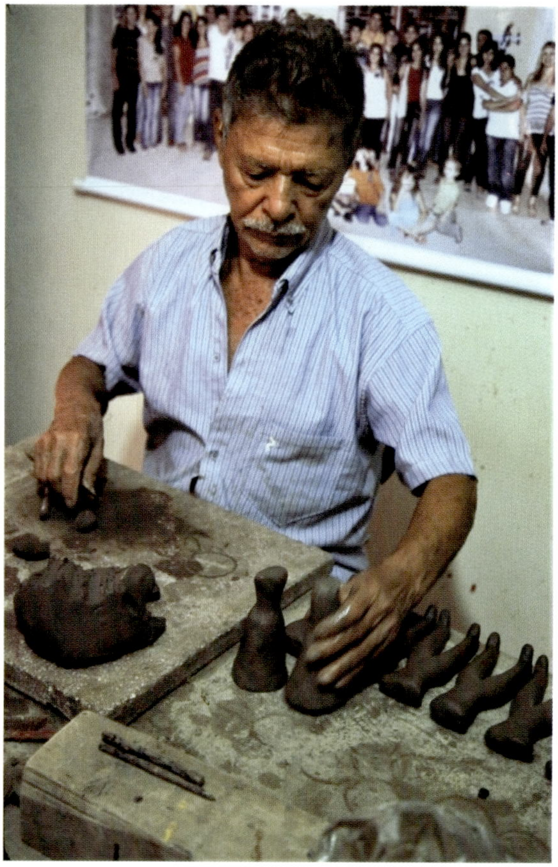

Luiz Antônio at work, 2015

Intimate shaping centers a shared process that runs back in time, past Vitalino's work and on to the little horses and bulls modeled by children sitting beside their mothers or grandmothers. Luiz Antônio would rather make than talk, and during explanations he often turns to demonstration, so having watched, we understand his practice and can say that, in general, he works in the way we described Luiz Carlos working back in the seventh chapter. He starts a figure with a tubular form, split below into legs, then adds a head, clothing, and arms. Luiz Carlos makes them one by one, one a day. So does Luiz Antônio, though more often than Luiz Carlos, he also makes several at once — oxcarts, say — shaping parts and then assembling a small group of identical forms.

The rest of the process is also generally shared. His pieces are dried and fired. Like the other artists, Luiz Antônio has a cylindrical, wood-firing, updraft kiln behind his shop, outside the back door, though his kiln is larger than usual and, closed into a dome, it is loaded through the side rather than the top. Then he leaves many of the pieces natural, like Severino's, but the majority get painted, like Manuel Eudócio's.

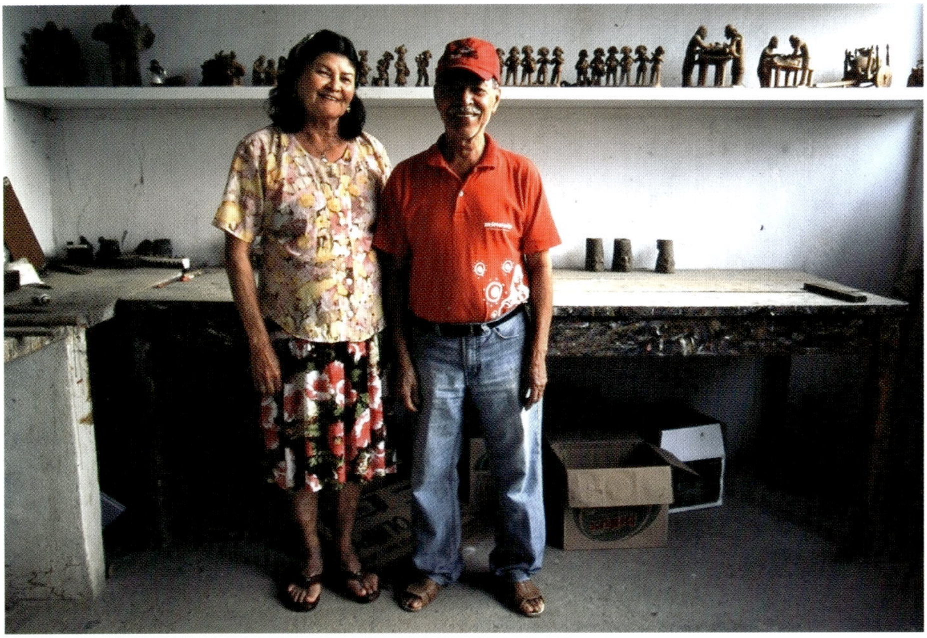

Odete and Luiz Antônio in the shop, 2014

For most of Luiz Antônio's career, the painting was done by his wife, Odete. When we interviewed Odete Maria do Nascimento Silva in 2015 she said:

"Right after I got married, I learned to paint. Because I really admired his art, right? And because of that I dedicated myself to the work, because he was already a good artisan. So I dedicated myself to this work.

"I painted and I made as well. It depended on the time. I made figures like his, not all of his, but the smaller ones I made. The agricultural laborers I really liked to make. There was still agriculture here when I came in sixty-two. So, I sought to make what I knew and what I saw others making. I watched them making things of this kind.

"It is beautiful work; it is the art of the people. It makes us want to do good in the world, and it makes us want to work in this art.

"So, I painted many years for him. But later, I had a problem with my health, so I stopped. Some six or eight years ago I stopped painting. And there is another person who paints for him now."

In its entirety, the sequence provides one clear view of traditional art. At the center of a shared, communal process through which continuity is achieved, there is an act of creation that brings pleasure to the maker and yields artifacts easily attributable to specific individuals. Continuity and creation also combine during the development of a distinct repertory.

Continuity is a matter of choice. Severino Vitalino was firmly committed to continuing his father's line, but he didn't make all the pieces that Mestre Vitalino made. He chose the ones he liked and wanted to make. Then the pieces invented by Vitalino and made by Severino formed the core of the collective repertory. When Antônio named the pieces that he and his brother Paulo make most frequently, he began with those invented by Vitalino and made by Severino, then he added the expansive contributions of Vitalino's collaborators. Zé Caboclo, his father, introduced *Maracatu*. His uncle Manuel Eudócio introduced *Bumba-Meu-Boi*. In Antônio's generation, his sister, Zé Caboclo's youngest daughter Marliete, refined *Maracatu*, and his cousins, Manuel Eudócio's sons Luiz Carlos and Ademilson, elaborated their father's *Reisado*. In the next generation, Antônio's daughter Amanda said correctly, "The tradition is always changing." Tradition is not defined by the absence of change but by the presence of continuity. Amanda acknowledged the existence of a core repertory established before her by Vitalino and Severino, by Zé Caboclo and Manuel Eudócio, when she termed her new scenes "not so traditional" — less deeply traditional, but not other than traditional.

Amanda's cousin, Carmélia's son Emerson, ensures continuity through his traditional process of making and firing, but he divides his repertory into the "traditional" (Lampião) and the "modern" (a soccer team). Luiz Antônio's great contribution to the widening repertory — parallel to the other gifts of his generation: Severino's selection, Zé Caboclo's *Maracatu*, Manuel Eudócio's *Reisado* — was to make the modern traditional. His argument begins with an old and generally accepted proposition: the subject, the content, of traditional art is the quotidian. Then he notes that Mestre Vitalino depicted the daily life around him, so following logically in Vitalino's line, later artists would depict the daily life around them, the life Emerson calls modern, and since the quotidian is always changing, traditional art, the record of the quotidian, is always changing, just as Amanda said. Continuity absorbs creative change; creative change yields continuity.

In creating a record of the quotidian, Luiz Antônio assembles the material evidence for a people's history of "our culture" that would be lost were it not for the efforts of the artists from Vitalino on. This is what he said when the recorder was going:

"When Vitalino started, he made the things he saw around him. They were new, now they seem old. Today it is different. So these different things we are making today, in time they will be *old* because the technology will have entered a new phase.

"The new things will be part of a story of what has passed. And that story is important. It is the history of Brazil, of the world. And if we didn't make it out of clay, it would not exist.

"All that exists is what is new. The past does not exist anymore. And the good things from the past, it is important to make them so they will remain, and later they will be seen as creative, as important in the lives of the people.

"I make things from yesterday, like I am making things from today that will later be seen as the things from yesterday.

"I make what I see around me. Every artisan has within him a method of encounter, a means of recording. If he does research, he can acquire much, and what he sees remains in the house of memory.

"So, if you travel, you will see things you did not yet see. And if he is a good artist, his mind grabs memories, and when he starts to work, he will say, Oh, I'm going to make what I saw.

"That is how it is, right? The mind of the human being, it records everything. It records much, as though it had been written down. And that is an incredible thing.

"And the mind suffers. When you begin to work, you trouble your brain. Things improve on the second try. Then the mind starts to go, and you make perfectly what you saw."

What he saw became art, and art — material culture —fills the voids in the written historical record that concentrates on the culture of the rich and powerful. The repertory that Luiz Antônio built reveals the interests of a back-country visual artist on a historical mission. Having twice surveyed the stock in his shop, we can arrange the pieces he makes into five main groups: classics, work, equipment, transport, and processions.

He makes the received classics of the collective core: memories of the bad old days in the Northeast (*Os Retirantes*, Lampião and Maria Bonita), musical delights (*A Banda de Pífano*, *O Trio Nordestino*, Gonzaga with the accordion, Vitalino with the *pífano*), and figures from the folkloristic performances of *Maracatu* and *Bumba-Meu-Boi*.

Where his energies fuse and focus, though, is in recording the quotidian in flux. Vitalino, he says, depicted the work and workers of his time, and Luiz Antônio's primary goal is to expand historically on Vitalino's theme. He has looked back, way beyond memory, to create a scene of slaves laboring on the plantation with a muscle-powered cane mill. From memory, he made an image, not quite historical yet, of a potter throwing on a kick wheel. Looking into these late days, he portrays bricklayers at work, and, about 1995, he altered

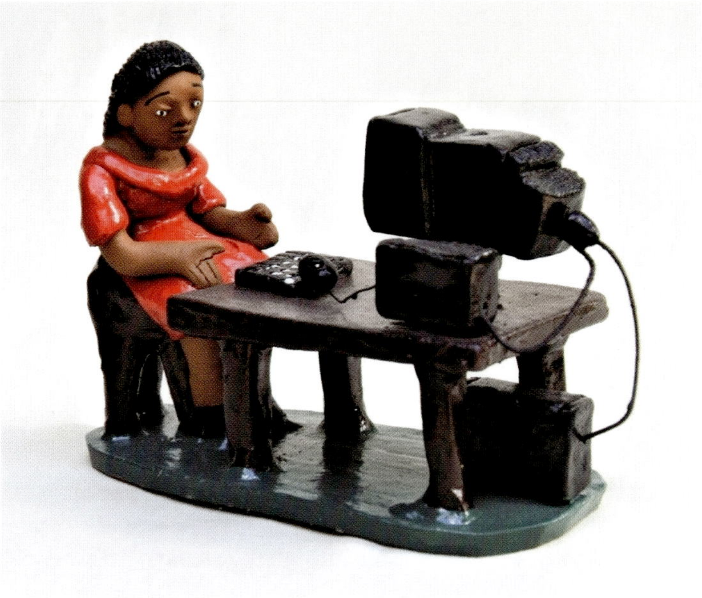

Working at the computer, by Luiz Antônio (17 cm long), 2015

the idea in the old image of a woman making lace to create a new image of a woman working at a computer, a big, blocky computer, and when computers got smaller and slicker, he held to his old image, so his depiction of the new transformed into a depiction of the old — a bit of postmodern nostalgia — just as Vitalino's renditions of the agricultural work of his era are now historical documents for the young and prods to reminiscence for the elderly. In Luiz Antônio's words, today's things become yesterday's things over time. In our words, his works, like Vitalino's and Marliete's, provide material evidence for the construction of a more democratic history.

His interest in the changing history of work led to the creation of his most famous piece. About 1980, Luiz Antônio read in the paper that the local government intended to replace wooden telephone poles with poles made of cement. He immediately celebrated the change with an image of a lineman working atop a cement pole. A sudden surprise in a predominantly rural repertory, an emblem of progress, a sign of the modern, it proved exciting, newsworthy, and it became his signal piece, made in many sizes. A large one stands in front of his shop. The piece brings Luiz Antônio private pleasure, for it is shaped like a cross and he is a devout Catholic. To the public, he feels, it aptly exemplifies his work. "So this guy," he says, "is attaching electrical wires on a cement pole, and I am making him out of clay. I make what I see people doing, working in their professions."

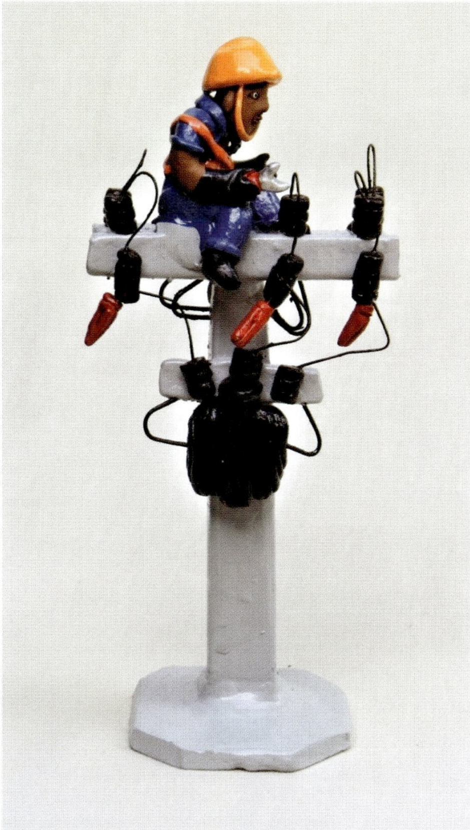

Lineman, by Luiz Antônio (22 cm tall), 2019

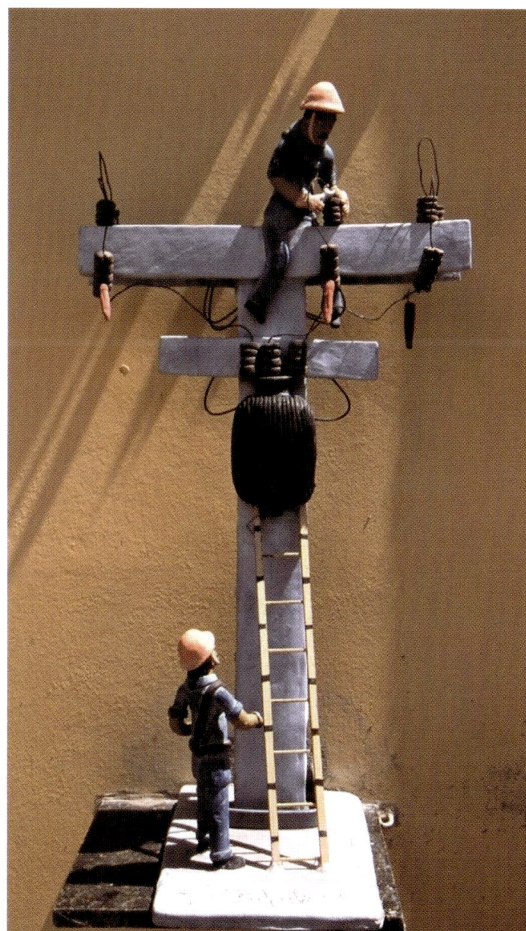

Large lineman by Luiz Antônio, outside the shop, 2015

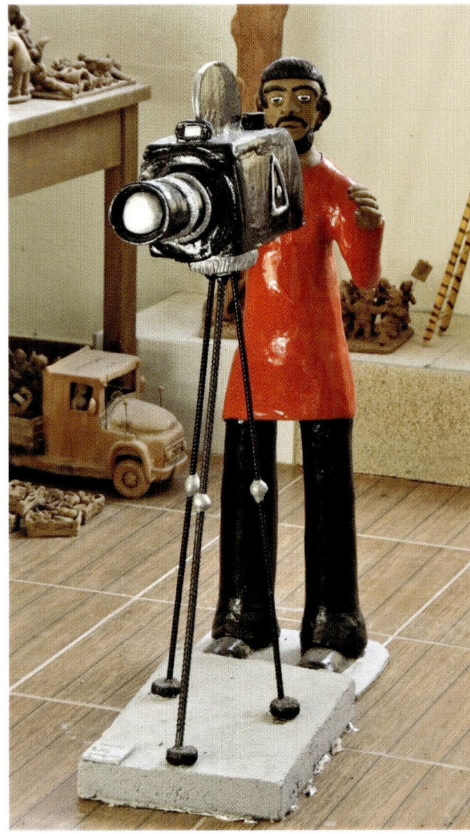

Cameraman in Luiz Antônio's shop, 2015

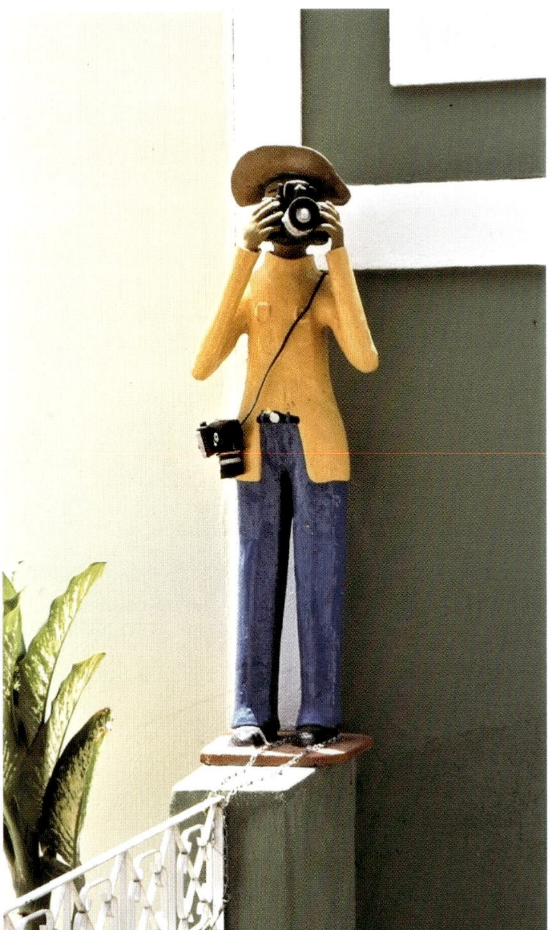

Photographer outside Luiz Antônio's shop, 2007

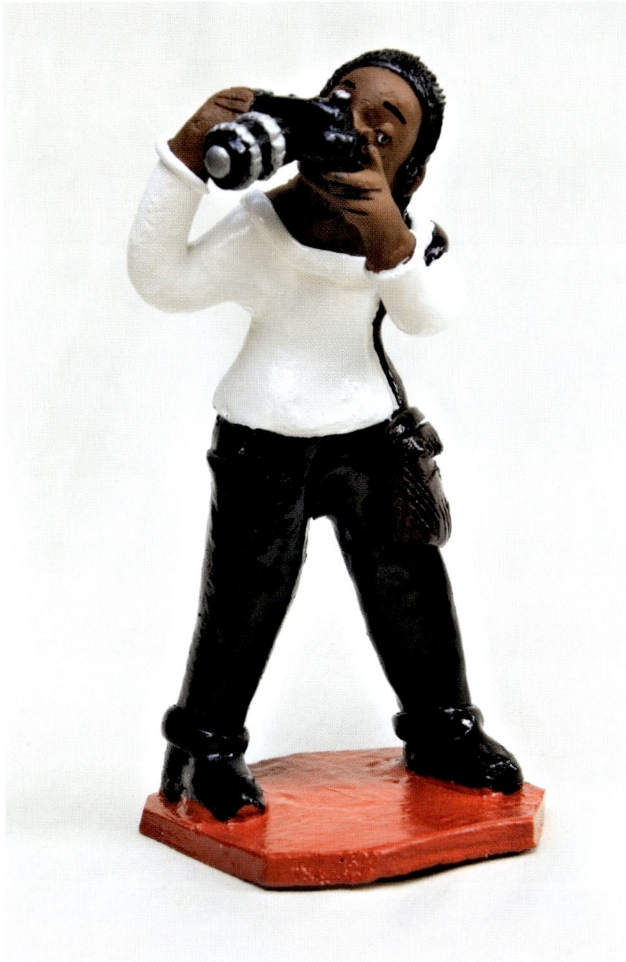

Lady photographer, by Luiz Antônio (17 cm tall), 2019

Like the cowboys made by Vitalino, the woman at her computer and the lineman on the pole are working in their professions, and Luiz Antônio represents a wide range of contemporary professions in shaped clay. He makes doctors and dentists treating their patients. He makes the musicians of the traditional Northeastern trio, and he also makes jazz bands and rock bands. Like Emerson, he portrays modern soccer players, the essential workers in the Brazilian sports and entertainment industries. Given his strong interest in vision, in capturing sights, it follows that Luiz Antônio would make a great many images of people at work with cameras — television cameramen and male and female photographers.

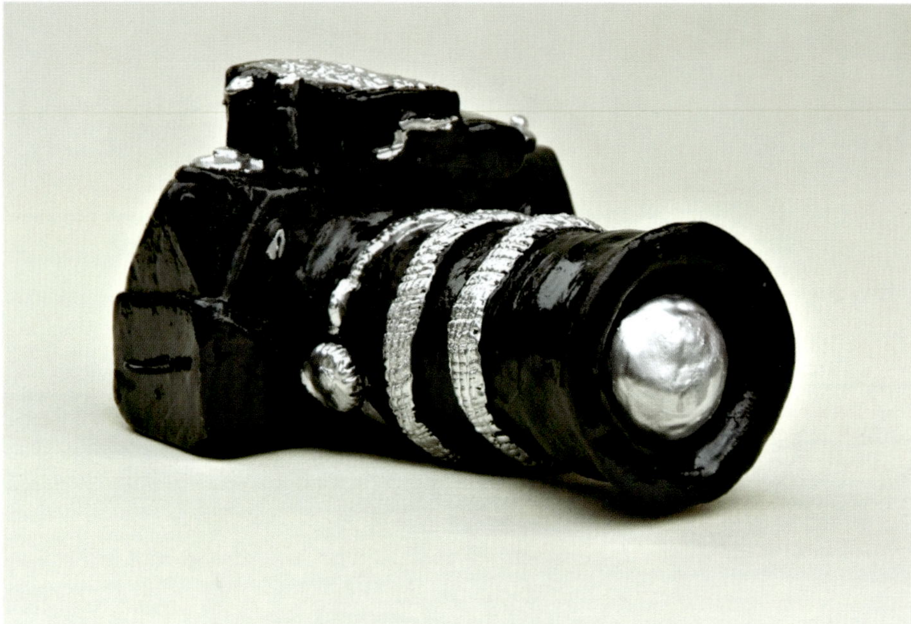

Camera in clay (18 cm long), 2021

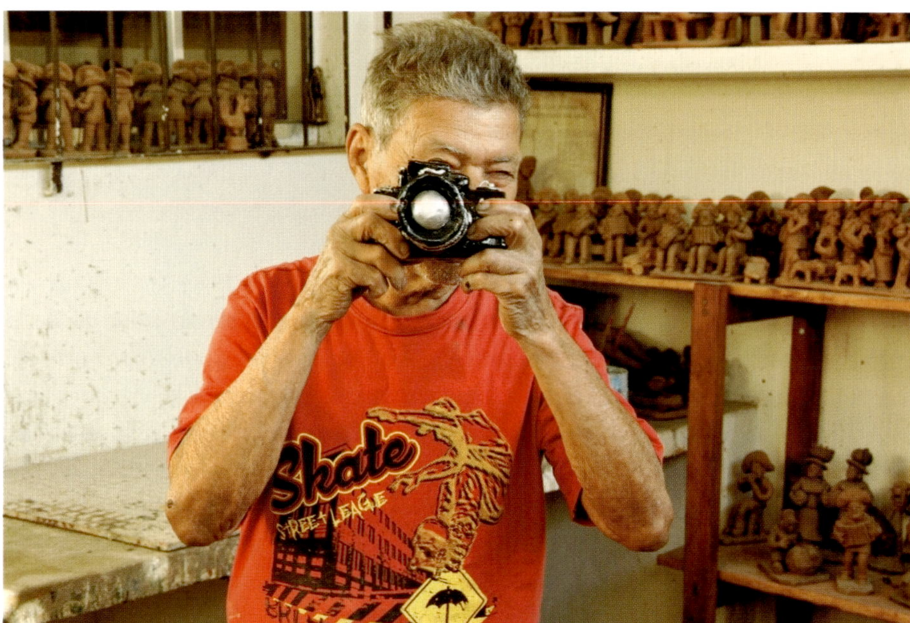

Luiz Antônio taking a picture of the photographer with his clay camera, 2021

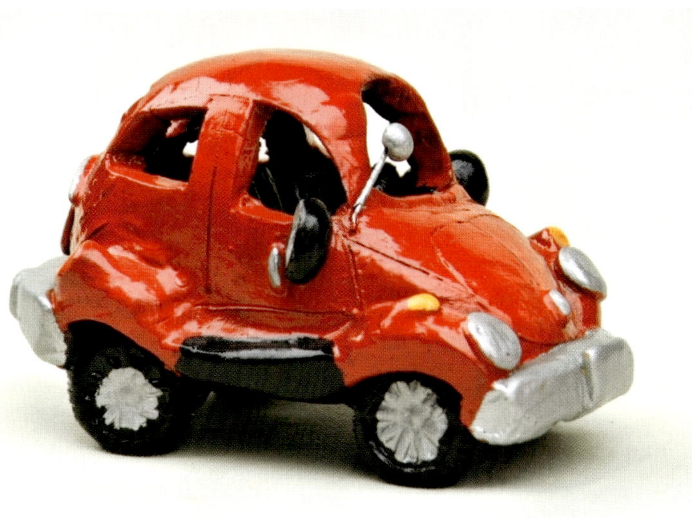

Volkswagen bug, by Luiz Antônio (15 cm long), 2019

Take a close look at those folks with cameras and you will see that what most interests Luiz Antônio are the most difficult, challenging parts of the piece, the machines. Clay is soft and supple, ideally suited to shaping the soft, rounded, flowing human form, but hard to control perfectly when rendering the sheer planes and sharp angles of industrial artifacts. Luiz Antônio, though, has conquered that problem, and he alone works in a third topical category, sculpting portraits of machines. He doesn't stop at the photographer; he replicates in clay the big, thirty-five millimeter SLR cameras that, once the top of the line, are now the dinosaurs of the digital age. His skill in representing the mechanical brought him early recognition with his piece *Máquina de Fazer Telha*, an exacting monumental model in clay of an archaic machine for making roofing tiles, now on display in the Museu do Barro in Caruaru. His sympathy with the machine and its operators appears as well in scenes of an old-fashioned flour mill and of a modern bakery, based on the one managed by his son, a pleasant place to stop for a snack, just down the street from Luiz Antônio's workshop.

Luiz Antônio's talent for depicting the machines he has seen enables him to trace the story of transportation from the obsolete oxcart into modern times with images of locomotives and airplanes, trucks and automobiles. His favorite, the Volkswagen bug, can't compete as a toy, he says, with industrial versions in metal that have doors that open and can survive through hours of rough, boyish play, but his little, round, red cars sell well to adults as amusingly cute works of art.

By following the quotidian line, Luiz Antônio found an entry for religion through the processions that are a common sight in the daily life of modern Brazil. In one image, he shows men and women, led by a monk, followed by a band, carrying a statue of Padre Cícero. In fact, he tells us, statues of the saintly priest from Ceará are not carried on procession, but the idea of the procession allowed him to include Padre Cícero, a hero he admires, in his repertory. In another, similar image, the people are carrying a statue of Christ bearing the cross. He makes them both in several sizes.

Luiz Antônio also acknowledges the presence of Candomblé, the Brazilian religion of African decent, in a less usual image of black women in white carrying a statue of Yemanjá, the *orixá* of the salt sea. Every year, on the second of February, Baianas, black ladies in full, immaculate white attire, carry a variety of images of Yemanjá through the crowds to the Atlantic coast in Salvador, making requests and praising the goddess who protected their ancestors during the dreadful voyage that dropped them into slavery on the Brazilian shore.

Within the tradition of the quotidian, set in motion by Mestre Vitalino, Luiz Antônio has gracefully gathered the modern imagery that is the source of his success, moving from farmers to photographers, from oxcarts to automobiles, and he has found a way to incorporate the sacred in renditions of processions, but, like Vitalino before him, he does not make statues of saints. His reasoning is different; he feels that the traditional practice of the *santeiro* demands command of esoteric knowledge he doesn't have — information from holy texts and, in particular, deep understanding of iconography.

Artists around him who have not been trained as *santeiros*, but do make the occasional saint, tend to restrict themselves to a pair of popular Franciscans: Saint Francis, the Father of Ecology, and Saint Anthony, who, born in Lisbon, is of particular importance for Brazilians with Portuguese ancestors. Their attributes of identification, essential to proper devotion, are not complicated. Saint Francis has a beard, birds, and a brown robe. Saint Anthony is tonsured, clean-shaven, and he holds a book with a baby on it. Manuel Eudócio, a professional of the quotidian but an amateur of the sacred, would be faulted by a *santeiro* for putting the book and baby on Anthony's wrong side, his right rather than properly on his left. Generally artists who are not *santeiros* avoid making images of Our Lady, which center the repertories of the *santeiros*, because they don't have a firm grip on the specific details of form and color that distinguish the numerous different images of Our Lady, one from the other.

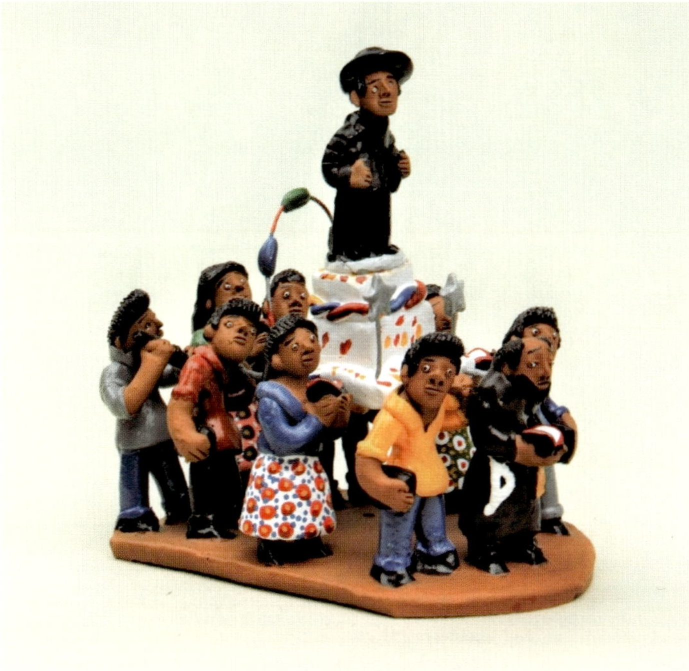

Procession for Padre Cícero, by Luiz Antônio (17 cm long), 2015

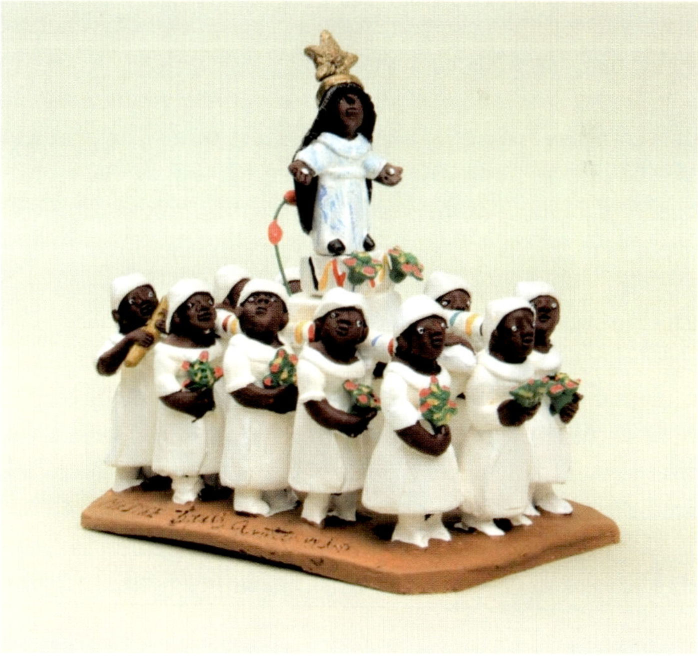

Procession for Yemanjá, by Luiz Antônio (20 cm long), 2021

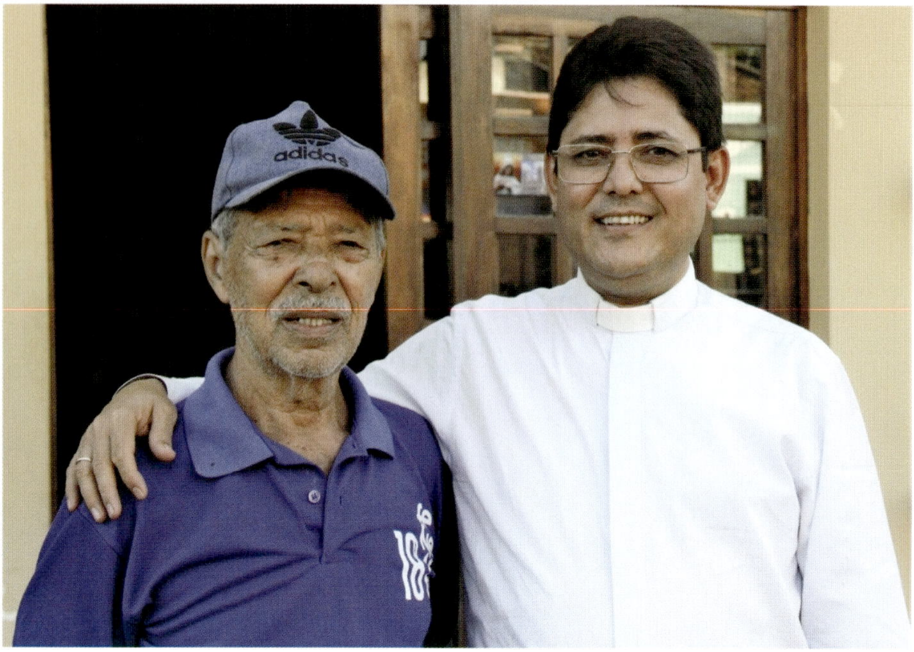

Luiz Antônio with his son Father Luiz Antônio Filho, 2019

So, being a good Catholic, Luiz Antônio follows Mestre Vitalino, a good Catholic, and he does not make images of saints. When we ask him directly about the sacred, he answers:

"Look, we make *Presépios*, we make processions with Christ. When Christmas comes we make Nativity scenes, big ones. The problem is this.

"When Vitalino came to Alto do Moura, he did not come with the aspiration of being a *santeiro*. He came with an aspiration to make rural scenes, like a man milking a cow. He did not come inspired by saints to be a *santeiro*.

"If he were a *santeiro*, then everyone in Alto do Moura would be *santeiros*. But he wasn't, so we are not.

"This is the reason why there are no saints. And the community makes the things of the Northeast, of the culture of the Northeast.

"But there are artisans who make saints really well, right? There is one here who was actually a *santeiro*. If he were to live here, the churches would not have plaster saints, but saints made beautifully by hand.

"He is now a priest in Bezerros, my son Padre Luiz Antônio Filho" — Father Luiz Antônio Junior — "and if he lived here, if he lived off the clay, he would be the *santeiro* of Alto do Moura.

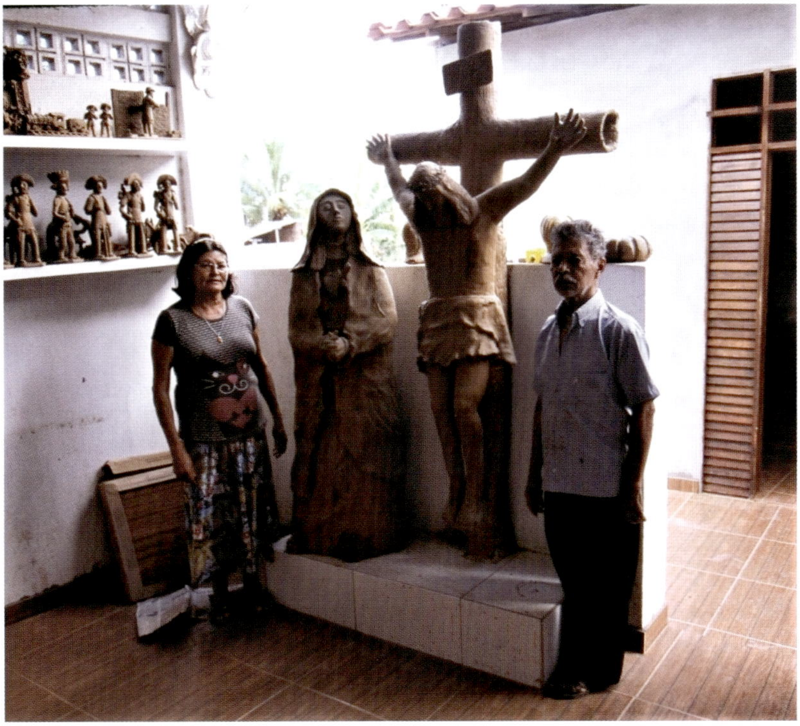

Odete and Luiz Antônio with the Crucifix in their shop, 2015

"Because he is inspired by saints. He makes spectacular saints. He makes Our Lady. He has everything recorded in his mind. All the questions of religion, he has the answers. He responds and responds correctly.

"He lives a life that gives him the answers. He has worked in art and he is someone who knows the Bible, who reads the Bible and reads the word of God, and already has everything memorized."

His son has the skills — and the knowledge — a *santeiro* needs. When we were first there a large Crucifix in clay, made by Padre Luiz Antônio, stood in the back of Luiz Antônio's workshop. It has since been installed in a lovely garden behind the shop.

In telling us about her ten children, Odete said, "By the grace of God, one of my sons, Luiz Antônio, received a *dom* to be a priest, a father of humanity. He lives in Bezerros, the Church of São José, the *Matriz*" — the Mother, the parish church — "in Bezerros.

"I am very pleased with him, right? A young man who found the correct path, which is the path of Jesus Christ."

A few minutes later Odete summarized, "I have seven boys and three girls. The girls don't work in the clay. One lives in São Paulo. Another is a teacher here in Alto do Moura. My boys, some work in the clay and they live here.

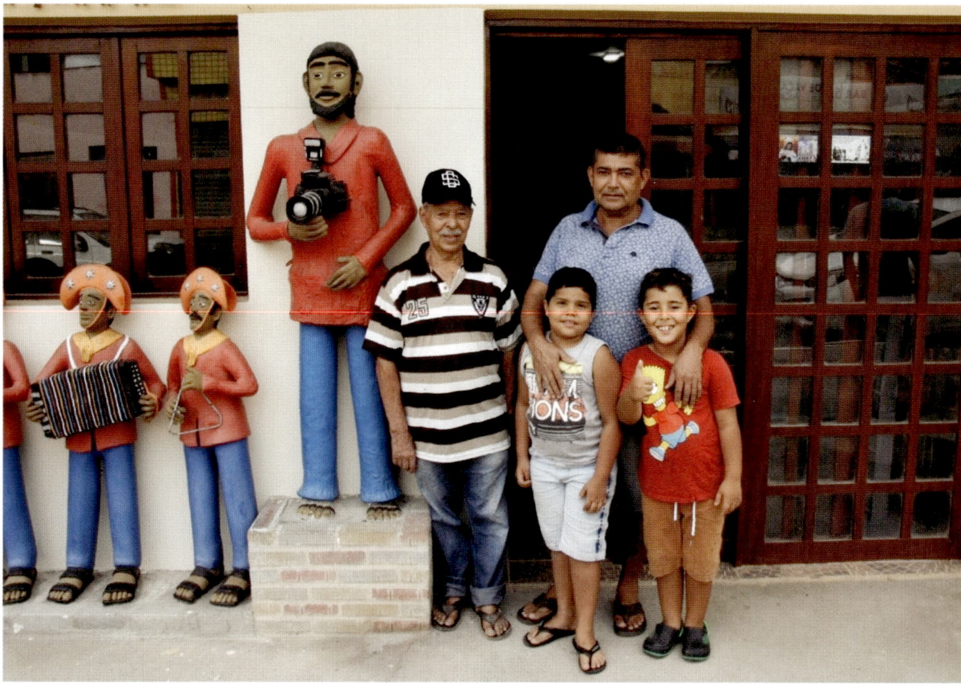

Luiz Antônio with his son Leonildo and two of his great-grandsons in front of his shop, 2021

"I am a mother to my grandchildren. There are many grandchildren, right? It is a comfort to me that most of my children live very near."

Odete's comfort is the direct consequence of the innovations made by the four masters of the second generation, the men who knew Vitalino and laid the foundation for the town's central repertory with Severino's selection, Zé Caboclo's *Maracatu*, Manuel Eudócio's *Reisado*, and Luiz Antônio's quotidian modern. Their artistic success was enough of a financial success for land to be bought, for the third generation to be established in place, so that individuals live near their relatives, and the families interact into a community. Across the street, Zé Caboclo's children live and work. Down the street, Manuel Eudócio's children live and work. Farther down the street, Severino's children live and work.

Here in Luiz Antônio's place, you enter a wide showroom with shelves of stock on both sides. He works at a big table in a room to the back. To the left, a passage through storage leads you out the back door to a museum. He talked about it when we first met and now, in 2019, it exists. The museum has not yet opened, its exhibits are not quite finished, so he asks us to take no photos, which is fine with us, and we wander with him slowly through it, taking notes.

Unusually Luiz Antônio has kept a representative collection of his work, from the beginning to the present, so his museum recaps his career and repertory. There are full sets of *Maracatu* and the *Reisado*; images of agricultural, medical, and industrial workers, including his famous lineman; displays of machines and vehicles, including a handsome old locomotive; and there are processions aplenty. There are also rare records in clay of historical events. One depicts the Formula One race car in which the famous Brazilian driver, Ayrton Senna, was killed in 1994. Another shows Lula, Brazil's president, addressing a crowd. Luiz Antônio also has a photograph of himself with Dilma, Lula's successor, standing in front of the Casa Museu Mestre Vitalino in Alto do Moura. Lula and Dilma are reminders of a happier time in Brazilian history when the Workers' Party was in command, not that long ago.

Outside, up the street from Luiz Antônio's big building, one of his sons has a store. Down the street, another of his sons has his bakery, and the Catholic chapel of Saint Joseph stands on land donated by Luiz Antônio. And there, down the street, you will find the workshop of his son Leonildo, who is, along with the the children of Severino, Zé Caboclo, and Manuel Eudócio, a creative force within the third generation.

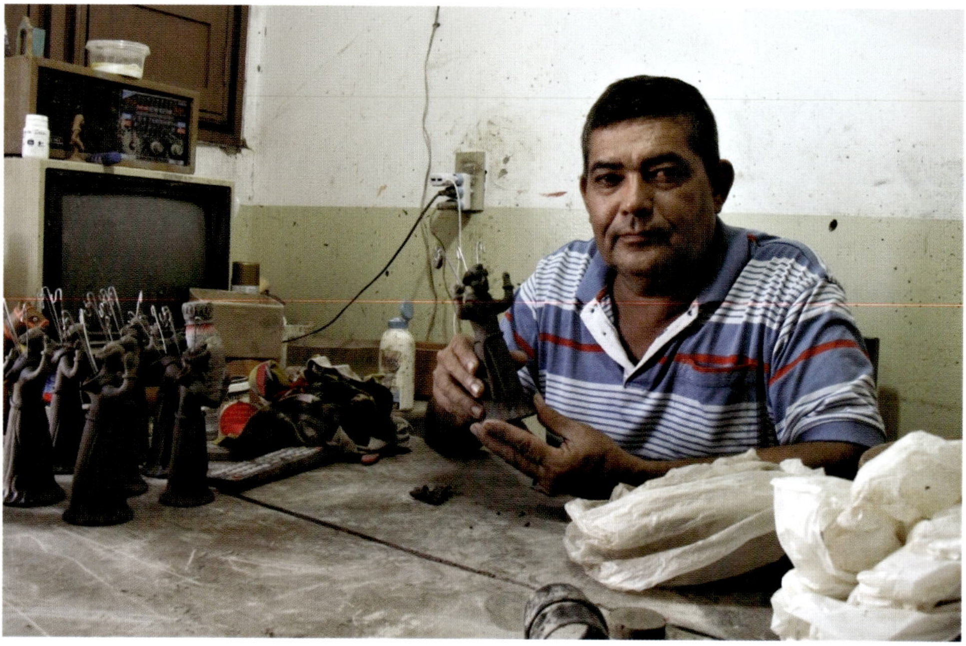

Leonildo making small statues of Saint Francis, 2019

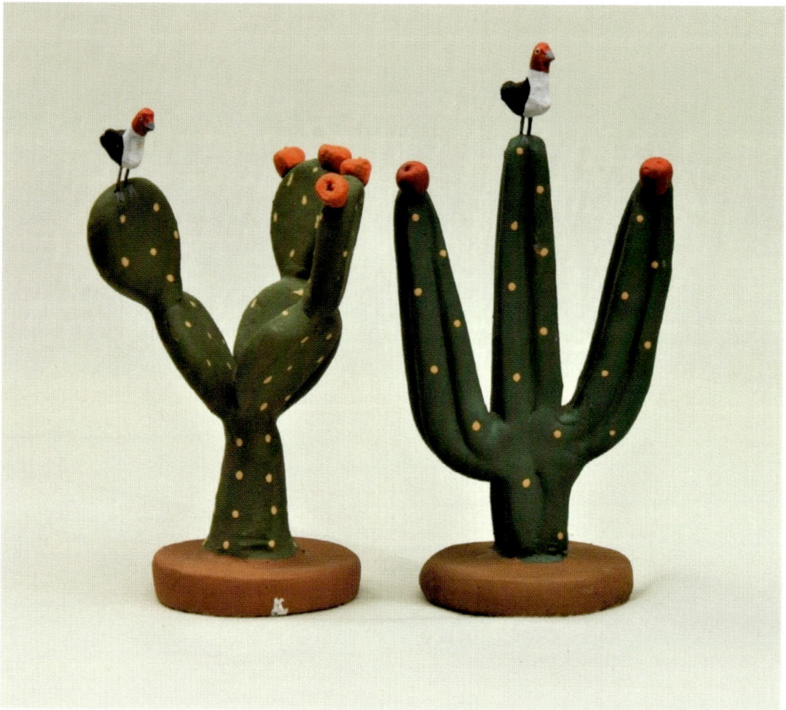

Statues of cactus, by Leonildo (16, 17 cm tall), 2021

15

Leonildo

Severino Vitalino told us about his father, Marliete told us about her father, Ademilson told us about his father, and Leonildo do Nascimento Silva tells us about Luiz Antônio:

"My father had a great importance in Alto do Moura, in the city of Caruaru, in Brazil, and in the world. A great importance.

"His importance is great, the legacy he left with us of teaching us his own art, of raising ten children in a period of difficulties. And with the work of his own hands.

"The artisan who is able to live off his own work — in this case my father — he *must* create. Create to be able to survive. Ideas came to him of creating new characters that were not in the one hundred and eighteen pieces of Mestre Vitalino.

"He created the Volkswagen bug. He created the photographer. He created machines. He made trucks, tractors, trains, the Volkswagen bug. All of the pieces I am talking about were creations of his. Nobody made them before.

"So, he comes to new ideas, and he also has difficulties selling his work. That is where the creativity of the artisan lives. To make new themes that can be sold to make a living. The lineman, the electrician, right? That is very creative.

"My father, he was creative, well known, an artisan who was invited to go to Japan to represent the city, the state, and Brazil."

The trip to Japan, in July of 1986, was a highpoint in his father's life, and Luiz Antônio had earlier told us the story:

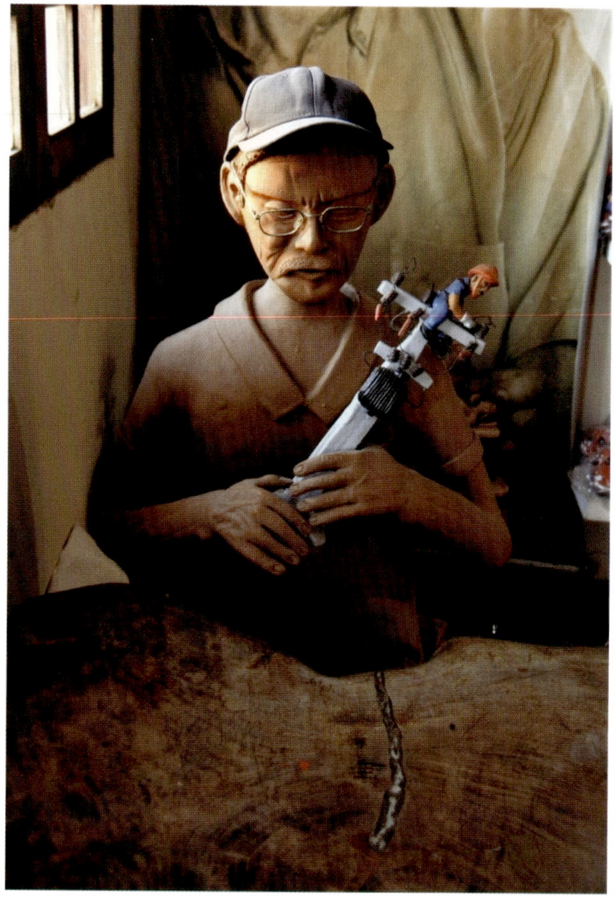

Life-size clay statue of Luiz Antônio, made by Leonildo and displayed in his father's shop, 2021

"The government of Japan asked for an artisan who knew how to make the statues of Vitalino. They came to my store:

"Are you Luiz Antônio?

"I am.

"Do you know that you are going to Japan?

"In that moment, I thought it was a joke, right? It was not. The Japanese asked for one thousand statues to take and sell there, right?

"I spent forty-six days there, and I made about three thousand pieces. I brought one hundred kilos of clay from Alto do Moura. The Japanese clay is weaker, so I mixed it with mine. Our clay is very good clay.

"So, I stayed there forty-six days. I made all of my creative works, and I made whatever the Japanese asked me to make."

Luiz Antônio told us that the Japanese loved his machines in clay, the German Volkswagen bugs in particular, and the trip lifted his reputation and led him to success, artistically and financially.

The lesson for Leonildo was that financial success follows creative action. He learned from his father in the way that children learn from their parents in Alto do Moura, and born in 1964, the second of the children, Leonildo recalls:

"Our father, he would ask us to pay attention to how he was making. And from there he would give us encouragement: No, no, don't do it like that. Do it like this, and it will be better — in terms of making, of firing, of painting.

"It was something passed down from generation to generation, and the parents give encouragement.

"So, in childhood, at ten years of age, I was already working. And the biggest encouragement was knowing that the products I made were selling, right? With the difficulties of that period, forty years ago.

"The products that I and my siblings made, there was a buyer for them. So, that encouraged us, so we could buy a bicycle or a book to study. It allowed us children to sustain ourselves.

"And then there was a point, when I was eighteen years old, that I had already decided on the profession that I wanted for life. And I even stopped my studies to give continuity to my *work* as a artisan, so I could create and raise a family.

"So, by eighteen years of age I was already thinking of marriage. I spoke with my girlfriend about marriage, and we got married. I had already built my house. And from there I provided for my family, and today I live off this *artesanato*."

From his father, Leonildo learned the process of artistic production, and he understood that he would have to find a route of his own to success:

"The pieces my father makes, we know how to make them too. We know how to give continuity to the works of my father. But between father and son, we have respect, let's say.

"Nobody is going to make the work of another artisan, right? Every artisan needs to create his own work.

"This doesn't mean that we don't know how to make what our parents taught us. One day when he departs for Eternity, I can give continuity to his work, so there's a sequence in his work.

"But I create new things no one has made. I make bigger things. It is a means to survive. One has to create to survive."

One difference between son and father is that Leonildo works often at a large scale, producing life-size images. A more significant difference is that Luiz Antônio, following Vitalino, marginalized the sacred themes that Leonildo brings to the center. He explains:

Christ

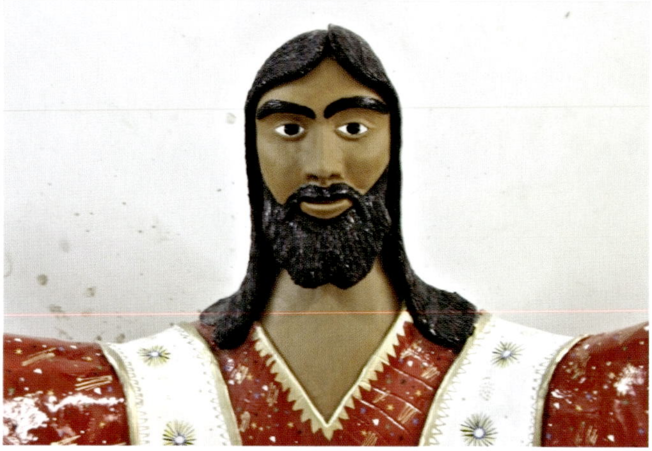

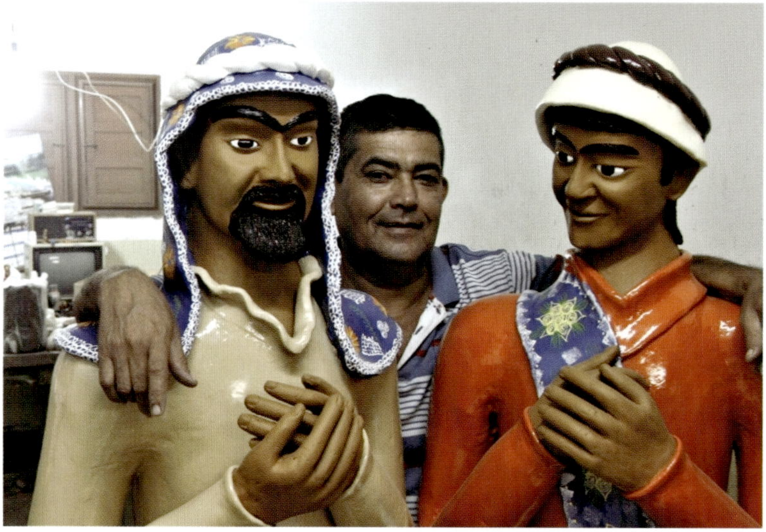

Leonildo among the Apostles

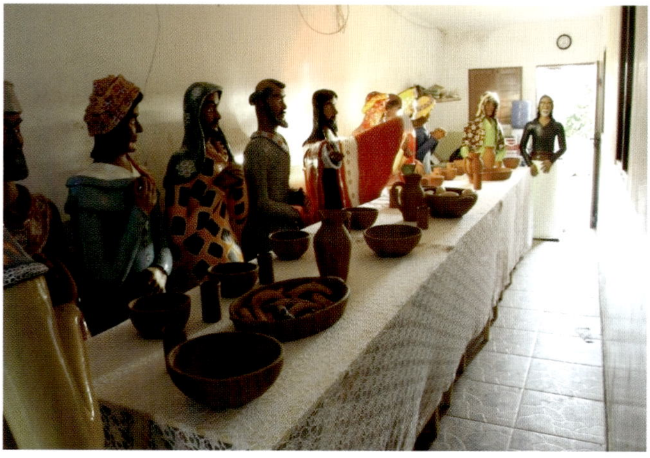

Leonildo's Last Supper, 2019

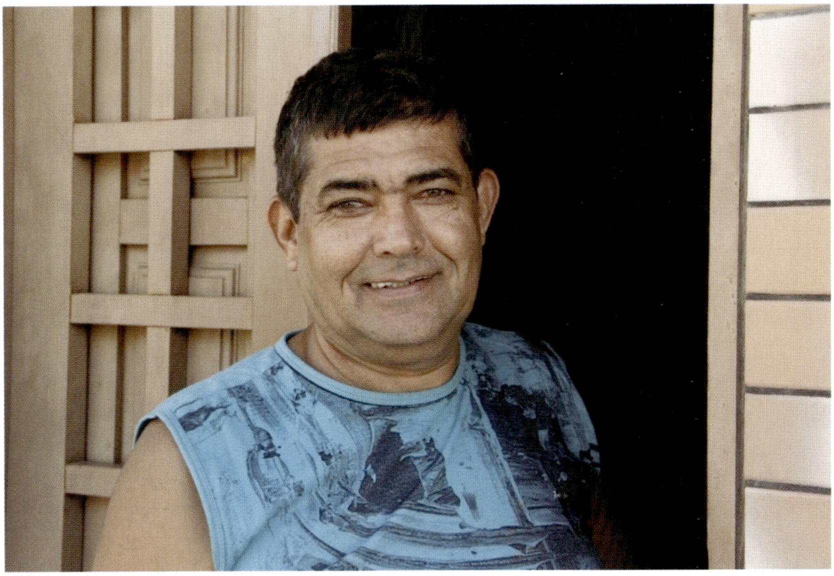

Leonildo, 2019

"Here in Alto do Moura, we have a tendency to continue the work of Mestre Vitalino, respecting the work that he created. Vitalino was not one to make religious pieces. More the quotidian, the day-to-day, like the *pífano* band, Lampião, agricultural laborers.

"But in the state of Pernambuco, you will find places that only work in religious themes. Like Ibimirim, where there is a style of work that is very much about sacred art, in wood. And Tracunhaém, which has a style of sacred art in clay.

"Here it is much more in the style of Mestre Vitalino, even though in the period of Vitalino there were other artisans who worked with religious themes: Zé Caboclo, Zé Rodrigues. These were two in the period of Vitalino who made religious themes.

"The people of that period were more religious than the youth of today, right? But Saint Francis, he sells in every period. Saint Francis, right? I make many images of Saint Francis. Images of the Last Supper, many works with religious themes, and there are collectors who seek these pieces."

Like his father before him, Leonildo depicts religious processions in clay. He has also made a scene of Mass in a church. Once we watched him making a great crowd of small images of Saint Francis, and he took a break to show us his life-sized rendition of the Last Supper — *Santa Cena* in Portuguese — that was set up in a narrow corridor beside his store.

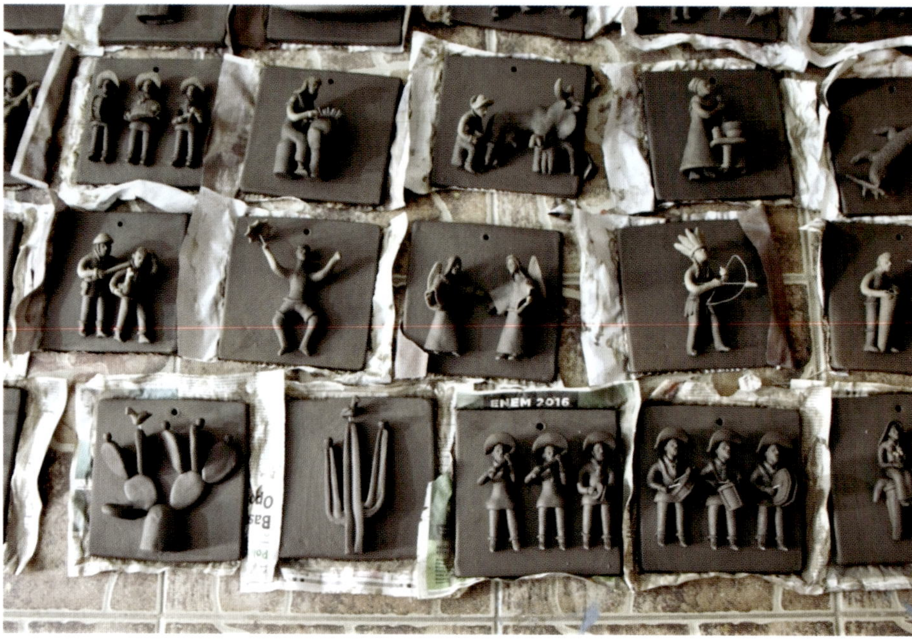

Leonildo's suite of tiles in progress, 2019

A week later we found Leonildo working on a new creation, a suite of one hundred tiles that will be left natural, unpainted, and sold as a unit to a collector. Each tile carries a scene in relief, plucked from the collective repertory, so, mounted together on a wall, they will present a symphonic recapitulation of Alto do Moura's artistic history. The tiles portray Vitalino's first pieces (the bull and the hunter of wildcats); they portray Lampião and Maria Bonita, Saint Francis, Padre Cícero, figures from Nativities, from *Maracatu* and the *Reisado*, many musicians, cowboys, an Indian, a priest, a dentist, a barber, a policeman, a farmer, a fisherman, women feeding chickens, making lace, working at a computer (an homage to his father), and there are tiles with cactus, a reference to his own work. Statues of cactus in clay, painted green and emblematic of the landscape of the Agreste and Sertão, are an innovation of Leonildo's and they sell particularly well.

That project kept him busy until the time came, in the middle of June in 2019, to pack his monumental Last Supper into his truck and drive to Brasília, over two days away by road, where Leonildo installed the set in the home of the lawyer who bought it.

Leonildo's big truck, parked behind his shop, in a lane beyond his kiln, is one component in the system of enterprise that he, an accomplished businessman, has assembled. Next to the narrow shop where he works, Leonildo has a bright, orderly store where he sells the pieces he makes as well as things made by other artisans in Alto do Moura who don't have outlets for sales of their own. The big truck allows him to distribute merchandise widely through Brazil. He says:

"I make within the day-to-day, the quotidian. And I also create within the imagination, that which comes to your imagination, your *thinking*.

"And that is what allows us to be able to live from the *artesanato*.

"The more that new things come — new ideas — and they are accepted by the public, the more profitable your work becomes.

"I make Saint Francis, processions, *Maracatu*, cactus. And from there I go to events to sell, events in other states.

"Since I live from *artesanato*, I can't just stay in my house, waiting for the customers to come to me. I have to go to them.

"I have three events in Brazil that I always go to. One is Fenearte. Another is the craft market of Minas Gerais in Belo Horizonte. The other is a market in Espírito Santo down south.

"This is a way for you to know new artisans, since artists come together from many states, from many countries. And these events are very good because you feel rejuvenated, you feel more motivated toward the work.

"Each region has its own style of work, right? Let's say, in Espírito Santo it is clay pots. In Caruaru it is figurative art. The customers from other states, they like our history of the day-to-day.

"They see the work, and they want to know the story of Lampião. Who was Maria Bonita? Who was Padre Cícero? So, we make the *history* of the Northeast. To tell it to others. To tell about the *Retirantes*.

"Today it doesn't exist. But it was an important occurrence, the emigrants escaping the drought of the Northeast. So, we make the family of the *Retirantes*, the old lady, these families leaving the Northeast for the South.

"It is the history of the Northeast. It is Lampião; he was a seeker for justice in the past. Today he does not exist anymore, but there was this history of the *cangaço*" — the bandit band — "of Lampião.

"So, when people see Lampião in the market, it is memorable, and everybody wants to buy one of these pieces.

"We make these pieces, and we tell the world our history, the history of the Northeast."

It is a history of hardship, of droughts and battles with the landlords; a history of work, of herding cattle and stringing wires from pole to pole, of feeding chickens and grinding corn; a history of entertainment, of costumed parades and musical performance; a history of faith, of processions through the streets; a history of artistic creativity in the dry and poor interior of Brazil.

Complications lie ahead, but with Leonildo we have come to the end of the four family lines most influential in Alto do Moura's ceramic production. Their work is art because it is made by hand with committed care. It is traditional because continuity and creativity combine in its making; old ideas are honored, new ideas are welcomed. In subject it is historical, avoiding the momentous events of written history in favor of a compensatory people's history of struggle, daily labor, and common pleasures.

Alto do Moura's artistic repertory accumulates through personal choices into a collective portrayal of the working-class worldview of the Brazilian Northeast.

16

Terezinha

At the bottom of Rua Mestre Vitalino, the sloping street of the artists, the last shop on the east is the atelier of Terezinha Gonzaga. Much as Mestre Vitalino pulled the figurative idea from the little bulls and lifted it into art, Terezinha has raised the old tradition of utilitarian pottery into excellence and commercial success, adding a dimension to Alto do Moura's work in the clay. Terezinha tells her story:

"I was born here in Alto do Moura. My father is Manuel Alexandre da Silva. My mother, Maria Gonçalves, was a market woman. She sold pots and little clay horses in the Feira de Caruaru. My father was an agricultural laborer and he made clay plates.

"As a very young person, I would accompany my father to the market. I would accompany my father to the market when I was about seven years old. We would go on a donkey cart, full of pots and pans. That was at one-thirty or two o'clock in the morning. And I would always accompany him.

"When he married my mother, he was already a bit elderly, right? He was already sixty years old. When I was born, he was already sixty years old, understand?

"Then he stopped going to the market, and I continued going with my mother.

"My mother would paint the little horses that we would make, that I would make, my sister would make, my brother would make. And Mother would paint them and take them to the market.

"And I also started to make my own things. I wanted my separate corner in the market to be able to earn my own money. And I would take the clay toys,

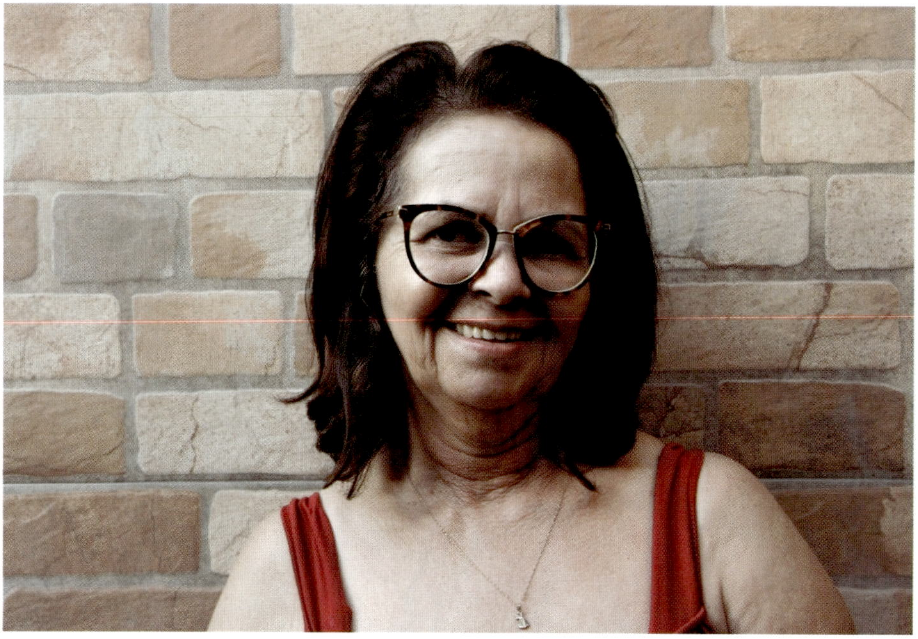

Terezinha, 2019

the little horses and little pots to sell. So, I would earn that money from the little horses, and I would buy something to bring to my father.

"Because I was very attached to my father. My father was my hero.

"In that period, my father would smoke, so I would buy tissue paper for him to roll cigarettes. It was better than corn husks. And my money would be enough to buy a twist of tobacco and rolling paper to bring to my father.

"So, I grew up in the market, working with my mother. Then when I was fifteen years old I met my husband. He is not from here; he was, in that period, living in São Paulo. And his mother, Dona Regilda, had married a man from Alto do Moura, and she was living here.

"So, in seventy-eight, he arrived, and the next year we met, and from there I got married.

"At sixteen years of age, I had my first son, and I have five sons.

"When we got married, I taught him how to work in the clay. I taught my husband how to work, for he did not know. And he became a very good *oleiro*" — throwing on the wheel — "making pots, vases. He used to make beautiful pieces, lovely, for decoration. He always worked very well. He had a *dom* for art in his hands, my husband did.

"Then he got sick.

"When he was thirty-five years old, my husband got sick. He got a degenerative disease. It is a disease unknown to medical science.

"So, my husband, thank God, he is alive. But he does not walk. He does not talk. He eats through a tube."

Terezinha took us to see him. In her spotless home next to her shop, José Gonzaga Simões lay in bed, breathing and no more. She calls him her angel. She feeds him, keeps him clean, and takes him for regular visits to the hospital where the doctors can tell her nothing.

His illness left her, a young mother, with five boys to raise and a large workshop to manage. Bold, energetic, and quick to smile, Terezinha was up to the task.

Terezinha's son Thiago told us, "My mother, her parents, worked in the clay. When she was little she saw her parents working in the clay, making pots to sell in the market. Then she dedicated herself to being an artisan to be able to maintain her children. There are five sons. And she dedicated herself to work in the art of clay so we could live." Terezinha said:

"I thank God for my sons. I taught them how to work. I taught them how to work, but I left them in peace. They could work, or study for another profession, but they chose toward *artesanato*. For which I thank God, you know.

"So, I could give continuity to my art, and I constructed my empire here in Alto do Moura — everything from the clay.

"And I thank God. I am successful, taking it all from the clay. Clay, art: if we make it with love, it multiples. And not only art. Everything that you do, if you do it with love, it will always multiply."

Terezinha pauses, looks back: "I thank my *father*, who taught me to work in this art. My father used to work on the wheel, making clay plates by hand.

"On the wheel, life taught me. I had the desire, you know. But today, really, I almost don't work on the wheel. My work is more manual. Today I have my son, Angelo, who works on the wheel. He has excellent production.

"Because my strength today is the *muqueca* pot, utilitarian pots for restaurants, from plates to pots.

"I make all types of pieces that are used in a restaurant. And, thank God, I don't have nothing bad to say. Of my art, I have only good things to say.

"Because clay is like a mother. It never tires of giving to us. It always has more to give. That's clay."

Terezinha's idea of art is clearly not restricted to the figurative. She makes figurative pieces and she makes useful pots. Both, when made by hand with love, are art. Marliete similarly considered the useful pots — made by women before Vitalino's arrival — to be art when they were made by hand with care. Art is not a type of product, but a drive within the creator that abides in diverse objects as a sign of dedicated humanity. With a skilled workforce around her, composed of her sons, Terezinha searched and experimented to increase the quality and commercial viability of utilitarian ceramic art.

One problem awaiting Terezinha's solution lay in the clay. She calls the local clay *massapê* and divides its processing into two phases. First, it is stepped down and kneaded with the feet. Then, in the past, little stones were picked out by hand and the clay was sieved; now a machine does that job. Maturing at a low temperature in the kiln, the clay is perfect for decorative figures and adequate for domestic cooking, but when that clay is used for vessels in a big restaurant, tableware is apt to chip and the cooking pots might crack at high heat, so Terezinha was off on a quest for a second clay:

"The clay for the figurative pieces, put that clay in high fire, and it breaks. It can't withstand the heat.

"To use it for cooking in a restaurant, the pot has to have a guarantee that when you put it in the fire with food, it will not break. I was worried that I was without a clay for the pots.

"Then I have a friend who has land here, and I felt that there was clay on it. I went and did an experiment and found that it is *excellent*, superb clay for the pots.

"So, this clay that I use to make pots, I call it *barro de formigueiro*" — ant-hill clay. "It is clay that can withstand the fire. It is clay that has more resistance to the fire.

"It comes from a different place, and it is completely different from the clay we use for the statues."

Two clays, suited to different needs: Terezinha is prepared for production. She sees her work as stemming from the work of the Indigenous people she calls *Índios*, Indians:

"The pot is very ancient, right? Because the pot, it came from far in the past, from really far in the past, you know.

"Now, the statues, no. The figurative statues were the creation of Mestre Vitalino. It was he who created it.

"I did not have the *pleasure* to know Mestre Vitalino, because in the year that I was born, he went to live with God. I was born in sixty-three, and he went to live with God in sixty-three.

"Now, the pot, the pot is more Indian, right? It comes from the Indians. Their art was marvelous, really very good.

"These pots come from the Indian women, because it was they who created it. These pots for *muqueca*, these pots I make.

"The Indians only worked manually. They didn't have the wheel. My father made pots. My father's father made pots. They also made pots, like the Indians, all by hand.

"And there was a gentleman named Biu dos Anjos. He used to make pots completely by hand. And another woman, Dona Lourdes. It has been a while since they went away to live with God.

"Now we have the wheel, but the Indians made beautiful pots completely by hand. And to fire, they would dig a hole and put the pots in. They would cover it with dirt and burn it. The Indians burned their pieces in a different way."

In Terezinha's shop, production in volume depends on two tools that the Indians didn't have, that were brought from Portugal, the wheel and the kiln. Her atelier divides into three main sections. At the center, in the middle of the middle, her third son, Angelo Gonçalves Simões, works at the wheel, meeting the highest standards of the production potter. He throws off the hump, creating identical forms, without a pause for measurement, at the rate of one a minute. Lined on wareboards, his pots rest on the shop floor, drying before firing.

A few steps from the wheel in a space behind, not outdoors but within the building, the big kiln stands. It is the same type as the others in Alto do Moura — cylindrical, updraft, wood-fired — but much larger. The firing chamber at the bottom is stoked, Terezinha says, with "light sticks from the country or leftover wood from the sawmill." The top closes into a dome with a chimney to carry the smoke away. A large loading port opens on the side to receive and release the pots. Terezinha describes the firing:

"There are eight hours of fire. The fire starts almost at zero degrees, just heating up. Then it starts to increase, increase, increase until the point we call the *cadear*.

"The *cadear* means you put a whole bunch of wood at once. Today we look through a little hole in the kiln to see if it is fired. Before, my father would know by the smell, a smell that is very different.

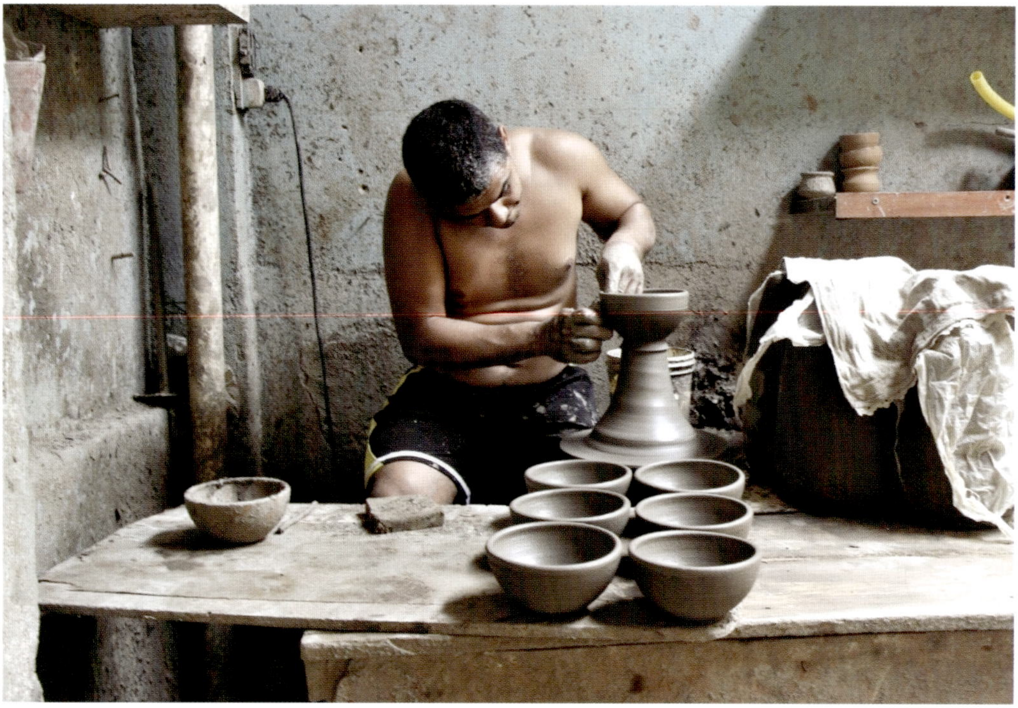

Angelo at the wheel, 2019

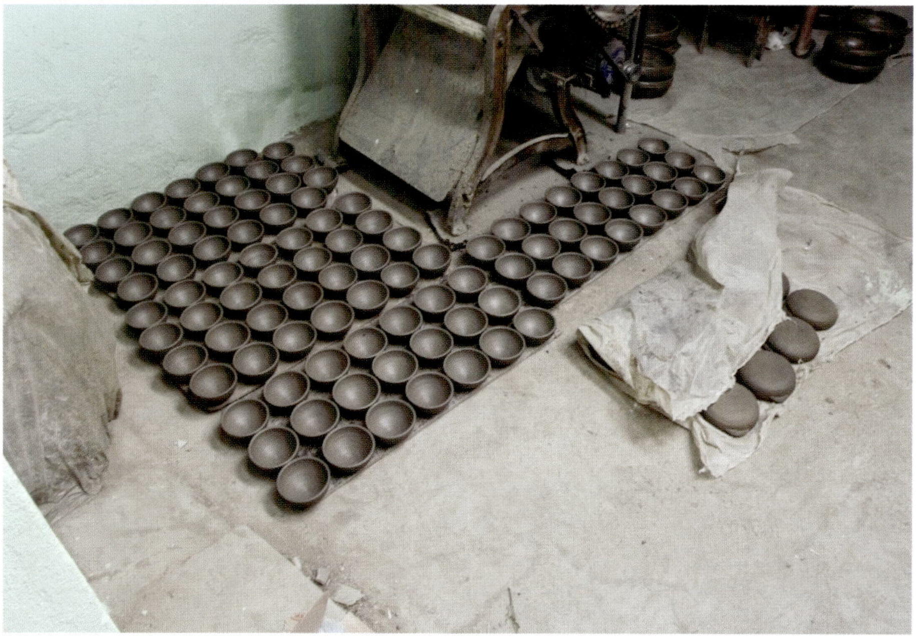

Angelo's bowls drying, 2019

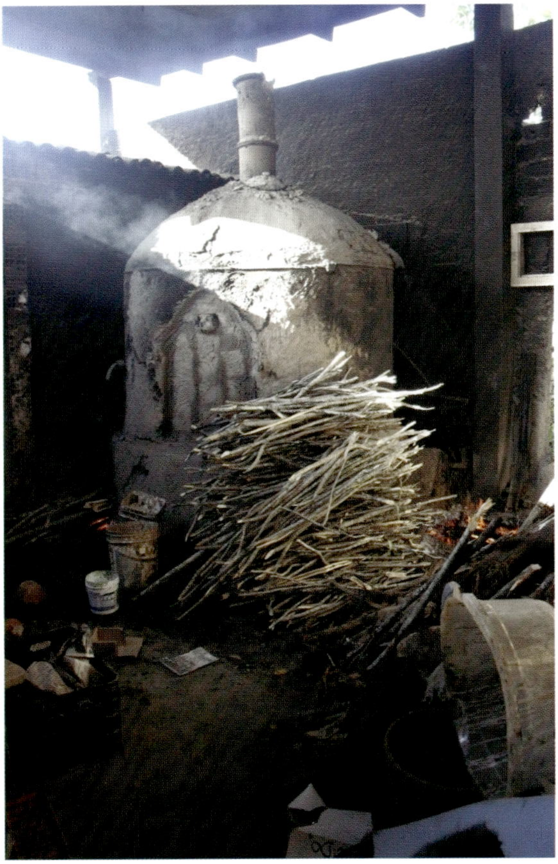

Terezinha's kiln firing, 2019

"Some people came with instruments, doing some research, and they said my kiln got up to nine hundred degrees. Then the clay vitrifies. Now, to burn: at seven hundred degrees it burns, it's ready.

"Then when you are finished, you can smother the fire. Put some green, wet firewood down there in the firing chamber. Smother it, and leave it, and the next day it is all black.

"It is all black."

These are the points to note. Recalling descriptions of firing by Luiz Carlos, Carmélia, and Emerson, you will understand that Terezinha's process follows the pattern of firing the figures, but it reaches peak heat two hundred degrees higher, so her high-fired pots of anthill clay meet the requirements of big restaurants. Then in her late, additional phase of smothering and smoking, her pots blacken in a reduction atmosphere, becoming distinctive and attractive. The hand-thrown, wood-fired, black utilitarian pot is, for Terezinha, the base of her success, aesthetically and commercially.

"In the past," Terezinha says, "for us to sell a single vase, we had to take it to the market in Caruaru. It was very difficult to sell.

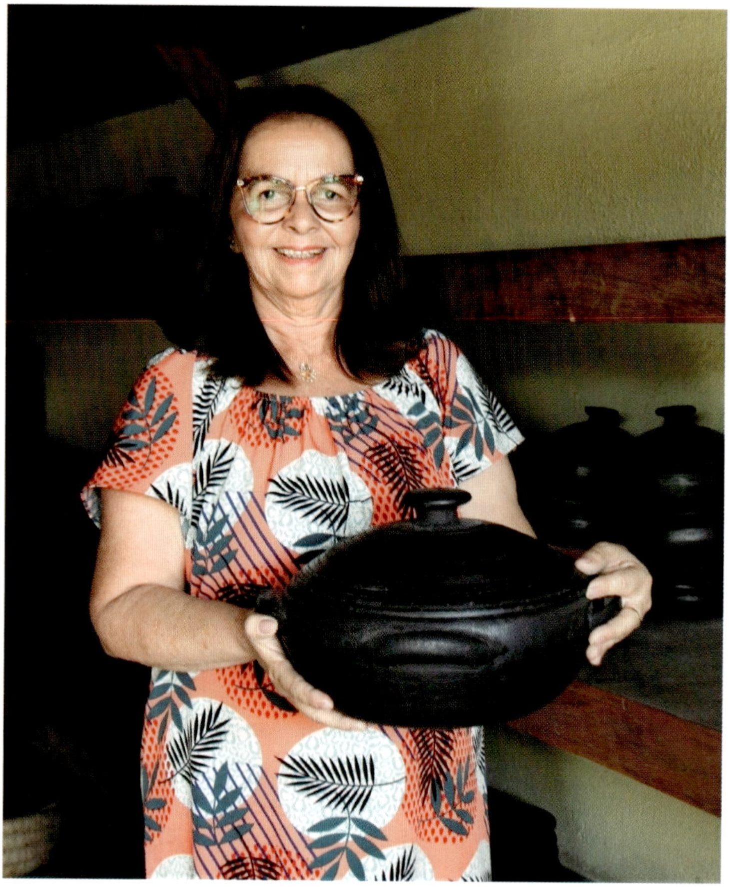

Terezinha with a black *muqueca* pot, 2021

"But now with my useful pots, with the beautiful black ones, all Brazil is seeking me. They send people here to make orders.

"I have customers in Brasília. I have customers in São Paulo. But really my strength is the restaurants in Recife.

"I have my line of really good restaurants in Recife that I deliver to. I have already sent my pots to Portugal, to Holland. So, I feel really happy, you know, happy inside my art."

The owner of a seaside restaurant in Recife wants Brazilian pots to cook and serve Brazilian food. The low, wide *muqueca* pot on the table holds *muqueca*, a spicy seafood stew. The restaurant's patrons might sense that this is regionally right, though they probably don't know just how right, don't know that, not far to the west, the pot was thrown out of local clay, and fired with local wood. But Terezinha does know and she is pleased with her art's success.

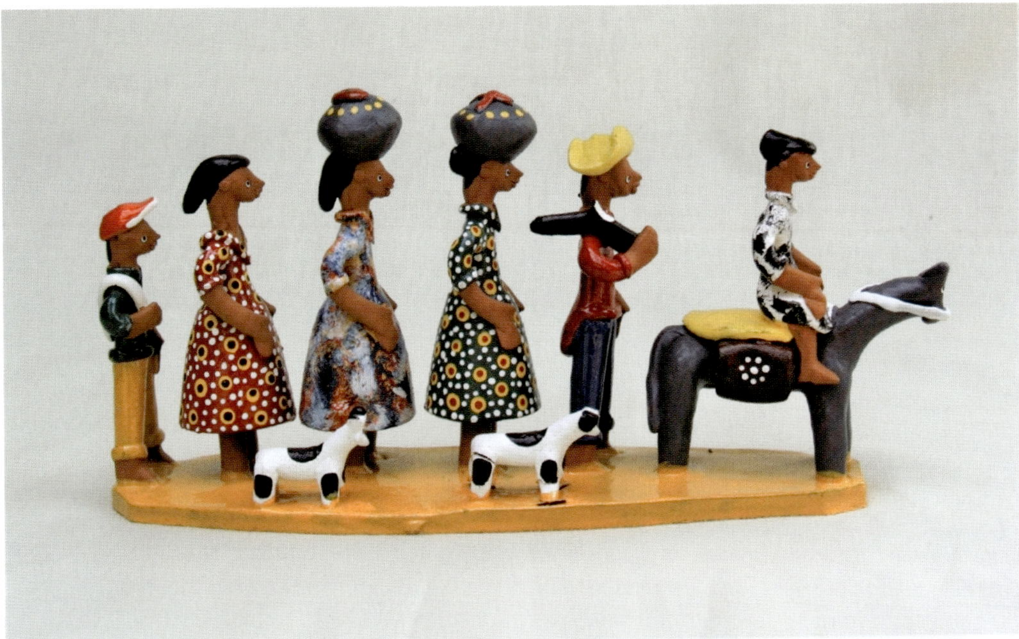

Os Retirantes, from Terezinha's shop (26 cm long), 2019

Through the center of her shop runs a line of production that begins with bare feet on raw clay and ends with a bowl on the table in a fancy restaurant, but the handsome black pot, the end of the line, is not the end of the story. Her atelier's section on the left begins with a wide showroom. Behind it Terezinha has her studio. "I make all kinds of figurative pieces," she says, and workers in her shop produce commercial-grade versions of Alto do Moura's classics — women at work, men making music, statues of Saint Francis, and she gave us her shop's rendition of *Os Retirantes*.

In a well-lit corner of her studio, a statue of Santa Terezinha, a favorite with Brazil's *santeiros*, stands near her wheel. Terezinha doesn't use that wheel to throw small pots but to make large ones that begin with a thrown base then grow in height through the manual addition of a multitude of coils, a technique used widely in the world to make pots too big to raise from the wheel in one smooth move. A big pot was the starting point for Terezinha's most famed creation, the *luminária*, a large jar pierced decoratively so that a light inside will shine a pattern into the dark. She tells us about it:

"I most like to make my own creations, pieces that I create. The *luminária* is my creation, it is. This *luminária*, I created it in ninety-eight. It was by chance.

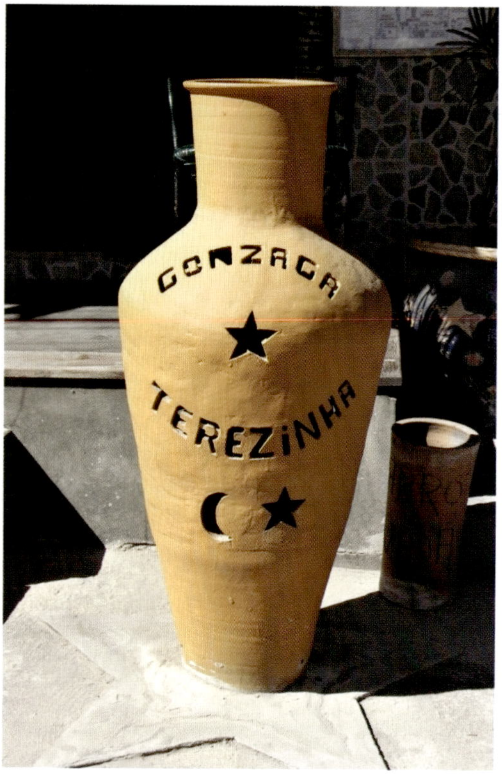

Luminária in front of the shop, 2019

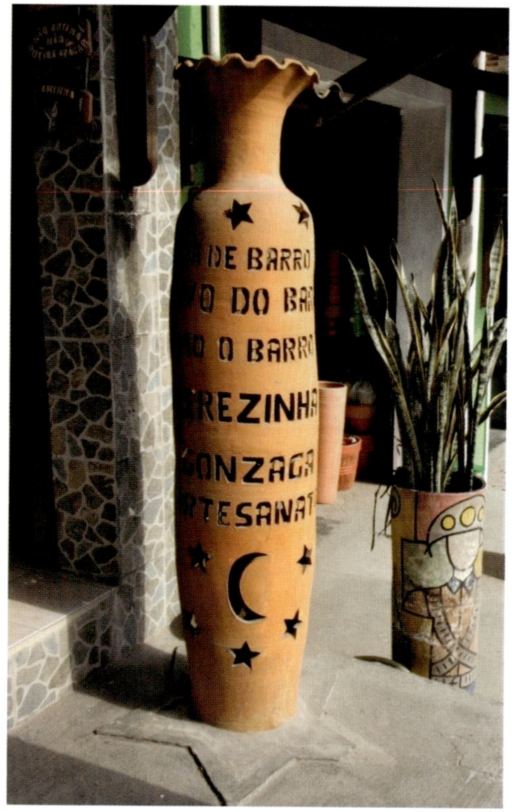

Luminária in front of the shop, 2021

"A government agency came and sponsored a course taught by the masters. It was me, it was Mister Manuel Eudócio, it was my brother Heleno, it was Marliete. A reunion of sorts.

"I participated, so they asked me to make something to do with *light*. Then in that moment, I created the *luminária*. And during that period, ninety-eight, ninety-nine, two thousand, I didn't make anything that people didn't want.

"I had an exhibition and during one night I received five hundred commissions for a *luminária*.

"Then my neighbor starts to make it. And another starts to make it. I am happy when I make a piece and my neighbor makes one almost the same. Because no one works exactly the same.

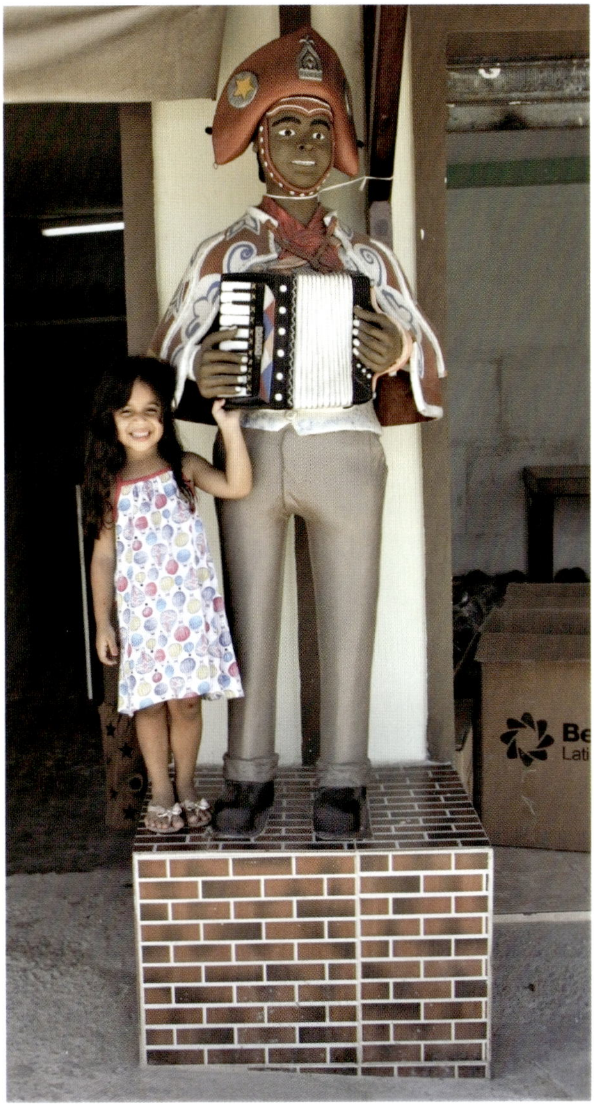

Gilliard's Gonzaga, with Genilda's granddaughter Clarice
Esther posing in front of the shop, 2019

"So, I am being useful. I am passing *ideas* to my neighbor, to my colleagues in art. That is very good.

"But it was my creation. The *luminária* is my creation."

In front of Terezinha's atelier, a large *luminária*, pierced with her name, stands to the left. Down to the right stands a life-sized statue of Luiz Gonzaga. It was made by her second son, Gilliard Gonçalves Simões, whose artistic name, Gilliard Gonzaga, affirms the connection to his mother and makes his statue of Gonzaga, like her *luminária*, an apt shop sign.

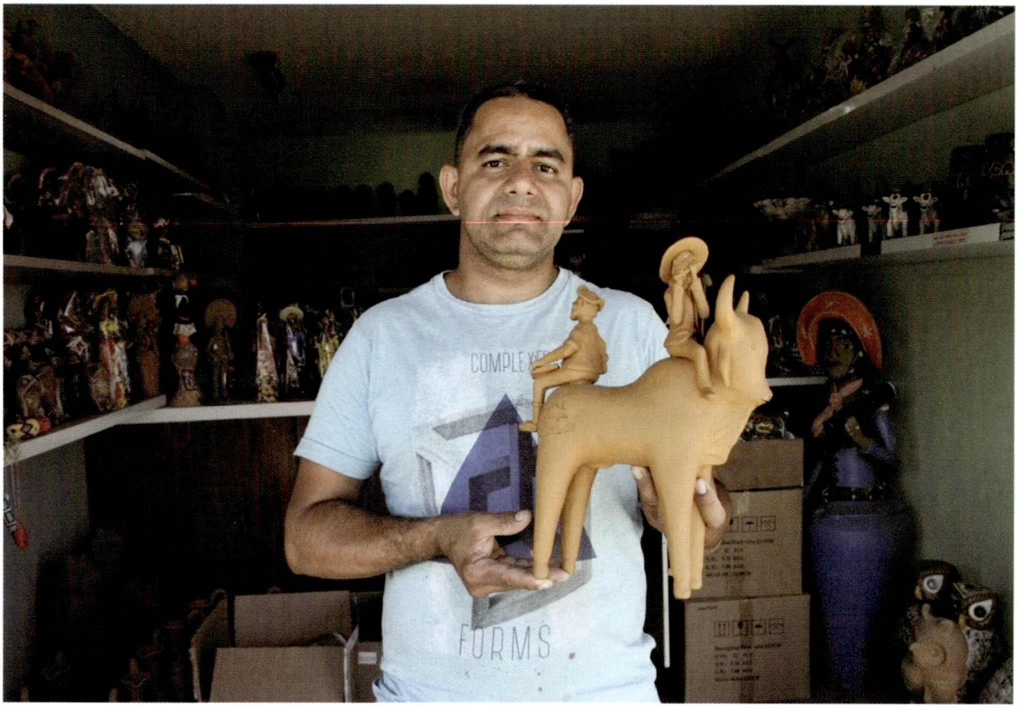

Gilliard with his statue of Galdino and Vitalino riding one bull, 2019

From his shop, the atelier's third section, Gilliard sells the figurative pieces he makes, drawn from the central repertory and left natural: Lampião, Padre Cícero, Mestre Vitalino. Then Gilliard also sells statues made by Joel, the son of Mestre Galdino, whose shop, now a museum, stands just across the street named for Saint Sebastian, a few steps to the south.

The portal at the entrance to Alto do Moura carries pictures of Mestre Vitalino on the right and Mestre Galdino on the left, establishing that, in this town, there are two distinctly different traditions of figurative creation. Gilliard reiterated that fact in 2018 with an image of two men on a bull, Vitalino in front, Galdino behind. Pairs on a horse or bull — bride and groom, Lampião and Maria Bonita, the Doutor and Dona Joana — imply unity, but Gilliard cleverly placed the masters back-to-back, holding different things in their hands, looking in different directions, to signal the radical differences between their traditions.

Alto do Moura is a small town, unified by ramifying social connections. After his first wife died, Terezinha's father remarried and Terezinha was one of the three children from his second family. He had two children in his first family. One was his son Heleno, a potter who worked where Terezinha now works, and he was the father of Luiz Carlos's wife Genilda, so a line of connection runs up the street to the north. Other connections run to the south, associating Terezinha's family with Galdino's, and we will follow along, turning our attention now to Alto do Moura's second figurative tradition — Mestre Galdino's — aiming to learn how such a small, tight place could accommodate work so different.

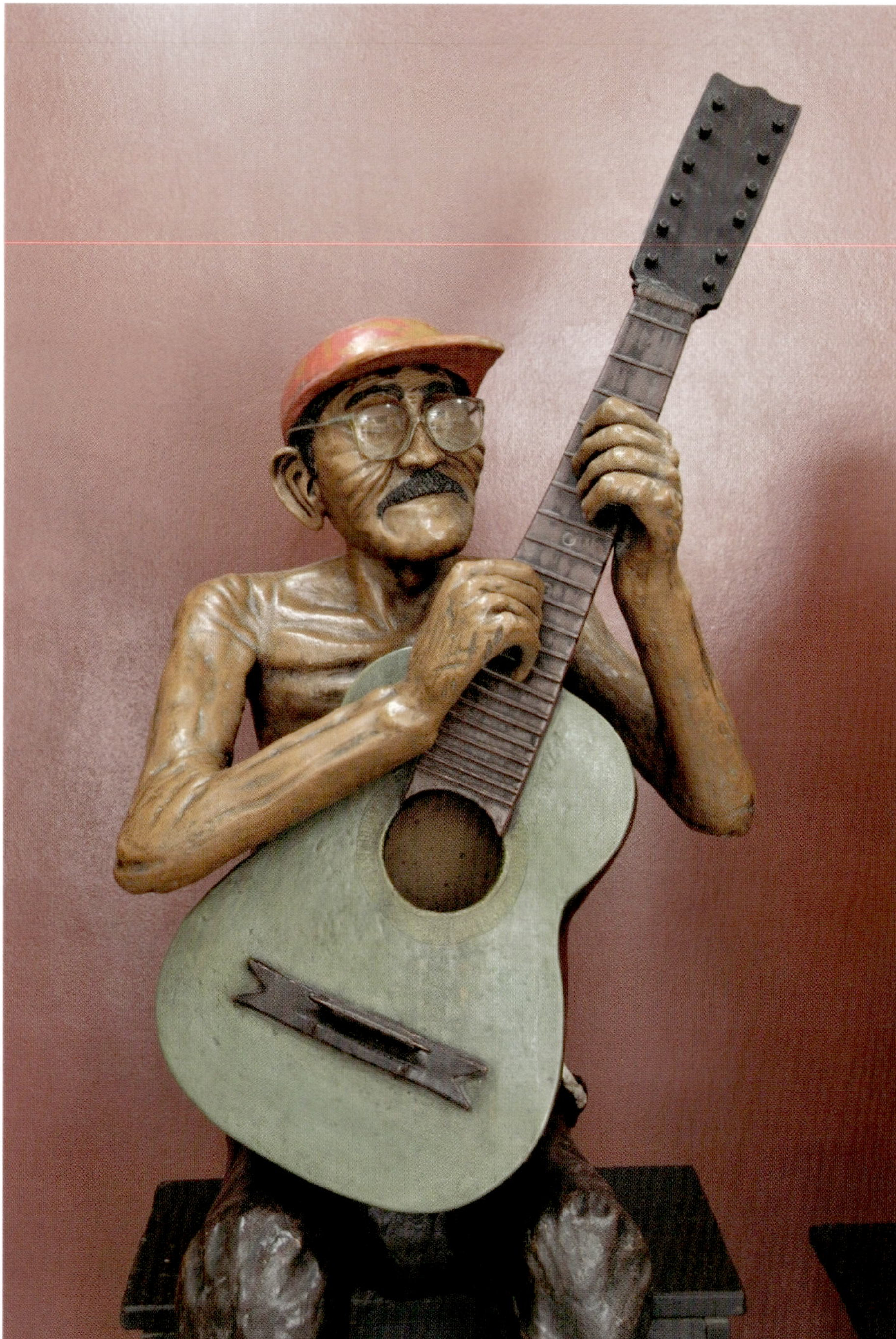

Mestre Galdino, a life-size statue in clay, made by Manuel Bernardo,
displayed in the museum, 2007

17

The Galdino Family

The simultaneity of distinct traditions is the question. Traditions different in process and purpose run smoothly in complementary union, side by side, through Terezinha's shop. To understand how two competitive figurative traditions, close in process and purpose, could maintain their difference over time in a place as small as Alto do Moura, we will begin with a comparison.

As in Alto do Moura, in the small Pernambucan pottery town of Tracunhaém, utilitarian production flows from its source among the Indigenous people and it has diminished, though not ended, while the weight of creation has shifted to the figurative. Here there are also two distinct traditions of figurative handwork in clay, both beginning in the twentieth century and attributed to specific progenitors. One descends from José Joaquim da Silva, called Zezinho de Tracunhaém. The other originated with three women working together, Lidia Vieira, Severina Batista, and Maria Amélia da Silva — we'll call it Maria Amélia's line for convinience. This is not ancient history. We interviewed Zezinho when he was seventy-five in 2014 and Maria Amélia when she was ninety-two in 2015.

Zezinho's line is dominant. This is not a subjective judgment, but a simple statistical observation. His tradition has reached beyond the family and gathered more followers, more practitioners, including his son Claudio, called Dinho de Zezinho; the men who worked in Zezinho's shop, Nilson Tavares and Antônio Alves Pereira, called Totinha; and men in the community without a direct connection to Zezinho, Antônio Pimpo and Joaquim Alves Pereira. By contrast, the artists of the other line come from the families of the progenitors:

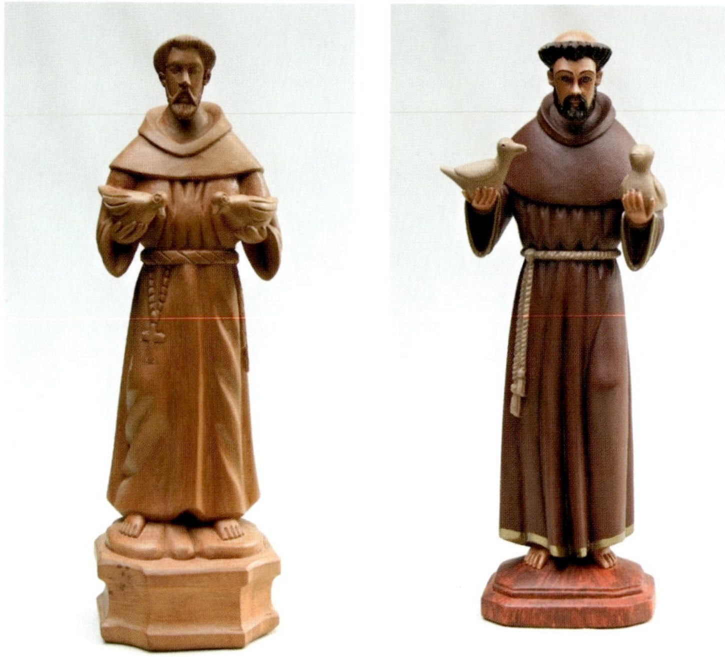

Saint Francis in wood from Ibimirim. Left: by Manoel Cordeiro (31 cm tall), 2015. Right: by José Bezerra (29 cm tall), 2019

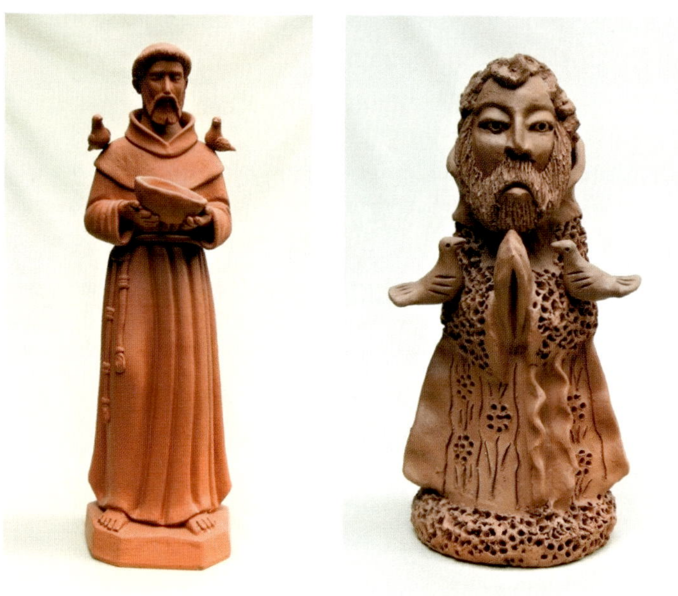

Saint Francis in clay from Tracunhaém. Left: by Totinha (52 cm tall), 2015. Right: by Mestre Zuza (33 cm tall), 2014

Maria Amélia's son Ricardo Félix da Silva and Severina Batista's nephew José Edivaldo Batista, called Mestre Zuza.

These artists all know each other, know and respect each other's work, and handle the clay, its shaping and firing, in much the same way, but the products in the two lines remain inviolably distinct. It would seem natural for traditions in proximity to interact and merge over time, but as Claude Lévi-Strauss demonstrates in his marvelous book *The Way of the Masks*, adjacent traditions can also recoil and purify into opposition. Tracunhaém's work, though unified in technique and saintly subject, divides clearly by size and, most dramatically, by form.

In Zezinho's line, figures range in height from fifteen centimeters to two meters. In Maria Amélia's line, they hover around thirty-two centimeters tall. But form is the key. Artists in Zezinho's line shape figures within the frames of baroque and neoclassical proportions — proportions they share with the *santeiros* of Ibimirim who work with wood. The bodies are four to six heads in height, and they strike the eye as anatomically plausible, close enough to reality. In Maria Amélia's line, heads and hands are much enlarged, the body is two or three heads tall. Visual accuracy has been traded for conceptual significance. Head and hands, thought and action, prevail.

On the hunt for origins, we would track Zezinho's line back to Europe and Maria Amélia's line back to Africa, just as we would trace the utilitarian line to the Indians, reaffirming the historical complexity of Brazilian culture. What matters to the artists in the present, though, is that two healthy traditions continue in Tracunhaém, and Zezinho's line is dominant because the more naturalistic work attracts more artists, and especially because it holds more appeal for more buyers.

Come home now to Alto do Moura, and you will find the same pattern: two figurative traditions — Vitalino's and Galdino's — with Vitalino's dominant because it has spread beyond his family to become Alto do Moura's, while only people named Galdino regularly create in Galdino's line. Works in Vitalino's line span from Marliete's miniatures to Leonildo's life-sized portraits in clay, while works in Galdino's style cluster in the middle range of size. Vitalino's line tolerates more anatomical distortion than Zezinho's, though the figures remain recognizably familiar, close enough to visual reality. But work in Galdino's line welcomes reconfigurations comparable to Maria Amélia's. In consequence, artists in Vitalino's line consider their work to be their own, but

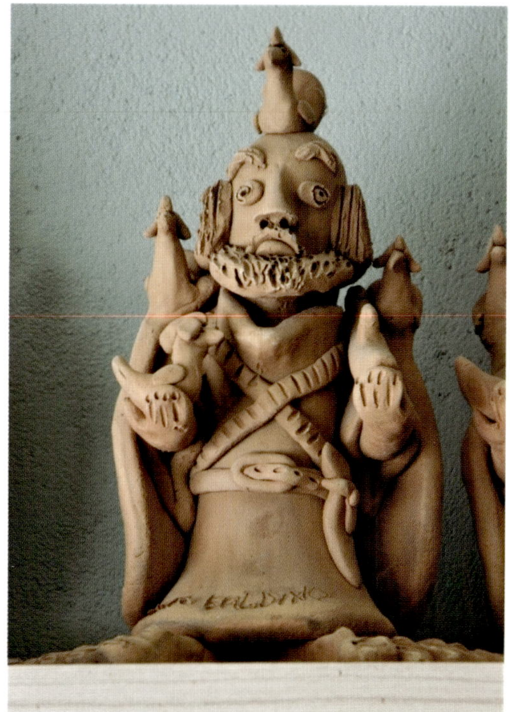

Saint Francis, by Joel Galdino, for sale in Gilliard's shop, 2019

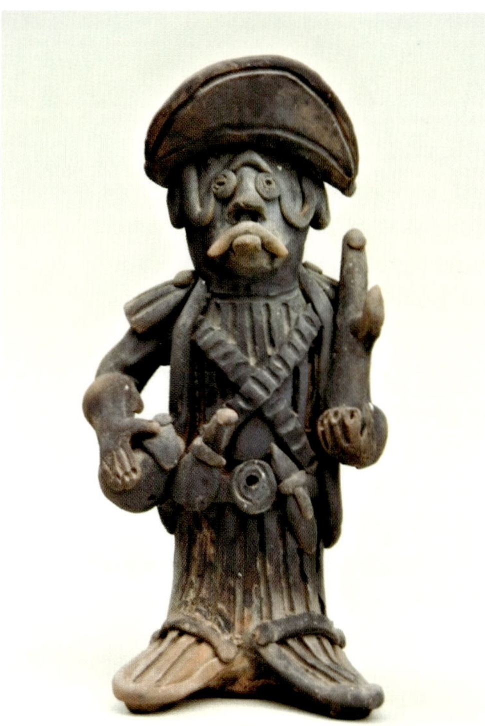

Cangaceiro, by Joel Galdino (32 cm tall), for sale in the Zé Caboclo family shop, 2019

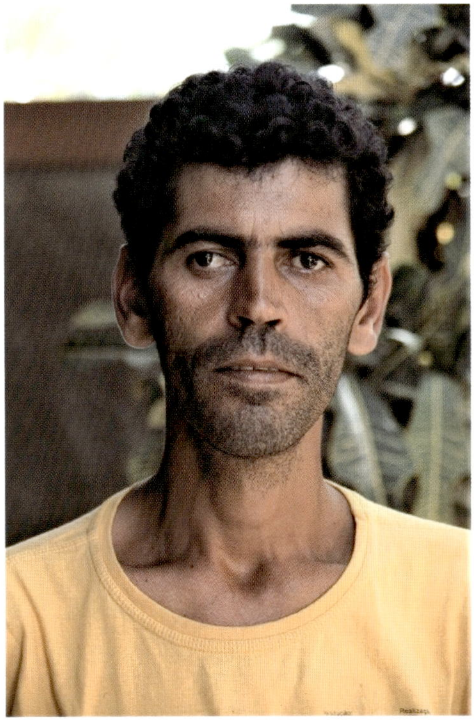

Joel Galdino, Alto do Moura, 2007

if someone unrelated to Galdino copies a Galdino piece, which Emerson has, it is so unnaturally distinct that it remains Galdino's.

Mestre Galdino died in 1996. We met his son Joel in 2007. Later Joel was troubled and out of touch, but examples enough of Joel's work remain in Gilliard's shop, and in the shop of the Zé Caboclo family, for us to be able to select pieces that share subjects with pieces in Vitalino's line and make comparisons to clarify the formal difference.

The heads are enlarged, the proportions close to the work in Maria Amélia's line. In Joel's Saint Francis, the body is two heads tall, reminding us of Mestre Zuza's work in Tracunhaém. (For contrast: the body of Manuel Eudócio's Saint Francis is four heads tall.) In an image labeled Lampião in large letters on the back — though sporting a moustache Lampião didn't have, it is more likely a *cangaceiro* from Lampião's back-country gang — the body is little more than two heads tall. (For contrast: the body of Luiz Carlos's Lampião is six heads tall.) Joel's Saint Francis and his *cangaceiro* both have enormous feet, obviating the need for bases, and both are extravagantly outfitted, Saint Francis with five birds (*santeiros* usually give him two), the *cangaceiro* with crossed bandoliers of lead and all the bulky equipment of war. Figures pitched much farther from reality erupt in Galdino's line, but this pair establishes the ground for design.

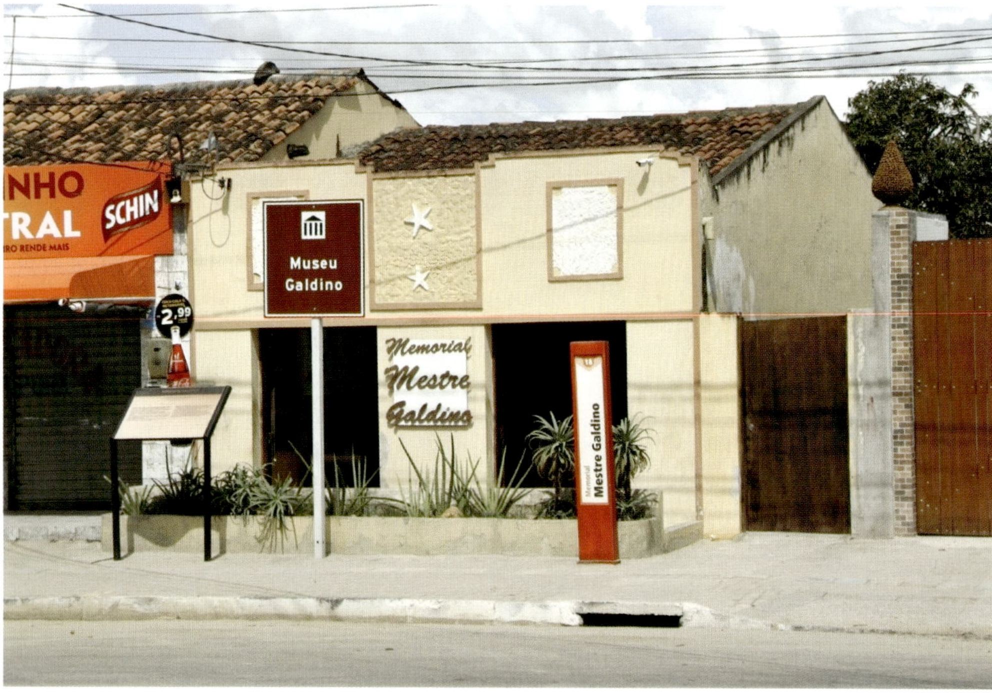

The museum dedicated to Mestre Galdino, Alto do Moura, 2019

Mestre Galdino's old shop is now a museum. Inside, a statue of the master at once pairs him with Vitalino and sets him apart: he is holding a twelve-string guitar, not a *pífano*. There is also a statue of Galdino's wife, Maria, along with works in cases and informative labels on the wall. Were you to walk, it is no great distance, from Vitalino's museum up on the main street and then downhill to Galdino's museum, you would pass the workshops of all the town's leading artists, as well as the private museums holding pieces by Luiz Antônio and Manuel Eudócio. In this public museum dedicated to Mestre Galdino, you would be welcomed by Terezinha's fourth son, Thiago Gonçalves Simões. It is his job to explain Galdino's life and work to visitors; he is the right guide to understanding.

Thiago

Learning from his mother and father, Thiago began working in the clay at the age of eight, and he continues to make both utilitarian and decorative pieces. In 2006, he also began working as a docent in the museum. In 2012, his wife, Maria Bárbara Rodrigues, joined him and he says, "We work here like cultural

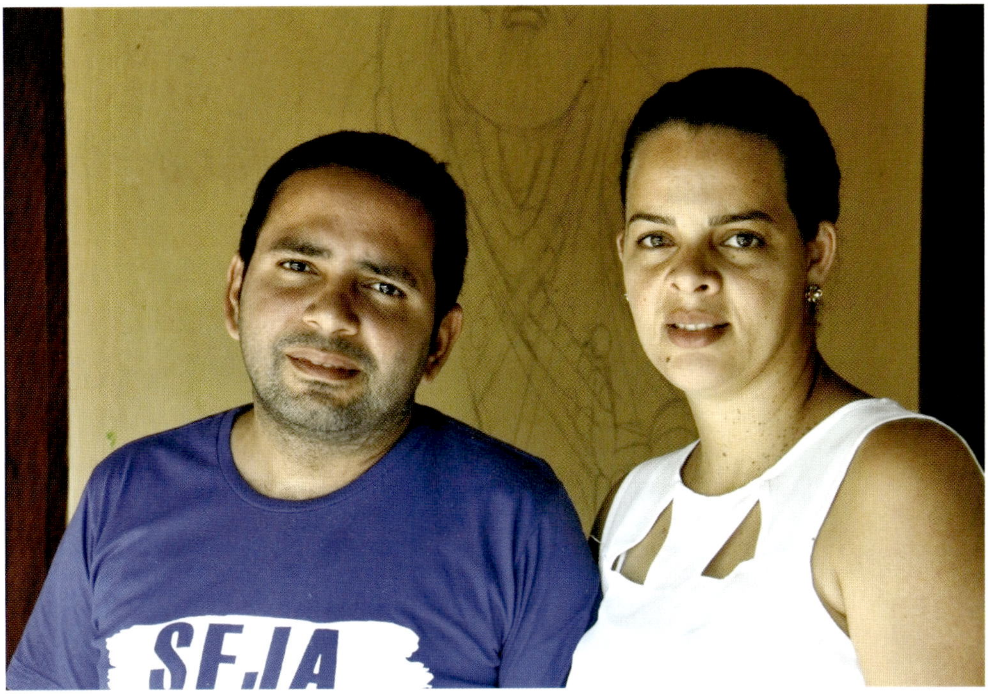

Tiago Gonçalves Simões and Maria Bárbara Rodrigues, 2019

agents. Together we give answers to the tourists through knowledge we gained by talking with people who lived with Galdino.

"I have no memory of him. I was very young in that period, a child. But I have learned through other people and through books. We transmit these bits of knowledge about Galdino."

Manoel Galdino de Freitas, called Mestre Galdino, was born in São Caetano, Pernambuco, in 1924. Synthesizing his sources, Thiago tells his story:

"Galdino came here, to Alto do Moura in seventy-four. He came as a construction worker, to work construction in Alto do Moura.

"He already knew about Mestre Vitalino" — who had died eleven years before his arrival — "and he was experiencing financial difficulties. He prayed, My God, I make so little money, make me a ceramic artist.

"And before that he had seen people who were working in the clay, who were making pieces similar to Vitalino's, who were followers of Vitalino. He said, I will get to know these people, to see the style of work they make.

"Then he went to the house of these people and said, Look, will you lend me a small piece, a ball of clay, for me to make a piece?

"Sure, Galdino, that can be done. I will lend it to you.

"Then he went to his place of work, sat down on the floor, prayed to God, and started to make a clay piece.

"Then he came to Alto do Moura to create a body of work that was totally different from the quotidian art that Mestre Vitalino had planted here in Alto do Moura and all his followers were making.

"So, he made a different kind of work, *surreal.* Surreal, with mythological monsters that nobody here had made.

"Many say that Galdino made these things through divine inspiration, right? He did not copy anybody. He said in a poem: In art, I owe only to God. Lessons I owe to no one.

"He did not copy anyone. He made through inspiration, through his own knowledge, through dreams.

"So, the tourists come. They go up top and see the pieces of Mestre Vitalino. When they get down here, they see those of Galdino, and they are entirely different.

"They ask, How does this man have that kind of inspiration to make these monsters? From where did this man get them?"

Answers to their questions — dreams, inspirations, intentions — lead toward an answer to our question about simultaneous traditions. As Thiago tells it, and there's no reason to doubt him, Galdino, for commercial and personal purposes, set out to create work that was distinctly different from Vitalino's.

Vitalino's work, dominant and profitable when Galdino arrived, is quotidian, *cotidiano*, founded on common reality. Galdino's is surreal. That word, the same in Portuguese and English, is generally and consistently used to capture the radical unreality of Galdino's creations. Galdino looked at Vitalino's work, then through contradiction, reversal, and transformative opposition, he intentionally invented a counter-tradition. The differences ran beyond reconciliation.

Galdino's figures, short in the body with gigantic, grotesque feet, depart from visual reality, and with two brave moves Galdino swept design into new, imaginative directions. In one move he concocted rebellious combinations. Sacred and quotidian traditions separate sharply in the Northeast, but Galdino meshed them aggressively, transgressively in a figure that is both the sweet, peaceful Saint Francis and the violent Lampião. It has the beard and birds of the saint and the weaponry of the outlaw. For another image, he ignored the historical constraints of the quotidian in a figure that blended a self-portrait with a portrait of Lampião (the source, surely, for Joel's *cangaceiro*).

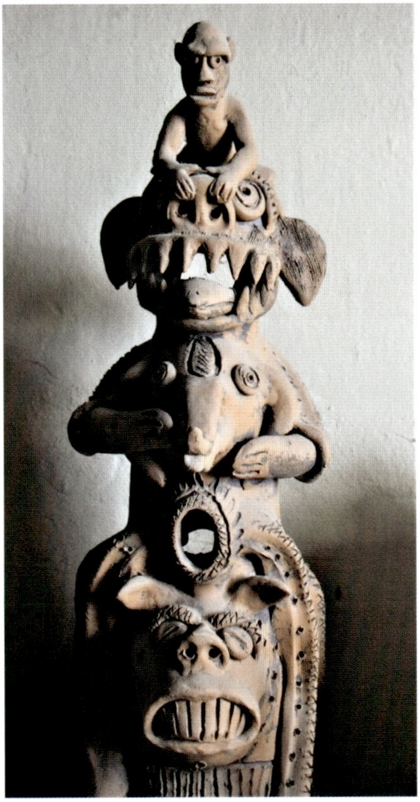

Carranca, by Joel Galdino, for sale in the Zé Caboclo family shop, 2019

In his second, more extravagant and notorious move, Galdino created the works Thiago called mythological monsters. Dream pieces, nightmarish and whimsical, they are conspicuously composed of rising piles of heads. While instantly recognizable as Galdino's, they manifest a spirit that is not his alone. They are called *carrancas*, identifying them with the fantastic figureheads on the boats of western Pernambuco that resemble the *Reisado's* Jaraguá.

But Galdino's works in clay are most strikingly like the works in wood made at Cachoeira in the interior of Bahia by Boaventura da Silva Filho, called Louco — Crazy. We are friends with Louco's son Celestino, called Louco Filho, Crazy Junior, so we know that Louco was a contemporary of Galdino's. Louco was born in 1932 and he died in 1992. Galdino was born in 1924 — though there are alternative sources that have them both born in 1929 — and he died in 1996. The difference is that when Galdino was getting started in Alto do Moura, in 1974, Louco was already famous. His works — predominantly cylindrical and pyramidal heaps of heads — had been exhibited widely and featured in Brazilian publications on Brazilian art. So, direct influence is possible, similarity is certain, and at least it can be said that Galdino's surrealism in Alto do Moura brought to the surface an undercurrent of back-country fantasy shared with Louco in Bahia and the carvers of figureheads in Pernambuco.

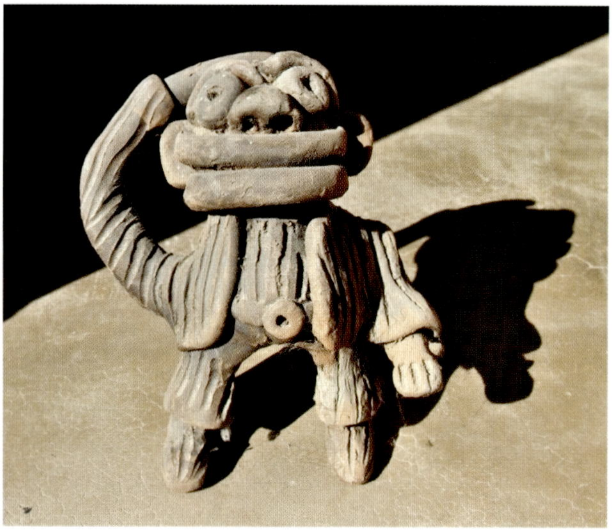

Mané Pãozeiro, by Joel Galdino, for sale in the
Zé Caboclo family shop, 2019

Galdino's most renowned work, analogous to Vitalino's bull or Luiz Antônio's lineman, is less weird, more caricatural. Made in defiance a decade after he came to Alto do Moura, it marks a turning point in his career. His reputation became national, like Vitalino's or Louco's. The piece is titled *Mané Pãozeiro*, meaning Manuel the Breadman. Thiago tells the tale:

"*Mané Pãozeiro* is the most famous piece of Mestre Galdino. It was made in eighty-four in São Paulo.

"Because an art critic criticized Galdino's art, finding it very ugly, and he said Galdino was not an artisan.

"Galdino returned to his hotel, feeling hurt, and he thought, I am going to show this critic that I know how to make art.

"He recalled his cousin who lived in São Caetano. He used to work in a bakery, selling bread, and people called him Mané Pãozeiro. And when he had financial difficulties he would put his hand on his head and ask for help. Then he said, I am going to make Mané Pãozeiro.

"So, he made it, and returning there to the art exhibition, he showed it to the critic: This is my work. It is *Mané Pãozeiro*. Since he was a poet, he made the piece and wrote a poem about the piece.

"Then he was honored and recognized as a major artisan. This was in eighty-four."

Thiago has diligently gathered the information, and during our long, meandering interview, he crafts a conclusion:

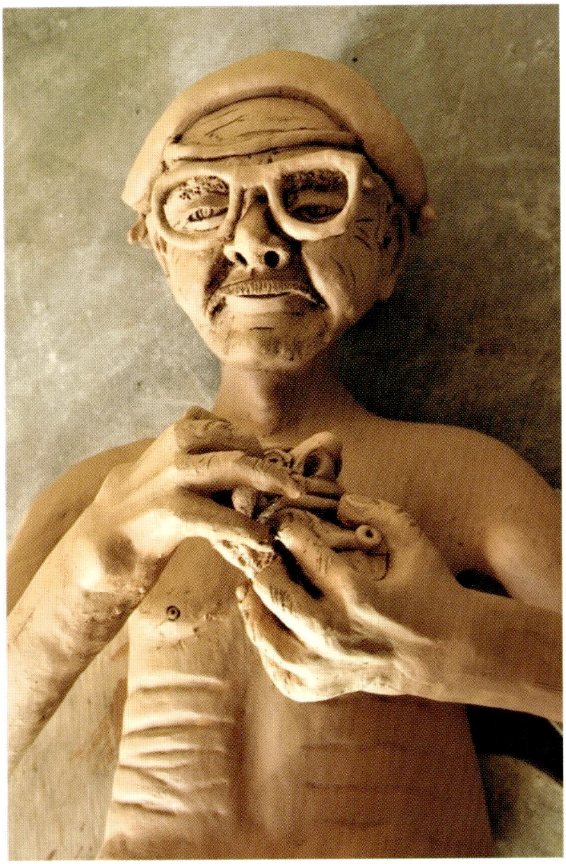

Mestre Galdino, a portrait in clay by Emerson, 2019

"Galdino, he was a ceramic artist and a poet. The tourists who would come here to talk with him, they said he was very sincere. Sometimes he would *give* pieces to the tourists out of friendship.

"Many people who have come here to visit the museum, they say he was very sincere. They liked him very much. Because he would joke with the people. He would recite poems to them.

"They would ask, Oh, Mister Galdino, how do you get the inspiration to make your pieces?

"Then he would say, Look, when I am at home, sometimes I look at the clouds, and I see the shape of a creature, of some strange thing.

"Then I go and I make the piece. Sometimes I have dreams, and I also make the pieces. And like that I go on shaping my work, making the pieces.

"He was really an artist. He died in ninety-six, due to heart problems. He would drink much too. Then he had heart problems and passed away. He left three sons.

"From his first marriage with Maria Rendeira" — Maria the Lacemaker, Marcionila Maria de Freitas — "he had three sons, which are Antônio, Jociel, and Joel. Antônio and Jociel have passed, and Joel is with us, right? He is still alive.

"My brother works with him because Joel is an alcoholic. He supports him, my brother supports him because Joel lacks control, right? Gilliard is his sponsor. He sells Joel's pieces.

"Because we have a store with an array of tourists to sell to. The tourists come to buy pieces of Joel's that are in the same line of Mestre Galdino.

"Joel's pieces are like his father's. When Joel got sick, he went to Recife. There he spent a month in the hospital, and precisely at that time some folks came from Recife, collectors of art.

"They came here to look for him, and at that moment he was not here; he was sick. They asked if I could make a piece of Mestre Galdino's. Then I made myself available and said that I could make it.

"And actually I made the most famous piece, which is *Mané Pãozeiro*.

"Always, you see, there are people who want pieces from Galdino's line. He is an artist still much admired, right?"

Now Mestre Galdino's line runs most smoothly through the hands of his nephew Luiz Galdino.

18

Luiz and George

Luiz Galdino owns one of the stores that line along the northern side of the main street in Alto do Moura. The front door opens into a wide showroom with a counter for sales in the back. A long corridor on the side runs to the rear, landing outside where a workshop stands to the left and a large pavilion opens to the right, ready for the festivities of June. All these spaces fill with a diverse abundance — statues small and tall, a bevy of *bonecas* — a riotous plenitude commanded by a single guiding mind. Luiz Galdino, the son of Mestre Galdino's brother, is the only artist who draws constant inspiration from both Vitalino's line and Galdino's. His is the right place to end our journey through Alto do Moura's creative complexity.

Out back, sheltered in the pavilion, there is another version of the half-figure of Vitalino with the *pífano* that Luiz Galdino made and placed next to the Casa Museu Mestre Vitalino, across the street. Here behind the store, displayed on a table, visitors find Luiz Galdino's take on a masterpiece invented by Vitalino and repeated, with plenty of personal touches, by those in his line. Characteristically, Luiz Galdino's *Os Retirantes* is the most different of all. It is large; the figures, standing on separate bases, form as usual into a rising and descending line, but they are unusually tall, thin, and roughly dressed. For the other artists, the first figure is the grandmother, riding a donkey and smoking a pipe, a figure so appealing and emblematic that Luiz Carlos has shaped her into an independent creation. Luiz Galdino's version has no old lady. A donkey is in the lead, bearing bundles, pots, and a basket of hens. The father follows, then the pretty mother, a bundle on her head, a baby in her arms, but the next two are not children. They are grown men, shouldering hoes, who have been

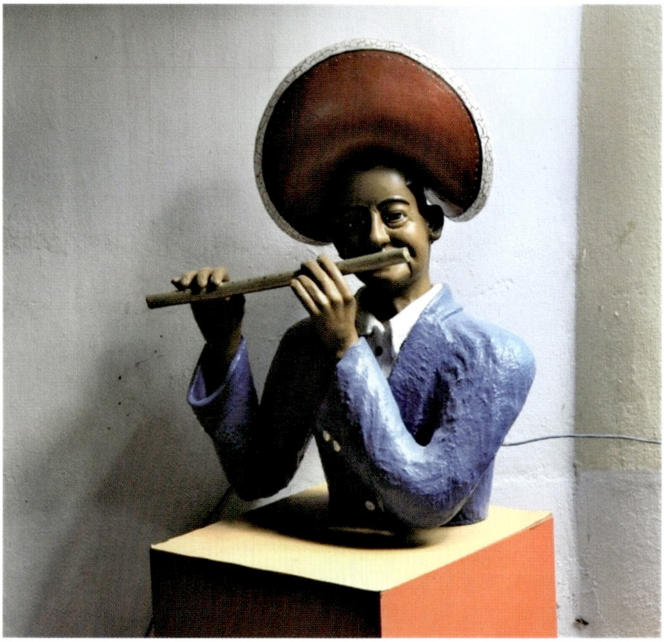

Vitalino with the *pífano*, by Luiz Galdino, a pair with the portrait at the Casa Museu Mestre Vitalino (see p.18), 2019

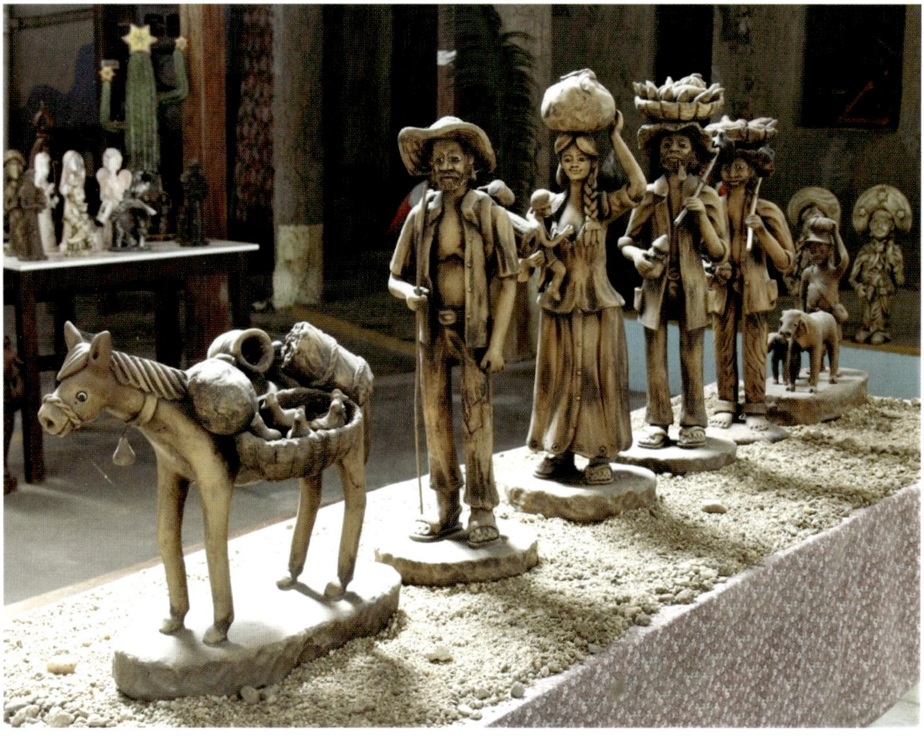

Os Retirantes, by Luiz Galdino, 2019

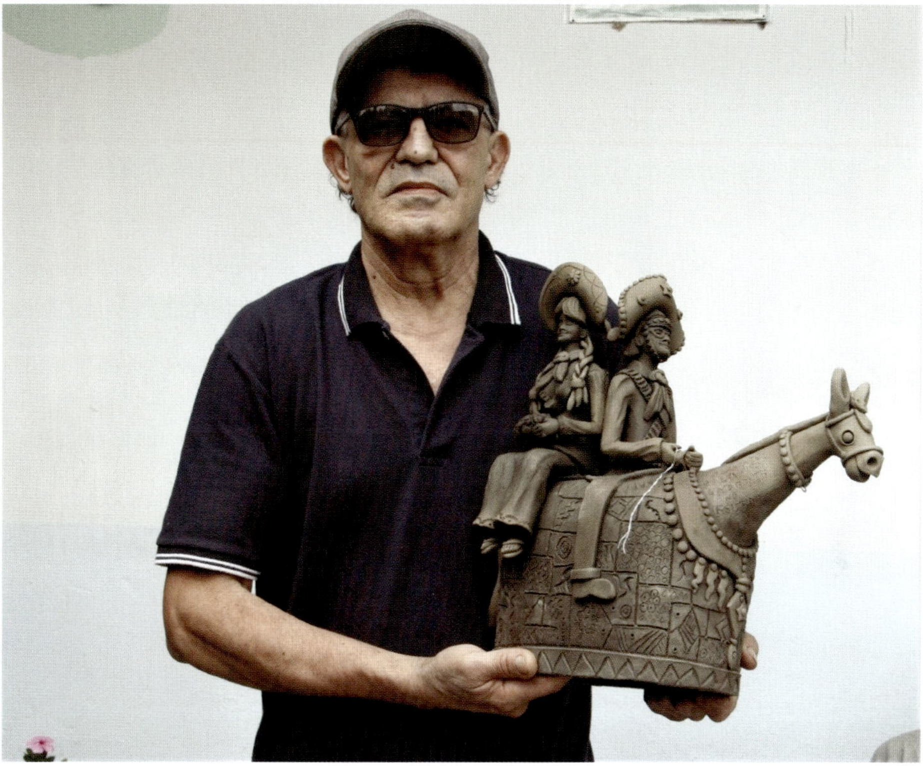

Luiz Galdino with his statue of Lampião and Maria Bonita riding the *Reisado's* bull, 2019

lifted out of the companion piece, *A Volta da Roça*. At the end a little boy walks with a calf and a dog. Neither painted with colors nor left natural, the piece is stained like Antônio's oxcart, a common finish for Luiz Galdino.

That's Luiz, all right: at once connected and off on his own. He belongs to no line, but his creations exhibit affinities with those of some of Vitalino's followers. Like Luiz Antônio he depicts contemporary workers and work. Through a series of images he illustrated the sequence of ceramic production in Alto do Moura, himself as the worker. Like Manuel Eudócio he enjoys repertorial play. In a recent piece he placed Lampião and Maria Bonita on the *Reisado's* Bull, where Manuel Eudócio placed the Doutor and Dona Joana, and where, in fact, nobody rode during the performance. Unlike Vitalino, but like Manuel Eudócio, Luiz Galdino portrays saints, most often the popular pair, Saint Francis and Saint Anthony.

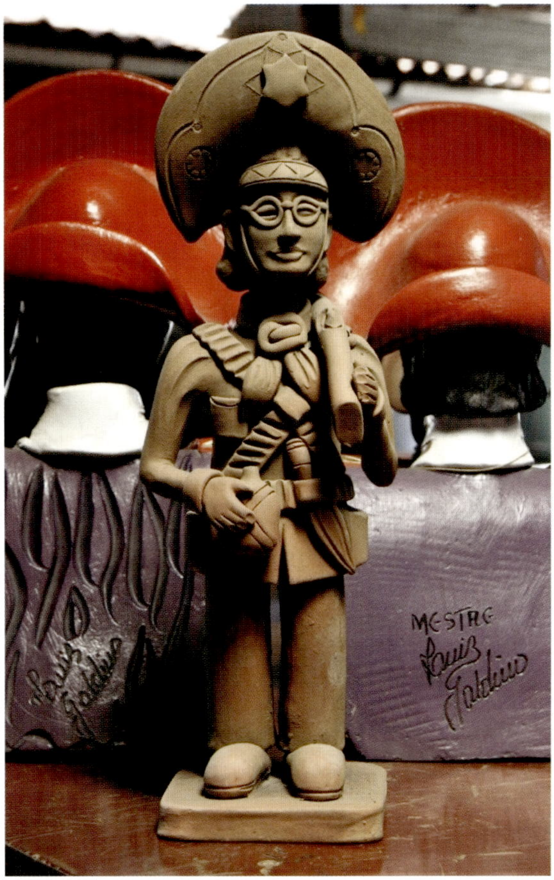

Lampião, Vitalino style,
by Luiz Galdino, 2019

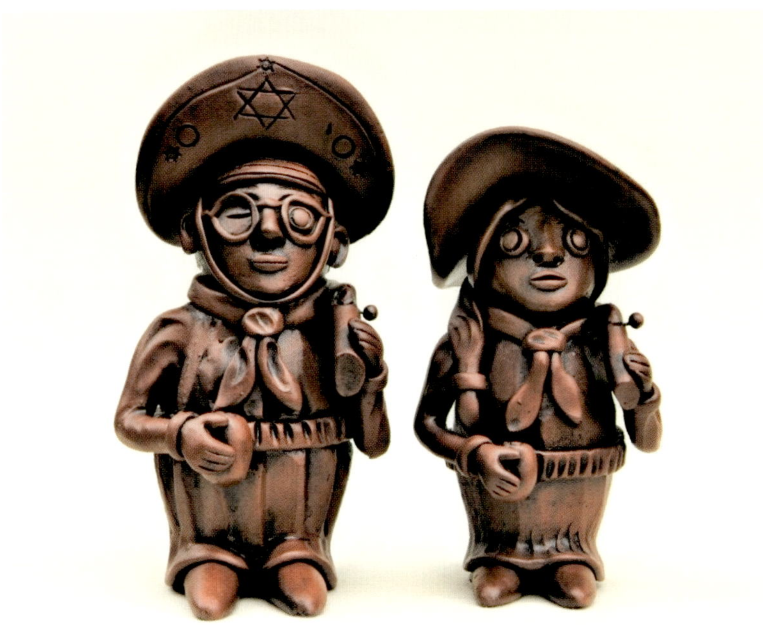

Lampião and Maria Bonita, Galdino style, by Luiz Galdino (24, 20 cm tall), 2021

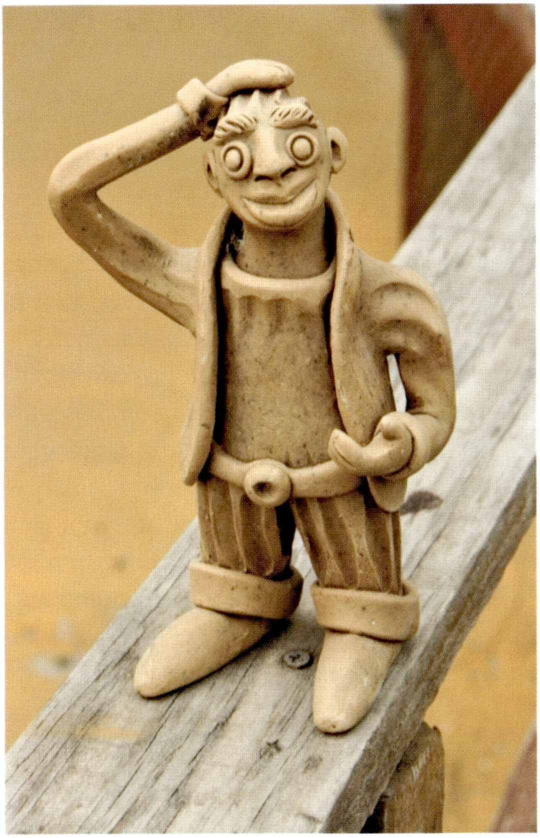

Mané Pãozeiro, by Luiz Galdino, 2021

When Luiz Galdino reaches back into his uncle's line, continuity is clear, but so is his particular presence. In repeating Mestre Galdino's famous *Mané Pãozeiro*, Luiz not only creates a lighter more finished piece, he stretches the figure toward more normal proportions; the body is three heads in height, not less than two. For variety Luiz uses Galdino's proportions for cartoonish images of Lampião and Luiz Gonzaga, though he also makes those two in proportions closer to Vitalino's.

Enter his store on the main street, and you won't find Luiz. At the counter, managing sales and ready to talk, you will find his bright, accommodating nephew, his brother's son, George. As a child George worked with his father, José Galdino, making useful pots, jars, and planters, but at fifteen or sixteen, drawn by the work he calls decorative and representational, he began painting his uncle's pieces. He still does, and now at thirty he conducts the face-to-face business and explains the stock's variety to customers. We interviewed him at length, and this is how George José Silva de Freitas introduces Alto do Moura, providing a clear overview:

"Originally, *artesanato* in clay commenced with Mestre Vitalino, who was the pioneer in the creation of figurative art. Soon after Vitalino came Manoel Galdino. These two, we can say, established the principal schools because both began with different styles, right?

"While Vitalino worked in depicting the culture of the Northeast — everything that takes place in our region, giving importance to the droughts, the lack of water, and the matter of Lampião and Maria Bonita — Manoel Galdino began with another tendency that was more surreal. It was an art that was more *abstract*, right?

"So abstract that there were pieces that he would make that even he didn't know the significance, right?

"So, he would leave it up to the interlocutor, the one who would see the piece and analyze it and say, Oh, this piece represents this.

"And then another would say, No, for me it represents this.

"So, like that it was a really abstract art, right? An art put out there so that the one who is analyzing the piece becomes its critic through the understanding that each person has about the world.

"And that is how it is. There are two principal styles. Then the second generation comes, of Luiz, my uncle, and my father. So they started giving refinement; we can say it like that.

"They started to improve the *artesanato*, they started to refine it, also in the matter of painting. In the past Manoel Galdino's pieces were the color of clay, raw, natural. There was no painting.

"And then they started giving it continuity. They started improving it and at the same time creating new pieces.

"And nowadays the entire neighborhood lives off the *artesanato*, right?"

George, with a grip on the rich local idea of tradition, doesn't describe continuity as repetition, but as a constant process of change, of refinement, improvement, new creations — and expansion. He goes on to say that the original two families have been joined by many more so that today the art helps to sustain, through its continuity, improvement, and expansion, seventy percent of Alto do Moura's population.

With regard to Galdino's line in particular, George says that today the one who works like Mestre Galdino is his son Joel, though, troubled by drink, he rarely works: "If he wants to work, the only one who works exactly like his father is Joel Galdino. Nobody else. Because that is an art that is very distinct.

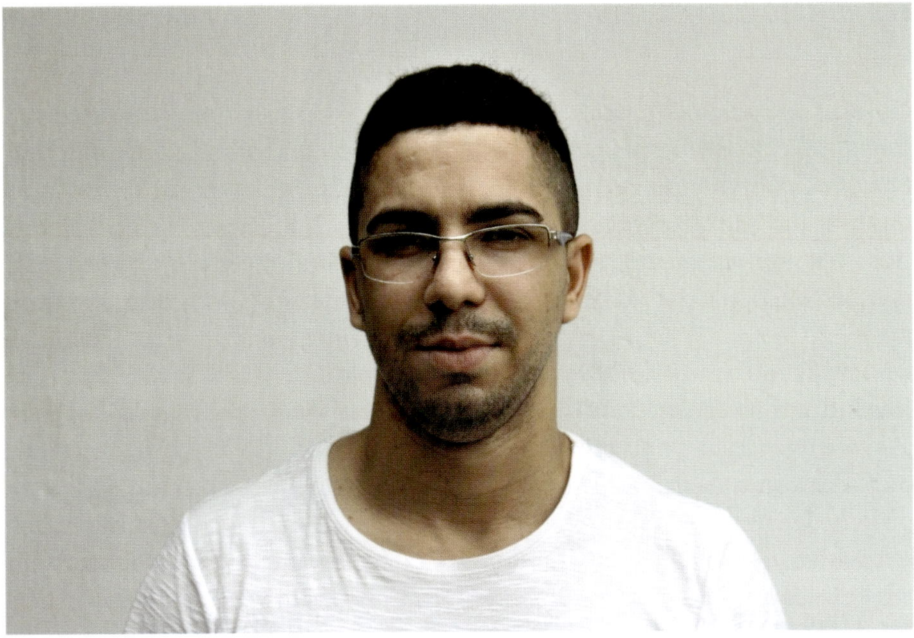

George José Silva de Freitas, 2019

"My uncle Luiz can do it. His work is excellent, but he makes so many things. And nowadays most people prefer to follow the Mestre Vitalino line, which is more commercially successful, the line of figures like the *forró* trio, Luiz Gonzaga, these things that represent the culture, you know.

"So, basically, at this time, the people focus on Vitalino's line and work within it because it is more commercial, more attractive to more people."

Consistently in Alto do Moura, as well as Tracunhaém, more artists and more of their customers prefer the work that is more natural in form and more familiar in subject. One line is dominant, made by more, sold to more.

In a position to know, George describes the business end of things:

"The appreciation for our art that exists in people's minds, it is strong. But now, in practice, when you talk with the artisans you find that, in reality, business is sliding down. I am talking about the matter of sales, right?

"Everyone appreciates, appreciates, but the majority of people who come into our ateliers, they don't buy. They satisfy themselves through a photograph.

"Nowadays, everyone has cellphones, they have their digital machines. So, they get here, find a piece beautiful. They take a photograph and leave. Nowadays it is like that."

Luiz Antônio complained comparably that in the past people entered his shop, inspected patiently, and bought a piece to take home, but now they come, don't bother to greet him, take a quick snapshot — a variety of digital theft — and flee. George continues:

"The sales are falling because of this, you know. It looks like people satisfy themselves by taking a photo of what they like, and not by having the actual piece.

"So, in this way I observe that, for the last five years, sales have fallen much. I am not going to say that the art will finish. It is never going to end. The *artesanato* will continue for the entire period of human existence on the earth, you know.

"But now the artisans tend to be discouraged, because they make many items, they work really hard, but, unfortunately, the sales, they are falling each year.

"This also has to do with the number of artisans. In the past it was a restricted number, right? In the beginning: Vitalino and Galdino. Then appeared the second generation. But nowadays practically the *entire neighborhood* is involved in *artesanato*.

"That is not bad. I am not condemning this, right? But while my uncle works with quality, making work that is well done, there is another artisan who is thinking about volume, about quantity. While my uncle makes ten, fifteen pieces, there will be another artisan who is making one hundred or two hundred per day.

"Obviously the finish will be different. There is a contradiction. One makes it well, the other makes in volume.

"I think that because of this the market is disturbed. And it is a matter of prices, right? Everyone is looking at the financial aspect of things.

"When customers get here, they like a piece and ask for the price, and we tell them. For example, this one costs one hundred *reais*.

"Then there are many people who will say to our faces, You attack us. This is robbery!

"I have heard that several times, people calling it robbery. It does not allow us to explain the price.

"Sometimes we try to explain. We say, This piece here was made by a master. The high price has to do with the finish. If you were to compare this piece here with that one there, you would see that the finish is much better. But, unfortunately people don't want to hear that. They declare it to be robbery and they go away."

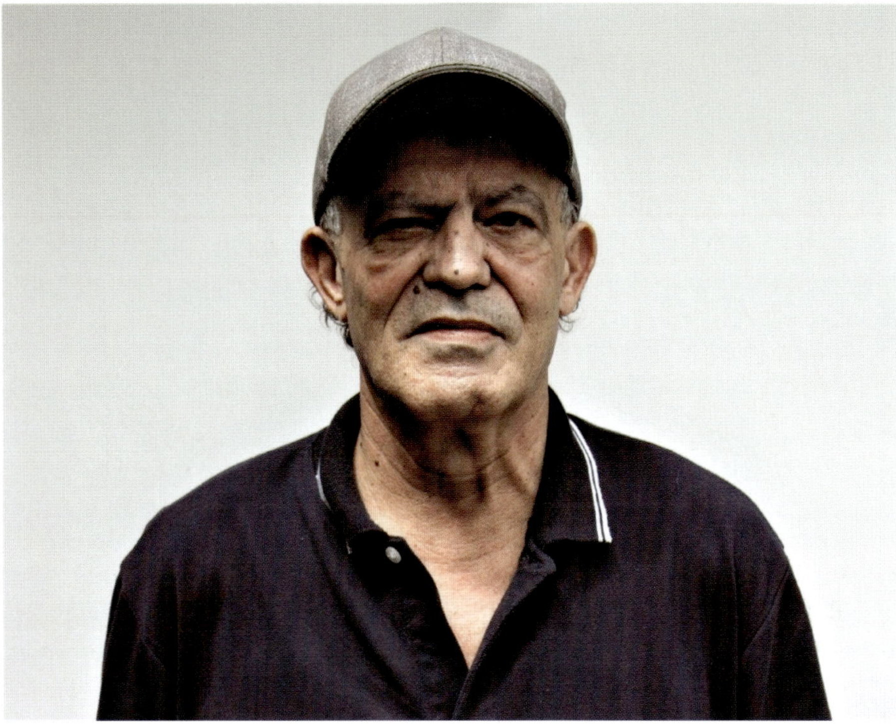

Luiz Galdino, 2019

George laughs and continues:

"If everyone knows how to make it, then go away and make it yourself.

"That's the thing, What we don't know how to make, we have to pay for. Obviously.

"For a personal example: we have a car, a motorcycle. When it breaks, do we know how to fix it? We do not. We have to pay a mechanic, right? The mechanic will resolve the problem in five, ten minutes.

"Why? Because he studied, he knows the entire machinery of the car.

"Some people don't value this thing of knowing, but the master has worked for a lifetime. He can make something quickly that others could never make. He deserves a higher price than he asks."

Luiz Galdino, the master who knows and makes, was always busy, elusive. He had no interest in answering the same old questions in another fleeting interview, but George convinced him that we were different and set up an appointment. Luiz asked us what we wanted to know. We answered by asking him what he wanted to say, and Luiz Galdino de Freitas was off, gathering enthusiasm as he took us on a looping trip toward understanding:

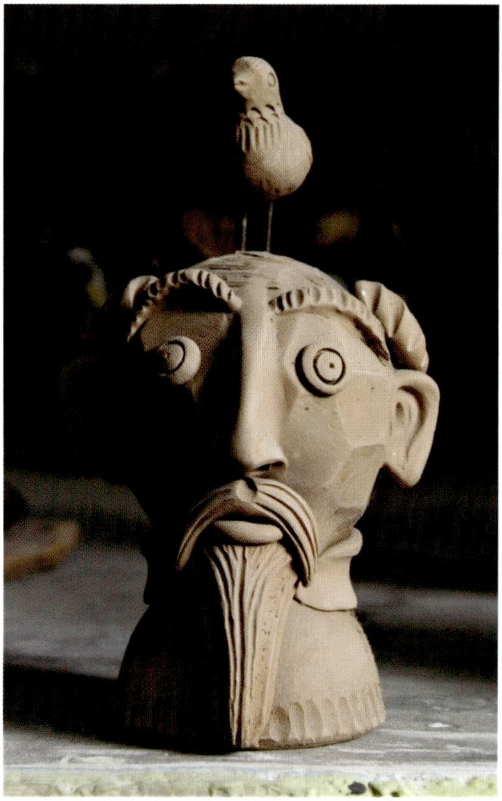

Saint Francis, by Luiz Galdino, 2019

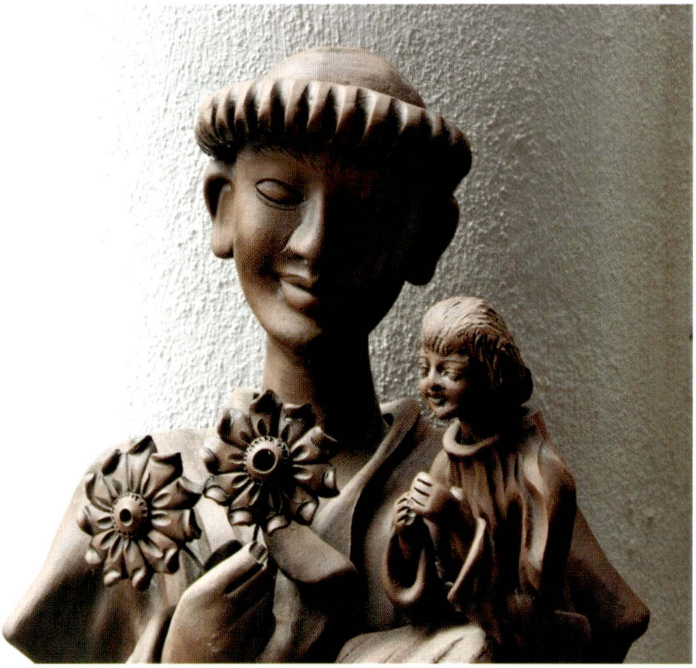

Saint Anthony, by Luiz Galdino, 2019

"Our roots are in São Caetano. My uncle Manoel Galdino, due to financial necessity, he had to dislocate from there. São Caetano is about twenty-three, twenty-four kilometers from here, from Alto do Moura.

"And he started working as a construction worker for the municipality, an employee. But he already had a notion of handling the clay, of making some *strange* things that would come to his imagination, an art that we can call surrealistic, right?

"He did not try to make what Vitalino was already making. He left the municipality and began working from home.

"Alto do Moura had a steady flow of visitors, and they started to praise him, to buy his works, precisely to give him support. And he started to loosen, to make more, and he died in the art.

"Now, he didn't die happy. He died in a state of disease. And where was the municipality? Where were the public powers to provide him some support?"

In those days, Luiz says, "Incredible as it seems, I was already at work, helping my mother with utilitarian ware. She made water jars, pots, vases. The family was needy, and she put me to work. I started with seven, eight years of age, making pots by hand, not on the wheel.

"And I noticed this already. By seeing the nimbleness in the art of Mestre Vitalino, I recognized that I had a distinct aptness for figurative work. Like my uncle, I also did not want to make what Vitalino used to make. I already had a tendency toward modernization. My touches today are different from the various followers of Mestre Vitalino, yet his is an art that serves me well.

"And if I try to make what my uncle used to make, I can do it. But I don't like to make copies. If I have to, I can make similar works, but always with different touches, right?

"But out of financial necessity we have to work in production to be able to survive. Like an assembly line; we could say it like that.

"So, someone who has a store says, Make twenty of these. So, we don't always work like an artist works. An artist makes one work at a time out of something in the imagination.

"The painful problem is to make money. That is true in all artistic realms, music too, for I am also a musician. I once made a vinyl disc, singing *forró*, you know. It was hard to sing and sell, and we must deal with many things to see if we can keep on surviving, sailing the boat, right?

"Here comes my complaint, because it is also part of the story, right?

"The work is like this. It is twenty-four hours, always attentive, you know. I work sixteen hours per day, so eight hours are for rest or maybe a trip to the city, but it has been a year since I have been to Caruaru.

"And life is like this.

"I wish that every day I could be creating a new thing. A different piece, never repeating, but we have to fill commissions from the stores to be able to pay our bills: water, electricity, food. Things of that kind. We have to work within these constraints.

"The pleasure would be immense if I could just make a piece and leave it there. Then begin another. That would be to live very well, you know.

"So, our art would give us great pleasure if things were like that."

Luiz Galdino has come to a conclusion. It is quiet for a moment, space opens for a question, and we ask about his creation of the portrait of Vitalino that stands beside the house museum. Luiz says, "It was I who made it. I was always a revolutionary. And I really like him." He points to a large image he made of Vitalino, selling at his stand and holding *A Banda de Pífano*, and continues:

"It looks really like him. It looks just like him, you know.

"It looks just like him, and he would sit like that at a little stand in the open-air market, here in Caruaru. It was his way; he would spread the little statues and remain there all day, Mestre Vitalino.

"I have a vague memory of him. This uncle of mine, Manoel Galdino, he had a little bodega, a little shop that sold sugar, milk, *pinga*" — *cachaça*, white lightning.

"So, Vitalino would walk around with the *pífano*. He would lean on the counter, start to drink, and then he would start to play the *pífano*. He didn't know how to play too well, but he would play anyway, right?

"So, a very strong memory I have of him comes from when a torrential rain fell. And the road was full of holes; there was no paving, no pavement.

"And with that fall of rain and him so drunk, he was stretched out in the street, the water was covering him up, and it had swept away the cloak he used to wear, a cape.

"And the *pífano* was lying there, and he was drunk, and I screamed, Hey, he is going to drown!

"The memory I have is very strong." (Luiz was about five.) "I was so scared, and such memories *mark* you, right? When you have a fright, it marks you.

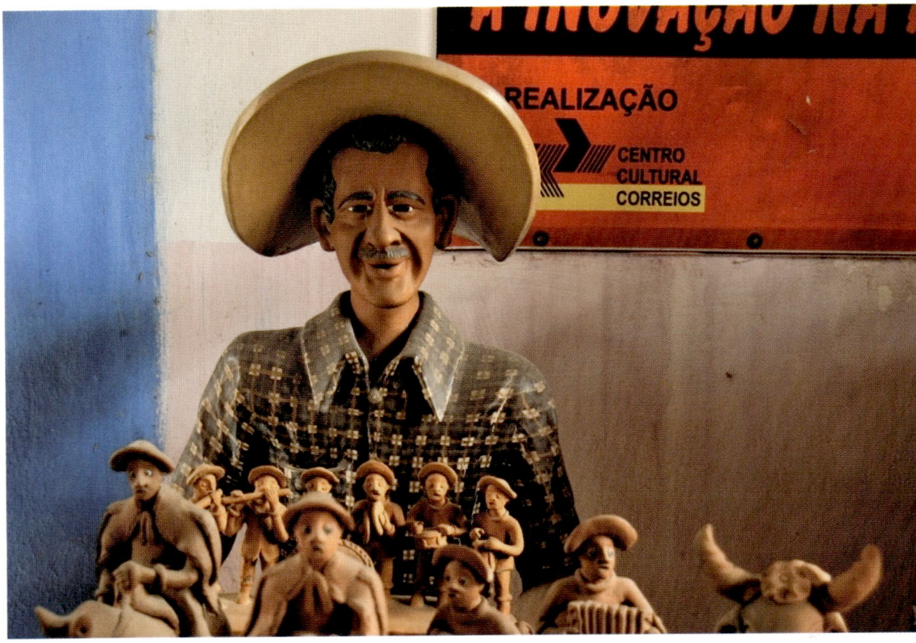

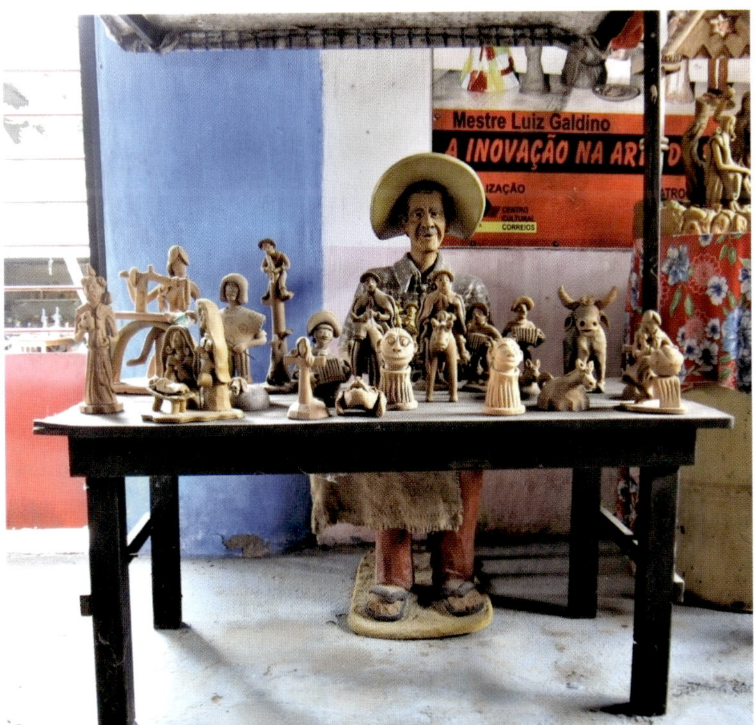

Mestre Vitalino in the market, by Luiz Galdino, 2019

"Anyway, there are memories. And another thing I want to say about Vitalino is that he was generous and charming.

"Because when the neighbors who wanted to deal with the clay started to imitate him, he let them set their tables near his in the market. And that made him very happy, right?

"Now, my uncle, no. To the contrary, he would create a piece, a work of art that he had created out of his own vision. He made that piece, and nobody could follow him. Nobody followed him because his work was totally different.

"So, I like both of them. But now I am giving much importance to Mestre Vitalino with much respect.

"Today, many generations live off Mestre Vitalino's art. This is what brings us food, enables us to survive in the end."

One line dominates as a result of the familiar, repeatable character of the work, the generous, genial character of the progenitor, and the wide, ongoing commercial appeal. Luiz has wound around again to the painful problem of money. Economic issues interest him and his expenses are high. Some artists, like Carmélia, work in their homes. Others, like Luiz Carlos, have shops by their homes. But Luiz Galdino has an expansive operation, a store on the main street with room for living above and space behind that brings him some rental income during the festivities in June. His profit has to support George as well. Now Luiz holds to the topic and says:

"Things are bad in this exact moment" — May 29, 2019. "So ten years ago we had a leader called Luiz Inácio Lula da Silva. He supported our art. Brazil took off and things were really good.

"But now another man has taken Lula's place, and Brazil has started to close itself, started to close itself. Things are bad, and our art — we are not earning much money.

"Then the youth, the young people are looking for work in business, or carrying sacks of flour or cement. They are looking for work to be able to survive. And they are leaving the art, so only the old ones are left.

"So, who is going to hire a worker who is sixty years old? So, these artists are going to have to swallow it and die in the art.

"But for the youth now, really, it is just a cellphone in the hand and the internet. They are seeking other things.

"And the demand for *artesanato* has decreased much. Much. Here in our region some people do come, but when they invented this thing so everybody was able to take a photo, that ended us.

"Now it is easy for people to take what I make. They arrive, don't even ask for permission, and they take my art before I have even sold it. That disturbs us very much.

"It is difficult. It is difficult.

"I don't like to mourn, but it's the truth. You have to tell the truth.

"So, let me explain things to you. I am modest. I don't have any cowardice. But I live outside of society here. This is part of my story too."

Luiz tells us that he lived for thirteen years in Recife, trying to make it as a musician, striving to promote and sell his own *forró* recording. He returned to Alto do Moura, having built from experience an understanding of commerce. Then, elected president of the Association of the Clay Artisans and Residents of Alto do Moura, Luiz set out to apply what he had learned to benefit his small town:

"Man, it is a heavy weight to deal with the community. But I began with a certain compassion, knowing that it was a hideous task. I assumed the presidency and began talks with the state government. I worked with barbaric drive.

"Around here there were still many small farms and the people were living from agriculture. So, I bought a modern harrow and a brand-new tractor. I modernized the Association, and I sought to bring happiness, hosting parties, dances for the people to unwind and let loose.

"Then comments started to circulate that I was doing all this to get rich.

"And I was living in a small, rented house, and this hurt me.

"I completed my two-year term, and left the Association. My successor was elected and until today the Association is in operation.

"And what else did I do? I created a cooperative with a much *wider* vision. I created a cooperative with a headquarters, and I got a truck to transport our merchandise to São Paulo, Paraná, Rio Grande do Sul. A very beautiful project.

"And I even went to Chile to promote our work in a market they have there at the Catholic University in Chile, which is a well-known market.

"And then during my international trip, they were talking against me.

"The cooperative ended because there was much jealously in the directorate, much jealously, you know.

"So then I disengaged.

"Then I said, You know what? I am going to take care of my own life. I stopped paying rent and bought this house. It was a hut, but I worked on it,

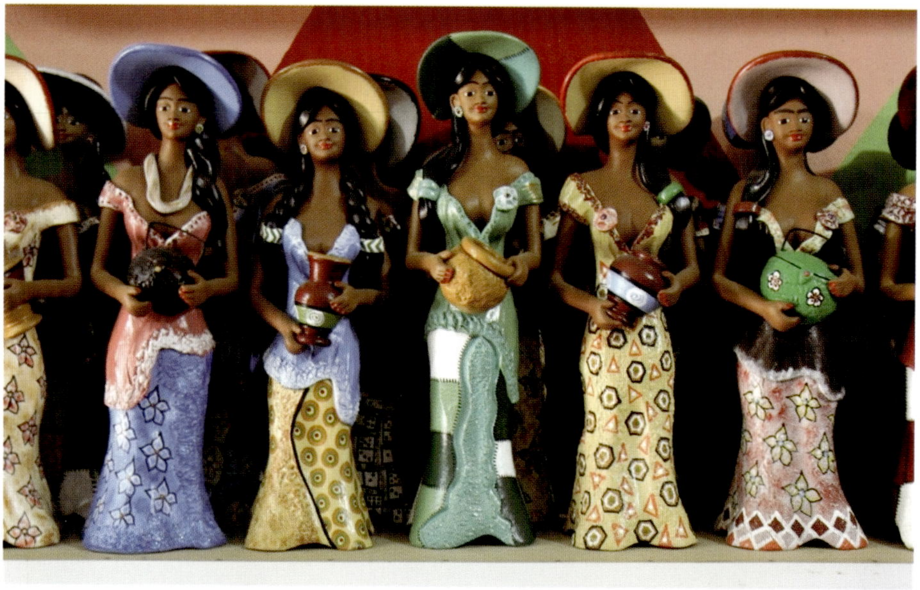

Bonecas, made by Luiz, painted by George, 2019

opened a store, and some money flows in to provide a background for my life, you know.

"It was a personal choice. I didn't have to fight with the mayor and the council members anymore. I learned to mind my own business.

"I isolated myself. I lived inside my house, every day creating a new piece.

"It was in that period when I created the *bonecas*."

So, the wheel-thrown, molded, and painted *bonecas* have arrived. Dates given by people for that event range from 1995 to 2008 — the inconsistency suggesting that business deals struck in private didn't become public knowledge. In the telling, the origin tale of the *boneca* is ordinarily framed in general terms, without specific names, but if a local individual is credited — or blamed — for introducing the *bonecas* to Alto do Moura, it will be Luiz Galdino, who lives outside of society, or Manuel Eudócio's son Silvano, who has a store a few doors along the street to the west and no longer lives in Alto do Moura.

Everyone has an opinion about the *bonecas*. Vitalino Neto hates them. Ademilson and Marliete dismiss them as art but acknowledge that they supply cash to people in need. Young men are more positive. Luiz Carlos's son Helton called the *bonecas* "a good thing," and Terezinha's son Thiago said:

"The *bonecas* were very good, because we started to sell more, much more. Many tourists, they would come to my mother's store and say, I want these pieces. They would arrive and already start buying. They would empty the store.

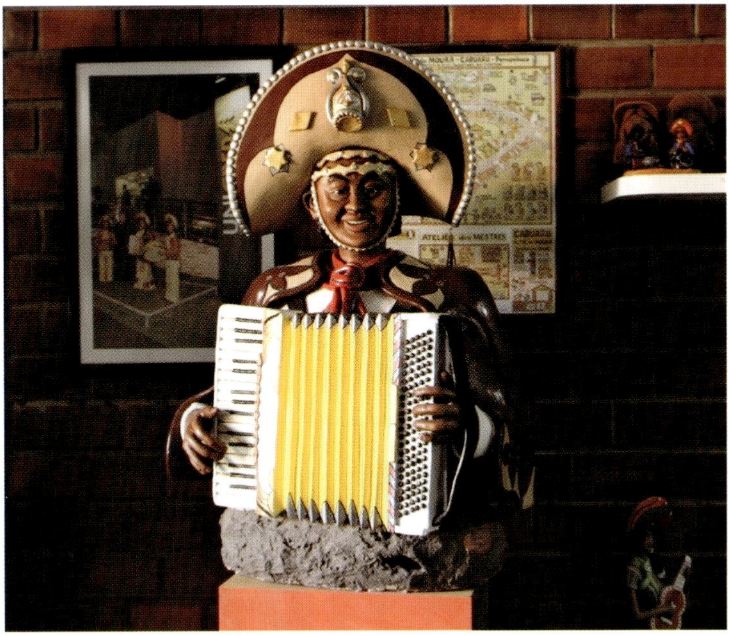

Luiz Gonzaga in the showroom of Luiz Galdino's atelier, 2019

"With time passing sales weakened a bit, but when it started in two thousand and three, it was very good. Many people balanced themselves here in Alto do Moura through these *bonecas*."

Luiz Antônio's son Leonildo, a man with a mind for business and an eye for art, advanced a nuanced argument, saying:

"The actual *boneca* is from the Vale de Jequitinhonha in Minas Gerais, a place like Alto do Moura. The *boneca* is a creation from there.

"But here in Alto do Moura, the artisans are quicker and they developed the piece more. It did not originate here, but the artisan of Alto do Moura has a tremendous capacity for creativity.

"So, the *idea* for the *boneca* is from Minas Gerais, but the painting is in the style of Alto do Moura. It is made of our clay and painted in our style, and many of our artisans survive from the sale of the *bonecas*."

Among the *bonecas* brought from Minas Gerais to serve as models in Alto do Moura, some were unattractively caricatural. They were copied at first but over time in the hands of Alto do Moura's artisans, the ladies became lovelier, their finish and painting finer. During the period of improvement, say 2007 to 2014, we noticed that *bonecas* replaced images of Lampião in the shops for travelers in the airports. Sales at the time were ascending swiftly, but since then they have slowly declined.

Luiz Galdino's repertory is extraordinarily diverse. *Bonecas* are certainly not all that he makes, but he can make them rapidly, George can paint them beautifully, and a stream of money follows them into his shop. Luiz remembers:

"The *bonecas* gave me better living conditions. We were living a bit fitfully, financially, economically.

"So, I saw that the Northeastern woman was being depicted despicably, with ragged clothes and no makeup.

"So, I got the idea of making her a real beauty, even when she was working, right? A cloth bundle on her head, carrying a child in her arms, yet beautiful, elegant, a smile on her face.

"Because we see photos of the populace of the Sertão, always suffering, right? Their clothes worn and torn.

"It is delightful to show the beauty of women. And the men, they shouldn't be left behind. So we have to make the men good looking too. It has to be like that.

"When I was making the *bonecas* more beautiful, a change came over Alto do Moura. Other places have this same human tendency.

"The neighbor who sees that you are doing well, he seeks to make what you are making, trying to see if he can make it too.

"This is also delightful. If it was not good to begin with, there would be no imitators.

"The *boneca*, she has done well for me. But I never escape from the actual history, here in the Northeast, in Brazil. I mean pieces like the bandit Lampião. I sell many Lampiãos.

"I am constantly shaping the clay with my hands. And when I am making a piece, I feel really good, because you are seeking, flinging your talent into the piece.

"And it is always interesting, always delightful."

Luiz swings his talk, back and forth, between financial pains and creative pleasures. This time he ends in delight, sitting in satisfied calm. We are all smiling, and he tells us that he was born in 1957 and recalls from earliest childhood a crisis of hunger.

"In Alto do Moura," he says, "we did not starve, thanks to the United States. Packages of milk, brown rice, a yellow kind of cheese, corn meal — all would come from the United States to Brazil to help those who were starving.

"So, I have affection for the United States. I am alive because of the United States, and I am sending big hugs" — *abraços* — "to the Americans.

"And I thank you and congratulate the two of you. You are happy, marvelous, and I end with a big hug for you from Luiz Galdino of Caruaru, Brazil."

Part Two

BEZERROS

Rural Bezerros

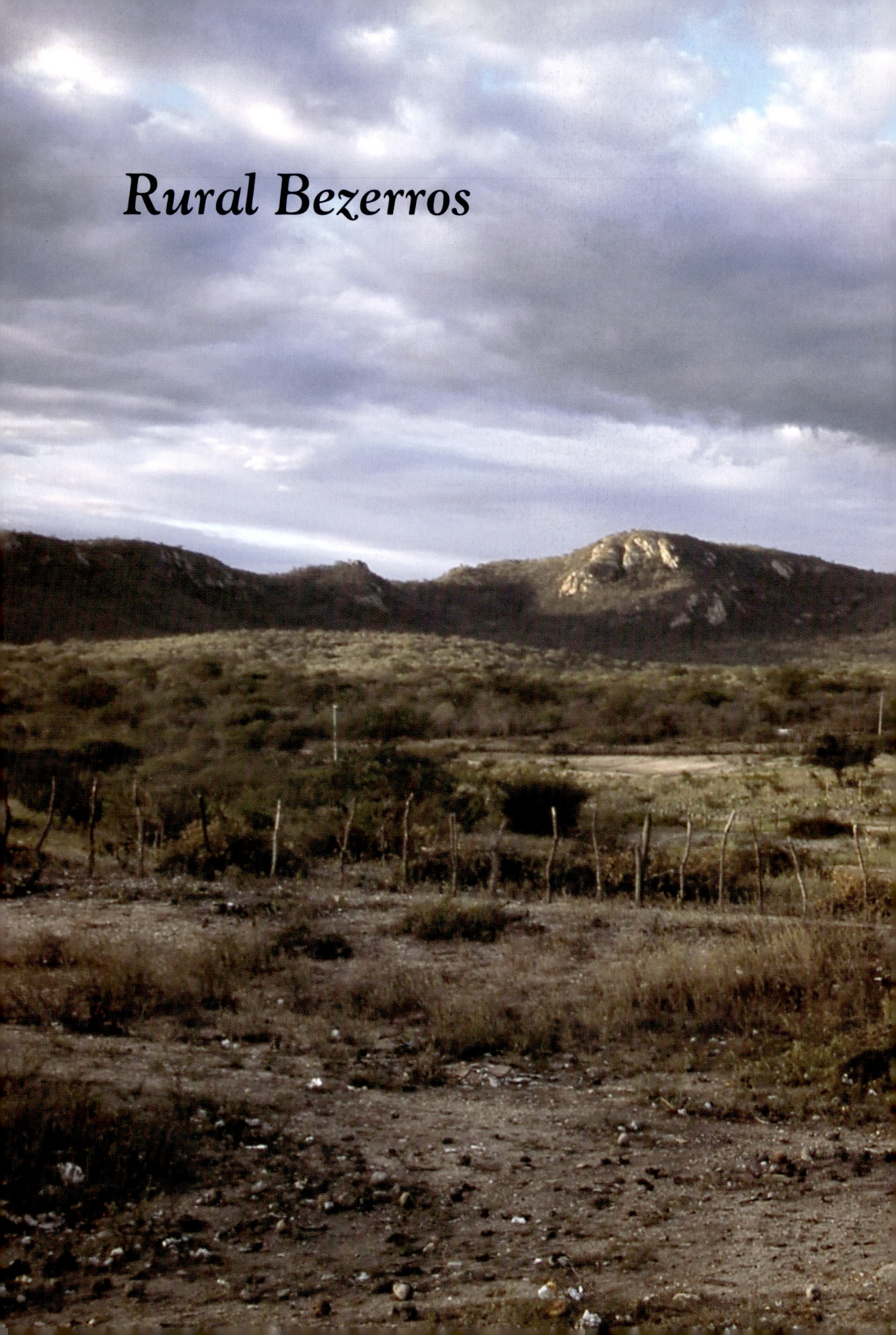

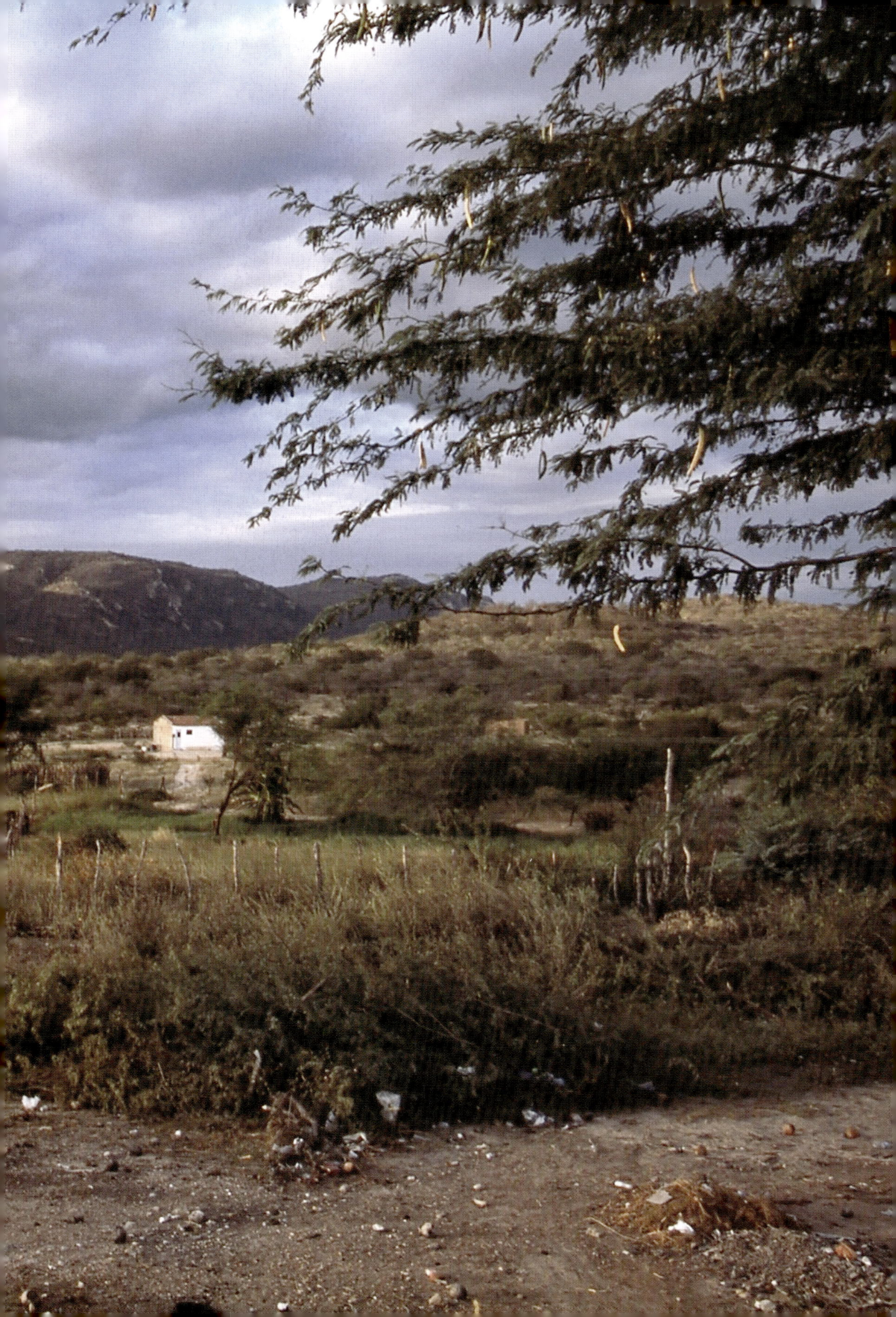

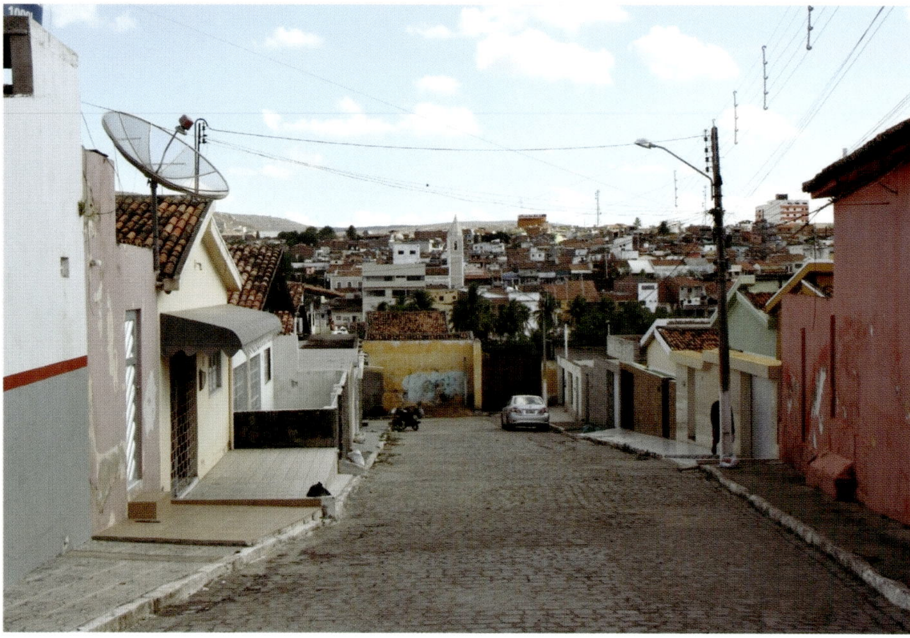

Bezerros: the city center, 2021

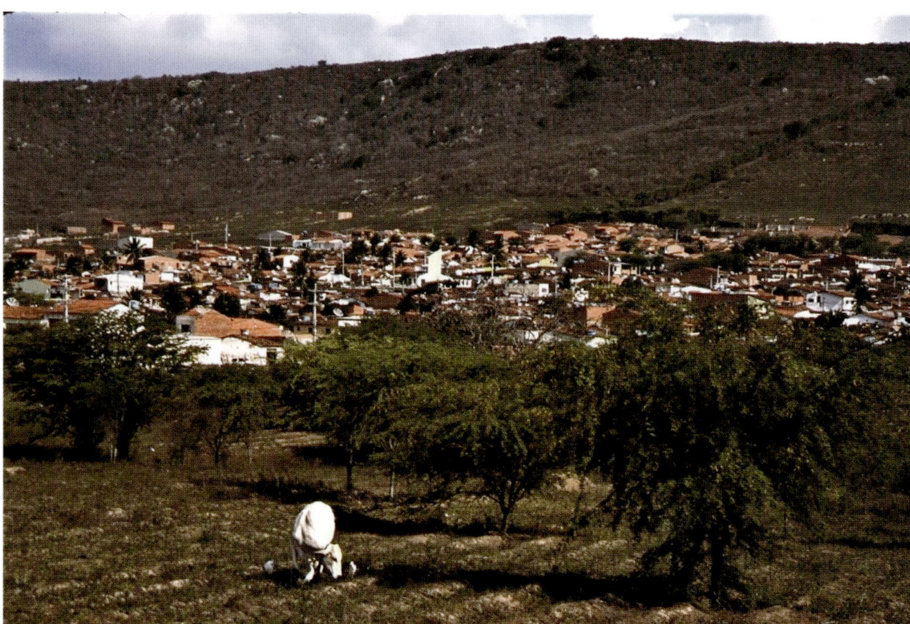

Bezerros: the southwestern outskirts, 2014

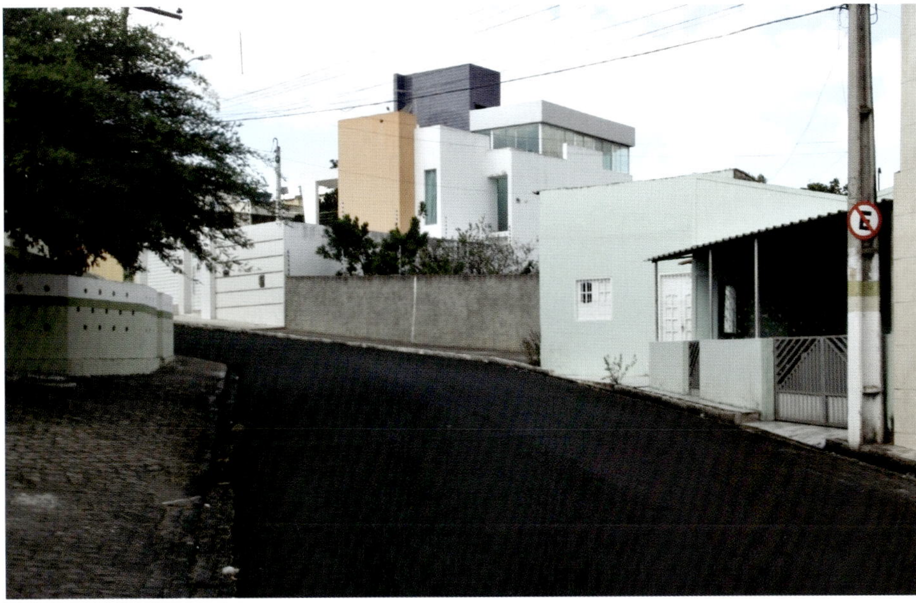

City street in Bezerros, 2021

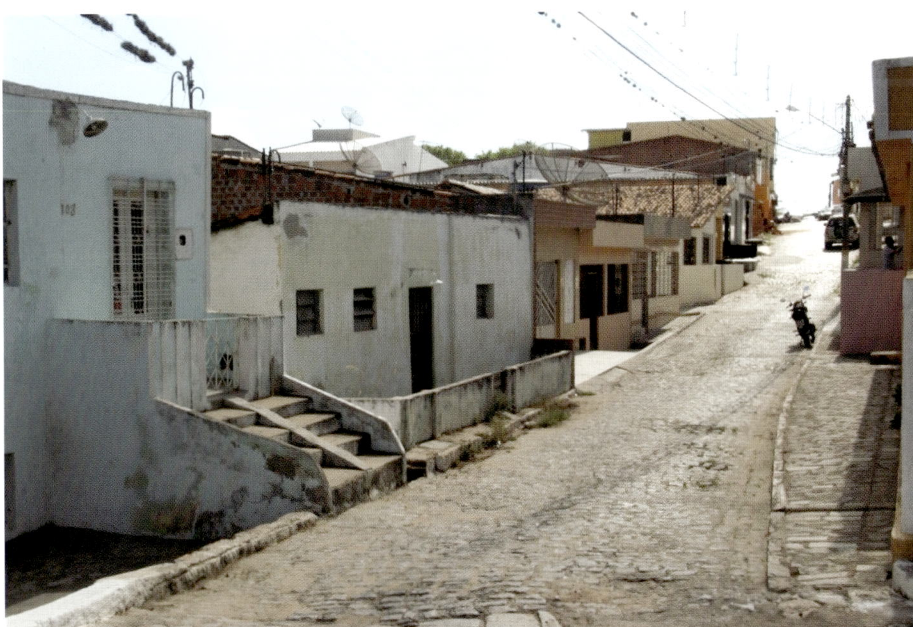

City street in Bezerros, 2021

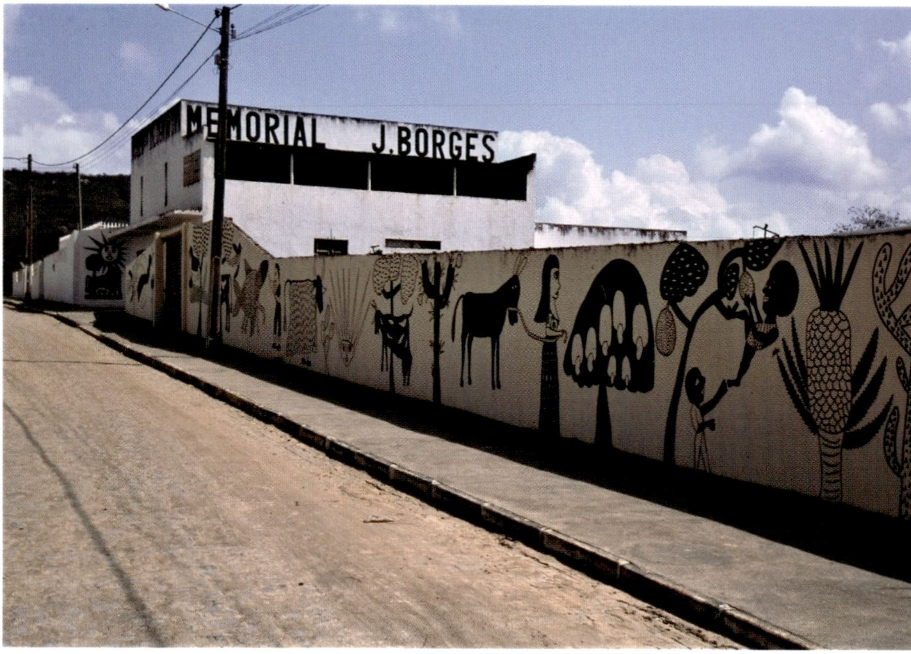

The J. Borges atelier, 2014

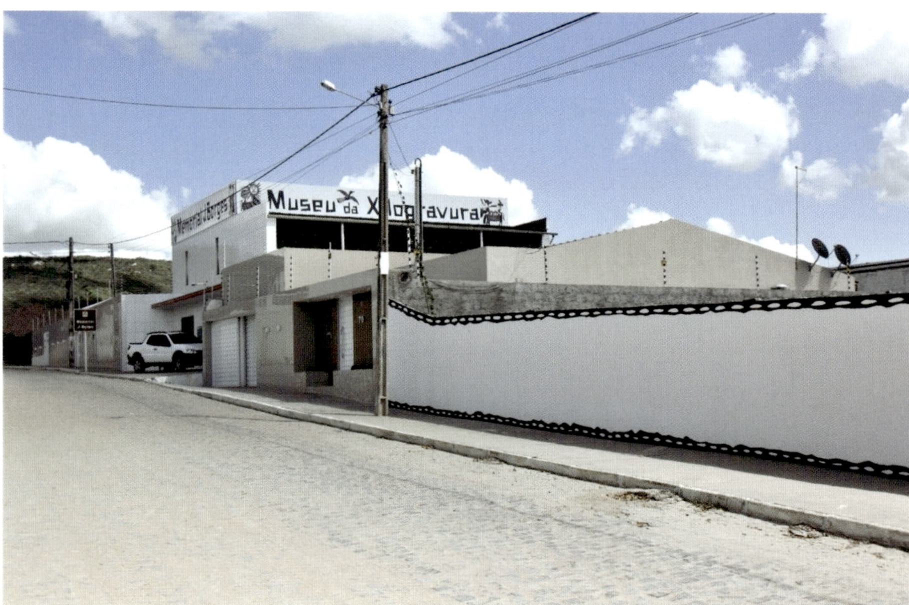

The J. Borges atelier, 2019

19

J. Borges

On the service road south of the highway that sweeps past Bezerros, there are five shops where woodblock prints are made and sold. Grandest by far is the shop of José Francisco Borges, called J. Borges, who holds a place in the history of woodblock art like Vitalino's in the history of quotidian ceramic sculpture. The shop stands uphill so its sign — black on white like a woodblock print — can be read at long range. When we were first there it read, Memorial J. Borges. Five years later, though there was no notable change in the man himself, it read, Museu da Xilogravura, Museum of Woodcut Prints. Like Mestre Vitalino's house museum in Alto do Moura, the shop is an anchor in space and a draw for visitors.

Uphill, the door on the shop's side opens into a spacious showroom, where goods in four categories are offered for sale. Shelves along one wall pack tight with chapbooks called *folhetos* or *cordels* — *cordels* because the *folhetos* were draped on strings, *cordas*, for sale in the market. Measuring in the neighborhood of eleven by sixteen centimeters, the *folhetos* carry stories, information, and advice in poetic form. Typically, they have a woodblock print on the cover; inside the poem breaks into three or four stanzas on each of eight consecutive pages. J. Borges is not the author of all the *cordels* for sale, but early in this century he claimed authorship of 251 titles, and he is still at it.

Within the showroom, stacked on tables or hung on walls, there are woodblock prints in a range of sizes, suitable for framing. They are the main attraction for visitors. In addition there are books illustrated by J. Borges and booklets he has written that don't conform to the format of the *cordel*. Then

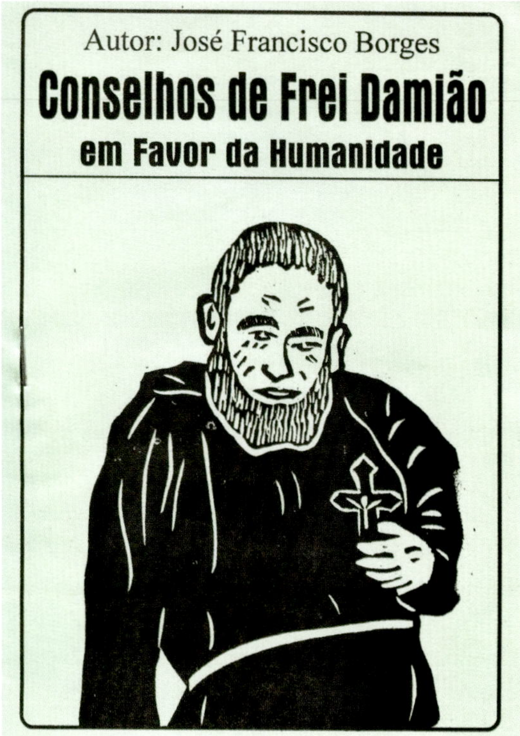

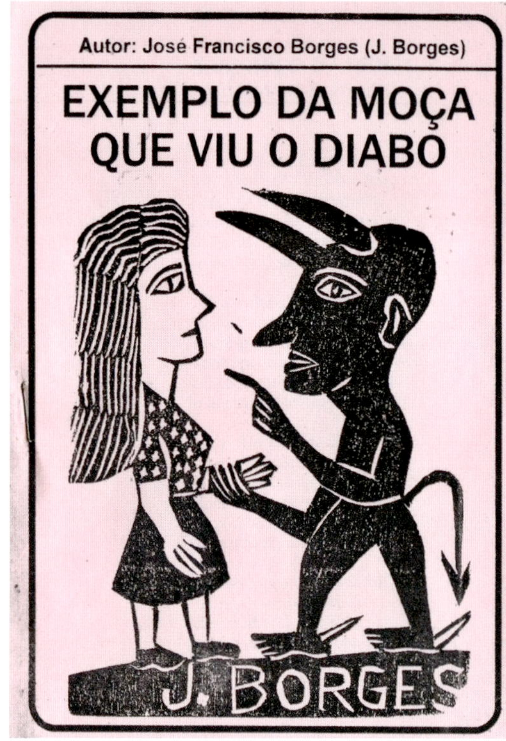

Cordels by J. Borges: Frei Damião's Advice, The Lady who Saw the Devil

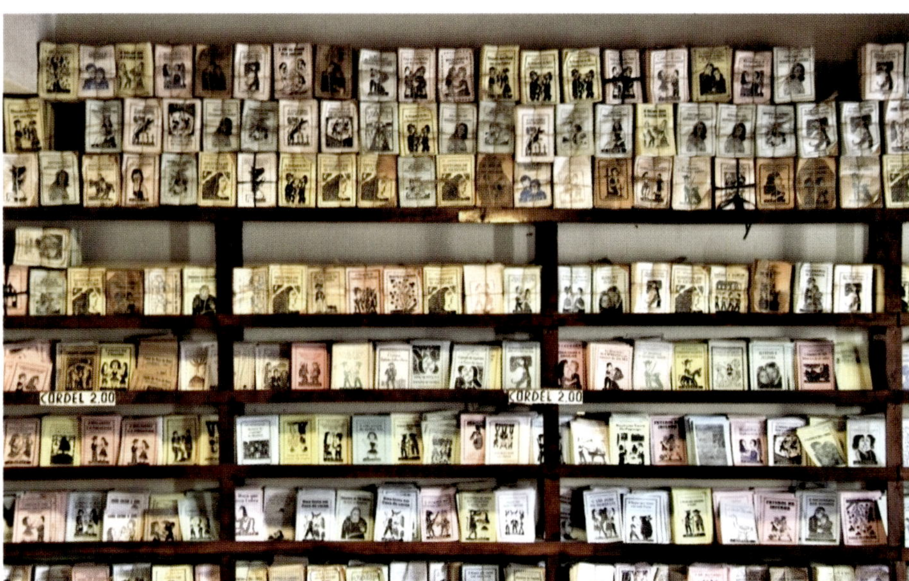

Cordels for sale in the atelier, 2019

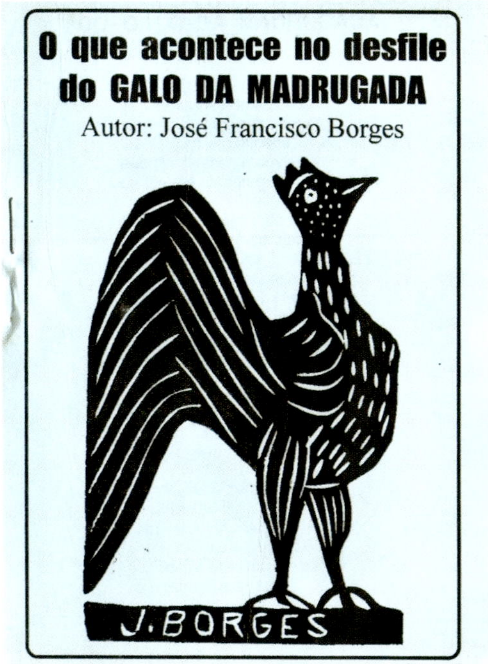

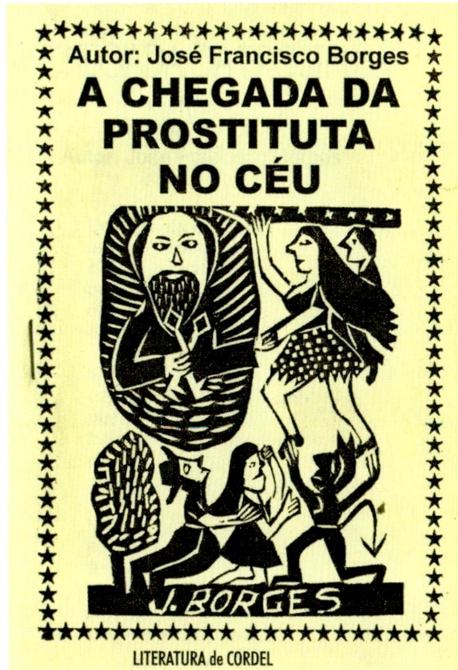

Cordels by J. Borges: Parade of the Cock of the Dawn, The Prostitute's Arrival in Heaven

the fourth commercial category contains items printed with woodblock imagery: magnets, tiles, tote bags, and notebooks.

Behind the showroom, another large space fills busily with young men and women at work, inking and printing. On the building's uphill side, a narrow gallery opens on the left, a narrow workshop to the right. A door in the back of the gallery leads toward the family's home, so the master can enter and turn left into the small, quiet workshop, sitting there to compose, to write the texts for *folhetos* on slim cards, each one cut to receive the stanzas for a single page.

Or J. Borges can come from the back and pass into the showroom to keep an appointment, sitting, say, at a big table to explain the *literatura de cordel* to a crowd of school kids who will get him to sign a *folheto* at the lecture's end, while their teacher wisely buys a few prints for the master to sign. They are not expensive. A small one costs only five *reais*, a larger one ten, the largest one ninety. For the equivalent of ten dollars, the teacher can take home a small treasured selection.

The shop's operation, from the purchase of materials through making to selling, is managed by the family. J. Borges has eighteen children, one daughter, seventeen sons, and some of the sons have wives who are quick with math,

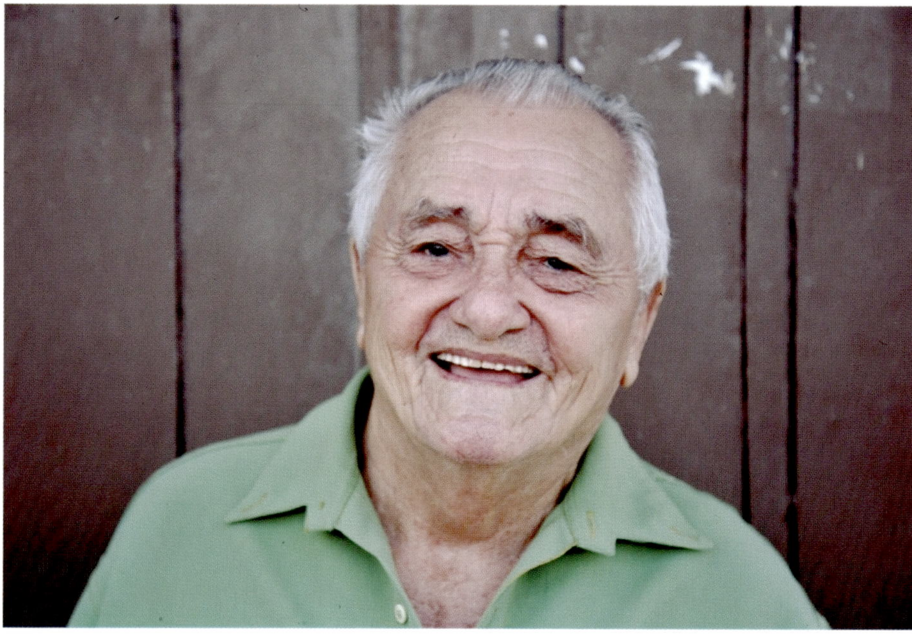

J. Borges, 2015

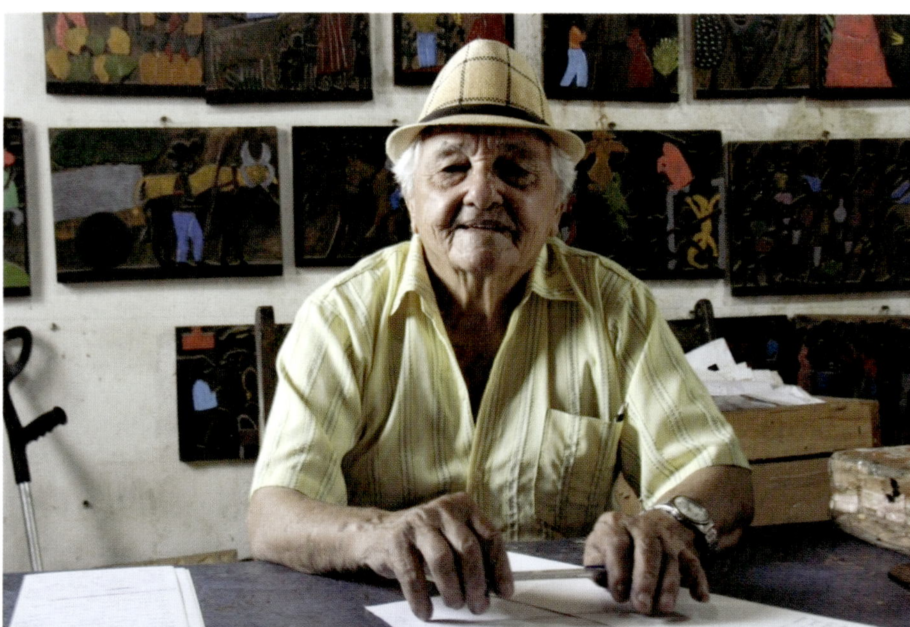

J. Borges, 2019

canny about business. Things rest in the capable hands of the next generation; J. Borges is only occasionally present. On our first visit, he was absent, and knowing he was seventy-eight, we chose not to call him out of his home and bother him with yet another interview. Eventually we chanced to be there a few times when he was too, and we found him to be relaxed and unhurried, witty and warm in conversation.

When we met J. Borges for the first time, we knew something about him from talk with his stepson J. Miguel and his nephew Severino Borges, but we had learned the most by reading his autobiographical writings, and we will let him introduce himself by translating the first section of one of them. It comes from a booklet he produced. Titled *J. Borges: Seu Perfil* — His Profile — it lacks bibliographical data, but from internal evidence the booklet seems to have been printed in 2008, and the text written around 1990.

For the record, this autobiographical piece was printed earlier, in 1996, in the excellent selection of his verse and works, *Poesia e Gravura de J. Borges*, edited by Silvia Rodrigues Coimbra. And a different autobiographical statement appears in *A Arte de J. Borges: Do Cordel À Xilogravura*, edited by José Octavio Penteado. Both books hold facts that enable enhanced interpretation.

So, here is the life that J. Borges wrote, broken into paragraphs at the points where he broke it into stanzas of six cadenced lines, *folheto*-style, toward the beginning, and then into paragraphs of prose for the rest of the way. J. Borges:

"I was born in the municipality of Bezerros, Pernambuco, on the twentieth day of December in 1935, the son of Joaquim Francisco Borges and Maria Francisca da Conceição, agricultural laborers in that municipality. With eight years of age, I was already working the land with my father.

"At the age of twelve, I was strong, smart, and healthy. From the farm in Sítio Piroca, very happy and entertained, I would go to sell the baskets that I myself had woven.

"I spent the day at the market" — in Gravatá a town to the east — "and in the afternoon I returned, bringing some pots my mother had bought and drinking brackish water from the wells I passed along the way.

"I would buy *rapadura*" — molasses candy — "and bread in the market, and that snack gave me the strength to climb the hill of Serra do Sapato that makes you very tired.

"And on that road I remember the big beautiful market and the girls with their hair bound in ribbons. That was my childhood for those who read and believe.

"In my pocket I already had a *folheto* by Pavão, bought from João de Lima for little more than a penny, and on arriving home that was my entertainment.

"I would lie in a hammock, reading and rereading the *folheto*, though time remained for me to go and see Fia, my first girlfriend who liked me very much.

"And every Monday I would go to school, taking a used book in a sack, blue pants, white shirt, and sandals.

"In ten months I learned to read, write, and count, during the best time in life for learning. Then I was forced to stop, schooling was finished, I could not study anymore.

"On leaving the school, I greatly lamented having to abandon the instruction of my teacher David Antônio Milanêz before I had learned division" — the last step of mathematical mastery.

"From that date on, I sold *jogo de bicho*" — the animal game, lottery tickets for gambling — "for three years. After that I began harder labor. During the summer I would go south in Pernambuco to work in the sugar mills. And I continued that until I entered the *olarias*" — the workshops for clay — "that made paving bricks and roofing tiles. After that I commenced to make wooden toys like Mané Gostoso" — a puppet that flips between sticks — "and miniature pieces of furniture, and I ended by making common furniture for adults.

"Gathering penny after penny, once I had 600 *cruzeiros*, I went to Recife and bought *folhetos* to sell in the markets of the region. This is in September of 1956.

"From then on I did a mix of work. I did not stop going to the markets with the *folhetos*, but in the middle of the week I worked in construction as a mason, carpenter, and painter.

"Always putting more faith in poetry, I ended up abandoning the other professions to dedicate myself with all of my power to the literature of the *cordel*.

"In 1964, I published my first original *folheto*, which was for me the realization of a great dream. Until that day I lived in timid insecurity about my writing.

"It was the veteran poet Antônio Ferreira da Silva, a colleague on the journey, who read that original piece and said: Go publish it; around here many are successful with work less good than yours.

"His words excited me to see my name as the author on the cover of a *folheto*. That was what I most craved as a new poet.

"With this first *folheto*, named *O Encontro de Dois Vaqueiros no Sertão de Petrolina*" — the Encounter of Two Cowboys in the Sertão of Petrolina (a town to the southwest in Pernambuco) — "and illustrated with a woodblock print by Mestre Dila of Caruaru, I had much luck, selling 5000 copies in 60 days.

"From then on I commenced writing with more enthusiasm, and unable to find printing plates for my *folhetos*, I decided to plane a plank of wood smooth and make my first woodblock print with a drawing of the facade of a church. I used it to illustrate my second *folheto*, titled, *O Verdadeiro Aviso de Frei Damião Sobre os Castigos que Vem*" — The True Warning of Frei Damião about the Punishments to Come.

(In 1965, J. Borges made his first woodcut, the abstract elevation of a church for the cover of his second *cordel*, a sort of back-country *Inferno* in which Frei Damião, Padre Cícero's successor, warns sinners of every stripe — drunks who don't provide for their families, nagging and jealous wives, brothers who lust after the sisters, mill owners who exploit the workers, Protestants who deny salvation for Catholics — about the horrors of the oncoming Day of Judgment.)

"This *folheto* brought me more income than the first one. Its immediate success inspired devotion in the public that surrounded me in the markets.

"Even today, 26 years later, if I print 5000 copies, I will sell them quickly. The *cordel* is not written by chance, because the poet works to express his imagination and gain success with his story, searching for a way to record the story and distribute it to the world beyond.

"This is why the *cordel* must be written in a way that touches the emotions of the people who will read or hear the tale, whether it is about love, slander, religion, politics, tragic events, suffering, revenge, or other themes.

"In 1972, the landscape painters Ivan Marquetti and José Maria de Sousa came from Rio de Janeiro, and when they were visiting me in Bezerros, they saw me making prints for the covers of *folhetos*.

"They really liked my work and ended up commissioning many prints in larger sizes with themes of my own choice.

"After receiving those prints, they became enthusiastic admirers of my work. They took the prints to show to Ariano Suassuna, a writer and professor of theatrical studies, and he was also enthusiastic about the themes that I had captured. In his opinion, I gained the name of *Melhor Gravador Popular*" — The Best Folk Printmaker.

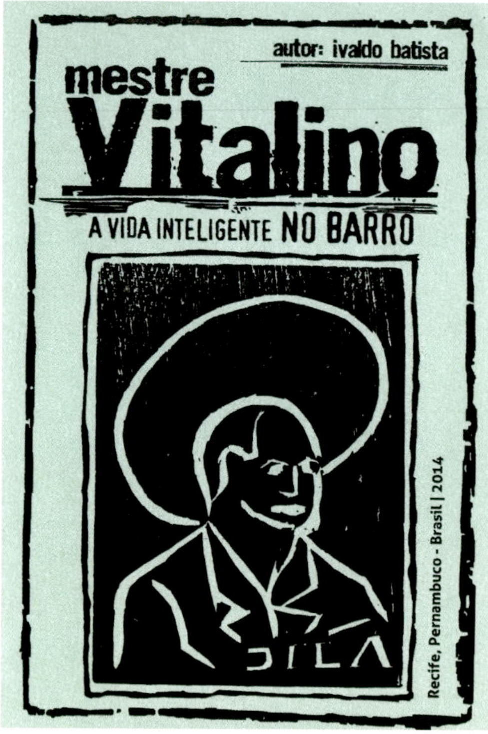

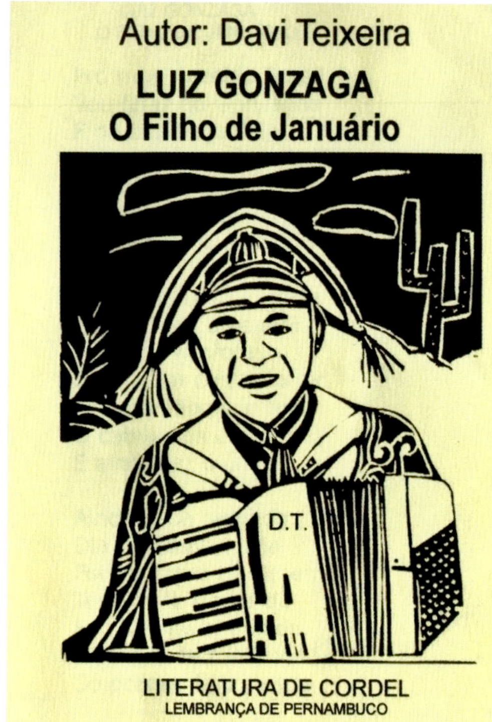

Recent *cordels* about Vitalino (2014) and Gonzaga (2008)

"This, for me, was and continues to be one of the best things that has happened in my career as an artist in the grand struggle of the day to day."

The life of the laboring man rolls through two key moments. In 1964, J. Borges became a creative participant in the tradition of the *cordel* that, in his view, began in Caruaru late in the nineteenth century and spread through Pernambuco, Ceará, and Alagoas, making the *folheto* a cultural marker of the Northeast, like Gonzaga's songs and Vitalino's statues — and there are *folhetos* in print today about both Gonzaga and Vitalino. In 1972, at the suggestion of sophisticated artists from the wealthy South, J. Borges doubled his production, beginning to make larger prints while continuing to make small *folhetos*. Six years later, in 1978, when Candace Slater was doing the research for her superb study of the cordel, *Stories on a String*, she talked with J. Borges. By that time, she reports, his big prints had achieved international acclaim, and she praises him for not moving to São Paulo to get rich, but remaining in Bezerros so he could continue with the *cordels*.

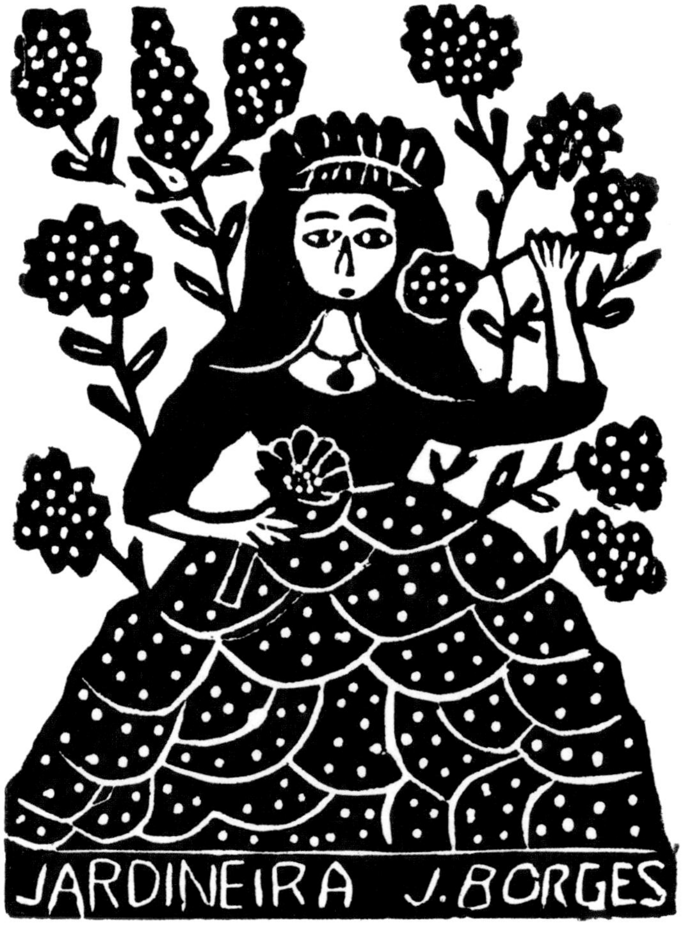

The Gardener, woodblock print by J. Borges (22 × 16 cm), 2015

The seventies were a time of change. Several of the *cordel* poets interviewed by Candace Slater feared that their tradition was nearing its end. Forty years after the publication of her excellent book, the *cordel* has, indeed, lost cultural centrality but new *folhetos* on new themes are still appearing. For J. Borges, the change in 1972 was one of the best things that had happened. The large prints brought him fame and comfort, but the shift to the print was for him a matter of expansion, like, say, Manuel Eudócio's addition of the *Reisado* to Alto do Moura's repertory. J. Borges made the new and kept making the old. For the woodblock artists of the next generation, though, the arrival of the print marked a change as dramatic as Vitalino's creation of the first quotidian clay statue. For them, the *folhetos* were left behind just as utilitarian pots had been left behind. Big prints pointed the way forward.

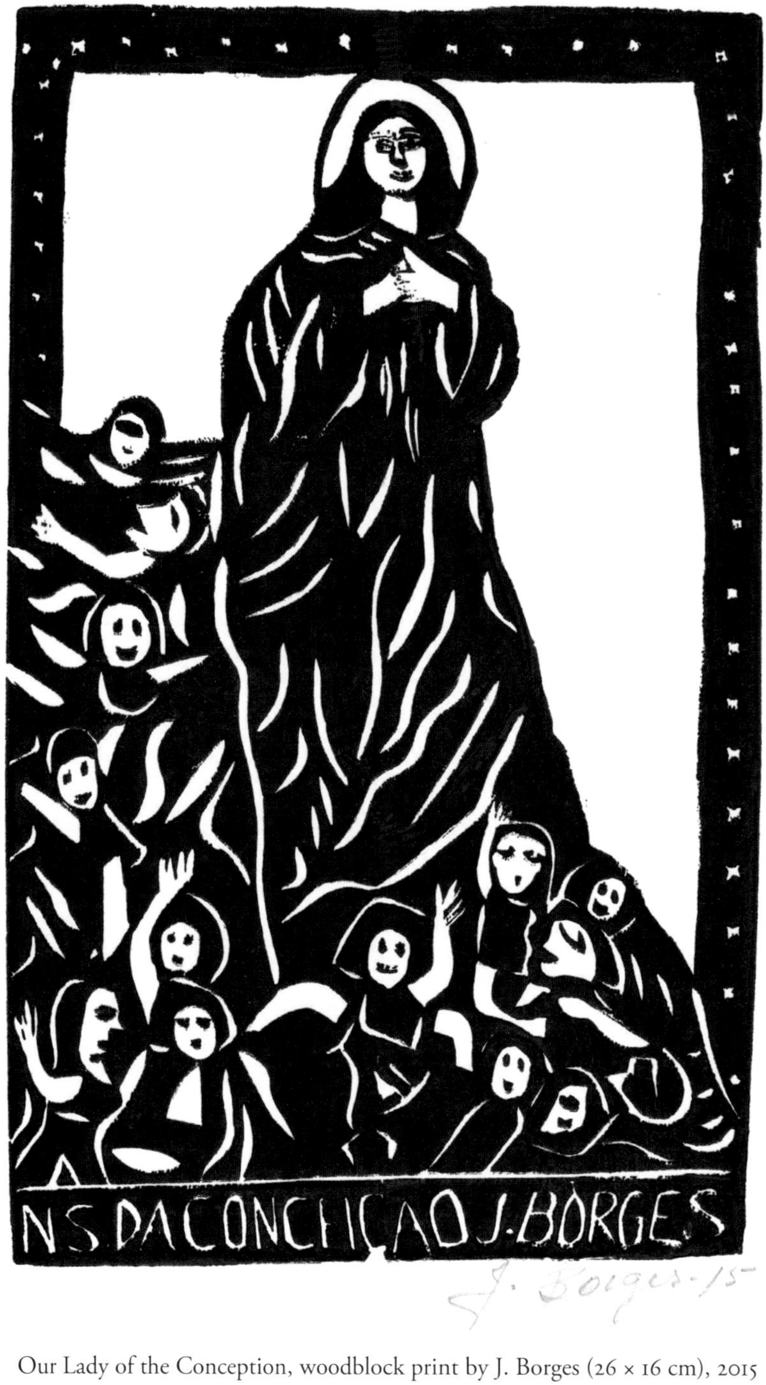

Our Lady of the Conception, woodblock print by J. Borges (26 × 16 cm), 2015

Late one afternoon in the spring of 2015, we are sitting in his shop with J. Borges. No tasks cry for his attention, and we ask him to tell us about change in his tradition. The recorder clicks on. He smiles, thinks, and then, a smooth and practiced speaker, he crafts an elegant statement, at once expanding and holding to the topic of change:

"In the nineteen fifties the demand for the *cordel* was great, you know. It was very great. The *cordel* was sold to ninety percent of the population.

"Almost everyone here was illiterate. They couldn't read, but they would buy *cordels*. Now, why buy it?

"Because there were many sellers in the plazas, in markets, during public celebrations. The sellers went where there were events, singing the poem of the *cordel*, reading it, explaining it, accompanied by gestures and much banter.

"The public would laugh and buy a *cordel*. But these people started to leave. The sellers started going away, and by the nineties the *cordel* came to the edge of the grave.

"But now the *cordel* comes toppling back, because the student population supports the *cordel* movement. The faculty, the teachers encourage the students, so I only sell when the students come.

"But in the markets, in the plazas, it is finished. The public today doesn't want it anymore. The old folks, they retired and died. The young ones don't want it anymore.

"Everyone today, they know how to read and they want paying employment. The others are scoundrels, bums who don't want to work.

"So, what has changed is the demand. The *writing* has also changed. It has changed much.

"Because today there are poets called urban poets, and they write nothing worthwhile. Their *cordels* are graceless, unappealing. They don't have rhyme, they don't have meter, they don't have sequence. The topic is mixed up. It makes the public crazy.

"So, the *cordel* has to have its limits, its metrics. It has to have strong rhymes. It has to have a *topic* that is well controlled. The episodes pick it up, one from another, going back to fetch it" — the topic — "and bring it forward, completing it to give dispatch to the story. If you don't do that, it's not a good *cordel*.

"And today what they write is a salad. They write from top to bottom, from bottom to top, and in the end they make a little booklet and call it a *cordel*.

"But inside there is nothing worthwhile. What I think has changed is this.

"Now, when the *cordels* were going down, the prints were coming up, and the prints brought change because they were sold to the elite. And from the seventies to now the print has popularized itself.

"After the print came, the *cordel* became somewhat popularized. And today the *cordel* sells some, but the print sells *too much*.

"Today who buys a print is everybody. In the past, only the erudite would buy a print, people who wanted a picture to hang in the home. They would buy it.

"But today the *masses* buy prints.

"I don't want to say that it was me, but I was the one who opened the path, from the seventies to now, making prints and selling them at the price of bananas — *cheap*.

"Because the public says, Your work is so well known, through the entire world, and why is it so cheap?

"And I say, Because I don't live off nature, nor do I live by selling one print a year. I want to sell every day.

"And if I am going to sell every day, then the print has to be priced low to be bought. So, the *doutor* and the farm laborer can both buy it. The high executive and the lowly factory worker both buy it. They all buy the prints.

"You must have a reasonable price, and everyone should know that they are *able* to buy it, right?

"And so the print popularized itself, and the themes of the print are the themes people want. The themes have not changed. In my case, the themes I explored in the seventies, I explore them today.

"I work within my region, what happens here and in the folklore of the region, and the legends, and the day-to-day of the people, the sadness and happiness, the celebrations. All of that I explore, so it never changes. In my case, it never changes.

"I have traveled abroad, and I have seen many beautiful things, but I want to make things from here. Those who come from elsewhere, they want to take home something from here.

"I represent the Northeast, the region of the Northeast. And what I have heard others say in the United States, in France, in all the places — I have heard that the richest place in terms of folk culture is our region of the Northeast in Brazil.

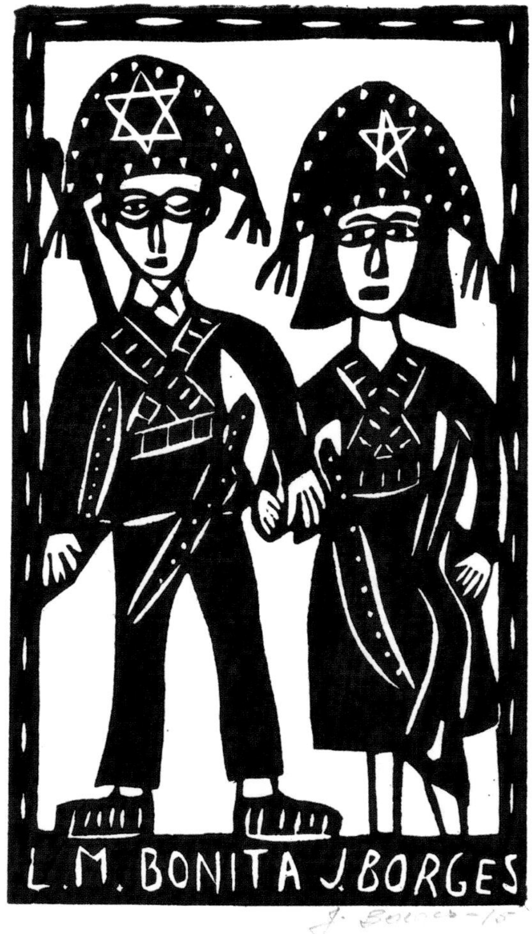

Lampião and Maria Bonita, by J. Borges (26 × 15 cm), 2015

"Because it was a region of suffering in the past. To be able to live then each person started to make something. One takes a piece of timber and makes a statue. Another takes a ball of clay and makes another statue. Another would take a slab of wood and make a woodcut.

"Everybody would make something, and that is why the tradition of art emerged. And now the children and grandchildren continue to make.

"So, we have Alto do Moura near Caruaru. It has more than a hundred years of *tradition*. From Vitalino to now, everybody is making perfectly.

"We have Tracunhaém with saints in clay. We have Passira with embroidery. We have Poção with lacework. And here the woodblock print is in command, here in Bezerros.

"We have much art in the Northeast. We maintain the tradition of the past, and those who explore the Northeast, they make the same things, though each one works differently.

"I make Lampião. I make it here on paper. He makes it there in clay.

"But it is the same thing."

With a great laugh. J. Borges stops. He is sitting, beaming with the satisfaction of a tale well told. We congratulate and thank him. He has given this book a central text that connects backward to the artists of Alto do Moura through attitudes and themes, while preparing, through an account of the prints, for the next generation of woodblock artists, first among them his stepson J. Miguel.

20

J. Miguel

The loose line of shops on the road begins with J. Borges on the east and ends with J. Miguel on the west. José Miguel da Silva, called J. Miguel, works in the shop that J. Borges established in 1982, a couple of decades before, blessed with success, he moved into grander quarters. In the old shop the ground floor was for work; the family lived upstairs. J. Miguel doesn't live here, though his pleasant sister Marli does live above, descending to mind the shop in his absence, and J. Miguel continues to work in the spacious old shop where he once worked with his stepfather J. Borges.

J. Miguel draws and carves at a table in the middle, lit by the light from the open front door. He rises to print at tables on the right, then piles prints for sale on a large table to the left. Woodblocks and tiles printed with woodblock designs line the walls. The road past his shop leads to the Centro de Artesanato where a big statue of Manuel Eudócio's Captain stands outside and galleries inside display Pernambucan masterworks from Ibimirim, Tracunhaém, Alto do Moura, and Bezerros. Heading to the Centro or returning from it, visitors often stop at his shop and, J. Miguel says, they like to buy in a place where they can watch the artist work and get him to sign the pieces they purchase.

We spent time in his shop productively, learning the woodblock process, and twice we interviewed J. Miguel at great length. J. Borges speaks in the manner he considers ideal for the *cordel*, proceeding energetically while holding tight to the topic. J. Miguel leaps over connections to linger on narratable episodes, prompting us to fill gaps with transitional facts to get his story told.

J. Miguel's parents lived in a village near Bezerros, and he was born in Bezerros in 1961. His father worked in an *olaria*, as J. Borges did in his youth,

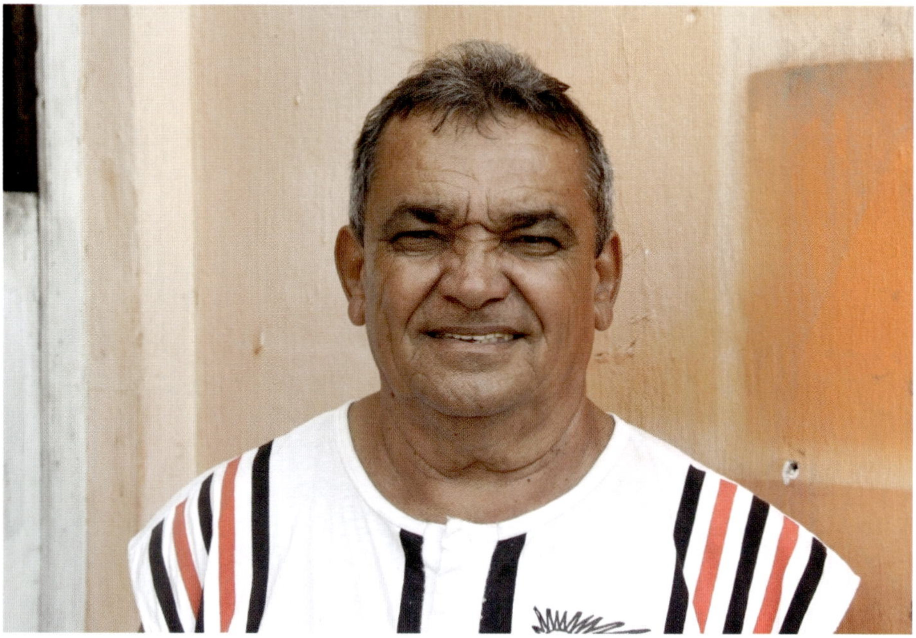

J. Miguel, Bezerros, 2019

making bricks and roofing tiles. When he died, his widow, Rita Maria, began laboring as a domestic servant in Recife where she met J. Borges. They married, she was his second wife, and she brought her three small children to live with him in Bezerros.

At the time, the shift to the print was about to happen, but it hadn't happened yet, and J. Borges was creating *cordels* and traveling to perform and sell them in the markets. Beginning at about eight years of age, J. Miguel occasionally traveled with him and he was helping daily in the shop. He recalls:

"I am his adopted son, but he is like a father to me, understand? He raised me. I grew up with him, and I have never worked with anyone else.

"I commenced, like, at less than ten years, but it was typographical work, right? Typographical work with my stepfather, typographical work. It had nothing to do with the woodblock prints.

"I was working with machines, presses, composing and printing the *cordels*. The illustrations I did not do at that time. I had no knowledge about how to make them. Who made the illustrations was J. Borges who also did the writing.

"I only did the typographical work, which was the part of the *cordel* done on a machine, understand? But every now and then I would take a little piece of wood and start drawing. I made some little pieces when I was ten years old, and I kept them."

J. Borges gave him scraps of wood to practice drawing, and helping in the shop with the printing of the *cordels*, J. Miguel became so interested that he snuck away to create a little *cordel* of his own, its tone admonitory and moralizing like his stepfather's second *folheto* in which Frei Damião warns of the punishments to come:

"I worked much with the *cordel* when I worked at the printing press with my father. And I invented my first story when I was still studying" — in elementary school.

"I took a piece of paper, wrote some little verses, and gave it a title: The Son Who Hit His Mother Visits Hell. I drew a boy, a man with a whip, and a woman being hit.

"It was not published. I signed it and put it in a little bag. If I had it today, it would be a relic. I did it all, man, the illustration and the story; there were four pages in my *cordel*."

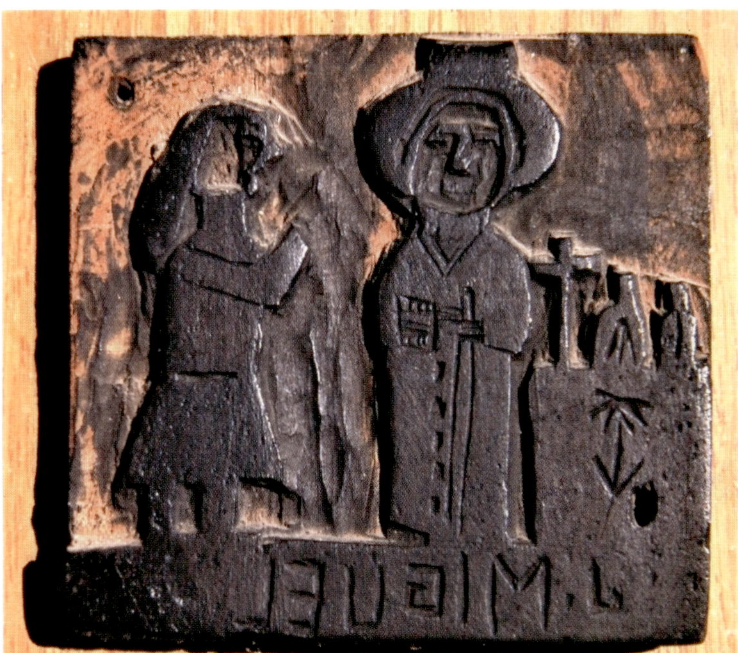

Woodblock with Padre Cícero, carved c. 1971 when J. Miguel was ten, 2015

Just like the artists of Alto do Moura, J. Miguel grew in an environment of serious work and exciting creativity, helping, imitating, and learning — not by instruction, but by sitting close, watching, and trying:

"I always kept my eye on J. Borges when he was making a woodblock. He was making and I sat next to him at the table. He worked at the table.

"And my mother said, If you want to try, take a little piece of wood and start learning.

"Oh, Mother, I said, I will start making. Then I made my first one. I drew it. I cut it.

"My mother showed it to him. It was a bird, *asa branca*" — the emblematic, white-winged bird of the Sertão.

"I was ten years old, and my mother showed it. She said, Zé, I want to show you this piece of wood, to show you what Zé is making."

J. Borges and J. Miguel both have José for their first names; both are addressed as Zé.

"Then he said, Yes, it is okay. Tell him not to cut himself. I always cut myself much. There's a secret to carving and if you do it wrong, the knife grabs your finger and rips the skin.

"All that blood. Ave Maria!

"He warned me often. I cut myself often.

"Then later he started to give me much support, and I started to advance.

"He encouraged me very much. My mother also, when she was alive, she also encouraged me much.

"And I had the complete support of J. Borges. He gave me a push, sold my little pieces, and publicized my work."

J. Borges gave J. Miguel's first woodcut to his close friend Giuseppe Baccaro who was building a collection of *cordels* for the Casa das Crianças, the Children's Home, which he founded in Olinda in 1970. J. Borges described Baccaro as a man born in Italy with a Brazilian heart. J. Miguel calls him "my first collector" and credits Baccaro, along with J. Borges, for giving him crucial support during a time of change for both his work and his tradition.

It is not part of his memory today, but it seems that J. Miguel made his first woodcut at the same time that J. Borges received his first order for large prints, around 1972, and it is certain that when J. Miguel was making his first small prints, J. Borges was making his first large ones:

"I made my first pieces when I was ten years old. At ten years I started.

"It was in the seventies that I started with little pieces. Later I started to make bigger ones. Bigger sizes, bigger.

"Then I started putting my pieces with his, here on a table. Tourists would come to him. Tourists always came here because they had knowledge of him. They would say, J. Borges, is this your work?

"No, it is J. Miguel's, my son. He is adopted, but I think of him as a son.

"Then they would buy it. That was good for me. It encouraged me much. I was already making prints in the seventies, so by the eighties" — when he was in his twenties — "I had a good series of big prints, thank God."

When J. Miguel was putting his pieces on his stepfather's table in this shop, just as the young Manuel Eudócio put his works on Vitalino's table in the market, the family gathered around the problem of a signature. J. Miguel is given the surname Borges in publications, on labels in stores and museums, and collectors frequently ask him to sign purchased prints J. Miguel Borges. He refuses; his name is da Silva. Early on, he signed pieces José M. Then in discussion with his mother and stepfather, he settled on J. Miguel. That caught the continuity, both being named José, but it skirted falsehood and permitted a distinct identity. He concludes:

"I made prints, many prints, my own. And I also made his. He would do the drawing and I would do the cutting.

"Then we stopped making the *cordel* because it wasn't selling anymore. That was in the seventies.

"Before that, some friend of his would say, Hey, this thing happened, you should write a *cordel*. Then my father would write it, make the illustration for the cover.

"After that it was only the woodblock prints, bigger pieces, and I kept on being interested, really interested. And I arrived at a point where I was making trips to Recife to sell my own prints. I also had customers in São Paulo, Rio.

"I started sending woodblock prints away, and I went on dedicating myself, right?

"I went from the printing shop to the big woodblock print. It has been thirty years or more, dealing with the prints, thank God.

"God first, the hands of J. Borges second, and today I live from art. And I like art. And I really like to make it."

Making is his pleasure. What he makes he calls art, but he doesn't call himself an artist. He is an artisan, making is his delight, and it is our topic now.

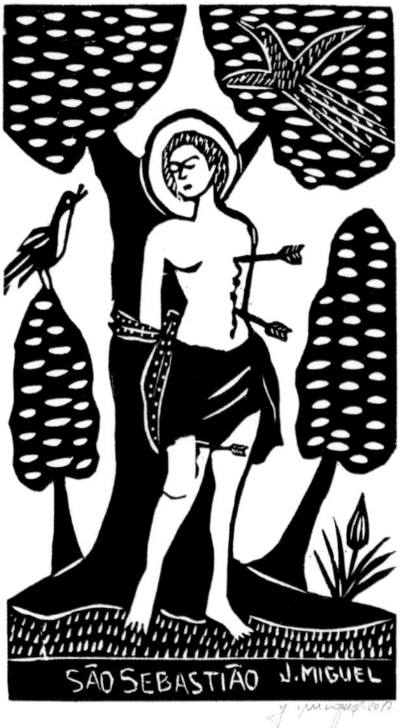

Saint Sebastian, by J. Miguel, 2017

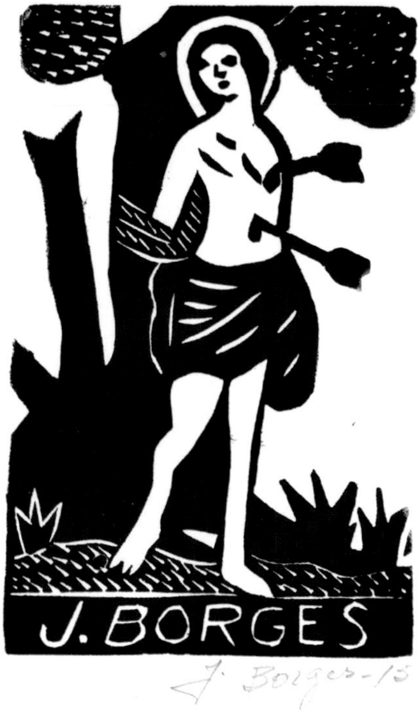

Saint Sebastian, by J. Borges, 2015

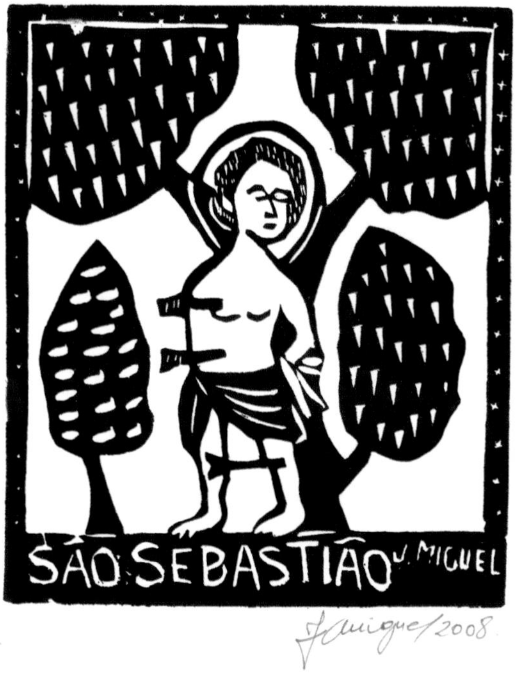

Saint Sebastian, by J. Miguel, 2008

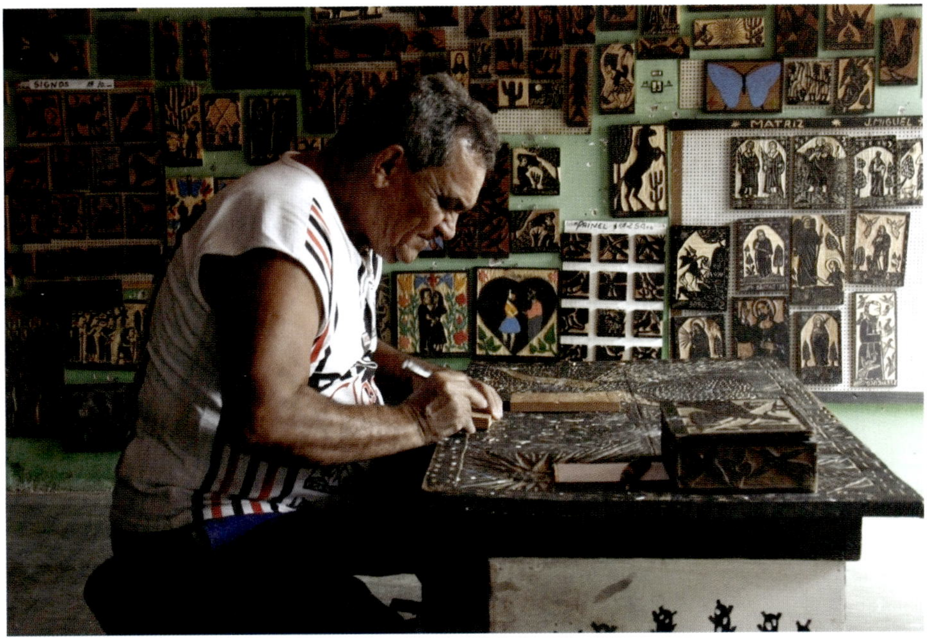

J. Miguel carving, 2019

J. Miguel begins with a board. The best wood is *umburana*, light and smooth in the carving, but the *umburana* trees that grow in the Sertão have become rare and endangered. Only the *santeiros* of Ibimirim are permitted to use *umburana*, so J. Miguel must content himself with splintery, knotty pine bought cheaply at a sawmill. It's the wood he can get and he planes and sands it smooth.

Some members of his family, J. Miguel says, draw a design on paper before setting to work, but he doesn't. He draws with a pencil directly on the wood, and he usually lifts the image out of his imagination. The unusual, very unusual, exception arises when he is commissioned to repeat an image from a photograph on a woodblock. Then he traces through carbon paper to get the proportions right. The common exception comes with the saints. He has to look at pictures to get the appropriate attributes. Even a professional *santeiro*, like Antônio Pimpo in Tracunhaém, will hunt through the internet to find the correct attributes for a saint he has not portrayed before. J. Miguel, by our count, has twenty-two saints in his repertory. He doesn't trace around found images, but he will look at a picture while drawing a saint for the first time, relying on his memory after that. Or, knowing the attributes, he will create a new image out of the imagination's wholecloth. His images of Saint Sebastian suggest his spread of options.

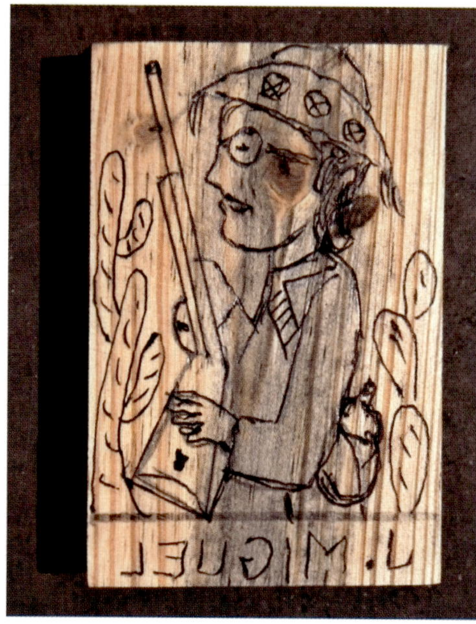

Lampião drawn on the block, by J. Miguel, 2015

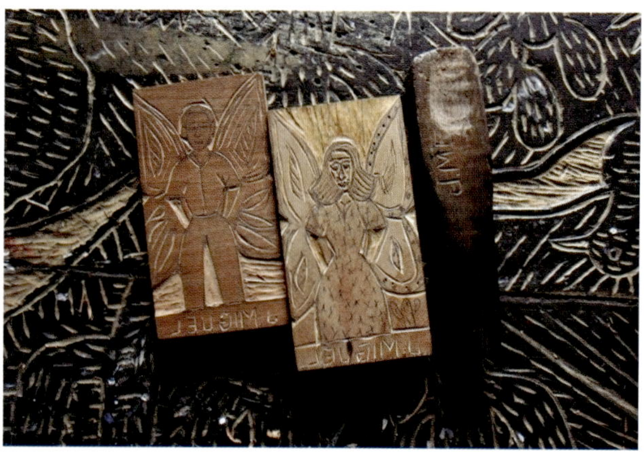

J. Miguel's carving begins with outlines, 2019

As for the others, the images drawn from his experience or from the familiar themes shared by Bezerros and Alto do Mora — Lampião, say, or the *pífano* band — they arrive fresh from the mind every time the pencil plays over the wood. Whatever the source, J. Miguel says, you have to remember that the print will reverse the block, so captions and signatures have to be written backward.

Now there is a drawing on the block. Cutting begins when J. Miguel uses a sharp knife to slice in and outline the figure. Then with a small gouge he drives toward the outlines to deepen the background so the lines stand in high relief to receive the ink. Then he hammers a battery of punches to get sparkles of detail in the standing sections. The aim is a clear-field print, the background blank, the figures sharp.

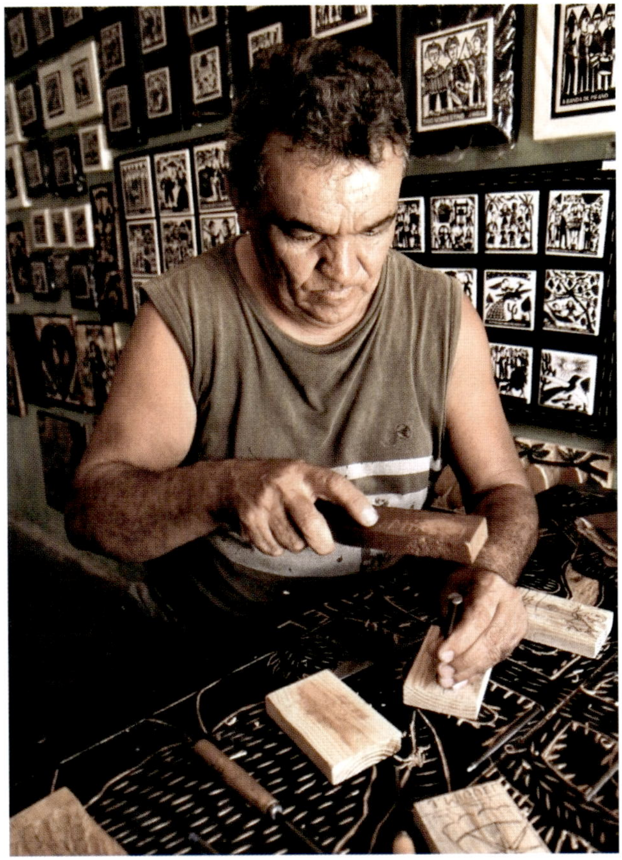

J. Miguel hammering the punch, 2015

The method, J. Miguel says, is the same for everyone, but everyone's hand is distinct: "You can take away the name and look at the print, and you know who made it. I can recognize my father's. My brother's I know, I know. I can tell by the physiognomy and the line, right?

"The line is always different."

Luiz Antônio put it like that in Alto do Moura. To the knowledgeable insider, the work of traditional art can always be attributed to a particular individual. Physiognomy is also a guide to difference in Alto do Moura. Paulo separated his work from his father's and his brother's by the body's shape. But line is the key in Bezerros. Drawn then cut, the line is the creator's implicit signature. From years of cutting the blocks that J. Borges drew, J. Miguel knows this stepfather's line intimately, and in comparison with his own he spots the lines of others immediately. A subtle eye, though, is not required, since the print is signed in the block, just as the statue of Alto do Moura is signed on its base. These are works of art, signed with pride.

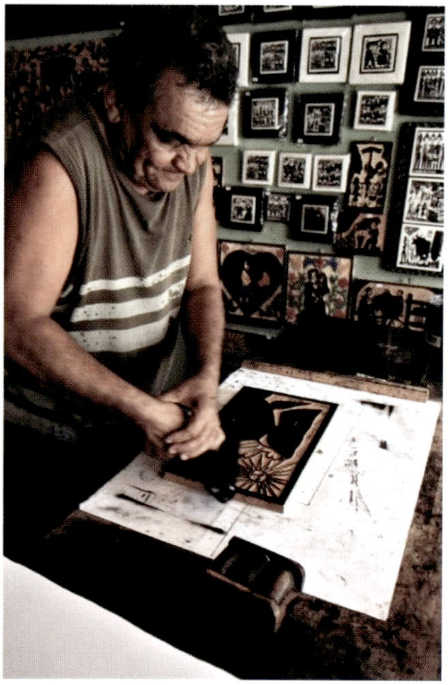

J. Miguel inking the *matriz*

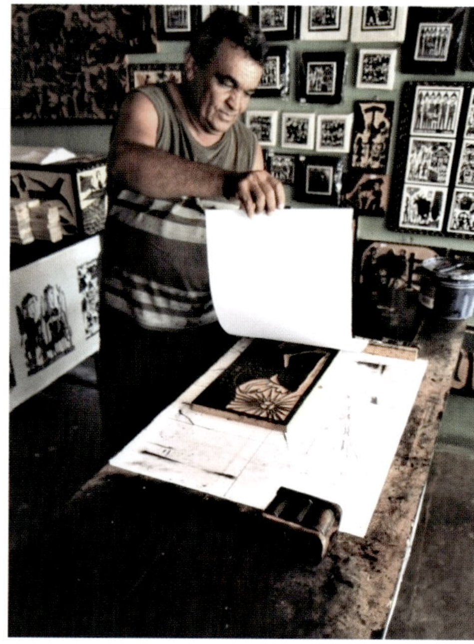

Placing the paper on the *matriz*

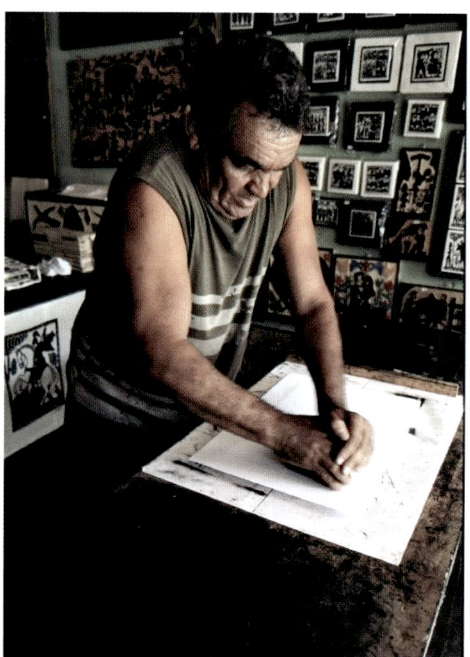

Printing with the *carrinho*

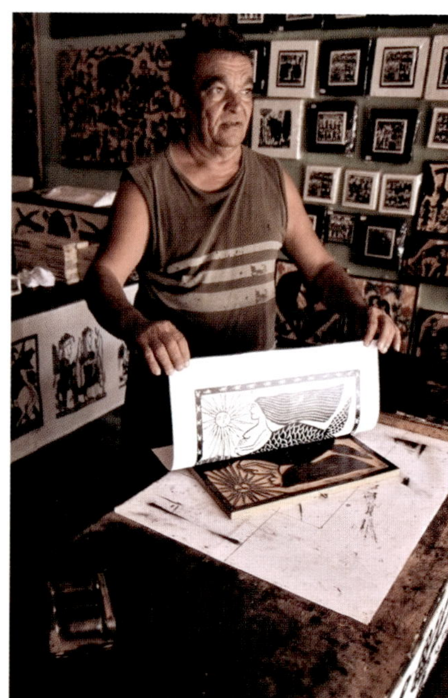

Peeling the print from the *matriz*, 2015

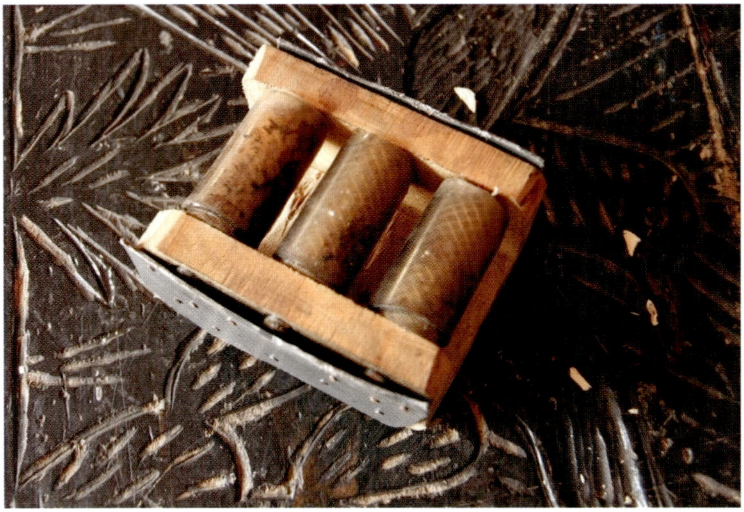

J. Miguel's *carrinho*, 2021

The cut block, the *matriz*, the mother of prints, is ready. On a bench to the right in his shop, J. Miguel has drawn two rectangles, one inside the other, separated by equal margins all around. He positions the *matriz*, cut face up, precisely within the smaller rectangle. Then with a small roller of the sort used for painting walls, he spreads black ink on a pane of glass and rolls the ink back and forth across the *matriz*. Next he takes a sheet of white paper, aligns it carefully within the larger rectangle, places it on the inked *matriz*, and begins running a *carrinho* — a little car composed of wooden rollers trapped in a frame — over the surface, side to side, bottom to top, bearing down hard with both hands to print the image. The ink is sticky, helping to hold the paper to the block. He peels the print away and hangs it from a clothesline in the shop to dry.

Since J. Miguel had plenty of practice when he was young, working at a mechanical press to print the *folhetos*, it might come as a surprise that he would employ such a manual, muscular method in printing, but it is used generally in his family.

The prints, like the covers of the *cordels* before them, were all black-on-white at the start. Then they were joined by colored prints, made not through a sequence of blocks in the manner of a Japanese master, but by painting sections of the *matriz* in ink of different colors and then printing in the customary way. With colored inks available, blocks can also be printed in solid colors other than black, blue or green most often. J. Miguel says:

"The black-on-white one, it was the original, from the beginning. Then they said to my father, Make a colored one. Make it so we can see what it looks like.

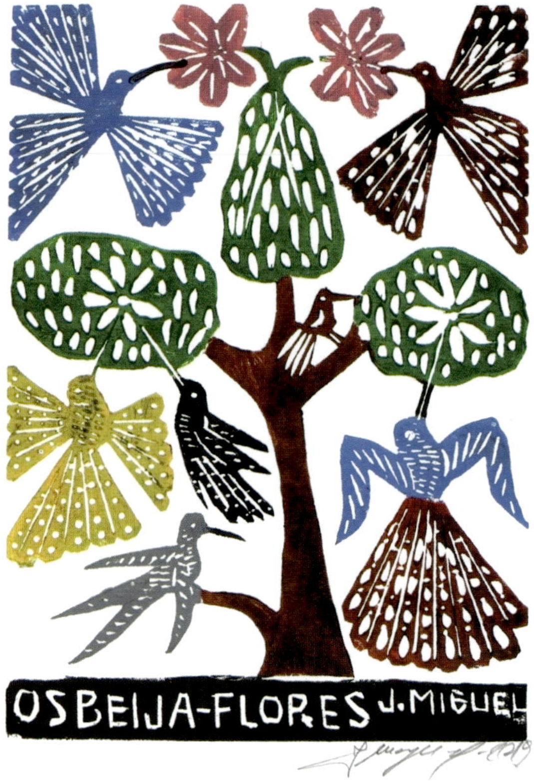

The Hummingbirds, by J. Miguel (26 × 19 cm), 2019

"Then he started to make colored prints. Then I accompanied him, right? That's it. I started making things of novelty, and they started asking for the colored one."

We ask when the colored prints began, and J. Miguel says he doesn't remember. Early in the nineties seems right. In 1996, J. Borges's friend, and J. Miguel's collector, Giuseppe Baccaro, who has since passed, wrote that the black-and-white print was J. Borges's masterwork because "between those two colors there are all the others and many more, both visible and invisible. I also believe that the more recent colored wood engravings are the result of commercial pressure."

J. Miguel can print a picture of rural work in black and white, add touches of color to a scene of the Sertão, and print a flight of birds in full color. Colored prints fetch higher prices and sell quickly, but they take much time. J. Miguel says he must maintain a large and diverse inventory to meet the needs of his customers, who generally care more about a print's topic than its art. So, he makes colored prints but many more of the quickly produced black-and-white ones. New prints in the old style dominate his repertory.

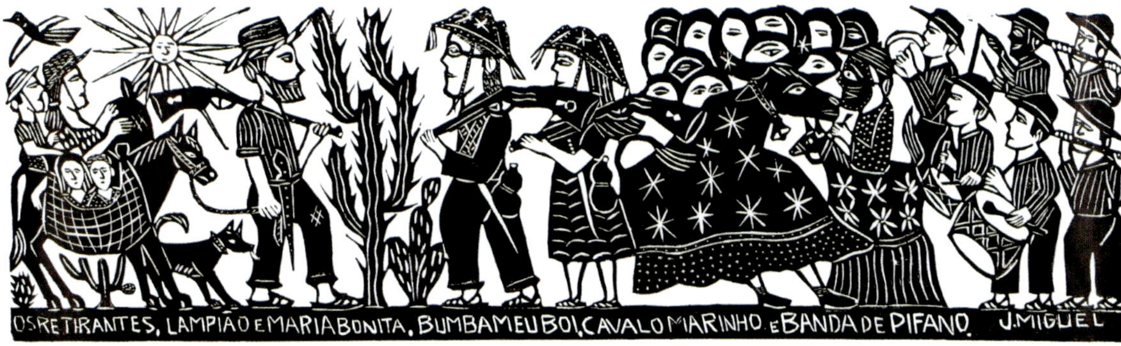

J. Miguel's overture (24 × 96 cm), 2014

The Woodblock Repertory

The wide repertory divides into *temas*, themes. J. Miguel created an introductory overture to his repertory by representing four themes in a single print ninety-six centimeters in length, trouble to the left, entertainment to the right. From the left, *Retirantes* enter to encounter Lampião and Maria Bonita. On the right, the *pífano* band plays and the Captain, Cavalo Marinho, meets the Bull in a performance of *Bumba-Meu-Boi*. These are central themes in both Bezerros and Alto do Moura. Those towns, separated by only forty kilometers, belong to the same region, the Agreste of Pernambuco. Their people live on the same dry, hilly landscape of small pastoral farms, sharing economic conditions, historical understandings, and musical taste, so it is logical that the artists would make, and their customers would like, the same images.

Open the issue to time, though, and it becomes apparent that when J. Borges turned from the *cordel* to the big print and was casting about for inspiration in 1972, Vitalino was dead but widely celebrated in print, Manuel Eudócio was energetically at work, Zé Caboclo was still alive, and Alto do Moura's expansive repertory had been consolidated for more than two decades. It offered a plenitude of themes that had proved commercially viable, themes J. Borges could adopt and adapt to a new medium.

When J. Borges listed the places where art is made in Pernambuco, he named Alto do Moura first, and by locating the origin of the town's tradition with Vitalino's creation of the hunter of wildcats in 1915, he accurately declared the art to be a century old. When J. Miguel visited the Casa Museu

Mestre Vitalino, he talked with Severino Vitalino who told him that he knew J. Borges well and greatly admired his work. The artists know one another, share a place, a culture, and join in mutual appreciation.

J. Miguel pictures all of the themes from his long overture in a variety of smaller prints that simultaneously exhibit affinities with Alto do Moura and reveal the differences that derive from his medium. For one, the statues in clay tend to frontality while the figures on prints — as his overture demonstrates — are apt to appear in profile.

On the long print, the six members of the *pífano* band play to the right in profile. The smaller prints of the *pífano* band are the only ones by J. Miguel that seem to have been developed directly from Alto do Moura's statues. On one print, all six stand frontally in a row. On another, four of the six pose frontally. In both, two play the *pífano*, three have drums, one a triangle. It is like that in Luiz Carlos's rendition in clay: six figures, all frontal, two with the *pífano*, three with drums, one with a triangle. And both J. Miguel and Luiz Carlos take care to make one of the musicians conspicuously African in descent, one out of six being a reasonably representative proportion for the dry interior of the Northeast; on the coast it could be six out of six, the instruments and music quite different.

The other musical ensemble, the *Trio Nordestino*, has a man in the middle with an accordion, a drummer to one side, a man with a triangle to the other. In Alto do Moura, the three share a base: they count as a single piece. Couples who dance to their music also share a base. Carmélia and Luiz Antônio shape them at a comparable scale, but they are almost never joined into a single piece with five characters. In his print, J. Miguel sets the trio to the right and shows five couples dancing *forró* during the festival of Saint John. Fifteen characters appear in his scene. A big scene with many figures is difficult to make in clay, very difficult to transport, but a scene is easily spread across a print's single sheet of paper, and the complicated scene, like the figure in profile, is a characteristic of woodblock art.

The same pattern obtains with *Bumba-Meu-Boi*. In Alto do Moura, the Captain, Cavalo Marinho, and the Bull are a separable pair, each created as an independent figure. J. Miguel joins them in a scene and gives them a crowded audience of eyes.

In Alto do Moura, the *Reisado* provided an opportunity for creative play. Manuel Eudócio lifted the Doutor and Dona Joana out of the cast and dropped them into a multitude of new situations. To J. Miguel, Lampião and

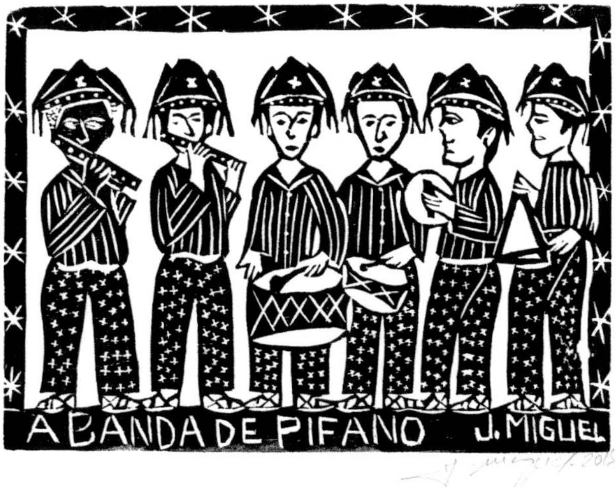

A Banda de Pífano, by J. Miguel (16 × 24 cm), 2015

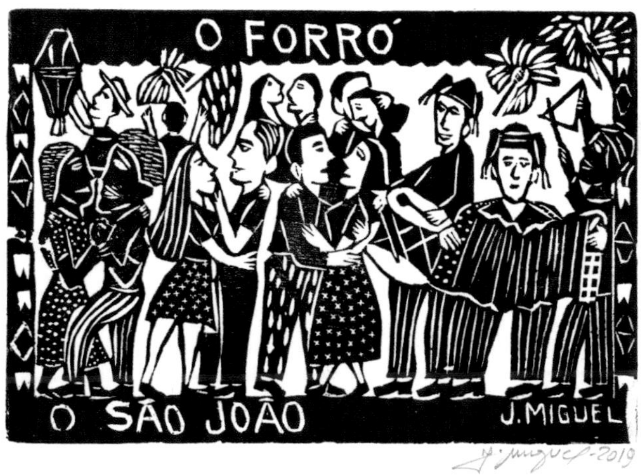

Forró dancing at São João, by J. Miguel (18 × 26 cm), 2019

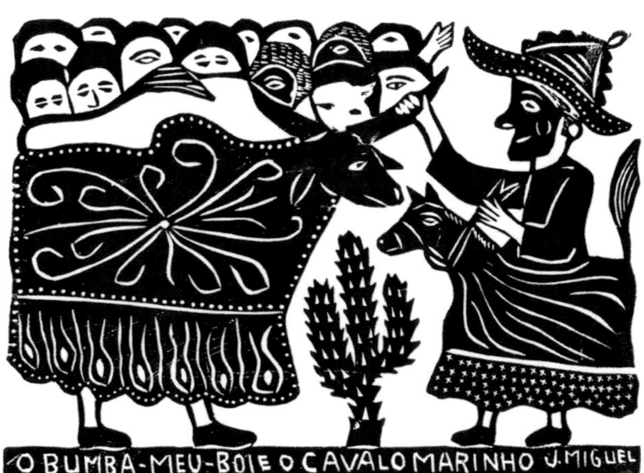

Bumba-Meu-Boi, The Bull and the Captain, Cavalo Marinho, by J. Miguel (19 × 26 cm), 2019

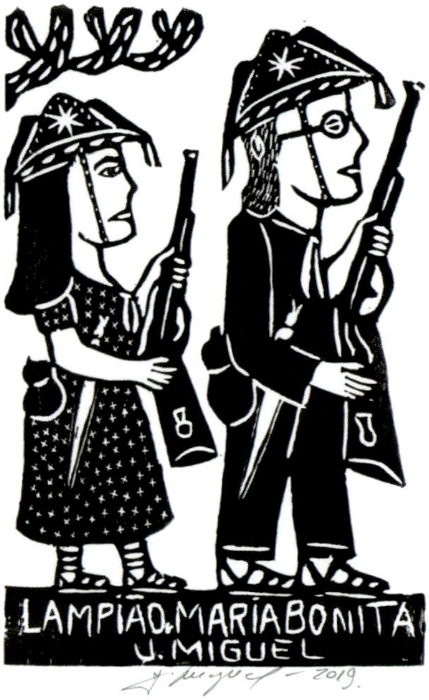

Lampião and Maria Bonita, print by J. Miguel (27 × 18 cm), 2019

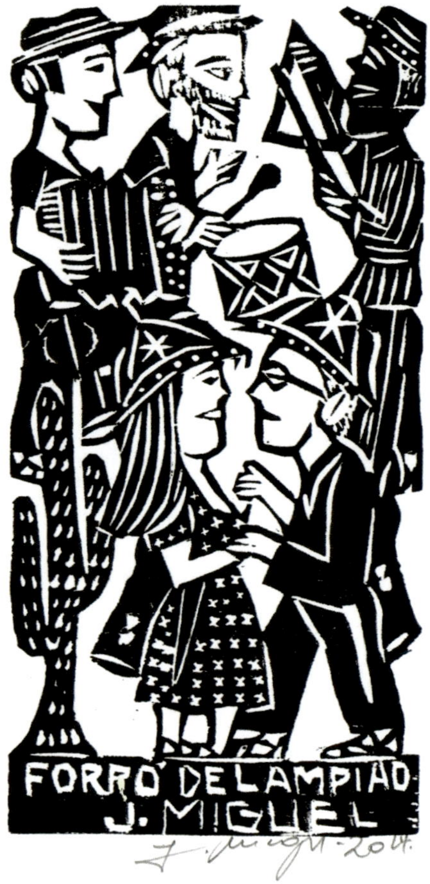

The *forró* of Lampião, by J. Miguel (23 × 12 cm), 2014

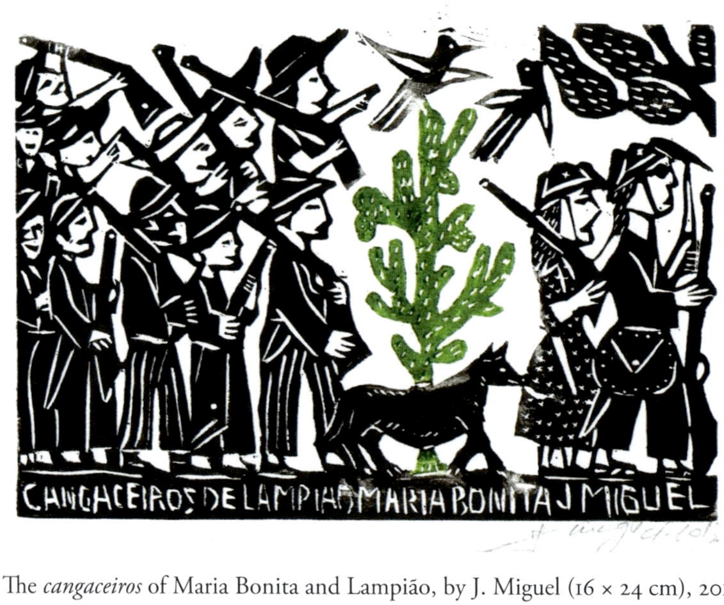

The *cangaceiros* of Maria Bonita and Lampião, by J. Miguel (16 × 24 cm), 2015

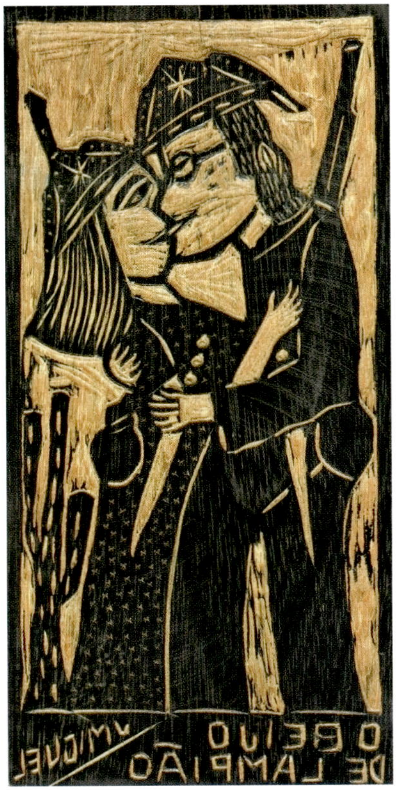

The Kiss, woodblock by J. Miguel (25 × 12 cm), 2019

Maria Bonita offer the same chance for fresh creation. In clay, they pose frontally. J. Miguel tends to pair them in profile and he puts them wherever he wants them. He pictures them in the Sertão, followed by the *cangaceiros* of their back-country squad. He pictures them dancing *forró* while the trio plays on. He says:

"I have my own style with the themes. I explore the same themes as my father. The only thing that changes is the drawing, the line. It can never be the same, the drawing.

"What he had, I have. *Bumba-Meu-Boi*, right? And themes of Lampião, Maria Bonita that he also made.

"But I think of new ones. I made the honeymoon of Lampião and Maria Bonita. I made the lunch of Lampião and Maria Bonita. There is the death of Lampião and Maria Bonita, but it did not come out too well.

"I made their courtship. I made both of them, Lampião and Maria Bonita, in the Sertão. I made a sun in the scrubland. And they are walking.

"I make many prints of them. If I think about Lampião and Maria Bonita, I will come up with something new.

"I have about ten, I have ten themes of Lampião. Even the Kiss of Lampião. I invented the woodblock print: The Kiss."

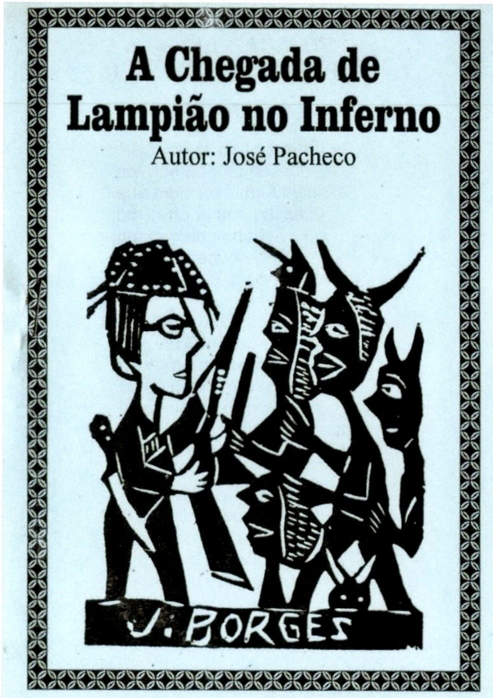

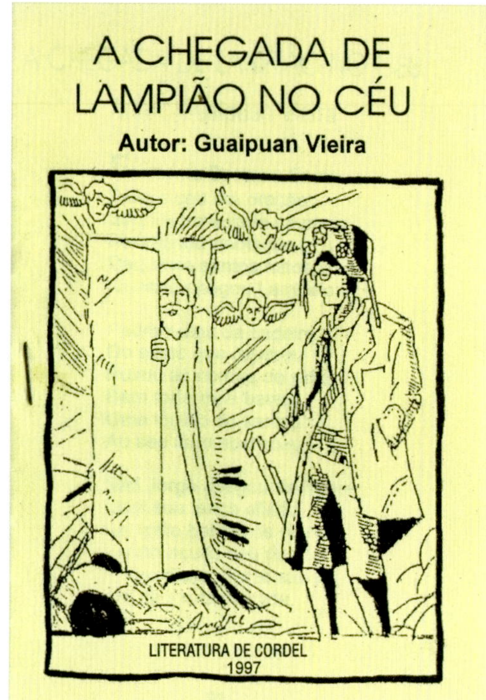

Cordels of Lampião arriving in Hell (2003) and Heaven (1997)

J. Miguel tells us that a couple from Recife stopped at this shop, saw the *matriz* of Lampião and Maria Bonita kissing, and commissioned him to use it in designing a wedding invitation for them. Another customer features in a story he tells, for which it is useful to know that a *cordel* by José Pacheco, *A Chegada de Lampião no Inferno*, The Arrival of Lampião in Hell, has often been reprinted, once with a cover by J. Borges, and Guaipuan Vieira answered with a *cordel*, *A Chegada de Lampião no Céu*, The Arrival of Lampião in Heaven. J. Miguel says:

"People say that Lampião was right. That he would take from the rich and give to the poor. I don't know.

"I think he was right, a hero. But he was also a bandit. I don't know which story to believe.

"There was an interesting person who came here, a fanatic of Lampião. I did not know him.

"He came, looked at my *matriz*, a woodblock that I had on the wall: The Arrival of Lampião in Hell.

"When he saw this work, he got angry, see? He got very angry.

"He looked at me and said, Miguel, how do you know he went to Hell? Mister Miguel, you have no idea.

"It is the story they tell.

"They tell it wrong. Why don't you make him arriving in Heaven?

"I said, You have given me a good idea.

"He said, I will come by on such and such a day at such and such a time.

"I said, I can't promise anything. But when he left, I talked with my wife and she said, Make it.

"I made a *matriz*, thirty by fifty. The Arrival of Lampião in Heaven. Saint Peter welcoming him. On the bottom: *cangaceiros* applauding.

"And I made a print. Time, it passed, and he showed up. He was passing by on the highway and he stopped.

"Do you remember me? I'm the Lampião guy.

"And I said, I made the work.

"He said, I don't believe it.

"I showed it and he bought it right away. This one I want. And he took it, a fanatic of Lampião.

"There are people who like that story. For me it has been a blessing. The story of Lampião, the Lampião who lived, we are selling it.

"If it weren't for Lampião and me selling the works, I would have no way to live.

"It is not a joke. I am living, thank God."

In his prints of Lampião and Maria Bonita, J. Miguel often captures bits of the landscape. Those bits always appear in his renditions of *Os Retirantes*. He doesn't borrow the characteristic contour of the *Retirantes* in clay, no grandmother rides in the lead, but he does depict a single family, father, mother, and two or three children. Their environment is a powerful presence, the cause of their exile, and the landscape itself holds interest for J. Miguel. He tells us:

"In the past, I would travel by bus, transportation by bus, to go by bus to Caruaru.

"So, I like to sit by the door of the bus to look out at the scenery, at the bush, to see the cattle, the drought, the plants, the birds, the hunters. These things.

"I based my work much on this, on seeing the scenery when I would travel by bus in that period. I would pass scenes of villages, of cattle grazing. I would see ranches, and I would see some of the oxcarts they used to have.

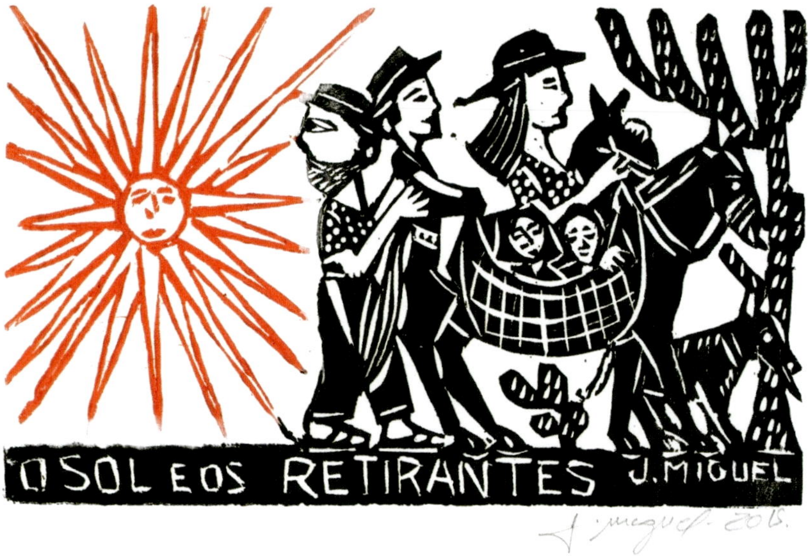

The Sun and the *Retirantes*, by J. Miguel (17 × 25 cm), 2015

"I would base my work on those scenes I saw from the bus, traveling. And that is why I would put into my work those things from the Sertão."

That is, J. Miguel developed an idea — an accurate idea — of the Sertão by observing the rural landscape of the transitional Agreste. It enabled him to provide backgrounds for images of Lampião and the *Retirantes*. More than that, it led him to create images of the land that lie beyond his overture of shared themes, occupying new repertorial territory where the techniques of the woodblock artist serve well, but the techniques of the sculptor in clay are inadequate. Luiz Carlos sometimes includes cactus in statues of Lampião and Maria Bonita. Leonildo comes close when he shapes cactus in clay to symbolize the landscape, but a comprehensive view, with cactus below and birds in the sky, is best left to the painter's brush or the woodblock artist's pencil and knife.

J. Miguel, in fact, doesn't record landscapes; he doesn't depict scenic visions as the painters in Salvador da Bahia, Iraquitan, Jó Silara, and Ubiraci Tibiriça, do. Instead, he selects key components — the blazing sun, the cactus, the famished cattle, the birds on the wing — and arranges them into artful, evocative compositions. He painted one for the front of the table where he sits to draw and carve, the first thing you see on entering his shop. Others are spread on woodcuts, some horizontally, a format fit to the vista, but his masterworks fill a vertical frame, a slice through space, ranging from nineteen to forty-eight to seventy-two centimeters in height.

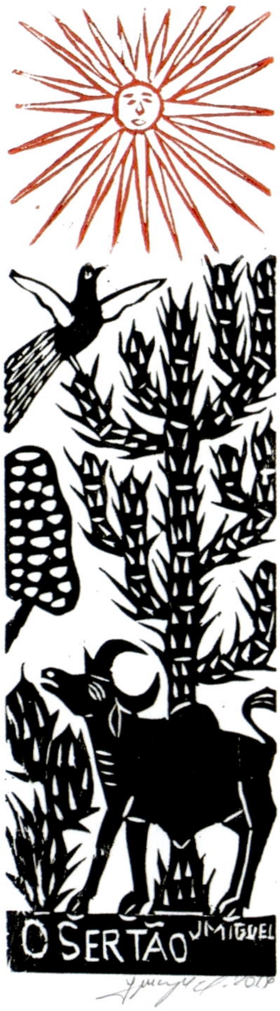

The Sertão, by J. Miguel (48 × 15 cm), 2014

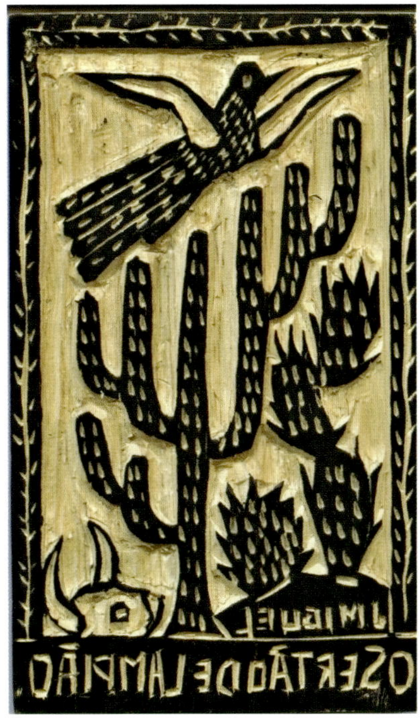

Lampião's Sertão, woodblock by J. Miguel (19 × 11 cm), 2015

One piece of the composition is J. Miguel's favorite of all images, *asa branca*, the white-winged dove of the Sertão. Prominent in every work inspired by the land, the white wing was pictured on his first woodcut, the one J. Borges gave to his friend Baccaro. J. Miguel says:

"What I like to make the most are birds, birds and cactus. The things of the Sertão.

"I really like to draw birds, the *asa branca*. It is the bird of the region. It has a secret which is the white wings. It only shows its white wings when it launches. When it is flying, then the white bottom of the wing shows. You notice from the bottom, looking up, that it is an *asa branca*.

"It has a secret, the white wing. You only notice when it is flying.

"It was the first thing I made in that period when I started to carve. *Asa branca* was first, the famous bird of the Sertão. It is the title of a song by Luiz Gonzaga."

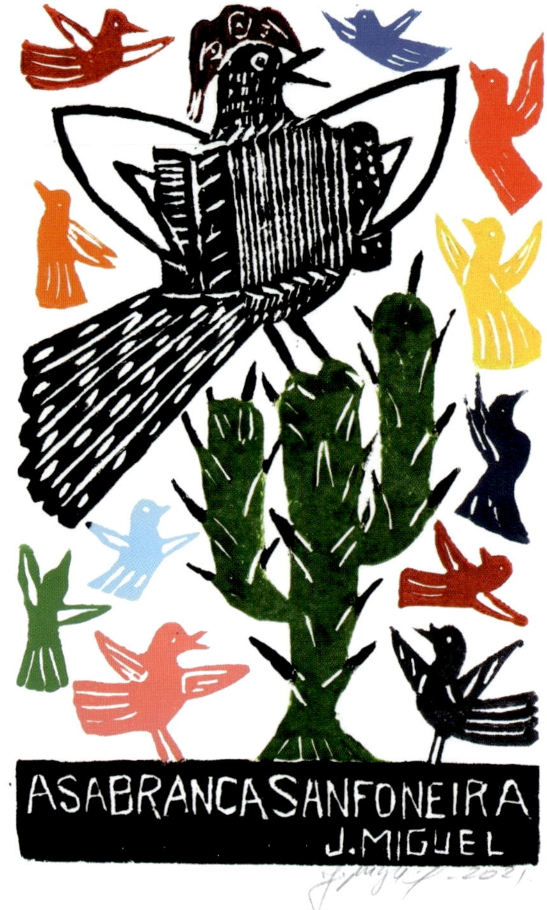

Asa Branca, Accordionist, by J. Miguel (28 × 16 cm), 2021

Gonzaga's melancholy "Asa Branca" is the anthem of the Northeast, the lament of a Sertanejo whose fields have burned, whose cattle have died, who must fly, like the white-winged bird, leaving home but promising to return. Whether driven by droughts or unemployment to find bad jobs in the big cities of the South, the exiles, the *Retirantes*, yearn for the Northeast; this is their song.

Beyond the shared territory of his overture, we have followed J. Miguel into the woodcut's own domain, coming first to images of the land and now to complex scenes of great size. Scenes with several figures appeared early in Vitalino's line; shops busy with workers became part of Alto do Moura's tradition. Luiz Antônio portrayed his son's bakery in clay. Luiz Carlos and Ademilson both inclined to the scenic. Luiz Carlos pictured his father in the midst of an interview. Ademilson made a barber shop. But J. Miguel was off on his own when he decided to double the size of the woodblock print and create his *carro chefe*, the flagship of his line, *A Feira Nordestina*, the Northeastern Market.

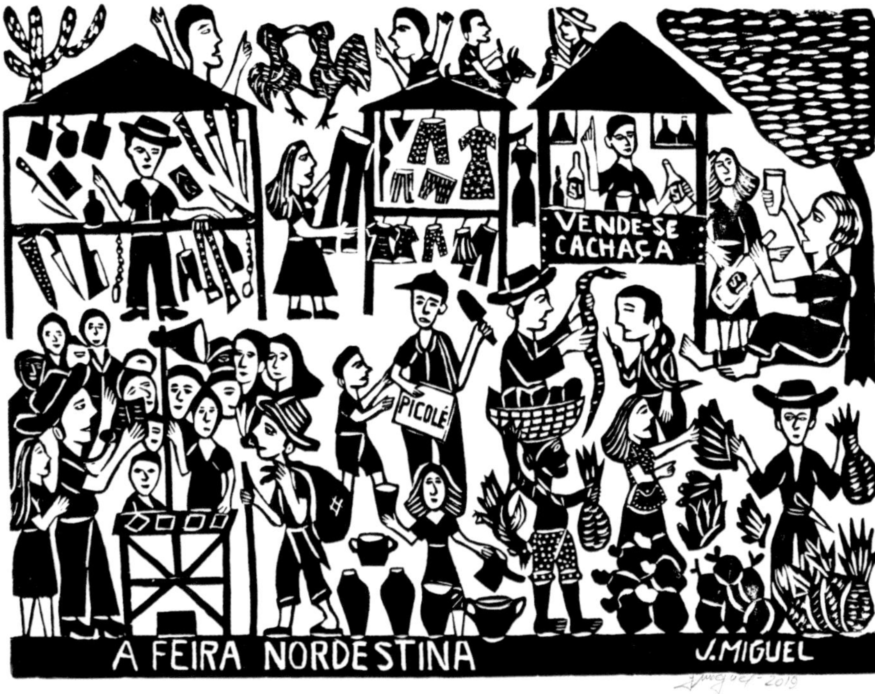

The Northeastern Market, by J. Miguel (38 × 53 cm), 2019

In shaping his wide view of the rural market, J. Miguel, like the painters of the cityscape in Salvador, blended the piled conceptual perspective, familiar to us from Turkish, Persian, and Indian miniature paintings, with the usual visual perspective conventional in Western art since the Renaissance. In the bottom row nearest to us on the left is a seller of *cordels*, a *cordelista*, intended as an homage to J. Borges. An ice cream vendor occupies the middle, and to the right men sell fruit and hold snakes. The snake-handler is a *curador de cobra* who inoculates people against snake bite by piercing the flesh with snake fangs and releasing snakes to slither over the patient's body. Above and beyond, slightly smaller at separate stands, a man sells knives, a woman hangs clothes, and *cachaça* is sold and consumed. At the top, behind the market, a cockfight excites a couple of men, then cactus on the left and a rider and hunter on the right imply deep space, the countryside in the distance.

The point is not that a scene with thirty-three figures can't be made in clay, but it would have to be microscopically miniature (possible for Marliete) or created as an installation (like Leonildo's Last Supper). This, though, is all on a single sheet of paper that can be rolled up, taken home, framed, and put on the wall. A masterpiece, slow to cut, quick to print, *A Feira Nordestina* has been a best seller for J. Miguel.

At the same grand scale, J. Miguel has printed images of life on the farm and life among the Indians, of Lampião and Maria Bonita, of *Os Retirantes*, *Bumba-Meu-Boi*, and *Papangu* — this last is doubly distinctive, being created with the techniques of Bezerros and representing a Bezerros tradition, unknown to the repertory of Alto do Moura.

Papangu is a costumed and masked procession with visits to private homes. In that respect it resembles the *Reisado*. It seems likely that the *Reisado* began as a procession to view Nativities displayed in homes on Epiphany, and the drama of death and resurrection was borrowed into the performance from *Bumba-Meu-Boi*. In some of the wide world's places, the drama remains essential and central. In others, the drama has been dropped, or it never appeared, and what endures is a march in masks that ends in a series of homes with a playful guessing of the identities of the costumed participants. J. Miguel says:

"The period of São João, it is busy in Caruaru. But not here. In Bezerros there is the tradition of *Papangu*. It only happens here. The town is full.

"People come here to have a good time in the streets, in the center of the city. People come to have a good time.

"Things are closed down, my shop is closed because it is Sunday. It begins on Sunday morning, goes on for Monday and Tuesday, but Sunday is really the day."

Manuel Eudócio participated in the *Reisado* he rendered in clay. J. Miguel participates in the *Papangu* he pictures in massive, colorful prints:

"Every year I participate in it. Every year I am part of it. It lasts three days, but Sunday is the main day that the gang performs the *Papangu*.

"We gather, me and my friends and relatives. A big part of *Papangu* is the masks. We buy them. Then everyone wears clothing of a different kind, or we all dress the same as a group.

"In an enclosed space, we get dressed and put on the masks. Some men dress as women, but women get dressed and come too, my wife, my sister.

"A few years past we all did homage to Luiz Gonzaga. I still have the robe I wore in homage to Luiz Gonzaga. It was photographed. Some tourists photographed it, right?

"On another year we did homage to J. Borges — like we did it for Luiz Gonzaga, understand?

"That's it. We get dressed and we go to the houses of friends, relatives, begging. Not for money, but for food and drink. *Cachaça*.

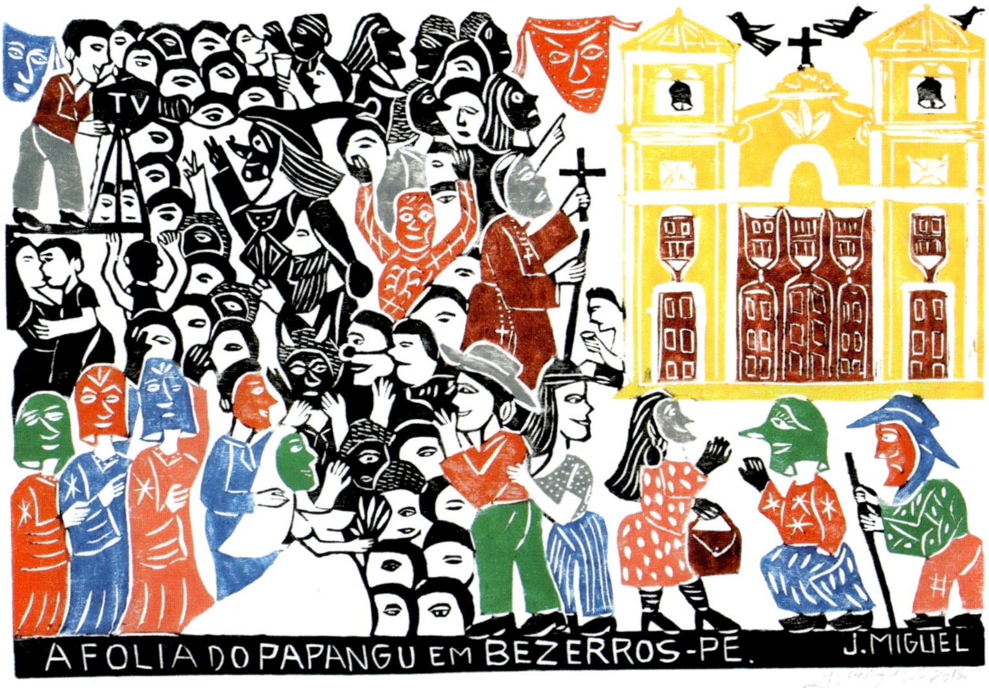

Papangu, by J. Miguel (37 × 56 cm), 2015

"We get there, all dressed. We get there at the house of a relative, or an acquaintance. We get there, we clap, then they let us enter. The people know it is a friend, but they don't know who it is.

"We arrive, dressed, with masks, walking different, talking different. Then they guess who it is. When you take off the mask: Oh, man! Is it you Miguel?

"Then there's a party with much drink. And then we leave for the road, to parade in the streets.

"Then on the street there are TV cameras. There are tourists taking photographs. From everywhere they come, Recife, Rio, São Paulo. The streets are full of cars.

"On Wednesday it is over. I only play on Sunday. All Sunday I enjoy myself with *Papangu*, drinking, but I can't stand much of it because the mask and robe are really hot.

"One time I gave my mask to a tourist, but the robe I kept, so I can remember the best party here, the carnival of *Papangu*. It is the tradition of Bezerros."

Papangu, complicated scenes, the land, and now the saints: these are distinctive traits of the woodcutter's art in Bezerros. As a result of the progenitor's

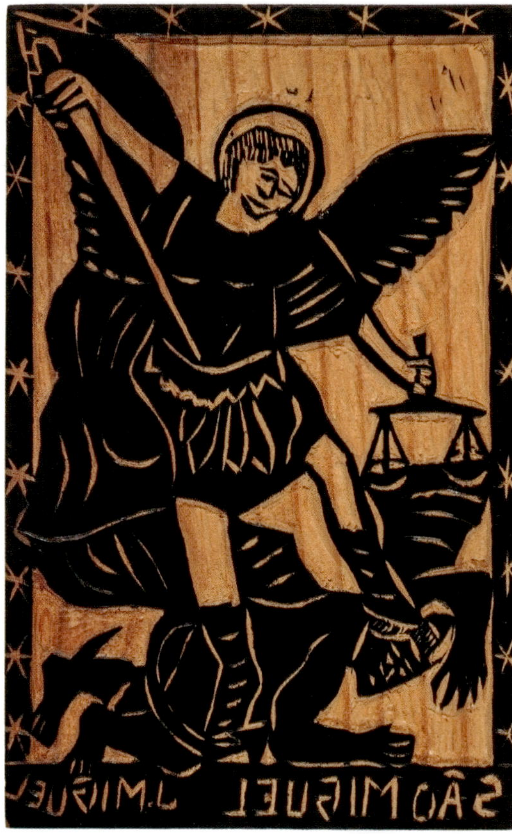

Saint Michael, woodblock by J. Miguel (25 × 16 cm), 2013

attitude, saints make only a shy appearance in Alto do Moura. But the progenitor in Bezerros welcomed the saints, so the repertory of saints depicted by J. Borges and then J. Miguel is far larger than Alto do Moura's and it aligns precisely with the professional *santeiro's* assembly of figures in Pernambuco — those shaped in clay by Dinho, Totinha, and Antônio Pimpo in Tracunhaém, those carved out of wood by Mestre Manoel, Nivaldo, and José Bezerra in Ibimirim, and those painted on canvas or board by Ricardo Andrade and Flávio Nogueira da Silva in Olinda.

The sacred repertory of the Northeast fills with beauty and power, not pity and pain. In Bezerros — and in general — first come images of Our Lady, most frequently Nossa Senhora da Conceição, Our Lady of the Conception, in one of two forms. She stands in the sky surrounded by angels or she takes the draped shape of Aparecida. Early in the eighteenth century, three fishermen cast their nets into a river in the southern state of São Paulo and they pulled in a statue, the body first, then the head. Assembled in a church, this statue, Nossa Senhora da Conceição Aparecida, was consecrated as the patron saint of Brazil and it is a steady source for the *santeiro*.

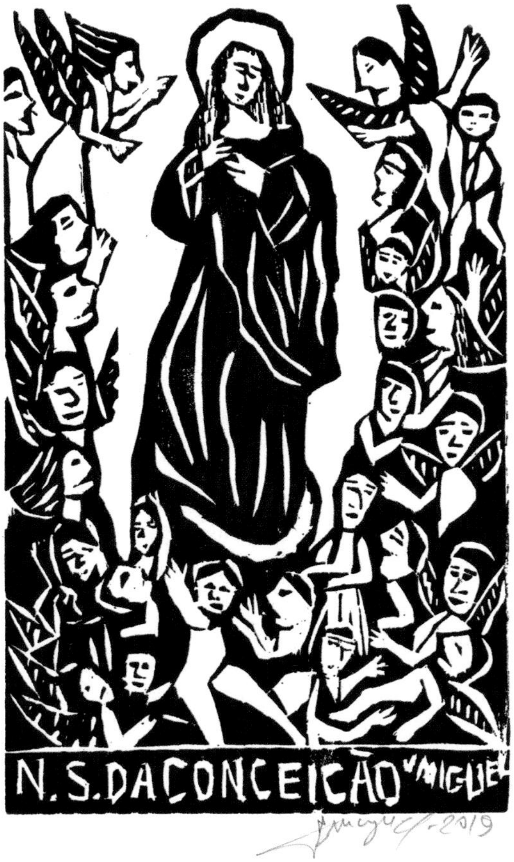

Our Lady of the Conception,
by J. Miguel (24 × 14 cm), 2009

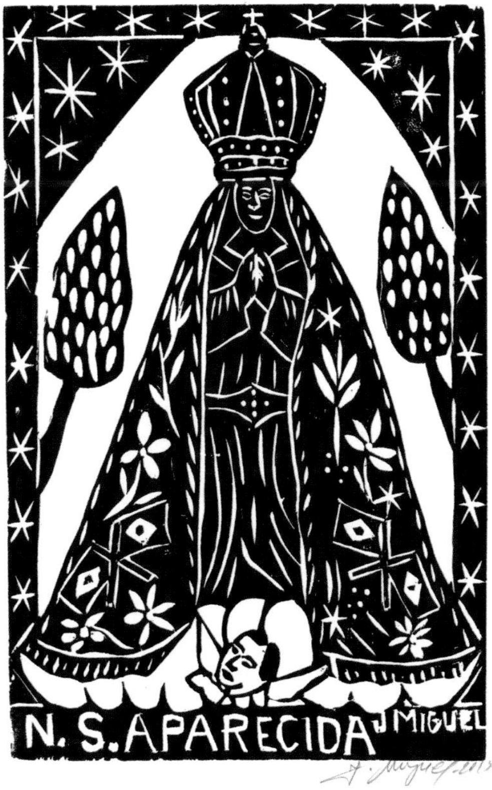

Our Lady Aparecida,
by J. Miguel (30 × 20 cm), 2017

São Benedito, by J. Miguel (23 × 15 cm), 2015

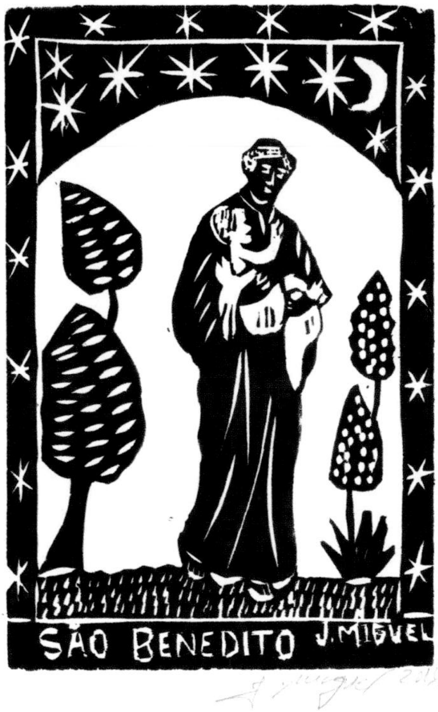

In the beautiful baroque churches of the Northeast, Our Lady stands beneath the Crucifix on the high altar. She stands centrally, too, in the repertory of sacred art. As the repertory widens in Bezerros, it includes the archangels, São Miguel, São Rafael, and São Gabriel. It includes the most popular male saints, São Francisco and Santo Antônio (also imaged by Manuel Eudócio and Luiz Galdino). It includes the most popular female saints, Santa Lucia and Santa Bárbara (also imaged by Marliete). And it includes São José, São João, São Sebastião, São Jorge, and São Benedito. A Franciscan, like Francisco and Antônio, Benedito was born to African parents in Sicily, and always imaged as black, he is revered in the Northeast where many people are, as he was, African in descent.

Candomblé, the Brazilian religion developed out of African sources, holds a pantheon of deities, called, using the Yoruba word, *orixás*, but also called *santos*, saints. The artists we know who only portray the *orixás* — the painter Francisco Santos and the woodcut carver Nilo dos Santos, both on the coast in the big city of Salvador — have repertories as large as those of the back-country *santeiros*. Catholicism and Candomblé come close in the Northeast. Plenty of people practice both, going to Mass in the morning and attending a Candomblé service at night. Both religions offer a comparable number of saints who answer personal devotional desires and, in some cases, mesh in identity.

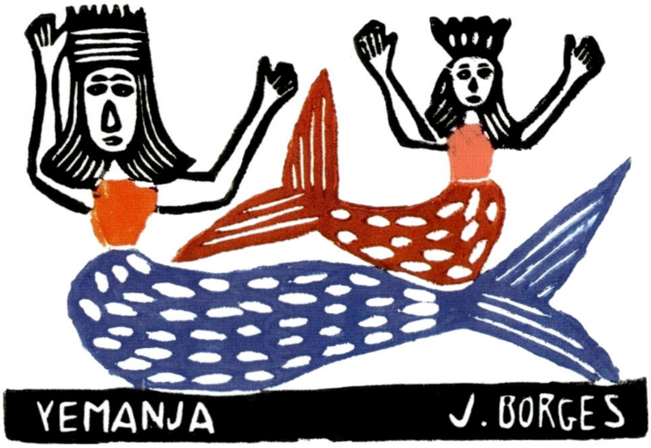

Yemanjá, by J. Borges (15 × 22 cm), 2015

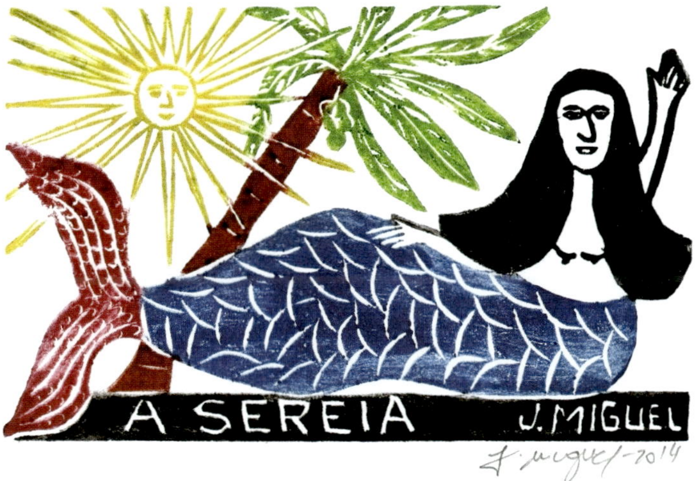

The Mermaid, by J. Miguel (15 × 24 cm), 2015. On another block J. Miguel names her Iemanjá.

Appreciating at a distance the presence and power of Candomblé, the artists of the deep interior choose to represent one of the *orixás*, Yemanjá, the goddess of the salt sea. Luiz Antônio shapes in clay a procession of her devotees. J. Borges and J. Miguel picture her in prints. The Candomblé artists show her in two ways: as a beautiful woman in blue emerging from the sea — the Star of the Sea, close to images of Nossa Senhora da Graça, Our Lady of Grace — or as a mermaid. In Bezerros, she is a mermaid, sometimes labeled *A Sereia*, The Mermaid, but always understood to be, for we have asked, Yemanjá.

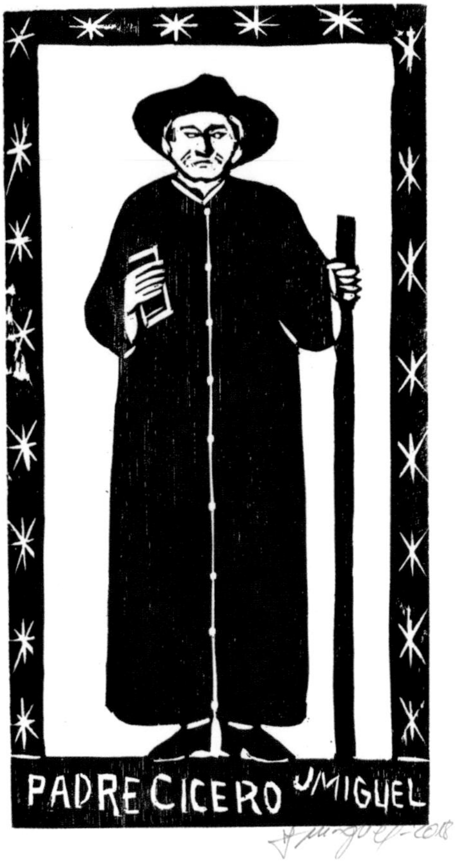

Padre Cícero, by J. Miguel
(28 × 15 cm), 2018

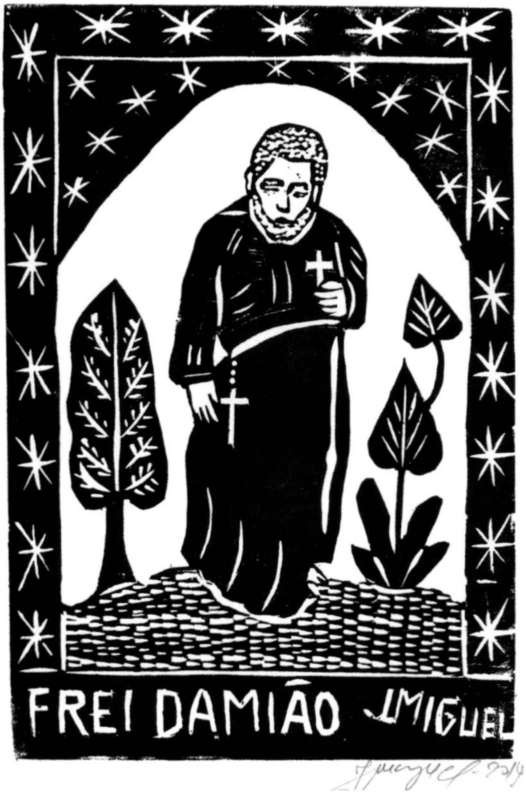

Frei Damião, by J. Miguel
(25 × 17 cm), 2014

The sacred line ends when we follow the saints and encounter the beloved priests. Padre Cícero, the subject of an excellent book by Candace Slater, is drawn by J. Miguel just as the artists of Alto do Moura shape him: frontally like a saint with his key attributes, hat, staff, and book. His successor, Frei Damião, the hero of J. Borges's second *folheto*, is pictured by J. Miguel much as his stepfather portrayed him on the cover of a more recent *cordel*, titled *Conselhos de Frei Damião em Favor da Humanidade*, Advice by Frei Damião on Behalf of Humanity.

J. Miguel has a talent for filling a frame with a balanced design, but the part of the work he most enjoys is carving the woodblock. If things had been different and he had truly become an artist, he says, he would be carving timber into monumental statues of saints. But like the artists of Alto do Moura, he began as a child, helping in the shop, then, following the familial line, he learned to like what the had to do, and he delights now in making the woodcuts. Selling is his concern:

"The people who buy are the people who like art. They are tourists, both Brazilian and foreigners.

"The people who value it come from São Paulo, from Rio. They come. From our region, fewer people value it. To live, what matters for me are people from elsewhere.

"The people who come here and like my work, they buy the prints. The price has to be reasonable to be able to sell it.

"The store owners in São Paulo, they put higher prices. They call me, and I send it. I give them a normal price, but I have no idea what they sell it for."

It is his work and, an honorable artisan, he does it well, but making a living is a day-to-day struggle:

"Thank God I have a space near the highway. Thank God there are people who know my work. People come here and they buy from me, help me. But there are weeks that I spend here when nobody comes.

"And what am I doing?

"And I remain here working. What happens? It seems that God helps. God is my only helper. But I am always battling. It's not like it used to be.

"There are weeks here when no people come. Nobody. You have to have patience, and it will be possible to survive.

"In the time of my father, the story is different. The media came searching for him. He is very deserving, understand? He was the creator. I am a worker.

"But God is good. God is on the case. The local road to the Centro de Artesanato passes right here in the front. The people who go to the Centro,

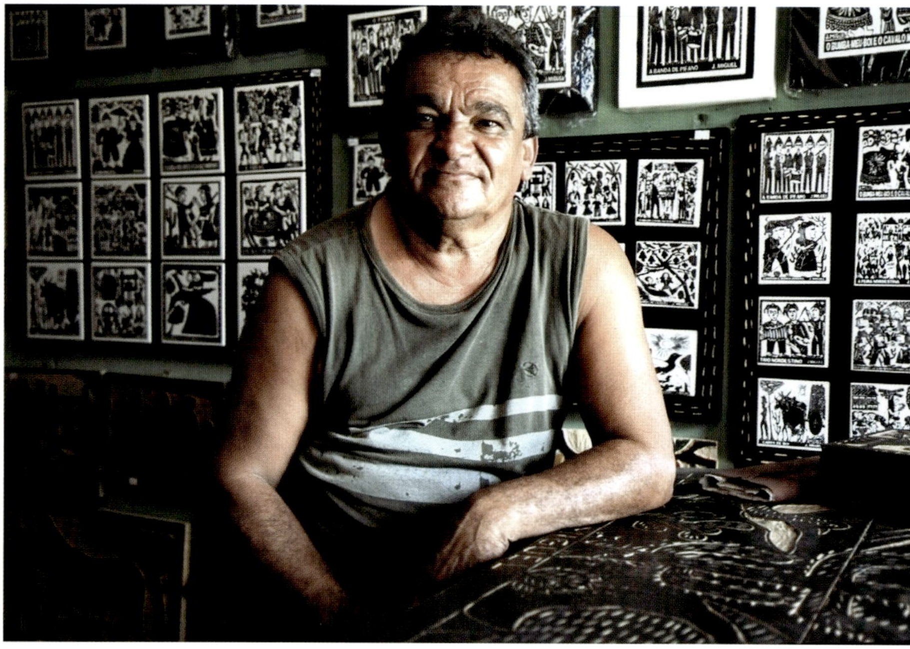

J. Miguel in his shop, Bezerros, 2015

they see my work. The girls" — in the gift shop — "tell them about me, and I am grateful. Then they pass by and stop: Oh, This is J. Miguel, the son of J. Borges.

"That's it. They stop, but I spend weeks without selling.

"Thank God I am surviving, but it is difficult. It is difficult today for everyone. Things are not so easy, right? The demand, it is going down, going down."

As demand declines, J. Miguel says, echoing Ademilson, only older people are buying. As demand declines, he says, echoing Marliete, the workforce is shrinking. His brothers, his mother's sons with J. Borges, are skilled but making little; "they are not obliged," he says, "to serve the tourists who come here to Bezerros." His brother Ivan has a shop next to his, but J. Miguel says he rarely sees Ivan there. J. Miguel's son Jefferson learned and showed early promise, a few pieces by him remain in J. Miguel's inventory, but he turned to other interests and more profitable work. Jefferson owns a car and continues to help by delivering J. Miguel's prints to stores in Caruaru and Recife.

The tradition, though, is not imperiled, he says, because his cousin Severino Borges creates fine prints in Olinda and J. Borges's youngest sons, Pablo and Bacaro, have infused their father's old shop with new energy. And J. Miguel has the *dom*. He will not stop.

Struggling in hard times, J. Miguel works with his wife, Raquel, crafting small tiles printed with woodblock imagery and coated with automotive varnish to get the look of glaze. Raquel also makes purses with woodblock designs, and these things sell in Recife. Like his stepfather, J. Miguel found that customers want to buy the carved and inked blocks. They are priced much higher than the black-and-white prints, even higher than the colored ones, and since he would rather carve than print, J. Miguel makes many blocks to sell, a benefit for us because we can acquire a few, helping him and getting pieces to examine and employ as illustrations.

Meanwhile, buyers or not, J. Miguel works every day, drawing, cutting, and printing to stock his inventory with hope. To end it all, J. Miguel said:

"My father was the creator. For me he is the master and the master teacher. I consider him to be the master of woodblock prints. He was my teacher, right? And, thank God, he is still alive.

"The family of J. Borges is very large. Woodblock prints, there are heaps of them here in Bezerros.

"And I thank God for the life here. My part is the cutting. I like my work, and life continues, thank God.

"It is bad, but it is good.

"And life continues, thank God."

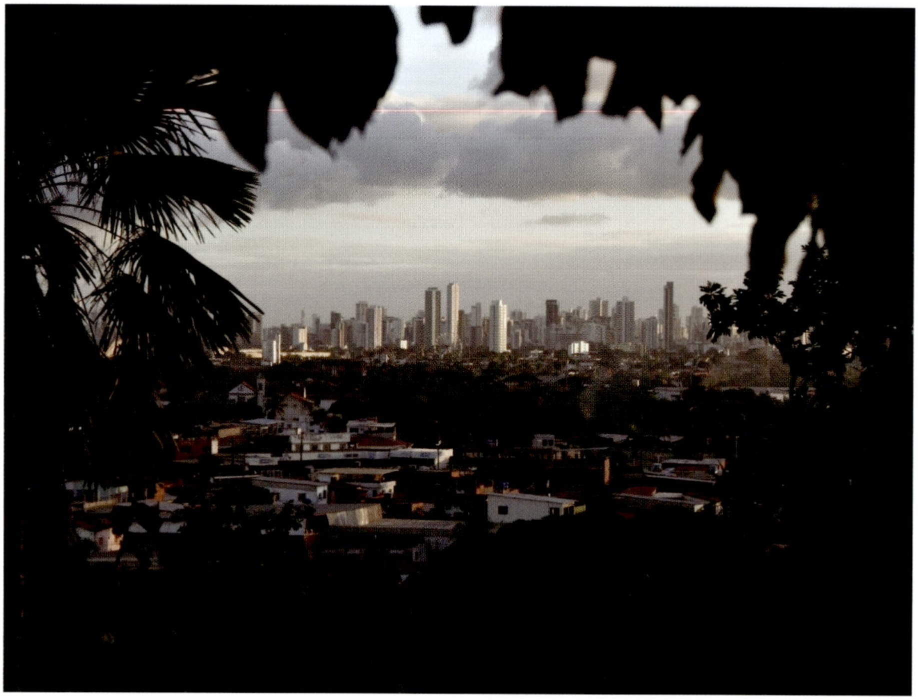

Recife, viewed from the high ground in Olinda, 2019

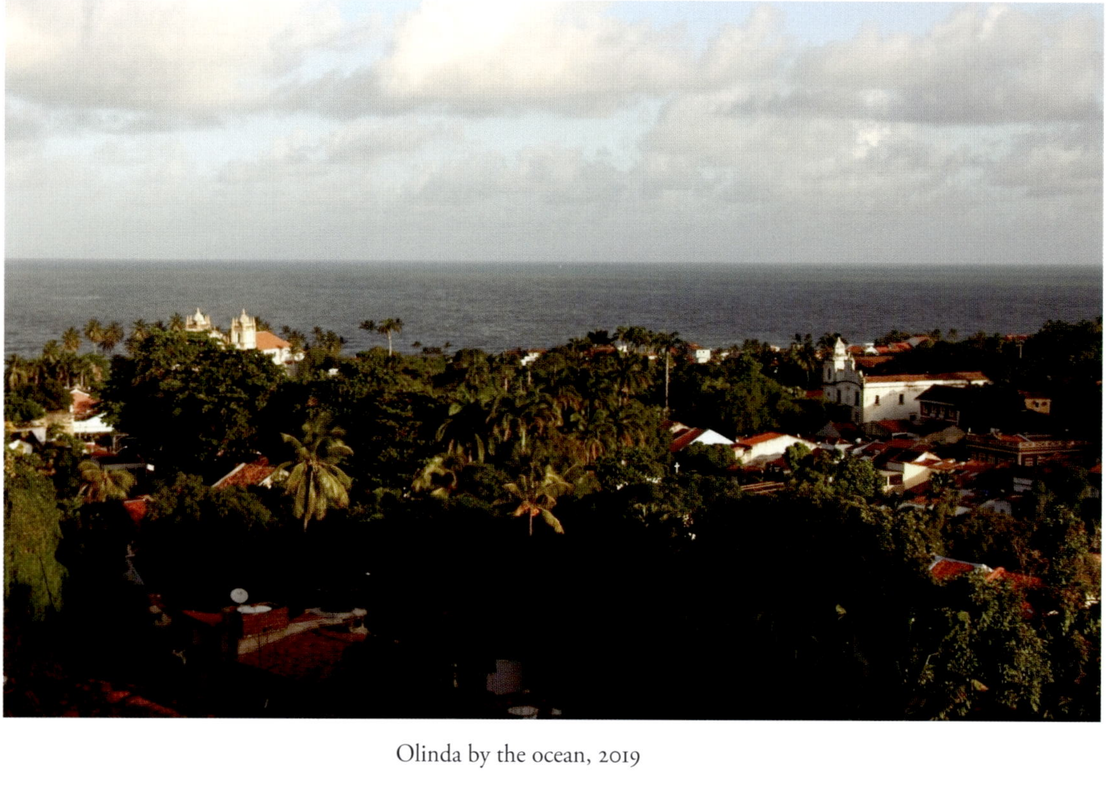

Olinda by the ocean, 2019

21

Severino and Ana Maria

Olinda lifts from the Atlantic and rises to a crest — like Lisbon, like Salvador da Bahia, the first capital of Brazil. Beautiful churches encircle the seaside slope, and the streets stream with fine old colonial houses, some converted into shops, restaurants, and convivial bars. It is a lovely historical place, attractive to tourists. Behind the ridge, on the sunset side of the city, the Largo do Amparo gathers commerce and fills the dip between two old churches. A long street leaves the Largo and heads northeast, running through a poor neighborhood, then just as it begins to rise it passes the trim, efficient home and workshop of Severino Borges, J. Miguel's cousin and J. Borges's nephew.

When he arrived in Olinda in 1996, Severino found a place rich with commercial opportunities. Fenearte, the grand *feira* for craft and art, takes place in Olinda every July. To the south, visible from Olinda's high ground, the vast city of Recife spreads to provide convenient venues for the sale of art. The most important of them for Severino is the repurposed old prison, the Casa da Cultura. Not long after his arrival, when he was making a delivery there, he met Ana Maria da Conceição. Both had been married before, were unmarried then, and now they are partners in life and labor. Since 2002, Ana Maria has managed two shops in the Casa da Cultura, where her diverse stock includes small pieces from Alto do Moura but features Severino's woodblock work. They are a tight, complementary couple. She says, "He knows how to make. I know how to sell." She is bright, cheerful, talkative. He is shy and quiet, industrious and thoughtful, an artist. Severino said this about art during our first interview in 2014:

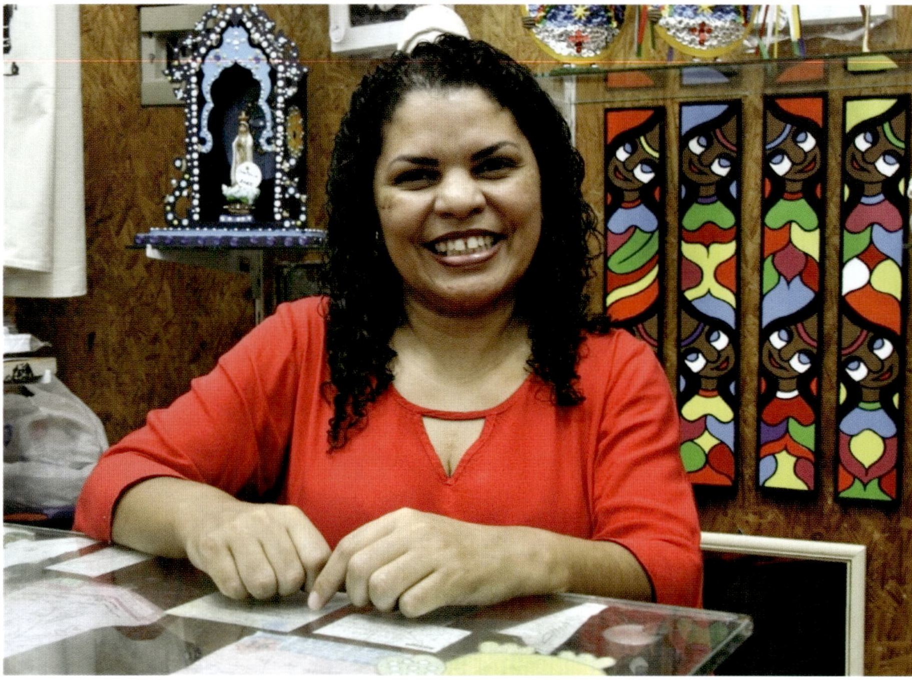

Ana Maria in her shop at the Casa da Cultura, Recife, 2019

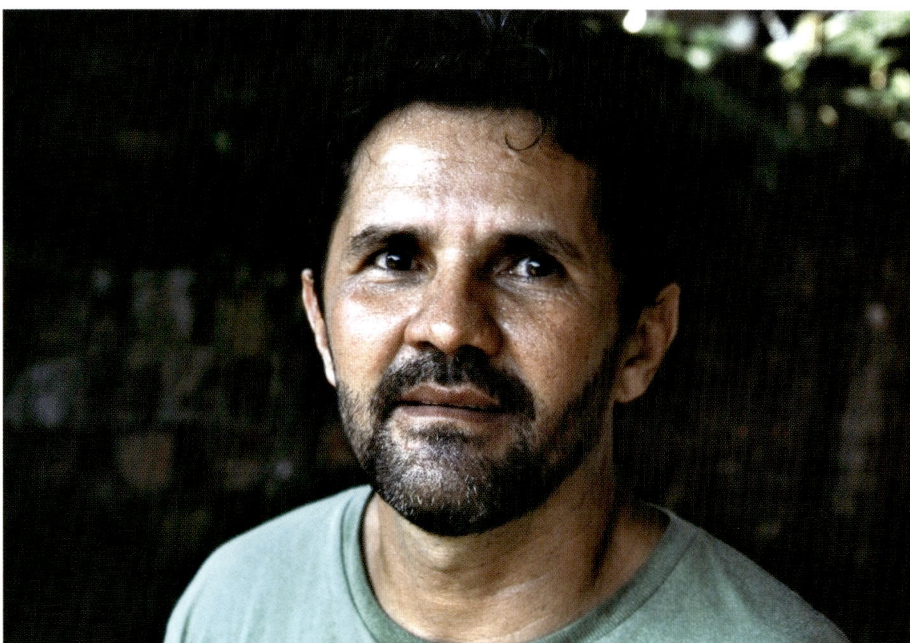

Severino Borges, Olinda, 2014

"My wife says, You are a dreamer. But you have to dream, no? If you stop dreaming, you stop making.

"You stop living.

"We can't stop dreaming, right? Our images come from the imagination, the imagination. We see things, but we create in the actual head.

"I look, then later I try to visualize the maximum possibility. I make a drawing and then I leave it behind and make it in my own way. And it comes out. A creation.

"The design is the first part, the idea. Then carving is second. If you draw well and are used to carving, then the *matriz* is good. The printing is easy. Anyone can do it.

"It takes agility. For you to make everything perfectly, the carving is essential. It is the most important part.

"And for me this art is everything, the whole importance. So, my life is art. Art is everything.

"Art is for everyone" — *Arte é pra todo mundo* — "and it is important. Important.

"There must be these crazy, dreaming people who make different things for the world.

"Art makes me happy."

Severino José Correia Borges was born on April 9, 1968, in Escada, a town in the coastal region of eastern Pernambuco. His father, Amaro Francisco Borges, was born in the municipality of Bezerros in 1939, in the place where his brother J. Borges was born in 1935. Severino says:

"My father was an agricultural laborer and a construction worker. When I was seven, Father had financial difficulties, and we moved to Bezerros where J. Borges lived, to see if he could improve the situation. My grandfather lived there. We went to Bezerros when I was seven.

"From there Father started making woodblock prints, there in Bezerros. He was a few years younger than J. Borges.

"Then I was raised like this. I was raised there, seeing them making.

"And even though I didn't understand much, I could see people coming to my uncle's house to see the prints. We were all boys, youngsters, and we didn't understand.

"We knew only that it was valuable, a thing that attracted attention in that period, seventy-six, seventy-eight.

"I was seeing that people would come, interested, and would buy something and take it away. It was a big production. Then Father also started to make.

"Then Father made the first print, and from there he started. J. Borges was making before that and he encouraged my father.

"J. Borges told him to make, and he started making. Father made out of his own desire.

"Father was illiterate. Then this Baccaro who lived here in Olinda" — J. Borges's close friend Giuseppe Baccaro — "started to buy his works in seventy-nine. And from there he started working.

"The difficulty was that Father was illiterate, and he was ashamed to go out and publicize his work, right?

"But my uncle, no. He was charismatic and extraverted. Uncle was a poet, he sang the *cordel.* He was free, and he had an immense importance in our art."

The simple story you hear is that J. Borges taught Amaro and Amaro taught his wife, Graciete Correia, who is called Nena, but Severino says, "I think it was she who taught him. My father's designs, many of them are her drawings. She directed his hand.

"In that period, he was busy. Father was a construction worker when he was making woodblock prints; it was not possible to make a living from the woodblock print in that period. She would improve his drawing, then he carved the *matriz.* It was she who gave him help, much help.

"She draws very well, and Father was doing the carving. Then Father said to her, You will have to learn to carve.

"I think Father was an enlightened being. He could foresee the future, many things in the future.

"He was illiterate, but he always talked about doing things for the theatre. He talked about mounting exhibitions in great museums, having never been to a museum.

"And he said to Mother, You will have to carve because I am not going to stay here much longer. I am going away.

"And she started to carve, learned it, and two years later he went away."

Amaro Francisco Borges died in 2005. His widow, Nena, lives in Bezerros, but, Severino says, she has no atelier and rarely makes. A few works by both of Severino's parents remain in Ana Maria's inventory in Recife, and they support Severino's opinion. Nena draws well and Amaro's prints, signed AF for Amaro Francisco, display delicate, decorative borders with flowers and birds, contributed by Nena Borges.

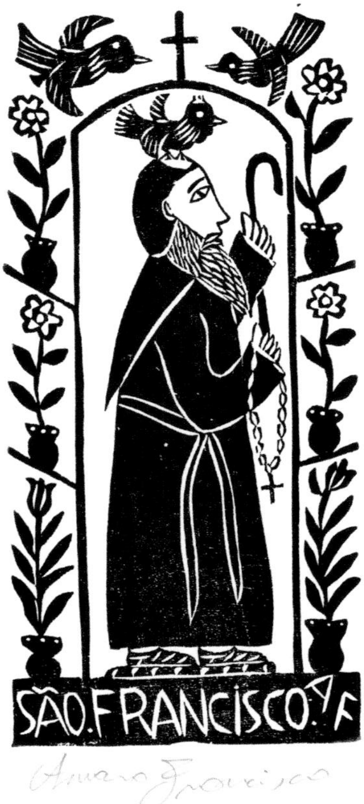

Saint Francis, by Amaro Francisco Borges (20 × 10 cm), c. 2000

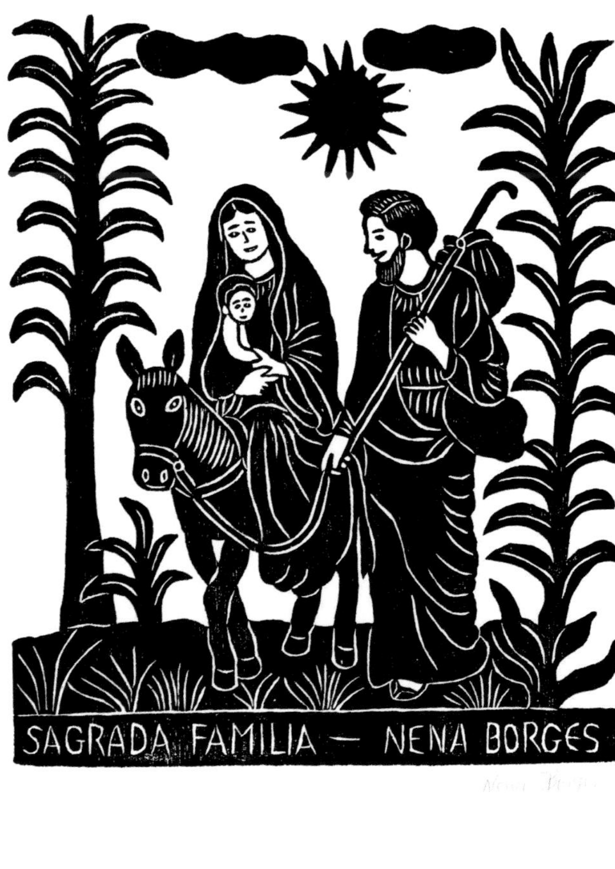

The Sacred Family, by Nena Borges (30 × 25 cm), c. 2015

Severino watched them work in Bezerros, but he was not drawn into participation. He graduated from high school, an unusual accomplishment for the artists of his region whose education was generally cut short by serious work in the family shop. On graduation at eighteen, Severino married. His father told him that a married man had to work, and he found employment in a plastics factory. He was unhappy, unsatisfied. In January of 1996, Amaro Francisco moved to Olinda, believing it to be a better location for making and selling woodblock prints. That summer he planned an exhibition and asked Severino to come and help him. Severino recalls:

"In ninety-six, Father came from Bezerros to Olinda. He came to work. In Bezerros at the time it was very weak. Woodblock prints were unsustainable. Then he came here.

"I quit my job in the plastics industry and came here to work with Father. I stayed here doing his work.

"Father said, You will work here for three months, and I will take responsibility for you. And in three months we will mount an exhibition.

"Then I started. I was producing for him. Nobody taught me; I had no apprenticeship. I bought the wood, got the paper, and had it all in my head. I would draw on the paper, then carve, and I made fifteen prints in three months. We mounted the exhibition.

"That is how I began. For two years I worked for him, then I went off on my own.

"That was the beginning. When I was in Bezerros, I did not make woodblock prints. I would visit J. Borges, visit my uncle, but I was never interested in making.

"I began when I came to help my father. He is my idol; he gave me much support. I began in Olinda, and I am the only one of the Borges family here in Olinda, The only one in this work. And my work, my art started in Olinda.

"I have been here for more than twenty years. But every fifteen days I am in Bezerros to see the region, to see what is difficult, to look, to do research. To talk with the country people, the people of the ranches.

"To talk with the older folks, the older folks who have the history, the stories for me to draw.

"I go back to drink at the source."

Severino's art flows from that source. He speaks first of its importance:

"The cover of the *cordel* illustrates a story in verse. The prints for the house show the folklore, the environment of the Northeast.

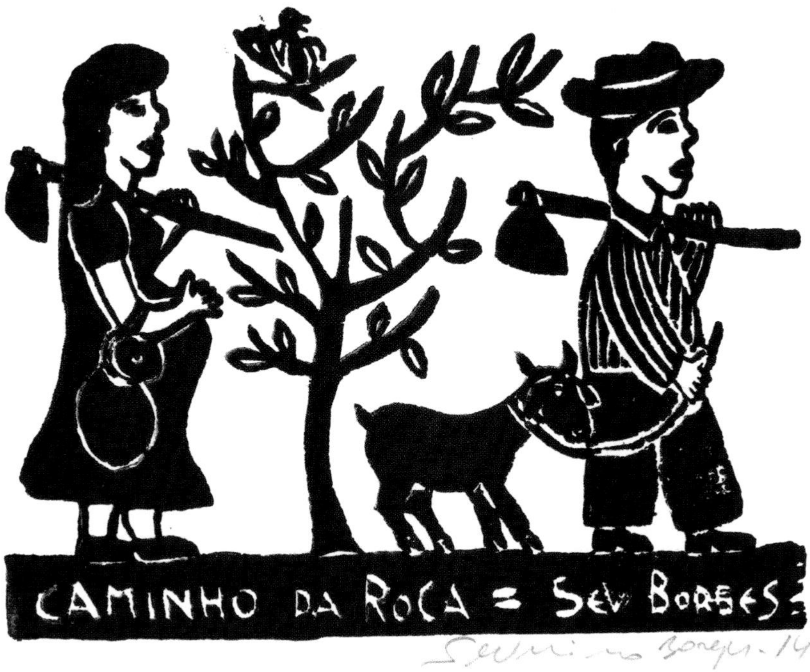

The Path from the Fields, by Severino Borges (13 × 17 cm), 2014

"My father worked in building construction and made woodblock prints on the side. Today, no. Today I work as a professional. I want to improve, to get better, right?

"J. Borges said it is good to tell a lie. The more we lie, the more the story becomes pretty, everything becomes pretty and people like it.

"We tell the tales of the people. I go to the interior and talk with someone and an idea emerges. It becomes a story.

"I tell the story of the day-to-day, the work, the dances. My art is geared toward the culture, toward the folklore of the region.

"It is so others can know it, so we can remember it. The Northeast has suffered. Outsiders are prejudiced against the people here. They discriminate against them. We are showing that the Northeast has many beautiful things. Many good things.

"And people like it. It is very important."

Severino's art flows from the source and finds its center where the repertories of Bezerros and Alto do Moura converge. He says, "We make the classics, Lampião, Luiz Gonzaga, the quotidian, the work on the farm. I have a print showing farm folks going to the fields, and another showing them coming back at the end of the day. Then there are the folkloristic ones, *Maracatu*, the dancers."

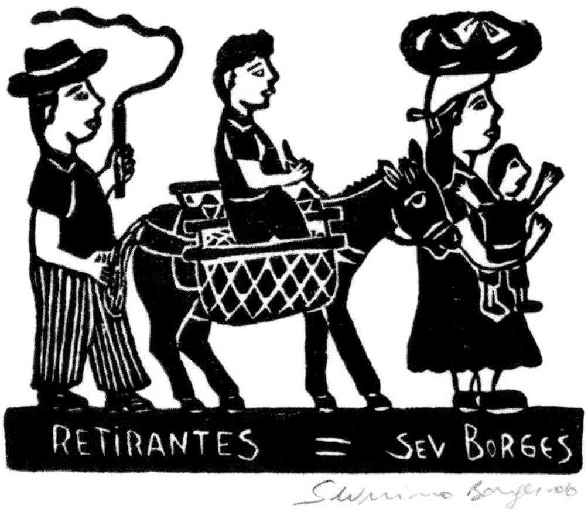

Retirantes, by Severino Borges (13 × 16 cm), 2006

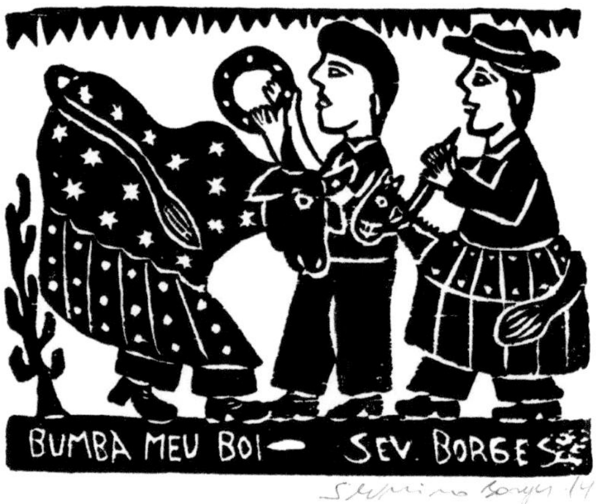

Bumba-Meu-Boi, by Severino Borges (13 × 16 cm), 2014

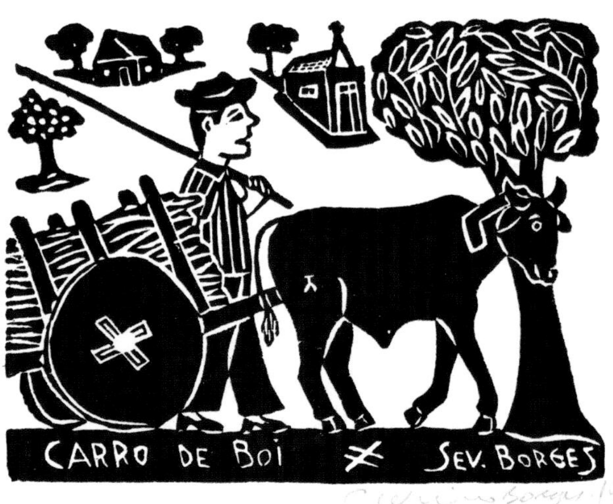

Oxcart, by Severino Borges (13 × 16 cm), 2014

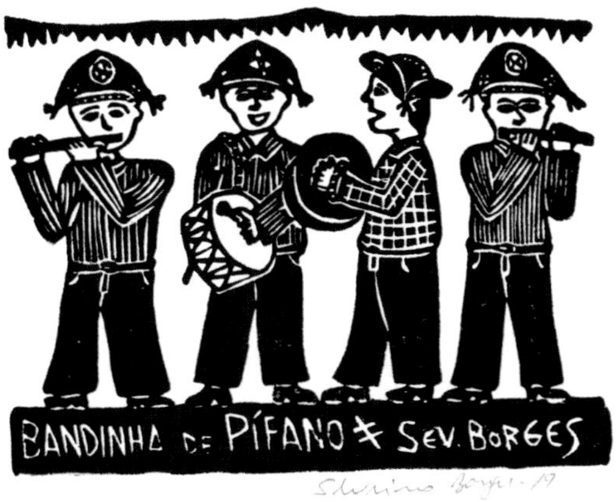

The Small *Pífano* Band, by Severino Borges (13 × 17 cm), 2019

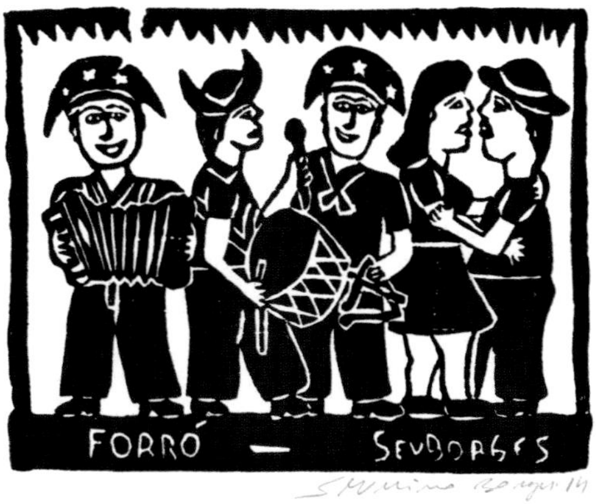

Forró, by Severino Borges (13 × 16 cm), 2014

Three times — in 2007, 2014, and 2019 — we took notes while looking through stacks of Severino's prints, most of them small, and — dividing them now as he does — we can list the ones that he has most consistently and abundantly made over time:

In the quotidian, rural set: *Retirantes* (father, mother, and two children, one mounted), *Carro de Boi* (the Oxcart), and *Caminho da Roça* (the Path from the Fields, husband, wife, and goat, the goat taken along so no one will steal it).

In the folkloristic set: *Ciranda* (children playing ring around the rosy), *Violeiros* (a pair of guitarists playing in a bar), *Forró* (the Northeastern trio with a dancing couple), *Bandinha de Pífano* (The Small Pífano Band, with four rather than six musicians), and then single images of the performances introduced by Manuel Eudócio and Zé Caboclo: *Bumba-Meu-Boi* (the Captain meets the Bull) and *Maracatu* (elaborate because Severino witnessed the performance and drew the image from experience, as J. Miguel drew *Papangu*, and not from images made by others).

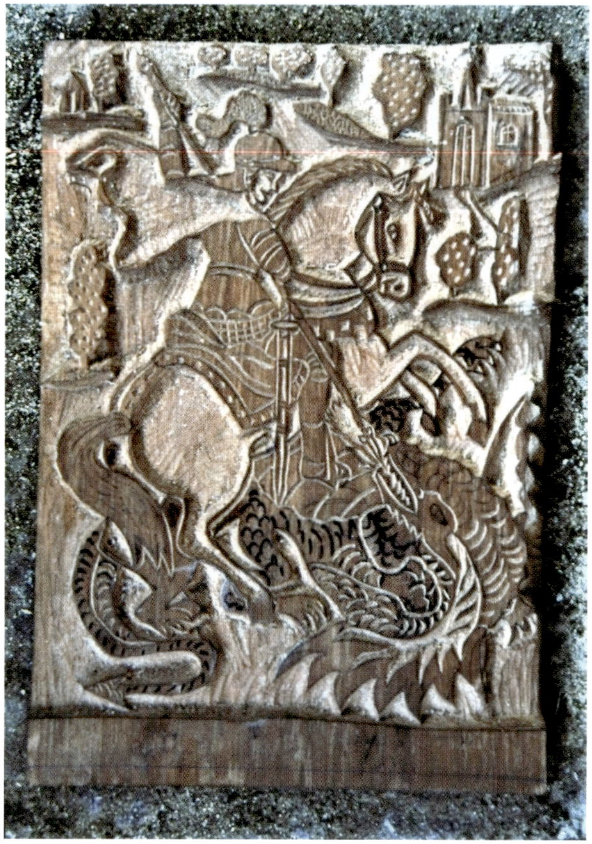

Saint George, woodblock by Severino Borges, 2014

Saints fill a third set, at the point where Bezerros departs from Alto do Moura. When we asked Severino about the sacred in 2014, he said:

"Of the religious ones I have a few, São Francisco and Nossa Senhora Aparecida.

"There is a customer of mine who has São Francisco by everyone. She has J. Borges. She has Amaro. She has Givanildo" — another woodblock artist in Bezerros. "I owe her a São Francisco. She does not want it only from one artist, she wants one from everybody.

"I have made a few saints on commission. But I am not ready to explore the religious theme, not yet.

"The moment has not arrived. I have not gotten the interest yet, right? I like it, but I have not begun this part of production.

"I work here alone, and since we have two stores" — in the Casa da Cultura — "I have to keep working to maintain the inventory. I told Ana that I am going to explore new things next year. That is maybe when the sacred part will come in."

When we ask about saints five years later, in 2019, Severino says:

"People now are asking for religious prints. What I did not make before, people are asking for it, the part with saints. And I am making it now. I make a collection of ten saints.

"I make São Francisco, Nossa Senhora da Fátima, Nossa Senhora Aparecida, Nossa Senhora Guadalupe.

"I went to Mexico. The devotion is great there for Nossa Senhora Guadalupe. It is a beautiful piece and I make it often.

"And the ones of Candomblé, Oxum, Ogum, Yemanjá, I am making these to market them. I lived in Bahia, in Salvador for three years, and I became interested."

Candomblé was developed out of African precedents in Salvador, early in the nineteenth century, then carried north to Pernambuco, south to Rio. Our friend Jorge Santos, who takes visitors to witness Candomblé services, estimates that there are twelve hundred *terreiros*, places for Candomblé worship, in the city of Salvador and four thousand in the big state of Bahia. It follows that Severino would take an interest in Salvador, and he continues:

"Yemanjá is the most popular, the one most worshiped here in the Northeast. Of the other *orixás* Ogum is the strongest.

"How do I say this? There is discrimination against the people of Candomblé, but it is a mystical thing of the people. There is mystery and beauty in the religion.

"Yemanjá is the most popular, and she is beautiful. Mermaids are beautiful, and she is a mermaid.

"This discrimination is wrong, and I am making the *orixás*. I am making the saints."

Severino is optimistic. The woodblock tradition, he says, is robust, but the demand is forever in flux and the artists must remain nimble and flexible. His father is his model. Amaro made prints on paper. Then when demand diminished, he also printed on tea towels, later returning to concentrate on the prints he never abandoned. In 1998, Severino printed on T-shirts. They were successful, and since then, while he has continued to make prints and feels that demand for them is rising again, he has also printed on a wide variety of wearable and usable items.

"The customers," Severino says, "they are pushing the creativity, and we are responding.

"They asked for a skirt. We made it. People ask for a vest. I make it. The pencil holders, we made them. Remote control holders, a tray — what arises from the customers we make.

"And then it sticks. Everything that you put woodblock prints on, it sells. Everything sells."

Severino's current success required him to double his command. A master of the handmade woodblock print, he has also — in the painstaking manner of the traditional artisan — mastered digital technology. In that, he is not unique but rare among the artists of the Northeast. It permits us to stay in touch, checking on the accuracy of the occasional fact, and we were able to send him a photographic portrait we took, and it is now featured on his website. That pleases us, just as we are pleased to see photos we took of Manuel Eudócio on the wall in Luiz Carlos's shop.

Follow now his double technique. Severino begins with a preparatory sketch on paper. If the piece has been commissioned, he can take a digital photo of the sketch, and send it through the internet for approval. Commissioned or not, the sketch precedes a drawing made on the block with a pencil, and then he works like J. Miguel, cutting around the figures, gouging out the background, inking the *matriz*, and printing it on paper by running the *carrinho* back and forth, up and down. The print is done.

When the image is destined to appear on fabric, for a tote bag, say, or a piece of clothing, Severino has found that if he uses the inked *matriz*, the print, depending on the fabric's weave, might be shaky or faint, so he takes a digital photograph of the woodblock print. It must be an actual, handmade print because the character of the image depends on the carving and printing; it can't be a black-and-white drawing. Severino owns a scanner, and he scans the print at a high resolution and sends it through the internet to a firm in Recife that converts it into a "silk screen" — the English term is used in Portuguese.

Severino draws, cuts, and prints the original in a bright room upstairs that affords a pretty view over Olinda. Downstairs in a studio, he takes the silk screen, inks it, and transfers the image onto a piece of cloth that a seamstress will cut and stitch into the final form. He says:

"Many people question whether a woodblock print on fabric is really a woodblock print. It is. It was carved on wood. We preserve the traces from the original on wood.

"It is just that it has been digitized, something modern. And then it was passed to the fabric. We did not have a means before to print so clearly on fabric."

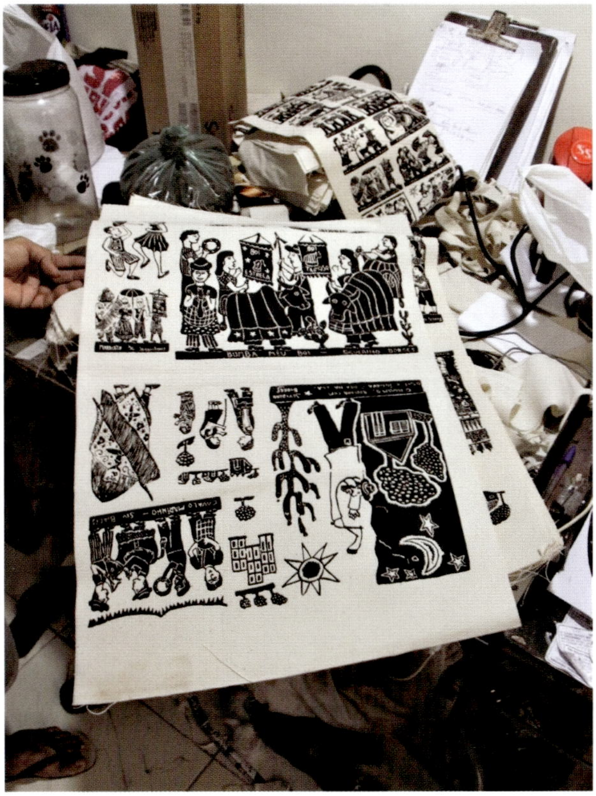

Printed cloth, awaiting the work of the seamstress,
in Severino's shop, Olinda, 2019

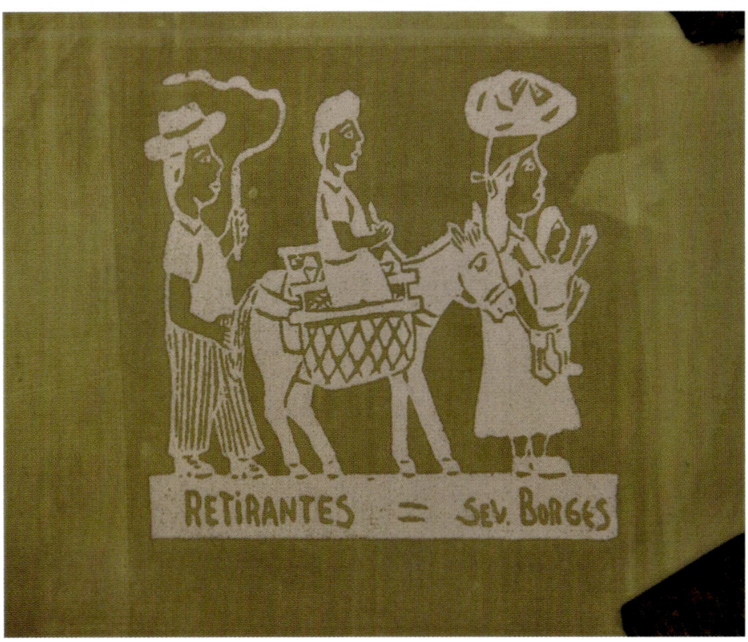

Silk screen for *Os Retirantes* in Severino's shop, 2019

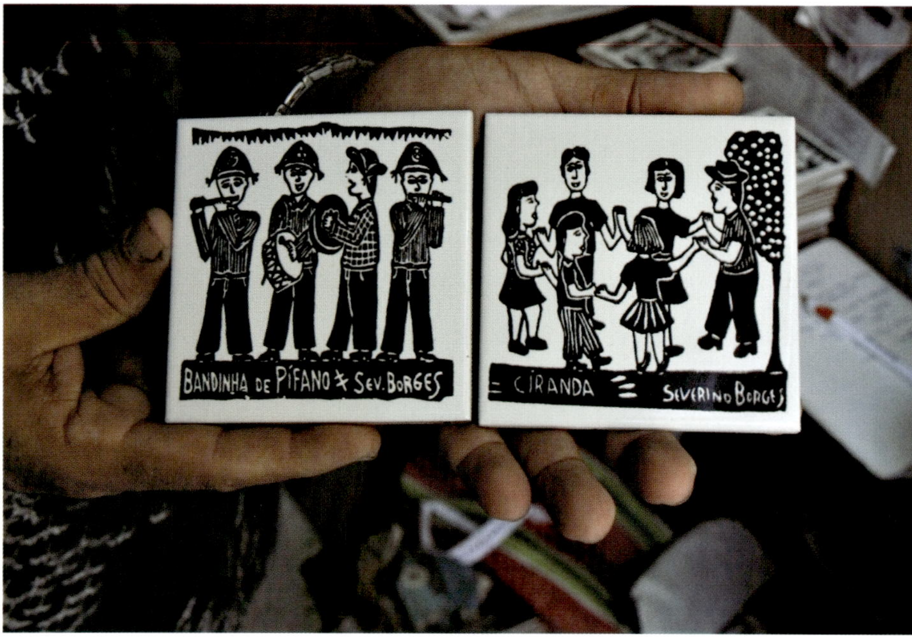

Tiles by Severino: the *pífano* band and children playing *ciranda*, 2019

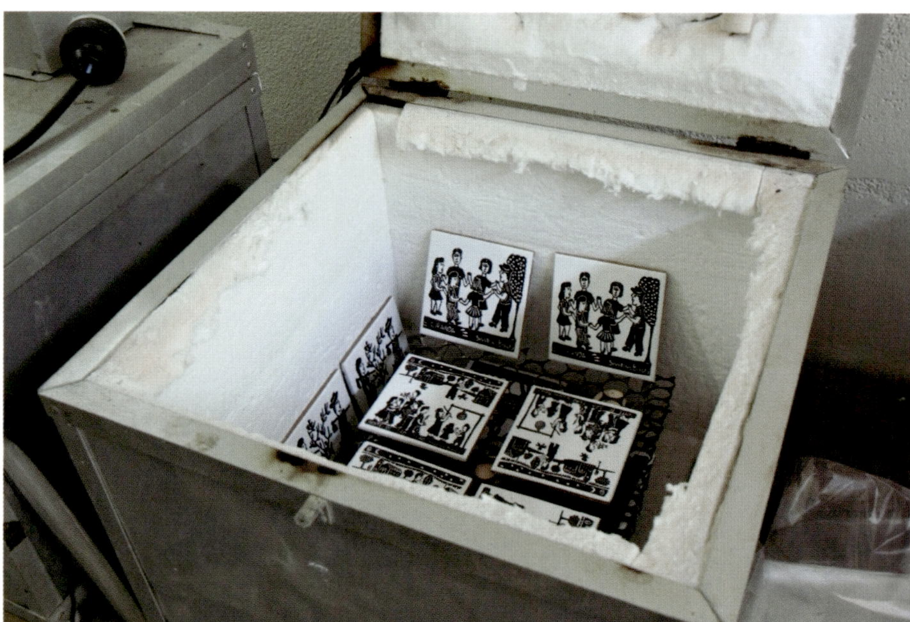

Tiles in Severino's kiln, 2019

Printing satisfactorily on tiles proved more difficult than printing on cloth. Severino's word for tiles is *azulejos*. Historically, *azulejos* were suites of blue-and-white tiles, technically *maiolica*, that were painted with sacred scenes in Portugal, then revetted to the walls of splendid baroque churches in Brazil, during the eighteenth century. Today the word simply means tiles, and tiles present woodblock artists with two problems.

Woodblock prints are usually rectangular, wider than tall, and if a woodblock design is digitally manipulated to fit on a square tile, the image will be distorted. Severino solved that problem easily by creating square designs, drawing, cutting, inking, and printing them, then photographing them to be made into silk screens. The other problem, harder to solve, is that if the design is transferred to a tile that is not subsequently fired, the tile will weather poorly, discoloring and disintegrating in an unstable, humid atmosphere. Severino knew that tiles were properly manufactured in Ceará, old tiles from Ceará are affixed to the facade of his shop, so he traveled north to Ceará to discover how it was done:

"I went to see a friend in Ceará. She made *azulejos* there in Ceará. Then she said, Let's make a partnership. You supply the designs. I will make the pictures" — on tiles — "and I will give you a percentage of the profit.

"Then I understood the partnership was one-sided, only she benefited. Then I said, No. I am going to try to make them.

"I will see if I can learn. Then I traveled to Curitiba" — far to the south in the state of Paraná. "When I got there I met a girl who painted ceramic pieces and burned them in a little kiln.

"I said, Will you teach me how to do this?

"Why, Severino?

"Because I want to make these *azulejos*.

"She taught me her style, which is the correct style for *azulejos*. Still, it took me six months of work before I got it right."

Now Severino buys tiles from a supplier of building materials. He silk screens them with the right paint — *tinta porcelana* — and places them in the electric kiln in his studio, lifting the heat for an hour to six hundred degrees, then holding the heat at nine hundred for an hour and twenty minutes. It took time and diligence, it took the artist's eye and the craftsman's caring hand, and Severino produces tiles with designs on the square and surfaces that will hold through tropical heat and lashing storms.

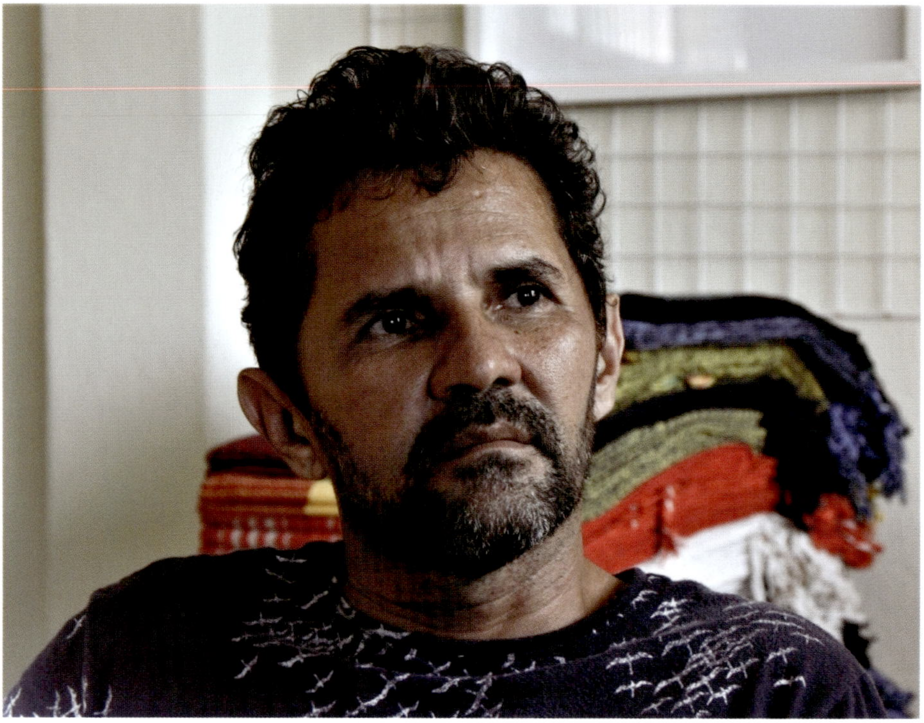

Severino Borges, Olinda, 2019

He knows the old, he knows the new, and balanced for contingency, Severino Borges is moving forward with confidence. Right now, in June of 2019, he says things are good:

"The *feira* here, Fenearte, takes place in July. It is the *feira* that sustains us all year round. I work for it from March to June, making products to sell. Then I make the commissions that customers request at the *feira*.

"I participate in Fenearte every year, and we have two stores in Recife, at the Casa da Cultura. Ana sells there, sales are good, and she learns every day what the customers want.

"She is selling and we are seeing the needs of the people. They say, Make this. And we make it.

"Once it was bags, but what they are demanding now is the colored woodblock print on paper. The colored one. My father made it, but it was forgotten for a while, right? Now it is returning, people are asking for colorful woodblock prints on paper, and I am making them, many of them.

"They are for the wall, and the consumption of the pure, colorful woodblock print on paper, it is great today.

"It is like this.

"You go to the modern. Then later you return to the classics. And the woodblock print never goes out of fashion. It never gets tired. People like it.

"The future is strong. It is strong."

Things are good in Olinda. In Caruaru, Severino's brother Silvo is a police officer, but he learned with Amaro when he was seven, he has arranged a shop in his garage, and when he retires from the force, he will return to making woodblock prints, and, Severino says, his prints are excellent.

In Bezerros, Severino says, Ivan, J. Borges's son, works in the town hall and his shop is usually closed. Givanildo, J. Borges's nephew, also has a shop that is often closed. J. Miguel, Severino says, was raised with J. Borges and he is energetically at work in his stepfather's old shop. But the big story is unfolding in J. Borges's grand atelier:

"In Bezerros, J. Borges has a big space, really good. They have an excellent atelier. They receive the students, the schools. They have many, profitable school-related dealings.

"Now the youngest sons of J. Borges have taken on the atelier of their famous father. It is a big responsibility.

"They drive everything, these two boys, Pablo and Bacaro. Their work is good. Pablo's work is really good. They are very responsible. They have given a lift to their father's work. Uncle is eighty-four years of age. They are giving a lift.

"I received it from my father and continued, with a very good *dom* to make very good work.

"And both of those boys are like that. They make very good work, both of them. There is new life in the atelier of J. Borges.

"Everything started with J. Borges."

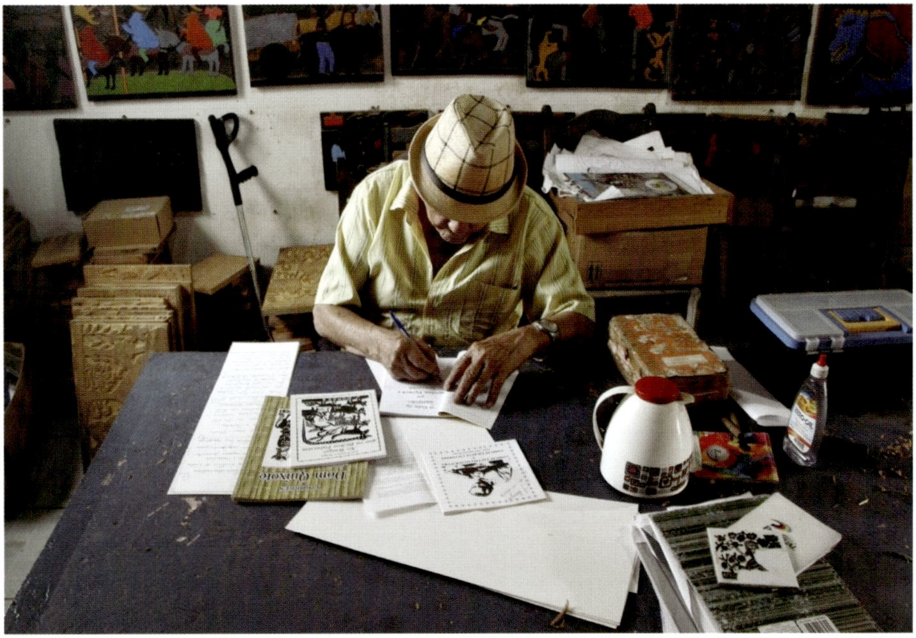

J. Borges at work in the atelier, 2019

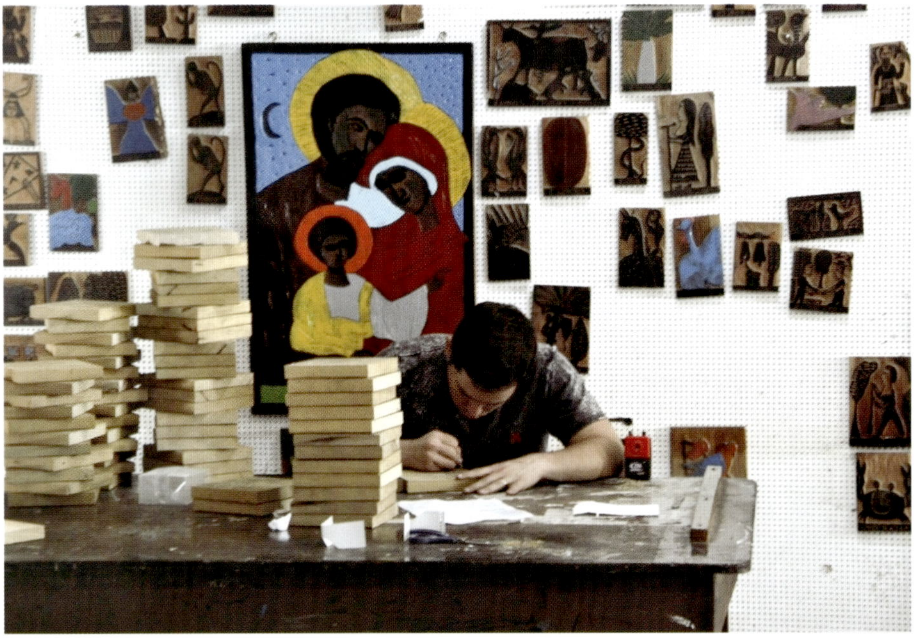

Pablo Borges at work in the atelier, 2019

22

Pablo and Bacaro

The next generation is in command, and Pablo is the man in the middle. J. Borges named his last two sons after helpful friends. Pablo was named for Pablo Stähli, a Swiss writer who lived in Recife, collected Pernambucan art, and mounted exhibitions featuring J. Borges. Joaquim Bacaro was named for J. Borges's friend and collector Giuseppe Baccaro, the spelling adjusted to Portuguese convention (the great Portuguese novelist José Saramago considered it a blessing that the double consonants of Italian were dropped in Portuguese). In June of 2019, when Bacaro was nineteen and Pablo was twenty-five, we sat with Pablo to bring the story up to date. Pablo José Borges began by saying:

"When my father had me, all of my brothers were much older, right? I was the youngest and I was raised inside the atelier.

"He would come here for work. The atelier was attached to the house, and I would go with him. Following him, I would get here and just play around. But when I was four or five years old I started to get interested. Always, since I was little, I liked to draw, trying to imitate him.

"But then, after four or five years of age, I already started trying to carve, right? I would take the wood, scratching it and trying to carve, but I ended up doing nothing.

"When I was still seven years old, I made my first print. It was badly made, of course, due to my age. But I made it, and my father's customers saw that I was interested, and someone bought my first one.

"I drew it and carved it, and my father said, Oh, he will be so happy. When I got home from school, there was the money, right there. Now I'm going to make more, I said, and then I started to make.

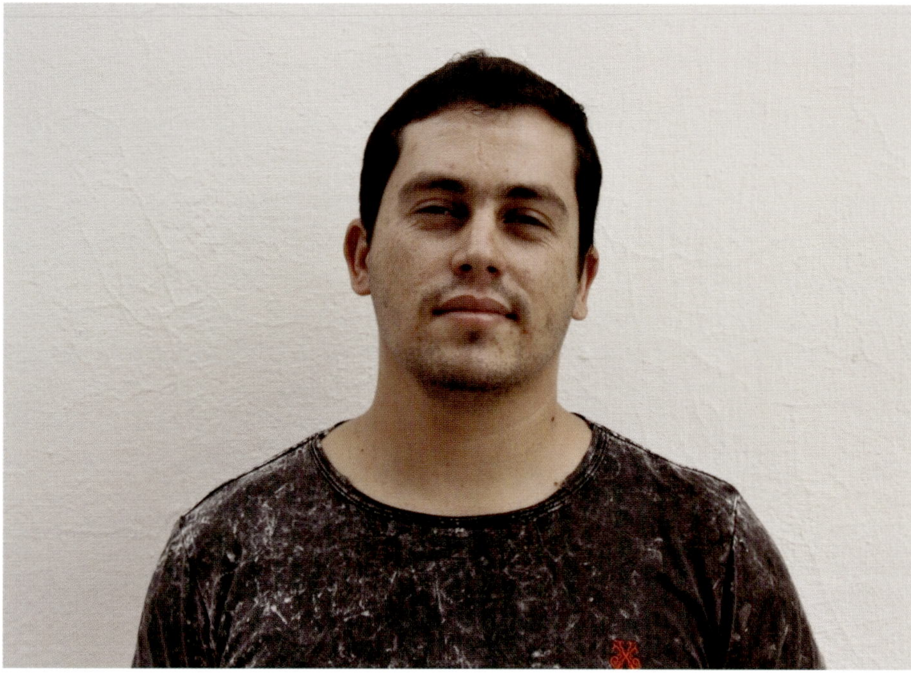

Pablo Borges, 2019

"My father said that it was not he who taught me. He said I learned by wanting to make. But it was he. He was my master, and still is.

"And it was from there I started, and until today, I continue to make. Today I am twenty-five years old, and I am giving continuity to his legacy."

Raised in the atelier, like the artists of Alto do Moura, Pablo began by playing, by wanting to make, and then, as Ademilson said, when the first piece is sold, the possibility of a career opens. A childhood piece by Pablo remains to be seen because at the age of eight he made a woodblock print for the cover of a *cordel* and it was reproduced on a postcard still sold in the atelier. The *folheto's* text is a letter in verse sent by Satan to George W. Bush, praising him for the genocidal violence of his war on Iraq. Pablo's print shows Satan wearing cowboy boots, the letter to Bush in his right hand and in his left one of the USA bombs that would drop to murder thousands of innocent civilians in Baghdad. The Brazilian boy had taken a stand against evil, and an adult now he continues his story:

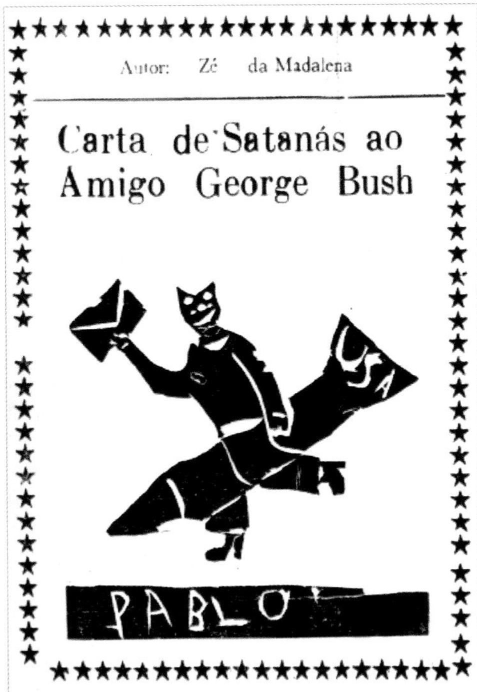

Postcard of the *cordel* Pablo illustrated (c. 2004), 2019

"When I actually decided to follow the legacy of the prints is when I had completed my studies and I was thinking about college, right?

"I thought about many types of subject to study in college. But I thought: My father is already at an advanced age, and there are eighteen children in total. I am number seventeen, and there is another, the youngest one, Joaquim Bacaro. Then what happens?

"It was only me and the youngest one who still lived here with him. And I wanted to help in some way, with this work that I know how to make.

"And I decided that, instead of going to college, I wanted to enter and continue my father's legacy, understand?

"It is not easy, of course, because when you are starting out, everything is difficult. For him it is different because he has a known name, and everything for him is easier now. But it was a tough struggle for him to get here, right?

"And I tried — I am trying — to follow his career beside him, and for me it is a bit easier because to every corner I go, I go with him.

"Other brothers of mine also make, but me and the youngest one, we are the ones who are living here with him, who are really trying to maintain everything that our father will leave behind one day.

"We are still following his legacy. We always portray the Northeast. We follow his themes, but we don't want to resemble each other. Everyone's work is a bit different.

"My father's work is more rustic. Mine is more specific, more detailed, understand? The difference is in the drawing, the drawing. The line.

"The carving ends up being the same, because it is carving wood, right? But the drawing, we can say, is an artistic identification. Every artist leaves a little bit of himself in his drawings.

"He has his drawing and I have mine. He works at one end of the table. I work at the other end. Always, every day, we work, but we never copy each other, and we end up with each one wanting his own things.

"It is always similar in theme, right? But the drawing is always different."

Pablo, like J. Miguel, locates the inevitable difference among artists in the line. J. Borges's line is free and energetic, Pablo's is smooth and confident, Bacaro's pulls verve from pop culture. And Pablo, like Severino Borges, locates creativity in the mind. "When it is a creation," Pablo says, "everything you think, you draw. The actual creation, it is all in the head. Then it is all actually created."

If, for a commission, Pablo must copy a picture, he works between hand and eye, concentrating on what he sees and surrendering much of his creativity to the image set before him. But when he works within the traditional themes, he has seen so many different renderings that he pulls from memory, creating an image in his head while he draws, focused on his hand in motion. This is a general trait of traditional art. The singer has heard the song so often, the artist has seen the image so often, that during performance the new piece arises from the self to become the performer's own, a personal blending of continuity and variability in the creation of an individual in a moment.

Pablo now tells us about the themes that connect him to his father and provide him with his resource for fresh creation. And since he is sixty-one years younger than J. Borges, thirty-five years younger than J. Miguel, the youngest of all the artists we interviewed, his statement is valuable in itself for carrying thoughts from the rising generation. Pablo says:

"Like my father, I seek to portray the Sertão, the Northeast of Brazil. In creation, we always portray the Northeast, the customs and the people from here. The characters, the folkloristic themes, and much more: Lampião, Maria Bonita, and the carnival themes, the festivities in June.

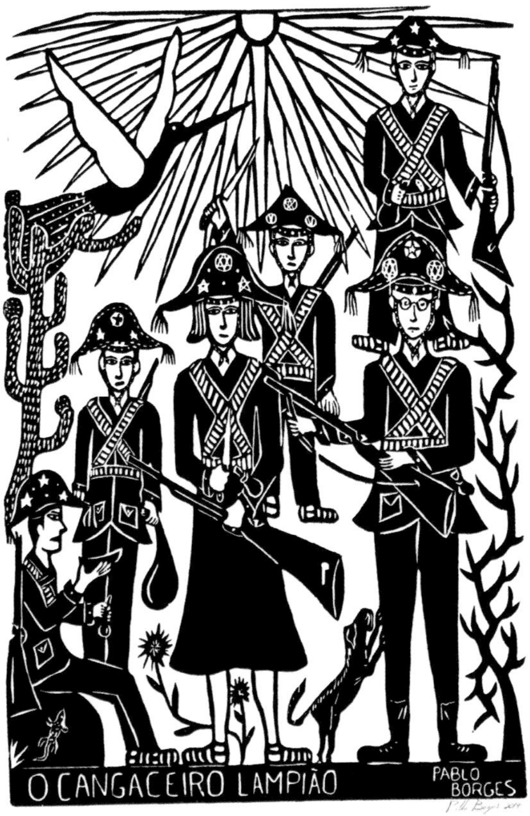

The Bandit Lampião, by Pablo (60 × 40 cm), 2019

"And it goes from there. See: Lampião, Luiz Gonzaga, and Padre Cícero, something that all of them have in common is that they were patriotic. They were people from the Northeastern end of the story.

"Luiz Gonzaga sang the entire Northeast. Lampião protected the entire Northeast. Padre Cícero was also part of it with his prayers, since he was the priest of the Northeast.

"And all of them were from the Northeast. Then it spread through Brazil, and even to the whole world. These three figures, understand? And since we work much with the Northeast, portraying the Northeast, we always have these figures at the tip of the pencil.

"And we try to make things to the taste of the customers, of course. But they — especially Lampião and Maria Bonita — they are always sought. It is because of history.

"Because Lampião, some people say Lampião was bad. But no. You learn the history of Lampião correctly, reading it, analyzing it, and you understand that he was just.

"He only found himself a bandit" — a *cangaceiro* — "he only turned into an outlaw, we can say, because a bandit came and murdered his entire family. Out of revenge, he became a bandit and murdered the family of the guy who had done this thing to him.

"And from there he became a captain and assembled men behind him. Then some coward betrayed him, and they killed him.

"Whatever we think, he was a man outside the law. He had to find a way, and he was good at fighting the soldiers. He made history, and he ended up turning into a myth.

"He became a mythic person of our region, a myth of the Northeast, and now of all Brazil.

"He is a symbol, because Lampião is a lamp that illuminates. And Maria Bonita was the name he gave her because he found her very pretty" — *bonita* — "and he said that was her name, Maria Bonita.

"In the gang of bandits there was Lampião, and fifty men, and there was one woman who was his woman.

"And they were Lampião and Maria Bonita. They turned into a symbol, right? A symbol of love. That's it."

A little later we ask Pablo about other aspects of his repertory. It was at this point in the conversation when some of the artists in Alto do Moura told us that they made no saints, but Pablo says that, while Northeastern themes prevail, he also explores "religious themes":

"I made my first religious print through a commission, and I found it very beautiful.

"It was Nossa Senhora Aparecida, and it was very beautiful. Very detailed. I put many details, and I said, Oh, man, I should make another saint. And I made many, and I have sold them, of course.

"The one I most like to make is São Francisco. My father also makes São Francisco. His name is Francisco" — José Francisco Borges — "but he says he likes to make it because São Francisco sells the best."

Pablo laughs and continues, "But I like to make it as a kind of homage to him.

"São Francisco, he is the Protector of Animals, right? And my fondness for animals has much to do with it.

"And the art of it: the saints make beautiful prints."

Change is the topic now, and Pablo begins with a sketch of J. Borges's career:

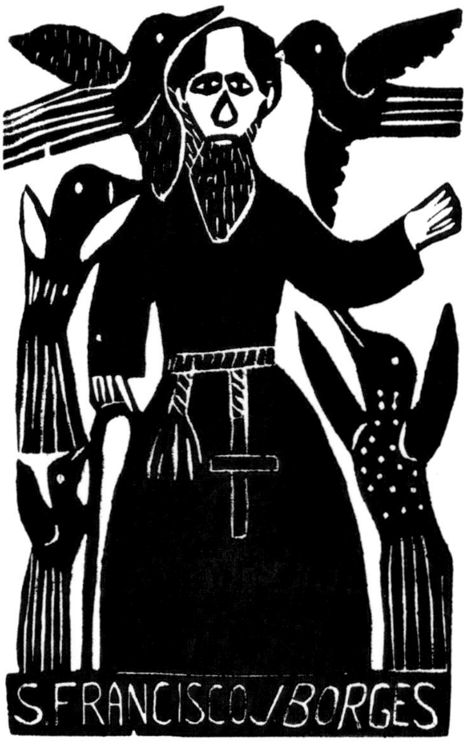

Saint Francis, by J. Borges
(25 × 16 cm), 2015

Saint Francis by Pablo
(49 × 20 cm), 2018

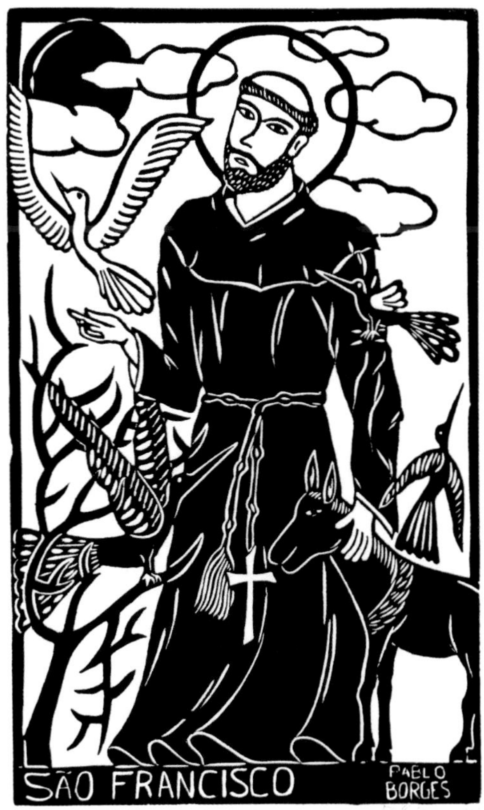

"My father studied for only ten months, and after that his schooling was finished; he got no opportunity to study again. At that time he fell in love with the *cordel* because there was no television and people would gather in the villages to read the *cordels*.

"And he fell in love with the *cordel*. From his ten months of schooling he knew how to read and he wanted very much to make a *cordel* one day. And he ended up making many *cordels*, right up to today, thank God.

"Then the woodblock print left the cover of the *cordel* and became decorative while his name spread.

"His name spread, and he started making the prints bigger, a little bit bigger, a little bit bigger, and they started attracting the interest of the galleries and the visual artists who saw his work. And from there it went.

"At first the print was black and white, right? Even today the woodblock print, the traditional one is black and white, but the desire of the people is ninety percent for the colored one."

Severino Borges also said that the demand is now for the colored prints. Pablo continues:

"My father is the one who developed the technique to use a single *matriz* to make both black-and-white and colored prints, and the colored one attracts much attention. Understand?

"It becomes a decorative art and many interior decorators seek it. And there are plenty of regular people who buy it to decorate their homes.

"Nowadays, we are commercializing it. If we make more, we can sell more, understand?"

Making more to sell more: the success of the colored print — the increase in demand and the increase in production to meet and stimulate demand — led to a transformation in the atelier and its workforce.

Up to this point, all the ateliers have been small in type, family workshops, their range in complexity illustrated in Alto do Moura. Amanda shapes the clay and paints her figures at a table in her home. Carmélia works in her home where her daughter does the painting. Luiz Carlos has a shop next to his house where he works with his wife who has her own line of production. In the Zé Caboclo shop, three men, two brothers and a nephew, work on their own projects but join in firing. Comparably, the woodblock artists, J. Miguel and Severino Borges, work alone, drawing, cutting, and printing, both of them helped in commerce by their wives. These are familial operations, the master — Marliete or J. Miguel — creating solo but gaining aid from close relatives.

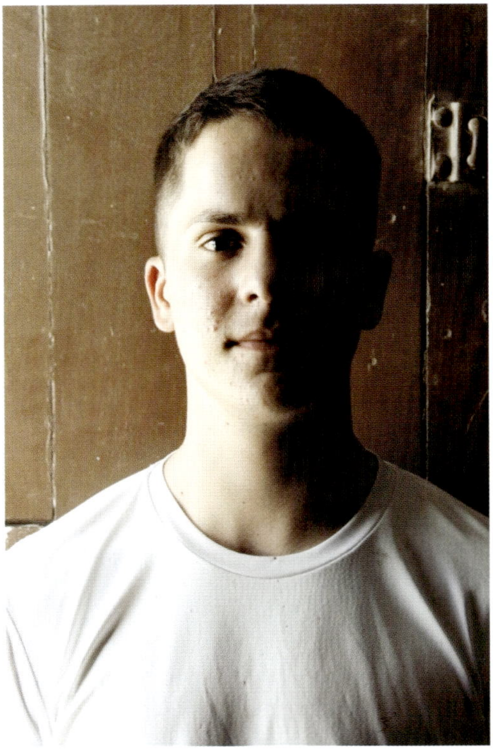

Joaquim Bacaro Borges, 2019

But the shop of J. Borges in Bezerros, admired by Severino Borges, is in its type a big atelier, characterized by workers hired from beyond the family and a clear division in labor.

Division in labor, essential in industrial production, was not a result of the industrial revolution, though division became part of the process of industrialization that, allied with capitalism, brought wealth to a few, misery to a multitude. But long before industrialization, big workshops had divided by rank and skill, and today in Portugal and Italy, in Turkey and India, in China and Japan, there are big ateliers where the work is done by hand in a preindustrial way but the workforce divides sharply by task. That is how it is in the big Borges atelier. It is all handwork, but the workers divide by responsibility in production.

There are artists who draw and cut the blocks. There are family members with specific duties, selling to customers, managing connections through the internet. And there are hired workers who ink and print the blocks.

The artists are three, Pablo says, "Me, Joaquim Bacaro, and my father. He still draws every day. In the drawing it is only we three. Then in the carving there are the three of us, plus two more. One is my uncle" — the brother of his mother, J. Borges's third wife. "Another is a brother of mine who knows how to carve.

"But the painting" — the inking of the *matriz* — "and the printing is a very slow process. If we were to print it ourselves, it would take too long, so we have people, friends and family, who help us.

"So, we carve the *matriz* and have it ready, and they do the painting and printing.

"When it started, this atelier here, it was very small. My father opened the atelier and he started teaching his son, and he raised two adopted sons. They didn't know how to make anything. Then my father went on teaching, teaching, and we have this big atelier.

"It started very small and now we have many to help us, family and friends. And we strive to make something that is very *well made*, understand? Because this attracts the customers, of course, and we divide the workshop: drawing, carving, printing, understand?

"Today I think there are twelve people working for us here. But the drawing, the only ones who draw are the actual artists."

In a simple summary, it might be said that design and production unite in the small atelier, but separate in the large atelier. That, though, would be too simple to capture the reality of the Borges shop or others like it. Here the artists are the designers. They always draw and usually carve the *matrizes* that others will print. That is their first responsibility, but they have others. They also handle the commissions. Pablo explains:

"For commissions we make an outline on paper. I make it, or my brother. My father does it, but he doesn't like it. We make a sketch and send it to the customer.

"He might ask us to alter the drawing, to add something that is missing. And we don't make it until he gives us the okay" — Pablo uses the English word and goes on:

"We transfer the drawing from the paper and naturally draw it on the wood. Then the carving comes.

"We don't usually number the prints. We make a run, sell it, then use the *matriz* again. But when it is a commission, we number the prints. We make the amount the customer wants, say one hundred. Then there will be one hundred numbered prints from that *matriz*, and it can't be used anymore.

"The *matriz* has a certain value, but it can't be used again, so we send the *matriz* to the customer, and it is finished.

"So, we charge a price for the *matriz* and send it with the run of prints the customer ordered. That's it."

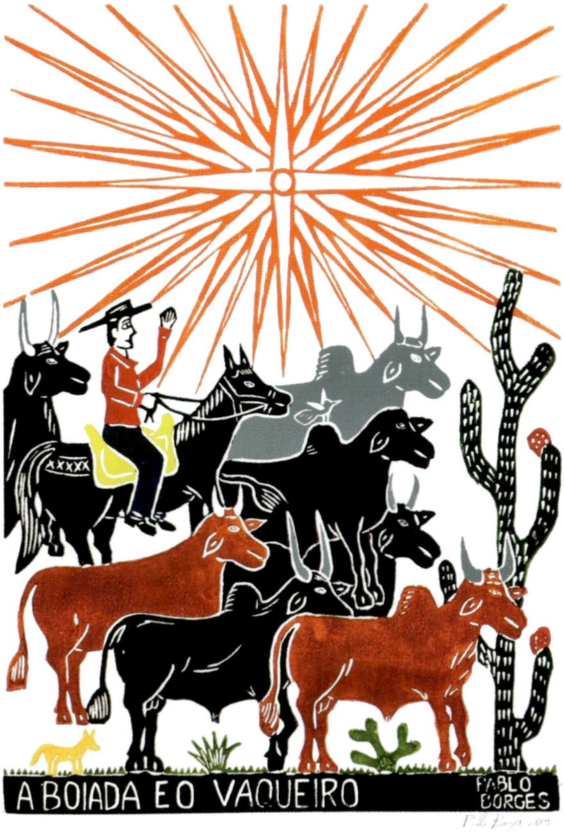

Roundup, by Pablo (49 × 34 cm), 2019

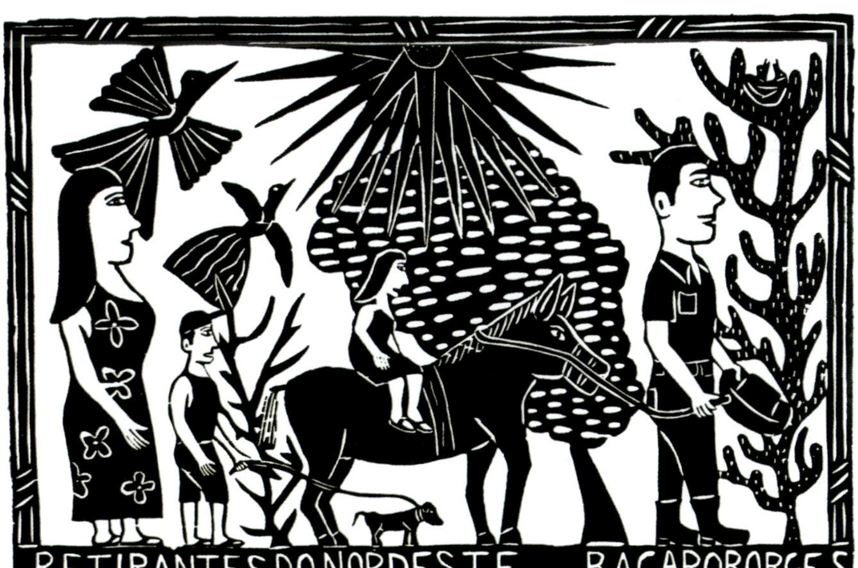

Northeastern *Retirantes*, by Bacaro (35 × 53 cm), 2019

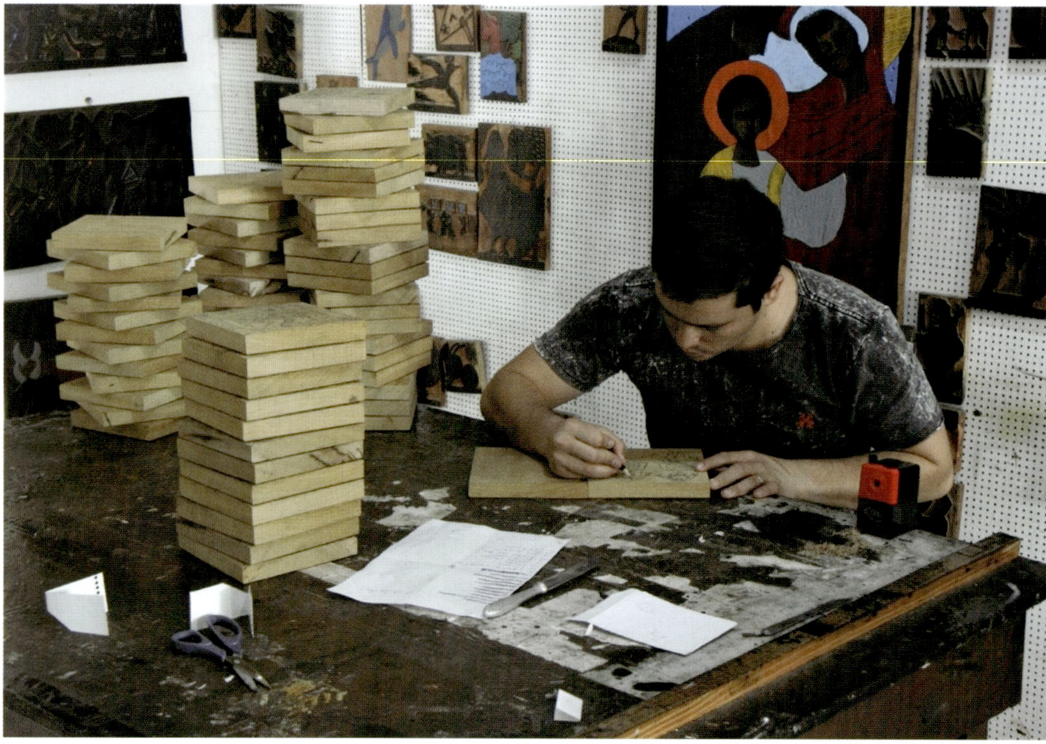

Pablo at work on his project, 2019

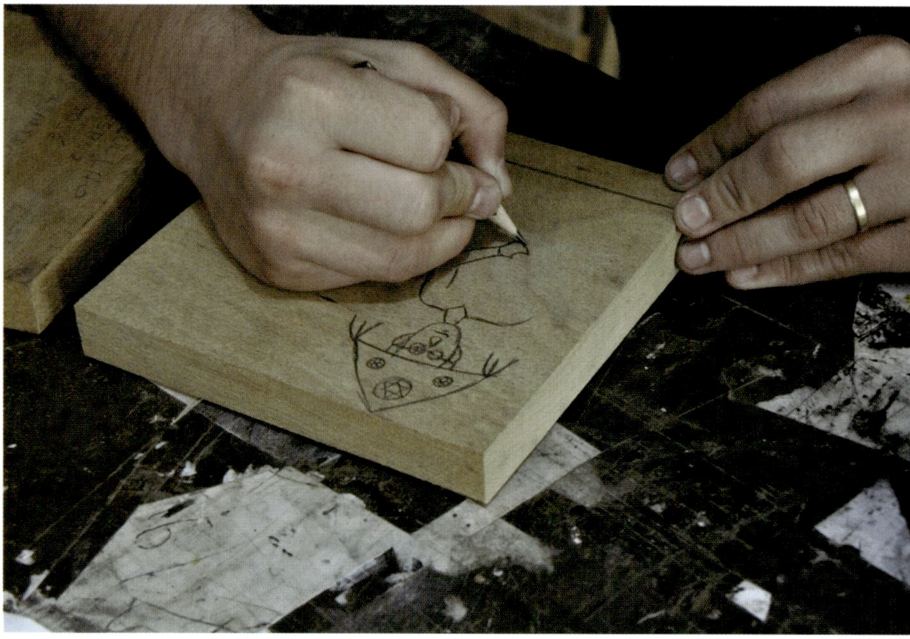

Pablo drawing Lampião on a block, 2019

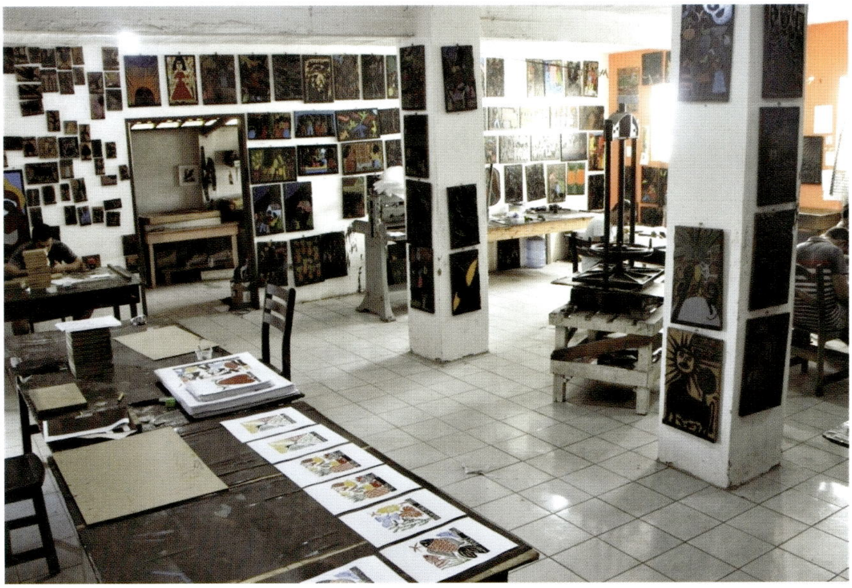

The atelier's place for printing, 2019

The artists design for the shop, respond to commissions, and they all have artistic projects of their own. They can work away from the crowd in a small shop to the side while the big shop fills with busy workers, painting and printing, but once when we were there Pablo set his table in a corner of the big shop, where he would be available to answer questions. No questions came. The workers, relaxed and active, knew what they were doing, and Pablo bore down on his personal project, intense in concentration.

Pablo's project was quite like the one that Leonildo had set for himself at the same time in Alto do Moura. This was not a matter of direct influence; rather, both were dipping simultaneously from the deep well of shared traditional imagery. Leonildo was working with clay, making small tiles in relief that exemplified the themes of the Northeast. Stacked beside him, Pablo had a big heap of small blocks, all the same size. On each he planned to draw and carve an image. Several, he said, would show Lampião and Maria Bonita in different situations. Others will picture scenes from the Sertão — cactus, the blazing sun, the white-winged bird — as well as musicians and dancers, *Bumba-Meu-Boi*, lovers, a heart, a fish, and Yemanjá as a mermaid.

Relying entirely on his memory, Pablo was drawing quickly on the blocks with a pencil, cutting a few before turning to draw others. Meanwhile the workers Pablo consistently calls friends, most of them about his age, were making the colored prints.

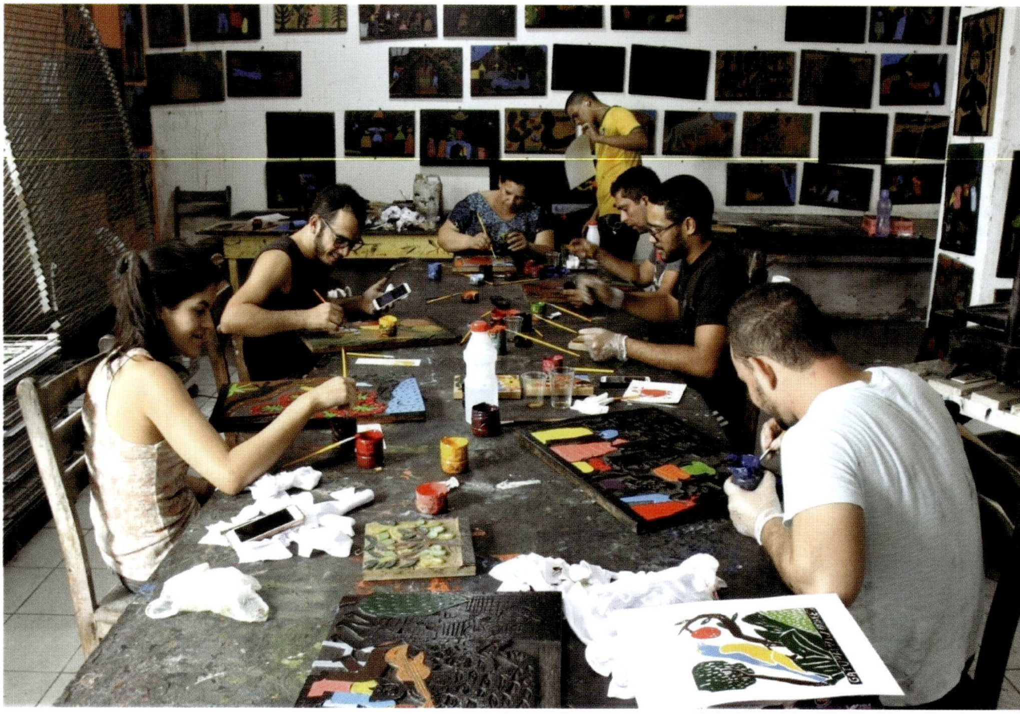

Around the table: Letícia, José, Jleyferson, Maria Célia, Emerson, David, Matias, 2019

Their space is wide, high, and bright. Around them the shop's walls carry a collection of *matrizes*, their titles written on the wall so they can be taken down, used, then replaced correctly to be used again. On the walls of the big shop we counted 242 large *matrizes* and 173 small ones. In the smaller shop to the side, where J. Borges sits to work, there are 230 big *matrizes* on the wall and another 62 in the gallery beside it. The total, more than seven hundred, testifies to the creative energy of J. Borges and his sons, and it introduces interest through diversity into the task of the team.

One time when we were there the team was reduced to the core four: Maria Célia da Silva, Emerson Otávio, José Jleyferson, and Matias Neto. On another day, Letícia and David joined them so six were sitting around the big table in the big shop. Chat and laughter were constant; all were working at a steady, easy pace on their own *matrizes* at different points in the sequence of the shared procedure.

They begin by cleaning the face of the *matriz* with a solvent, removing dried crust but leaving enough of the old color to guide their painting. They

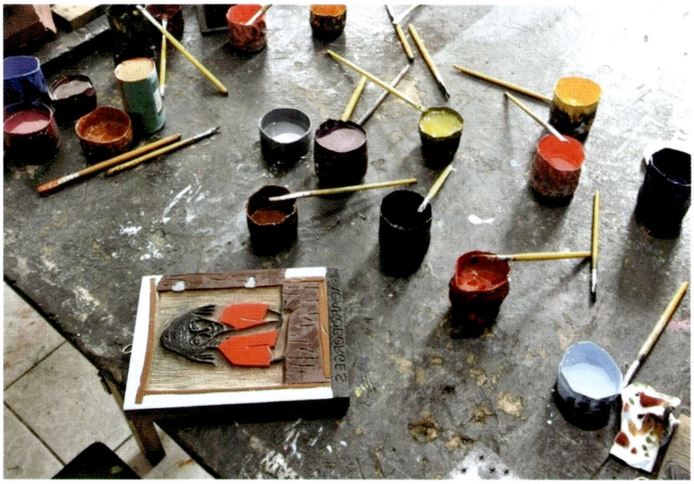

Ink and brushes, 2019

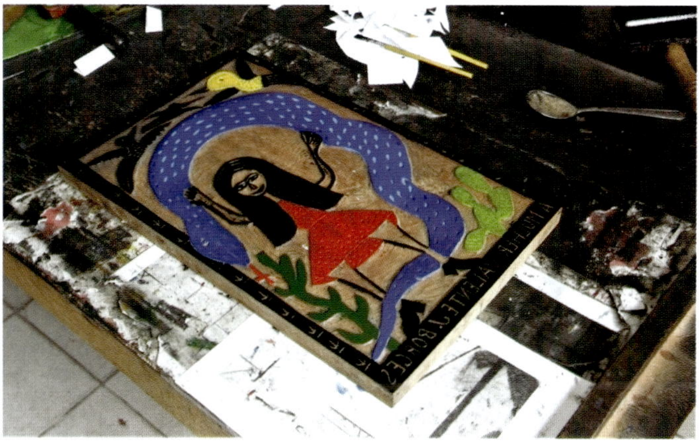

Inking in progress on a *matriz* by J. Borges, The Brave Woman

deepen narrow grooves, then using small rollers — but watercolor brushes more often — they paint the *matriz* with the tinted inks that Pablo's uncle, José Venancio, called Dedé, mixes and prepares. They coat the raised sections between sharp cuts with solid blocks of color. Then, once a *matriz* has been painted, Maria Célia, Emerson, or José print on tables to the side, working in exactly the way that J. Miguel and Severino do: placing a sheet of paper on the inked face and driving the little car of rollers over it.

One inking will yield two impressions. After that the *matriz* will have to be cleaned and painted again, or it will be thoroughly cleaned before being used for a black-and-white impression. Undated, the *matriz* can be used for many years to make new prints that might be dated in pencil to the year of printing. Printing seems the final step, but it is not. The print must be inspected and retouched with ink, usually by Matias, to meet the shop's exacting standards.

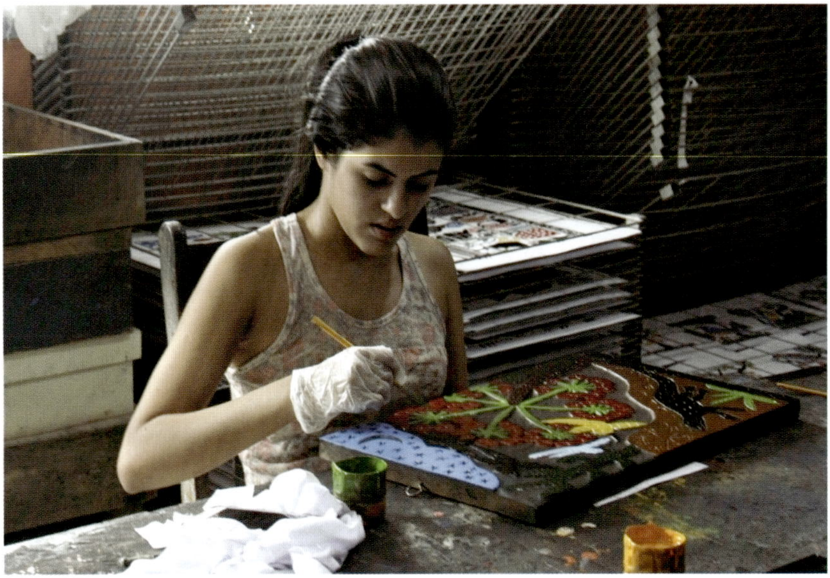

Letícia Santos painting

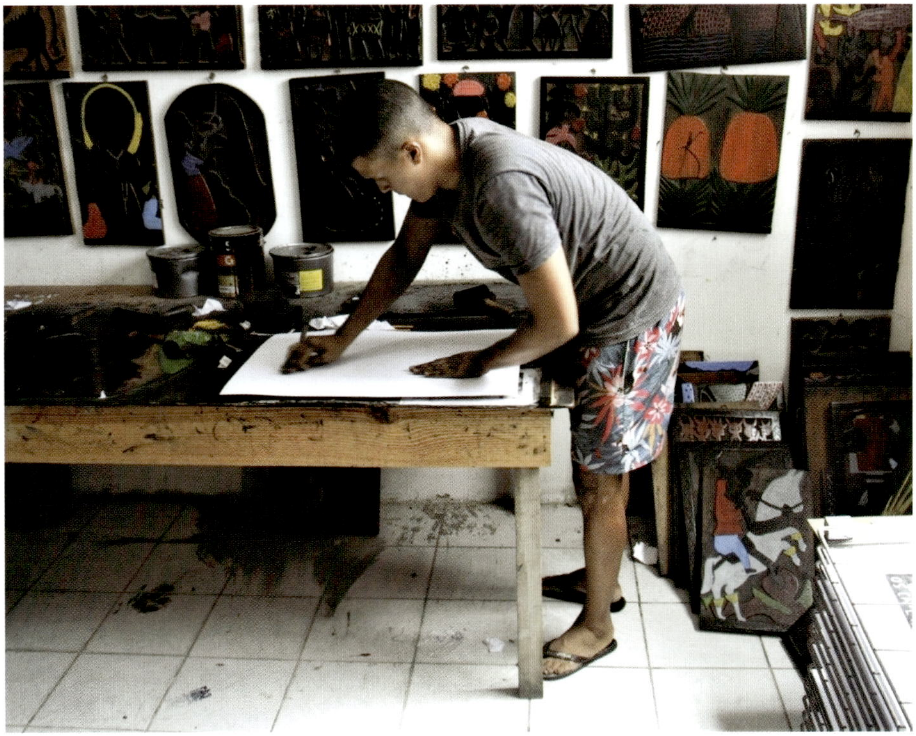

Emerson Otávio printing

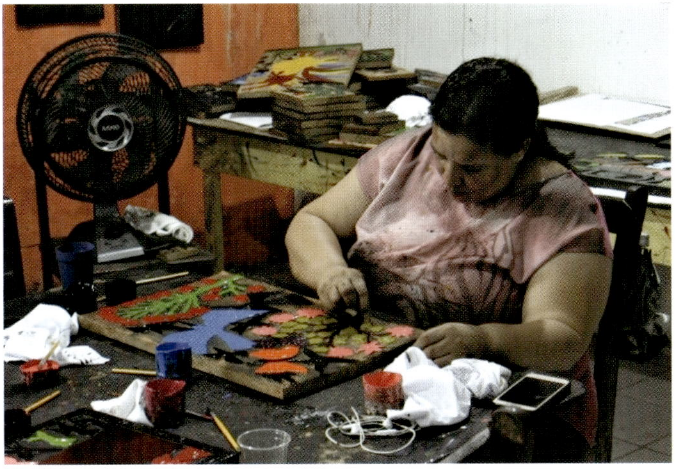

Maria Célia da Silva painting

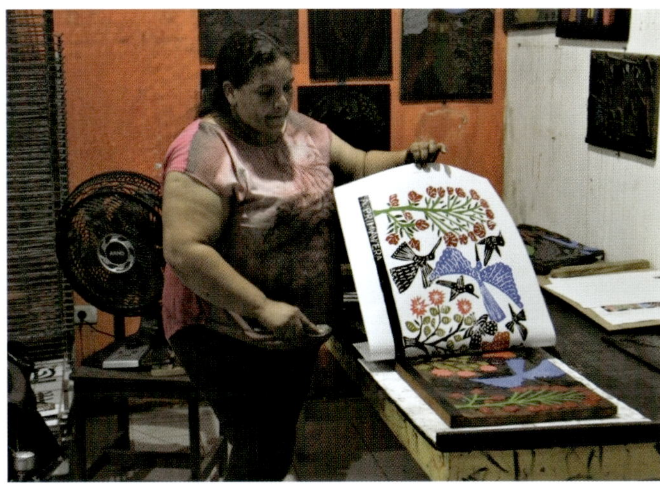

Maria Célia printing from a *matriz* by J. Borges

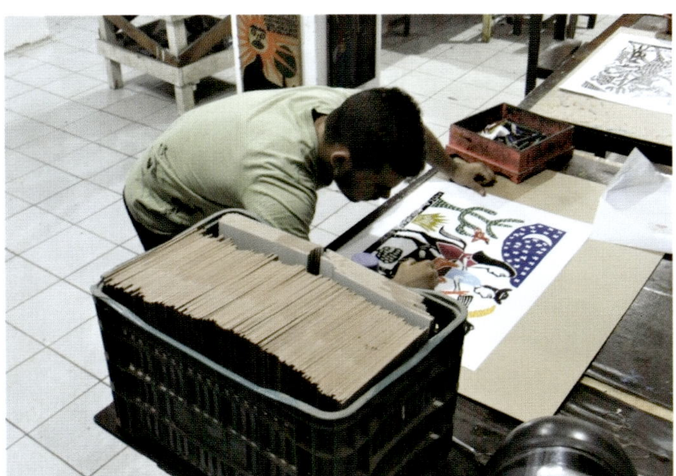

Matias Neto retouching a print by J. Borges

Colored prints in abundance now center the atelier's production. To one side lie the artists' personal projects. To the other, there are commissions and the licensing of woodblock images for commercial use on bags and clothing and boxes. That job is managed by J. Borges's stepson Antônio Carlos Rufino da Silva whose quick and clever wife, Edna, controls communication over the internet and deals with the customers who show up at the shop in Bezerros.

All of this flowered from the bright, particular genius of J. Borges. Pablo concludes:

"Our future is strong. Everything, of course, is due to my father's name. He is eighty-three years old, soon to be eighty-four. I know that the human being does not live forever, but I wish he could live for another one hundred years, or another two hundred.

"My father always said to me, Don't work for financial gain, nor to make a name for yourself. Work because you love it.

"That was something I learned from him. The artist lives in *creation*, understand? My father has an *immense* talent for creation. He has a really good head. He is a poet too. He is a very good person and he created an art that is famous.

"He eternalized the woodblock print. It will never die, understand? There is growth in the woodblock print. There is interest in every part of the entire world.

"And it has ended up that he is a living symbol. I think that he has become eternal.

"We can say that he eternalized himself."

23

The Work Goes On

On the twenty-second of April in 2020, not long after the Covid pandemic hit, J. Borges appeared on Pernambuco Globo television to recite the poetic text of a new *cordel.* Medical matters hold a small but significant place in the tradition of the *folheto*, and J. Borges shaped his comment on the current crisis into loosely rhymed couplets, which transcribed and translated run like this:

> This coronavirus
> appeared there in China.
> It spread all over the world,
> leading to death and destruction.
> And science until this day
> has not discovered a vaccine.
> With this unhappy disease,
> the whole country is held back.
> There is no cure, no remedy,
> and the whole world is blasted,
> And the doctors recommend
> for us to stay at home.
> It has been two weeks
> since I closed the atelier.
> I keep waiting for good news
> to appear.
> There has to be some exit
> to prevent the world's death.

A year and seven months later we are back in Bezerros. Pablo tells us that his father, who will turn eighty-six in December, is healthy and well. J. Borges was not infected with the virus, though Pablo was. He felt pain in his legs, lost his sense of smell, and tested positive. In isolation, young and strong, Pablo swiftly recovered, but at first the pandemic was hard on J. Borges. An active, extraverted man, he was stuck in the house — a complaint registered in his poem — and he suffered depression, though now he is fine, and with the majority of people vaccinated, Pablo says, things are returning to normal.

The recorder is running, and we ask Pablo to describe how the time has passed since we saw him last. Always clear and articulate, Pablo says:

"Look, this virus, it came as a surprise to the whole world, right? The whole world was with their hands tied, unable to react when it came.

"And for us who work with *art*, with tourism, who travel *much* — everything paused.

"We *stopped* doing everything. The atelier closed; we were obliged to close it. For some eight months, I think, we were closed.

"We were working inside, but without receiving any visitors, right? The tourists were very scarce because, most likely, they couldn't get here. When they wanted to come, the authorities would not allow them.

"And so we ended up having to adjust ourselves to sell, to show what we did through the internet.

"This in some ways was good, because we adjusted and we were able to achieve a *better* cash flow.

"Because we used to wait for the customers to come to us, and today we go to them, understand?

"We *show* it" — on the internet — "they request it, and we send it in the mail. The majority are private customers, but we have store owners too.

"And now in this month of November — and I hope from now on — things are returning to normal.

"We are already open, have been open for some time now, and the tourists are returning. Actually we receive tourists from the entire world.

"First, only the tourists from Brazil were coming. Many people from São Paulo would come, but now foreigners are coming as well. That's it.

"Sales are now about eighty percent of normal. But it is returning to normal, and it is very strong.

"We have plenty of work to do."

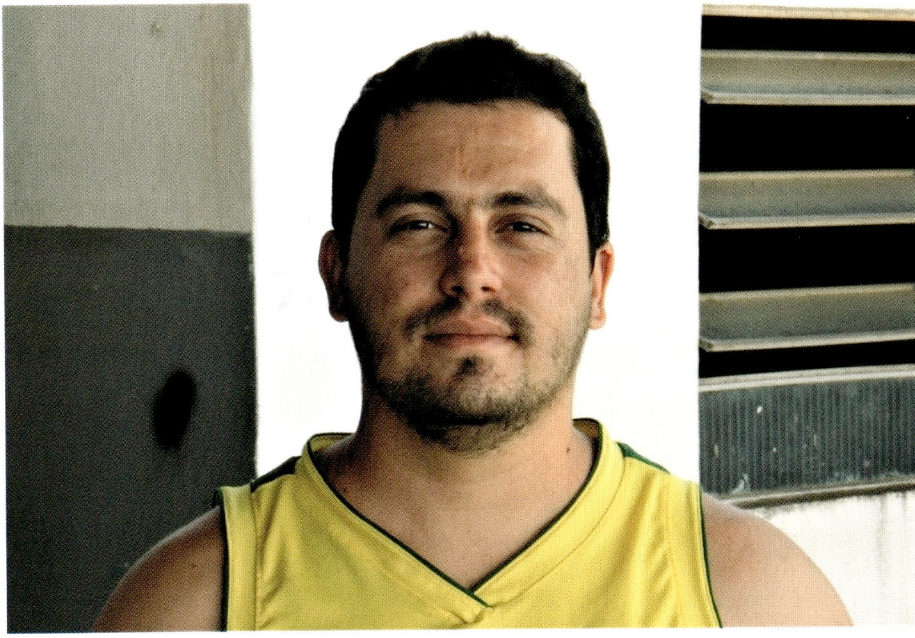

Pablo Borges, Bezerros, 2021

During the pandemic, Pablo says when we ask, the atelier received commissions, especially from medical professionals, for prints with Covid-related themes.

"Of course, we did it," he says. "Now, all of them were commissions, right? We never kept any of them for ourselves. We made some, but we never carved blocks to use ourselves.

"Look, the pandemic was not a good thing.

"My father said we have to work on commissions, but he refused to create anything to do with the virus. What he wanted was for it to pass away.

"And now it is passing.

"We worked on commissions, but made nothing to exhibit here.

"And now that things are calm, we don't want to be looking at things that remind us; we don't want to remember all that, understand?

"God willing, this will *disappear* for good."

Down the road to the west, J. Miguel also closed his atelier. There was, though, no time for rest. He took his tools home, and helped by his wife, Raquel, his son, Jefferson, and Jefferson's wife, Simone — the men carving, the women printing — J. Miguel drove energetically forward. He sent prints to

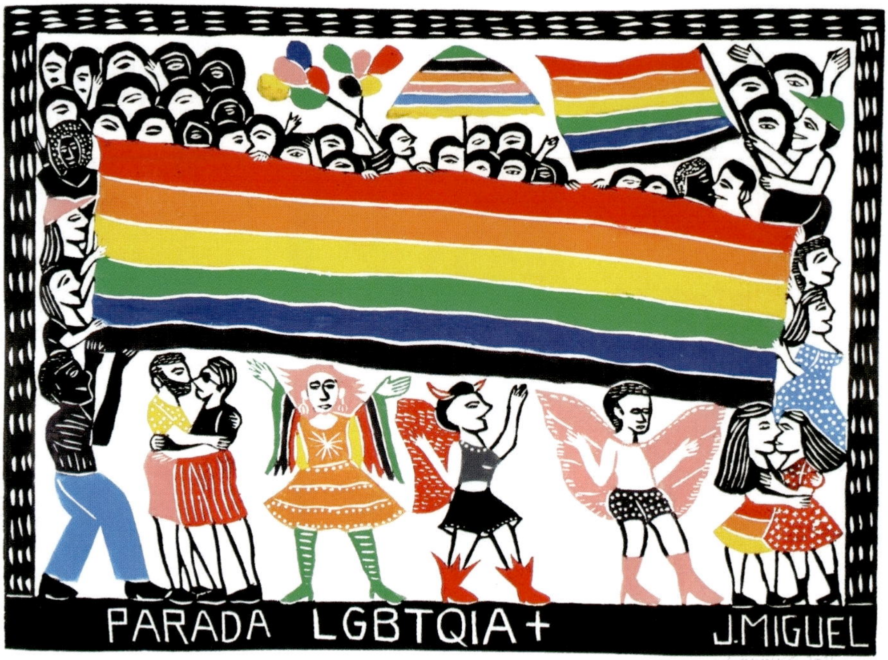

Gay Pride Parade, by J. Miguel (39 × 54 cm), 2021

stores in Recife and Rio, and he built his stock with innovations to meet the increased demand that, he had to hope, would follow the pandemic.

He, too, created no scenes with Covid themes. He made a set of blocks to tell the story of Christ's life. Aware that customers often choose prints with personal significance, J. Miguel made a full set of the astrological signs, and he expanded his collection of images of professions, adding new occupations and more women. He had always depicted women as teachers, now added lawyers, doctors, and psychiatrists. His son suggested a fresh and fashionable topic: the celebration of gay pride. Then working at the scale of his popular print of the Northeastern rural market, J. Miguel placed male and female couples embracing beneath the grand sweep of the rainbow banner. It was immediately a commercial success.

J. Miguel's shop was closed, locked up tight, for seven months. When at last he opened the door and beheld the mess inside he nearly wept. Then he went to work, framing a partition to divide his space, so the shop's front, where prints are made and sold, would be tidier, more attractive. He painted the door in the partition with cactus and white-winged birds, and he painted the front of his table for work with a scene from *Bumba-Meu-Boi*. He was ready to greet the crowds of customers that the pandemic's end would bring.

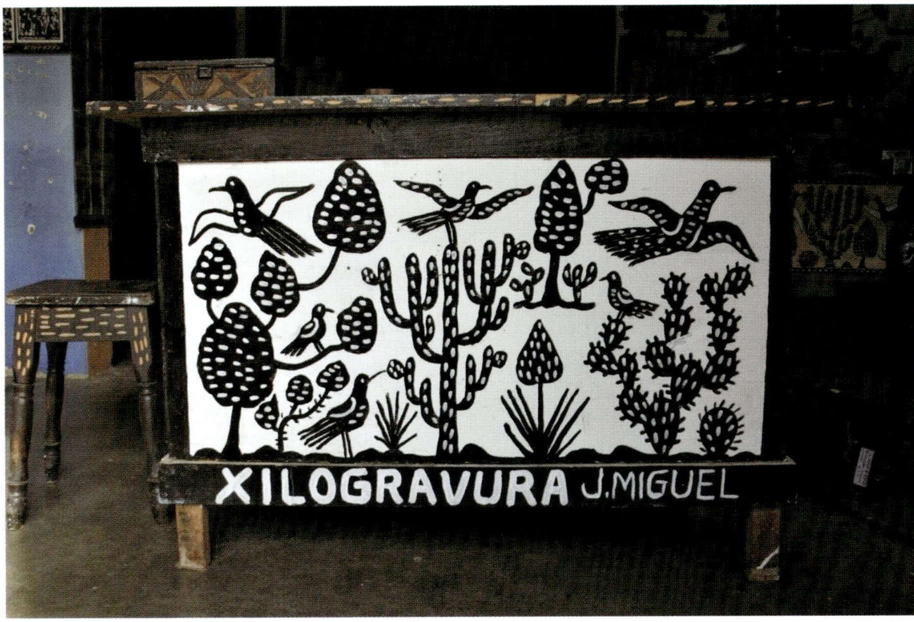

J. Miguel's table, 2019

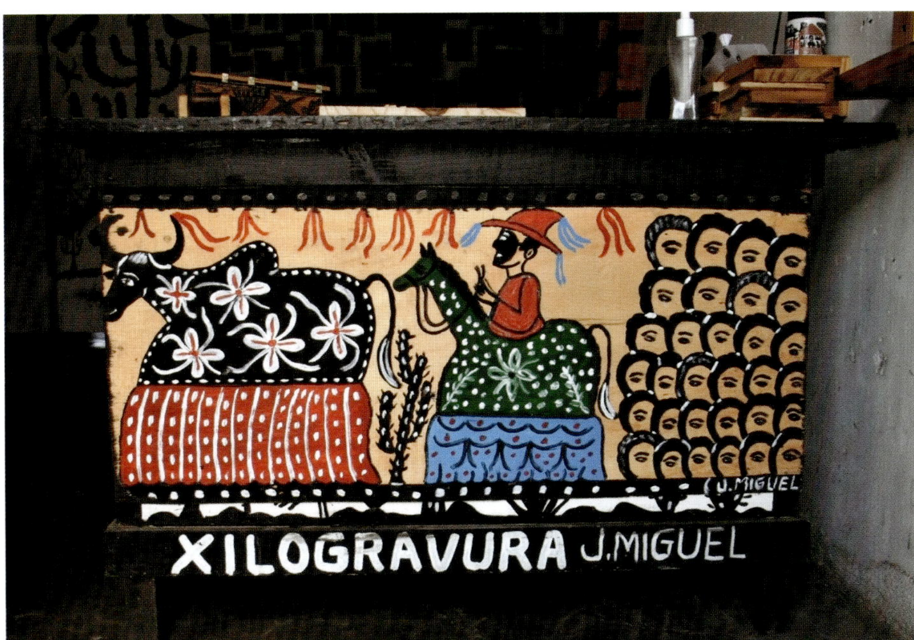

J. Miguel's table, 2021

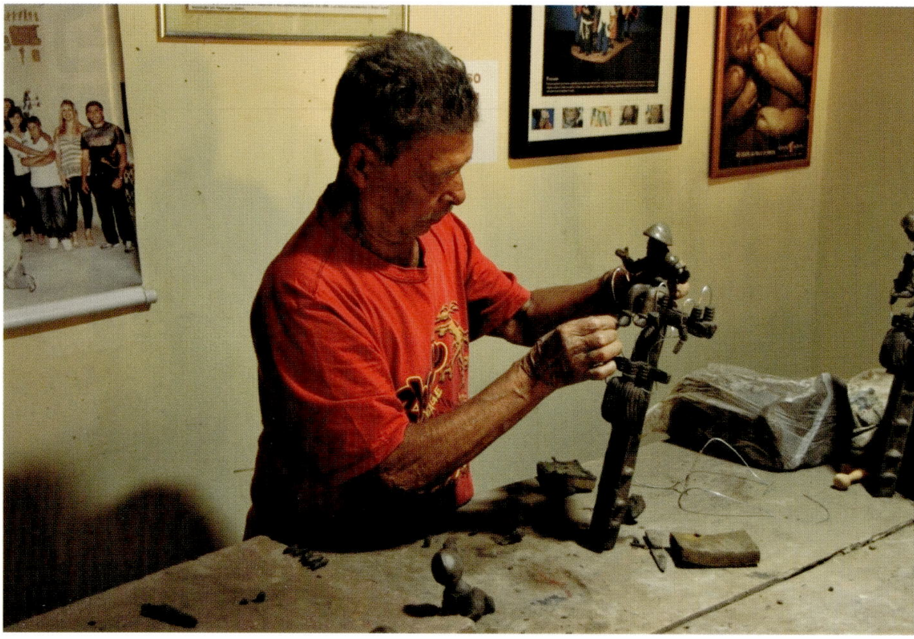

Luiz Antônio creating another lineman, Aldo do Moura, 2021

In Alto do Moura, Marliete went into action, running errands — to the grocery store, the bank, the pharmacy — so her elderly relatives and neighbors could stay safely at home. She felt pain in her joints, lost her appetite, and tested positive. Then, twice vaccinated, she rested, recovered, and continued to serve others, bringing her aged brother José, who had been hospitalized for a month, into her home so he could receive constant care. Her brother Antônio told us that he was vaccinated to protect his neighbors. "I took a shot for the community," he said. Undefeatably cheerful and bright, Marliete said, "We can't lose faith. We can't cower; we have to stay at work."

Across the street, Leonildo did what he could to keep his parents safely at home. His mother, Odete, would cleverly sneak out to visit friends, but his father, Luiz Antônio, was perfectly happy to remain in the shop, the clay running through his hands into oxcarts and processions, musicians, photographers, and linemen working atop cement poles.

Down the street, Ademilson lost his sense of taste. He didn't bother with a test, but quarantined himself, and, delighted to have time alone in his shop, he pitched into a phase of energetic production and witty innovation. He made statues of Lampião and Maria Bonita, of Vitalino with the *pífano*, of all the characters from the *Reisado*.

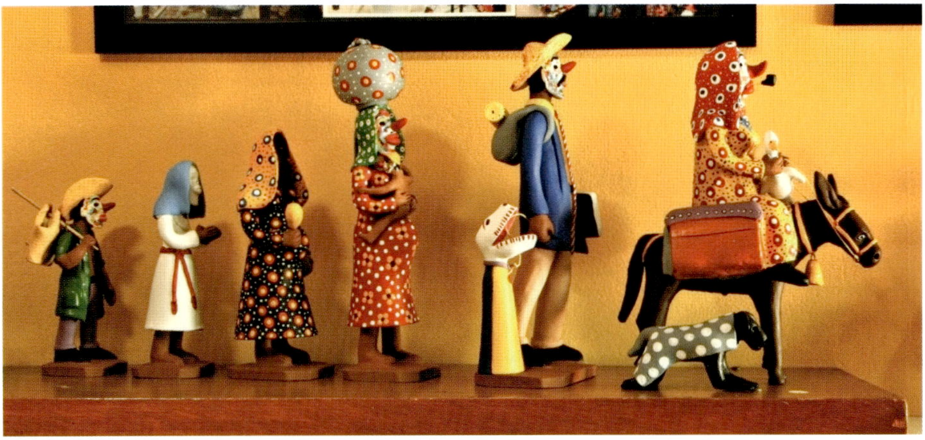

Reisado Retirantes in Ademilson's shop, 2021

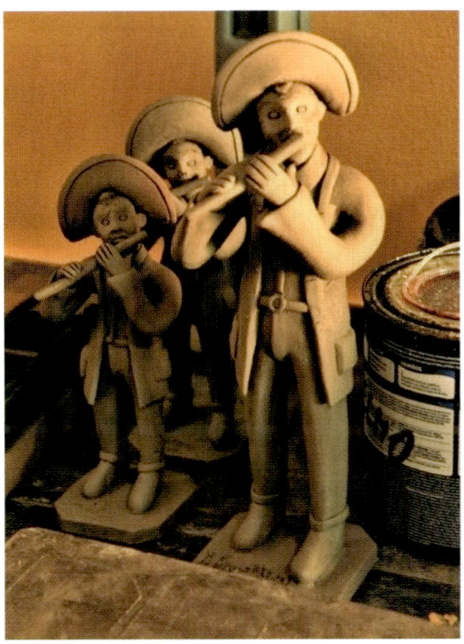

Images of Vitalino with the *pífano*, in progress in Ademilson's shop, 2021

His revered father, Manuel Eudócio, was a master of repertorial play, and during the pandemic, Ademilson upped the ante. Alto do Moura's prime, classic piece, the hunter of wildcats, was first made by Vitalino, then by his son Severino, then by Severino's son Emanuel, and most recently by Emanuel's ten-year-old daughter, Stephanie. Ademilson parodied it into a surreal joke. He replaced the hunter with a farmer searching for straying stock, and at the top of the tree he dropped a big, bewildered white cow. In this moment for creative action, Ademilson made for the first time a full version of the *Retirantes* with all the people replaced by masked characters from the *Reisado*. A surprise, uniting the dark and bright sides of life, it prompted a laugh with every glance.

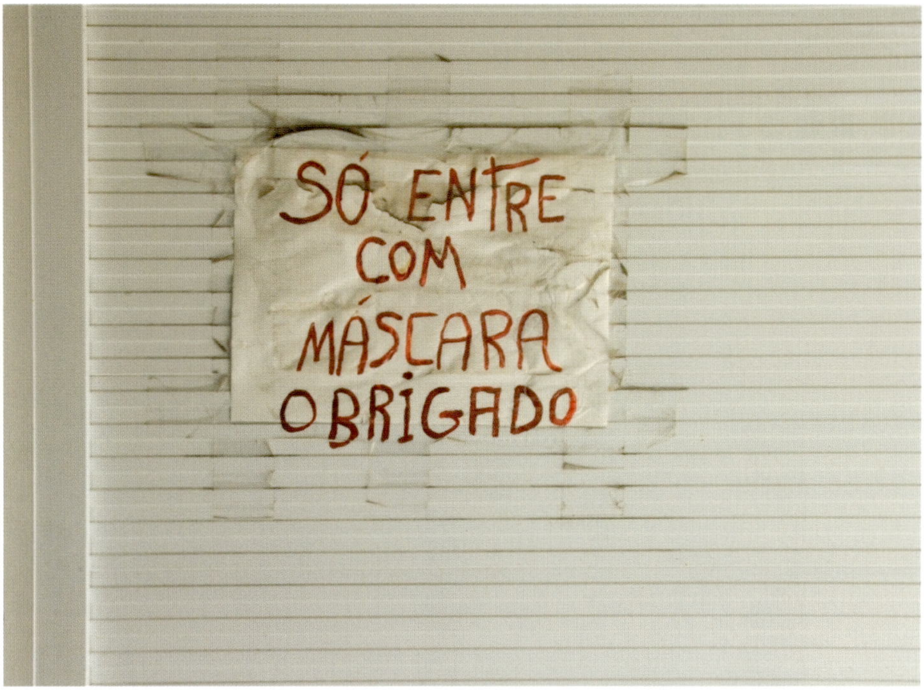

Sign on the door of Luiz Carlos's shop, asking visitors to enter masked, 2021

On the other side of the street, the big doors of Luiz Carlos's atelier bore signs thanking visitors for entering only if masked. Outside in front stood a statue of Luiz Gonzaga; inside in the back, Luiz Carlos and Genilda worked busily at their tables.

During the pandemic, Luiz Carlos had two points of concentration. A man fond of animals, he made bold statues of bulls in two styles, one in the smooth form developed by Vitalino and called *Boi de Vitalino*, the other in a more naturalistic form, based on close observation. Luiz Carlos favors the scenic option for representation, and during this slow period he carefully crafted a scene of Vitalino at his table in the market crowded round with customers.

Down at the bottom of the street, Terezinha had held her fragile husband within the loving circle of life. She and her sons had kept the big kiln burning, filling the shelves with stock, with rotund black *muqueca* pots and upright statues of Saint Francis, aflutter with birds. No one made artful objects that, in their representational forms, would force them to recall the pandemic; it will pass as other horrors have.

Vitalino's bull, by Luiz Carlos, before firing, 2021

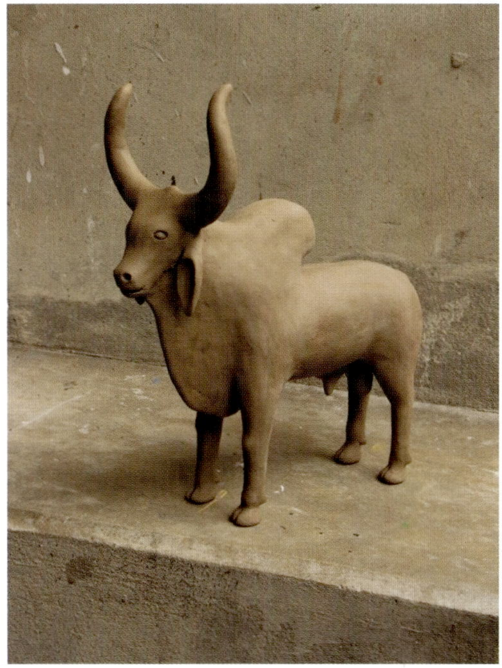

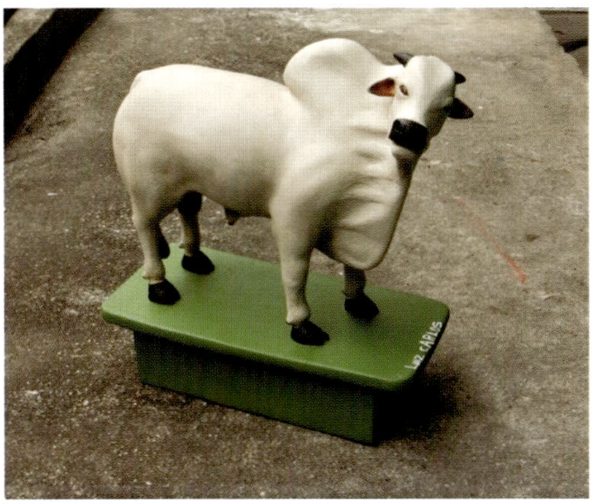

Bull, by Luiz Carlos, 2021

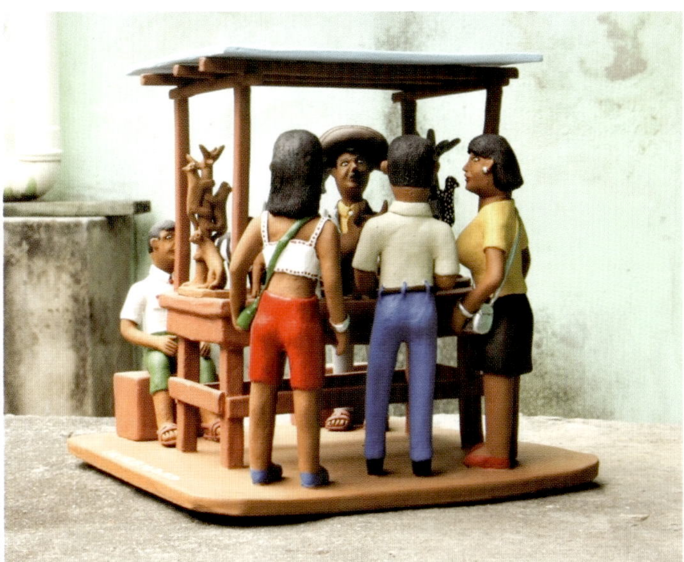

Mestre Vitalino's booth in the market, by Luiz Carlos, 2021

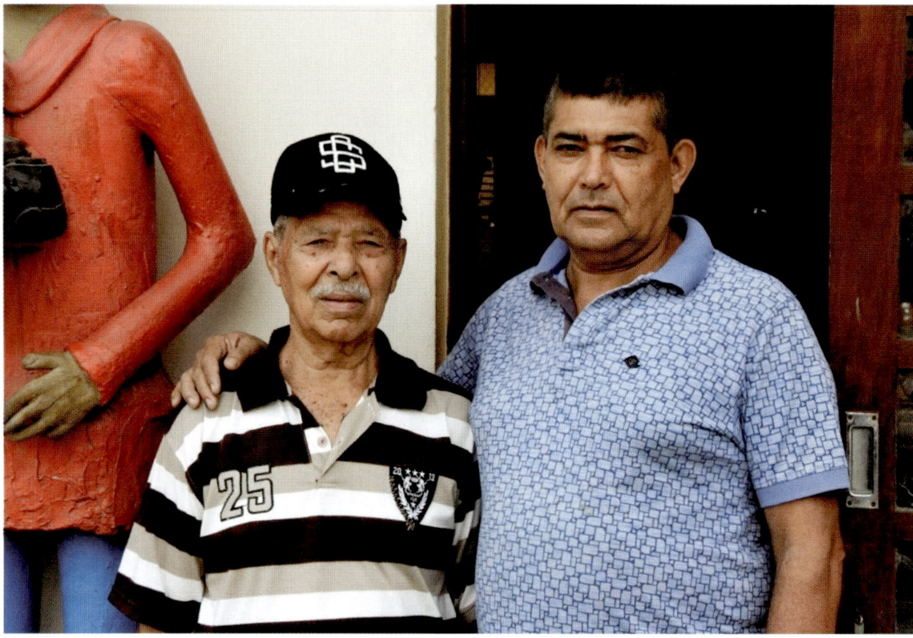

Luiz Antônio with his son Leonildo, 2021

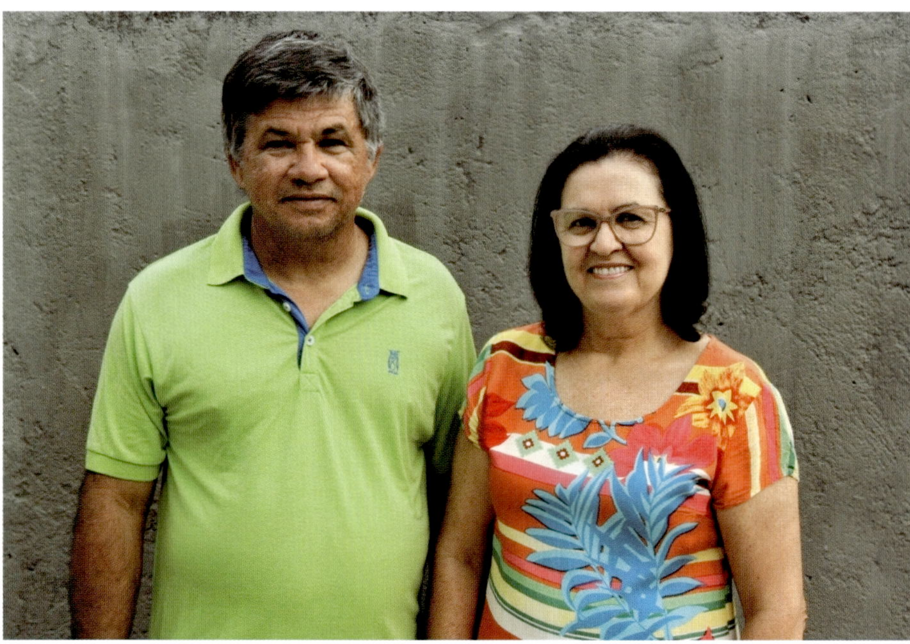

Marliete with her brother Horácio, 2021

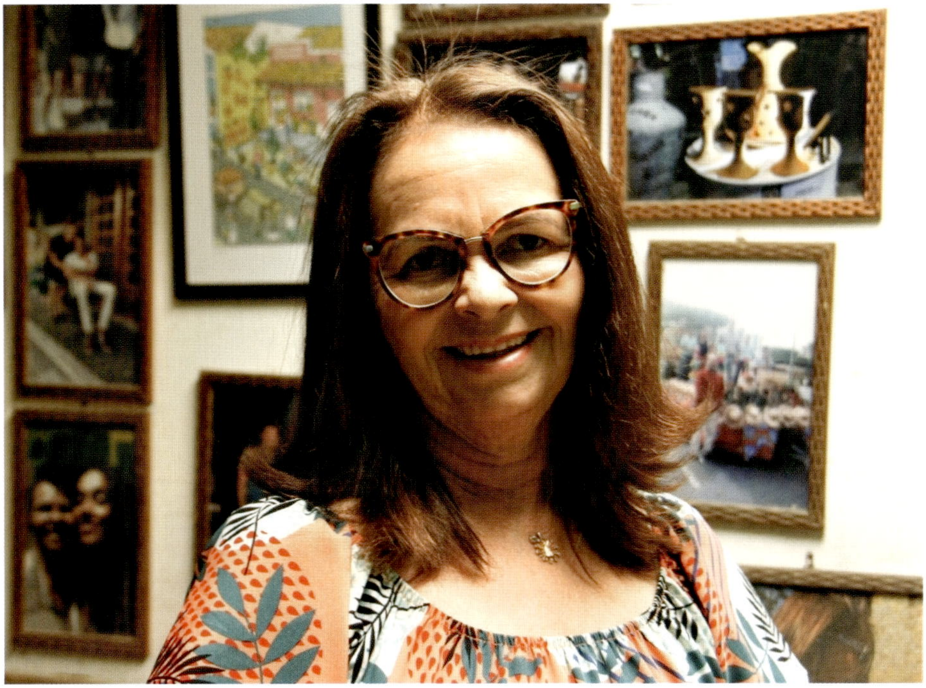

Terezinha, 2021

These are people who are used to hard times. They know how to endure. Community is an experiential reality for them. They know how to join in helpful, cooperative action.

Meanwhile, government officials offered some encouraging support. In 2020, Luiz Antônio was named a Living Patrimony of the state of Pernambuco. Preparations for the ceremony delayed progress on the museum behind his shop, so this time when we walked through it with Leonildo and Luiz Antônio photography was permitted. We took pictures of a big pair of Lampião and Maria Bonita, a scene of work in his son's bakery, and a massed procession for Yemanjá.

In 2021, Marliete was also named a Living Patrimony of the state of Pernambuco. A grand poster celebrating the award hangs in her orderly studio. Also in 2021, Terezinha was named a Living Patrimony of the city of Caruaru. It was a triumph for the women and beneficial reinforcement for Terezinha's argument that utilitarian pots can be works of art. We chanced to be there when, beaming, Terezinha left for a celebratory interview on television.

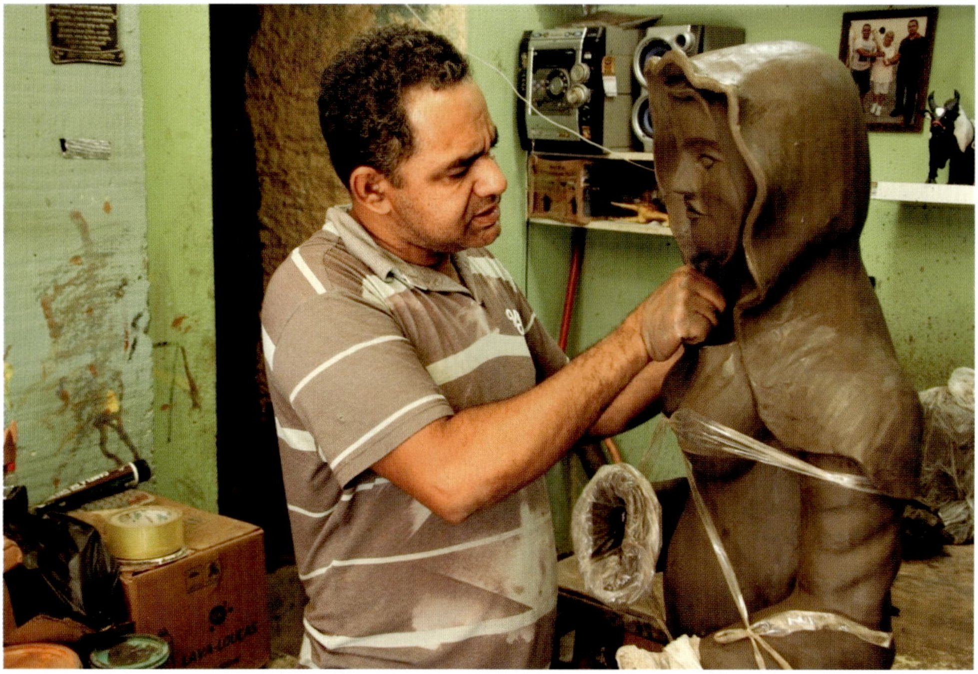

Gilliard at work, shaping a figure for a large Nativity, 2021

And so the work goes on. In his shop at the edge of Bezerros, J. Miguel is carving a big *matriz* so he can print a new image of Adam and Eve in the Garden. In Alto do Moura, in the Casa Museu Mestre Vitalino, Emanuel is shaping clay into a statue of his grandfather playing the *pífano*. Carmélia has just returned from a successful sale of her family's work at the Casa da Cultura in Recife. Luiz Carlos is painting a big batch of the *Reisado's* most popular figures, the Captain, the Bull, and Jaraguá. In Terezinha's shop, her son Gilliard is creating life-sized figures for a Nativity, commissioned by the government for the coming Christmas season. Up the hill, Luiz Antônio, deep in his eighties, is steadily at work, crafting another cruciform pole to hold aloft another hard-working lineman.

Their work, diverse in method, congruent in subject, gathers to represent the worldview of the Northeast: the environment, the labor, the entertainment, the heroes. Collectively their work exhibits the characteristics of folk art.

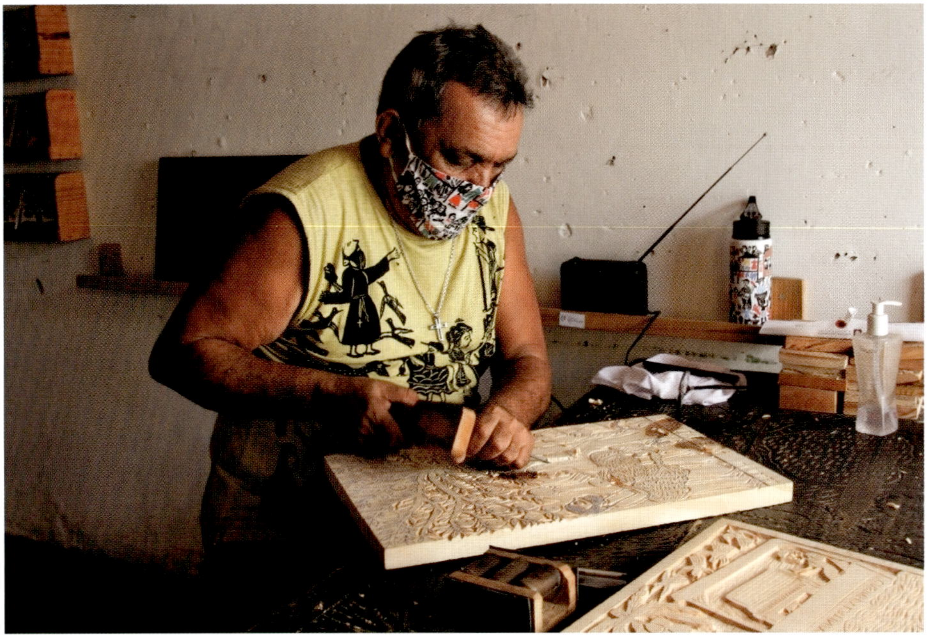

J. Miguel at work, carving the block for a print of Adam and Eve, Bezerros, 2021

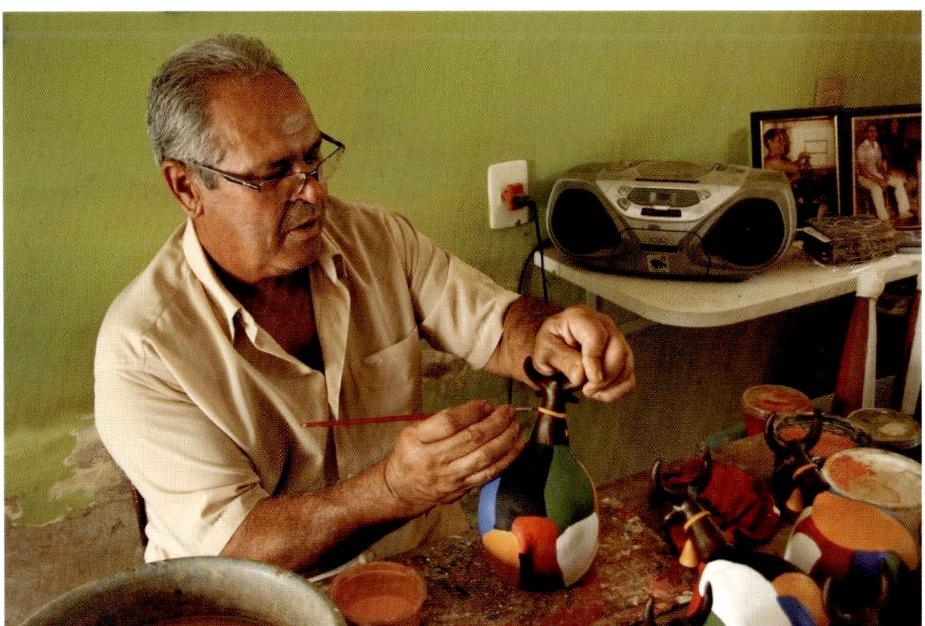

Luiz Carlos at work, painting figures from the *Reisado*, Alto do Moura, 2021

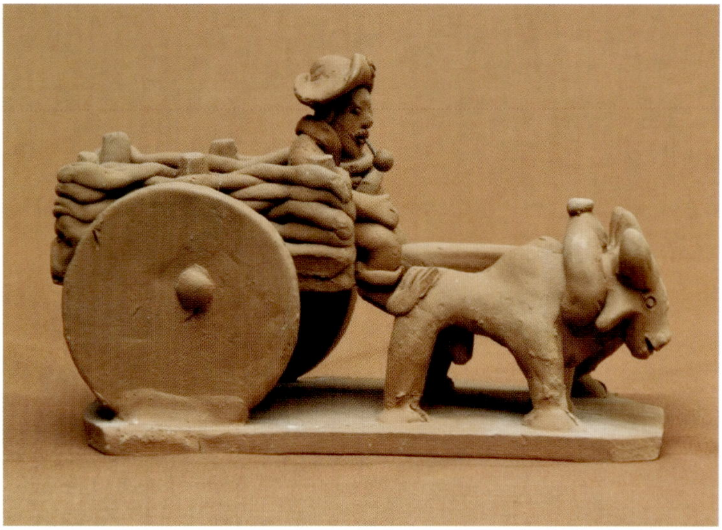

Oxcart by Luiz Antônio, 2015

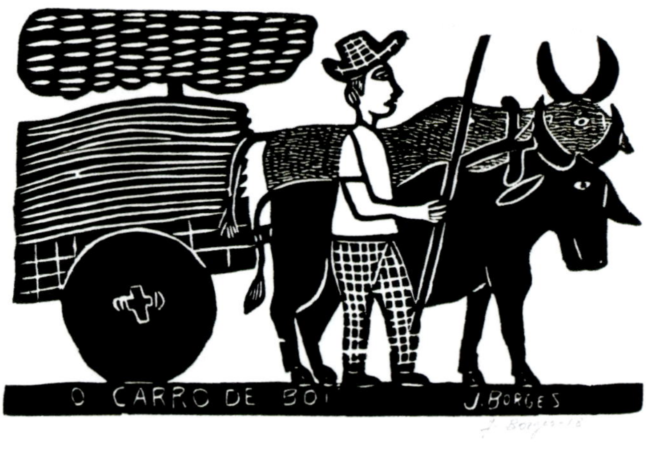

Oxcart by J. Borges, 2018

The way to folk art is not to accept the centrality of what is called fine art — an accumulation of privileged opinion — and then to pick bits from the margins to answer the obligation to inclusion. A productive procedure will begin — not end, but begin — with a medium that approaches universality, reaching deeply in time and widely in space. The Neolithic gifts of ceramics and textiles offer the best options and the goal is to discover within them patterns in the quest for excellence.

That is our task now, and relying on our own work in the field, we will locate the general characteristics of folk art.

Part Three

Folk Art

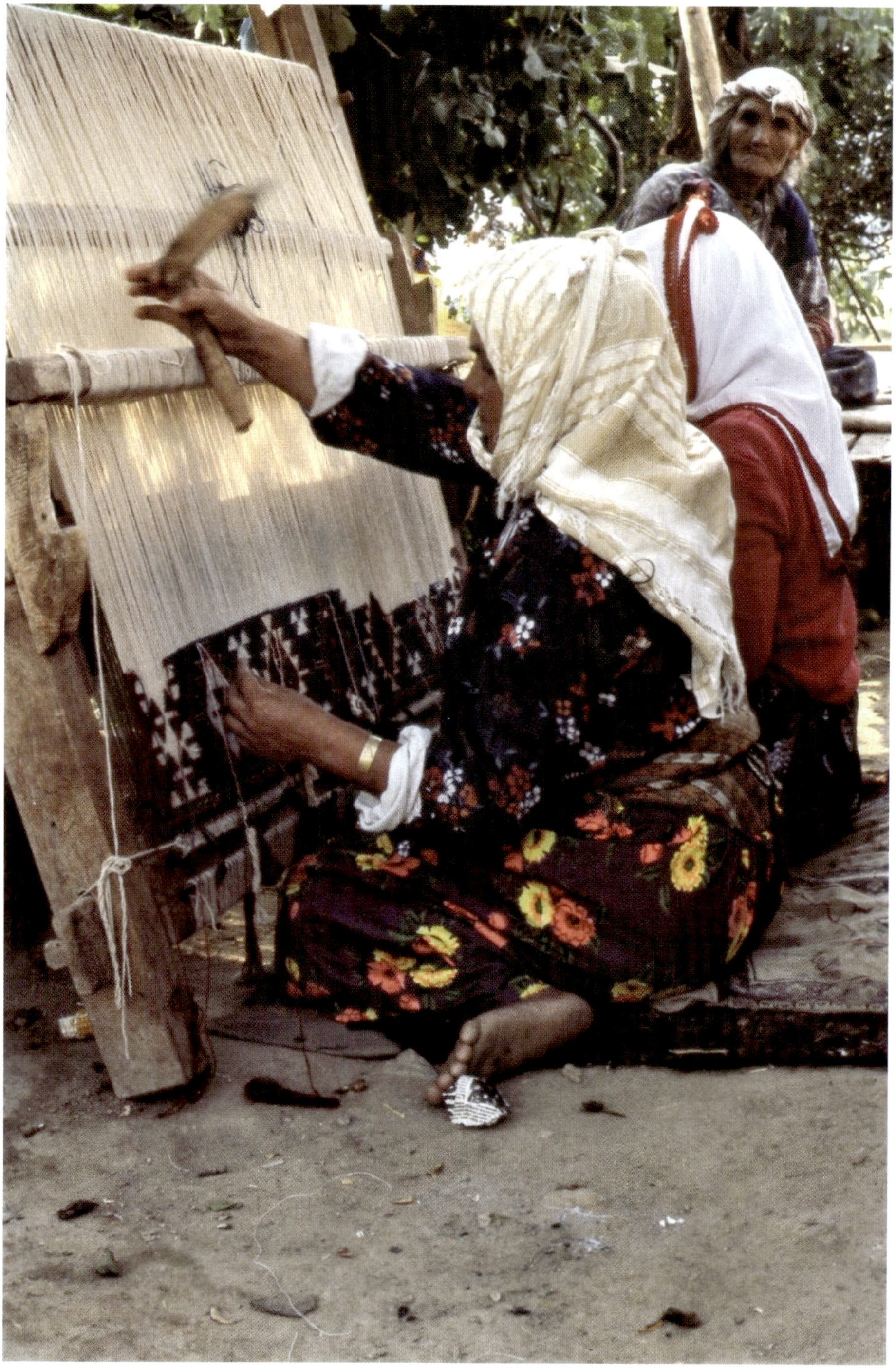

Eşe Coşgun watching her daughter and granddaughter, Fadime and Emine Akdağ, weaving a kilim, Güneydamlar, Manisa, Turkey, 1989

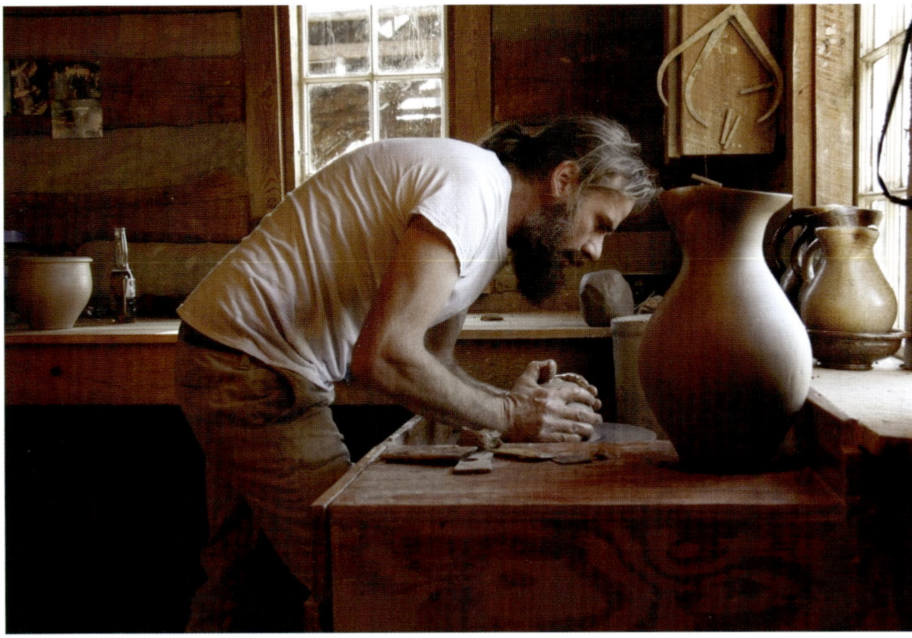

Daniel Johnston at work, Seagrove, North Carolina, 2018

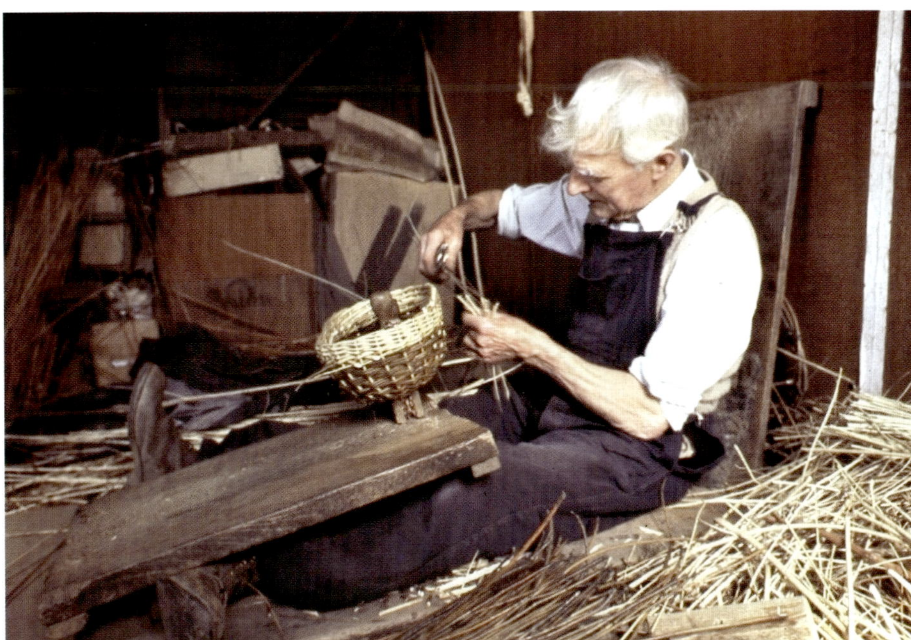

Stan Lamprey at work, Braunton, Devonshire, England, 1978

Sun Xiuqing with a vase she made, Pengcheng, China, 2000

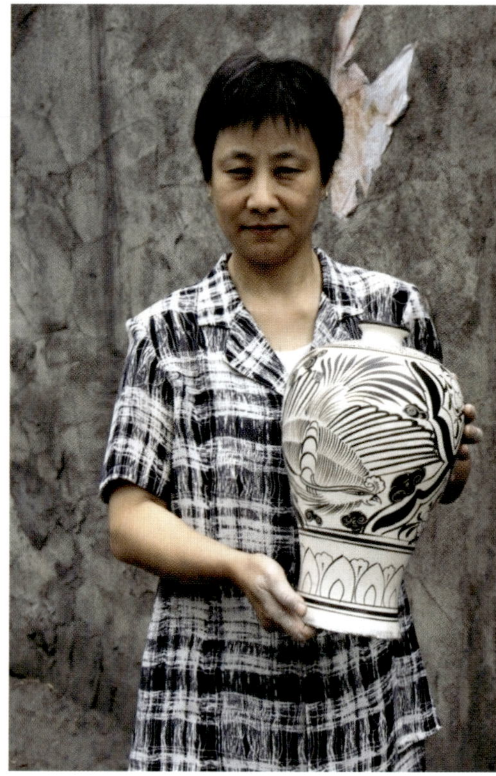

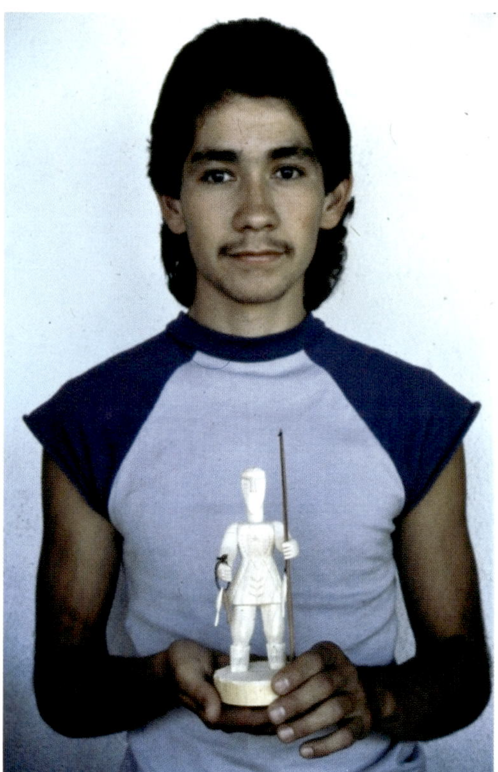

Rafael Lopez Córdova with his carving of San Rafael, Córdova, New Mexico, 1987

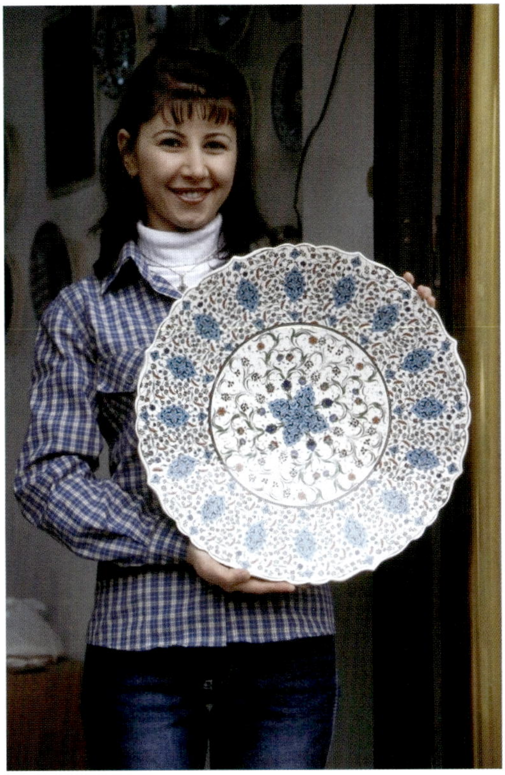

Kadriye Tosun with a plate she painted, Kütahya, Turkey, 2001

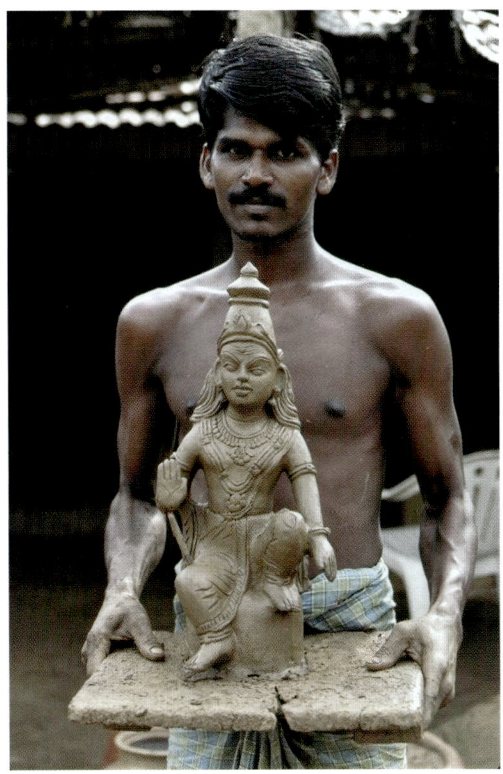

N. Murugan with his statue of Ayyanar, Manamadurai, Tamil Nadu, India, 1999

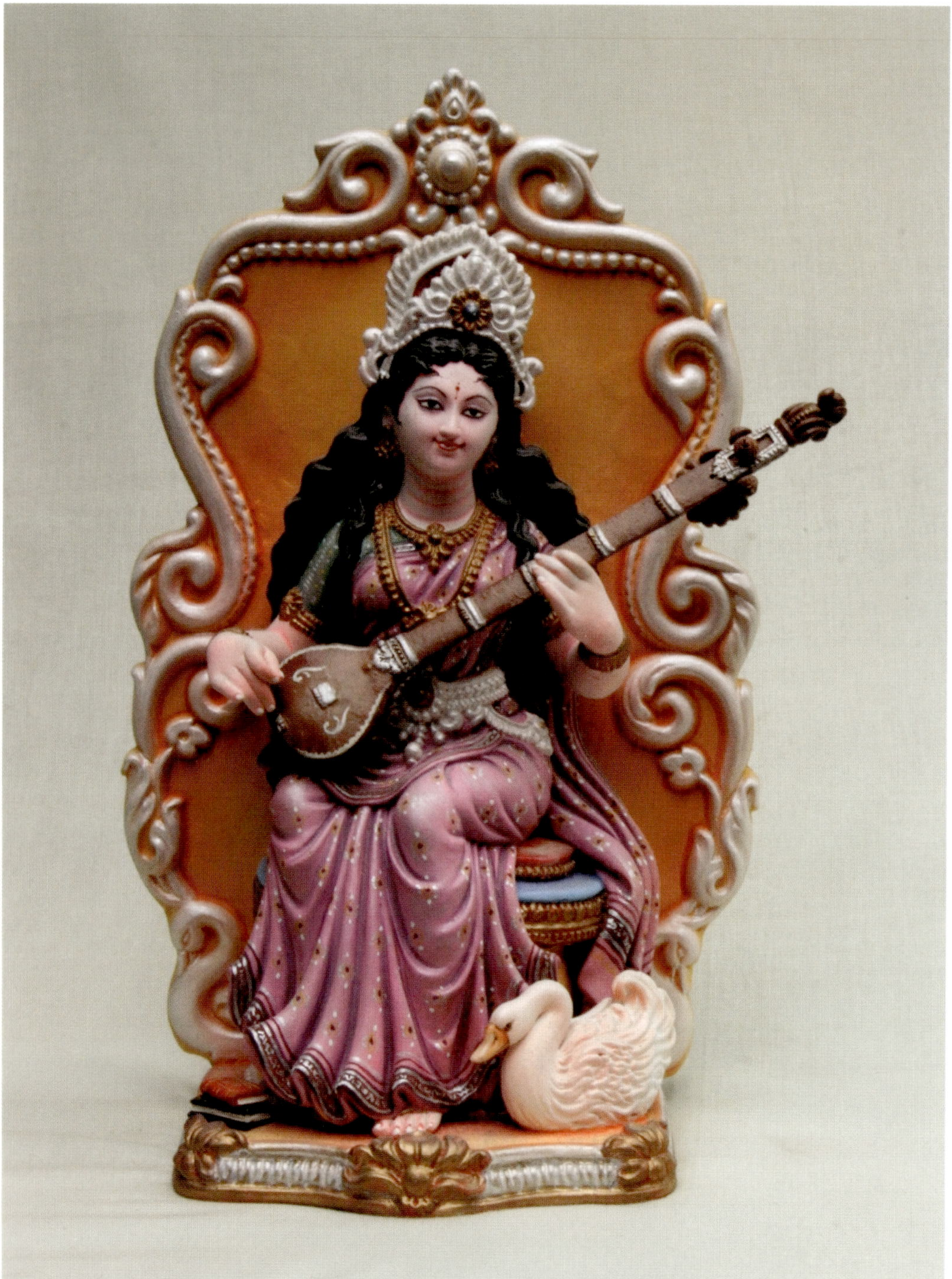

Saraswati, a statue in clay of the goddess of wisdom (36 cm tall),
by Haripada Pal, Dhaka, Bangladesh, 2000

24

Performance

Fieldwork on five continents has brought us into alignment with Noam Chomsky's definition of humanity as complexly creative. A biological endowment unites humankind, invalidating arguments of superiority based on race or gender or caste, and radically separating human animals from all others. Chomsky is a linguist and linguistic research provides him a grand resource for contemplation, but during his search through speech for thought, Chomsky has occasionally noted parallels between the thought that leads to speech and the thought that leads to artifacts. When, with Robert C. Berwick, Noam Chomsky turned to evolution, those parallels proved crucial.

The universality of language implies great depth in time, but there are, of course, no linguistic data from deeply enough in time to aid evolutionary speculation. Archaeological evidence is all that remains. It reveals that creatures had skeletons like ours 300,000 years ago, but it was not until 80,000 years ago, before the African exodus, that they had minds like ours. They created decorative artifacts, so presumably they had language. The mind capable of art is the mind capable of language. That mind is our universally human *dom*.

This inner creative force, shared by speakers and makers, by all of humankind, is the capacity to convert a finite set into an infinity of results. It is the employment of grammatical rules to generate an infinity of statements, the use of architectural rules of design to generate an infinity of buildings. It interests us to find echoes of Chomsky's concept in the field, not corroborations but signs of minds at work on comparable problems.

A pertinent entry to Hindu thought was offered by Haripada Pal, mystic and sculptor of sacred statues in Dhaka, Bangladesh. Haripada's image in clay of Saraswati, the goddess of wisdom, the incarnation of mind, has two prime attributes: her tool, the *vina*, a stringed instrument, and her *vahana*, the swan who, able to separate the milk from the water in liquid mix, symbolizes the mind's dynamic of discrimination and division. In the beginning there was the single sound: *om*. Saraswati split the single sound into several. Then using her *vina*, Saraswati arranged the separate sounds into the musical scales that human beings have employed in creating an infinity of different melodies.

The Muslim calligrapher Muhittin Serin in Istanbul developed a congruent argument in defense of his art. To those who feel his art is limited, being based on a small set of letters, the Arabic alphabet, Muhittin replies that the letters are few but they can be formed differently, since calligraphers before him created a range of distinctly different hands, each with its own formal rules. Calligraphers can choose from among the hands, which he likened to musical scales. Then in creation the calligrapher can combine the letters into a vast variety of words that can then be combined into the creation of an infinity of texts, each possibly different in its overall artistic configuration.

Built biologically into the brain, our common humanity must be inferred from sensate data. The inner capacity to erect sets and transform them into an infinity of texts, melodies, and artifacts is a latent potential, realized into the world through particular performances amid particular conditions. These performances range from simple sentences to *Finnegans Wake*, from lullabies to *Messiah*, from the decorated dibble stick to *Guernica*. Turning to our work, to existential ethnography, we need to map the territory of performance.

The analytic field of performance is organized around two key points of contact: between the performer and tradition and between the performance and circumstances.

On top of the universal human capacity, genetic chances and life's experiences accumulate to render all people unique individuals who must unify the personal and cultural dimensions of the self in order to realize their latent creative potential. Turkish artisans describe this complicated process as smooth, nearly natural, when they say that everyone is born into a place that has a distinct *hava* — an air — an environment of sounds and sights, of traditions. During growth that air is constantly inhaled. It circulates within, fusing with the self, so when it is exhaled in creation, the product, song or pot, inevitably and simultaneously represents the individual and the individual's shared tradition.

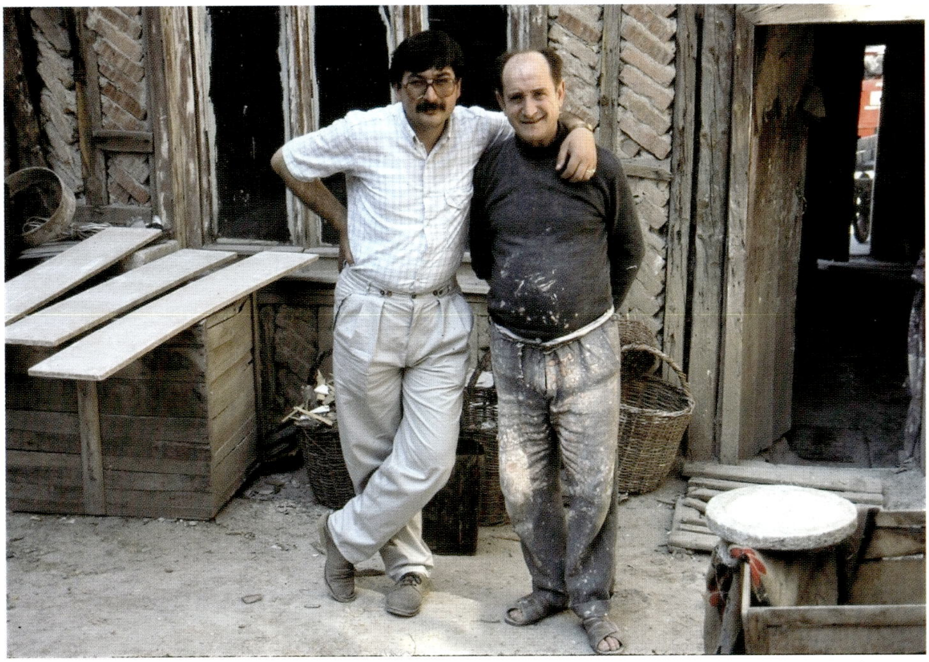

İbrahim and İhsan Erdeyer, Kütahya, Turkey, 1989

Poetically put, that process eventuates in a successfully situated performer. It fits the experience of İbrahim Erdeyer, one of the artists who articulated that graceful formulation. İbrahim is a master of ceramic art, born in a town, Kütahya, where exquisite ceramics have been made for more than five hundred years, raised in the workshop of his father, İhsan, a master potter. İhsan has passed, İbrahim continues.

Look closely, though, and the process seems to be as much a matter of choice and commitment as it is of natural development. Consider the facts from another pottery town, Alto do Moura. Not everyone raised in a shop full of clay became, like İbrahim Erdeyer, a master. Six of Zé Caboclo's eight children followed him. Five of Manuel Eudócio's ten children followed him. Four of Luiz Antônio's ten children followed him. All of Severino Vitalino's thirteen children learned the craft, but only two became artists. The big families of that generation helped to ensure continuity; with children aplenty, a few would surely choose to follow. For some who began early and continued, however, it did not feel like a choice. They had no other option, but once they began in earnest and acquired a taste for the work, it was a choice to commit themselves to creation and constant improvement. And they were satisfied. Marliete, Zé

Caboclo's daughter, spoke for them all when she said, "This is what delights me: to be always learning, always improving." Ademilson, Manuel Eudócio's son, said that the artist lives "a life full of pleasure." He concluded, "Art is life."

The smaller families in the next generation, and the increase in occupational options, meant that there were fewer who chose the artist's life. But Amanda, Antônio's daughter, said that when she has a free moment, "I run to the table and work." And Carmélia's son Emerson said, "I feel happy in this art." It is like that, too, among the current generation of woodblock artists. Pablo, J. Borges's son, said, "The artist lives in creation." Severino Borges, Amaro's son, said, "Art makes me happy."

For the artist, the performance, the actualization of the innate potential for creation, is a matter of intention, of a choice to commit the self. For Noam Chomsky, linguistic theorist and wise political critic, the actualization need not be elegant — grammatical errors and baby babble are instructive — it needs only to supply evidence of the biological brain that unites humanity and invalidates racism. For Dell Hymes, linguist, folklorist, and poet, who placed the idea of performance at the center of contemporary folkloristic practice, the actualization is a performance that unites nature and will, revealing the fullness of the human being in acts of personal commitment — intended acts that might yield an artfully ordered narrative by a Native American woman, or maybe an opera by Busoni. Hymes's example of a perfect performance was Emily Dickinson composing a poem alone in her room.

Folklorists following along — inspired by Chomsky and Hymes (as well as a host of others) — we begin ethnographic inquiry at the point where people are in command. Our goal is to expand the record, welcoming missing persons into presence — missing usually because of their class or race or gender or nationality. We don't concentrate on their limitations and failures, but on their competence, on the topics that interest them, on the creations of which they are proud. We intend to document and celebrate them in the fullness of their humanity, in the instants of their excellence.

Our work entails two main tasks that happen at once but divide to provide an existential understanding of the performances that center comprehension. We listen, gathering biographical information as people explain their learning, their social associations, their personal takes on a collective tradition. We watch, gathering information on the process of production, coming to understand how intentions are achieved and conditioned in creative performance. Let us now sketch a series of performances that will increase in complexity.

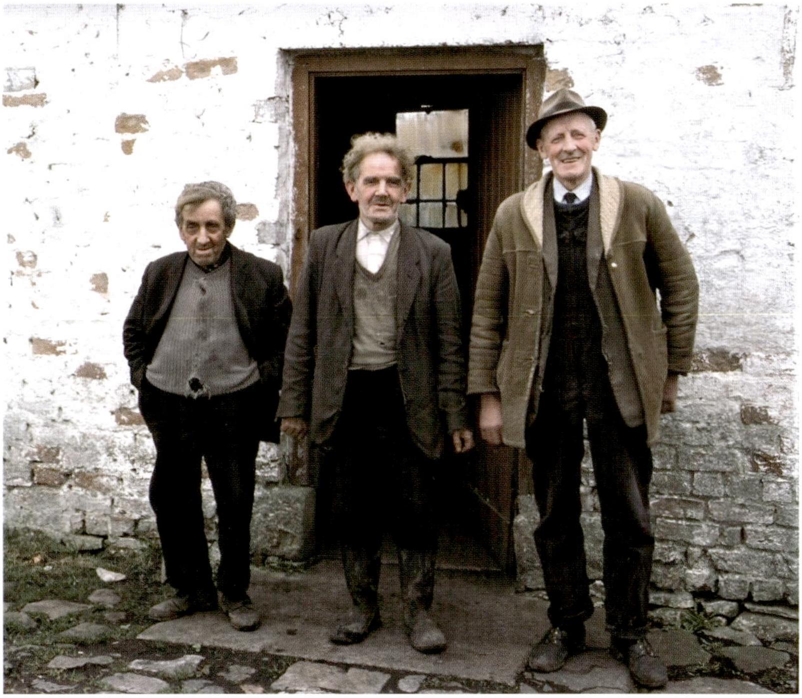

Joseph Flanagan, Peter Flanagan, and Tommy Love at the Flanagans' home, Ballymenone, County Fermanagh, Northern Ireland, 1976

It is dark, late at night by a small fire in a house on a ridge in the Irish borderland. The *ceili*, the night visit of neighbors, is nearing its end. The others, Packie and James, have gone. Tommy remains. "Give us a song, P," he says. Tommy Love is sitting to the left of the glowing turf smolder. Peter Flanagan is sitting in front of the fire, his brother Joe to the right. Tommy plays the fiddle, not as well as Peter, but Peter's old hands have hardened with labor. He can't play well enough to please himself, and he has channeled his love for music into singing. Tommy knows that, so he asks for a song, not a tune. Peter rocks forward, looks down into the fire, and sings a sweet song, "If I Was a Blackbird," a song that he knows Tommy likes, a song that suits the melancholy moment of a late night separation. "Good man, P," Tommy says, and after a last mug of sugary, milky tea, Tommy rises and goes, walking down, then over the hill to the south, to the thatched house he built on his small, impeccable farm.

Now Peter drops into a familiar but more complicated scene. On a Sunday night, when bars are closed in Northern Ireland, Peter has come a few miles south, crossing the border to a public house in Swanlinbar. He is standing at the counter with a glass of black stout in his hand and a desire to sing in his head. At last someone asks for a song and he steps forward, a small man in a loose black suit. The crowd is loud. He knows few of the people personally, but he knows enough to lift an appropriate song from his deep repertory. Behind him, a small group of quiet, fashionably dressed young men stand in a cluster. These are the lads who play in the game, the Provos who are fighting to eradicate the border they crossed to get here. Before him, older farming men have come from the south for a night of drink. Married couples sit with drinks in a parlor across a narrow corridor. Peter's audience, crowded close, is male, Catholic, republican. Now the men around him call for quiet. "Listen, this man is going to sing."

It is smoky, still noisy. Peter chooses a "political" song, a song of the long Irish struggle. He identifies with the sentiments, but he most wants to sing and he needs a song the crowd will accept. He doesn't choose "Sean South," the favorite of the young men, nor "Kevin Barry," the favorite of the older men. To please himself Peter selects "O'Donnell Abu," an unusual song rich in poetry and historical reference, and he sings it in his own style, enunciating the words clearly, carrying the melody forcefully, restraining melisma. When he starts, the shop falls suddenly quiet. When he stops, he gets a clap. "Good man, Flanagan," they shout. He steps back to the counter smiling, and the racket rises again. Peter is pleased with his performance, glad to have chosen a song that won general approval, but hoping most to have impressed the other singers who are present, two men out of the sixty or so in his audience: Marty Crudden and Owney McBrien, who have, like Peter, come south, as Marty put it, "mad to sing."

Desires meet circumstances in performance, raising the question of which aspects of the scene are contextual, conditional. The political and economic conditions that concern historians were influential when Peter sang. The political conditions of the Irish borderland in Peter's day, in the time of the Troubles, constantly rattled the brain and they determined Peter's choice of the sort of song to sing in public. The economic conditions were subtler, but they brought on Peter's poverty, the absence of electricity in his dark, cold house and the work he had to do as a landless laborer, which wrecked his hands, preventing him from playing satisfactorily the fiddle tunes by Michael Coleman that rolled around his head. More relevant were the social conditions, stressed by Richard Bauman in his writings on performance. In the private event of the *ceili* at home and in the public event of the gathering in Swanlinbar, differences of social knowledge and social connection yielded differences in artistic action.

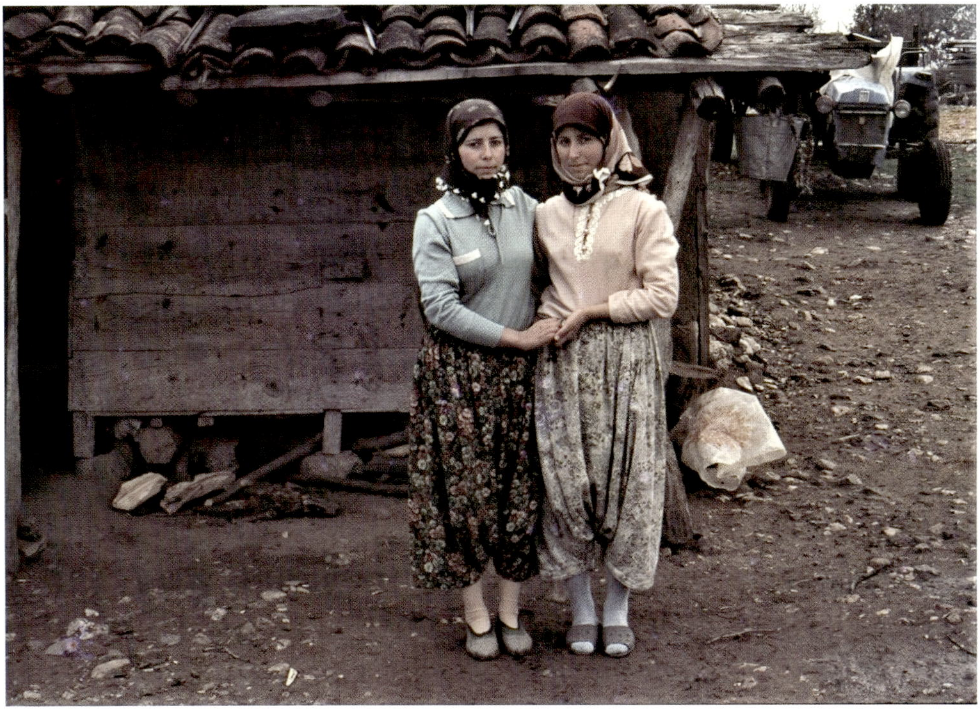

Aysel and Hanife Öztürk at home, Karagömlek, Ezine, Turkey, 1985

But the force most potent in shaping the events was the personal passion Peter developed over a lifetime of musical experiences, listening to his father Phil, a master of the flute, marching as the youngest of the musicians in his local fife-and-drum band (the Irish equivalent of Brazil's *pífano* band), and performing in response to numberless requests from neighbors and strangers in bars.

In oral performance, the creator and the consumer are normally face to face. Reaction, positive or negative, expressed or hidden, is immediate. In material performance, the creator and consumer are normally separate. Reaction is delayed. In both, though, a communicative loop, maybe quickly, maybe slowly, conditions future creations, just as past reactions conditioned past actions during the ongoing sequence of performances. A delay in reaction is but one of the differences in the complexity of material performance.

The loom stands before the window in one of the two rooms in Mehmet Öztürk's house in Karagömlek, a village in western Anatolia. Mehmet's daughters, Aysel and Hanife, are sitting together at the loom, weaving a carpet. Earlier Aysel sat here with her mother, Hörüye, learning. Now she sits here with her younger sister Hanife, teaching. Hanife is contributing her effort in exchange for Aysel's instruction. Aysel is the master: their carpet will be hers. She might keep it, but she will probably sell it, converting cash to gold, and — textiles or gold — her wealth will be stored in an ornate dowry chest that will go with her, a personal source of economic power, when she marries and leaves the village. Villages are exogamous and in time, courted by the son of the owner of the sawmill in Bozeli, Aysel will marry well.

Aysel and Hanife are weaving their mutual affection into a carpet. Space widens around them, and through their place a chain of acts has led to this moment. Out at the edge of the village, beyond the tilled fields, a rocky, infertile landscape sustains the sheep that Mehmet tends with his remarkably smart black dog. Agricultural land is tight, rocky land is wide, and the people here say that this is no land for farmers; life depends on *hayvancılık* and *halıcılık*, animal husbandry and carpet production. The sheep are sheared. Their wool is combed, then spun into yarn by Hörüye, using a drop spindle. Next the yarn is dyed in a vat above a fire, and it is ready for the loom.

A carpenter in the village, Salih Darıcı, crafts the looms; they cost one and a half times the price of a carpet. The houses are small, so when the loom is not in use it is knocked down, disassembled, and left outside. The houses cluster close, people know what is happening, and when the time comes to weave, a team of older women suddenly appears to wind the warp, affix it to the rolling beams, lug the parts into the house, and erect the loom, leaving the weaver the tiresome task of lashing the heddle.

The loom stands before the window. Color by color, Aysel and Hanife tie tight rows of knots on the warp between shoots of weft. They have no cartoon, no drawn plan. The carpet comes, they say, *kafadan*, from the head, and when thousands of knots have been correctly tied into one of the seven complex symmetrical designs they hold in their heads, the carpet is cut from the loom, ready for use. Its destination, most likely, is one of the region's three weekly agricultural markets, probably on a Friday in Ayvacık.

Early on the day of the market, the weavers, all of them women, most of them young, gather to set the prices: an optimistic price to ask, a bottom price to hold during bargaining. Along with that information, the carpets go to market with a few of the older weavers. Selling takes place in public on the streets where farm produce is also sold. All are watching while a middleman spreads the carpet on the street, kicks over a corner to check the quality of the weave, and names a price. The weaver counters, the prices bounce back and

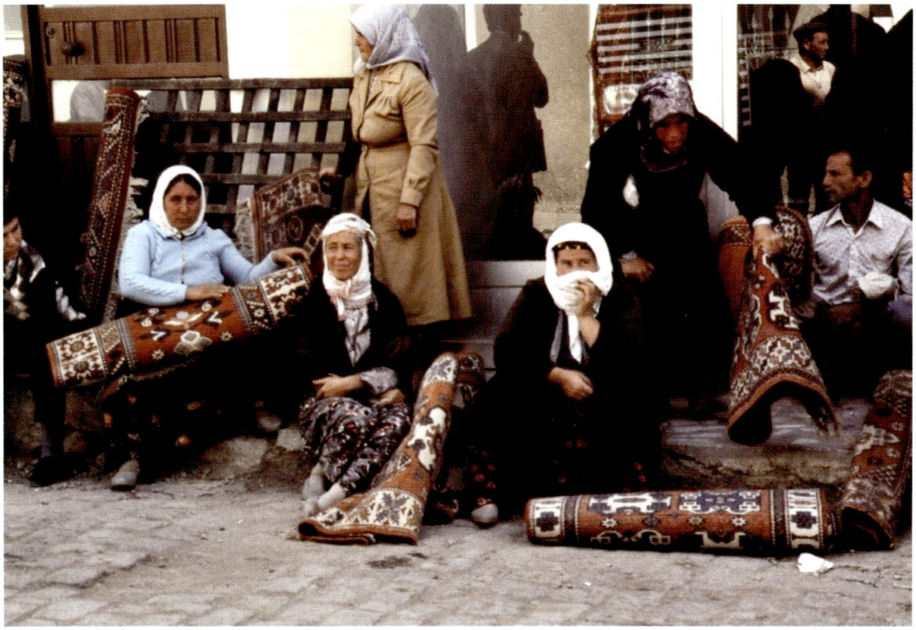

Carpet market, Ayvacık, Turkey, 1990

forth, getting closer, but they don't drop below the price at which the weavers have agreed to hold. The others watch to be sure that the one pressured during bargaining will not break the price, accepting a small sum that would disrupt their shared economy.

Selling is done. The middlemen bundle the rugs onto a bus and take them to a big city, Istanbul or Izmir, where they sell them to merchants who will sell them to customers who might also be merchants who will sell them in cities in the Middle East, Europe, or the United States. The weavers will share their profit with their families, probably donate a bit to the new mosque under construction in the village, but about half of their winnings will be invested in bracelets of twenty-two carat gold. They don't want paper money that loses its value during inflation. They want gold and they have set their bottom price by the international price of gold, reported in the newspaper. "Art," they say, "is a golden bracelet" — a reward, an adornment, a lasting beauty.

The piled oriental carpets woven by rural women in Turkey, appreciated widely in the world, issue from a complex procedure. Align Aysel's process for weaving woolen carpets in Karagömlek with Carmélia's process for shaping clay figures in Alto do Moura, and the salient features of material performance become clear.

The natural environment, possible to ignore in oral performance, provides a foundational condition in material performance. At the edge of Aysel's village, on rocky land, sheep grow the wool that will be processed into the yarn Aysel uses in weaving. At the edge of Carmélia's town, the ground holds the clay that will be processed into the substance she uses in shaping her statues.

Aysel and Carmélia both work at home in a social environment of learning and teaching, assistance and creation. Carmélia learned from her father and siblings. She taught her son Emerson, her niece Amanda, and her daughter Olga, who assists her by painting the clay figures. Aysel learned from her mother and she taught her sister Hanife, who assists her in weaving. Maybe in the future Aysel will teach her daughter, Yasemin, in the village of Bozeli.

Carmélia's creations go to the market in a city where they are bought by merchants for resale. Aysel's creations go to the market in a town there they are bought by merchants for resale. Their prime buyers are not random customers but people in the trade whose financial success depends on general understanding, whose choices and prices provide immediate information about current demand, information that will condition the next round of creation.

Aysel calls her work good. It is not strenuous and fatiguing like work out in the fields. She is inside, sitting down, her sister or a friend chatting beside her. Time it not wasted, every minute is preserved in a knot on the warp, nor is time a burden. Aysel forgets time in the intense concentration that her work requires, work in the flow that is engaging in the moment, rewarding at the end.

Carmélia says she loves her work. She and Aysel are both admired by their peers for the excellence of their skill. Aysel says *sanat*, Carmélia says *arte*, they both call their work art.

25

ART

ART, THEY SAY IN BRAZIL, is for everyone. Grounded in the creative potential shared by all of humankind, developed through learned techniques and driven by commitment, art springs from need and seeks excellence.

The physical needs of humanity are food, clothing, and shelter. All launch art. Food begins with a minimum of nutrition and lifts toward the aesthetic extravagance of festive feasts. Clothing begins with a wrap of hide and lifts toward carefully crafted items of apparel arranged into attractive outfits, billows of fabric and feathers. Shelter begins in a cave, expands into a vast variety of dwellings, and ends in humanity's grandest works of art, sites of social assembly: the Cathedral at Chartres, the Hagia Sophia in Istanbul, the Selimiye in Edirne, the Minakshi temple in Madurai, the Todai-ji in Nara.

To illustrate the diversity of possibility, we will sketch the range of the potter's art, an adjunct to the need for food that has for millennia supplied vessels for cooking, transport, storage, and service; chances are that ceramic bowls and plates held your breakfast this morning. Now, having begun with the clay in Alto do Moura and trusting that pottery provides an approach to world art as fruitful as painting does to European art, we will stick with the clay while creating a typology of the ceramic art of our day in order to reveal an exemplary medium's variety.

An Art of Form and Surface

The first option in ceramic art is to perfect the hollow forms and impervious surfaces of utilitarian pots, and we will settle first into a place where that possi-

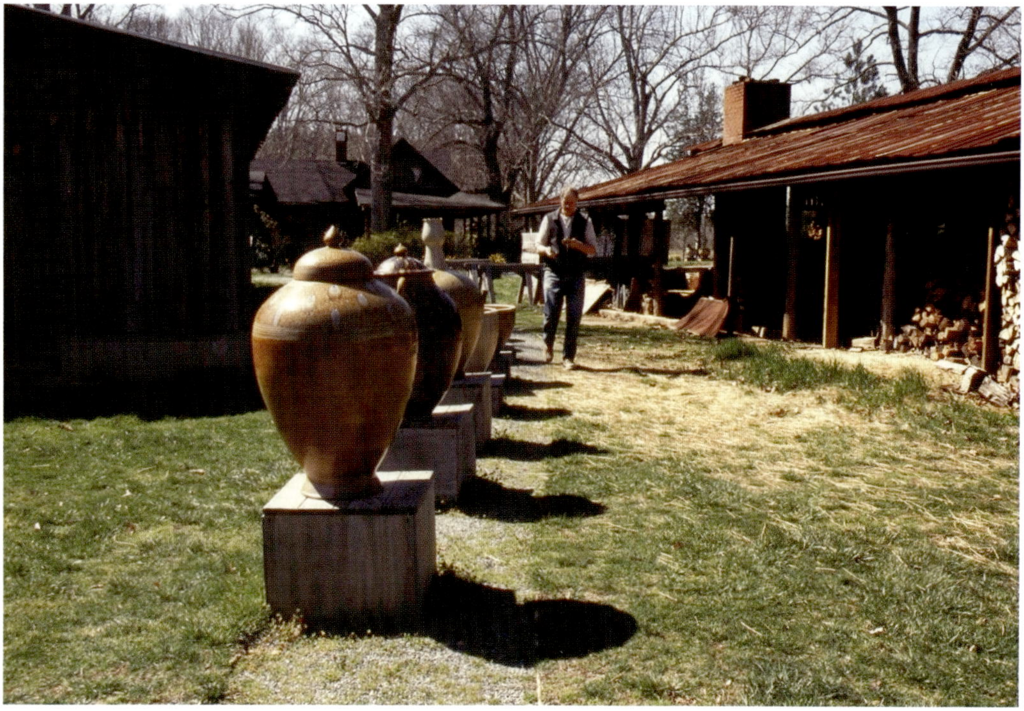

Mark Hewitt on his farm, between the workshop and kiln shed, Pittsboro, North Carolina, 2008

bility has been explored for far more than a century and continues to focus the effort of numerous potters who link into a loose community of working artists.

North Carolina's Piedmont, transitional like Pernambuco's Agreste, rolls between the Atlantic coast and the Appalachian highlands, carrying a wide dispersed landscape of white churches, small farm houses, and the workshops of potters who throw local clay on the wheel, shaping forms that rise and swell smoothly. At work in the log shop he built, Daniel Johnston explains that the pot's power spins from its central axis, reaching for the taut curves he compares to those of a healthy young body. The pot stands on the wheel. Daniel names its beauty with the human virtues of generosity and grace.

The pot's visual appeal is set in beauty and enriched by scale. Journeys to the East, to Thailand, Korea, and Japan, have yielded technical inspiration for Carolina's potters. Employing a method similar to Terezinha's in Alto do Moura, a method perfected by potters in Japan, Mark Hewitt and David Stuempfle in North Carolina throw the base form on the wheel, then add thick coils that circle the widening circumference. Daniel Johnston uses a Thai technique of small coils attached into rings that are piled, stretched, and shaped into form.

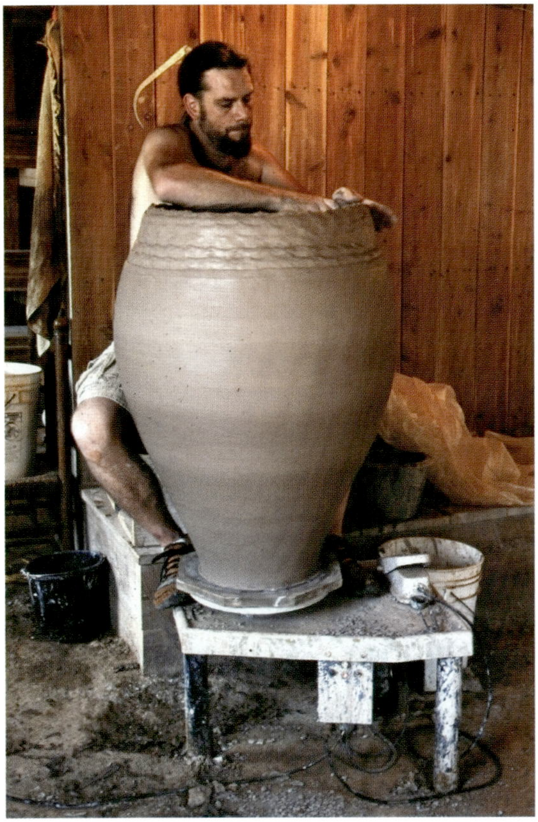

Daniel Johnston coiling a big pot, Seagrove, North Carolina, 2012

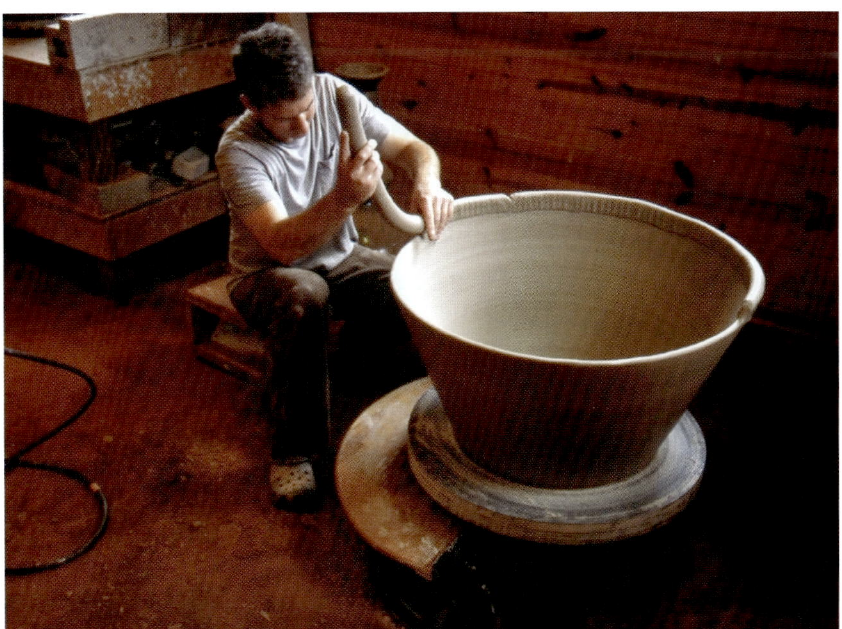

David Stuempfle coiling a big pot, Seagrove, North Carolina, 2013

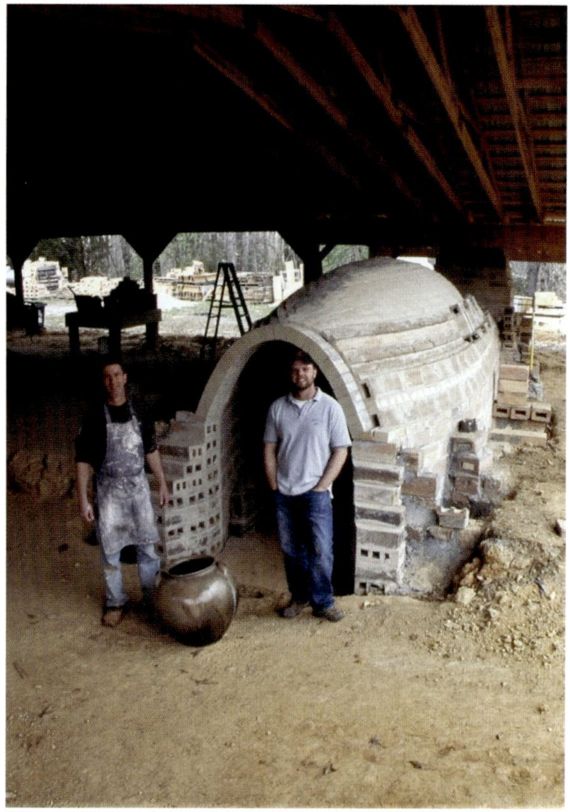

David Stuempfle and Chad Brown at David's kiln, Seagrove, North Carolina, 2010

Their big pots run past two feet in diameter and rise to four, five, six feet in height. They stand as silent, monumental presences, idealized representations of utilitarian pots, just as ancient Greek statues were idealized representations of human bodies.

Big pots need big kilns — big pots and big kilns are signal attributes of the current phase of development in North Carolina. The old local kiln, the groundhog, was small, low, and fired frequently. The new kilns are, like the groundhog, cross-draft and wood-fired, a firebox at one end, a chimney at the other, but they are much larger and they have portals for side-stocking along their flanks to increase control of the heat. Normally they are fired only four times a year: twice before shows where pots are sold in North Carolina (in March before the show in Hickory, in August before the show in Charlotte), and twice before the times when customers are most apt to visit the potteries (in May before the summer, in November before the Christmas shopping season).

Alto do Moura's earthenware fires in a day. Carolina's stoneware takes a week. On Tuesday the kiln is loaded with rows of big pots and shelves of small ones, separated by gaps aligned with the stoke holes on the sides. At dawn on Wednesday the fire is lit, and the kiln is fed through its mouth with slabs of pine while the heat rises slowly until the side-stoking begins and the heat reaches its peak of 2300 degrees fahrenheit on Saturday afternoon. For two days the kiln cools down, then on Tuesday, a week after it was loaded, the kiln is opened and the pots are spread for inspection.

The pots differ from kiln to kiln, from potter to potter. As it is with the statues of Alto do Moura and the woodblock prints of Bezerros, the initiated can look at a pot and name its maker. For all their variety, though, the pots are united by an aesthetic that brings a stately, symmetrical form into exciting tension with a wild and free surface, the consequence of time in the fire and the chosen glaze. Two glazes are traditional in the Piedmont.

To the east in the Piedmont, around the small town of Seagrove, salt enters the hot kiln, vaporizing to fuse with the silica in the clay and glaze the pots. Invented in medieval Germany, taken to England late in the seventeenth century, salt glaze was used by potters in the nineteenth century from New England through Pennsylvania to North Carolina. Today in the Piedmont, Ben Owen and Chad Brown create robust salt-glazed pots with surfaces invigorated by lively motion in the downward flow.

To the west in the Piedmont, in the Catawba Valley, an alkaline glaze containing wood ashes is preferred. Ash glaze belongs to Asia, and as the story goes, early in the nineteenth century, a prosperous potter in South Carolina read an eighteenth-century account of making pottery in China. Landrum was his name, and he introduced the ash glaze that then flowed through northern Georgia into the western Piedmont of North Carolina where its runny, rich colors were enhanced by pieces of glass that melted and streaked into the downward flow. Today Matthew Hewell in Georgia and Kim Ellington in North Carolina use ash glaze to get vibrant, active surfaces. Then taking the next step in the quest for surfaces of exhilarating complexity, Mark Hewitt and Daniel Johnston combine the two glazes. Late in firing, Daniel blows both salt and ash through the stoke holes along the sides of his big kiln. The salt makes a mottled field for the swift run of ash. Meanwhile, David Stuempfle gets marvelous results when he adds no glazes but fires long and hard, letting the flame and flying ash in the turbulent kiln produce beautiful surprises.

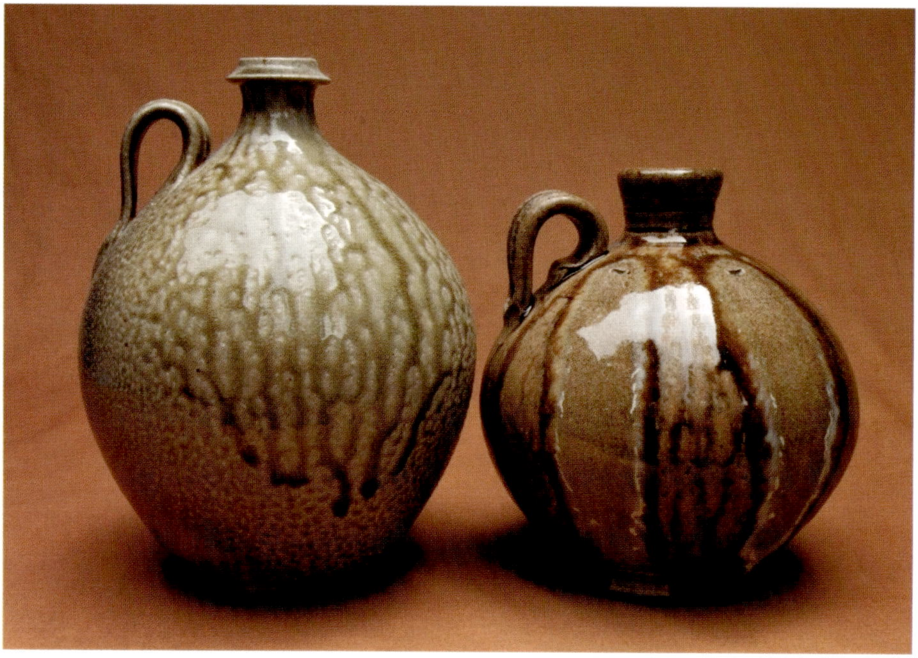

Small North Carolina jugs. Left: salt-glazed by Ben Owen, 2004.
Right: ash-glazed with glass runs by Kim Ellington, 2013

The potters get their surfaces by relaxing control and welcoming the accidents that they want but don't know they have achieved until the kiln is opened. This artistic procedure is fully understood by Carolina's potters, though it has no name. It does have names in Turkey. When weavers, like Aysel Öztürk, use hand-spun, naturally-dyed yarn that wavers in value and hue, they get accidental but desired variation on the surfaces of their carpets; they call is *abraş*. When potters, like Mustafa Baydemir, mix damp, tinted slips and let them flow to decorate earthenware surfaces, they call the effect *ebru*, likening it to the marbled paper that is an old and highly valued art, advanced by Necmeddin Okyay and Mustafa Düzgünman, and regularly practiced in Turkey today. Artistic work of this kind is probably most familiar to Americans from the dribbled and dripped paintings made by Jackson Pollock.

Daniel Johnston commented that the surfaces of his pots resemble Pollock's paintings. Step back, take a wider view, and it becomes clear that the traits of Carolina's pots — abstract forms, altered scale, nonobjective decorative surfaces — align with the traits of the twentieth-century art called modern, which began in Europe with revolutionary acts by Kandinsky and Picasso

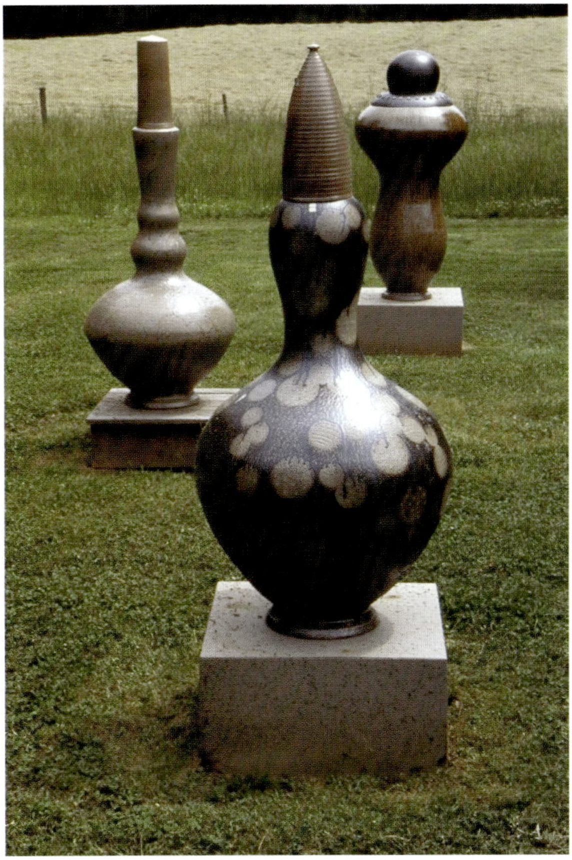

Big pots by Mark Hewitt, exhibited on his farm, Pittsboro, North Carolina, 2013

(who shared appreciation of African art) and matured in the United States with the abstract expressionists (who shared appreciation of Native American art). These similarities, perhaps subliminally, guide collectors of art toward North Carolina's pottery, but for the potters themselves the inspiration comes, not from the famed paintings and sculptures of the modernists, but from the pottery made earlier in the South, notably by Isaac Lefevers and Daniel Seagle in North Carolina and by Thomas Chandler and David Drake in South Carolina — all of them at work before 1860.

This point about deep regional connections was made in the first major exhibition of North Carolina pottery. Mounted at the North Carolina Museum of Art in 2005, it was curated by Mark Hewitt and Nancy Sweezy and accompanied by an excellent catalogue they wrote, *The Potter's Eye*. Mark Hewitt was born in the old English ceramic center of Stoke-on-Trent, where his father and grandfather were potters before him. In search of a place with good clay, abundant wood for firing, and a vital society of working potters, Mark married and settled in North Carolina in 1983, becoming in time the most influential of the region's potters and an expert on the region's historical tradition.

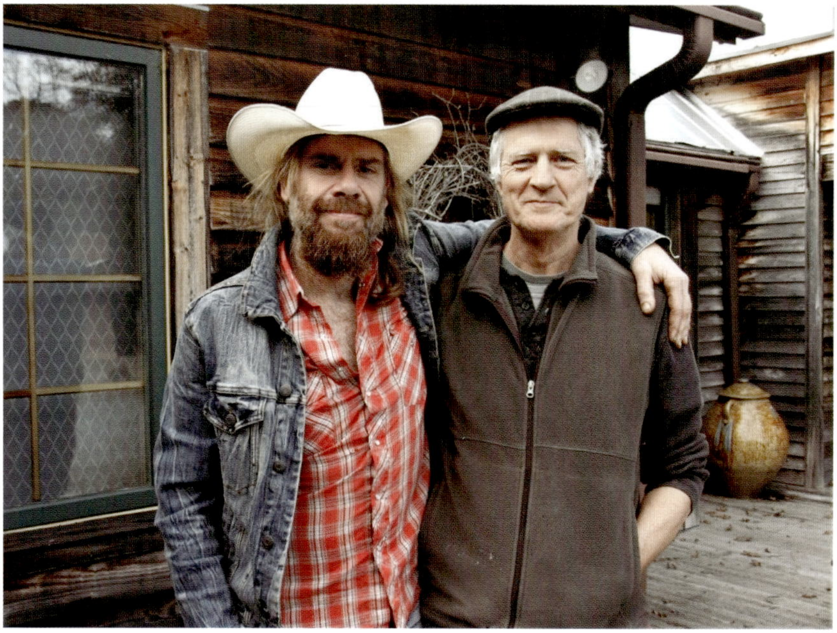

Daniel Johnston and Mark Hewitt, Pittsboro, North Carolina, 2019

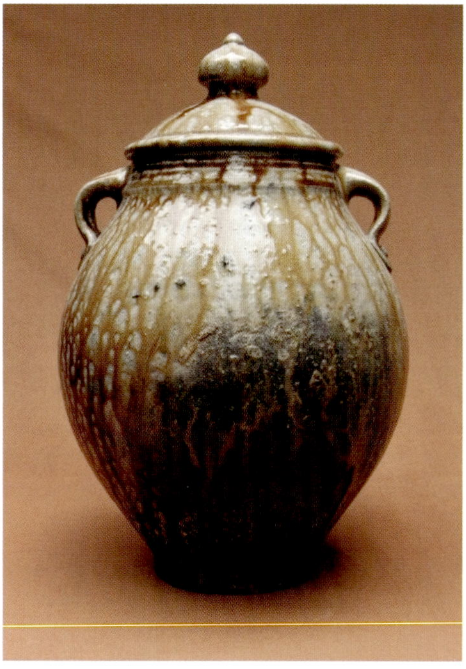

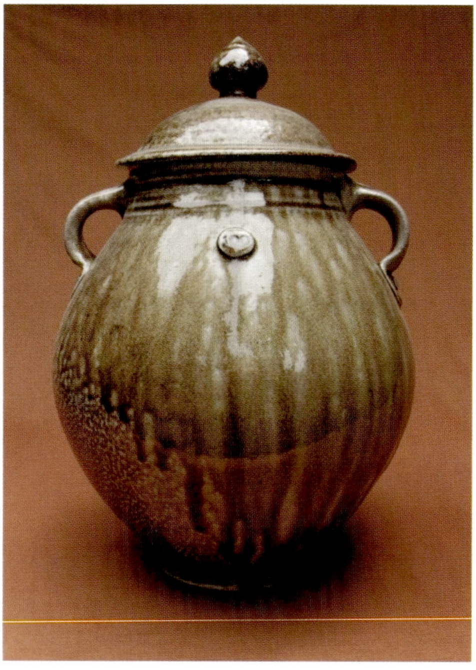

Lidded jars from North Carolina. Left: by Daniel Johnston (34 cm tall), 2012.
Right: by Mark Hewitt (35 cm tall), 2019

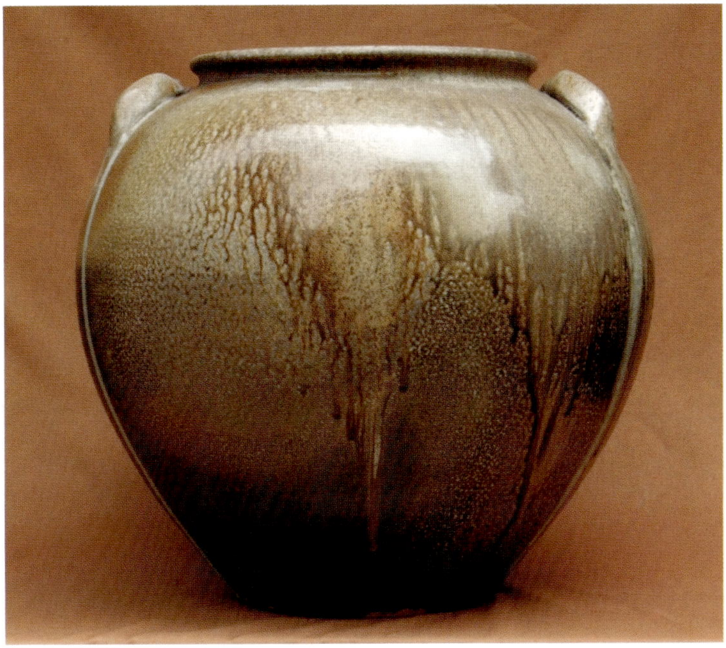

Big pot by David Stuempfle, inspired by Isaac Lefevers (56 cm tall), Seagrove, North Carolina, 2012

The exhibition featured the leaders of the moment: Kim Ellington, Mark Hewitt, Ben Owen, Vernon Owens, Pam Owens, and David Stuempfle. Around their works, historic pots were gathered from many places to stimulate comparisons and suggest connections. The modern star of the show was a gigantic pot by David Stuempfle. The historical star was a big pot, given much space in the catalogue, by Isaac Lefevers, who enlisted in the Confederate army and was killed in action in 1864. After the show, David Stuempfle made a big pot like the one Lefevers made, not a copy, the accidental richness of is surface could not be copied, but an homage to a master long gone.

Continuity in tradition is commonly secured along family lines — in Alto do Moura, from Zé Caboclo to Antônio to Amanda; in the Owens family in North Carolina, from Melvin to Vernon to Travis. As society loosens, formal arrangements compensate. Grateful for his apprenticeship with the great Michael Cardew in Cornwall and wishing to pass it on, Mark Hewitt instituted formal apprenticeships in North Carolina, training many of the leaders in the state's next generation: Alex Matisse, Joseph Sand, and Daniel Johnston, and Daniel in turn took on apprentices, training John Vigeland, Bill Jones, Andrew Dutcher, Charlie Hayes, and Natalie Novak. The work goes on.

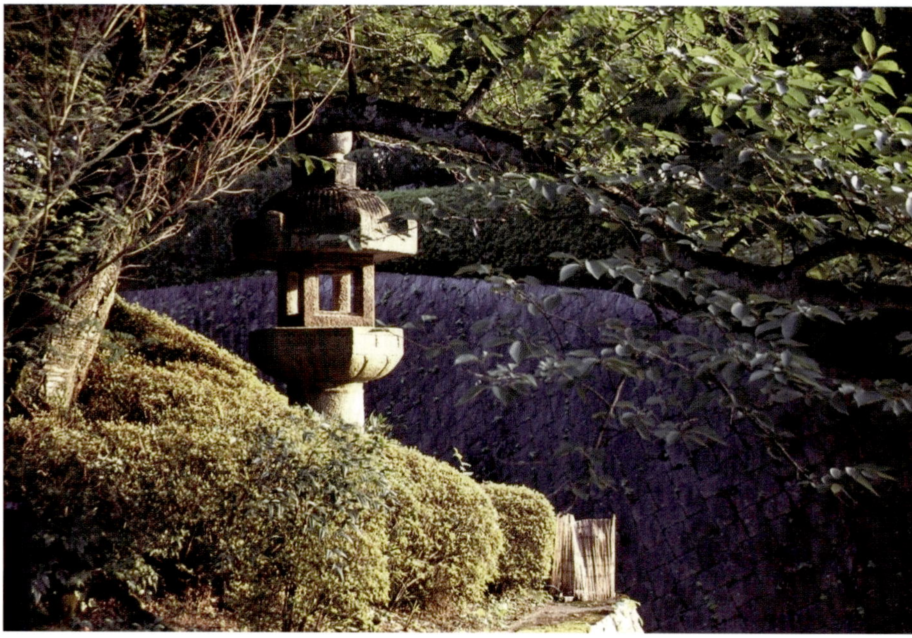

Garden at Kiyomizu-dera, a Buddhist temple in southeastern Kyoto, 2005

For a second instance of the first option, in which form and surface make art, consider the pottery embedded in the Japanese tea ceremony.

As it is performed in our day, the tea ceremony — *chanoyu* — retains the pattern that was formulated by Murata Shukō in the fifteenth century and perfected by Sen no Rikyū in the sixteenth century. Rikyū wrote that *chanoyu* begins when water is fetched and firewood is gathered. Then the water is boiled, tea is prepared and served to the guests. It is, he wrote, "a Buddhist spiritual practice." Both Shukō and Rikyū were trained in Zen Buddhism, both had associations with Daitokuji, a Zen temple in Kyoto, where on the grounds around the prayer hall there are twenty-three sub-temples, beautiful Zen gardens, and eight famed tea houses. Kyoto is still the center. Zen thought frames the ceremony; Zen and tea, it is said, have the same flavor.

Zen teachings provoke inner revelations, and an experience of *chanoyu* in performance, directed by the aesthetic called *wabi*, leads toward a Zen understanding of the world. *Wabi* is a plain, unpretentious, and relaxed beauty, a counter to arrogance through respect for humility. *Wabi* welcomes the imperfect (the cracked and repaired bowl), the incomplete (the moon glimpsed through clouds), and the subtle (a tuft of grass in the snow). Displayed in every

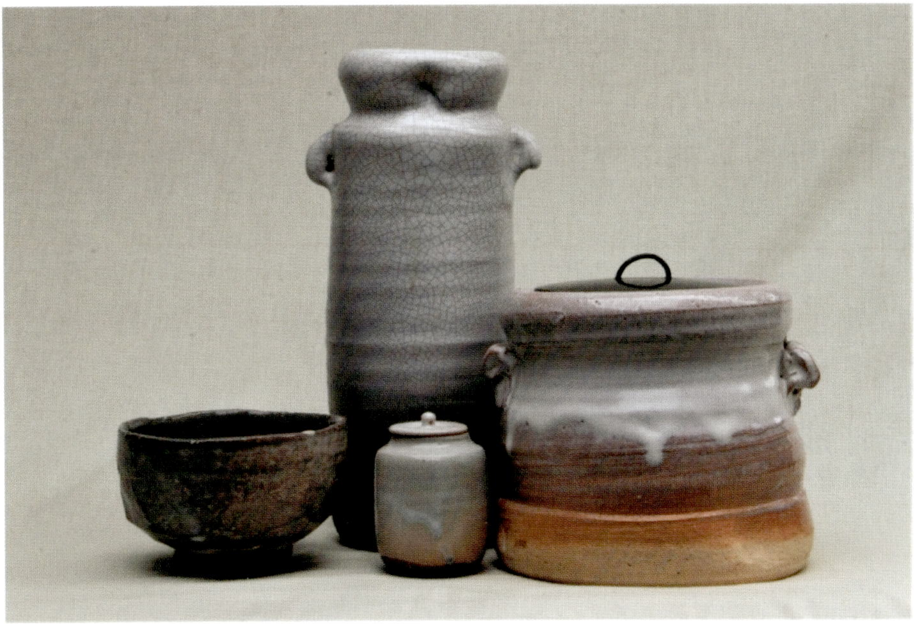

Tea ware from Hagi, Japan. Tea bowl by Agawa Norio, 1999. Vase by Matsumura Takuo, 1998. Tea caddy by Matsumura Takuo, 2005. Freshwater jar by Kaneko Nobuhiko, 1998

aspect of the ceremony, *wabi* becomes clearest in the ceramic vessels chosen for use. Early on, the favored vessels were *karamono*, opulent Chinese objects, but the taste shifted in the days of Shukō and Rikyū to *wamono*, the simpler, rougher, unadorned — *wabi* — pots made in Japan.

In Japan, that is, Buddhism provides the philosophical foundation and *wabi* supplies a name for creations in the first option for ceramic art, the useful works that rise directly from the potter's essential acts of shaping and firing.

During the slow, quietly convivial ceremony, time is taken for appreciation of the pieces in use. A vase stands in an alcove, a step above the floor where the host and guests sit, facing each other. Below a calligraphed scroll on the alcove's wall, the vase holds flowers, not arranged formally in the tradition of *ikebana*, but casually in the *wabi* way. In front of the host — on our first time, a delightful monk at Daitokuji — the smallest, most precious piece, a tea caddy with an ivory lid, holds powdered tea. To his left, a large jar with a black lacquered lid holds the water he boils, pours onto the tea in a bowl, whisks into a foam, and hands to the first guest who drinks and passes it along. This is the basic ceramic set: vase, caddy, freshwater jar, and tea bowl.

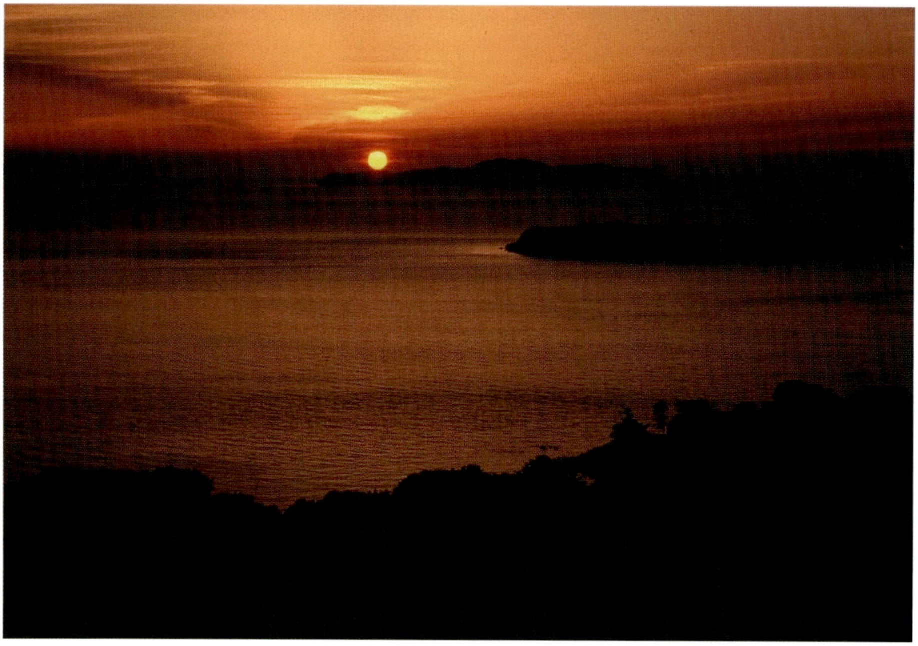

Sunset at Hagi harbor, 1998

The beginner — today most likely a young woman taught in a school — might buy a matched set at a department store in a city or a big atelier in a pottery town. But the practiced master, whether a monk at a temple or a woman at home, wants a mismatched yet harmonious collection of old and new pieces made in different centers of production, each with its own distinctive clay, handling, and style. Tea ware has been made in many places, in Shigaraki, Bizen, Iga, Seto, but it is proverbially put that for tea ware Kyoto is first, Hagi is second. In Kyoto, Sen no Rikyū's friend the potter Chōjiro invented the hand-built, low fired *raku* tea bowls that have been made for centuries in the city. Hagi is a city by the sea at the far western end of the main island that carries the old capitals of Nara and Kyoto near the middle and the current capital of Tokyo at its southeastern bend.

At Hagi, the Miwa family has the name and fame, but Hagi's distinctive pottery — Hagi *yaki* — is made in about a hundred shops, and many artists make tea ware, including Kaneko Nobuhiko, Matsumura Takuo, Sakakura Seichi, and Agawa Norio. At the city's edge, Agawa Norio has a bright workshop next to his house on the banks of the Hashimoto River that runs to the sea. In every phase of his work, Agawa Norio is aided by his sprightly wife, Motoko; they are a couple in action like Luiz Carlos and Genilda in Alto do Moura.

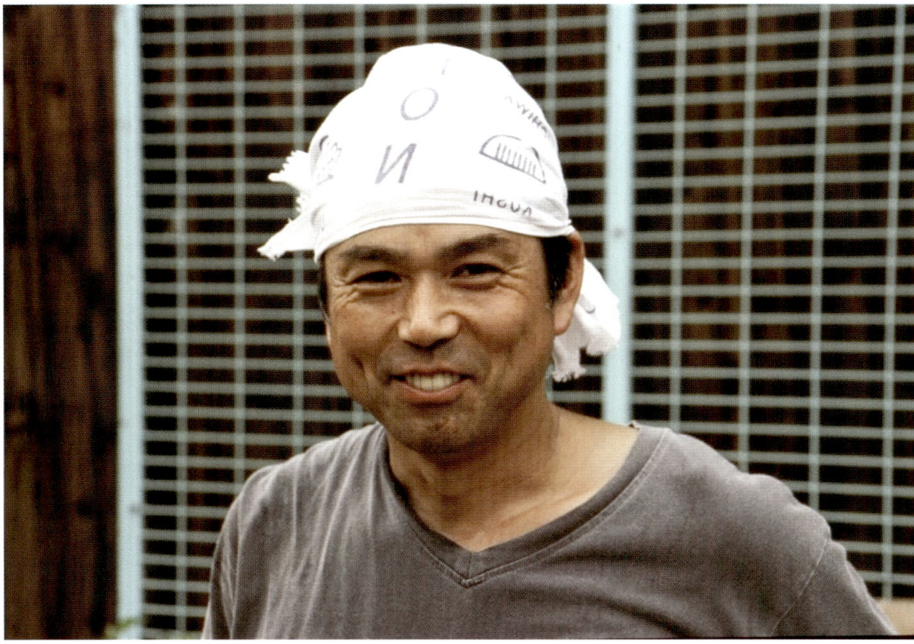

Kaneko Nobuhiko, Hagi, Japan, 2001

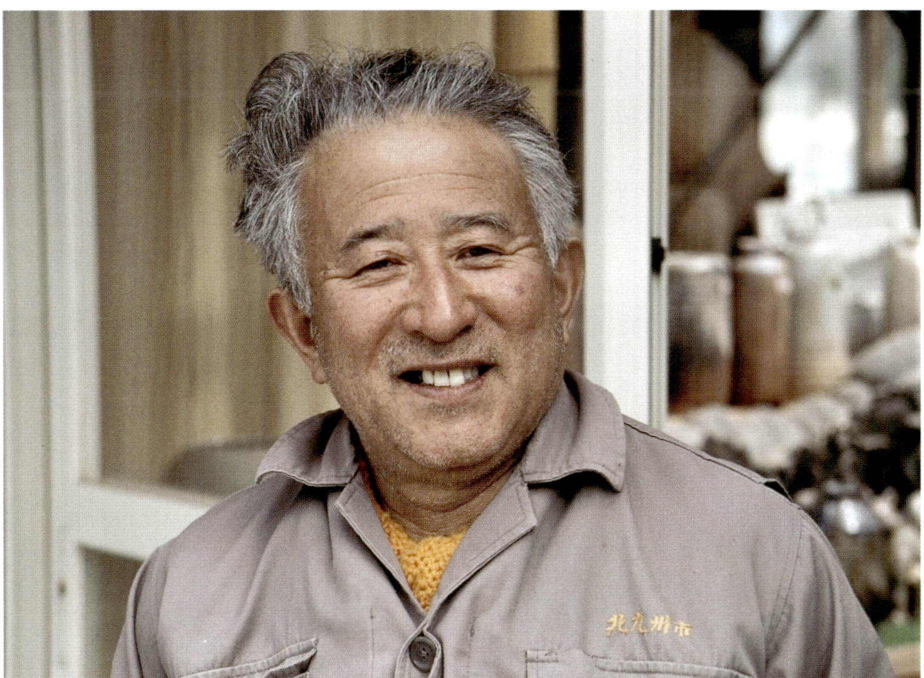

Agawa Norio, Hagi, Japan, 1994

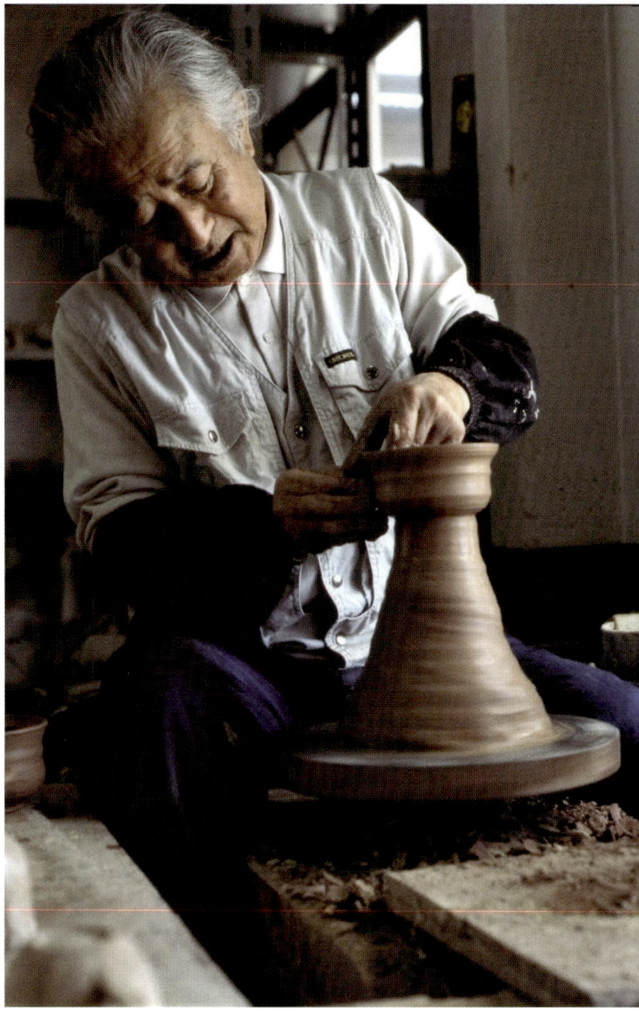

Agawa Norio at the wheel, Hagi, 1998

Agawa Norio works at the wheel lit by a window in the back of his shop, and having taught himself he says that if you can throw a tea bowl on the wheel, you can do anything. A pug mill and a kiln stand at the far end of the shop, a long table fills the middle, and a stove warms the front where retired men gather in the afternoons. While Agawa Norio works on, cheerfully, constantly, Motoko supplies them with hot green tea while they talk. Most amusing among the regular guests is a man who keeps his treasured collection of Agawa Norio's works safely packed in the trunk of his car and wears the black cap and jacket of a baseball umpire, commenting on the conversation with an ump's calls on the field: Foul ball! You're out!

North Carolina's pots oppose a controlled, smooth and symmetrical, form with an uncontrolled, free and surprising, glazed surface. Tea ware in Agawa Norio's hands is *wabi* and wild from start to finish. He has two clays: *Mishima*,

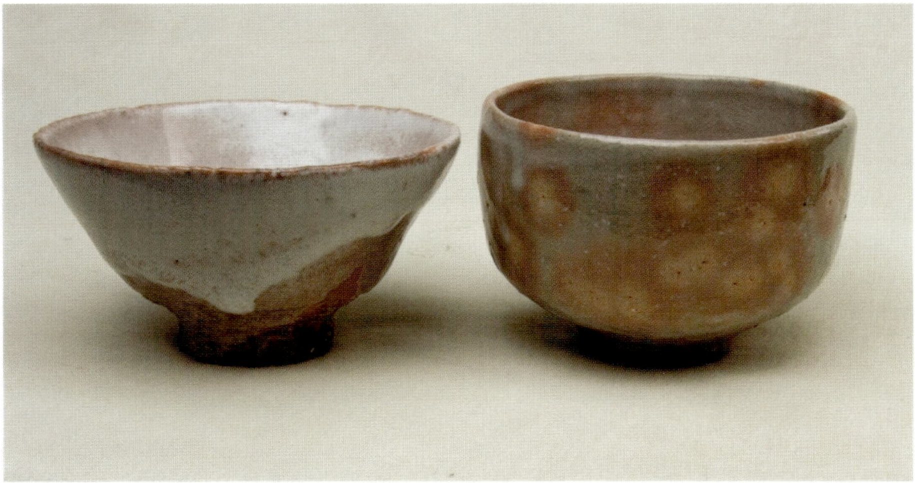

Hagi tea bowls. Left: flaring, with the rice-straw white glaze, by Kaneko Nobuhiko, 2001. Right: cylindrical, with the firefly surface, by Sakakura Seichi, 1998

a red clay from an island to the north, and *Daido*, a yellow clay from a railroad cut to the south. The yellow clay can be used alone, but the red clay must be mixed with the yellow to take form. He can blend the two into a range of tones from pinkish yellow through ruddy buff to warm brown, or he can fuse them loosely to get accidental streaks of color like the old English marbled ware. When preparing the clay, Agawa Norio carefully removes the tiny bits of stone. Then he puts them back, spreading them evenly through the clay so the kiln will give him the "firefly" effect of specks nimbed with orange on a gray field, or he bunches them for gritty clumps on the surface.

Agawa Norio throws off the hump. He centers a towering truncated cone of clay on the wheel and shapes forms from the spinning top, as Angelo does in Terezinha's shop in Alto do Moura. Agawa Norio marks the length on the hump, presses down and pulls up, shaping a cylinder, then he sweeps a spiral over the surface with a loop tool to begin a vase.

Let's follow a tea bowl. There are two basic forms: one flared wide like the Korean rice bowls once used for tea in *chanoyu*, the other with sides rising more vertically. In shaping the form, he uses a throwing stick to give the interior a ribbed richness, and he grooves the exterior with the tracks left by his fingers in motion. Then he cuts the bowl from the tower top with a wire and places it on the wareboard beside him. Once it has dried enough, Agawa Norio returns the bowl to the wheel, slices the surface with irregular facets, vertical counterpoint to the horizontal course of his fingers. Then he turns the bowl over, attacks the bottom and carves the footring. A key feature that prompts comment during *chanoyu* performances, the footring is chopped and notched, a definitive trait of Hagi *yaki*.

Agawa Norio uses two slips, a white kaolin and a dark gray made out of clay from Seto. In many traditions, slips provide a smooth and consistent primer, but he splashes them in patches so the pot's clay is randomly revealed behind the slips as the moon is revealed behind scudding clouds. Slipped, the bowl is ready for its first firing at 800 degrees centigrade.

After its first firing, the bowl is slipped again, the dark sections darkened still more with the gray slip, heavily loaded on a calligrapher's brush. Then it is glazed. An alkaline glaze, blended of feldspar and ashes from wood and straw, coats the bowl with a pale, shiny background. The foreground, Hagi's signal effect, comes from the "rice-straw white." Agawa Norio gets rice straw from farmers in his neighborhood. Then he burns it, not to ashes, but to black charcoal, and mixes it with his usual ash glaze to get thick flows of a smoother and richer white. Now he grips the bowl by the footring, dips it quickly in a vat of glaze to coat the exterior, pops it at the surface to fill the interior, swishes it back and forth to thicken the glaze on the rim, and then flips it over suddenly so the thicker white oozes down over the lighter coat beneath, white upon white. The bowl is ready for its last agony in the kiln.

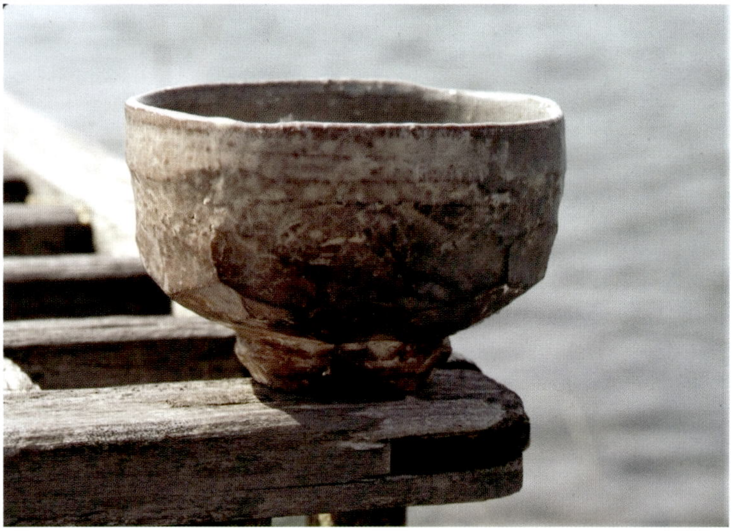

Tea bowl by Agawa Norio, 1998

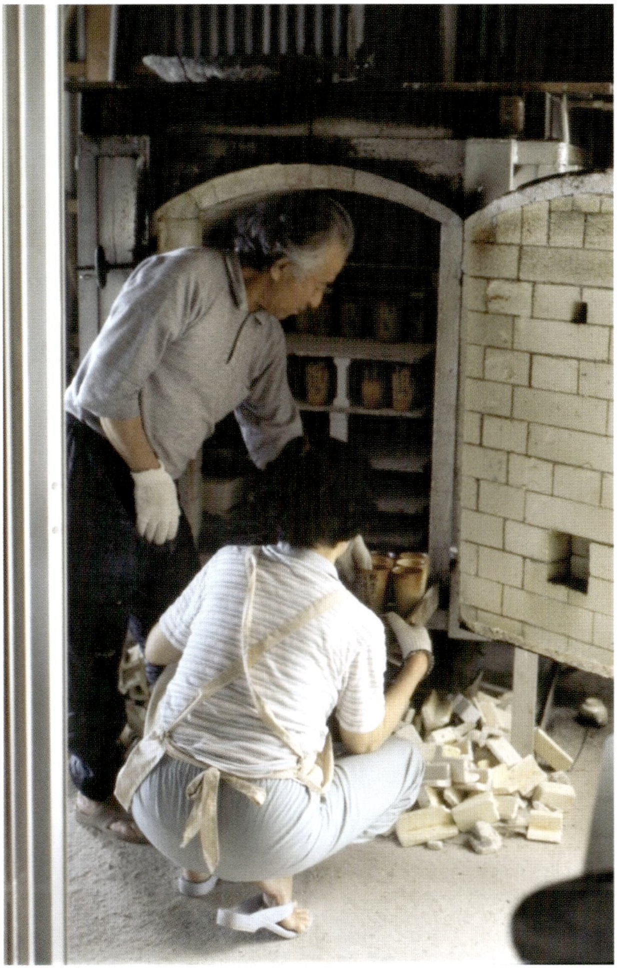

Norio and Motoko opening the kiln, 1998

When he was young Agawa Norio worked at a wood-fired climbing kiln, and he remembers with scant pleasure the endless labor of cutting wood for stoking. Some potters in Hagi have returned experimentally to firing with wood; one is his neighbor Nishimura Shuseki. But like most of his colleagues, Agawa Norio uses a convenient gas-fired kiln. For their second and final firing his works remain in the kiln for eight to twelve hours while the heat ascends to the stoneware peak of 1250 degrees centigrade. To get dramatic effects, comparable to those of wood-firing, Agawa Norio shoots air into the kiln, withdraws it, then shoots it again, so that bouncing between the oxidation that brings out the yellow and red colors and the reduction that yields a dark melancholy tone, his works exhibit surprising diversity when the heat descends past 300 degrees and he opens the kiln's door.

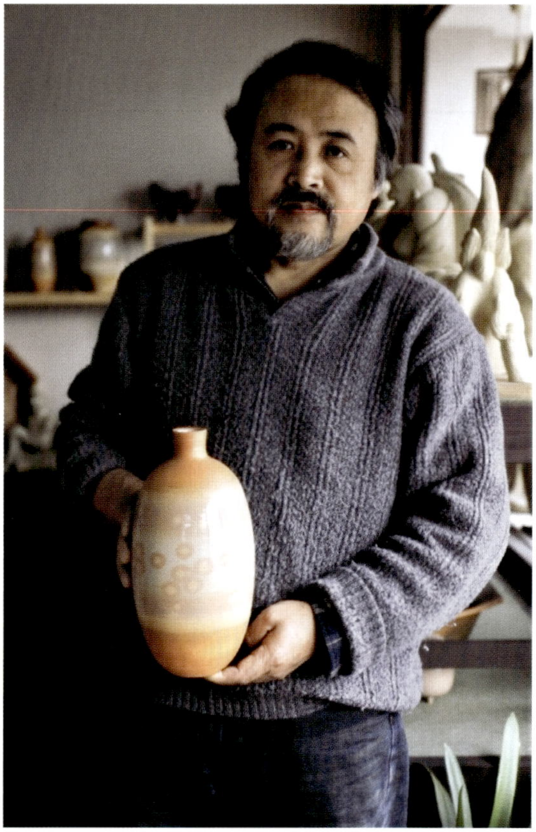

Matsumura Takuo with a vase he made, Hagi, 1999

The results, he says, are owed half to his intentions and half to God's will. Working at the big Jozan atelier in Hagi, Kaneko Nobuhiko says that when you put your works into the kiln, they leave you. The kiln owns them now and does whatever it wants. In his tidy shop in Hagi, Matsumura Takuo says the beauty of the pots depends upon accidents in glazing and firing. You never know what will happen, he says, but you work to make accidents happen. Their thinking finds a match among the potters who fire with wood in North Carolina.

The masterpiece in Hagi has a rough surface of clay, spilled with the smooth rice-straw white — the look of a spume of sea foam on a gravelly beach. That, though, is not the end. Hagi *yaki*, they say, matures through seven phases. It is shaped, slipped, fired, glazed, fired, and then put to use. In use, handled and filled again and again, the white bowl darkens, darkens, slowly turning a beautiful black. Then it cracks. The cracks are filled with golden lacquer, so the image of white foam on gravel converts into an image of a lighting flash in a dark storm.

An Art of Ornamented Form

The second option for ceramic art entails a distinct phase of decoration. Some potters in North Carolina — Matt Jones and Kate Waltman consistently, Mark Hewitt frequently — decorate their pots, and Japan abounds in decorated ceramics. Oribe, Sen no Rikyū's follower in *chanoyu*, invented a free, offbeat variety of decoration that continues to be practiced in Seto. Japan's splendidly painted porcelain — Kakiemon and Nabeshima — has been made since early in the seventeenth century at Arita on Kyushu, and later in the seventeenth century Arita's technical tradition was taken north to Kutani. All of this work remains vibrantly vital, but we will now treat a different pair of traditions, again one American and one Asian, both deeply rooted in history and robust today. First, the earthenware made in the Native American communities in the southwestern United States, then the ware called *çini*, made at Kütahya in the mountains of western Turkey.

Pots made around Seagrove in North Carolina and at Hagi in Japan are comparable in technique and taste: a wheel-thrown form is invigorated by intended accidents in the kiln. Pots made in the pueblos of the Southwest and at Kütahya in Turkey differ radically in method but find accord in the aesthetic quest for excellence in tight control.

In Alto do Moura, Terezinha described the pots made before her by the Indians in the interior of Brazil, saying they were made by women who had neither wheel nor kiln, but built their pots by hand and fired them outdoors. After he had completed his monumental *Mythologiques*, demonstrating among other wonders the cultural congruence of the Indigenous people of South and North America, Claude Lévi-Strauss kept to his task in smaller books. In one of them, *The Jealous Potter*, he affirmed the unity of the Native American pottery traditions in North and South America. The traits Lévi-Strauss noted were Terezinha's — traits still basic in the Southwest.

The potters are predominantly women. The greatest artists, like Nampeyo at Hopi, have been — and remain — women who build their pots by hand, without a wheel. The main change has come in firing. Some pots are still burned outdoors in heaps beneath fuel, but more are fired in electric kilns with conspicuous aesthetic results. Since fewer pots are spoiled or lost in firing, the artists will not have wasted their time if they linger long over a particular piece. The decoration has become finer, more intricate, more demanding, satisfying, and rewarding.

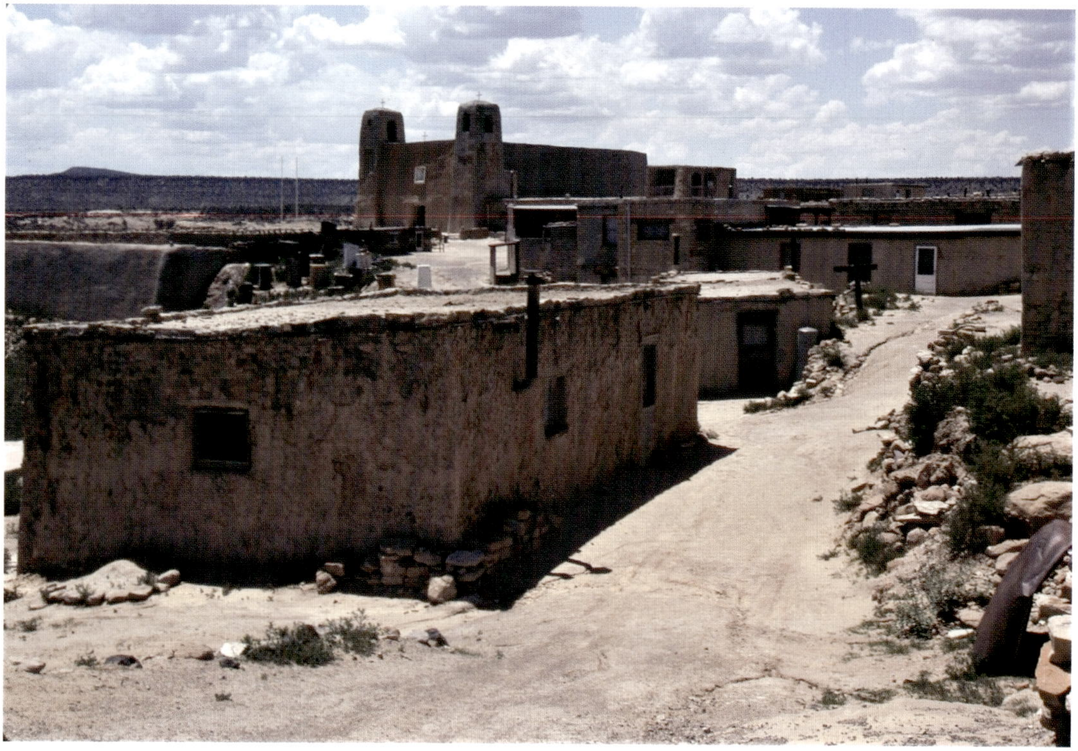

Acoma, New Mexico, 1987

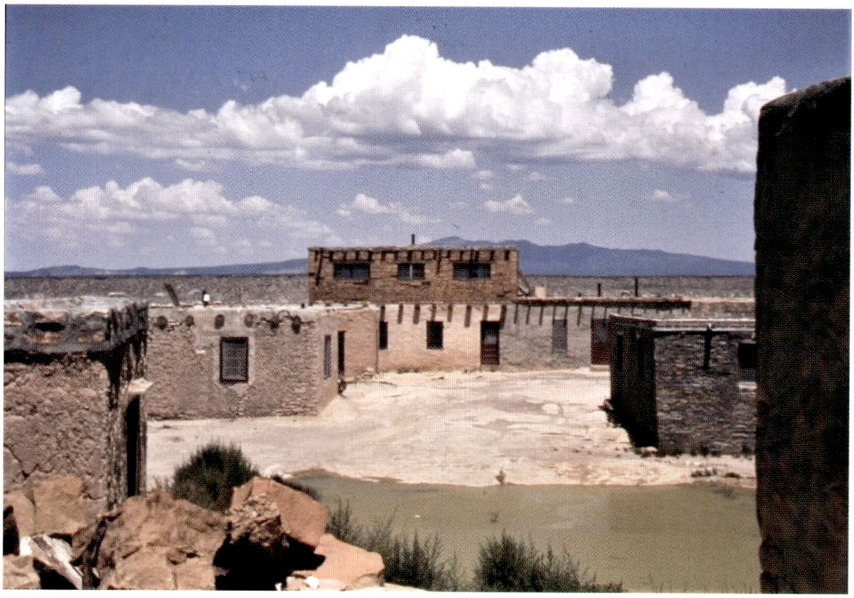

Acoma, New Mexico, 1990

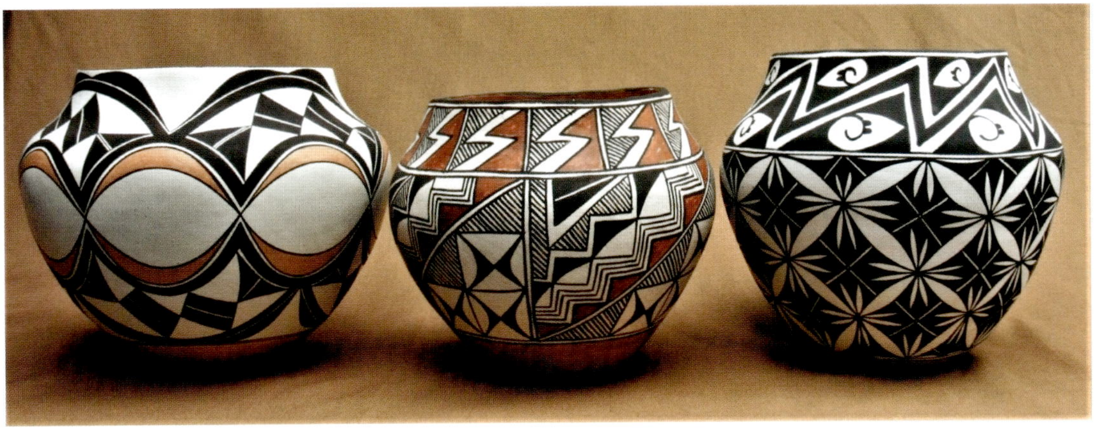

Geometrically-decorated Acoma jars. Left: by Franklin Peters, 2019.
Center: by Frances Torivio, 1986. Right: by Larry Chino, 2006

The basic techniques are similar, pueblo to pueblo, but decorative differences enable easy attribution to specific communities: Hopi, Zuni, Acoma, Laguna, Santa Clara, San Idelfonso, Cochiti, Santo Domingo, Zia. The work, both shaping and decorating, is especially fine at Acoma.

Established more than eight hundred years ago, the pueblo of Acoma is the oldest continuously occupied site in the United States. The pueblo rides on a high mesa. When the first Spanish invaders saw it, in 1540, they declared Acoma to be the world's greatest stronghold. The pueblo on high, they call it Sky City, crowds on sacred ceremonial occasions, but most people live in places below, where gardens are tended and pots are made. Unencumbered by bulky equipment for production, the potters work, like Carmélia in Alto do Moura, in small domestic spaces, within the flow of daily familial life.

A survey at Acoma in 1974 listed fifty-six professional potters, all of them women. Change since that time has led to the inclusion of some men (just as the third generation in Alto do Moura includes some women). When Lucy M. Lewis, Acoma's most famed master, passed in 1992, her work was carried on by her skilled daughters, Emma and Dolores, and by her burly, witty son Andrew. Her son Ivan married into Cochiti pueblo, learning and practicing Cochiti's distinct style. Listed in the 1974 survey, along with Lucy Lewis among the eighteen masters, Frances Torivio's daughters Maria Lilly Salvador and Wanda Aragon are among the artistic leaders today, and Wanda's husband, Marvis makes works of his own. Marvis said that men at Acoma have always made pottery, but only the vessels for sacred ceremonies that were never offered for sale.

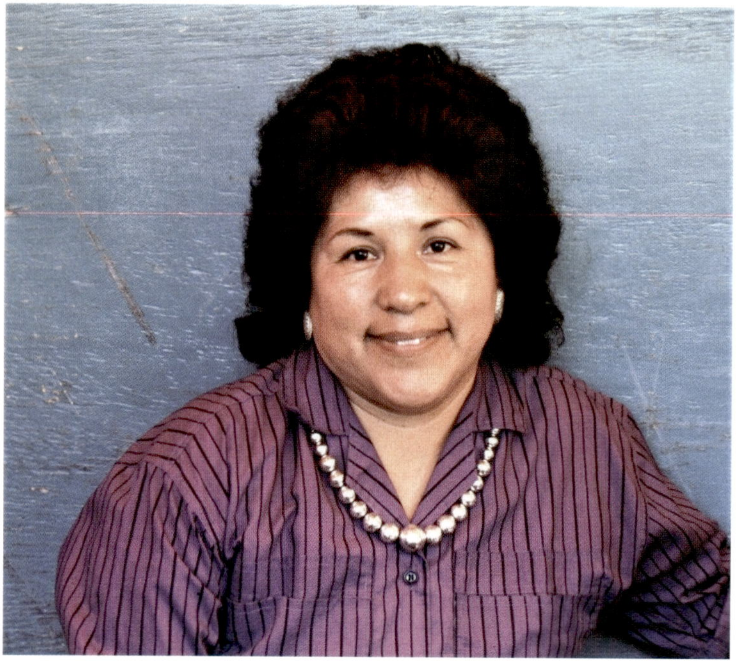

Maria Lilly Salvador, Acoma, New Mexico, 1988

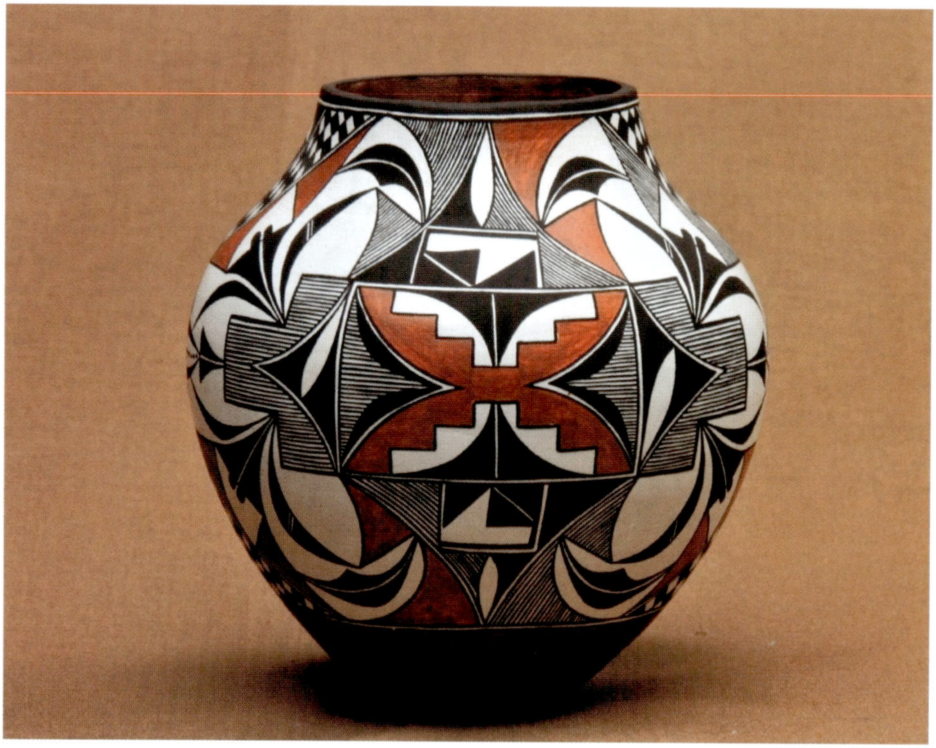

Miniature jar, by Maria Lilly Salvador (4.5 cm tall), 1996

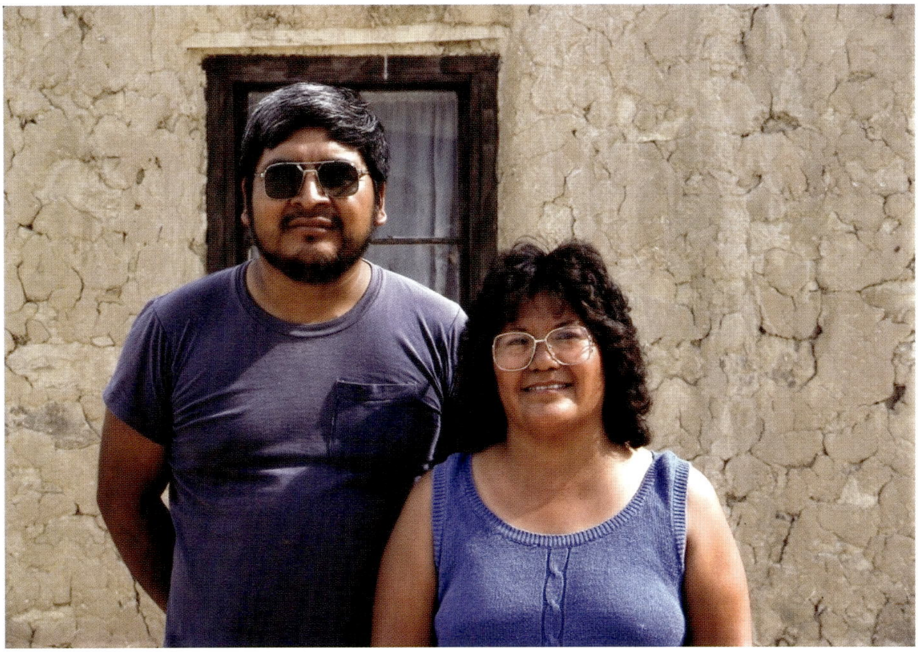

Marvis and Wanda Aragon at home, Acoma, New Mexico, 1987

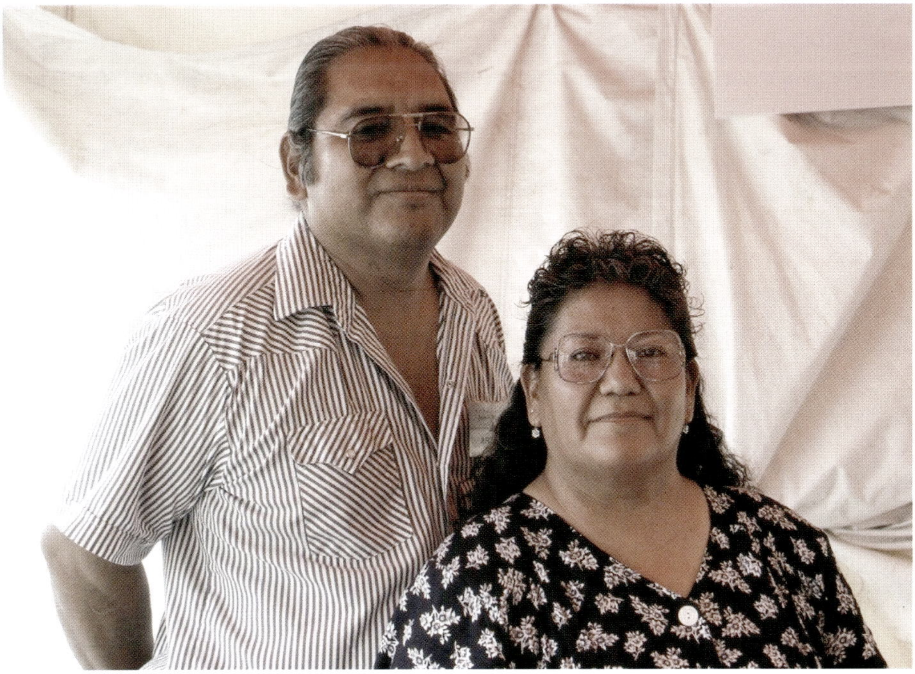

Marvis and Wanda Aragon on the road, at a Native American arts fair in Indianapolis, Indiana, 1996

A close couple, partners in action like Norio and Motoko in Hagi, Marvis and Wanda go together to dig the clay, the flesh of Mother Earth, at locations on the community's land unknown to outsiders. The clay comes in hard gray lumps that are dried, broken, dampened, and kneaded with the feet, quite like the *massapê* clay of Alto do Moura. Another step, though, is necessary at Acoma. Centuries of pots made and broken have scattered the land with shards that are collected, crushed, and mixed into the clay for temper. New pots absorb ancestral memories.

Wanda Aragon sits at a table in the room next to her kitchen. She has clay in her hands and a form in her mind — a jar of the kind once used to carry water up to the pueblo. The jar rises from a narrow foot, spreads wide, and rolls over the shoulders to a short, wide neck. Wanda's jars range from big ones, nine inches tall, through a middling size at six inches, down to miniatures, three inches in height. Hand-built, Wanda's pots can't be metrically symmetrical, but they aspire to a perfection of the sort that Mark Hewitt achieves on the wheel in North Carolina: a balanced form, a smooth surface, and walls so thin that the pot's light weight is a surprise when you lift it.

Wanda rolls a ball of clay and pinches it into a rough bowl, something like Kyoto's *raku* tea bowls. She lifts and settles her bowl into the bottom of a broken old pot, the mother of the new one, then she adds coils to get a cylinder that she paddles into smoothness and spreads outward into form. Once it is dry enough, she lifts the new pot out of the bottom of the old one, then scrapes and polishes the surface, smoothing it and smoothing it more.

The pot is gray, the gray of the clay that will be hidden, inside and out, beneath natural slips in three colors: white, red (a rich russet-orange), and black. First, Wanda coats the form with white, providing eventually a canvas for painting, a clean background for a display of ornament, providing now a ground for planning the grammar of her design. Like many artists, she sketches with a pencil, the marks of which will burn away in firing.

Here is one of her favorite plans. Wanda quarters the design, creating four equal segments that assure a unity of scale on the pot as a whole. She splits each segment with a vertical line, correctly centering a bilaterally symmetrical motif that descends from the top and exits toward the bottom. Then on the lines that separate the segments, she positions a similar motif that rises from the bottom and exits toward the top. The division into four segments has become lost into a sequence of eight motifs that, alternating high and low, circle the jar in a continuous flow. Horizontal unity is set with a foundational line near the

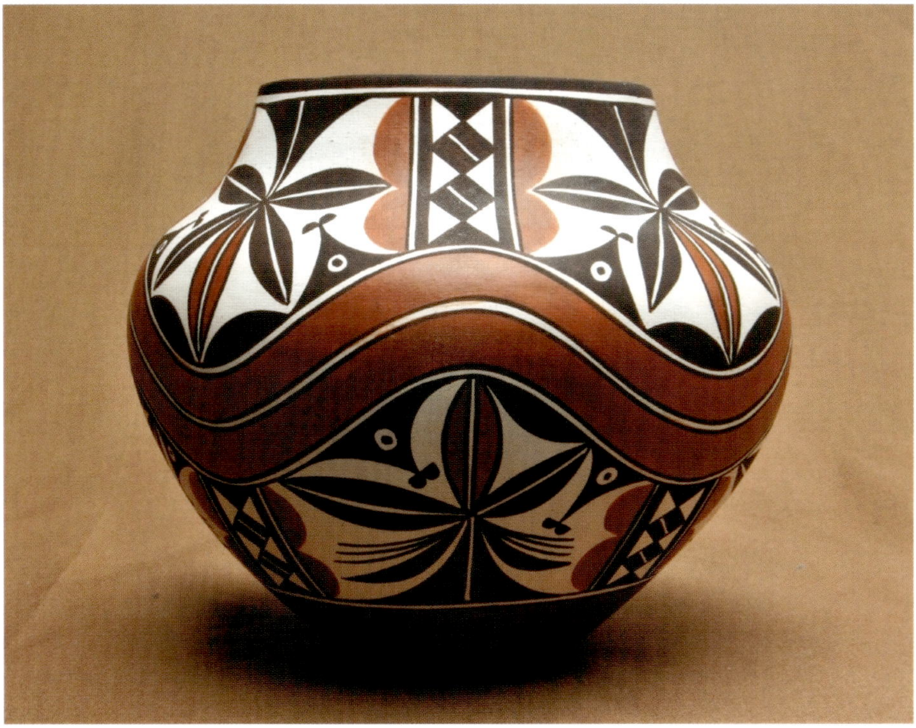

Jar, by Wanda Aragon (14 cm tall), 1996. This jar and the one on the next page were designed with versions of the same geometric plan.

pot's bottom and a wave that sweeps the pot below the descending motifs and above the ascending motifs, so the vertical segmentation of the beginning has yielded to an endless horizontal ring around the pot, circling forever like the days, the seasons, the years.

Planning is done, the difficult, demanding execution begins. Wanda uses a supple filament from a yucca leaf as a brush and outlines her design in black. Her black is mixed with a vegetable gum so it will stick to the pot, just as Genilda's paint in Alto do Moura is mixed with white glue. Wanda uses no tools to guide her, no rulers or squares, but she miraculously maintains lines that are thin and even, perfectly vertical, smoothly curvaceous, working with the exactitude of an engineer making a technical drawing. Then she paints the base, below the bottom line, with her red and fills the pattern with coats of red and black to get consistently solid, unshaded hues. Nothing rough, nothing accidental or wild, Wanda Aragon's jar will join Acoma's assembly of geometrically ornamented masterworks, characterized by astonishing precision.

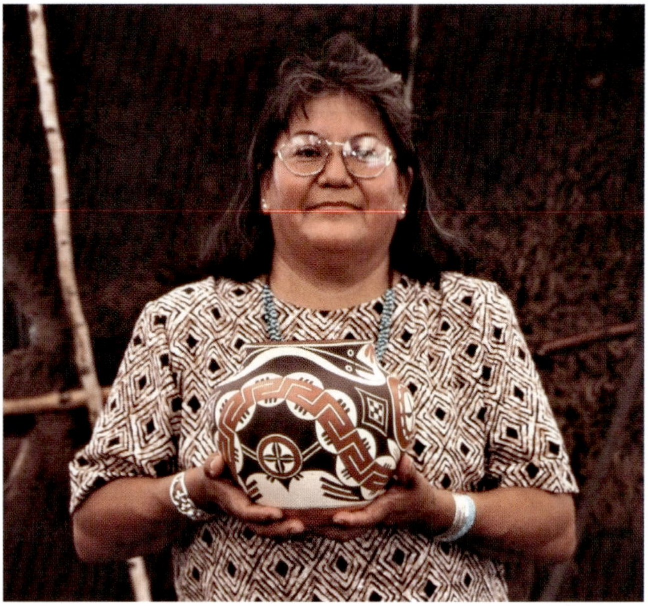

Wanda Aragon with a jar she made, 1998

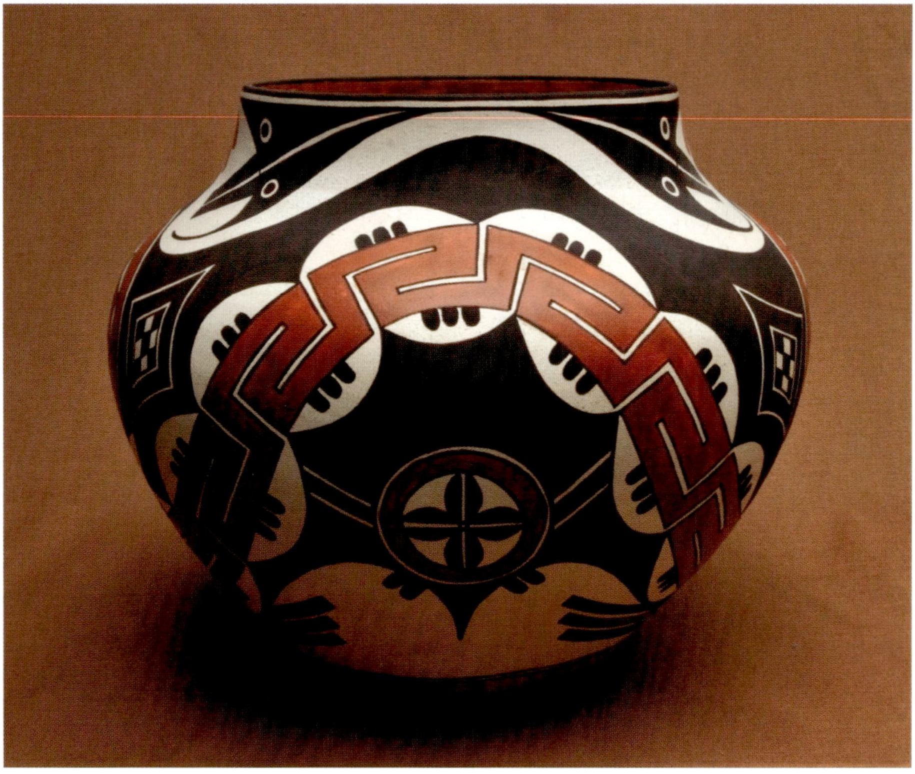

Jar, by Wanda Aragon (20 cm tall), 1998

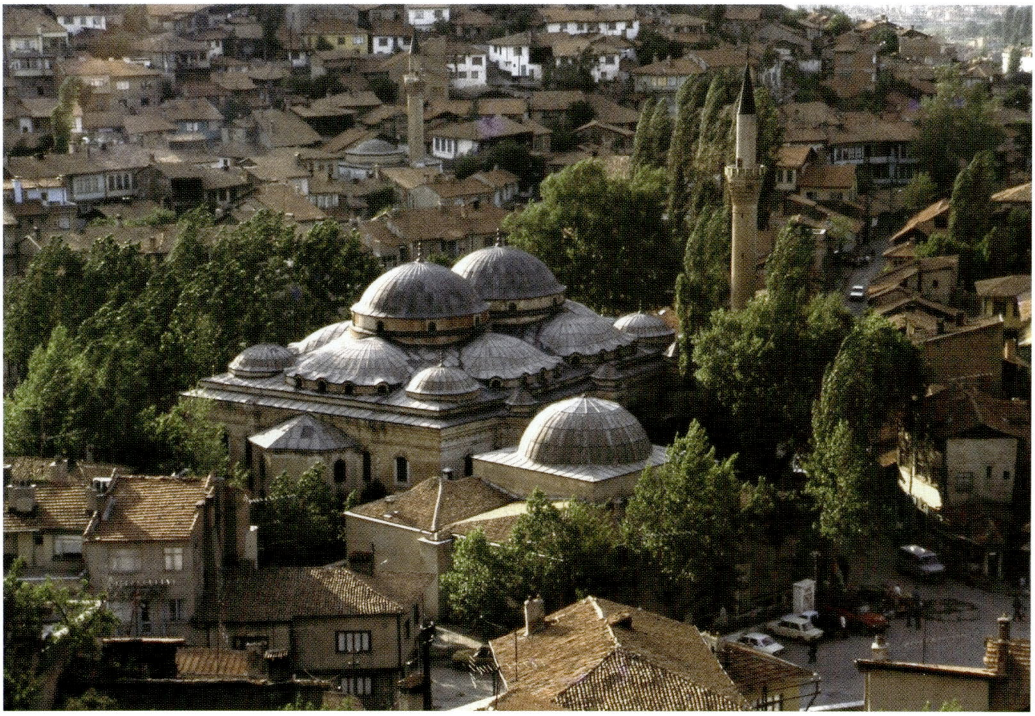

Kütahya, Turkey: Ulu Cami and the market district, 1987

Precision in ornament aligns Acoma's pottery with Turkey's *çini*. Inspired by the stunning wonder of Chinese porcelain, *çini* was perfected through experimentation at the Ottoman apogee, during a period that began with the conquest of Istanbul in 1453, extended through the reign of Süleyman the Magnificent, called Kanuni, the Lawgiver, and then ended with the death of Süleyman's son and successor, Selim, in 1574. In that era, *çini* was made in several places. Today it is identified with one of them, Iznik, where the tradition failed in the eighteenth century, but it continued in the mountain town of Kütahya, where the oldest dated piece was made in 1529 and the tradition rolled along through change after change until, following the War for Turkish Independence, in the violent aftermath of the First World War, it came to a stop.

At the beginning of the twentieth century, half of Kütahya's workers were Armenians. They were called away to repair the tiles of the Dome of the Rock, and their descendants, with Marie and Neshan Balian in the lead, continue to make *çini* in Jerusalem. The Armenians were gone. Mehmet Emin, Kütahya's central master, had been killed in the war. The shops were closed, and in the early days of the new Turkish Republic, the old tradition seemed at an end.

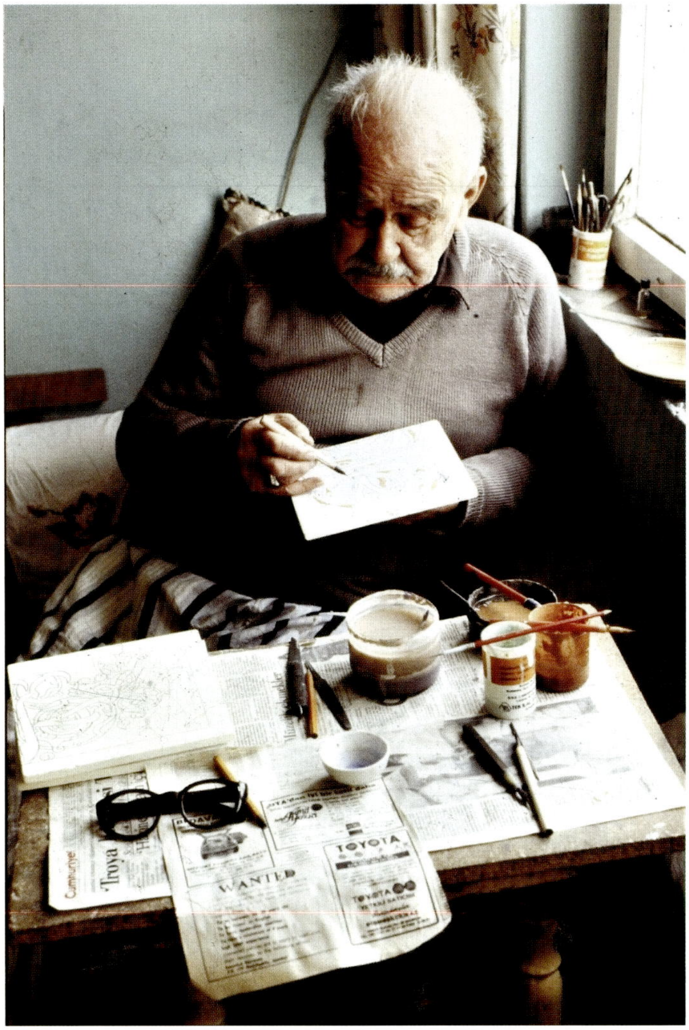

Ahmet Şahin, painting tiles at home, Kütahya, 1994

Traditions don't take care of themselves. In 1927, two young men, Ahmet Şahin, then twenty, and Mehmet Emin's son Hakkı Çinicioğlu — Son of the Çinici, the maker of *çini* — formed a partnership and announced the opening of a new atelier. On the next day, Ahmet Şahin said, the line of eager workers stretched around the block.

One shop became several during the nineteen-fifties, and in the eighties, Kütahya had twenty-three big ateliers, more than a hundred small ones, and a hundred retail outlets, providing the livelihood for forty thousand people. By that time, Ahmet Şahin was widely acknowledged as the city's *son usta*, its ultimate master. A talented practitioner, he was the city's chief designer, its soul and guide.

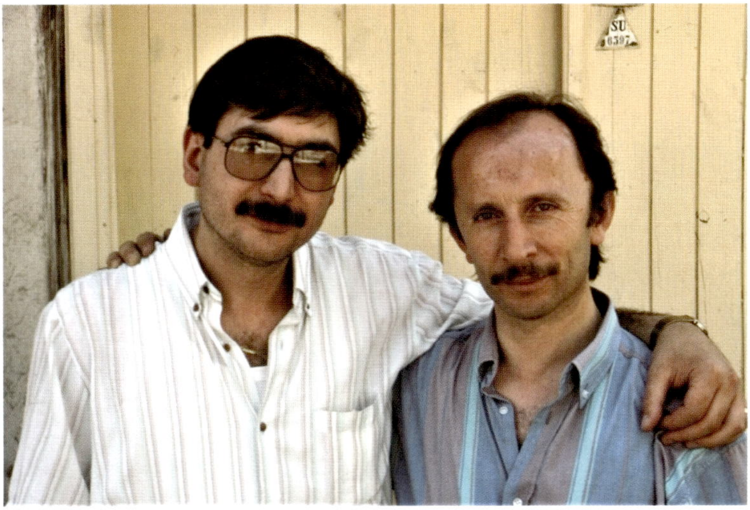

İbrahim Erdeyer and Mehmet Gürsoy, Kütahya, 1993

İbrahim and Mehmet, 2007

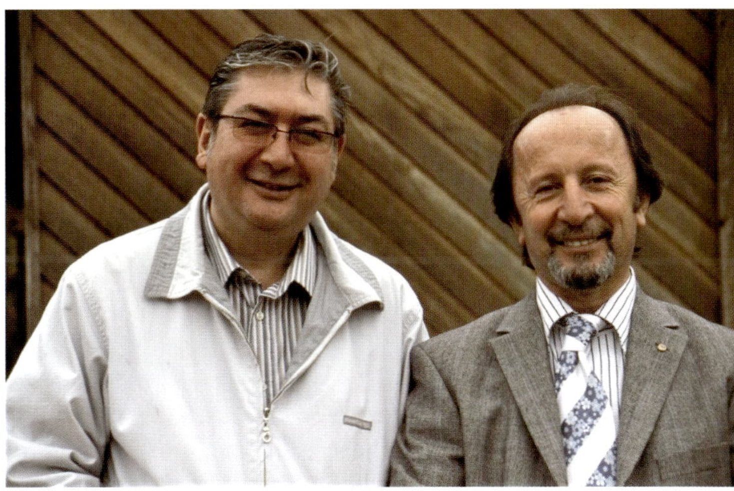

His family followed him into his art. Ahmet Şahin's sons, Zafer and Faruk, became excellent and innovative creators. Zafer's son, Ahmet Hürriyet Şahin, and Ahmet Hürriyet's supremely skilled wife, Nurten, joined the artists of their generation in the drive for evolving excellence. Ahmet Şahin said that, being a master, he was obliged to teach, without recompense, all who came to learn, and until his death in 1996, they came constantly. The masters of the next generation, Mehmet Gürsoy and İbrahim Erdeyer, humbly, respectfully sought the master's advice.

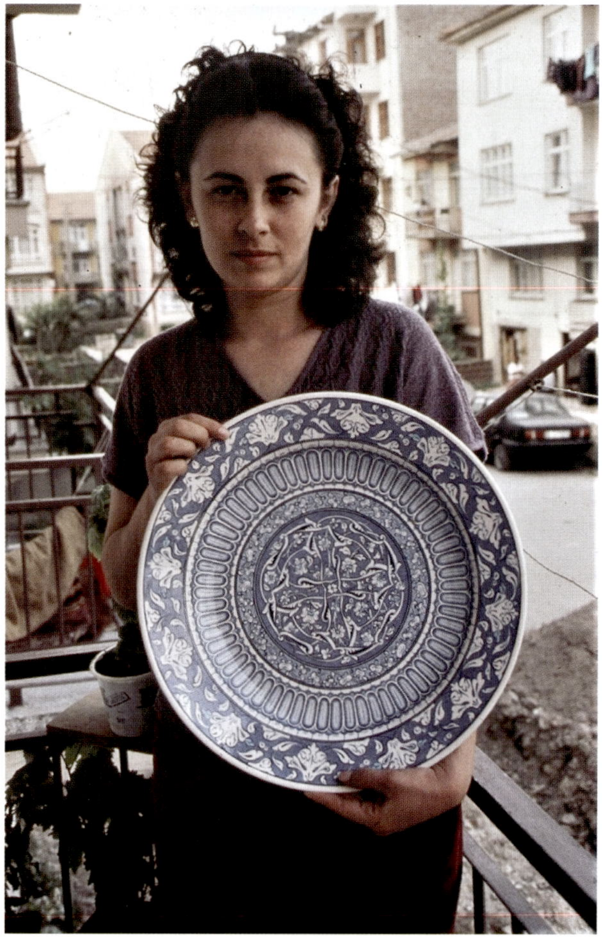

Nurten Şahin with a geometric plate she painted, Kütahya, 1993

Early in the twentieth century, *çini* was imperiled. Late in the century, Kütahya could boast a grand gathering of artists, committed to tradition and distinct in their personal styles: Sıtkı Olçar, Hakkı Ermumcu, Mehmet Gürsoy, İbrahim Erdeyer, Nurten Şahin, Mehmet Koçer, İsmail Yiğit, Kerim Keçecigil, Saim Kolhan. The complexity of their creative performance was built on the efficiency of the big ateliers, where the tasks were divided as they are in J. Borges's atelier in Bezerros.

The ateliers split into two sections. In one, men — young apprentices and old masters of the wheel — do rough and dirty work with the substance of creation they call *çamur*, mud. In the other, a mature master directs the clean and patient work of painting, done mostly by young women who are, at once, learning and making the city's common ware. *Çini*, cognate with china, names the ware and the shops where it is made. The old Metin Çini at the center of town and Özen Çini, one of ten at the edge, shelter both sections in big, rambling workshops. Other ateliers position these functions in separate buildings.

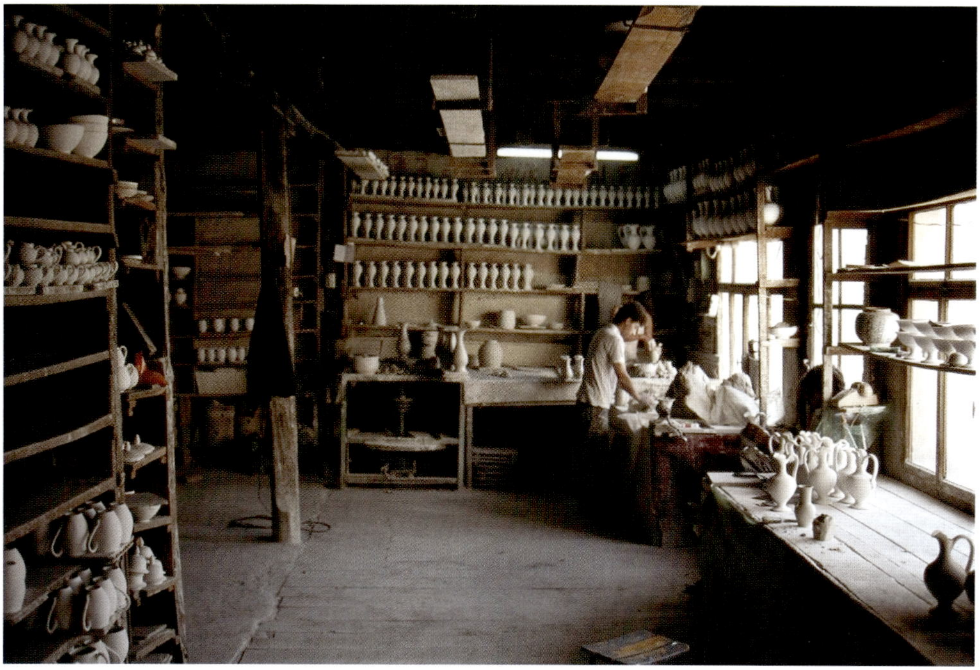

The atelier's space for the clay, Nakış Çini, Kütahya, 1994

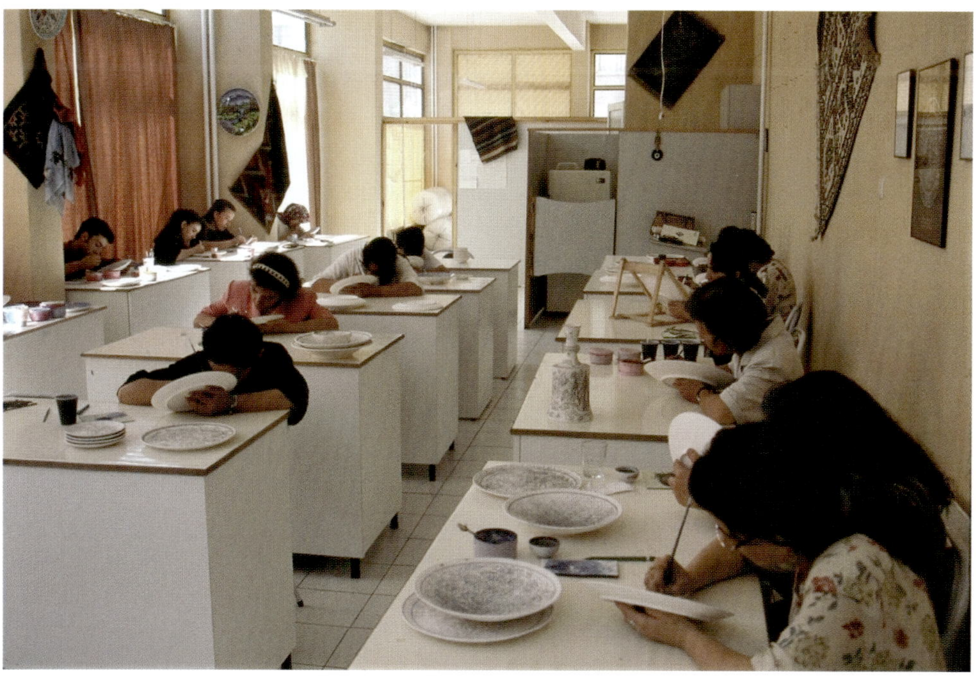

The atelier's painting studio, Doğuş Çini, Kütahya, 1996

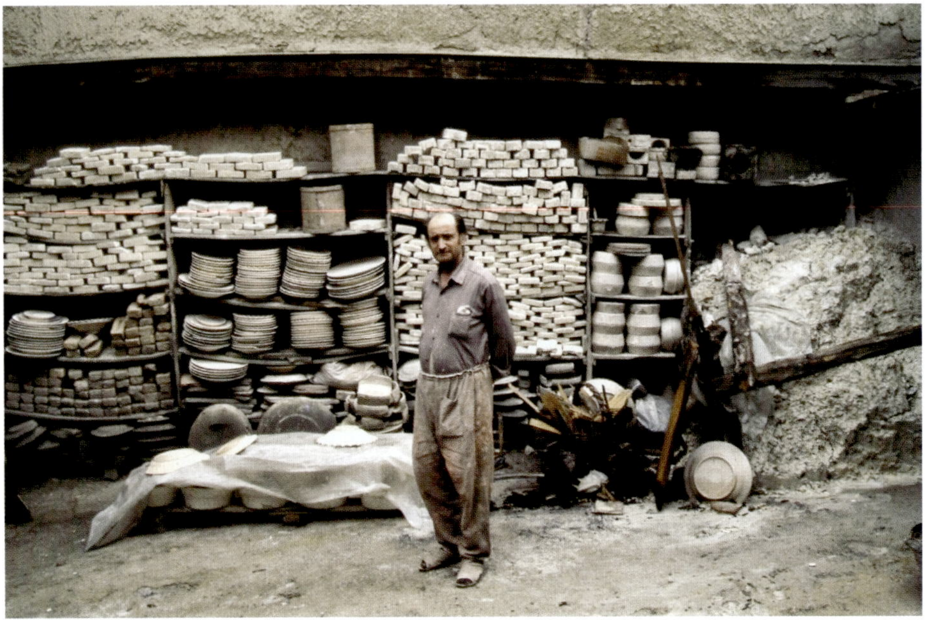

İhsan Erdeyer, Süsler Çini, Kütahya, 1987

Süsler Çini, a plastered half-timber building, was designed so that the *çamur* moved smoothly counterclockwise from processing, through shaping, to firing. Ali Özker established Süsler in 1950. İhsan Erdeyer joined him in 1968 and became the shop's master in 1974. As master of the works, İhsan directs the workforce and manages the materials — not a simple task.

Many ceramic traditions are based, like Alto do Moura's and Acoma's, on a clay dug in the neighborhood and refined for use. Kütahya's *çini* body, though, is a complex composite. Half of the substance is a local white kaolin called *dümbüldek* that fires lower than the kaolin used for porcelain. Next comes crushed quartz that adds strength and sparkle. The higher the amount of quartz, the harder the work, the higher the quality of the finished piece. Next chalk is added to whiten and bind the mix. Then two clays are added for plasticity, a bit of sand for strength and hardness. These materials are blended, blunged into a slurry, then strained through three cloth sieves, increasingly fine in mesh; the last is called the silk. The resultant white liquid steeps in a pool for three months, then, after it has dried in plaster forms, the paste is twice milled, then kneaded and balled, ready for shaping.

Kütahya's main products are three. Tiles, *karolar*, are molded to sheathe the interiors of new mosques being built throughout the nation, and some are masterworks, single or assembled into panels, for fountains or homes. Hollow-ware, *dik mal*, is thrown on the wheel for vases in abundance and a few magnificent mosque lamps. Plates, *tabaklar*, are jiggered on the wheel. At Süsler that is İhsan's job, and plates are his shop's primary product. They are not destined for the table; they will hang on the wall, contributing beauty and meaning to the home.

The shaped form is slipped with a mix of kaolin and quartz, creating, as at Acoma, a clean white ground for a virtuosic exhibition of ornament. Then after a first firing, the process of decoration begins with a drawing on a sheet of paper that is pricked along the lines of the design with tiny holes. It is not a stencil of the sort employed in some Portuguese ceramic ateliers, but a pounce like those used by the fresco masters of the Italian Renaissance. A tiny bag of charcoal rubbed over the paper deposits a dotted pattern on the tile or plate, centering the design, establishing its proportions, and guiding the brush.

As at Acoma, painting begins with long, slender sweeps of the brush that outline the design in black. Then it is filled with color. Mineral powders mixed with slip provide a wider, brighter palette at Kütahya: red, blue, green, and turquoise, but not today the yellow, common around the Mediterranean, that was used in Kütahya during the eighteenth century.

That process is everyone's. Through repetition, painting the familiar designs they are given, young workers come to competence, making the shop's common ware that is sold wholesale. There is exceptional work too. When a truly excellent young artist emerges, as Kadriye Tosun did at Süsler, she — it is usually a young woman — will be granted the right to paint and sign works of her own. And most ateliers have a master who creates *özel*, special, works that serve as models of excellence for the whole atelier and get sold individually at high prices.

The master who invents original designs and paints them with exquisite exactitude might be a man like Mehmet Koçer at Altın Çini or Mehmet Gürsoy at İznik Çini, and it might be a woman like Nurten Şahin at Doğuş Çini. At Süsler it is İhsan's son İbrahim. So, Süsler Çini, not unusually, has three masters: the master of the works, İhsan Erdeyer; the master of the wheel, İsmail Değirmencioğlu; and the master of art, İbrahim Erdeyer.

İhsan glazes each piece. Then, when enough have accumulated, he fires them, and he fires about twelve thousand annually. The top of his kiln appears as a hole in the shop's floor, the oculus of a deep domed cylinder. İhsan climbs down a ladder and slowly, calmly arranges the plates his apprentice hands down to him. In the lower two-thirds of the kiln he builds shelves and

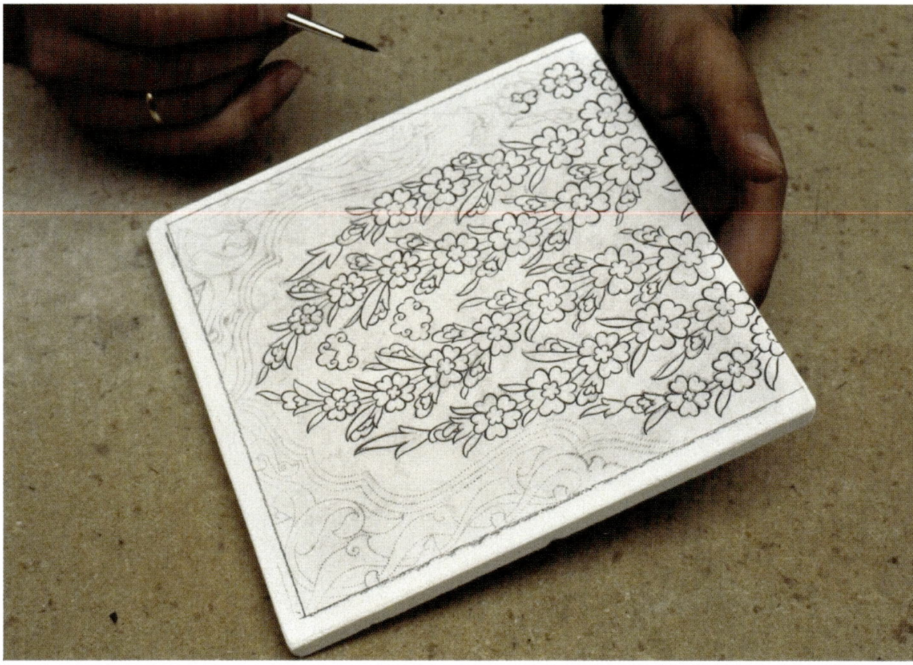

A tile pounced, outlining begun

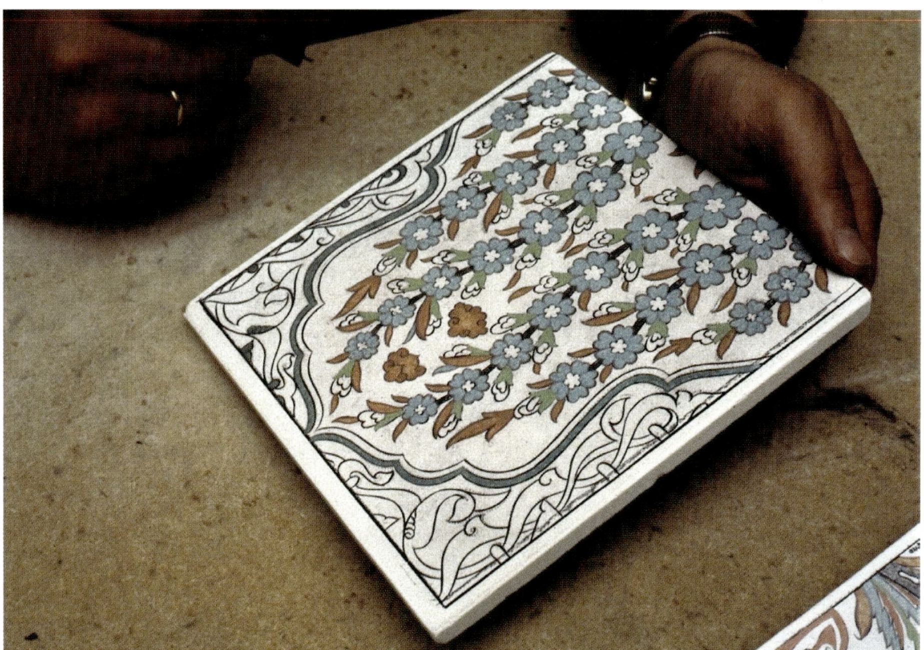

A tile outlined, painting begun, by İbrahim Erdeyer, 1991

places on them the "cooked," painted and glazed, plates, encased in saggars. The upper third holds the "raw," slipped but unpainted, plates that will receive the heat most slowly at the start, most violently at the end. He caps the hole at the top, seals it with mud, descends along a stair, and begins stoking the firing chamber at the bottom of the kiln with dry pine slabs, the wood also preferred in North Carolina. Peeking through a sliver of glass in the kiln's wall, İhsan gauges the temperature entirely by eye, by the flame's color and the smoke's amount.

For valid environmental reasons, the municipal government has decreed that no new wood-fired kilns can be built in the city. The shift to electric kilns, as at Acoma, is underway. The old masters grouse about diminished depth in the fired surface. The young masters are pleased by the loss of fewer pieces in firing, and, using pyrometers, they can supply centigrade numbers for the sequence in Süsler's kiln.

For two hours, the heat is held below 200 degrees. Then for four hours it rises to 600, when the quartz converts. At that point it is swiftly pushed to 865, when the great flame rises, rolls over the top, and pours down the walls to the bottom, where the smoke escapes through flues to the chimney that runs up the shop's wall. If the heat doesn't reach 865, the colors will be dull. If it passes 960, the colors will run. So the heat must be held — a delicate, difficult task — between those numbers for four more hours. On the next day the kiln cools slowly to prevent crazing in the glaze, and on the third day the kiln is opened.

Acoma's colors are earthy, Kütahya's are bright. Hagi's look is foam on a beach, Kütahya's is a scatter of jewels on snow. The pieces are finished, and the question of benefit rises. In North Carolina and Japan, the potters, most of them men, exercise their bodies and engage their minds completely in the work — the personally fulfilling work William Morris called good — that brings them their livelihood. At Acoma it is important that women make and sell pottery because many of their husbands have cyclical spiritual obligations that prevent them from holding steady, nine-to-five jobs; pottery finances the continuity of the pueblo's ancient religion. In Kütahya, the young women who paint in the ateliers, like the young women who weave in the villages, gain through pay the financial independence they will take into marriage, assured in strength and ability.

For the consumer, for the one who owns and lives with *çini*, Mehmet Gürsoy describes the benefit as an increase in awareness that rises, step by step, up an inner stairway of enlightenment. On the bottom step, the eye is excited aes-

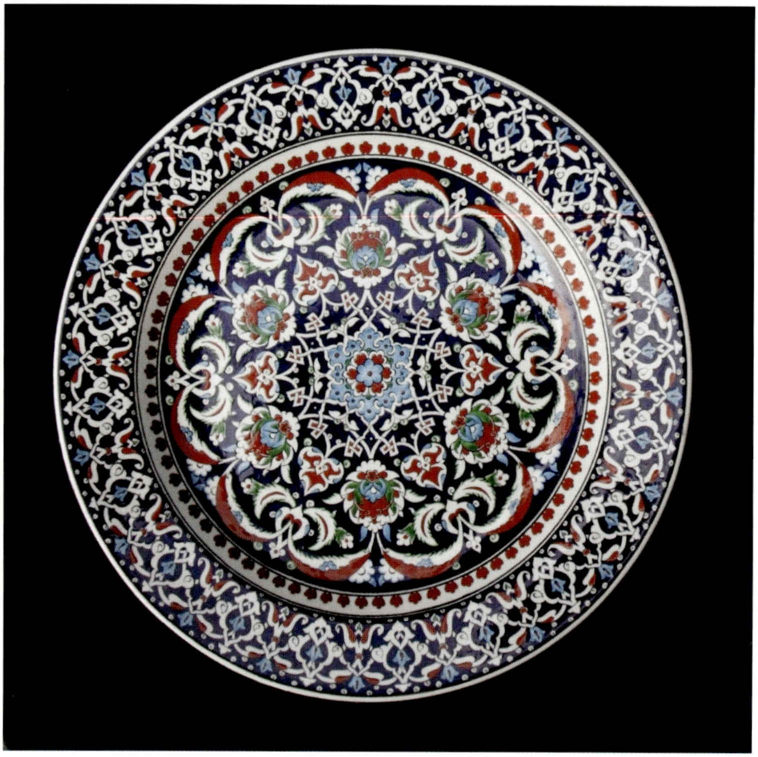

Geometric plate, by İbrahim Erdeyer (43 cm), Kütahya, 2007

thetically, pulled in by careful craft and bright colors. The mind then follows the eye onto the second step, coming to understand the tradition of creation to be historical, its source lying in the glorious Ottoman past when political order was governed by Islamic precepts. Then the soul rises in wonder to the top step where the designs are contemplated to reveal their spiritual significance.

The designs collect into four key categories, each rich with differences and clear in focus. One, the hardest to paint, is geometric. It expands symmetrically from the center, outward toward infinity, evoking the encompassing order of God's creation, from the perfection of the atom to the whirl of the farthest stars in the universe. For the Muslim, God is without form — no body, no gender, no old man's beard. God is beautiful and loves beauty, Mehmet Gürsoy says, and the closest one can come to a representation of God is a beautiful, abstract, impeccably geometric image of the eternal workings of God's will.

A second design, less tedious, more pleasant to paint, is floral. Mehmet says to note that the flowers are not naturalistic. These are not the flowers that

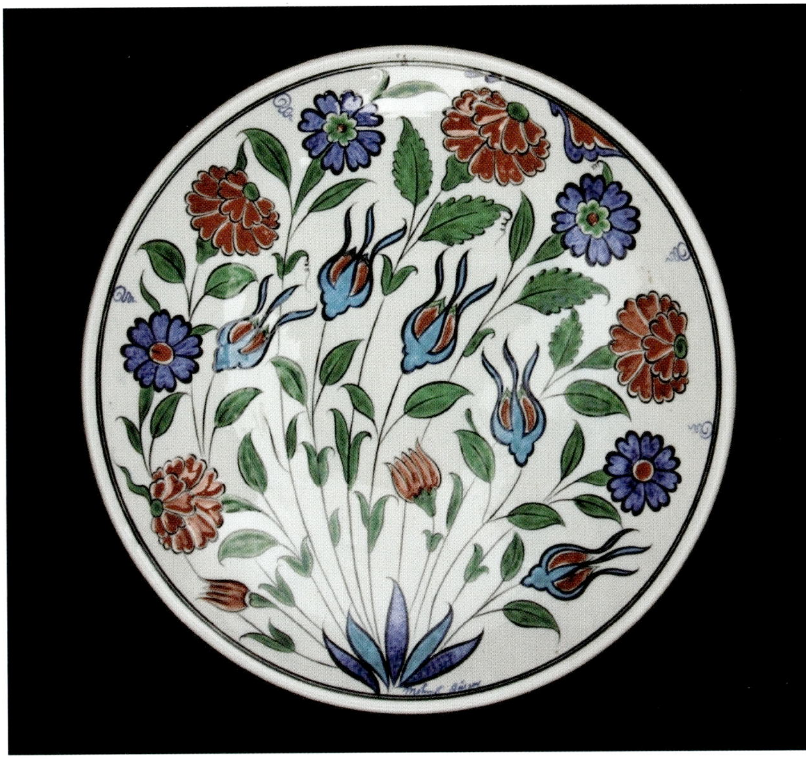

Floral plate, by Mehmet Gürsoy (26 cm), Kütahya, 1991. See too p. 509

wither by the roadside. They have been abstractly perfected to be symbolic. They stand for people, not for their trivial, imperfect bodies, but for their beautiful immortal souls. The flowers, different in their varieties, all grow from a single root at the bottom of the design. The root symbolizes God's will. It is God's will that people are different: some are roses, some are tulips; some are men, some are women; some are white, some are black. God wills it so, and people, different at birth, grow into the world to be blown differently by the winds of chance, swaying into an asymmetrical, but harmonious pattern. The design is a plea for human unity. People are inherently different, but they should join in mutual respect, understanding that they are, all of them, God's creatures.

In a third design, a fantastic bird joins the flowers. This is a plea for an ethical, traditional art. The bird is the artist, who, different in innate ability, could fly free into opulent isolation, but chooses to remain down among the flowers, the people who share the tradition and need the delight of art in their workaday lives.

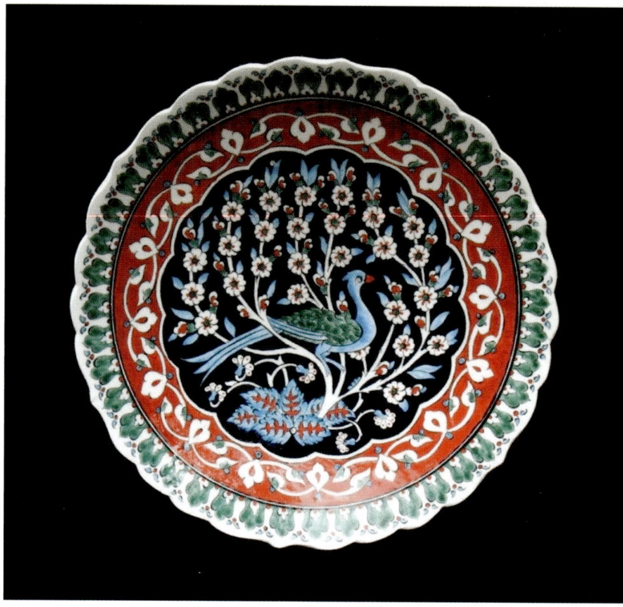

Plate with a bird among the flowers, by İbrahim Erdeyer (29 cm), Kütahya, 2002

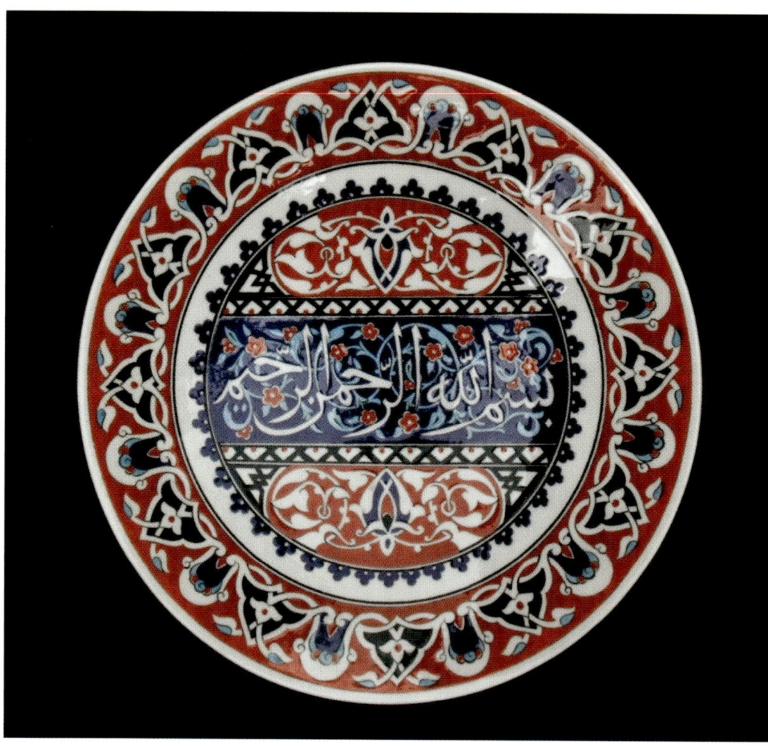

Plate with the *Besmele*, by Nurten Şahin (25 cm), Kütahya, 2000

The fourth category of design is calligraphic. The artist borrows the work of a famed calligrapher, rendered in the Arabic script, usually in the *sülüs* or *talik* hands, and enhances it with ornament on a tile or plate. The text might read that all human necessities flow from God. More often it is the *Kelime-i Şahadet*, the Muslim profession of faith: There is no god but God, and Muhammad is the messenger of God. Most often it is the *Besmele* — In the name of God, the Merciful, the Compassionate — the opening formula of the Holy Koran and a prayer for beginnings. Plates with the *Besmele* hang above the door so people venturing into the errors of a new day, leave knowing that God is compassionate, merciful.

Mehmet Gürsoy and his close friend İbrahim Erdeyer bring this section of the writing to a coherent close. In 1991, they were invited to come and demonstrate their craft at the opening of a major exhibition of Turkish art at the Museum of International Folk Art in Santa Fe, New Mexico. Like many Turks, they have a special interest in American Indians, feeling a deep kinship because Native Americans left northeastern Asia and went east to settle the Americas, and Turks left northeastern Asia and went west to settle in Anatolia. During their free time, Mehmet and İbrahim visited the pueblos. They were profoundly moved by the old churches, finding them sweet with the serene spirituality of old Turkish mosques. Curious, naturally enough, about the pottery, they were disappointed by its quality until they got to Acoma.

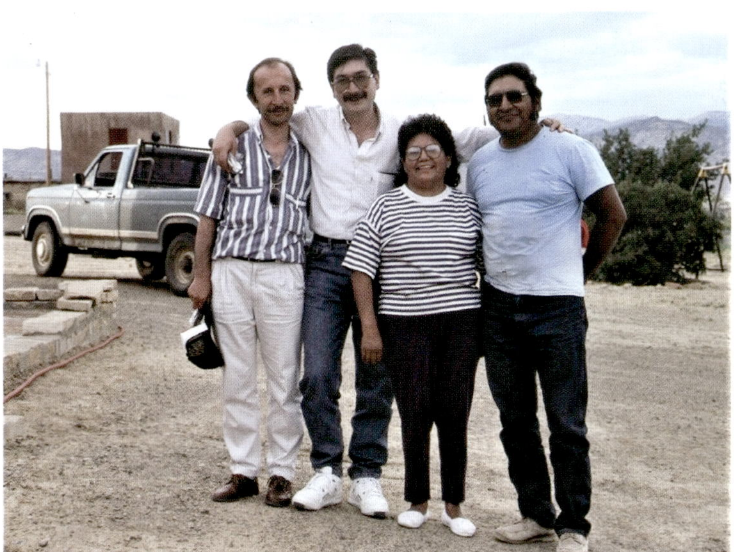

Mehmet Gürsoy and İbrahim Erdeyer, Wanda and Marvis Aragon, Acoma, New Mexico, 1991

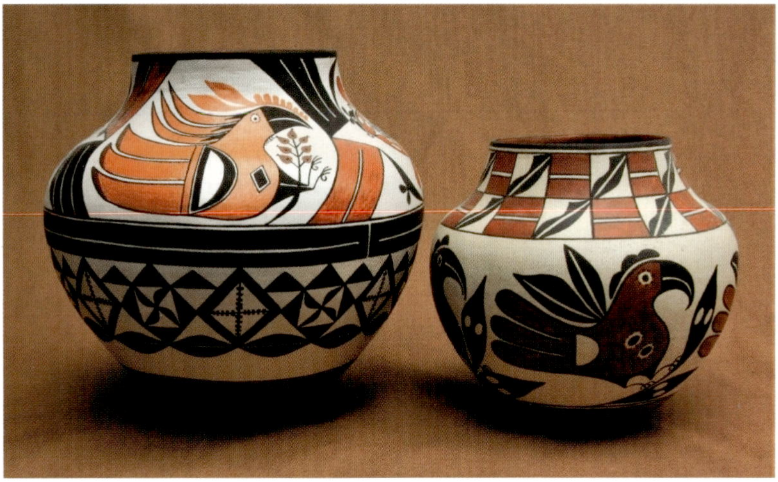

Parrot pots from Acoma. Left: by Lilly Salvador (17 cm tall), 1997.
Right: by Wanda Aragon (13 cm tall), 1998

When they met the sisters Lilly Salvador and Wanda Aragon at Acoma, Mehmet and İbrahim lifted their pots — potters always want to feel pots, looking is not sufficient — and, holding them like newborn infants, they marveled first at their technical excellence, the smooth surfaces and thin walls as delicate as eggshells. Then they approved of the painting, the confident black outlines and solid infill of color.

Mehmet and İbrahim agreed that artists in Kütahya and Acoma strive toward the same aesthetic goals, and then, not surprised, they commented on the compatibility of the repertories. Most of Acoma's pots are decorated geometrically, as many of Kütahya's are. At Acoma, as at Kütahya, the representational impulse in decoration extends to birds and flowers, but stops short of the human figure. Worldwide it is remarkable, yet logical, that many ceramic designs feature the birds of the air and the flowers of the hillside, nature's parallel to the artist's reach for beauty. The parrot accompanied by flowers is an emblem of Acoma, just as the roadrunner is an emblem of the pueblo of Zia.

The similarity with Kütahya seems to cease with the calligraphic designs, but the most usual of them, the *Besmele*, is a prayer, and the artist's act at Acoma is a prayer. Lilly says that when she is painting, her mind fills with moisture, essential to life and precious in her desert place. Details in the geometric designs are calls for water: the stepped patterns are clouds, the white spots are snow, the diagonal lines are rain, the points swell with dampness into lush leaves. All of our designs, Wanda says, are prayers for rain.

An Art of Figurative Form

Clay is supple; it takes form and holds it. Little Vitalino playing with scraps of his mother's clay, little Manuel Eudócio playing with scraps of his grandmother's clay, little Maria Amélia playing with scraps of her father's clay in Tracunhaém — all of them shaped the clay into little animals. It seems nearly natural for clay in the hand to convert into creatures, and in all four of the traditions we have treated so far, each one centered on useful forms, figurative works appear out at the edge.

In the southeastern United States, those figurative pieces are face jugs. Early in the nineteenth century, African American potters enslaved in South Carolina modeled useful jugs into heads with staring, toothy faces. The idea drifted along the trail blazed by ash glaze, through northern Georgia, into the western Piedmont of North Carolina, then on west as far as Alabama. A peripheral, occasional whimsy among white potters, the face jug met the taste of collectors of folk art and helped to sustain the Southern pottery tradition during hard times in the nineteen-seventies and eighties.

Burlon Craig in North Carolina and Lanier Meaders in Georgia, both of them now gone, made face jugs in astonishing numbers. Burlon held to his pattern, varying his work by size and glaze. Lanier slowly, steadily sought greater realism. Many joined in, quickly establishing distinct personal styles easily recognized by collectors, and sometimes stretching for the amusingly

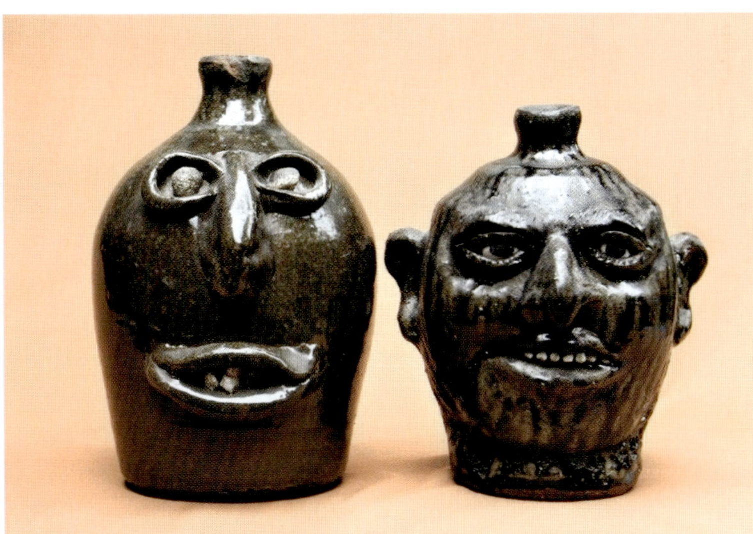

Face jugs by Lanier Meaders, Mossy Creek, Georgia.
Left: 26 cm tall, 1967. Right: 22 cm tall, 1991

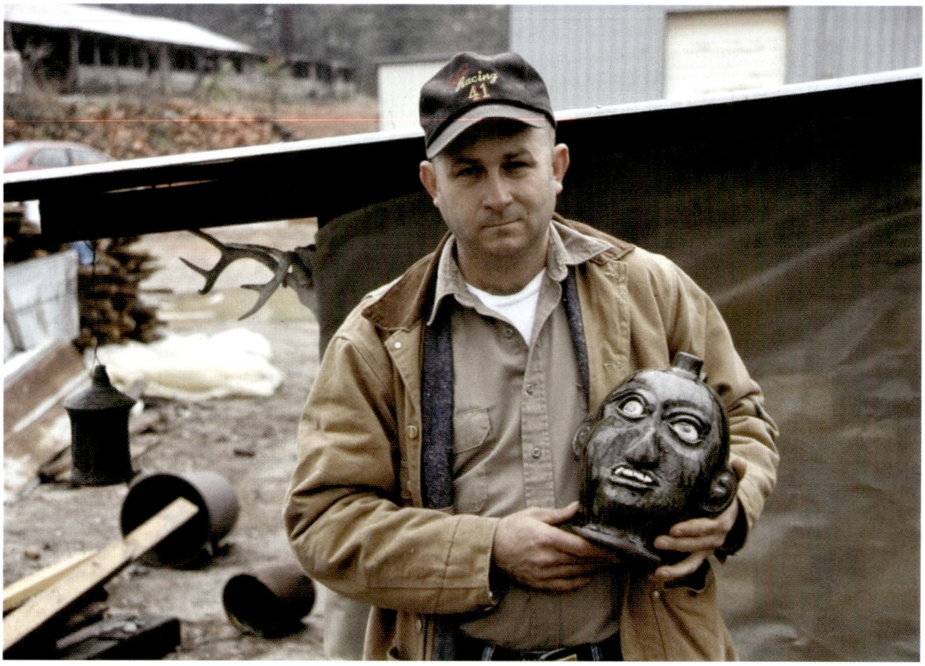

Chester Hewell with a face jug he made, Gillsville, Georgia, 1994

grotesque in the jugs they called ugly. In a humorous aesthetic reversal, Southern country men will praise a growing boy, a hunting hound, an old pickup truck, or a jug for being ugly. Making those jugs, the potters made some money and had some fun during long days of hard work.

Lanier Meaders, who made his first thirteen face jugs in 1967, was joined by his cousin C.J. and his brother Reggie, by Reggie's son David, David's wife, Anita, and C.J.'s son Clete. A bit south in Georgia, at Gillsville, Chester Hewell, who learned how to make face jugs from Lanier in 1974, was joined by his mother, Grace Nell, and his sons, Matthew and Nathaniel. In Carolina's western Piedmont, many followed Burlon Craig, notably Kim Ellington and Charlie Lisk, and face jugs were taken up in the eastern Piedmont by Melvin Owens and Sid Luck.

Time passed. In Georgia, Matthew Hewell thought about it, abandoned ugly jugs, and turned exclusively to the sleek, beautiful utilitarian forms of his tradition. In North Carolina, Kim Ellington, who once made many but now makes few, said that face jugs get more attention than they deserve. That atten-

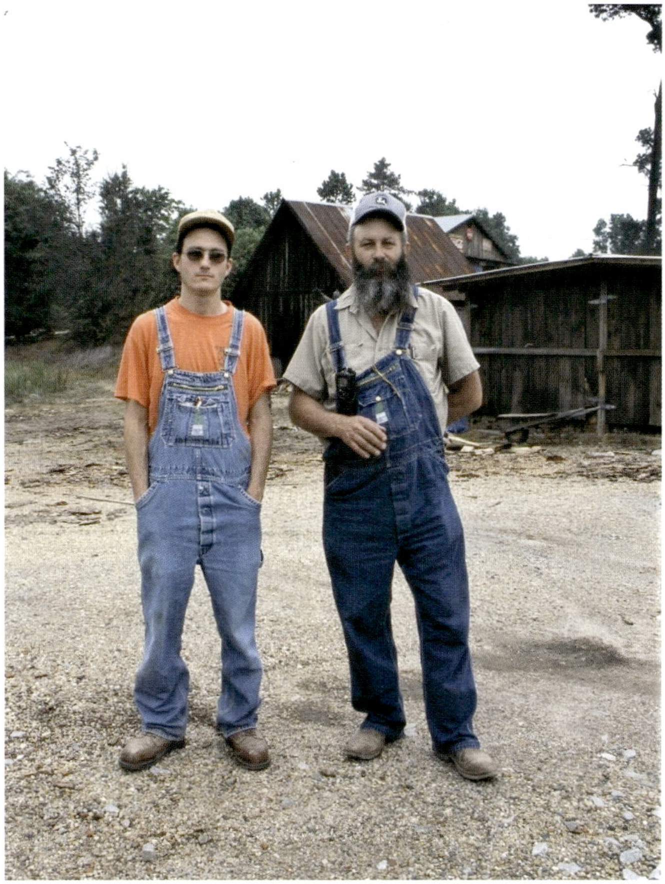

Matthew and Chester Hewell, Gillsville, Georgia, 2004

tion registers in publications that could lead you to believe that the face jug is the prime pot of the South, when it was a beneficial, but marginal distraction within a tradition that centers on the graceful forms and lively glazes of the pots made by Matthew in Georgia, by Mark, Daniel, and David, by Ben, Kim, and Chad in North Carolina.

American writings, guided by narrow representational interest, could mislead you about the Southern tradition, and writings on Japanese pottery, fixed on the *wabi*, will not prepare you for the fact that many of the masters of tea ware also create sculpture. Agawa Norio, Matsumura Takuo, Higaki Hachirō, and Tsuchitani Dosen in Hagi, and Katō Susumu, Maekawa Denko, and Masuda Shigeyuki in Seto all make statues in clay.

When the basic ceramic ensemble of *chanoyu* — vase, caddy, jar, bowl — extends to vessels for incense, it affords a figurative possibility, since the incense burner can take the shape of a lion and the lids of the tiny incense cases are usually modeled, most often with the twelve animals of the year, from rat to

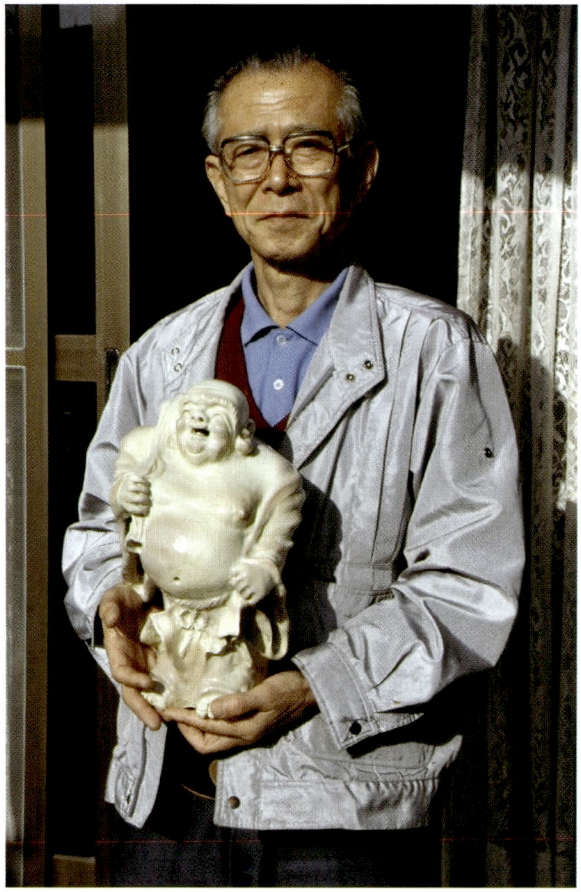

Higaki Hachirō with his statue of Hotei, Hagi, Japan, 1999

pig. Agawa Norio's brother, Higaki Hachirō, is a marvel of the miniature when he makes the containers for incense, and Hachirō joins the other potters in making large statues out of clay.

They work differently. Matsumura Takuo uses molds. Some are his own, others were made by Nakano Geirin, an inventive, eccentric potter in Hagi's recent past. Katō Susumu plans fastidiously and builds his forms with neat, circling coils. Agawa Norio shapes and joins slabs bravely in the air. Their methods differ, but their repertory is coherent.

Lions, the temple's guardians, are made in pairs, seated in Seto, pouncing in Hagi. The lion of the right opens her mouth. The lion of the left has his mouth closed. Mouths open, then closed: together they are making the sound of the beginning: *om*. Agawa Norio's goal for life was to make the best lion in Japan. He studied the old stone lions at the temples. He scrutinized the lions made in clay by Nakano Geirin. He wrought through delight to triumph.

Agawa Norio examining a lion by Nakano Geirin, Hagi, 1999

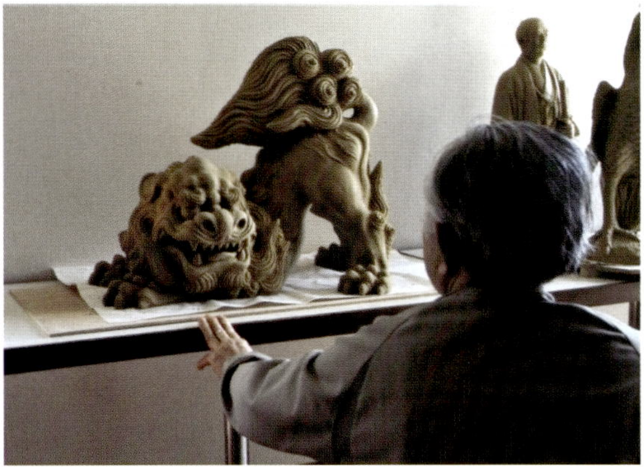

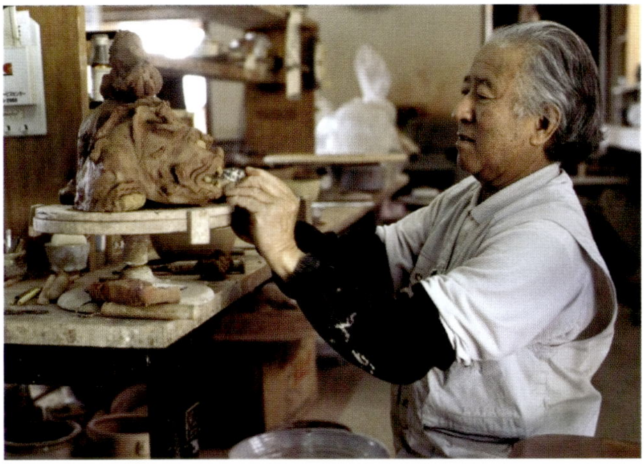

Agawa Norio making a lion, Hagi, 1998

Lion of the right, by Agawa Norio (24 cm tall), Hagi, 1998

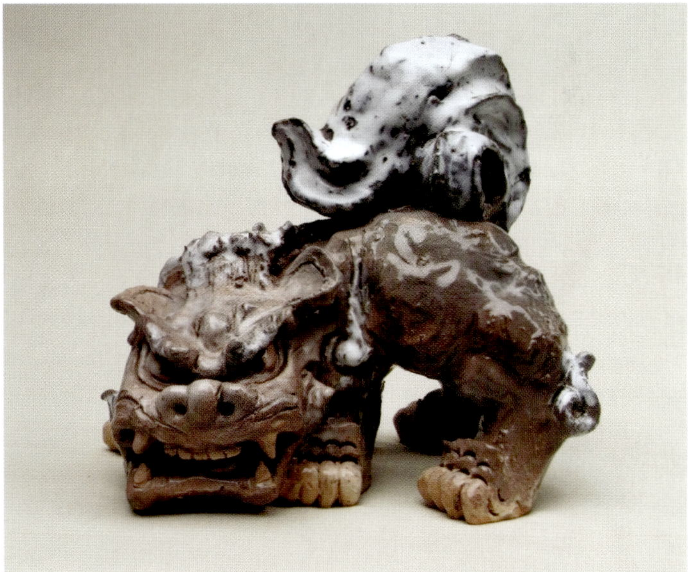

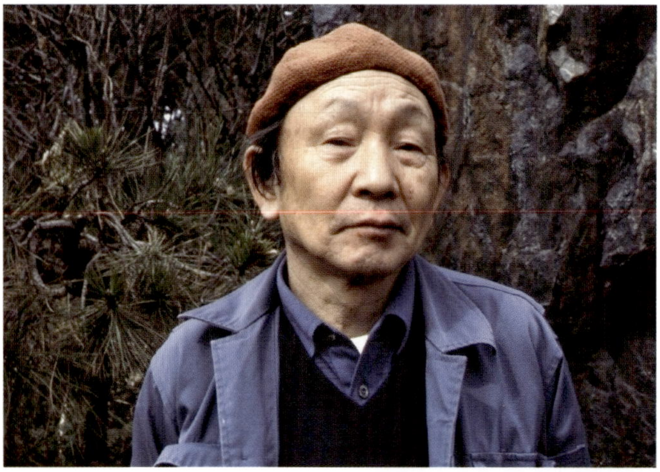

Katō Susumu, Seto, Japan, 1999

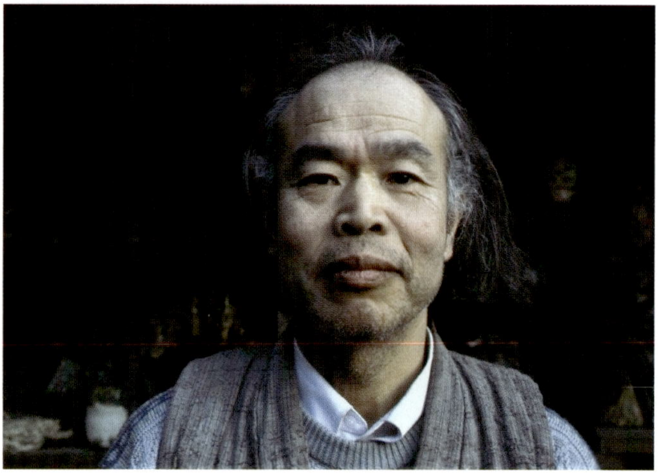

Maekawa Denko, Seto, Japan, 2000

The core of the collective sculptural repertory is occupied by the seven lucky gods, gathered since the fifteenth century from different sources and the popular patrons today of different professions. Plump, happy Hotei was a Chinese Zen priest who died in the tenth century. Fukurokuju and Jurojin are Chinese deities of wisdom and longevity. Bishamon and Benten came from India where Benten, the only goddess in the assembly, was Saraswati, the goddess of wisdom. Saraswati's *vina* became a lute in Japan, and Benten's domain became art rather than wisdom. The working pair, Daikoku the carpenter and Ebisu the fisherman, are generally thought to be Japanese in origin. The potters in Hagi and Seto depict them all in clay, though Hotei, Daikoku, and Ebisu, who associate with happiness and prosperity, and Jurojin, who associates with long life and learning, appear most frequently.

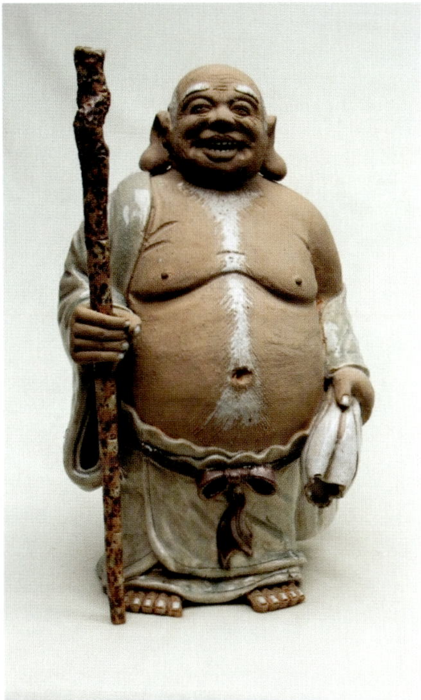

Hotei, by Katō Susumu (36 cm tall),
Seto, Japan, 2001

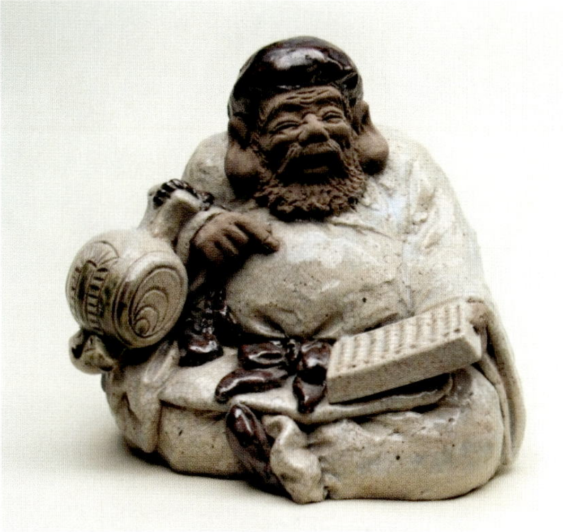

Daikoku, by Shigeyuki Masuda (23 cm tall),
Seto, Japan, 2005

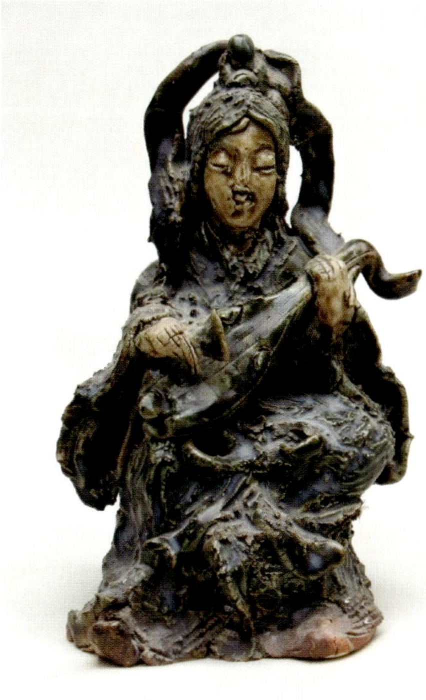

Benten, by Maekawa Denko (20 cm tall),
Seto, Japan, 2005

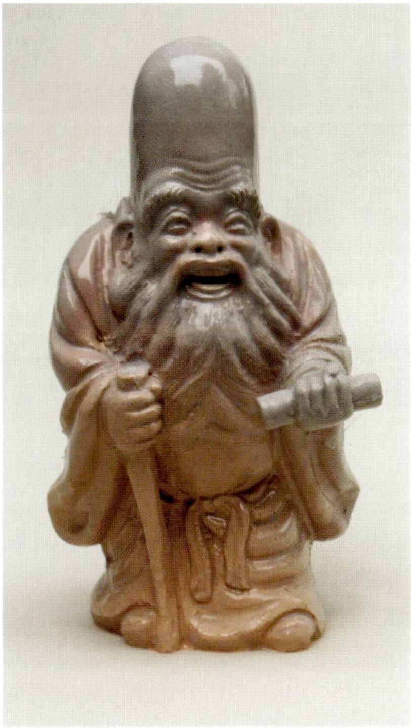

Jurojin, by Matsumura Takuo (25 cm tall),
Hagi, Japan, 1998

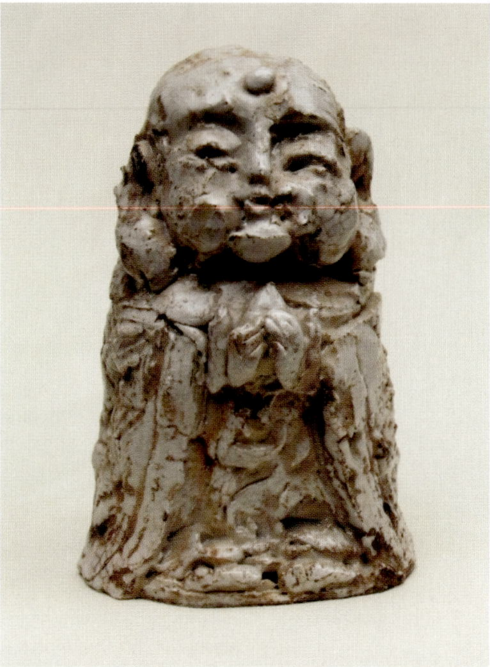

Jizō, by Maekawa Denko (15 cm tall), Seto, Japan, 2005

Some potters shape additional images. Agawa Norio and Masuda Shigeyuki portray the brooding Daruma, the first Zen patriarch who brought Buddhism from India to China. In his rough, vigorous style, Maekawa Denko depicts Jizō, the guide on the path who protects stillborn and aborted babies on their otherworldly journey.

The sculptural tradition of these potters in Japan centers on the sacred, just as the sculptural tradition does at Tracunhaém in Brazil. In Acoma and Kütahya, where the painted ornament orients to the sacred, figurative work is unusual and secular.

In New Mexico, Cochiti is the pueblo with the strongest figurative tradition. When Ivan, the son of Acoma's master Lucy M. Lewis, married a woman from Cochiti, he learned from her mother and rose to excellence as a creator of the human figures that have been made at Cochiti since late in the nineteenth century.

Cochiti's influence suddenly expanded when Helen Cordero altered the old figure of a singing mother into a new image of her grandfather telling stories to the children sitting in his lap and on his shoulders. Her storyteller, the first one made for a collector, appealed immediately to tourists and writers. Helen Cordero was soon joined by more than thirty potters at Cochiti, including Ivan Lewis and his wife, Rita, and her storytellers spread swiftly to other pueblos where they were copied, altered, and parodied.

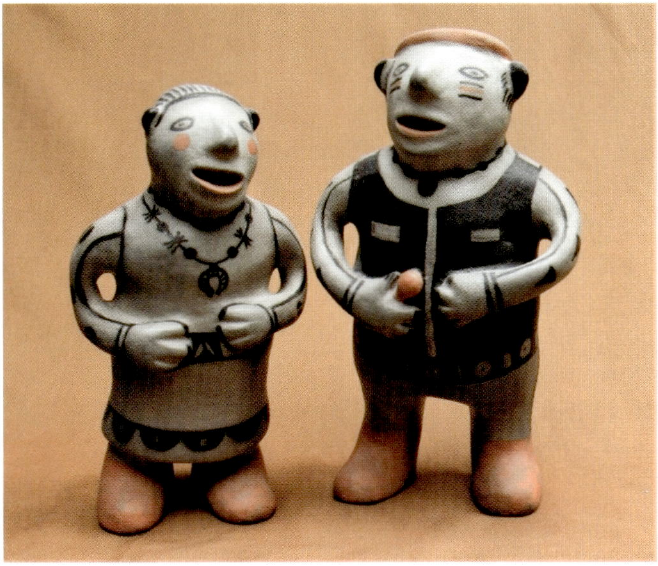

Singers, by Ivan Lewis, Cochiti, New Mexico (19, 23 cm tall), c. 1985

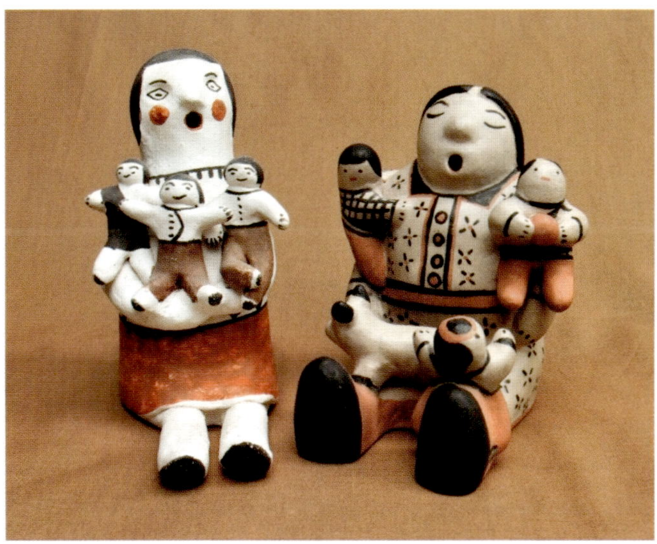

Storytellers. Left: by Frances Torivio, Acoma (15 cm tall), 1988.
Right: by Ivan Lewis, Cochiti (13 cm tall), c. 1985

At Acoma, Wanda's mother, Frances Torivio, a free spirit, was the first to make storytellers, though hers were women, not men. And at Acoma, Ethel Shields innovated playfully with the storyteller idea, making statues of bears telling tales.

Storytellers and face jugs proved simultaneously successful. Helen Cordero made the first storytellers in 1964; Lanier Meaders began making face jugs only three years later. During the nineteen-seventies and eighties, potters in the southeastern United States, most of them men, made crowds of face jugs, and potters in the southwestern United States, most of them women, adopted storytellers as they wandered from Cochiti to Jemez, Santo Domingo, San Idelfonso, and Santa Clara, to Acoma and Zuni. Storytellers and face jugs are still made, but the figurative urge has relaxed, and the young artists, east and west, are furthering the excellence they discover in the old grooves.

As for Kütahya, recent innovations have been mostly of a technical sort, leaving the geometric and floral designs intact. Human images remain largely absent, which is not the consequence of a prohibition. The Holy Koran only commands the believer not to worship statues. That injunction engendered convulsions of iconoclasm in the Eastern church when Islam appeared along the southern borders of Byzantine territory. The eventual solution was a compromise. Saints in the Eastern church are painted as frontal icons but not rendered as statues in three dimensions.

In a reliable text preserved in tradition, the Prophet advises Muslim artists to ally the decorative with the useful. Kütahya's dominant works follow logically. Paintings are made on usable plates, even though the plates will be hung on the wall and not used on the table. There being no universal prohibition, plates were painted with depictions of men and women during the eighteenth century in Kütahya, and they were recently reproduced as historical curios by Sıtkı Olçar and Ahmet Hürriyet Şahin.

More remarkably, since early in the twentieth century, a few artists in Kütahya have used the materials and methods of *çini* to mold and slip, paint, glaze, and fire small bright statues. In our time they have been made by two men — two out of thousands. One is Tahir Konakçı, who makes utilitarian earthenware at the edge of town and has a small studio for sculpture in the market beside Ulu Cami, Kütahya's great mosque, built late in the fourteenth century, then rebuilt in the sixteenth and nineteenth centuries. The other is Ömer Cesur, a skilled and clever master who delights in creating copies of antiquities that trick the eye. Their statues represent wedding couples, rural people in the old-fashioned attire still seen in the villages, and the heroic bandits of western Anatolia — the *zeybekler* — who make an exact parallel with Alto do Moura's images of Lampião.

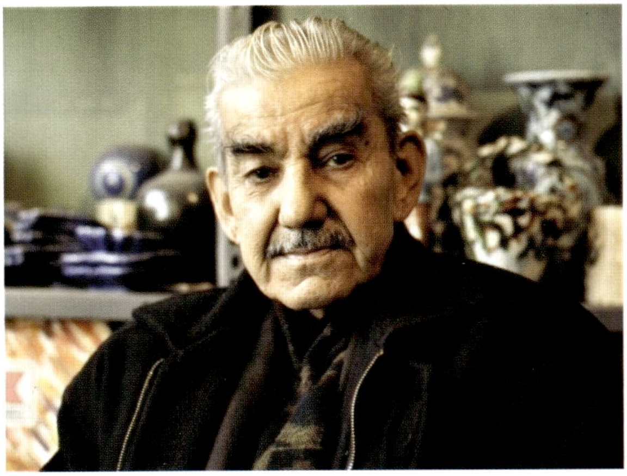

Tahir Konakçı, Kütahya, 1999

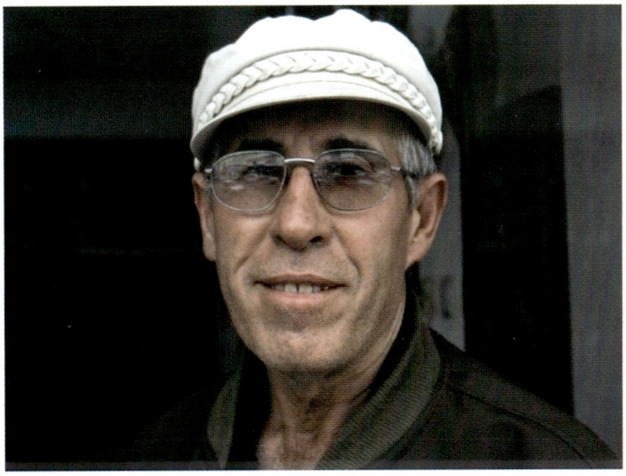

Ömer Cesur, Kütahya, 2004

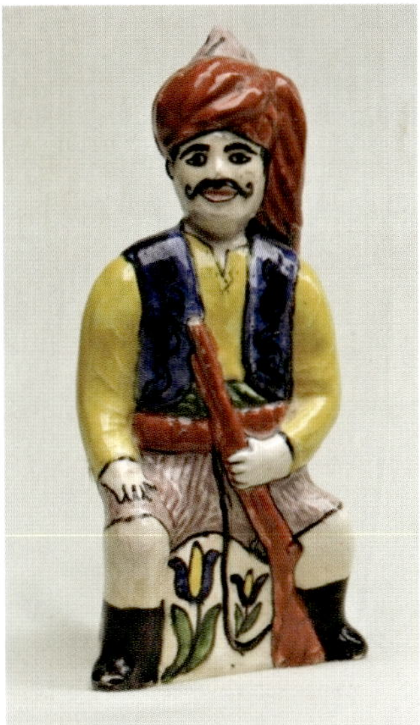

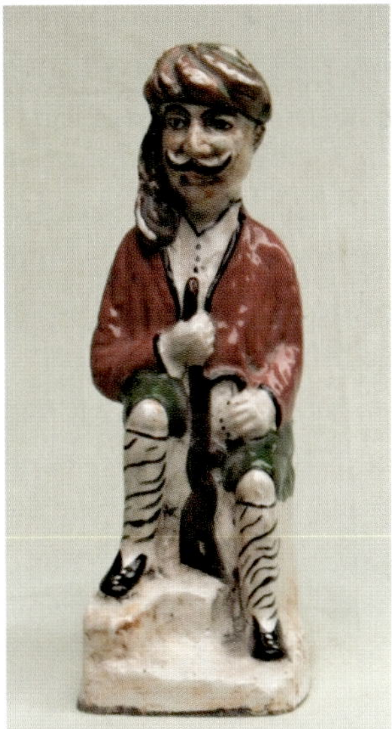

Zeybekler. Left: by Ömer Cesur (19 cm tall), 1997.
Right: by Tahir Konakçı (24 cm tall), 1999

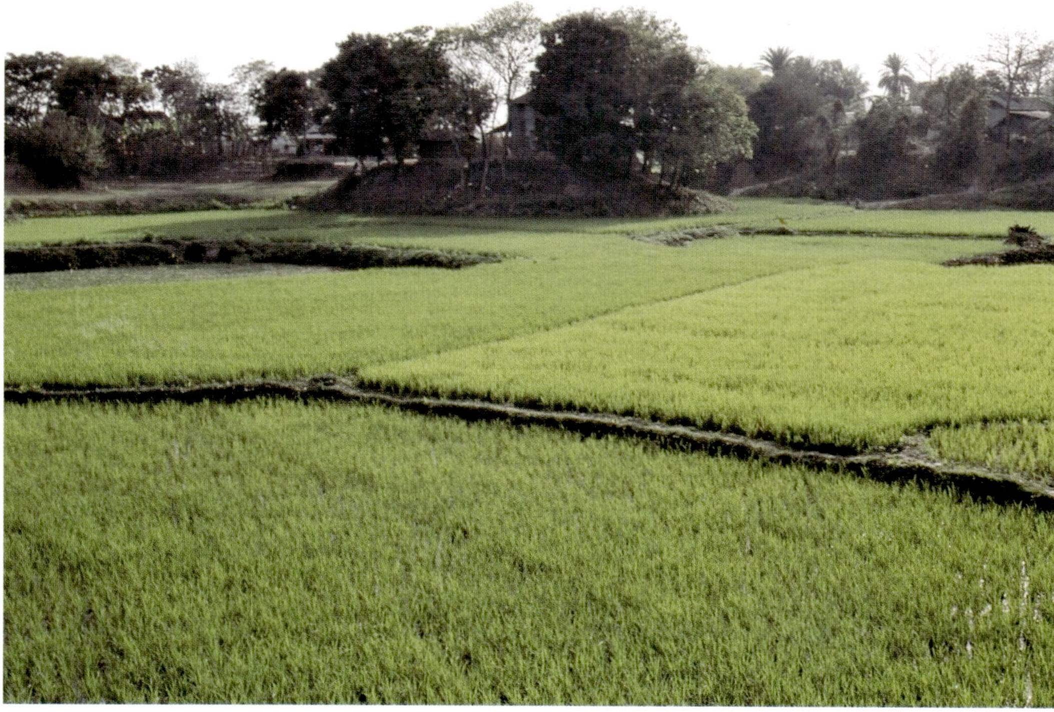

Bangladesh: the landscape of the delta, 1995

The quotidian figures of Kütahya and Alto do Moura are similar in size, style, and subject. What is normal in Alto do Moura, though, is exceedingly rare in Kütahya. One of our purposes in this chapter has been to sketch a wide realm of production within which Alto do Moura can be set. In the four traditions treated so far — from the east and west of the United States, from the east and west of Asia — figurative forms comparable to Alto do Moura's are peripheral.

This chapter will end by coming closer to Alto do Moura through treatments of traditions in which figurative and useful forms have shared centrality for centuries or figurative forms have risen to dominance when utilitarian forms failed. Bangladesh is a good place to begin.

Mighty rivers, flowing with the melt of the Himalayas, twist and split in their run to the sea. Built by their silt, the vast delta of Bengal, the central territory of Bangladesh, is relentlessly flat. Every elevation requires an excavation; headloads of soil, dug and borne, mound into the earthen platforms that lift the villages above the seasonal floods. Wide fertile fields surround the villages, yielding three crops a year, and potter's clay in abundance lies nearby. The nation holds sixty-five thousand villages. In six-hundred and eighty of them, and in the Rayer Bazar district of the capital city of Dhaka, potters make the utilitarian vessels needed in millions of homes. Most of the citizens are Muslims, but most of the potters are Hindus who belong to the craft-caste of the Pals and share the same surname, Pal.

Their clay, dug at the riverside, comes in two kinds, one black and sticky, the other white and sandy. The two are champed with a spade and mixed, six parts black to ten parts white, and then built into a little hill, a *stup*, that is shaved down, trodden, and rebuilt five or six times, becoming smoother with each repetition. Then the clay is shaved into leaves, dusted with ashes, shaped into discs, and kneaded with the feet twice before it is patted into cylinders, ready for use. That tiresome, complicated process is normally accomplished by couples, like Shachindra and Saraswati Pal in the village of Kagajipara, working together at home.

For daily household use, their chief products are the *patil*, a bowl for cooking food, and the *kalshi* for transporting water. An ancient tile discovered archaeologically proves the *kalshi's* form to be at least two thousand years old. That form meets need perfectly: it is spherical to contain the maximum volume, the walls are thin so the pot is light, and it is capped with a collar so it can be hooked in the crook of the arm and pressed into the hollow of the waist for carrying. *Kalshis* are made differently by women and men.

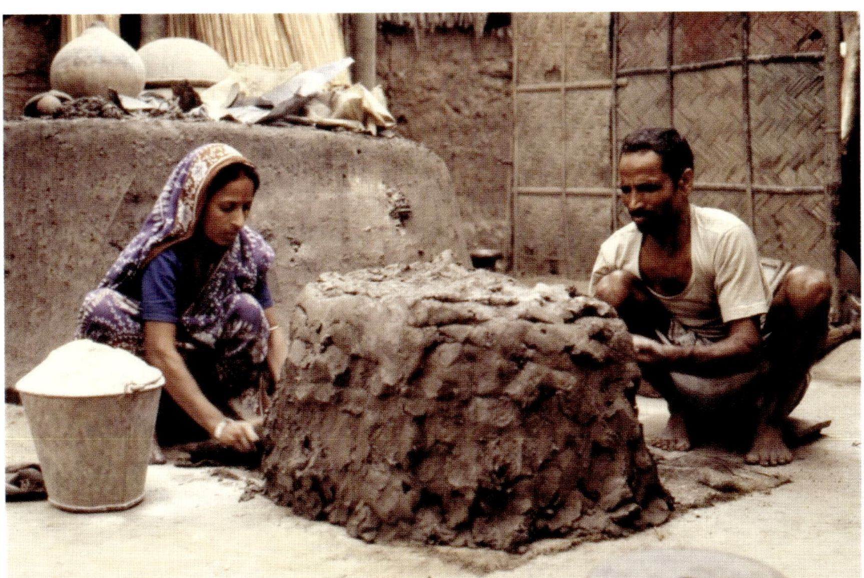

Shachindra and Saraswati Pal, preparing the clay, Kagajipara, Dhamrai, Bangladesh, 1995

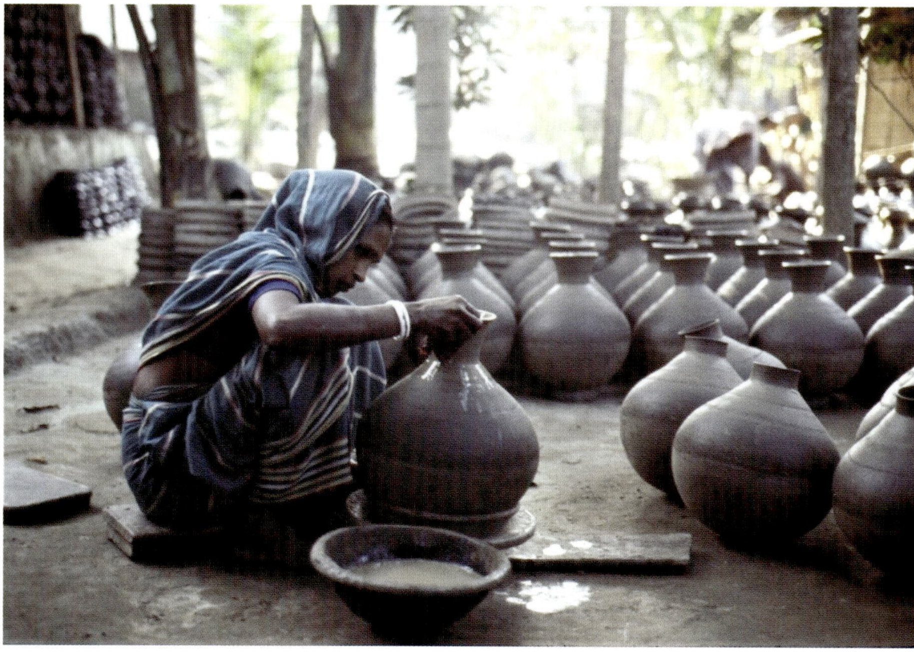

Parul Rani Pal coiling a *kalshi*, Kagajipara, 1988

Women work much as women do in the pueblos of the southwestern United States. Parul Rani Pal presses clay into a *para*, a dish that serves her as the bottom of a broken old pot serves Wanda Aragon. It embraces the damp clay and assures symmetry in the rising form as Parul adds coils, smoothing and shaping the walls. When it is dry enough, she lifts her pot, places it in a larger *para*, and continues adding, smoothing, and shaping coils to complete the form.

Meanwhile, Bajan Chandra Pal, a muscular young man, is working nearby. He centers a tower of clay on the big *chak*, in size and form like a wagon wheel. Bajan whirls a stick in the spokes, gets the big wheel spinning, throws the top of a *kalshi*, then its bottom, and leaves another man, Bijoy Kumar Pal, the job of paddling the parts into the form Parul gets by coiling. The men's process, she says, is quicker but harder on the body.

The buildings of the village, clustered around open spaces for labor, flow along paths into unity. People live close and cooperate in firing. The kiln is like the firing chamber of a large, circular, updraft kiln. Its dished top slopes to a slitted monitor that breathes fire. There is no upper chamber. Pots are piled

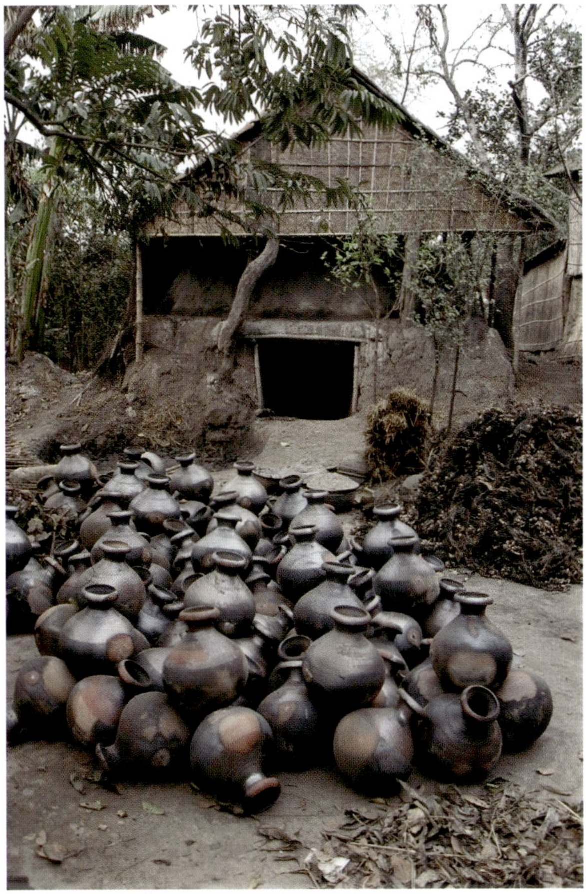

Kiln, Norpara, 1996

on the top, large toward the middle, small around the edge, and then they are covered with split sticks leaned vertically, then rice straw, and finally a coating of damp earth. For two or three days — it depends on the size and number of the pots — wood, bamboo, and nearly anything flammable is fed through the kiln's mouth while the heat, judged by eye, reaches earthenware maturity. If the mud cover over the pots is undisturbed, black pots will emerge from an environment of reduction. If holes are poked through the coat, oxygen will increase, and the pots will come out a pinkish tan. There is no difference in utility, but an effort is made to get the differences in color that satisfy differences of taste among the people who will buy and use them.

So, the pots are done, ready to be shipped to market through the delta's riverine mazeway, but the story has only begun. In the villages, about a tenth of the potters dedicate themselves to figurative work. All of them are men. Some

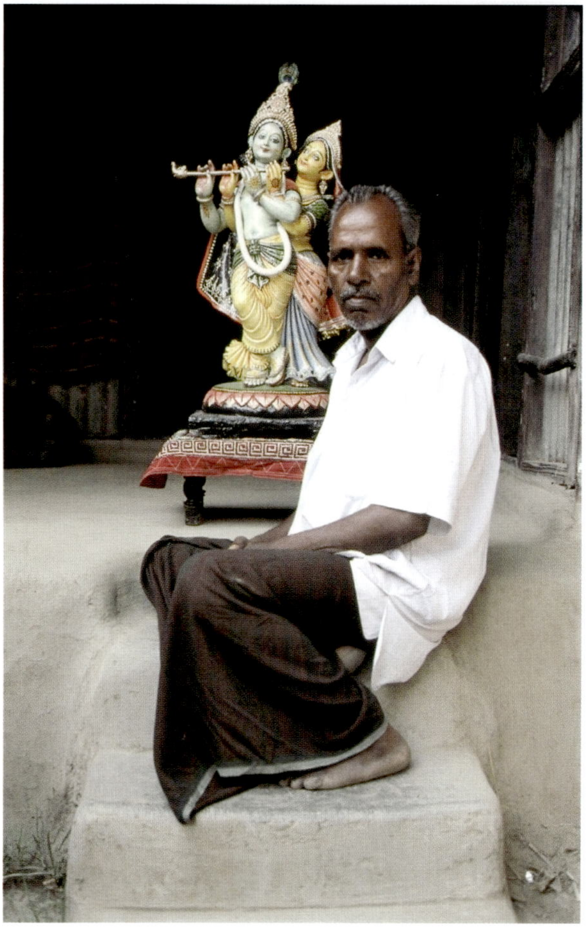

Babu Lal Pal, with the *murti* he made of Radha and Krishna, Khamarpara, 1996

carve tiles with regional imagery as Leonildo does in Alto do Moura. Others shape clay into large animals as Luiz Carlos does in Alto do Moura. But most of the artists for most of the time create *murtis*, statues of the Hindu deities. Before the sequential, cyclical times for *puja*, for the worship of particular gods, the villages are bustling with sculpture, with artists making small statues for domestic altars and large statues for temples and public locations.

Some of these masters of the figurative have gained reputations that widen beyond the home place: Amulya Chandra Pal, Ananda Pal, and Basanta Kumar Pal in Kagajipara; Nepal Chandra Pal in Kakran; Babu Lal Pal, Maran Chandra Pal, and Narayan Chandra Pal in Khamarpara; Nimai Pal and Narayan Pal in Manikganj; Maran Chand Paul and Lal Chand Pal in Rayer Bazar. The greatest of them is Haripada Pal, who was commissioned to create a portrait bust in clay of the father of the nation, Bangabandhu Sheikh Mujibur Rahman. It stood first in an exhibition of Bangladeshi traditional art that opened in 2000 at the National Museum in Dhaka.

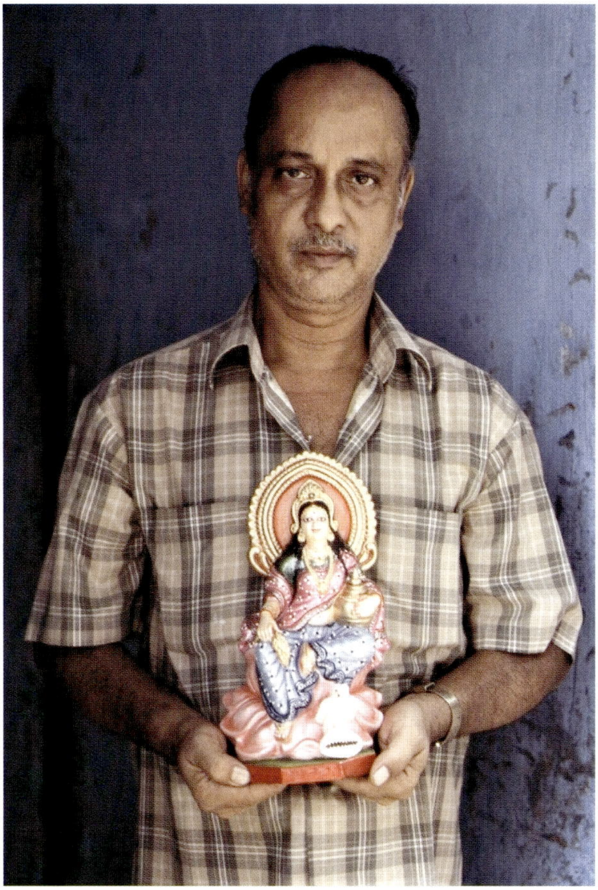

Haripada Pal with his small image of Lakshmi, Shankharibazar, Dhaka, Bangladesh, 2001

Haripada was born in the village of Norpara, where he was taught to make *murtis* by his beloved grandfather Niroda Prasad Pal, the third in a familial line of famed sculptors. Wishing to learn more, Haripada came south to Dhaka, then went west to Calcutta, apprenticing with Bangladeshi masters in Kumortuli, renowned for its monumental clay images of the gods. Then he went east to Tripura and north to Assam, learning more before settling in Dhaka and opening a workshop in Shankharibazar. South in the city, not far from the waterfront of the Buriganga, Shankharibazar runs along a narrow street, walled by tall buildings, that has a Hindu temple at each end, and another in the middle.

The clay comes by boat from the village of his birth, and, assisted by his uncle Jatish Chandra Pal, Haripada shapes it into images of the deities for worship in *pujas*. They are not fired; flames would destroy the inner power that abides in their dampness and opens the path for prayer. Small, inexpensive statues are made in large numbers, normally by Jatish in molds made by Haripada. Finer, more costly small statues for domestic worship are made by Hari-

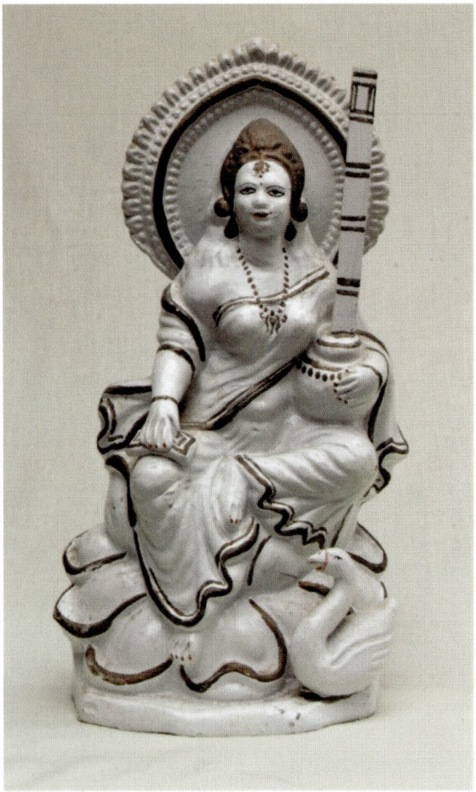

Saraswati, handmade clay statue by Haripada Pal (30 cm tall), 2001

Saraswati, molded clay statue from Haripada's shop (29 cm tall), 1996

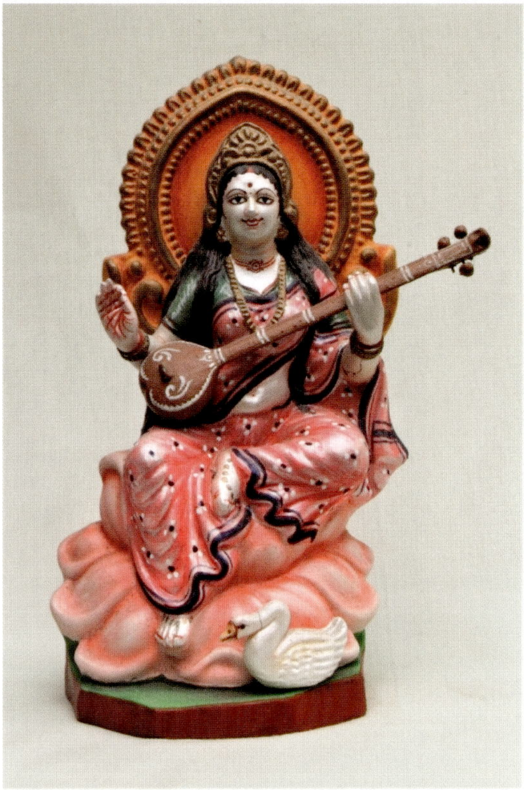

pada, working alone. The grand *murtis* for public settings, standing from three to beyond six feet in height, begin with a bamboo armature, wrapped with rice straw, bound into form with twine, and then coated with clay. Strengthened with chopped straw, then fibers of jute, the clay is slowly, patiently shaped toward perfection. Once it has dried enough, the *murti* is coated with thickened white paint, then delicately colored.

His creations, Haripada says, unfold from two traditions: from the technical tradition of manufacture he learned from his grandfather, and from the mystical tradition of interpretation he learned from a saintly ascetic, Surdendra Chandra Sarkar. Material and spiritual traditions blend for Haripada Pal in Dhaka as they do for Mehmet Gürsoy in Kütahya. Haripada says his work is a prayer, a part of his devotion. "Everyday I am making the body of God. The *murti* is a blessing and a benefit to the people."

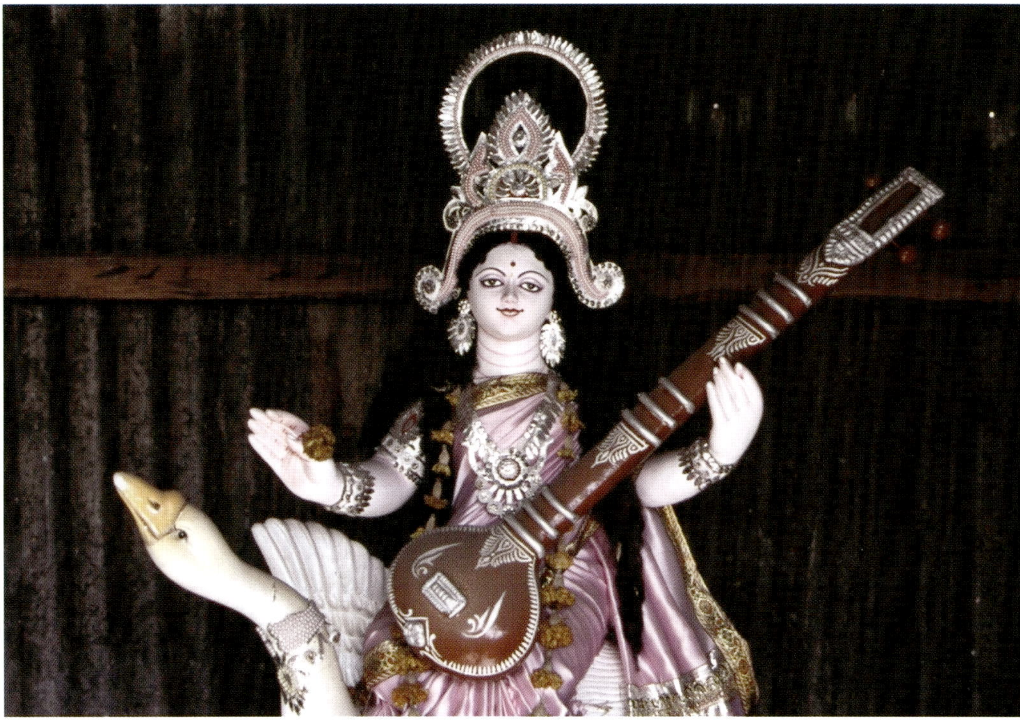

Saraswati, large *murti* by Haripada Pal, installed for *puja* in the village temple of Norpura, 1996

Haripada calls the *murti* a mediator. It functions to open a communicative channel between the human and the divine worlds. The process begins with prayer, with mantras of praise that bring a specific image into his mind — a divine revelation. God's gift, the life force in his body, enables Haripada to hold tight to that image during creation. The life force, the *atma*, in his body is the same as the life force in the soil that makes it possible for seeds to germinate. Life force spreads, too, through the clay in his hands, so while he is pressing the clay, shaping and smoothing it, the life force in his body springs through the tips of his fingers and fuses with the life force in the clay, effecting a reunion of the *atma* scattered through the universe. As his hands move in the clay, the life force, the power, in his *murti* steadily increases, and as his hands move, Haripada gratefully, responsibly responds to God's gift of his innate talent by striving toward an unattainable perfection, doing the best he can do, which is the universal obligation of the artist. And as his hands move in the clay, while his *murti* becomes steadily more powerful, it also becomes steadily more beautiful, and beauty is basic to the *murti's* communicative mission.

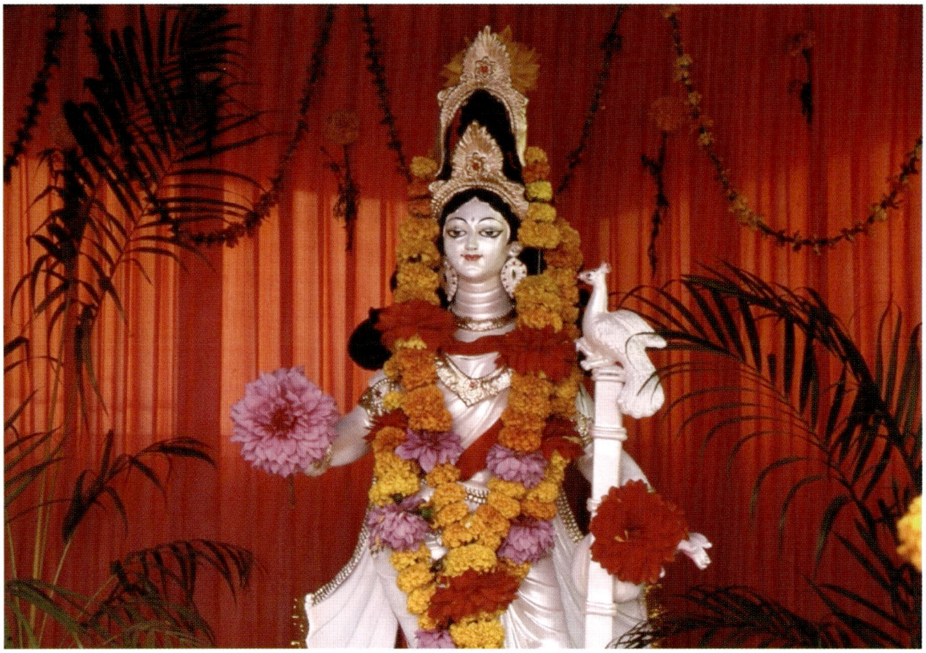

Saraswati Puja, Dhakeswari Mandir, Dhaka, Bangladesh, 1995

When the *murti* is installed for worship — let's say for Saraswati Puja at the Dhakeswari Mandir in Dhaka — the priest recites the same mantras of praise that brought an image into the artist's mind. Now they call the goddess who, flattered by the beauty of the image prepared to receive her, descends into the clay. The devotees, drawn by the *murti's* beauty, press close, taking *darshan*, connecting eye-to-eye with the goddess. Union through the eyes, and through the dampness in the bodies of the statue and the worshipers, opens the channel of communication. The goddess receives the praise she wants. The devotees can ask for the boons they want. Since Saraswati is the goddess of wisdom, requests befit her domain. A mother will ask for her daughter to succeed in school. A young teacher will ask for tenure in the university.

For the *murti* there are two ends, both exemplified by images of Kali made by Haripada. Kali, he says, can appear in one hundred and eight different forms. When she is the goddess in rage, wild and beyond contact, she carries a sword in her left hand. When she has a sword in both hands or only in her right, she is Rakshakali, approachable to all, and that is the *murti* Haripada created for the Shankharibazar Kali Mandir, close to the place where he lives and works. Shaped of clay, ornamented by the goldsmiths of Tanti Bazar, this Kali, standing in a temple, will remain as long as the priest recites every day the mantras of praise that brought her into the clay and keep her there.

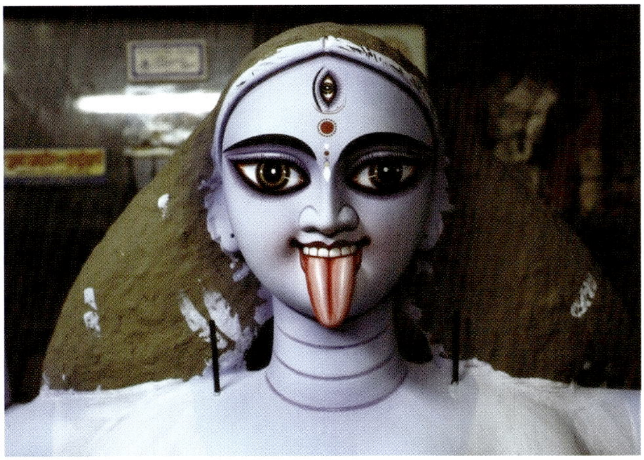

Rakshakali painted

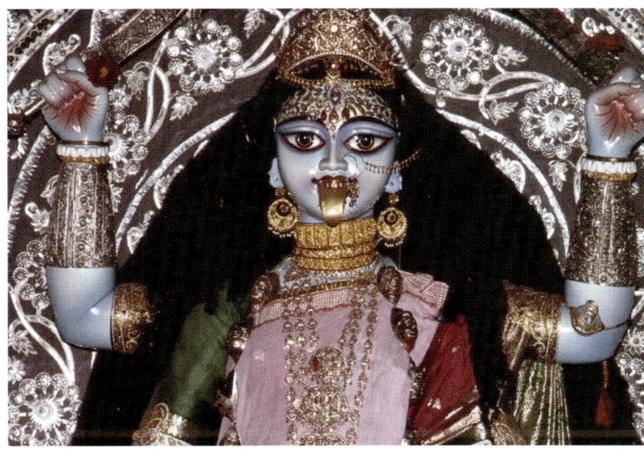

Rakshakali ornamented

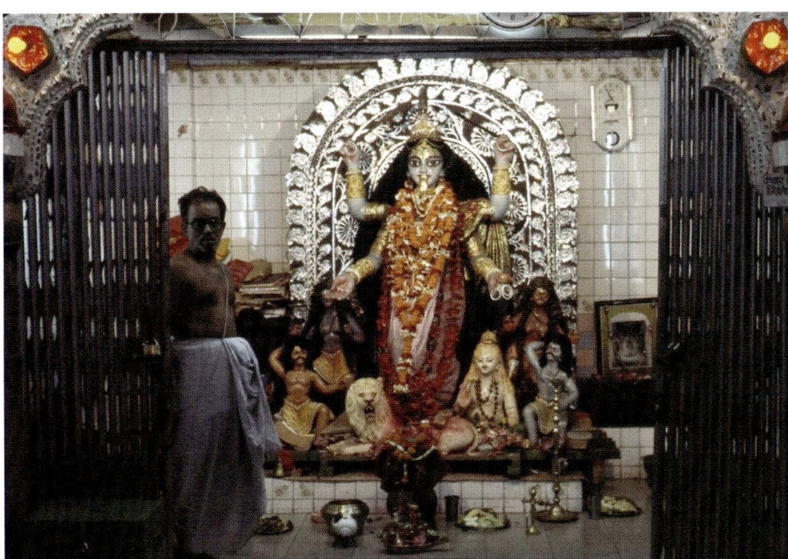

Rakshakali, by Haripada Pal in the Shankharibazar Kali Mandir, 2001

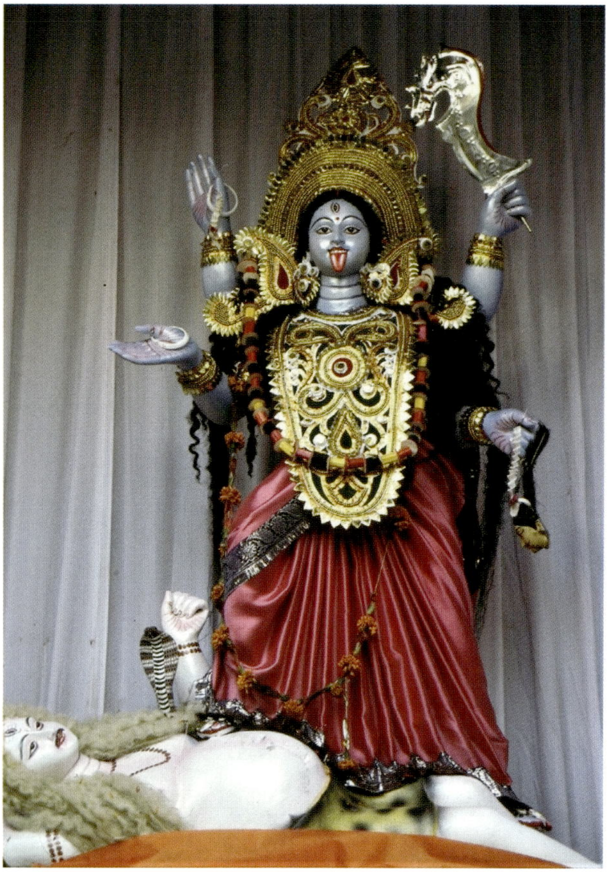

Shamakali, by Haripada Pal,
Shamakali Puja, Shankharibazar,
Dhaka, Bangladesh, 1998

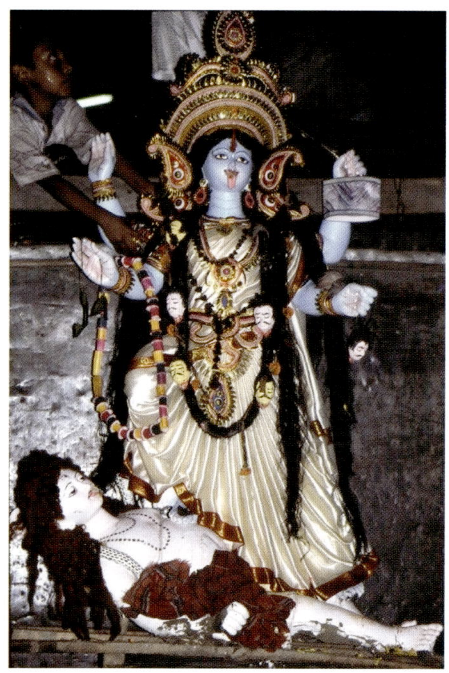

Shamakali sacrificed in the
Buriganga on the last day of
Shamakali Puja, Dhaka, 1998

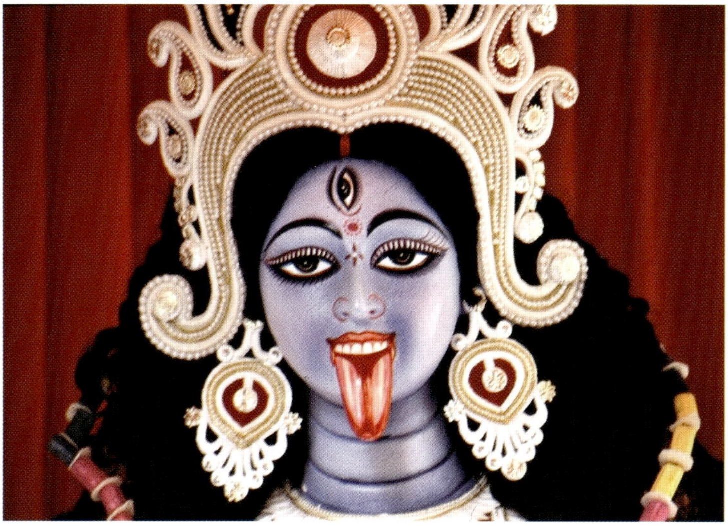

Shamakali, Shamakali Puja, Tanti Bazar, Dhaka, 1998

Shamakali is the goddess in the instant of awareness. Rampaging through the world, intent on destroying evil but wildly destroying everything in her path, Kali, oblivious, stepped on the body of her husband, Lord Shiva. With the sword still in her left hand, realizing the wrong she had done, shocked, her tongue rolled out of her mouth. Her tongue is the sign of her awareness, her readiness to help humankind.

During Shamakali Puja in one October, thirty-four large statues of Kali, eleven by Haripada Pal, stood along the streets of Shankharibazar and the adjacent Tanti Bazar. On the *puja's* last day, all those *murtis* were gathered and carried through the night in a jubilant procession that ended on the banks of the Buriganga. There they were put in boats, taken far from the shore, and slid into the river, sacrificed in running water. The unfired clay will melt and mingle into the river's silt. Carried downstream and accumulating along the banks, that silt will become the substance out of which the *murtis* of the future will be shaped, in a symbolic reenactment of the endless cycles of reincarnation.

Every year a new display of the central sacred images is installed at the Dhakeswari Mandir, Dhaka's main temple. Tall in the middle stands Durga, the goddess in supreme power, calmly, suavely killing the Buffalo Demon. Her children stand to the sides: her daughters, Saraswati, the goddess of wisdom, and Lakshmi, the goddess of wealth, and her sons, Ganesh, the lord of beginnings, and Kartik, the dapper deity of war. All of them have *pujas* of their own that differ in dates, duration, and the intricate rules for proper performance, but all of their grand *murtis* begin in damp clay and end in running water.

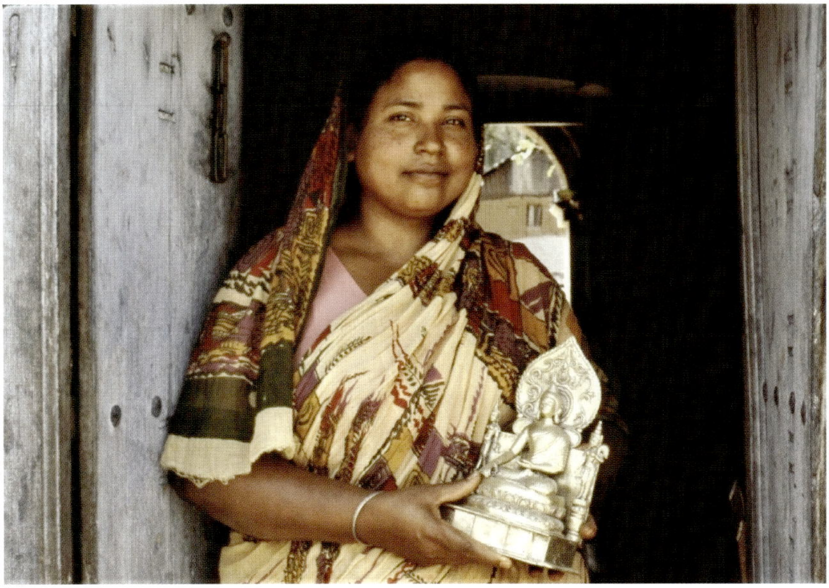

Rashida Musharraf with an image of the Buddha that Gauranga Pal modeled and she cast in brass, Dhamrai, Bangladesh, 1995

Sacrificed, the greatest Bengali works of art are gone, lost into the flow, leaving to historians the difficulty of understanding the art from the smaller works of lesser significance that were cast permanently in metal. Fortunately, in Bangladesh at least, the artists who shape clay into *murtis* are also the ones who shape wax for casting. In the village of Kagajipara, this is the specialty of Ananda Pal and his brother Gauranga. Ananda's personal style is distinctively energetic, but he begins with a prayer, receives a vision, and proceeds as he would with clay, shaping an image in wax that is coated with clay. When the clay is fired, the wax melts and runs out, leaving a delicate void that will be filled with molten brass. The clay is cracked away — every image is unique — and the tedious task of filing and finishing the brass figure begins.

Dhamrai, a town north of Dhaka, is a center for metal casting of several kinds. Here Hossain Musharraf began casting images in the lost-wax process. When he died, his apprentice Ahmad Ali and his wife, Rashida, continued the work, and they were later joined by Mohamad Babul Aktar Chowdhury. All of them are Muslims, but Rashida says that no one in the Muslim community objects to her manufacturing these gods of other people. Shaped by Hindus, cast by Muslims — emblems of the complexity of Bangladesh — some of these statues will be bought as souvenirs by officials in foreign embassies, but others will stand in the cluster of images on the altars of Hindu temples.

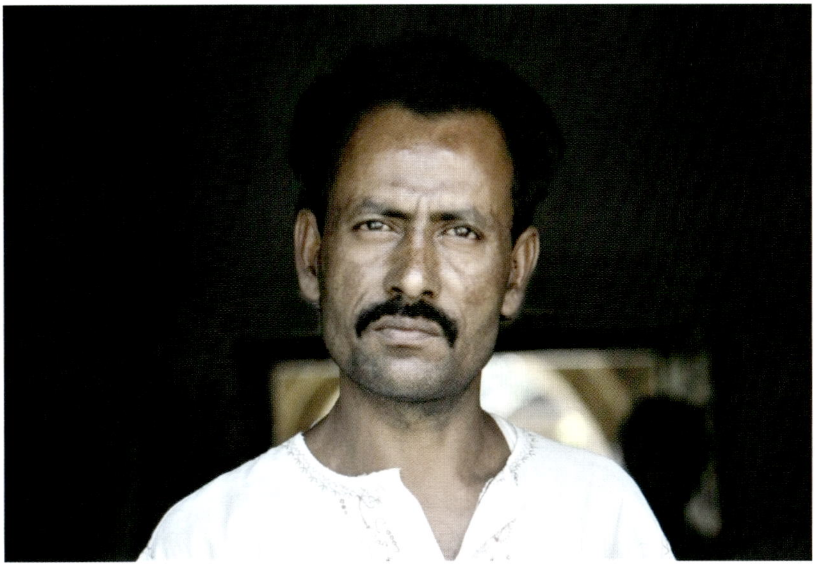

Ananda Pal, Kagajipara, 1996

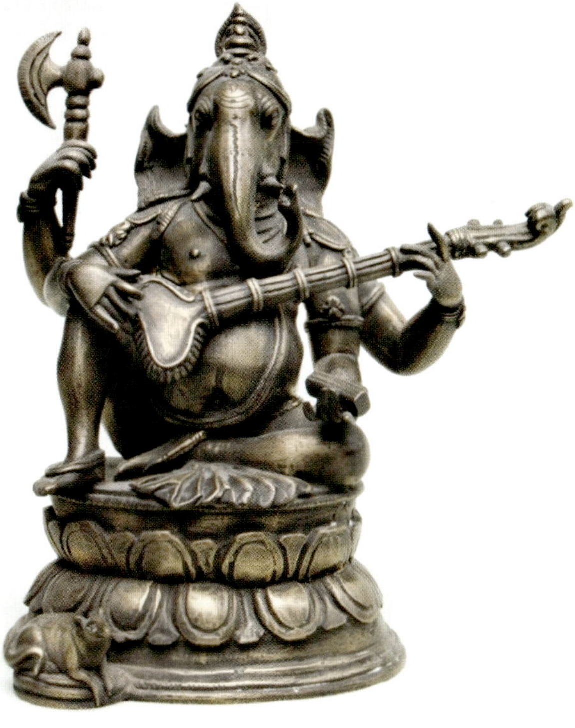

Ganesh, modeled in wax by Ananda Pal, cast in brass by Mohamad Babul Aktar Chowdhury, Dhamrai, Bangladesh (23 cm tall), 2013

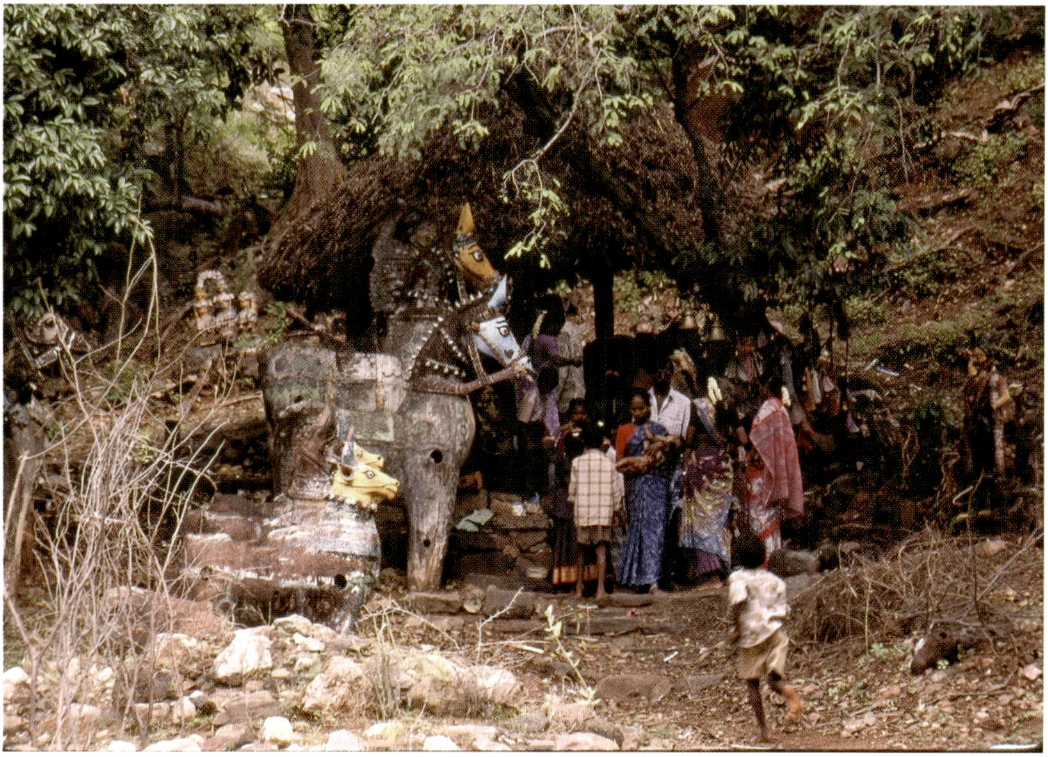

Manjamalai Ayyanar temple, Tamil Nadu, India, 1999

Hindu traditions of figurative work in clay are especially rich, rooted deeply in time, continually vigorous, and as a result of the polymorphous and localized nature of the religion, remarkably diverse in practice. It would be a pleasure to report on fieldwork in Tamil Nadu, at the southern tip of India, where a ceramic artistic tradition centers on the god Ayyanar and includes gigantic votive horses in fired clay. But we will swing to the final topic, to figurative traditions, which, like that of Alto do Moura, flourished when utilitarian pottery failed. José Saramago, the great Portuguese writer who won the Nobel Prize in 1998, will lead us in.

In Saramago's superb novel *The Cave*, an elderly potter finds that the market for his useful pots has come to an end. His loving daughter suggests making small statues in clay. They search through books for inspiration, work hard, and their statuettes are given a trial in the market. Judged old-fashioned, they fail, and the potter's art is over. Their mistake was making images that were merely decorative, lacking in local significance. The Brazilian examples show that careful craft is not enough. The quotidian images in Alto do Moura movingly record local history in a time of change. The sacred images of Tracunhaém strengthen Catholic commitment in the context of Evangelical opposition.

Saramago's potter was denied the right to significance because the writer didn't locate him in Portugal, but in a nameless place, a bit like Portugal but, finally, not like any place in the world. He had no resource of meaningful tradition around him. That is a characteristic move for José Saramago. He often sets people in abstract space, weak in particularity, in order to pose and explore a human problem. Suppose everyone started to go blind, or two men were identical in appearance. If there were a society without crime, what need would there be for government? The problem raised in *The Cave* is large, general, crucial. What can the working man do when his hard-won skills are no longer needed, when neither his body nor his mind finds satisfaction in the labor that brings him no more than not enough pay?

The potter's options reduced to a collapse into boredom or an escape into the unknown. Had he lived in Portugal, though, he would have had other choices.

When José Saramago graciously led his reader through his country in *Journey to Portugal*, the landscape flooded his text with historical and cultural significance. The rambling writer was on a quest to sharpen his eye. Beginning in the far northeast, he stopped to inspect every church, favoring the Romanesque and rustic; he visited every museum, examining the statues, paintings, and ceramics. The closer Saramago got to Lisbon in the southwest, the more he commented on the tiles, and once in the city he visited the Museu do Azulejo, "a precious place," and to understand *azulejos*, he says, is to understand "what it means to be Portuguese" — to be, like Saramago, at once earthy, pleasant, and suave. He doesn't remark that those tiles were shipped to Brazil in the past. Old Portuguese *azulejos* still carry sacred significance through the interiors of the baroque churches in Salvador, where Saramago visited his colleague the Brazilian novelist Jorge Amado. Nor does Saramago note that *azulejos* of quality are still made in his city of Lisbon.

Set in an industrial neighborhood in Lisbon, the Fábrica Sant'Ana divides into sections like the big ateliers in Kütahya. On the ground floor, men begin the process by shaping the clay, molding pieces or jiggering them on the wheel, and they end the process with big kilns. They used wood until late in the twentieth century, use gas and electricity now. Upstairs the pieces are painted — overglaze like *maiolica*, not underglaze like *çini*. In one studio,

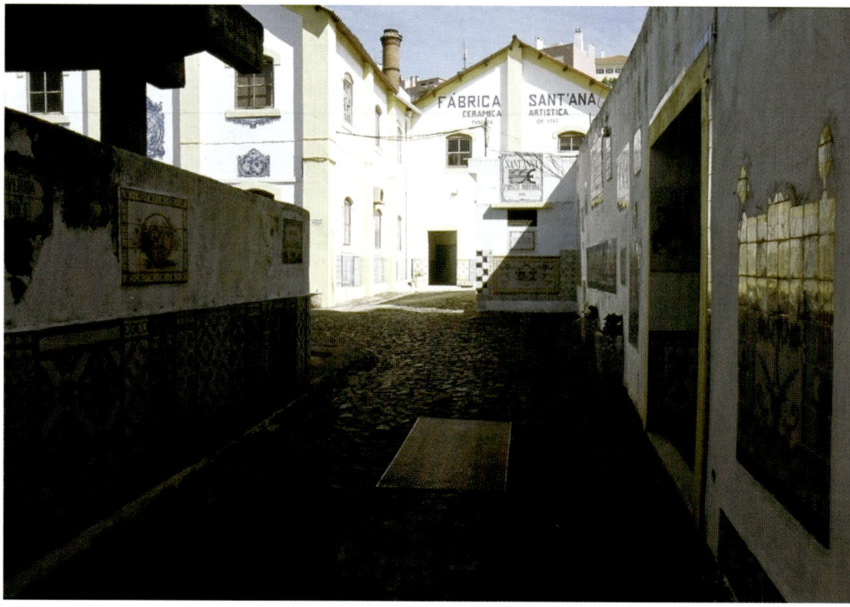

Fábrica Sant'Ana, Lisbon, Portugal, 2013

about thirty women and exactly one man paint tableware by hand. In another, the master Maria da Graça plans and paints *azulejos*. She draws a design on paper, pricks it into a pounce, as they do in Kütahya, and then she paints the tiles, blue on white, taking care to shade the human figures into lifelike presence. A sweet, shy artist, Maria concentrates on the sacred, making large suites of narrative tiles, destined now, as in the deep past, for churches, and she paints single tiles, portraying Our Lady, a youthful Saint John, or Saint Anthony who was born up the hill in Lisbon.

The shop — advertised as the last artistic tile factory in Europe — was established in the middle of the eighteenth century. The products, once shipped to Brazil, go now most often to northern Europe and Japan. It is a big operation, high in energy and quality, so if Saramago's potter had lived in Portugal, when his local market failed he could have found worthwhile employment in the capital city. More to the point, being a potter he would have known (as Saramago did) that there were two centers in Portugal — Barcelos and Estremoz — where small figures were shaped in clay. A bit of research in place or in books would have shown the potter and his daughter which figures were commercially viable — not the random international figures they chose to make, but the regionally meaningful quotidian and sacred figures made in both Portugal and Brazil.

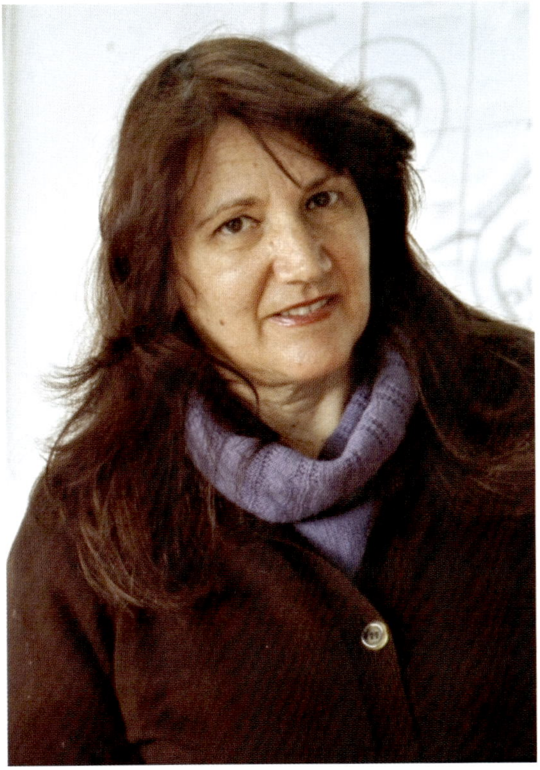

Maria da Graça, Fábrica
Sant'Ana, Lisbon, 2013

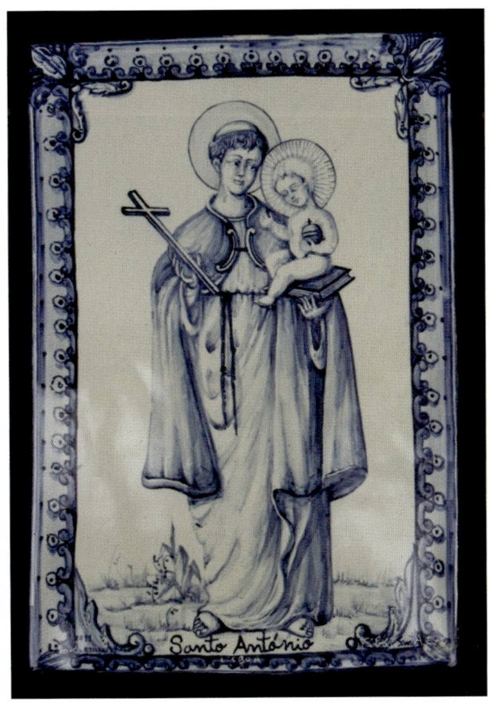

Santo Antônio, *azulejo*
by Maria da Graça (35 × 23 cm), 2011

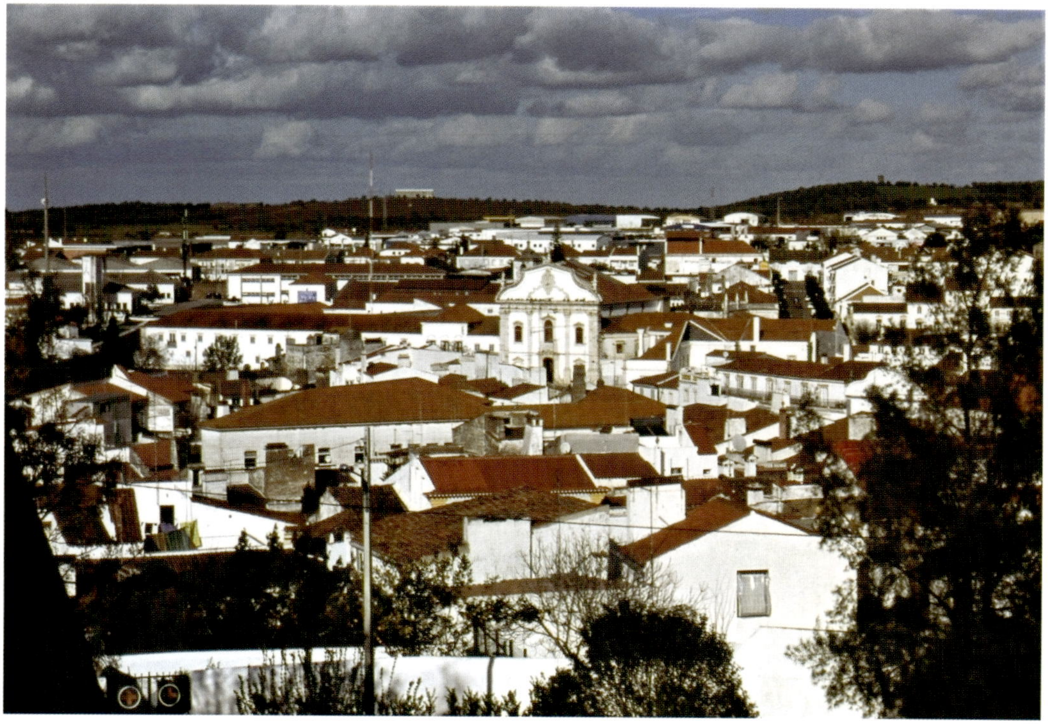

Estremoz, Portugal, 2013

In Estremoz, to the east in the country, the Irmãs Flores, the Flores Sisters, work in a bright, tidy shop. Maria Inácio Flores shapes the small figures by hand, using molds for the faces as they do in Alto do Moura when crafting *bonecas*. After they are fired at earthenware temperature in an electric kiln, Perpétua Flores paints the figures. Their nephew Ricardo Fonseca works beside them. His work is especially fine, and his aunts call him their hope for the future.

The Flores Sisters make quotidian figures of hunters and fishermen, of street vendors, of women making and baking bread, of people eating and drinking together. And they make sacred statues of Nossa Senhora da Conceição and of Sant'Ana Mestra, an image of Mary learning to read at her mother's knee that has long been popular with Brazil's *santeiros*.

Brazilian depictions shift nearer to the naturalistic, but the Portuguese and Brazilian repertories are thematically close. The Flores Sisters know about the work of Vitalino and for years they have wanted to visit Brazil. When Alto do Moura's own Marliete saw the work of the Flores Sisters on one of her trips to Portugal, she recognized the similarity in subject and declared the work of the sisters to be beautiful.

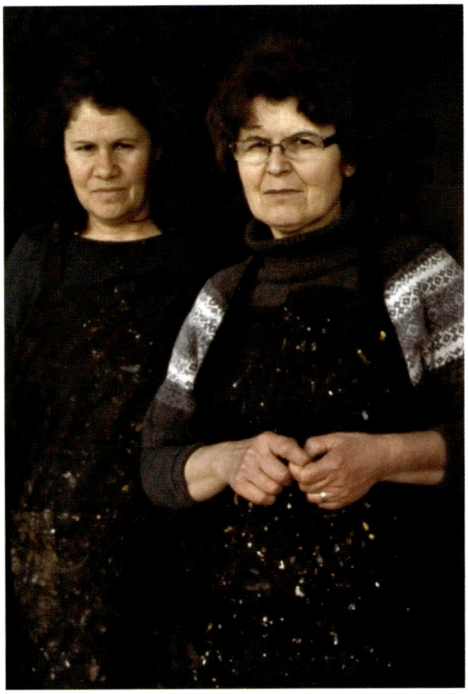

The Flores Sisters: Perpétua and Maria, Estremoz, 2013

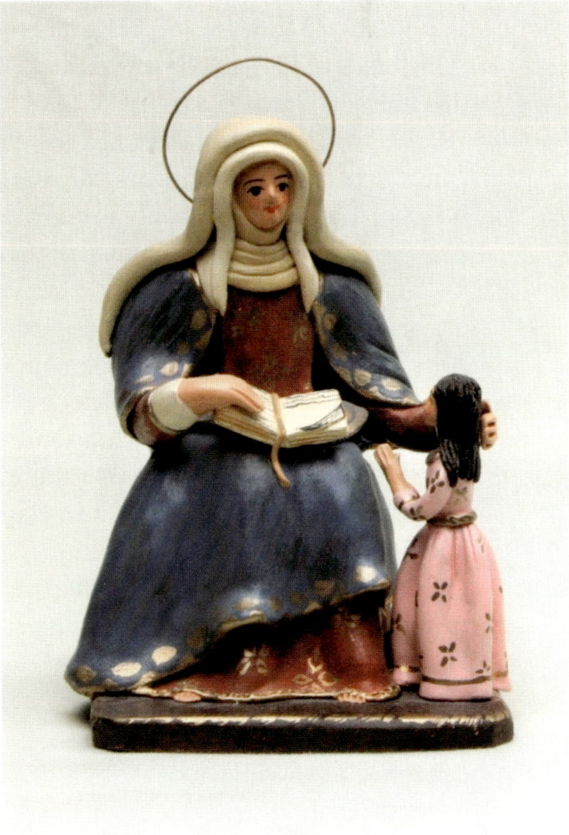

Sant'Ana Mestra, by the Flores Sisters (21 cm tall), 2013

Similarities are clear, and the easy explanation would be that Portuguese people brought a tradition that took root in Brazil. But a wide gap opens in time between the colonial era and the creation of quotidian figures in clay. Historical evidence calls for more nuance. What the contemporary potters certainly share is the crisis brought on by the global spread of cheap industrial products. Handmade utilitarian pots can't compete. Even in poor, rural Bangladesh, plastic containers are pushing the handsome old pots toward oblivion. That's the predicament in Saramago's *The Cave*. Pottery sinks into death — or it rises into new life as art.

The quest for art is double. It involves a look back, perhaps far back, to discover inspirational qualities in old works, and it involves a move forward toward excellence by perfecting useful forms and glazes, or by perfecting the decorative and meaningful patterns on useful forms, or by perfecting figurative forms. Those figurative forms are most likely to achieve the desired excellence in environments established by religions that incorporate images in worship: Hinduism, Buddhism, and Catholicism. Western art reached a figurative peak in the days of Donatello, Verrocchio, Michelangelo, and Bernini — in Catholic Italy.

In Portugal and Brazil what the modern workers in clay share are these conditions: competition from the industrial products that bring wealth to a privileged few, and the daily experience of life in a predominately Catholic place. It follows that Manuel Barbeira in Barcelos, Portugal, and Luiz Antônio in Alto do Moura, Brazil, would respond to their scenes by making similar images in clay of the holy processions that pass frequently through their streets. Most important in history is the tradition of making images of the saints that the Portuguese brought to Brazil.

In the seventeenth and eighteenth centuries, saints in Brazil were occasionally shaped in clay, some by great masters like Frei Agostinho da Piedade, but there is no evidence of a direct connection between colonial and modern figurative work in clay. The tradition of carving wooden saints and then painting them, however, has continued in an unbroken line for more than four centuries, and by the eighteenth century the workforce had become distinctively Brazilian. Salvador's greatest master, Francisco das Chagas, was an enslaved artist of African descent, and the greatest master in Minas Gerais — the most famous artist in Brazilian history — Aleijadinho, was the son of a Portuguese carpenter and a woman of African descent. Of the leading *santeiros* in northeastern Brazil today, not one of them is purely Portuguese in ancestry; they

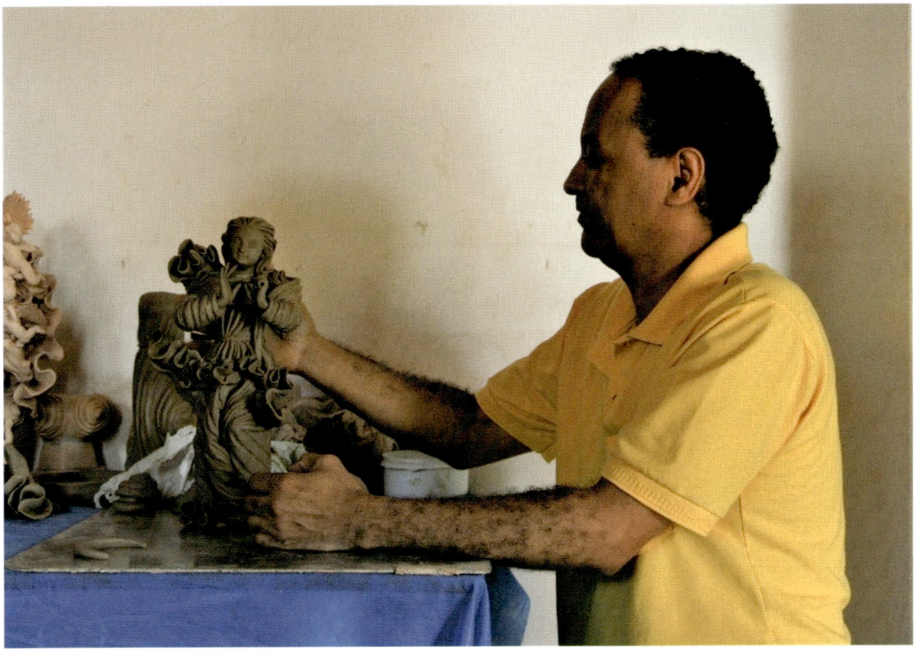

Rosalvo Santana, shaping clay into an image of Our Lady, Maragojipinho, Bahia, Brazil, 2018

all come from what the Brazilian novelist Jorge Amado called "the good old Brazilian mixture."

The general result of the strong Brazilian carving tradition is that people in church see three-dimensional, polychromed images, standing ready to receive prayers and provide inspiration to the rare artist. When Rosalvo Santana, the son of a potter, went to church with his mother in the Bahian pottery village of Maragojipinho, the wooden statues he saw inspired him to create exquisite images in clay.

That seems to be the story. As the demand for utilitarian ware declined, people who knew how to work with the clay saw the beautiful statues in church, saw daily life changing around them, and then made figures of clay in Portugal, Brazil, and Mexico.

The story ends where it began. There is no better example of the shift to the figurative, when utilitarian demand declined, than Alto do Moura. This chapter's logic would locate Alto do Moura right here, so the best — though highly improbable — thing for you to do is to treat this book so far as a circular narrative, returning to the beginning and reading straight through until you reach this point again, before turning to the next chapter.

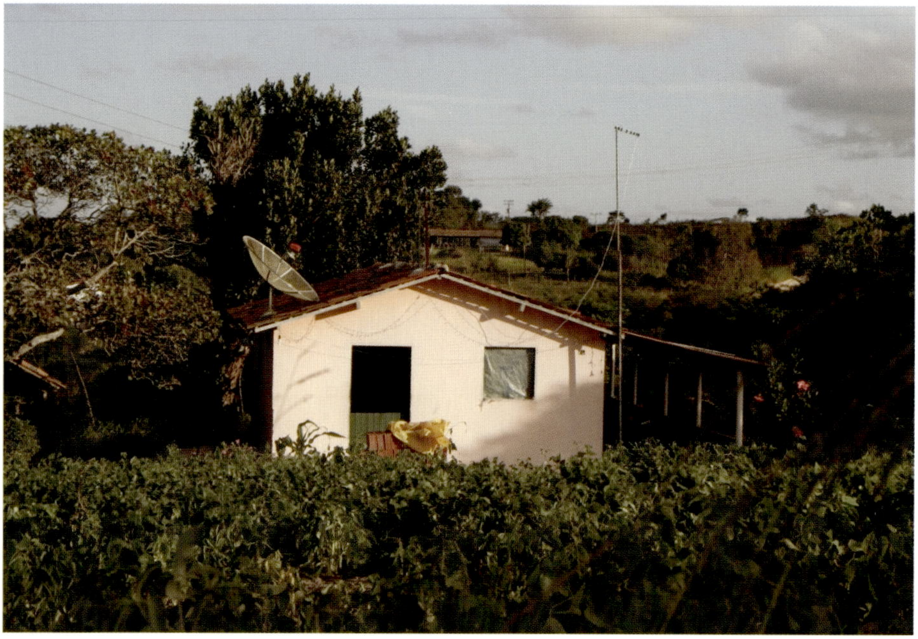

Northeastern house in the Agreste of Pernambuco, 2019

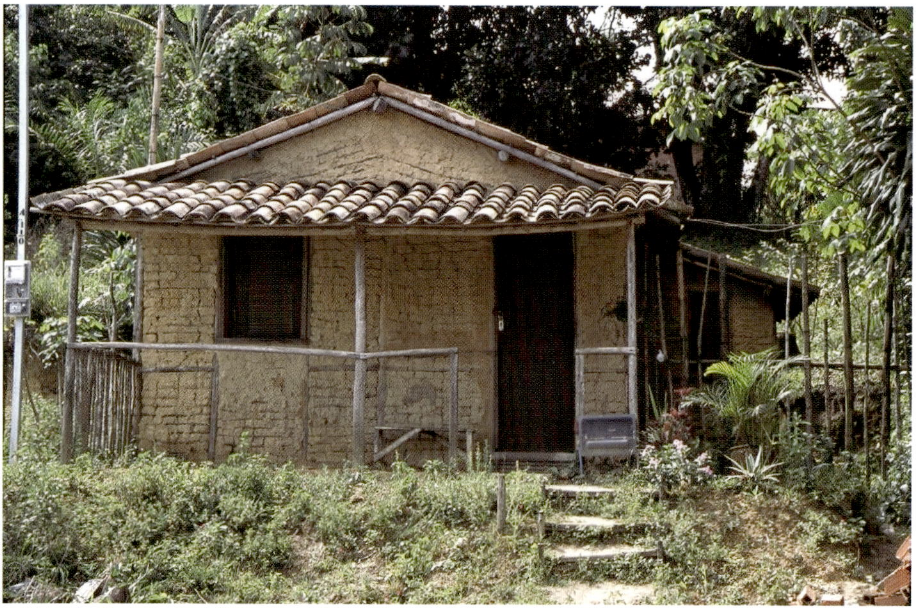

Northeastern house in the Recôncavo of Bahia, 2015

26

Production in Place

Back again in Alto do Moura, this time on the hunt for general principles, we can say that art begins at home, and here the home is a house of a particular type. In a single story it contains a narrow sequence of rooms. The first, a parlor, and the last, a kitchen, widen from wall to wall. Connecting the first to the last, a corridor runs along the side, past one or more small bedrooms. In the Brazilian Northeast, the house is usually built in the countryside with the gable aligned from front to back, and in the small towns and big cities with the gable aligned side to side, paralleling the street. Plain in the country, ornamented in the city, the house holds to some variation of its flexible plan.

Houses of this kind tend to appear where Indigenous, European, and African cultures meet — in northeastern Brazil, in the Caribbean, and in Louisiana. Carried northward from New Orleans, along the Mississippi and Ohio Valleys, this dwelling, clearly unlike the French and British buildings around it, is called the shotgun house in the United States.

Ubiquitous and unremarkable in the interior of Pernambuco, this house required no modifications to become a site for creation. When, in 1959, he had accumulated wealth enough, Vitalino built a house of the usual rural sort in Alto do Moura, and he needed only to add a kiln in the yard to have a place to work. In her house on the long street named for Vitalino, Carmélia clears a space to work in the kitchen, and out the back door she has her kilns.

To the west in the Sertão, in Ibimirim where the material is wood, the craft is carving, and the art is sacred, the workers live in houses of the same type. Their homes add a forecourt on the front, in proportion like the porches on country houses, in appearance like suburban garages. Here in the forecourt,

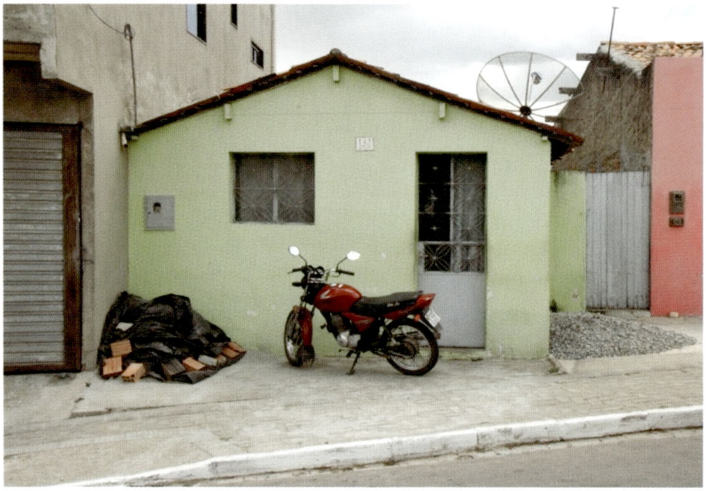

Northeastern house,
Alto do Moura, 2021

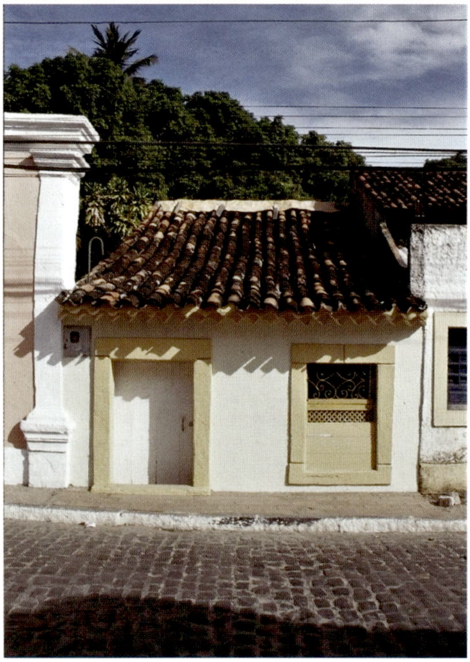

Northeastern house, Olinda, 2014

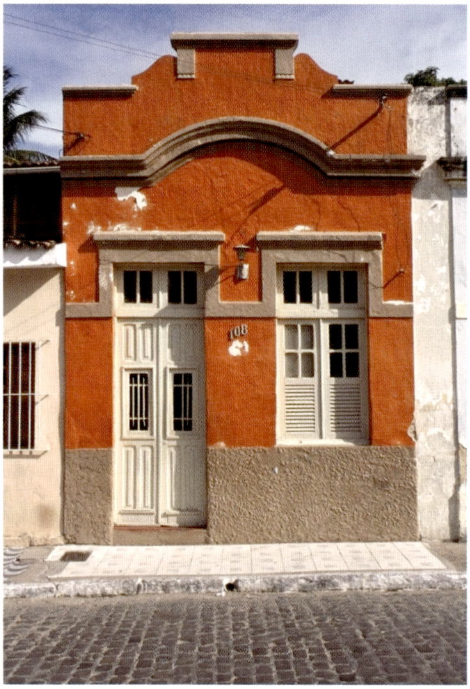

Northeastern house,
Salvador da Bahia, 2007

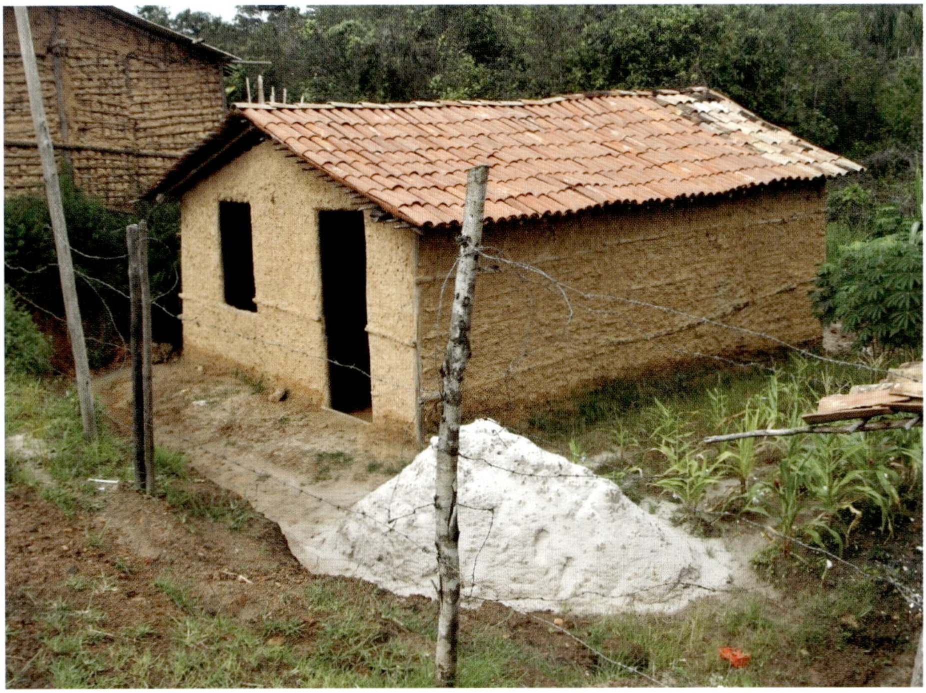

Northeastern house under construction, Maragojipinho, Bahia, 2018

the artists — Mestre Manoel Cordeiro, Nivaldo Gomes dos Santos, and José Bezerra — sit in the breeze to do the fine carving, wave to their neighbors, and spot the occasional customer. Beyond the kitchen, out in the backyard where kilns stand in Alto do Moura, they have small shops for rougher, heavier work in wood.

In 1953, realizing the mistake he had made by moving to Caruaru, Manuel Eudócio returned to Alto do Moura. Then he built a convenient architectural frame for his work. Beside his house, on a plot of the same dimensions, he added a workshop. A door in the back wall gave him smooth access to his kilns. A door in the front wall provided cooling cross-ventilation and gave him immediate access to the street where he received deliveries of clay and welcomed visitors. He placed a big table for work in the back of the shop, lit by a window in the back wall, but bringing the clay into shape doesn't require this much space. Selling does.

In Caruaru, Manuel Eudócio learned that it is best to sell directly to his customers. In his new shop, to one side, shelves on a long blank wall displayed his finished pieces for sale, and the front door opened, not into his home, but into a place for commerce. Visitors could meet the artist, watch him work, look through the stock, and, he said, they would always buy something. J. Miguel said the same thing in Bezerros. Mestre Manoel said the same thing in Ibimirim, and the forecourts in his town functioned like Manuel Eudócio's shop, affording a place to work, greet customers, and exhibit pieces for sale.

When he lived in Caruaru, Manuel Eudócio sold to merchants for resale. His profit was pinched, demand was narrow. If artists like Genilda and Vitalino Neto work on a commission from a businessman, they are obliged to make, over and over, the few pieces that are known to sell quickly. At work in Olinda, Severino Borges benefits because Ana Maria sells his woodblock works directly to customers in the Casa da Cultura. She sees what they buy and hears what they want but haven't found, and the information she gathers, Severino said, drives his creativity. In selling directly, Manuel Eudócio learned from his customers, and he taught them. The loop of performance closed, and he brought them into accord with his wishes. He wanted to work in Vitalino's line, and he wanted to make new things. His original creations, his introduction of the *Reisado*, doubled the size of Alto do Moura's repertory: more variety in the creative act, more variety in the stock for sale.

For making and selling, Manuel Eudócio had his own shop. He made what he wanted to make and he made it when he wanted to make it. His home was nextdoor, separated from his shop by only a wall. He wasted neither time nor money commuting from the place where he lived to the place where he worked. He walked out of his kitchen and into his shop: his commute lasted for less than a minute. Shifting easily back and forth, he began to work when he wanted to begin, paused for a rest or a meal when he wanted to, then quit when he wanted to quit. He had no boss to give him directions or blunder awkwardly into his process. External information — about demand in the market, say — refracted through his brain to become his own decision. With no middleman between him and his customers, with no boss to push him around or cut into his profit, Manuel Eudócio was free to do what he wanted to do when he wanted to do it.

He was free, free in the way that John Ruskin said artists must be free — free to express themselves and make their own mistakes. In place, at home, Manuel Eudócio did what he wished, and he gained the aid of his family. His wife painted his pieces, and when she died his daughter took up the task. His sons helped him, and by helping, watching, and listening, they learned.

In the next generation, his sons Luiz Carlos and Ademilson numbered among the art's leaders. A few steps uphill, Luiz Carlos arranged his space as his father had, a house and shop side by side. A few steps more and Ademilson has his home. His shop stands across the street, a short walk downhill.

Two observations will carry us from Alto do Moura toward general principles.

First, when life and work unify efficiently in place, as they do on a small farm, one master makes the prime products, directs the labor, and receives support in a familial environment of cooperation and education. That could seem patriarchal, but the work is structured in the same way whether the master is a man, like Manuel Eudócio, or a woman, like Terezinha, Socorro, Carmélia, or Marliete. Terezinha works with her sons, Socorro with her daughter-in-law, Carmélia with her son and daughter, Marliete with her sister-in-law and her nieces. Cooperative work tightens the familial bonds that hold and expand while generation follows generation in place, and the art, at once, achieves continuity and enables personal expressivity — the key traits of folk art.

And second, the architectural forms that unite families in life and work can take different configurations. Manuel Eudócio was the first in Alto do Moura to build a house and a shop on a single site. He set them side by side, and Luiz Carlos followed him. But Luiz Antônio piled them, with a shop for creation and sales on the ground floor and space for living upstairs. That piled form was chosen by Luiz Galdino in Alto do Moura, by Antônio Pimpo and Dinho de Zezinho in Tracunhaém, and by J. Borges for his old shop in Bezerros, where J. Miguel works today.

Life and labor unite differently in centralized courtyard plans. In the remote and beautiful village of Kınık in the mountains of northwestern Anatolia, slip-decorated earthenware is made in more than a hundred shops, then shipped throughout Turkey. Osman Kaya's place is typical. On the long, curving main street, across from the mosque, a door opens into the shop where Osman and his partner Mustafa Baydemir work at wheels, side by side, in the light of a wide window. A door in the back of the shop gives into a shed that shelters a barrel-vaulted, wood-fired, updraft kiln. Beyond the kiln, a wide courtyard contains an oven for baking bread and offers space for piling and processing the clay. Walls run along its sides and the courtyard is closed in the back by the big house where Osman and his wife, Hüsniya, raised their four children. Past the house, a passage leads out of the courtyard, uphill to the fields; Osman, like most of his neighbors, is both a potter and a farmer. The courtyard's main entry is a big double door, wide enough for an oxcart or a tractor, that opens from the street into a runway next to the shop.

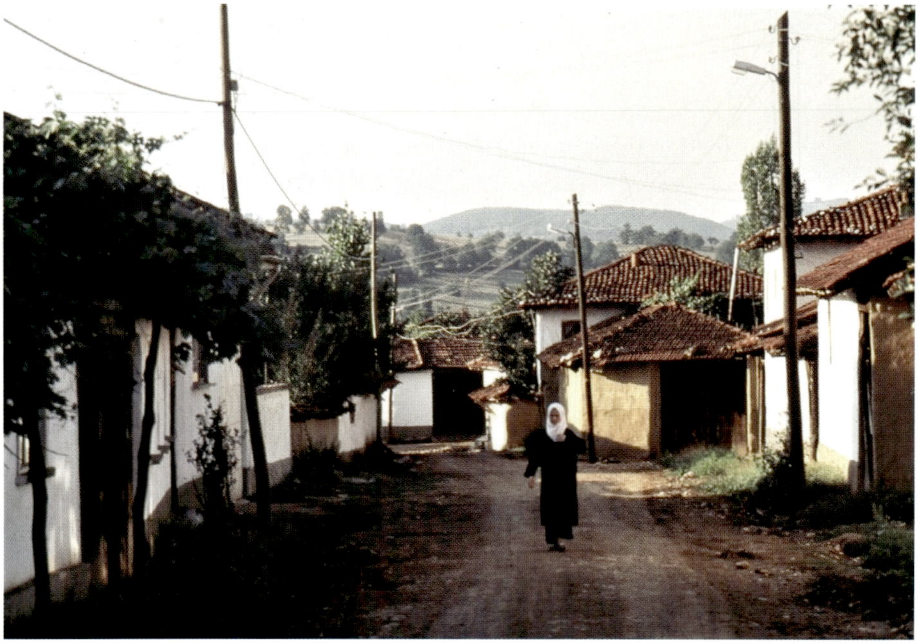

Kınık, Bilecik, Turkey, 1995

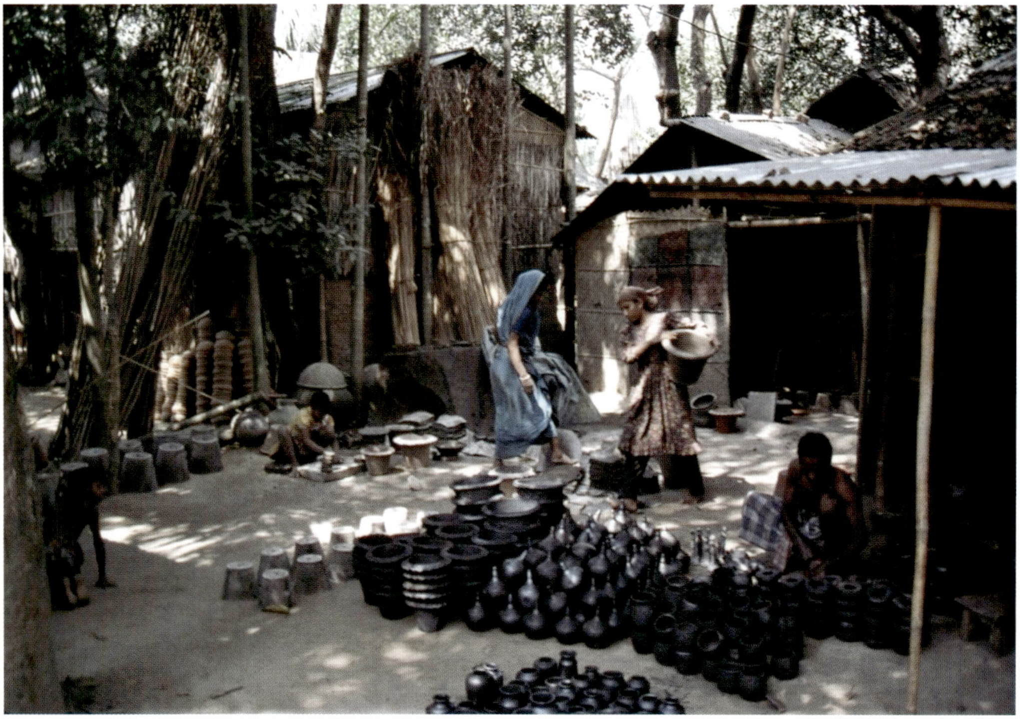

Space for work, Kagajipara, Bangladesh, 1996

The Kınık courtyard plan is trim and tight, a rectangular walled unit built with others into neat rows along the streets. The courtyards in the pottery villages of Bangladesh are splayed and gapped. Small buildings for sleeping, cooking, and storage stand apart to admit the breeze and permit easy motion from the home to the kiln, and they gather into a loose square around a central open space for familial work, for processing the clay and making the pots.

When the Bangladeshi plan is transplanted from the village to the city, it compresses and distorts in limited locations. Maran Chand Paul's place for living and working in Dhaka's Rayer Bazar squeezes onto an irregular plot. The courtyard swings around the end of his house then runs beside it, following a narrow route, gathering the kiln, and ending at a workshop that stretches along the street.

Space is tight in the village, very tight in town, but where space widens and the farmsteads scatter in the Piedmont of North Carolina, the potters, Mark Hewitt and David Stuempfle, still gather the house, shop, and kiln into tight unity. Comfort and efficiency are the goals. The proximity of the shop to the kiln — the connection between throwing and firing — is the key to efficiency. On Daniel Johnston's place, way back in the country on a rough dirt road, the shop he built and the kiln he built stand as close to each other as the shop and kiln do in Osman Kaya's place in the village, or in Manuel Eudócio's place in the town, or in Maran Chand Paul's place in one of the world's largest cities.

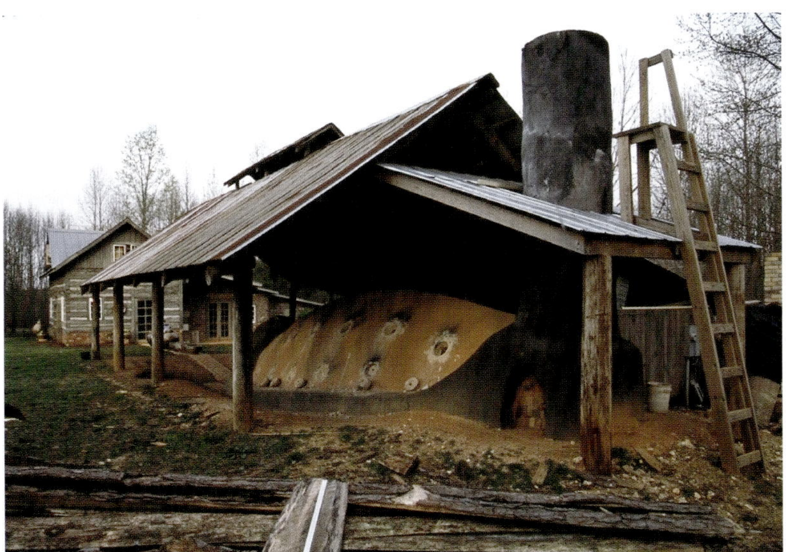

Shop and kiln aligned on Daniel Johnston's place, Seagrove, North Carolina, 2016

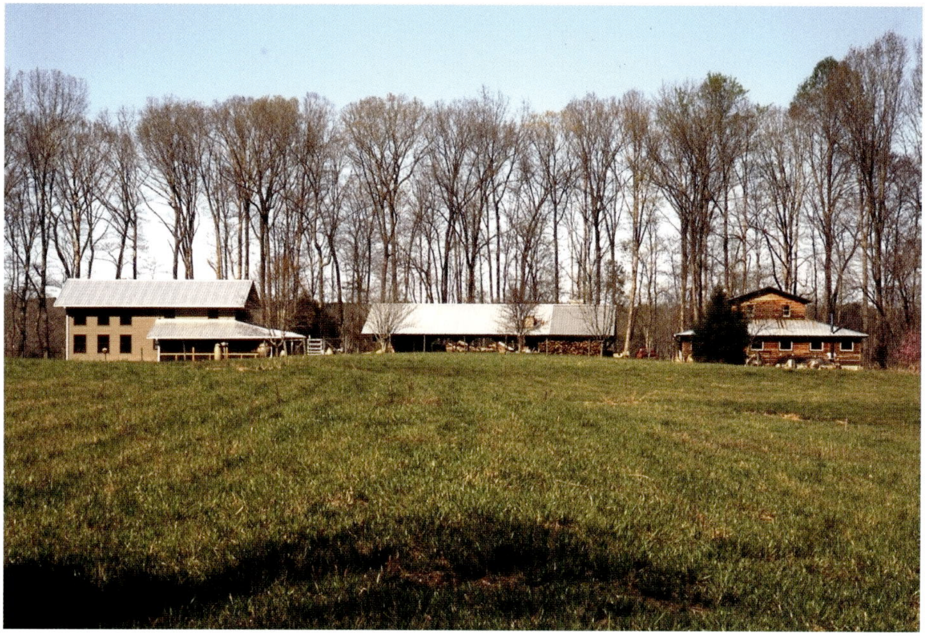

House, kiln shed, and workshop aligned on David Stuempfle's place,
Seagrove, North Carolina, 2016

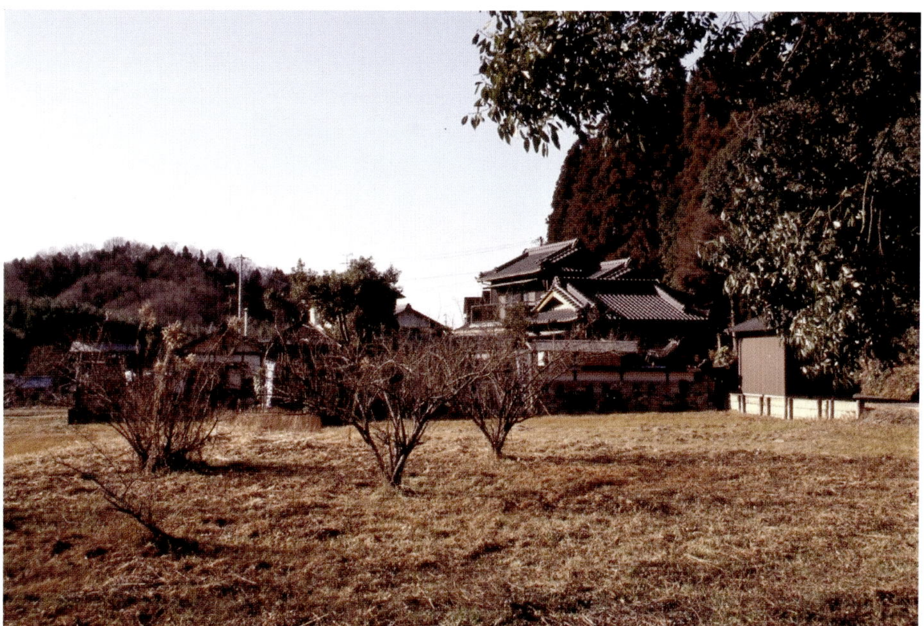

House, workshop, and kiln gathered on Maekawa Denko's place, Seto, Japan, 2005

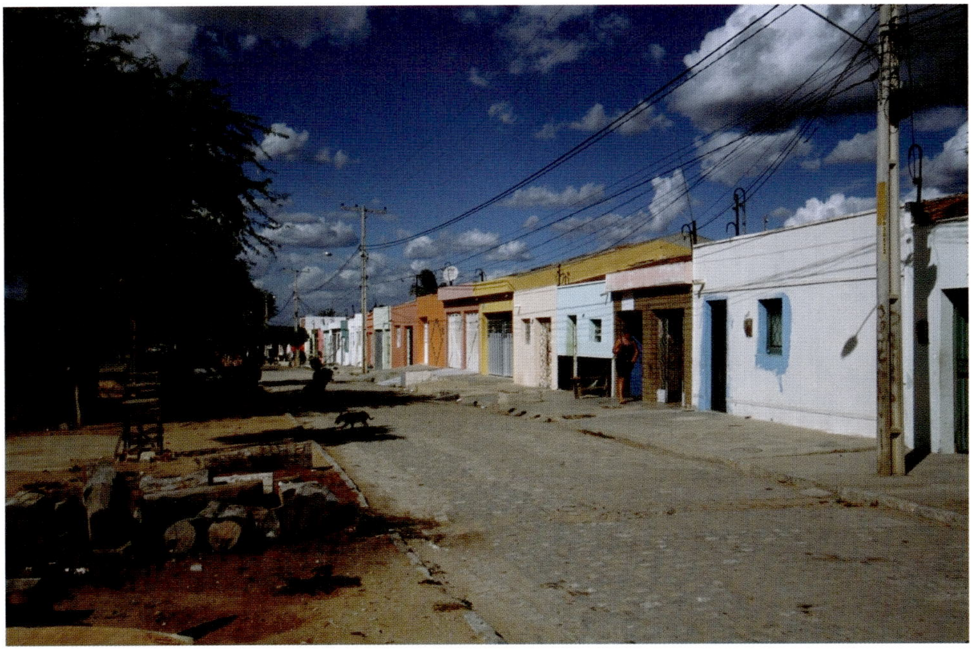

Rua Inés Rolim, the street of the carvers, Ibimirim, Pernambuco, 2015

Architectural configurations vary, but for comfort in life and efficiency in creation it matters most that the home, shop, kiln, and place for sales occupy the same plot. It is like that in the west, in England, for the potters Clive Bowen and Svend Bayer in Devon, and like that in the east, in Japan, for the potters Tatebayashi Hirohisa in Arita, Agawa Norio and Matsumura Takuo in Hagi, and Katō Susumu and Maekawa Denko in Seto.

Now widen the view. All the artists in Alto do Moura live and work on the same street, the Rua Mestre Vitalino, and in Ibimirim, all the artists live and work on the same street, the Rua Inéz Rolim. Familial networks knit into larger, more inclusive communal networks, and the artists have formed communal associations for mutual benefit. Control of their materials is a primary concern. Alto do Moura's association owns the clay banks beside the Ipojuca where only members of the association can dig the clay that is processed on the street of the artists and delivered to all the shops. In Ibimirim the artists joined to secure their right to use *umburana*, a rare local wood, soft and smooth to carve, that only they are permitted to use. It is the best wood for carving woodblocks, but woodblock artists like J. Miguel must content themselves with pine, and other *santeiros* are left with cedar, which takes form beautifully but is harder to work. Piles of *umburana* on the street signal the homes of Ibimirim's carvers.

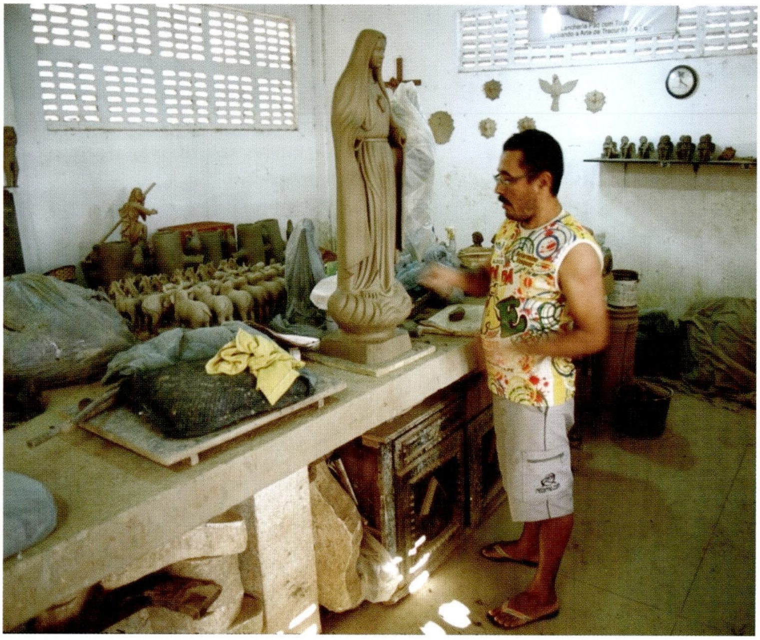

Antônio Alves Pereira, called Totinha, at work in the cooperative Centro de Artesanato, Tracunhaém, 2015

In Tracunhaém, the artists work in a section of the town that swings elliptically around two points: the Church of Nossa Senhora do Rosário and the Church of Santo Antônio. Within their space, they have established a communal center, the Centro de Artesanato, where the artists' works are sold and where artists who lack shops and kilns at their homes can work in clean studios and use the collective kilns.

Common problems and procedures unify the neighborhoods of artists in Pernambuco, yielding the sense of communal destiny that Marliete praised in Alto do Moura. Experience in Pernambuco positioned us in small towns — at the center of a spatial series with rural villages to one side and districts in big cities to the other.

When rural agricultural villages draw together around a single craft, art joins with cooperative labor in the fields and participation in religious ceremonies to promote collective solidarity. Women making pots in their homes in the pueblos of New Mexico and women weaving carpets in their homes in the highland villages of Turkey contribute crucially to collective identity and enterprise. Villages in Bangladesh concentrate on a wide variety of artful products: pottery in Kagajipara, bell metal vessels in Uttar Dariabad, fine extra-weft textiles in Rupshi, decorated split-cane prayer mats in Madhya Chandpur.

Urban districts also cohere around certain crafts. Pottery brings unity to the Kiyomizu district of Kyoto, weaving unites the Sonarpura district of Varanasi, woodworking unites the Tahtakale district of Istanbul. The shift in scale to the city generally brings two changes in its train, both exemplified in the city of Kütahya.

For one thing, the artists rarely live where they work (as they do in villages, and small towns). They live in highrise apartment buildings and travel to work. Familial connections hold but they prove less important for social coherence than the collegial connections among workers. Kütahya, like Alto do Moura, has a workers' association for collective benefit, though the most important cause for coherence lies in the circulation of artisans among the shops. Partnerships shape and break, new shops rise, old ones fall, and workers seeking advancement and artists seeking new opportunities move from one atelier to another. Their motion brings technical and aesthetic unity into the art and social unity into the city.

In the cities, first, collegial affinities prevail, and second, big ateliers become more numerous, and they assemble their force for work from widely beyond the master's family. In Kütahya, there are more small shops than large ateliers,

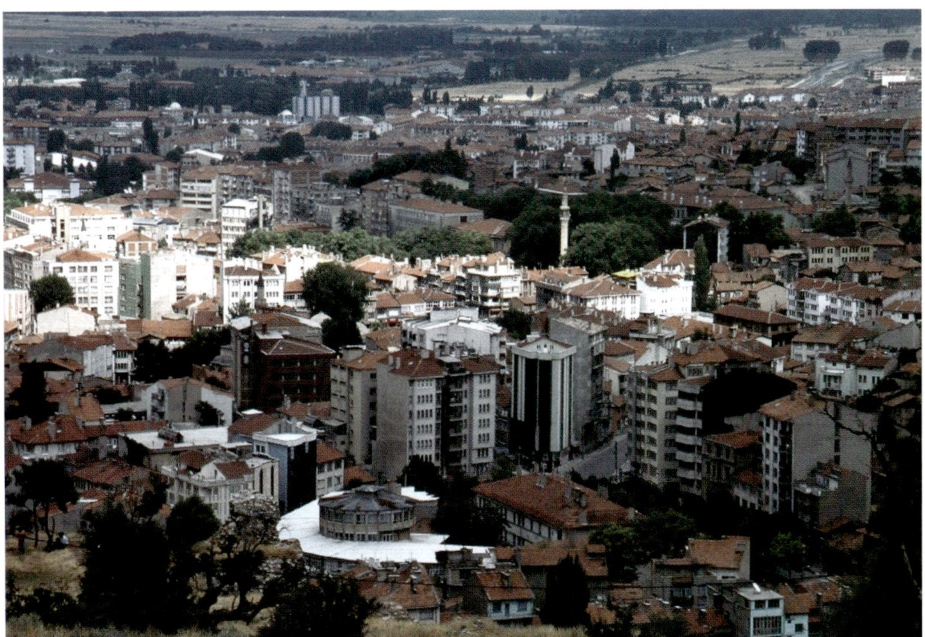

Kütahya, Turkey, 1997

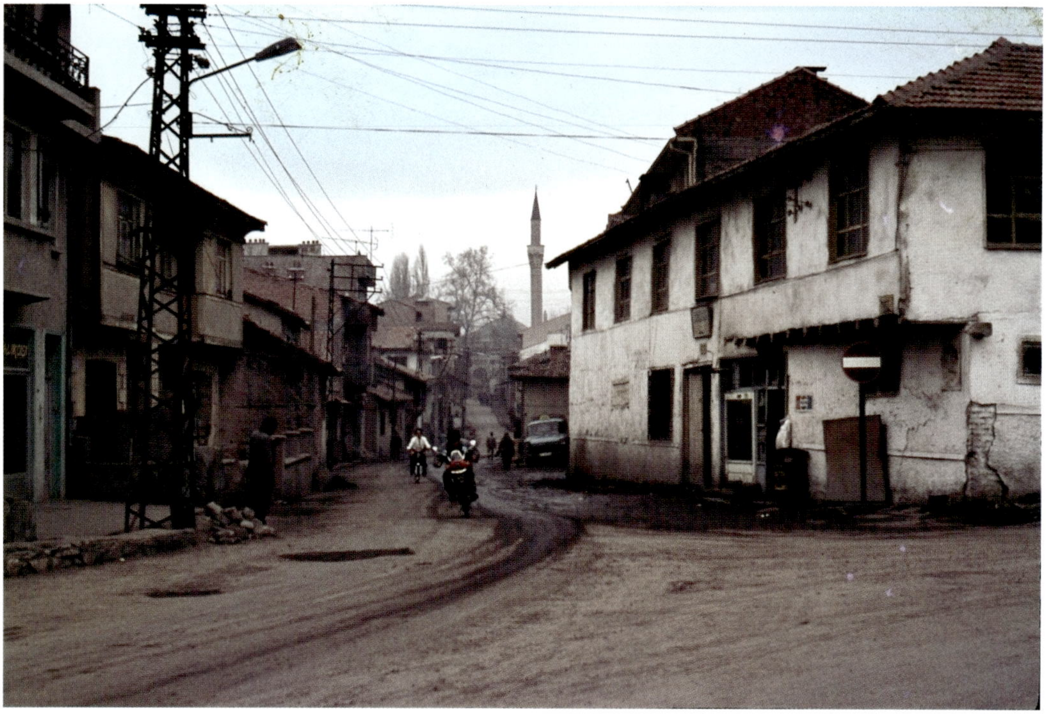

Large ateliers cluster in Eski Sanayi at the edge of Kütahya, 1985

the ratio around four to one, but the small shops depend on the big ones. In the past, mature women picked up pounced plates at the atelier, worked at home, and then returned the plates painted; some of these women gained local reputations for excellence. More recently, the artists in small shops bought bisque-fired plates or tiles from large ateliers, painted them, and, before the days of the electric kiln, returned them for glazing and final firing.

Pernambuco hints at the traits that typify the big urban atelier. In Alto do Moura, Paulo, Antônio, and Emerson work in the Zé Caboclo family shop, not far from the places they live. Normally each man works on his own artistic project, but occasionally, while Antônio concentrates on his own creations, the others make lesser things of little more than commercial value, and the shop's production diversifies as it generally does within large ateliers. In Kütahya, the ateliers — divided into sections and gathering a large workforce diverse in skill — can produce a full range of things for sale, from superb and expensive masterworks, through commercial-grade versions of painted plates and tiles, right on down to souvenir ashtrays. The variety in production that usually scatters through different small shops in Alto do Moura tends to unify in the big ateliers of Kütahya.

Smooth motion in collaborative labor requires momentary adoption of roles of the sort that separate sharply in big shops. At Bezerros in J. Borges's atelier, the artists divide from the workers. The artists — J. Borges, Pablo, and Bacaro — work on projects of their own and they design the blocks that the workers paint. In Kütahya, the artists — İbrahim Erdeyer at Süsler Çini, say, or Mehmet Gürsoy at İznik Çini — make their own masterworks, and they create the designs the workers paint. In both places, in Brazil and Turkey, the workers paint and chat together in big, clean spaces, bringing their own tasks to completion. It is not a regulated, industrial, assembly-line scene. In Kütahya, the girls in the shop put a favorite tape in the box and take a break to dance.

Continuity and Creation

Art flows from deep human desires. One desire is for connection, for connections between the generations that become connections among colleagues and register in art as continuity in time and consistency in space. The other desire is for freedom, for the right to satisfy the self in work, in creations that register in art as signs of the presence of distinct individuals.

The desires for connection and freedom, for collective continuity and personal creativity, can be argued into conflict, but they merge without tension in small family shops as a consequence of the process of learning.

The child is born into a home where the most interesting thing that happens is the creation of art. She sees her parents busily engaged. She plays with their clay, learning its feel, then watches, imitates, and matures into a creator whose work is continuous out of filial piety and personally distinct because her process of learning — based on watching and trying, guided by a few orientations but no formal instruction — opens the road to her own quest for excellence. The outsider sees her work and knows it comes from Alto do Moura; the insider knows it was made by Marliete.

In a familiar and productive domestic environment, loose learning enables self expression. The artists of Alto do Moura and Bezerros make that clear. At question is the learning process in a big atelier.

The young woman who will become a successful worker in a big shop in Kütahya has missed the first phase of open learning. If she had been born in a village home with a loom at the center of action, she would have played with scraps of dyed wool and watched her mother and big sister while they worked.

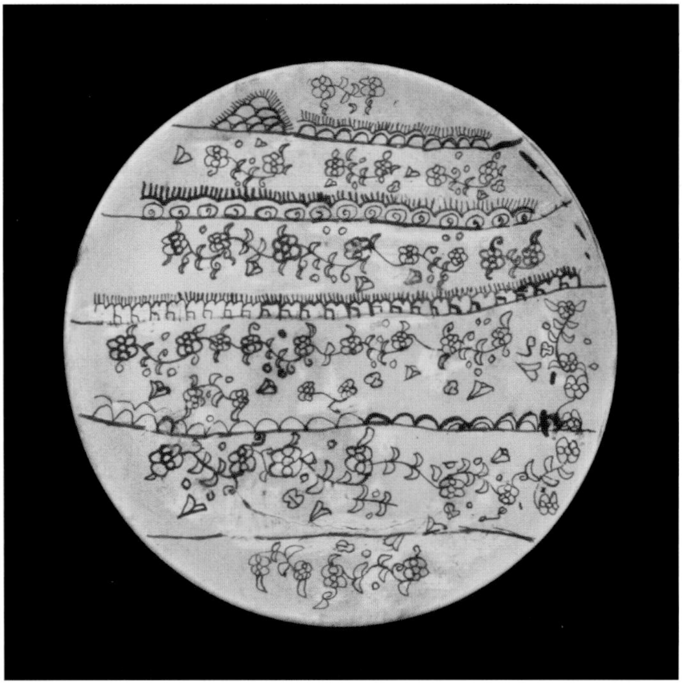

Beginner's practice plate (31 cm), Özen Çini, Kütahya, 1985

When she was tall enough to sit at the loom, she would already know what to do. The weavers consistently say that they weren't taught; they learned to weave just as they learned to talk — by being attentively present. Then sitting beside her mother she would begin the second phase of her life of learning, when between the ages of sixteen and twenty-four, before her marriage, she would work diligently within the youthful sisterhood of weavers to accumulate the wealth that would go with her when she married.

In Kütahya, the young woman enters the atelier at the beginning of this second phase in life, and she has to start from scratch. She is given a defective, blank, once-fired plate, a little pot of paint, and a brush. By doodling over the plate's surface, she teaches herself, getting the feel of the materials and learning the foundational hand skills. It is not easy. The paint, tinted slip, is thick. The brush is unwieldy, wide at the base to hold enough paint for long strokes, thin at the tip to leave a consistently fine line behind. The long lines in *çini* don't accumulate through a series of hesitant stabs; they sweep with the grace of a single motion. Once she can manage that, she can begin to paint over the designs pounced on plates. Her first efforts are cracked and trashed with slight comment. She knows the next ones must be better. She examines the examples of excellence hanging on the shop's walls, tries harder, and she starts to paint plates that can be sold as factory work for low prices.

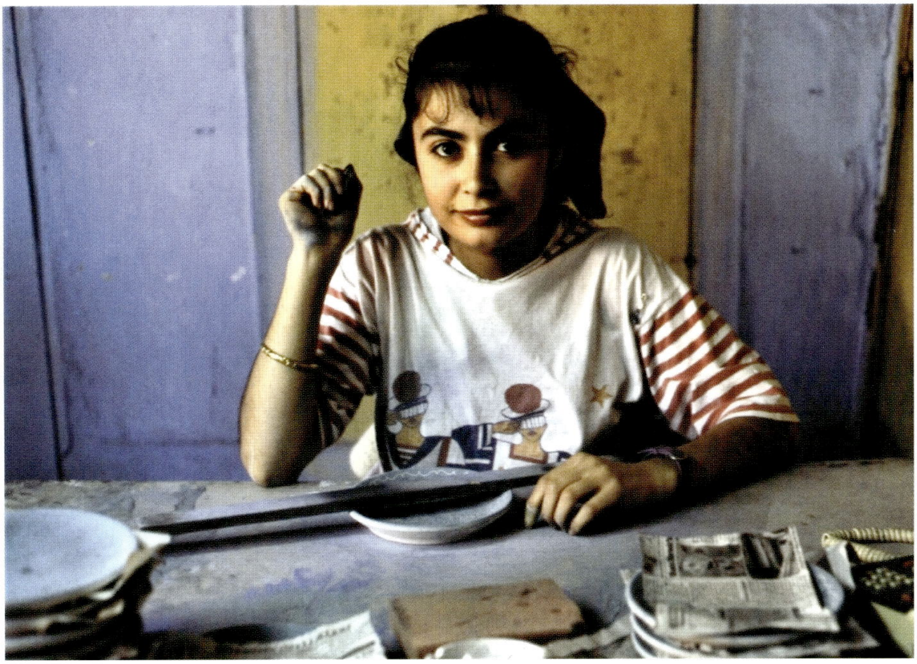

Filiz Kök, painter, Süsler Çini, Kütahya, 1994

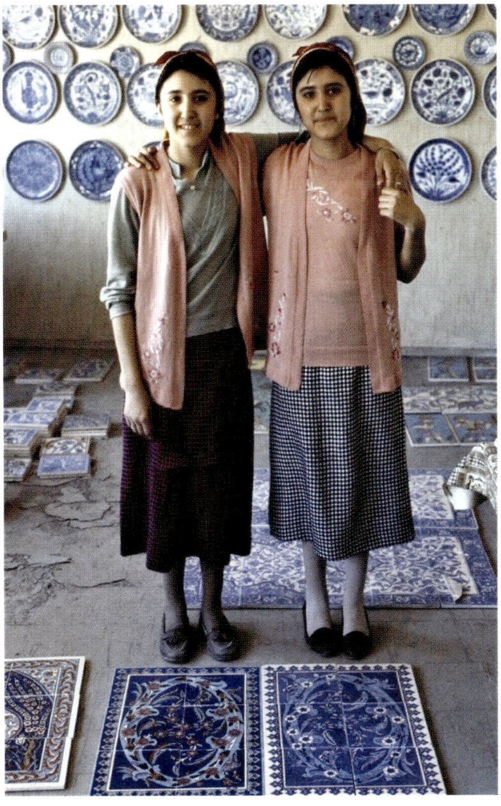

The Dönmez twins, Emine and Meryem,
painters at Işıl Çini, Kütahya, 1989

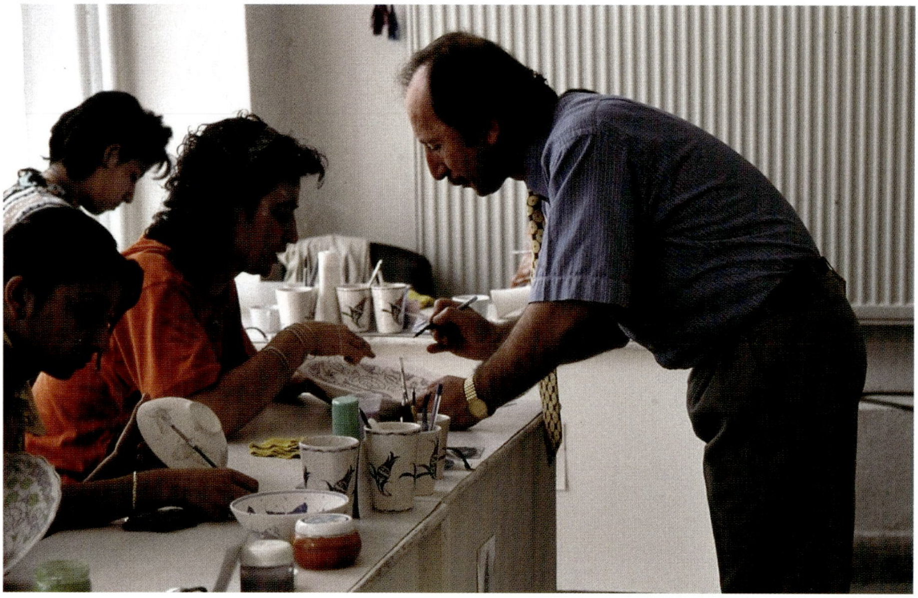

Mehmet Gürsoy teaching, İznik Çini, Kütahya, 1997

Mehmet Gürsoy is both a leading artist and a great teacher. He taught in a school before he dedicated himself to art. Taking a break from his own fastidious work, he strolls through the shop where the young women work at separate tables, pausing to answer the occasional question about technique. Periodically, Mehmet chooses a plate that one of them has just finished. Ignoring the flaws, he isolates its points of success, and, addressing them all, Mehmet offers a clear aesthetic orientation, but no instructions, leaving them to find their own ways forward.

Then married and mature in life's next phase — when only the weavers who love the art will continue steadily in the villages — many of the women who learned in the urban ateliers will leave the craft behind, but a few will work from home, a few will open their own small shops, a few will become teachers in big ateliers, and one, perhaps, will become a renowned master like Nurten Şahin.

Shifting in space and medium, we will offer a second instance. Edival Rosas lives with his wife, Izaura, above their shop on a steep street in the Pelourinho district of Salvador. Edival is the greatest carver of sacred images in his big city, and in his estimation one of the three best in Brazil. Outside of the city at Jauá, Edival has a shop where he works with an assistant on big projects, most of them commissioned by churches, and there he trains his apprentices.

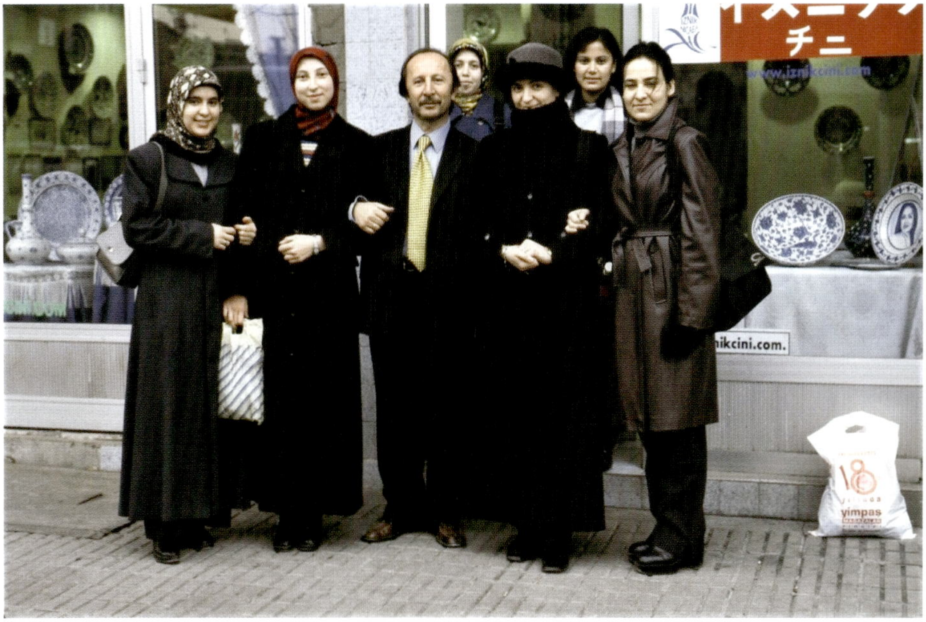

Mehmet Gürsoy with the young women of his atelier, Kütahya, 2000

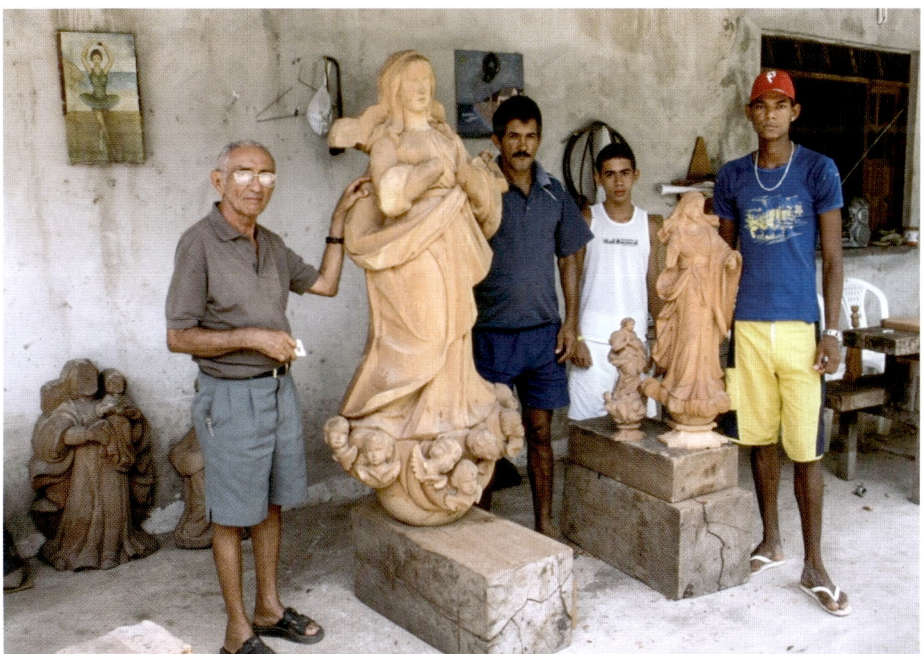

Edival Rosas with a statue of Nossa Senhora da Conceição in progress. His assistant Antônio, Antônio's son Victor, and Edival's apprentice Leandro join him at his shop in Jauá, 2007.

The boy in Jauá, like the girl in Kütahya, begins by getting a feel for the materials and tools. He starts with a stick of cedar in his hands, learning how it feels to cut with the grain, and then across the grain. Next, looking at a small statue and holding a piece of cedar in the same size, he draws no guidelines with a pencil, but using only a carver's sharp tools, he attempts a copy. That done, he begins to work beside Edival on a large image. Edival's statues of the saints range from less than thirty centimeters to more than two meters in height.

Knowing that the apprentices are shy around the master, Edival gathers all of them to watch while he demonstrates a stage in the process to the most advanced one among them. Then the inexperienced apprentices watch while the more experienced one works, and they teach themselves by emulating his motions. So it goes, slowly for years, until all of them can start and finish a large wooden saint on their own.

Edival Rosas contends that teaching with verbal precepts is hopeless. The apprentices can learn only by watching and working with the tools in their hands. He concludes that, at the most, forty percent — less than half of what a carver needs to know — can be taught. Far away in Japan, Agawa Norio argues that only the easy things can be taught. The difficult things must be learned in solitary struggle.

That is, in the small family shop and in the large atelier, art is, at last, self-taught. And that must be so if, as Marliete and Luiz Antônio said in Alto do Moura, the work of art can be immediately identified as the creation of a particular individual.

Art is conventionally divided into the taught and self-taught. Artists can certainly succeed without instruction, so long as they have access to inspirational models. Mestre Galdino in Alto do Moura is one in a great host of examples. But even if they begin with formal instruction, their art will become, through personal drives for excellence, self-taught. Consider writing. Writers are taught the alphabet, their compositions are corrected in school. They might even go so far as to take classes in creative writing at a university, but their effort will become creative only by reading much, writing much, and heeding the inner voice William Faulkner called the cop in the head. Through repetitive practice and harsh self-criticism their writing becomes self-taught.

Craft can be taught. Art, as Agawa Norio said, results from a solo struggle. The final work entails both. In Kütahya, the clay form is craft, its painting is art. In Alto do Moura, the clay form is art, its painting is craft.

Things are complex but clear on the ground. Creations issue from performances by unique individuals in specific locations. Continuity comes from willed acts of acceptance and transfer that can be traditionalized into collective heritage. The artists of Pernambuco know that, while there were others before, their lines of action stem from particular progenitors.

The acknowledged progenitors — Dona Zefinha in Ibimirim, Zezinho in Tracunhaém, and Vitalino in Alto do Moura — established the main lines in their towns by passing their art to members of their families and also to artists from beyond their families. In the secondary lines of Tracunhaém and Alto do Moura, the artistic tradition remained within the families of the progenitors, as it did in Bezerros.

This is a tradition of one type, begun in the twentieth century by remembered progenitors in places where works of art from the distant past don't survive in sufficient numbers to provide alternative inspiration or provoke revivals.

Revivals take many forms. The variety of revival that is enmeshed in a second type of tradition does not involve an appropriation of the alien. It is, instead, what the great Nigerian writer Wole Soyinka called selective retrieval when he was encouraging African artists to return to African sources. Retrieval is the word we need for acts of revitalization that entail returns to historical works from traditions that the artists consider to be their own. The old works become direct communications from the dead to the living. The modern artist, connected in place to historical works through continuity in technique — through carving, say, in Africa and Brazil — receives the message and retrieves from the works of the elders the inspiration required for aesthetic progress.

Back in Kütahya, the cruel war is over, the work has stopped, and Ahmet Şahin is about to partner with Hakkı Çinicioğlu and become the prime progenitor of the contemporary *çini* tradition with an act of retrieval that echoed an act of retrieval by Ressam Hasan Özkurt in Mehmet Emin's atelier thirty years earlier. Their selective retrievals overleapt the intervening era to concentrate on the ceramics from the Ottoman cultural zenith in the sixteenth century. They found their inspiration in the *çini* tiles revetted to the walls of the old mosques where people frequently gather for rest and prayer.

The artists who followed Ahmet Şahin in the twentieth century refreshed their vision with visits to two mosques in Istanbul, both designed by Mimar Sinan, arguably the greatest architect in world history. One is the mosque of Rüstem Paşa, built in 1561 at the bottom of the street of the long market

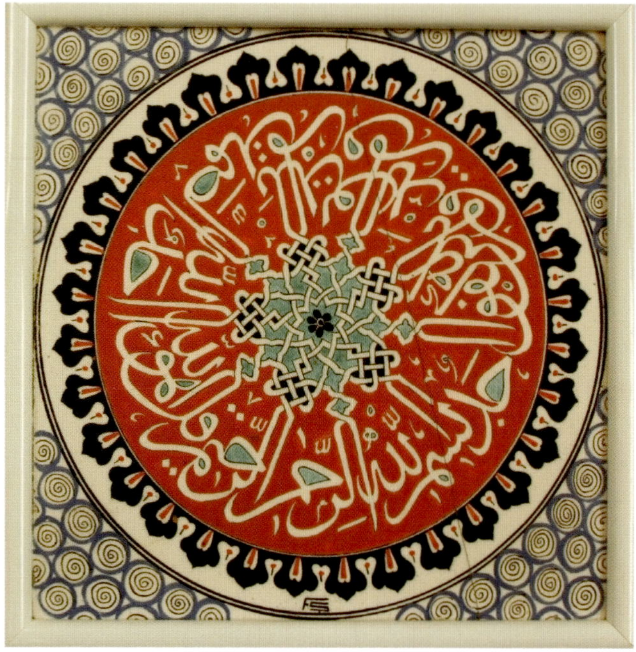

Çini tile by Faruk Şahin (22 × 22 cm), c. 1980, inspired
by the tiles in the mosque of Sokollu Mehmet Paşa

that rolls down through the district of Tahtakale. The tiles inside Rüstem Paşa clearly came from several different workshops during a period of experimental development. The other, across the old city in the neighborhood of Kadırga, is the mosque of Sokollu Mehmet Paşa, built ten years later when the tiles had reached perfection. Ahmet Şahin's son Faruk took his inspiration for a masterpiece from the tiles that flank the *mihrab* in Sokollu Mehmet. On a large tile he painted a circular calligraphic design that contains the text of sura 112 from the Holy Koran. Made about 1980, cracked but still magnificent, Faruk's tile hung on the wall of his beloved father's shop.

Beginning in the nineteen eighties, a rising tide of lavish publications with excellent photographs swept a treasury of historical options into Kütahya's ateliers. The modern repertory stretched around its sixteenth-century center.

On a pleasant evening in Kütahya, Mehmet Gürsoy, İbrahim Erdeyer, and Nurten Şahin gathered to drink endless tiny, tulip-shaped glasses of red tea. Their talk turned, as it always does, to their work.

All of them had created original designs of their own and painted designs created in the two generations before them. Still, they agreed that they most enjoyed painting floral designs with antecedents in the sixteenth century. Most

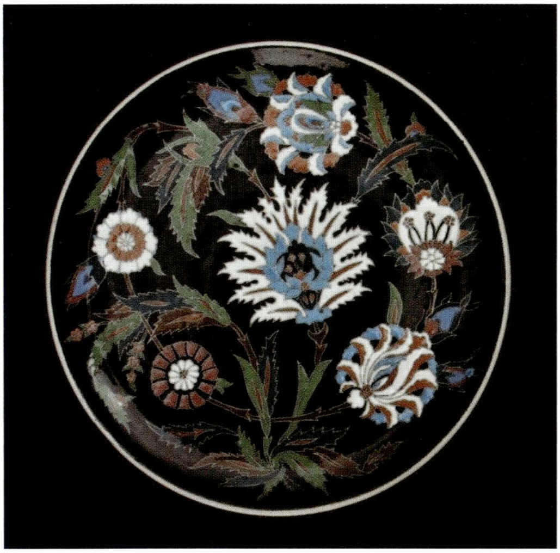

Çini plate with the whirling floral design, by Fuat Tuzcu (30 cm), Kütahya, 1987

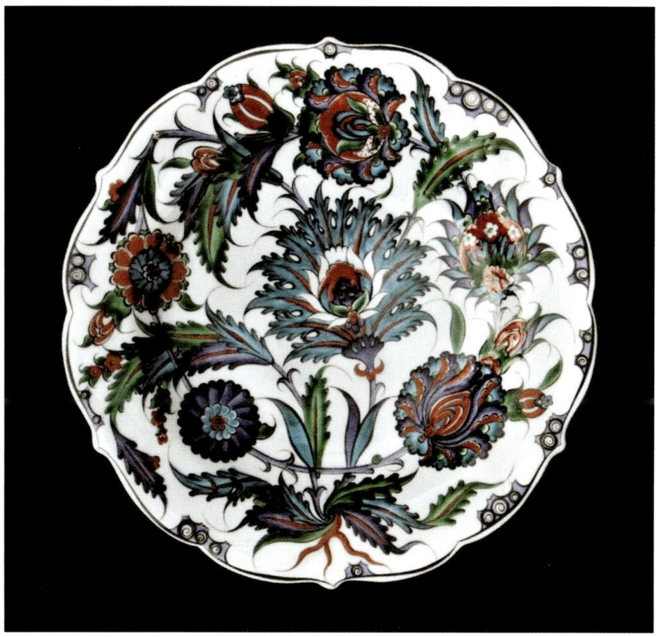

Çini plate with the whirling floral design, by Mehmet Gürsoy (30 cm), Kütahya, 2007

of those designs had long belonged to their repertories, but all of them most enjoyed painting a whirling floral design from a rare plate, created around 1545, held in a private collection, and pictured in several books. Adjusted by many artists to suit themselves, this design, vigorously executed in blue and white or in the full palette, appears on the plates featured in Mehmet Gürsoy's repertory, and he still featured the design in 2021, more than twenty years after that conversation.

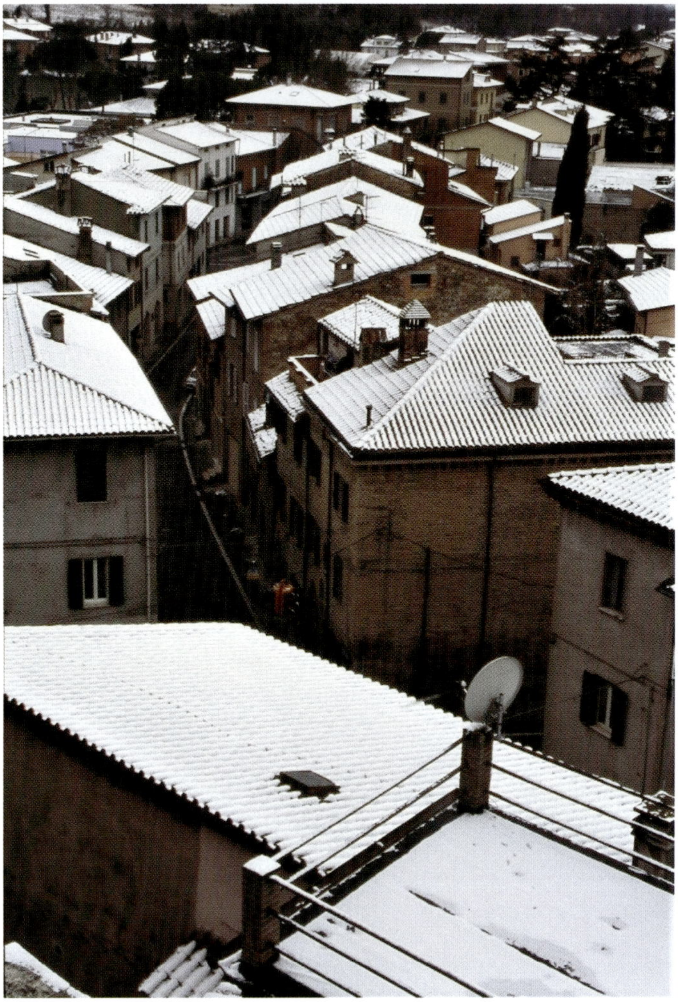

Deruta, Italy, 2012

Kütahya's pattern is matched in Deruta, a hill town near Perugia in Umbria. Deruta's art is *maiolica*. Like *çini*, *maiolica* is complex and rich with artistic potential. Plates are pounced and carefully painted, but the process differs. The fired *çini* plate is painted, coated with lead glaze, and then fired again. The fired *maiolica* plate is coated with white tin glaze, then painted and fired again. *Maiolica* differs in technique, palette, handling, and subject, but the lines of historical development run in accord in Turkey and Italy.

In İznik and Kütahya, and in Deruta, Faenza, Montelupo, and Gubbio, the art rose from the middle of the fifteenth century to its peak in the sixteenth century, the period of Sinan in Turkey, Michelangelo in Italy. Then it slowly drifted, shifted, weakened, or failed until a movement for revitalization began late in the nineteenth century — in Deruta as in Kütahya. In Deruta, Ubaldo Grazia, the son of the master in the town's main atelier, joined with the artist

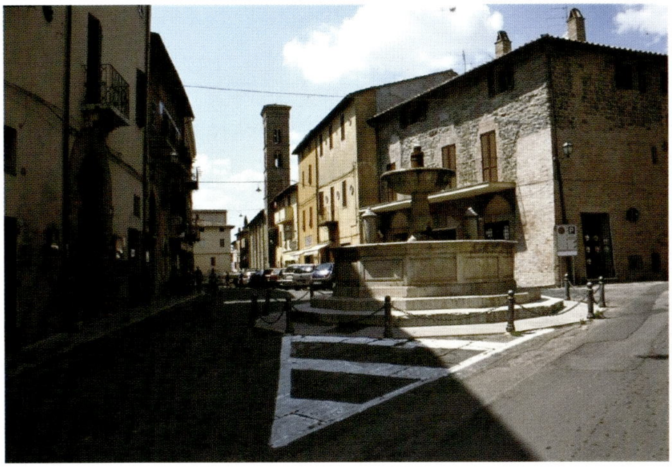

The plaza on the hilltop, Deruta, 2011

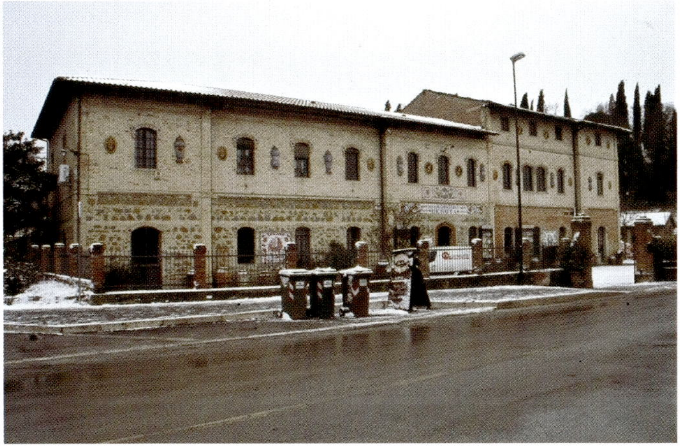

The Grazia atelier, Deruta, 2012

Alpinolo Magnini in the first decade of the twentieth century to mount a full-bore retrieval of the excellence of the sixteenth century, just as, less than twenty years later, Hakkı Çinicioğlu, the son of the master of the city's main atelier, would join with the artist Ahmet Şahin to recover — in a more perilous moment — the excellence of the sixteenth century for Kütahya.

Early in the twentieth century, the Grazia atelier was one of three workshops in Deruta. A century passes. The big Grazia atelier stands to the left on the road into town. Thirty-five more shops, mostly small familial operations, stand along that road, and another thirty-two stand up on the hill. The plaza on top has a fine museum dedicated to Deruta's historical ceramics. Opened during the phase of revitalization in 1901, the museum provides an instructive welcome to visitors and it holds a host of inspirational models for the town's artists.

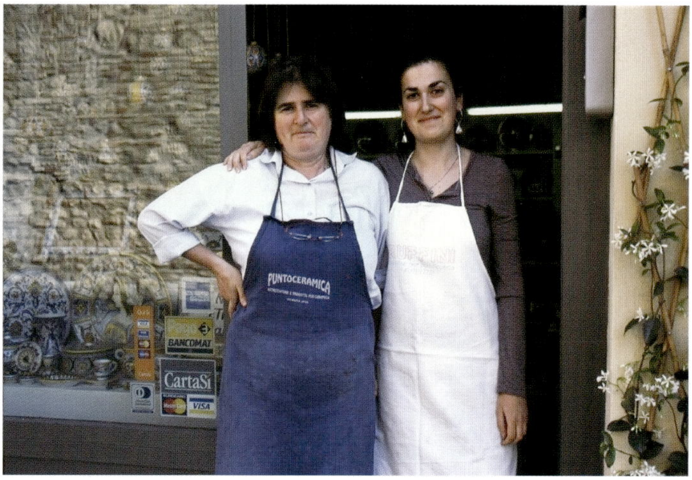

Chiara Bonini with her mother
Graziella, Deruta, 2011

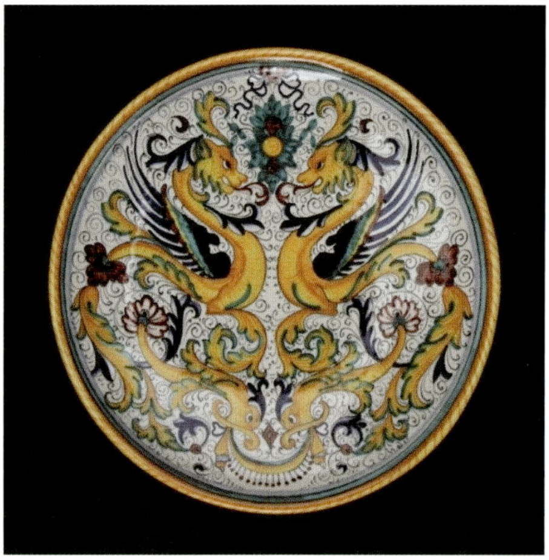

Grotesque plate, by Chiara Bonini
(28 cm), Deruta, 2011

Forever in flux, the repertories of the artists in Deruta, like those of the artists in Kütahya, widen beyond the sixteenth-century center, but four lines of action in Deruta link to the Renaissance.

In one line, Chiara Bonini, at work in the Nuova Etruria shop, paints symmetrical grotesque designs on white backgrounds for tableware, paints so well that her plates can be bought to hang on the wall. The designs are called grotesque because, about 1480, they were discovered in grottoes, in fact buried rooms from Nero's palace in Rome. Quickly adapted for interior decoration, grotesque designs were used by Raphael to ornament the Vatican Loggias in 1519. Evocative of the Renaissance, the designs are called *raffaellesche* more often than *grottesche* in Deruta. These Raphaelesque designs, generally dark in tone, were popular for *maiolica* masterpieces in the first half of the sixteenth

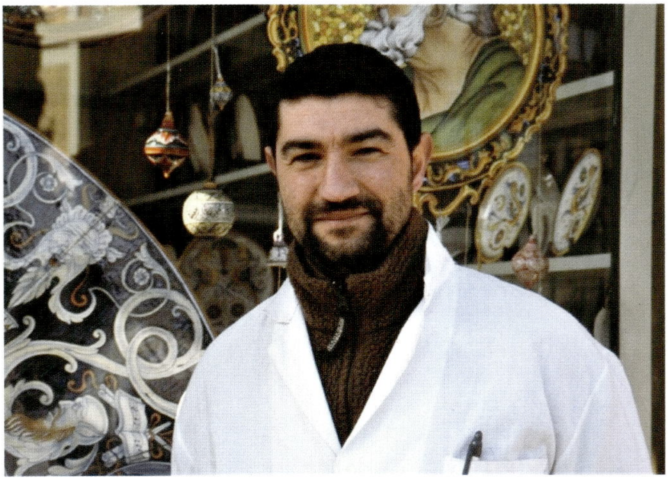

Gianni Marcucci, Deruta, 2012

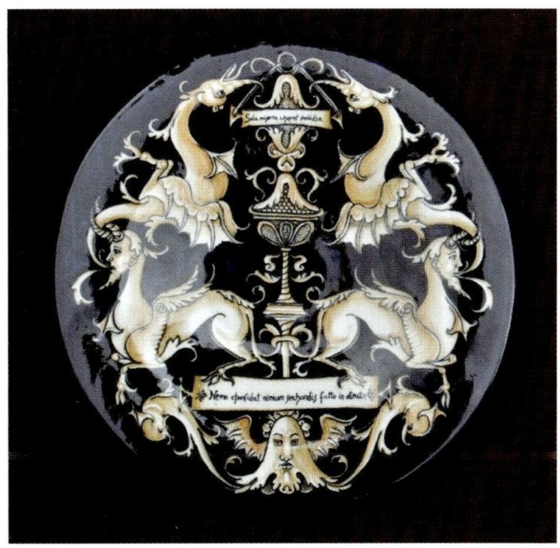

Gianni's replication of Francioli's plate (31 cm), 2012

century. Then painted on white grounds through the seventeenth and eighteenth centuries, the designs are used for fine tableware today in several Italian places of production.

At the foot of the hill, in the bright Marcucci family shop, Gianni Marcucci, an artist of great skill, connects to the Renaissance along two lines. He borrows from paintings by the masters, by Botticelli, Raphael, and Michelangelo, to create beautiful plates for the wall. And Gianni fastidiously replicates several of the antique plates made in Deruta. One of them, a grotesque masterwork on a dark blue background, was painted by Nicola Francioli in Deruta about 1525. On display in the Victoria and Albert Museum in London, the original has been featured in many books.

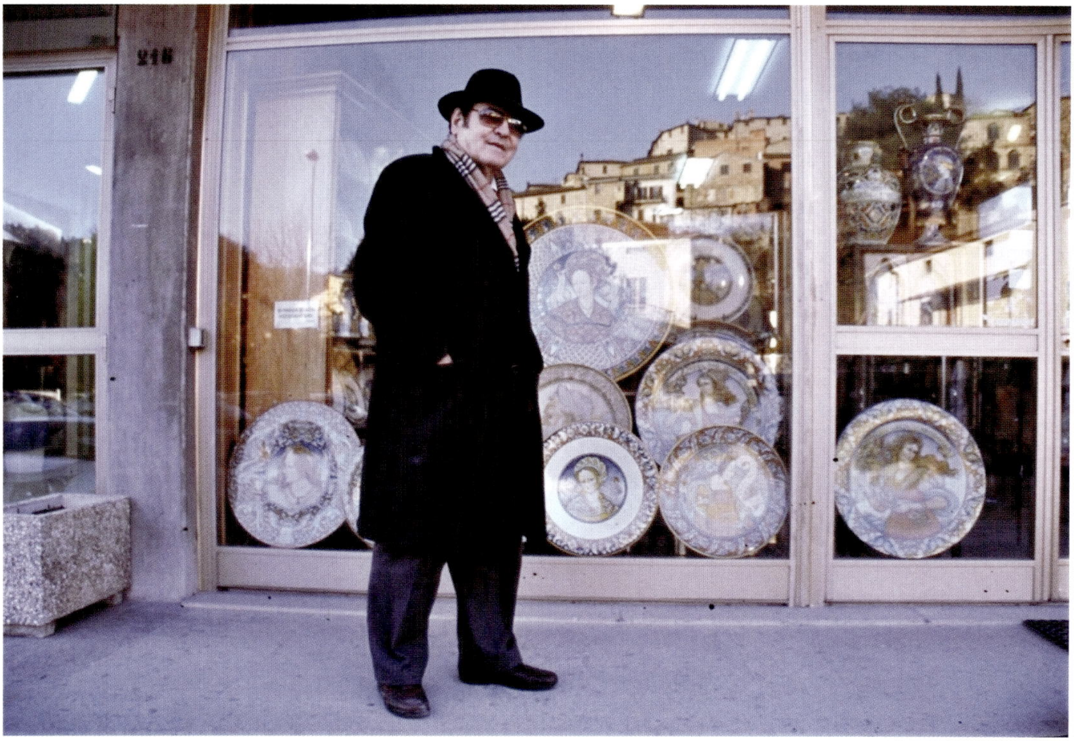

Antonio Margaritelli in front of his shop, 2012

The fourth line is Antonio Margaritelli's. He is the one man, they say, who works like the old masters. Chiara Bonini works in a line that flows through many Italian towns. Chiara's source is the tradition she shares with her mother, Graziella, and her brother Yuri. Gianni Marcucci works like many of his colleagues in Deruta to bring old art into new presence. Gianni's source is the historical record. Antonio Margaritelli finds his sources within himself.

Born up on the hill, Antonio apprenticed in the Grazia atelier, then worked in the shop beside the master Virgilio Spaccini before venturing off on his own. His shop, just down the street from Gianni Marcucci's, has a showroom in front and a space for creation behind, where he has worked for more than thirty years with his assistant Maria Tomassini. Maria uses Antonio's pounces to paint the borders for Antonio's plates and to paint plates with geometric designs, an underappreciated variety of abstract art that appears on historical *maiolica* and is painted excellently today by Maria in Antonio's shop, by Lorella Binaglia in a shop down the street, and by Anna Tiacci in the El Frate shop up on the hill.

Beginning early in life, Antonio visited construction sites in Deruta to pick through the mud for shards. His big collection of ceramic fragments prompts

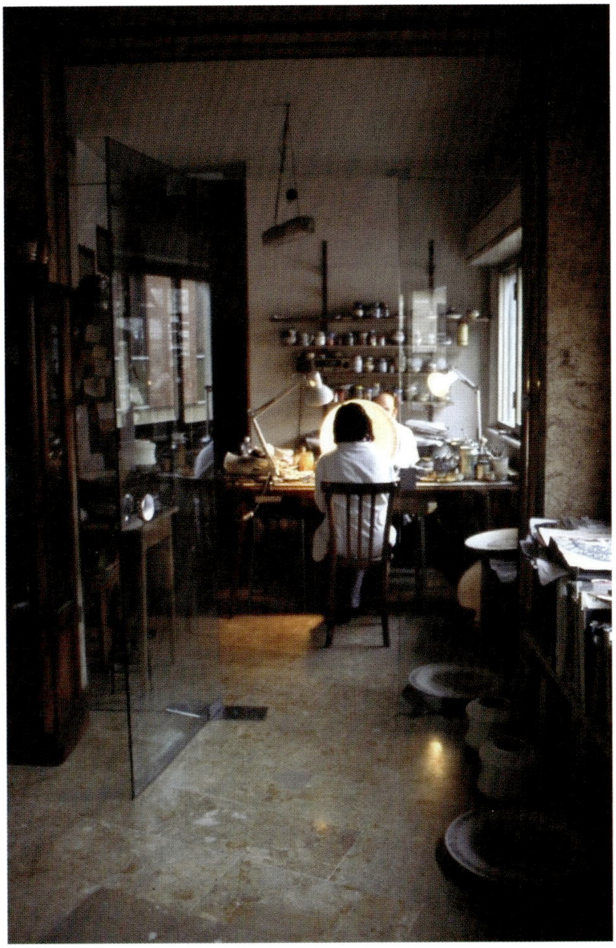

Antonio and Maria at work in Antonio's shop, 2012

richer profiles for plates and finer forms for standing ware like *albarelli*. He also has a big library — the *maiolica* bibliography is vast — and he knows the history. In creation, Antonio adheres to the generic categories of the past, but he innovates freely within them, making no copies, so his images of Saint Francis or his portraits of beautiful women gesture to history but remain insistently his. He draws from his mind, pricks his designs, and when he paints over the faint pounced traces, he departs spontaneously; every work is different. Confident in design, Antonio is most proud of his *colore*, the subtle range of hues in the paint he makes out of oxides and applies with grace.

In his shop's basement, Antonio has a gas-fired kiln. He fires first at about a thousand degrees centigrade. Then he glazes, paints, and fires again at a slightly lower temperature. And then he fires a third time, at a still lower temperature in a reduction environment, where the smoke from burning gorse blesses his work with the dark sheen of the best historical *maiolica* — the final touch of perfection.

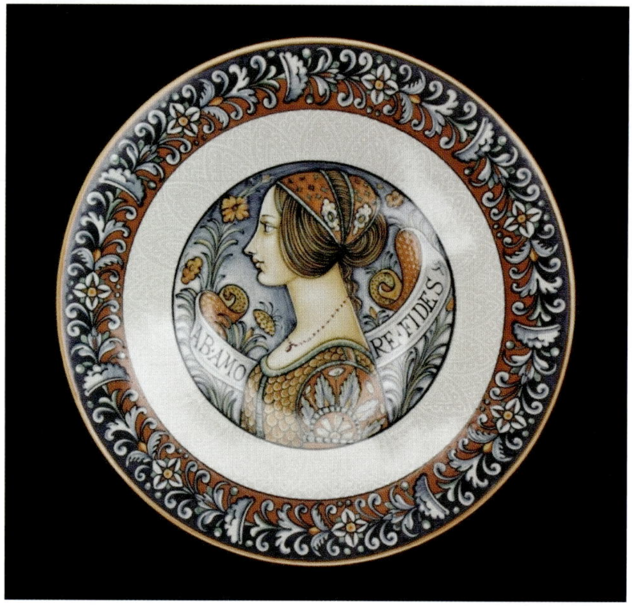

Maiolica plate by
Antonio Margaritelli
(35 cm), Deruta, 2012

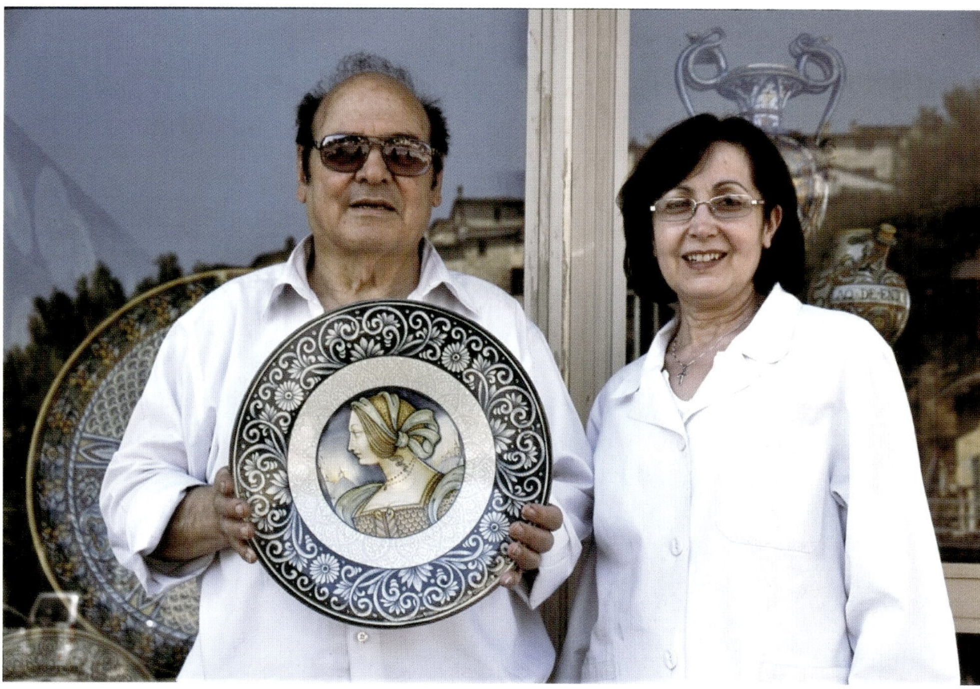

Antonio Margaritelli and Maria Tomassini with a new plate (35 cm), Deruta, 2011

Antonio Margaritelli says his work comes from his experience and passion. It comes from within, like the work of Ahmet Şahin in Kütahya who said that he spins his designs out of his gut just as a spider spins her web.

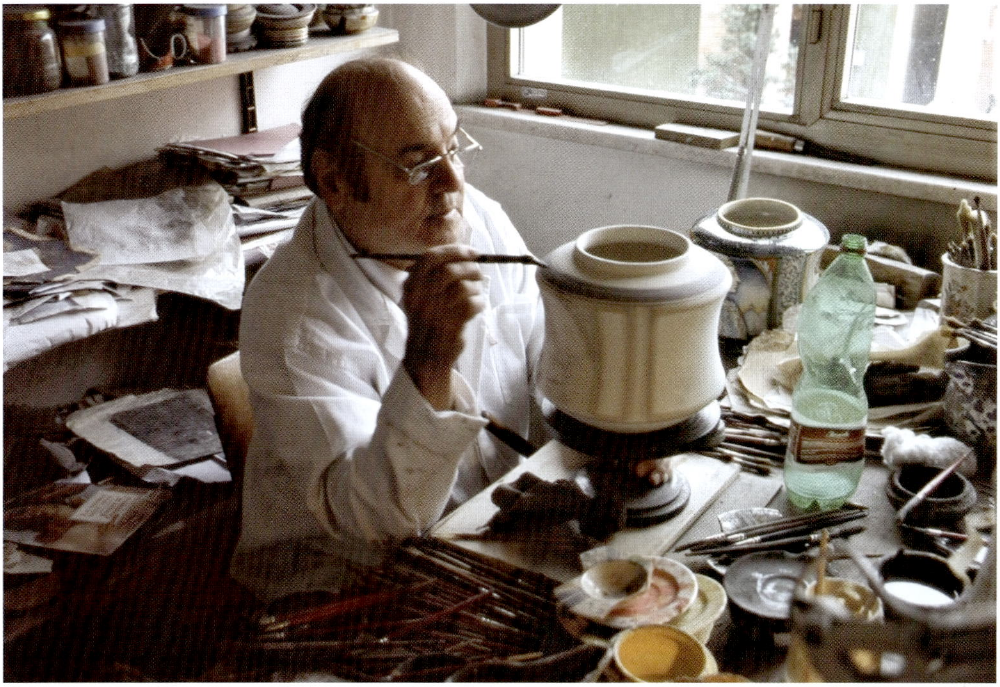

Antonio Margaritelli painting an *albarello* in his shop, Deruta, Italy, 2012

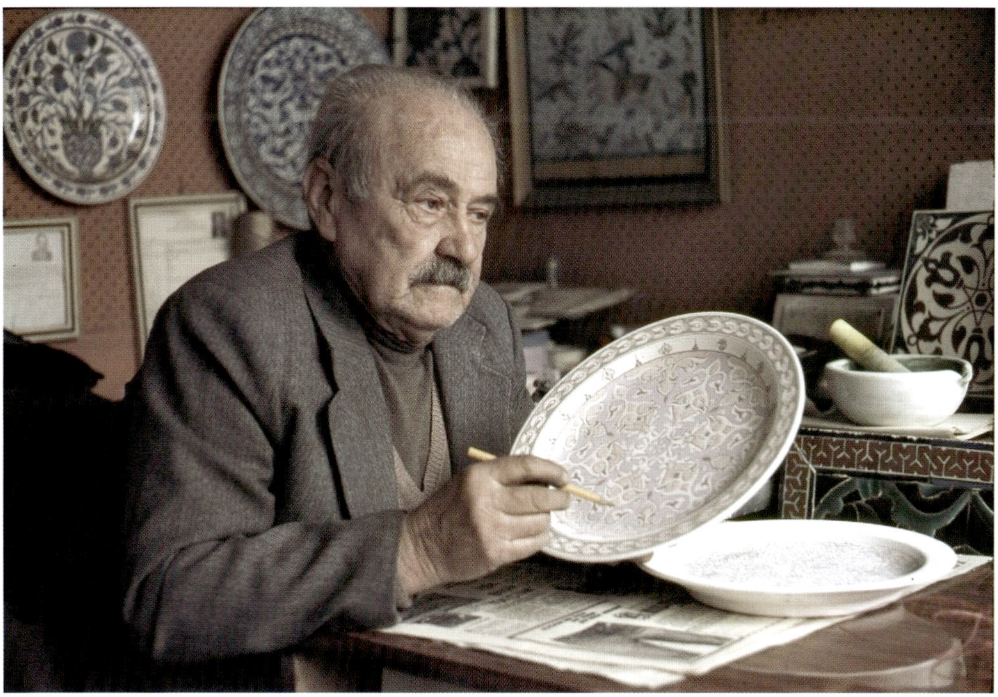

Ahmet Şahin in his shop, Kütahya, Turkey, 1985

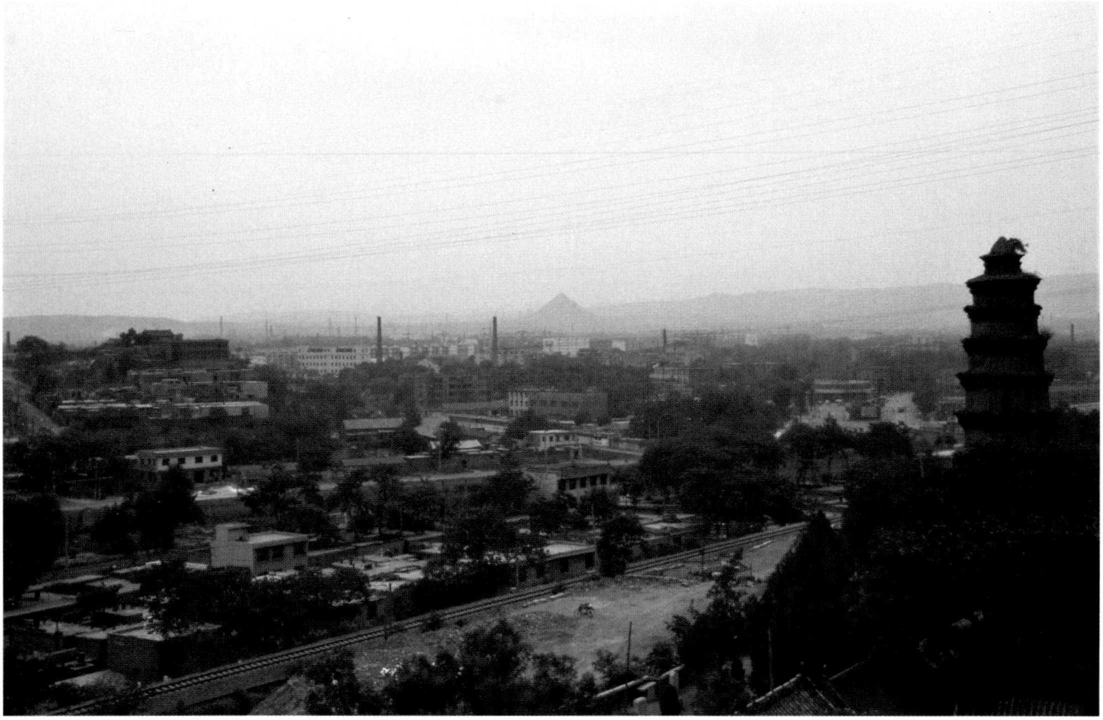

Pengcheng, China, 2000

For a third instance of retrieval in motion come to Pengcheng, a town near Handan in northeastern China. Pengcheng's art, a stoneware called *Tz'u-chou*, was made in more than thirty locations in northern China between the tenth and seventeenth centuries. Eventually abandoned in most places, it endured in Pengcheng to be revitalized later in the twentieth century as *çini* and *maiolica* had been revitalized earlier in the century.

The *Tz'u-chou* retrieval in Pengcheng is now in the hands of a small circle of artists who work in separate shops with members of their families: Liu Lizhong with his two sons, Ren Shuanghe with his son and daughter, Sun Xiuqing with her husband, and An Jiheng with his wife. They cooperate in firing and all hire additional help. Mr. An's shop is the largest, an atelier with ten employees, including a man to throw the pots, another to shave them, and a young woman to paint them.

Liu Lizhong, their leader, explains that the work continued through the twentieth century in as many as a hundred shops where utilitarian pots in vast numbers were speedily produced, using shortcuts like molds and jiggering. Competition from industrial products diminished demand in the nineteen-fifties, and with the Cultural Revolution of 1966, artistic work was prohibited.

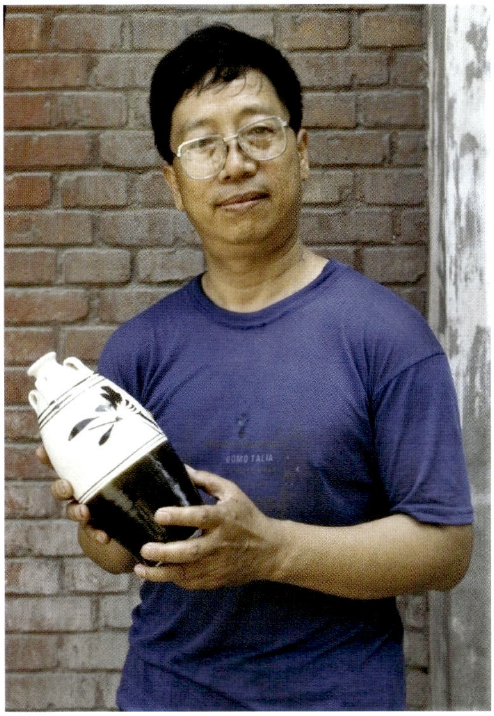

Liu Lizhong with a slipped and painted bottle he made, Pengcheng, 2000

An Jiheng with a sgraffitoed vase he made, Pengcheng, 2000

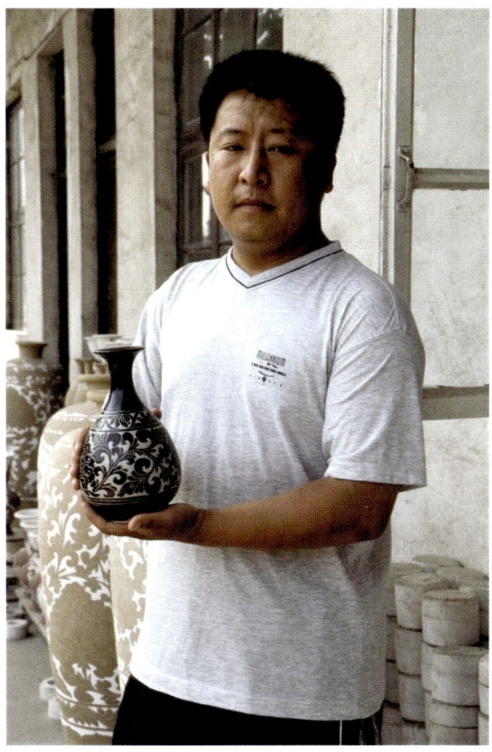

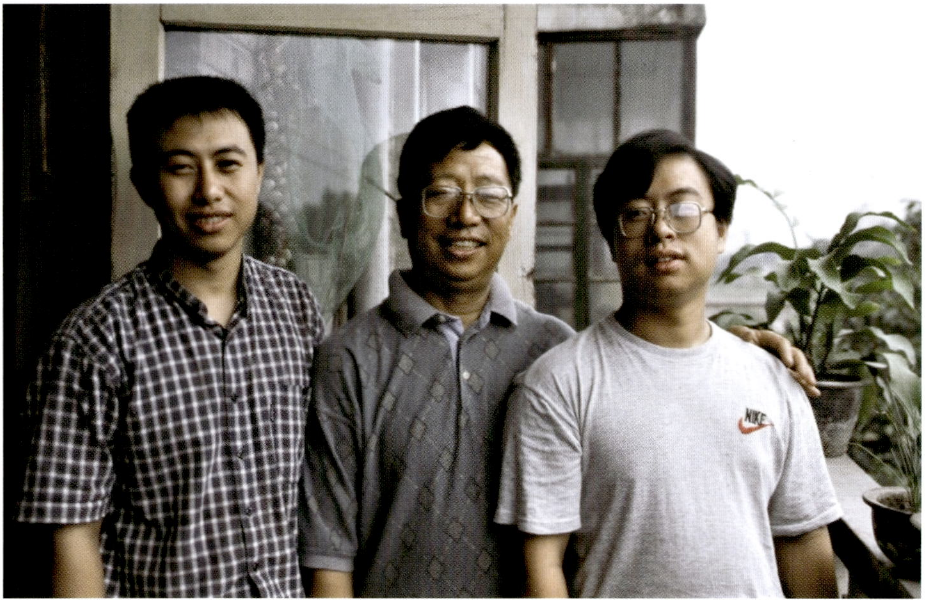

Liu Lizhong at home with his sons Pengrun and Pengju, Pengcheng, 2000

Mr. Liu defines his art as made entirely by hand and decorated with the techniques of the *Tz'u-chou* masterpieces created between the tenth and thirteenth centuries. Early in his twenties, he had begun to learn from a great master, the third in a famed sequence, but during the Cultural Revolution he was forced to find employment as an electrician. Then as the Cultural Revolution came to its end around 1976, Mr. Liu joined with others in a vigorous, concerted act of retrieval.

It was not easy. They were left with shadows. The pot, Mr. Liu says, is a shadow of the potter. The old potters are long gone. They must be met in their shadows, learning how to learn from them through the shadows they cast far in the past. The old potters' works — avidly sought by collectors in Japan, Korea, and Europe — are too valuable, too expensive for today's potters to own, so they collect shards, as Antonio Margaritelli does in Deruta, and Mr. An displays his collection of shards on a wall in his shop. Mr. Liu has also filled notebooks with excellent drawings of old pots and their ornament. From these shadows of shadows the modern masterworks of *Tz'u-chou* are born through the inventive effort of Liu Lizhong and his colleagues.

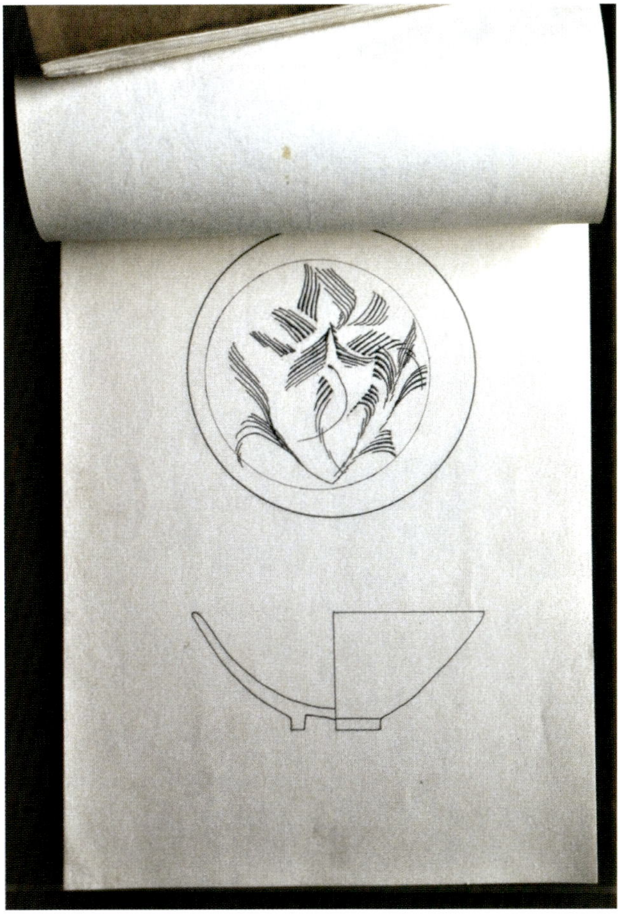

One of Liu Lizhong's notebooks with drawings of historical ceramics, Pengcheng, 2000

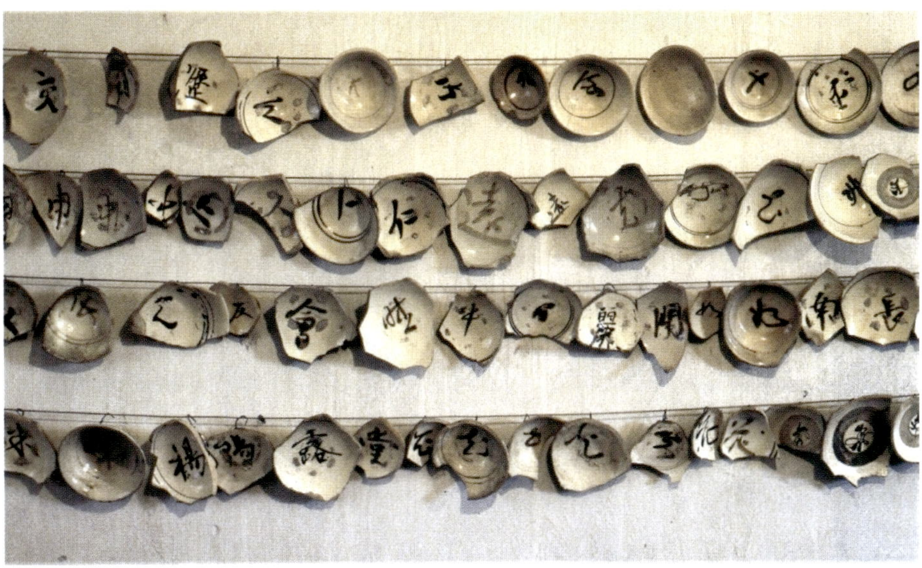

An Jiheng's collection of shards, displayed in his shop, Pengcheng, 2000

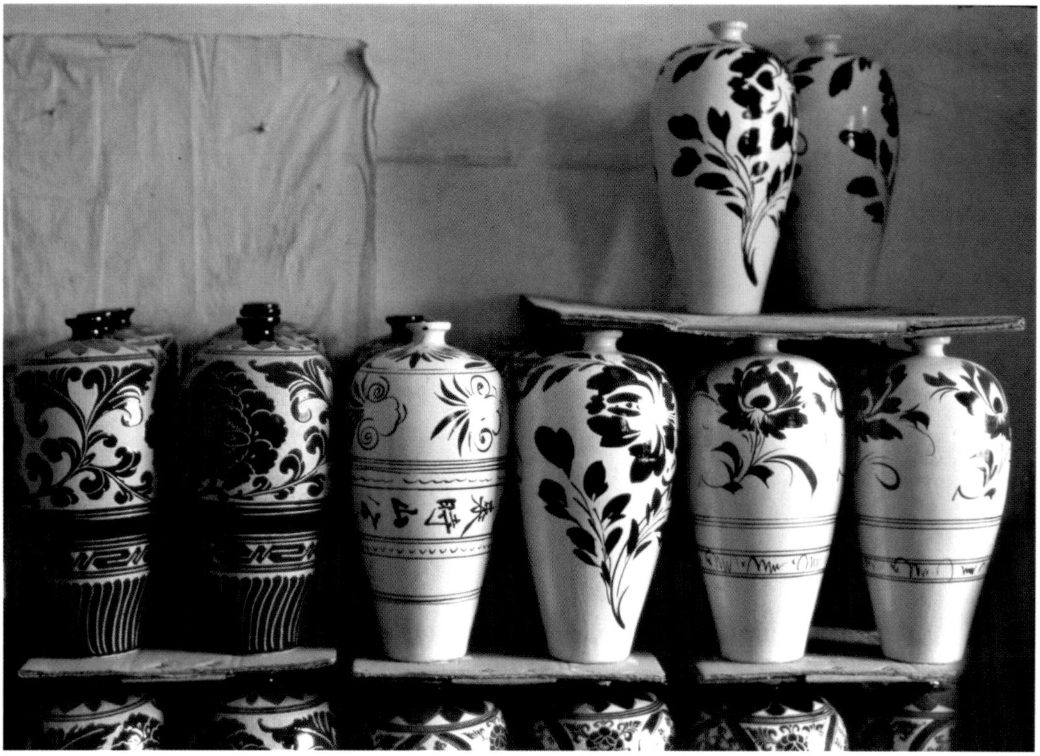

Tz'u-chou ware made by Liu Lizhong and stored in his shop, sgraffitoed to the left, painted to the right, Pengcheng, 2000

Their work's foundation lies beneath their feet in the seams of coal used in firing and the seams of clay they shape on the wheel. The pot, ultimately glazed and fired at 1100 degrees centigrade, is decorated today in three main ways.

In one, the gray pot is coated with white slip to provide, as in Acoma, a clean white ground for the brush in motion. Loaded with iron oxide in solution, the brush plays freely, gracing the surface with a spontaneous array of black figures from nature, flowers most often. In a second technique, the white slip is covered with a coating of brown, iron-rich slip that will blacken in firing. Then the brown slip is sgraffitoed, incised with a sharp wooden stylus to outline the usually floral figures. Then using a slim wooden chisel, the artist scrapes away the background between the figures, revealing the white ground beneath. This ancient technique is difficult and rare, though it has a parallel in the historical slipware of Devonshire in England. The third technique achieves the look of the second more easily. The brown slip is coated directly on the pot's gray body. It is sgraffitoed — incised and scraped — so the figures stand in low relief, and then the spaces between them are painted with white slip.

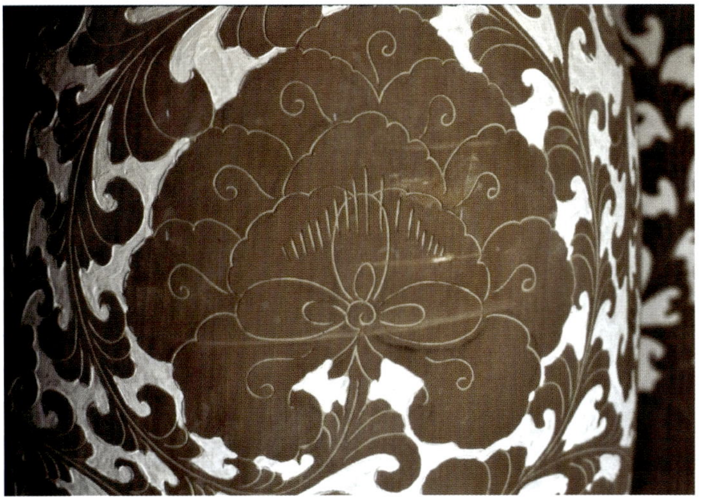

Sgraffitoed surface before glazing and firing in Ren Shuanghe's shop, Pengcheng, 2000

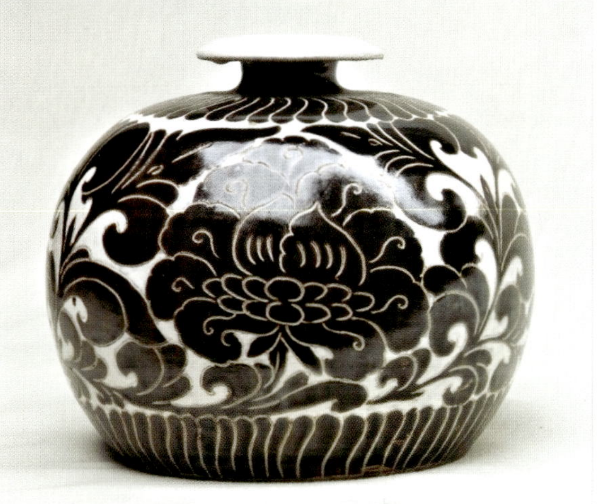

Glazed and fired *Tz'u-chou* bottle, by An Jiheng (15 cm tall), Pengcheng, 2000

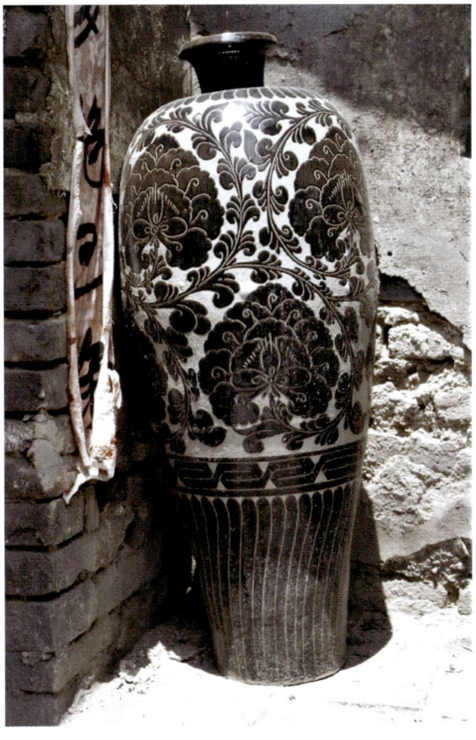

Tall, sgraffitoed *Tz'u-chou* jar by Ren Shuanghe, Pengcheng, 2000

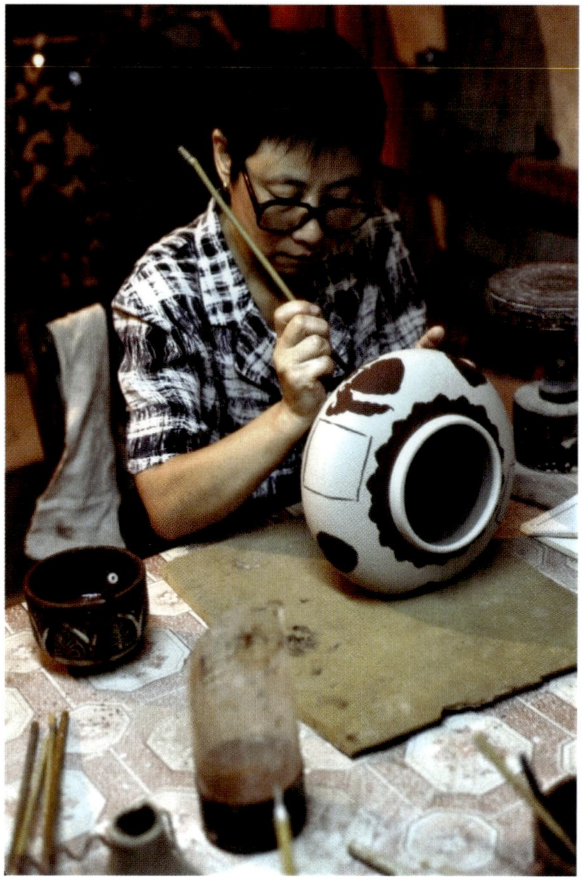

Sun Xiuqing painting an urn, Pengcheng, 2000

Loose in its brushwork, tight in its carving, Pengcheng's art is united by its black-and-white tone and diverse in its forms. *Tz'u-chou* ware has always included large works, and today gigantic sgraffitoed pots are made in An Jiheng's and Ren Shuanghe's shops to decorate gardens and fine restaurants. Sun Xiuqing specializes in making and painting urns for the ashes of the dead, specific commissions that include brief biographies and photographic portraits of the deceased. She and Mr. Ren also shape images. Figures have long been a minor part of the *Tz'u-chou* repertory. During the Cultural Revolution, they were statues of Mao Zedong; today they are most apt to portray Shou Xing, the deity of learning and longevity called Jurojin in Japan.

In Kütahya and Deruta, the artists look back to the high points of their traditions in the sixteenth century. In Pengcheng, they look even farther back in time. All of them gather inspiration from the past to move toward increased excellence in the future.

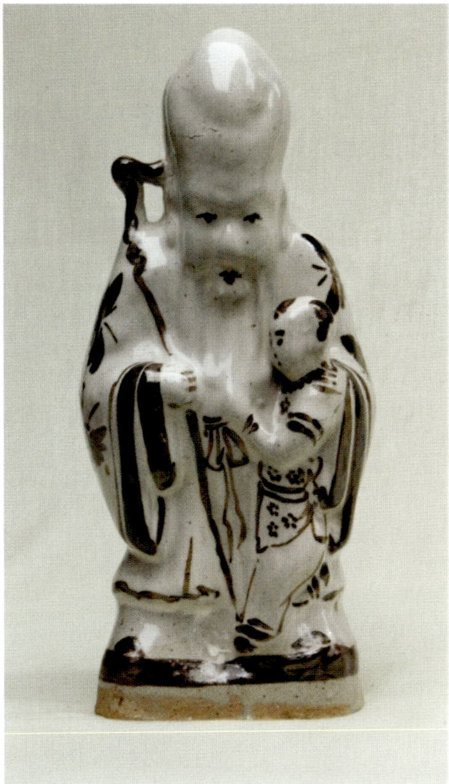

Shou Xing, by Sun Xiuqing (26 cm tall), Pengcheng, China, 2000

Tradition

Tradition is a name for both the received resource and the subsequent process of creating the future out of the past. These acts of receiving and creating bring continuity between the people of the past and those in the present who share the resources and processes that guide forward motion while contributing to social solidarity and satisfying personal desires.

In one of its characteristic contours, tradition moves through direct contact, person to person. Scholars, often being teachers, are apt to describe the process as teaching, though evidence from the field suggests that it would be more accurately understood as learning — learning from a master, rather than teaching a student. In Ibimirim, the center for sculpture in the Sertão, there was a carver of wooden saints before, João Desilda, but Dona Zefinha Paulino was the progenitor. Her husband, Pedro Ferreira da Sousa, learned from her. Nivaldo Gomes dos Santos learned from him, and then José Bezerra de Morais learned from Nivaldo. Another twisty route of direct contacts leads from Dona Zefinha to Mestre Manoel Cordeiro.

In a second of tradition's patterns, technical continuity provides a base for innovative moves. One move, demonstrated in Kütahya, Deruta, and Pengcheng, involves returning along the technical line to learn through artifacts from the unknown artists of the past in order to improve future production. In a second move, continuity in method provides a supportive frame for original departures. Manuel Eudócio, working in Vitalino's line, expanded Alto do Moura's collective repertory through his creative addition of the *Reisado*. Luiz Antônio, also following Vitalino's line, added modern images: women working on computers rather than making lace, electricians rather than farmers. Comparably, artists in nineteenth-century France held to their pictorial techniques while altering the imagery in a way that can be retrospectively read as a quest for the modernism of the twentieth century.

A third pattern in tradition rises from the appropriation of an alien technique to achieve a continuity of subject; tradition runs through topics rather than methods. The Nigerian painter Prince Twins Seven-Seven will lead us in. His father named him Bamidele, his grandmother named him Olaniyi, but when he took to the road as a fantastic dancer he named himself Ibeji Meji-Meji, Twins Seven-Seven, for he was the sole survivor from his mother's seven sets of twins. And, as the direct descendant of a king, he is permitted the address he prefers: Prince.

At the age of twenty, in 1964, Prince danced into the town of Oṣogbo, attracting crowds for the sellers of Superman Tonic, a cure-all concoction of river water and spices. One day in Oṣogbo, having nothing to do, he wandered into a studio where Georgina Beier was teaching art to young African men. Prince watched, then called for pen and paper, and starting in a corner he filled a brown sheet with an ink drawing, *The Devil's Dog*. Ulli Beier, Georgina's husband who had lived in Nigeria since 1950, said that the drawing, Prince's first, already bore the distinct Twins Seven-Seven stamp. Within six years, Prince's works had been exhibited in Europe and he was a famous man, launched on a life of travel and trouble.

Prince painted on canvas, learned etching, and invented his own method, the sculpture's painting in which a painting on a board is cut out and then glued to another board painted with the background. He used these foreign and novel techniques to depict, preserve, and revitalize the culture of his people, the Yoruba. Prince's career developed while Wole Soyinka was advising African artists to return to African sources. They knew each other. Soyinka was ten years older, but they were comrades in a cause, Yoruba men on a mission.

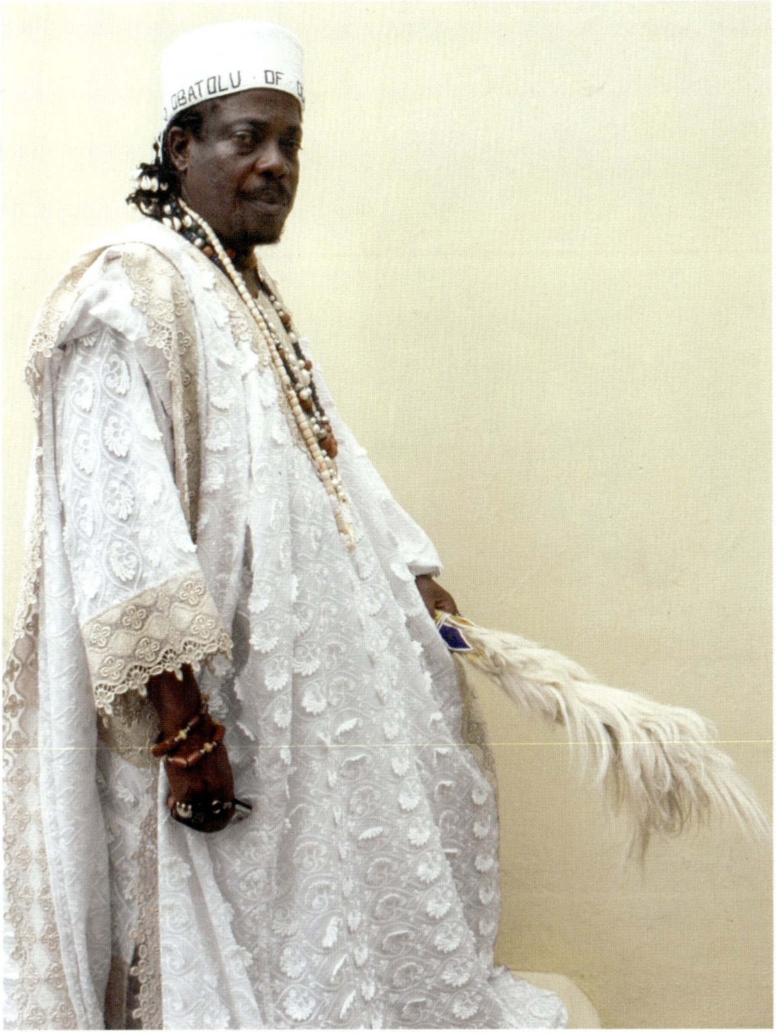

Prince Twins Seven-Seven, Ibadan, Nigeria, 2006

Wole Soyinka brought vitality into the old tradition through writing. Prince Twins Seven-Seven did it through painting.

Surveying the scenes of change around him, Prince can descend into melancholy. In one sculpture's painting, *The Last African Mask*, he identifies with the masked dancers of the old religion who stand in sad array, ignored by the people who sleep in the darkness behind them. Or he can turn critical. In *The Beginning of the End*, an alien priest holds a gigantic book, one page from the Bible, the other from the Koran, while a silly bird, representing the native people, recites without understanding texts from the intrusive religions. Prince's mother was a Christian, his father a Muslim, but Prince is a believer, devoted to the old faith.

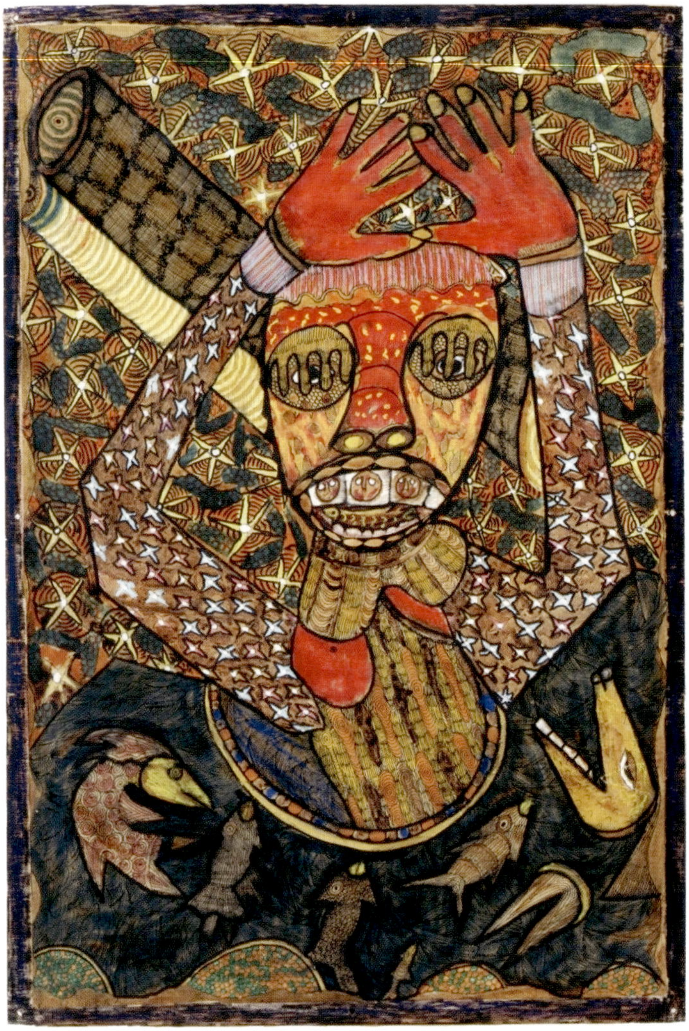

The Dream of the Abiku Child, by Prince Twins Seven-Seven (102 cm tall), 1967

One line through Prince's wild repertory carries the theme of his devotion to Ọṣun, the *orịṣa* of the sweet water. When he was born, his mother, Madam Mary, anxious to keep her boy in the world, went to a diviner who told her to give her son Ọṣun's water to drink. She dipped from Ọṣun's lake, Omielja, in Ijara where he was born. He lived, and in 1967 pictured the event in *The Dream of the Abiku Child*. The *abiku* is a child born to die, sent by the spirits again and again to torture the parents, but this one lives, rising to spiritual life from the dark water, alive with the fish that symbolize the powerful presence of Ọṣun.

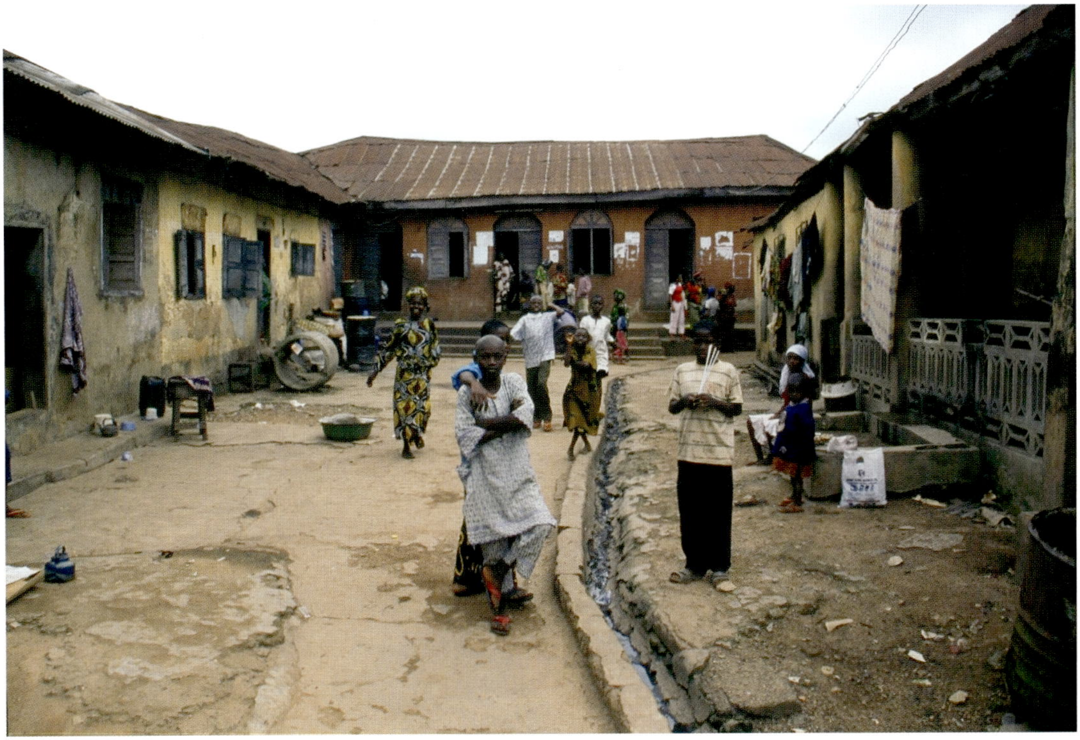

The palace, Ibadan, Nigeria, 2006

Prince's devotion to Oṣun is a personal obligation, displayed daily in the white clothing he wears, and it is a familial obligation. His great-grandfather, a military man who was the king of Ibadan for two years late in the nineteenth century, was named Oṣuntoki, meaning Oṣun is worthy of worship. Oṣuntoki's tomb remains in the old earthen palace in Ibadan. In the courtyard behind the palace, Prince's father, Aitoyeje, was born. In the courtyard in front of the palace, Oṣuntoki's descendant Chief Busari, though a Muslim, maintains the shrine to Oṣun where a priestess, Iyaoṣun, officiates on sacred occasions.

How could Prince not believe that Oṣun led him to Oṣogbo where his artistic career began? Oṣogbo is the capital of Oṣun state in the Yorubaland of southwestern Nigeria, and the River Oṣun flows past the town. Here in Oṣun's place Prince made his home — though base of operations would be more apt, since he was always on the move; his last great burst of creative energy took place far away in the city of Philadelphia during the first decade of the twenty-first century. But he built and decorated his rambling house on the outskirts of Oṣogbo, and on the outskirts of Oṣogbo, not far away, stands the prime shrine to Oṣun.

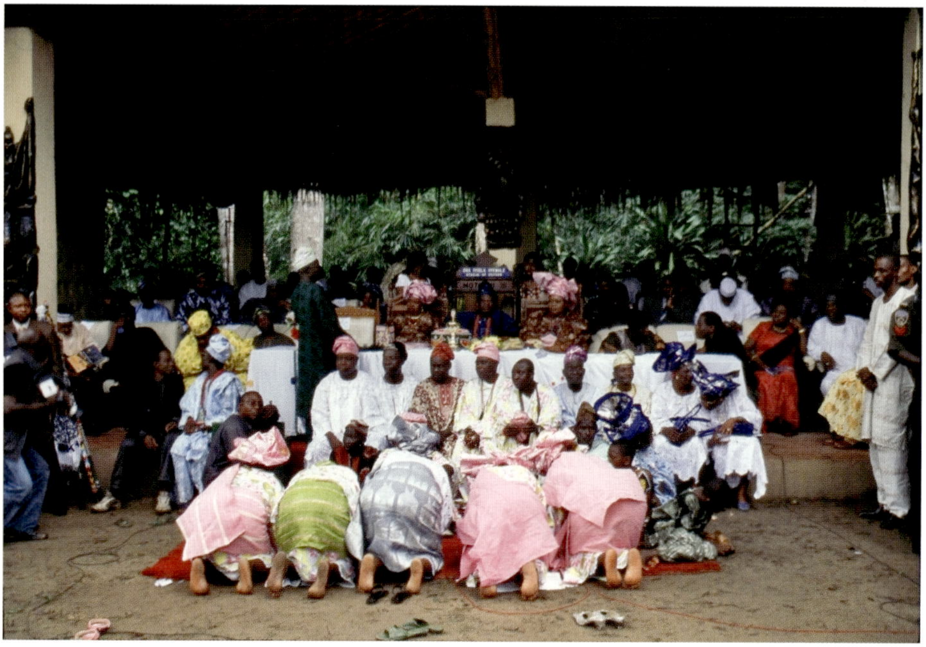

Reverence to royalty, Oṣun Festival, Oṣogbo, Nigeria, 2006

On the final Friday in August, the Oṣun Festival brings thousands onto the grounds around Oṣun's shrine. The drummers arrive early on the morning to lead Prince into the crowd that flows toward the pavilion where the royal family sits to be honored by groups of costumed dancers. A break for political speeches precedes the climax of Egungun, the dancer of the ancestral dead.

Through the day people turn away to pass through the gate to the thatched shrine. Removing their shoes, their bare feet on holy ground, they move in a tight line to meet the twin priests of the shrine, Aji-Ogbe, who give them a pinch of spiced yam and a sup of Oṣun's sweet water. In communion, they take the goddess into themselves and then squeeze through the slim slit of the gate, as though reborn. At the day's end they gather on the banks of the river, dipping sips of healing water and watching the river run on its way to the sea.

The river is Oṣun; she is a flow of sweet water. When a rainbow arcs in the sky, the fish swarm to give her form, and then they disperse. In Prince's numerous portraits of Oṣun, she takes the form of a woman or mermaid, and he takes care to show that her body has been shaped by a momentary assembly of fish. She is not necessarily beautiful. The notion that she is a goddess of beauty

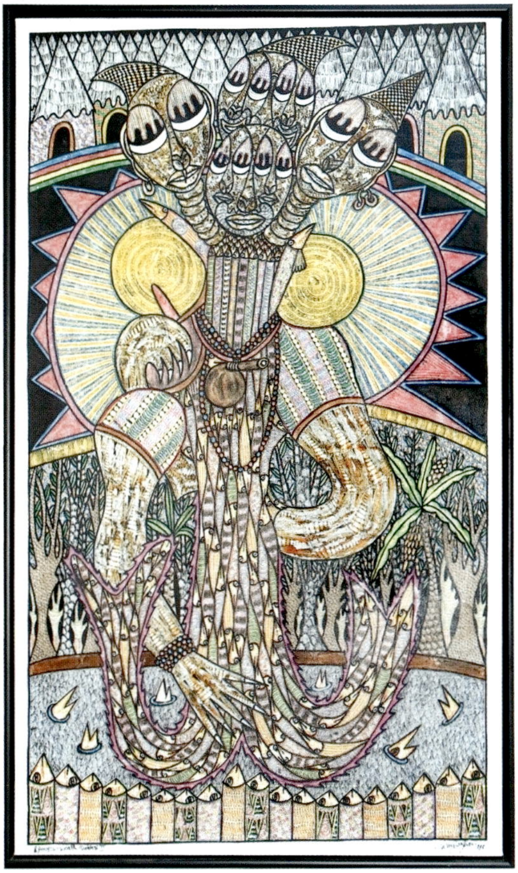

Rainbow Wealth Goddess, by Prince Twins Seven-Seven (141 cm tall), 1989

and love, a sort of Yoruba Venus, is, Prince says, the view of the uninitiated. As an initiate in her cult, he knows that she can be beautiful but she is certainly powerful, and her powers bring fertility, health, and wealth to her devotees.

In a masterwork from 1989, *Rainbow Wealth Goddess*, Prince employs a characteristic compositional format. Ọṣun rises into a vertical form in front of a background divided horizontally into zones, with a village at the top and water at the bottom, below a forest. Fish in the water sweep up to shape the split tail of a mudfish that joins into a narrow body with the long arms Ọṣun uses to help women, like Prince's mother, and their babies, like her son. Then above an explosion of light, Ọṣun has the four faces that govern the weather during the year's cycle of seasons. Her eyes have the slitted lids that allow her to see simultaneously into the world that people can see and into the world that is invisible to humankind.

This is not something that Prince has seen in the world. He has seen it only in the deep invisible world of his imagination. His inner vision was realized with foreign methods, with the pastels and oil paints on canvas that enabled cultural continuity in imagery. His painting is a celebration of the old religion of his people and a profession of faith to the *orịṣa* who gave him his life and art. Tempted by the contentious political powers of Ṣango, the deified fourth king of Oyo, Prince Twins Seven-Seven struggles to hold to the peaceful creative powers of the artist, granted to him at birth by one of Ṣango's deified wives, Oṣun.

Protected by Olokun, the god of the salt sea, Oṣun crossed the wide ocean with her people when they were thrown into slavery on the Brazilian shore.

Back home in Brazil, we will welcome Francisco Santos into the story, an artist whose creations align with Prince's: new in method, old in topic.

Francisco Santos has his wide, bright studio on an upper floor in an old building in Pelourinho, the historic center of Salvador da Bahia. Rolling down from a ridge then rising again to carry nine splendid churches, most of them built early in the eighteenth century, Pelourinho is an architectural treasure, a draw for tourists. Some come from Europe, a few from the United States, but most of them come from southern Brazil. Their best souvenir is a work of art, and in 2016 we counted eighty-two places where art was sold in Pelourinho.

The great sculptor Edival Rosas lives here, but the artists are predominantly painters whose works on canvas can be easily rolled up and taken away. Ubiraci Tibiriça paints the lush, natural landscapes of the Native people. Jó Silara paints the rural Bahian scene. Iraquitan Gomes da Sá paints the piled cityscape of Pelourinho. Ricardo Miranda paints portraits of black heroes. And Francisco Santos is Salvador's leading painter of the Candomblé deities.

Born in the home of a carpenter, Francisco was making drawings with scraps of charcoal at the age of seven. At fifteen he was taking lessons in a state school of art. It was in the nineteen-sixties, and the other students were painting pictures of Pelourinho, then in the midst of architectural restoration. Francisco alone chose to paint the *orixás* of Candomblé. Baptized a Catholic, he was the only one of his parents' ten children who went with his mother, an initiated participant, to Candomblé services. A little boy, thrilled and entranced, he stayed up all night to witness the whirling beauty of the ritual.

Candomblé, Francisco says, is the prime instance of the *cultura Afro-descendente*, the Brazilian culture of African descent. Developed out of African resources, right here in Salvador, Candomblé centers on a pantheon of Yoru-

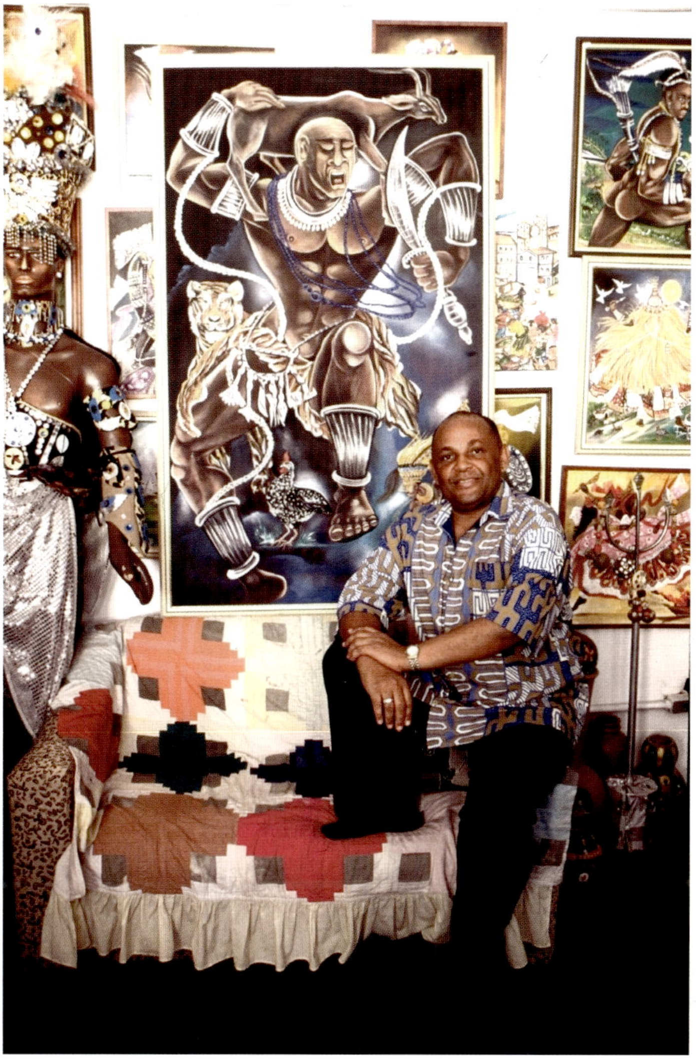

Francisco Santos in his studio, Pelourinho, Salvador da Bahia, 2009

ba gods: Xangô (Ṣango), Ogum (Ogun), Oxalá (Obatala), Oxum (Oṣun), Yemanjá (Yemoja), and Yansan (Oya). The *orixás* are also called *santos*, and they syncretize with saints, so in the past people could worship their old gods through images of saints, and today people who attend both Catholic and Candomblé services can inwardly praise as they please. Most consistently Yansan can be Santa Barbara, but Xangô can also be Saint Jerome, Ogum can be Saint Anthony, Oxalá can be Christ, and Oxum and Yemanjá can syncretize with various images of Our Lady.

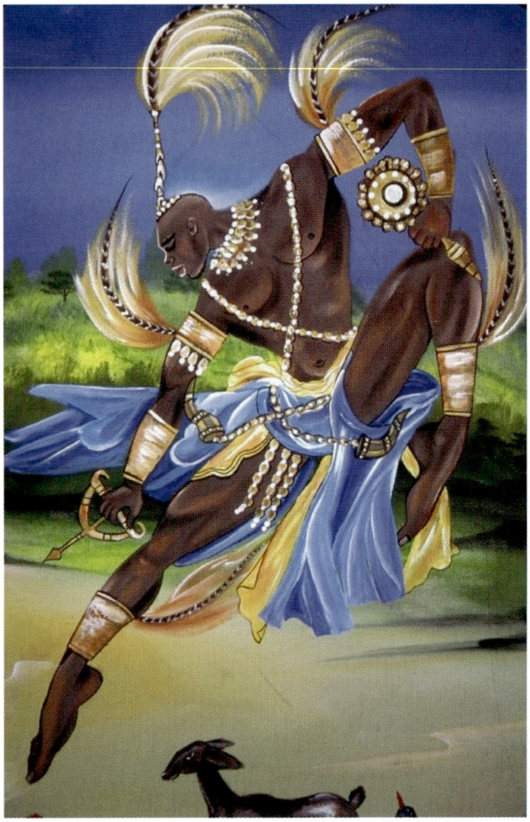

Logum-Ede, the youthful Ogum of the seaside, a painting in Francisco's "African" style, 2014

Francisco portrays the *orixás* in two ways. In the style he calls African, knowing that the *orixás* are beautiful embodiments of natural forces in motion, he shows them with perfect brown bodies, flung from the earth in dance. Francisco, like Prince Twins Seven-Seven, is a famed dancer and he draws from bodily memories to bring the gods out of his imagination. More usual in his repertory, though, are images based on observation in the Candomblé *terreiros*.

Drums set the tempo for the dancers who move in a counterclockwise circle. Slight shifts in percussive pattern signal different *orixás*, acknowledged by the dancers with slight shifts of motion as they continue — more women than men, all dressed in white — circling the wide hall's central post, a symbol of Xangô, the lord of justice. As time passes, one *orixá*, then another, comes down from Orun, descending to ride a devotee who shutters in possession, leaving the quotidian world behind. She — it is usually a woman — is taken by her friends into a back room where she is given a dress in the color of her *orixá*, gold if it is Oxum, and an emblematic *ferramenta*, a golden mirror if it is Oxum.

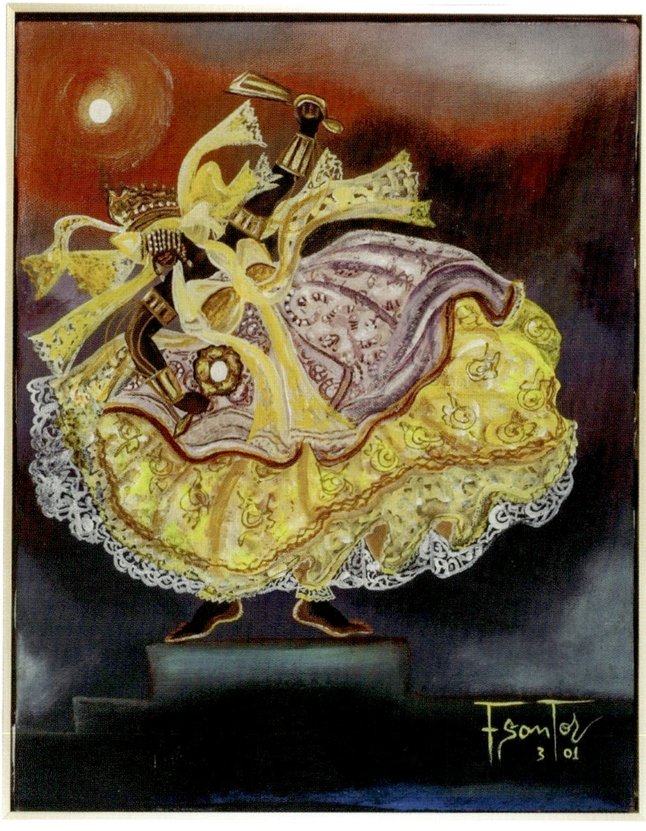

Oxum, a painting by
Francisco Santos
(50 × 40 cm), 2001

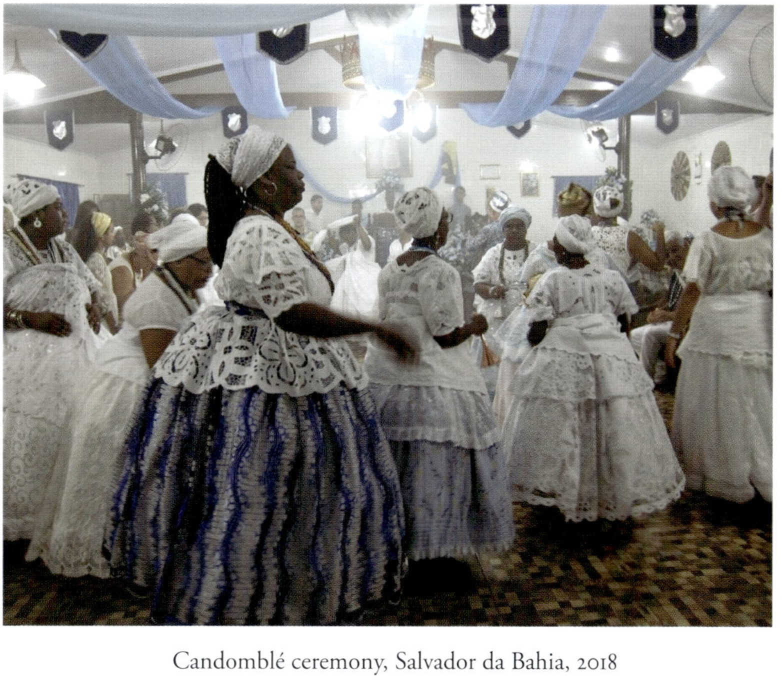

Candomblé ceremony, Salvador da Bahia, 2018

Now Oxum, she returns to the great hall where the people in white still circle to the beat of the drums and the people in possession swing to rhythms of their own with inexhaustible energy. A burly man, wearing a helmet and carrying a sword, is now Ogum, the celestial smith, and he dances in masculine power to honor the enthroned priestess of the *terreiro*. A gay man, liberated in the blue silk gown of the goddess Yemanjá, spins with grace. Several women in Oxum's gold transfer divine blessings by embracing the spectators, men on the right, women on the left. The great circle dance will go on for hours. Then the service will end, long past midnight, with a feast, when all will dine together in communion.

Francisco watches, understands, then in solitude he paints. His most usual images don't show an *orixá* lifted from his imagination — like his "African" figures or Prince's *Rainbow Wealth Goddess*. Instead, they represent an *orixá* through a dancing devotee of the kind he has seen throughout his life. It is wrong, he feels, to depict the *orixás* in static, iconic frontality like saints. The *orixás* are forces of nature in motion, and dancers in motion logically follow. In the churches, the saints appear in wooden, polychromed statues. In the *terreiros*, the *orixás* appear in the bodies of the dancers. The dancer's movement is the first indicator of the *orixá* whose color and *ferramenta* are the keys to identification — in the *terreiro* and on canvas.

The *terreiro* is plain, impeccably clean, unadorned. It is unlike the church with its statues of saints on the high altar and in four or six altars along the sides. The only image theologically essential in Candomblé is Exú, the Yoruba messenger of the gods, the force of connection between the earth and the sky. Made of iron by José Adário dos Santos, Samuel Rodrigues, or Jorge Pacheco, one or more statues of Exú are seated in the *terreiros*, hidden out of sight. *Orixás* on display are uncommon: still, paintings of the deities by Francisco Santos hang in about twenty *terreiros* in Salvador, including all of the noble old houses: Casa Branca, Ilê Axé Opô Afonjá, and Gantois.

Though once reviled — and reviled still (as Catholicism is) by the Evangelical minority — Candomblé is now a widely valued aspect of Brazilian heritage. Francisco Santos makes it his business to expand understanding by bringing the *orixás* into the public. He supplies inexpensive photographic prints of his paintings to the stores where Candomblé beads and props are sold. He has published two small paperbacks with photos of his paintings: *Africa Bahia*, in 2000, with sixteen *orixás*, beginning with Exú and ending with Oxalá, and *Os Deuses do Panteon Africano*, in 2004, with seventeen *orixás*, beginning with Oxalá and ending with Exú.

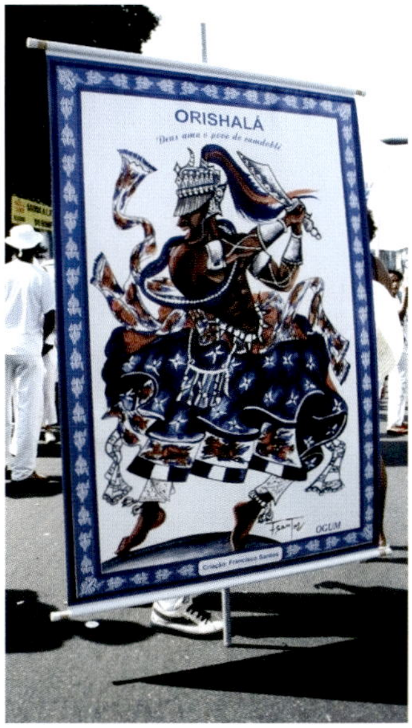

Banner of Ogum, by Francisco Santos, ready to lead the walk of faith, 2007

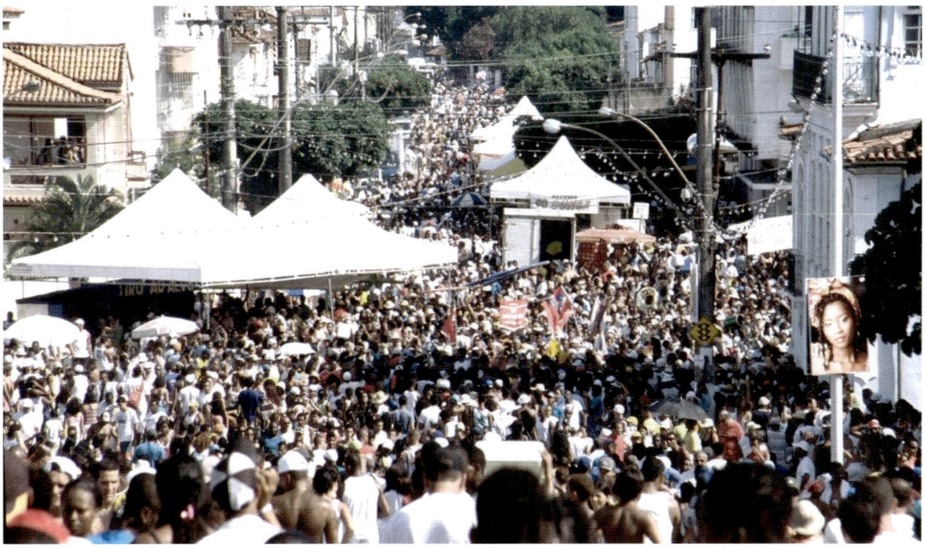

Salvador's grand walk of faith, 2007

Early on a hot January morning, banners painted by Francisco Santos with images of Oxalá and Ogum wait in the hands of the men who will lead Salvador's great walk of faith, the Lavagem do Bonfim. It begins at the waterfront, at the Church of Nossa Senhora da Conceição da Praia, where the priest welcomes the people of Candomblé and says the long, hard walk will wash hatred and sin from the soul. The vast crowd, dressed in white, surges behind the banners and bands, then marches north through the streets for eight hot kilometers to the Church of Senhor Bom Jesus do Bonfim, the Lord of the Good Death, who is, at once, Christ for some, Oxalá for others.

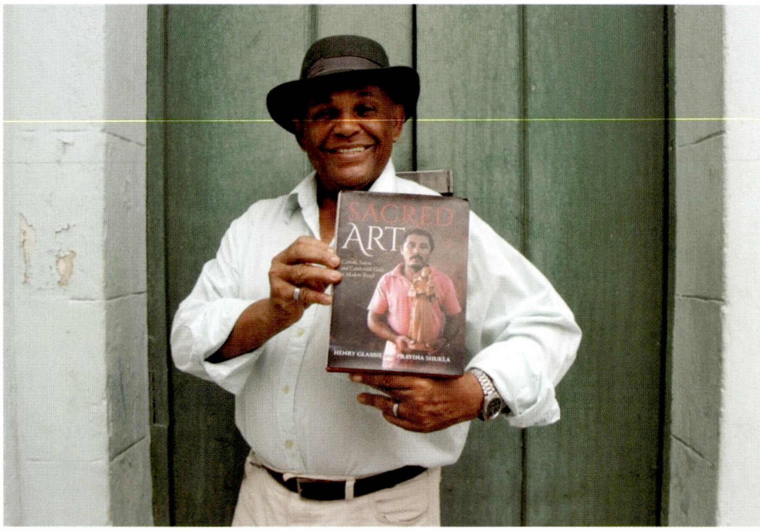

Francisco Santos with his copy of *Sacred Art*, Salvador, 2018

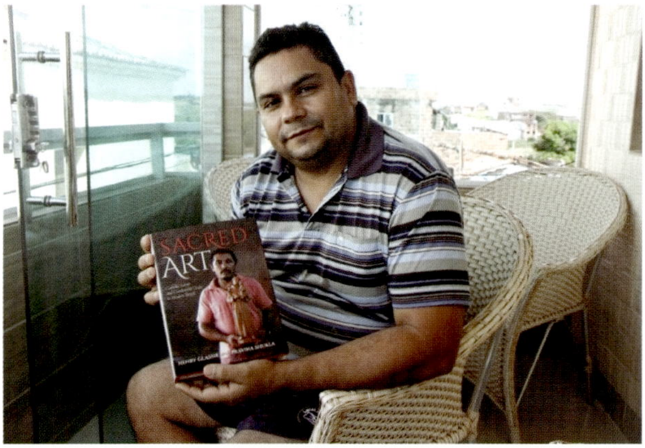

Antônio Pimpo with his copy of *Sacred Art*, Tracunhaém, 2018

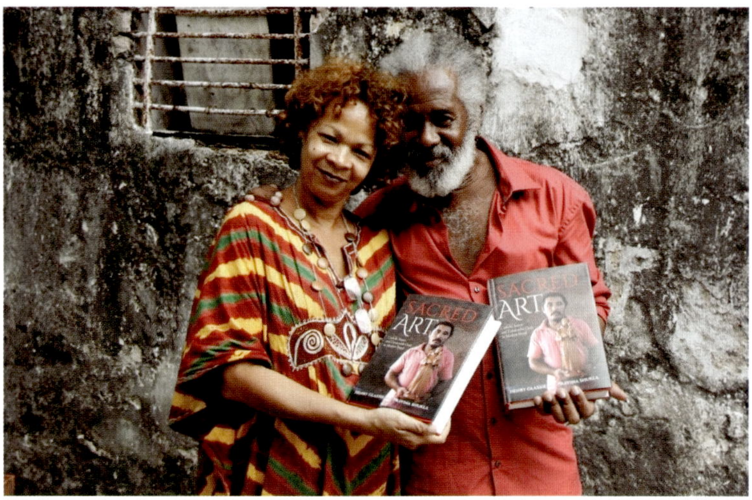

Maristela dos Anjos and Nilo dos Santos with their copies of *Sacred Art*, Salvador, 2018

Francisco Santos, whose banners led the procession, is one of the artists in Bahia who depict the *orixás* with the methods used to portray the saints in Pernambuco. In Pernambuco: Flávio Nogueira da Silva paints the saints on canvas in Olinda; Mestre Manoel and José Bezerra carve the saints out of wood in Ibimirim; Mestre Zuza and Antônio Pimpo shape the saints out of clay in Tracunhaém; and J. Miguel and Pablo Borges depict the saints on woodblock prints in Bezerros. In Bahia: Francisco Santos and Adilson de Jesus Santos paint the *orixás* on canvas in Salvador; Celestino Gama da Silva and Wallace Araújo Silva carve the *orixás* out of wood in Cachoeira; Maristela dos Anjos shapes the *orixás* out of clay in Salvador; and Nilo dos Santos depicts the *orixás* on woodblock prints in Salvador.

All of them were celebrated in our book, *Sacred Art: Catholic Saints and Candomblé Gods in Modern Brazil.* In this book, searching for the spirit of folk art, intending to demonstrate what it is, not what it is not, we began with quotidian imagery in Pernambuco, swung wide to gather comparisons, and returned to Bahian sacred art, having come to two conclusions.

The first, particular conclusion lies in the worldview of the Brazilian Northeast, represented through the collective repertory created by the region's artists.

Start with the quotidian clay figures of Alto do Moura, where the saints are peripheral. Add the repertory of Bezerros. A second method, the woodblock print, appears, and the number of saints increases to match the sacred repertories of Ibimirim to the west, where a third method, carving in wood, appears, and Tracunhaém to the east, where the clay statues elaborate in form and increase in size. At this point, the *orixás* of Candomblé are present, but still marginal. A reach to the centers of production in the coastal cities, Olinda in Pernambuco and Salvador in Bahia, adds a fourth method, painting on canvas, and brings the number of *orixás* up to match the number of saints.

The collective repertory is complete. It pictures the land (dry to the north, green to the south), the people (the good old Brazilian mix), their work (agricultural and domestic, industrial and medical), their music (*forró* and marching bands), their processions (secular and sacred), their heroes (artists, musicians, and rebels), and then the saints and *orixás* of their devotion.

The second, general conclusion swings from Brazil to the wide world, locating the center of artistic action at the point where continuity and creativity combine, where the old and the new connect, where personal expression and collective order interlock in fruitful satisfaction.

Here at the center, folk art becomes a revelation of the human, based on a universal biological endowment for creation, and performed amid conditions to merge the desires for personal freedom and social unity.

Another day is upon us. Once more Marliete and Ademilson are shaping the clay, Severino and Pablo are carving the blocks, Edival and Samuel are bringing the divine into visibility. Time is flowing through their hands into art, and life goes on.

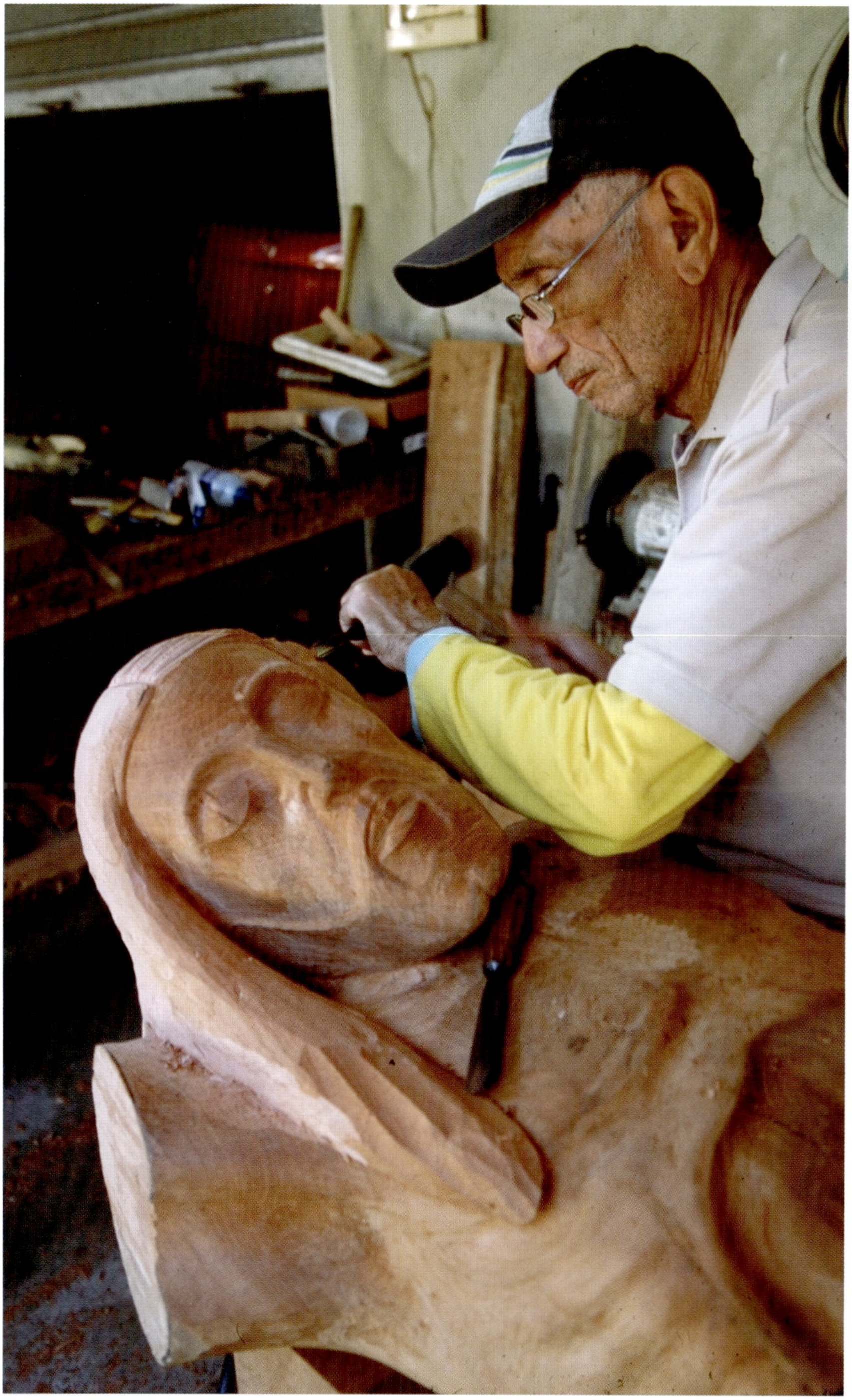

Edival Rosas carving an image of Christ, Jauá, 2016

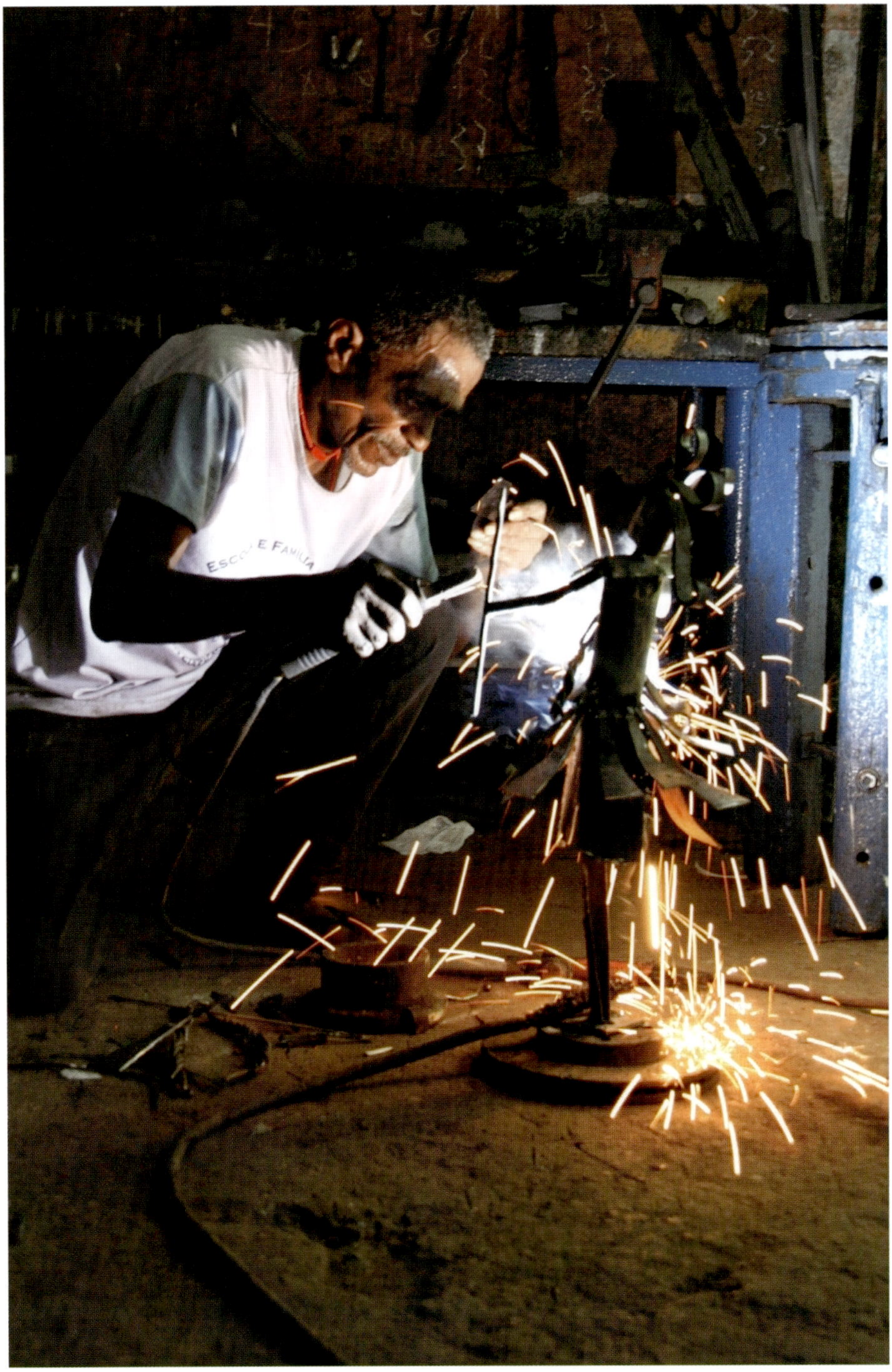

Samuel Rodrigues forging an image of Oxóssi, the Candomblé lord of the hunt, Salvador da Bahia, 2018

Acknowledgments

INDIANA UNIVERSITY HAS THE OLDEST department dedicated to folkloristic scholarship in the United States, and Indiana University Press has long served as a prime source of books on folkloristic topics. Over the years we have worked with a series of excellent directors at the Press, John Gallman, Peter-John Leone, Janet Rabinowitch, and now Gary Dunham. Trained in anthropology, Gary understands and welcomes writing by folklorists, and he gracefully managed the production of this big book of ours.

Production entails problems for friends to solve. The colors being truer, we shot on film as long as it was possible, and Michael Finger digitized our photographs so they could be manipulated toward accuracy. We are grateful to Mike, to Tony Brewer, and most grateful to Jennifer Witzke, a skilled designer at the Press. She printed our text, then Henry cut up the pages to position the pictures so the words and images could flow harmoniously together, and Jennifer prepared the design for publication. Working with Jennifer is a pleasure; she is an artist and a dear friend.

Out in the field, where the book is little more than a raggedy thought, we were helped in many ways by the people we met. Language is a clear instance of a problem to overcome. Pravina speaks English, Hindi, Portuguese, and Spanish. Henry speaks English, Turkish, and Italian. His Bangla, though, is weak, and he was helped by colleagues in Bangladesh, Firoz Mahmud and Shafiqur Rahman Chowdhury. In eastern Asia, we relied on colleagues, Takashi Takahara in Japan and Wang Juan in China.

This book fills with the names of creative people we befriended, but here we wish to acknowledge a few who proved especially helpful.

In Pernambuco: Luiz Carlos and Genilda, Ademilson, Marliete, Carmélia, Emerson, Antônio, Leonildo, and Terezinha in Alto do Moura; Luiz Rufino in Caruaru; J. Borges, J. Miguel, and Pablo Borges in Bezerros; Severino Borges and Ana Maria, Flávio and Coquito in Olinda; Manoel Cordeiro, Nivaldo, and José Bezerra in Ibimirim; Nando, Totinha, and Antônio Pimpo in Tracunhaém.

In Bahia: Edival and Izaura Rosas, Jó Silara, Ricardo Miranda, Ubiraci Tibiriça, Francisco Santos, Nilo dos Santos, Maristela dos Anjos, and Samuel Rodrigues in Salvador; Celestino Gama da Silva in Cachoeira; Rosalvo Santana in Maragojipinho.

In Japan: Agawa Norio, Kaneko Nobuhiko, and Matsumura Takuo in Hagi; Katō Susumu, Shigeyuki Masuda, and Maekawa Denko in Seto; Tatebayashi Hirohisa in Arita.

In China: Liu Lizhong, Ren Shuanghe, An Jiheng, Sun Xiuqing, Wang Juan, and Lu Jang.

In Bangladesh: Haripada Pal, Maran Chand Paul, Amulya Chandra Pal, Rashida Musharraf; Sirajul Islam, Showkat Ali, Shamsuzzaman Khan, Sultana Nahar, Firoz Mahmud, Shafiqur Rahman Chowdhury, and Shipra Sarkar.

In India: Hemant Khanchandani, Hashim Ansari, Chaman Lal, and Anand Kumar in Banaras; B. D. Soni and Kerati Ram Bhat in Rajasthan; N. Murugan and Alagar Chettiar in Tamil Nadu.

In Turkey: Ahmet Şahin, Ahmet Hürriyet and Nurten Şahin, İhsan Erdeyer, İbrahim and Ayşe Erdeyer, Mehmet Gürsoy, Sıtkı Olçar, and Ömer Cesur in Kütahya; Osman Kaya and Mustafa Baydemir in Kınık; Muhittin and Vildan Serin, Yusuf Sezer, Sait Bayhan, Ahmet Sefa, and Mustafa Sargın in Istanbul; Mehmet, Hörüye, Aysel, and Hanife Öztürk in Karagömlek; Ahmet, Rahime, and Fatma Balcı in Ahmetler.

In Italy: Antonio Margaritelli, Maria Tomassini, and Gianni Marcucci in Deruta; Marino, Marzia, and Tonia Parllanti in Montelupo.

In Sweden: Kersti Jobs-Björklöf, Mats Widbom, and Lars Andersson.

In England: Clive and Rosie Bowen, Svend Bayer, and Ernie Hartnoll in Devon.

In Ireland: Hugh Nolan, Peter Flanagan, Ellen Cutler, Michael Boyle, Vincent Woods, Miriam de Búrca, Patrick McCabe and Margot Quinn, Louis de

Paor, Pat Collins, Colm Hogan, Bob Brennan, Tina O'Reilly, Bryan Gallagher, Marion Catheart Maxwell, and Barney Devine.

In the United States: Marvis and Wanda Aragon, Wayne and Lilly Salvador, Gloria Lopez Cordova, and Karen Duffy in New Mexico; Mark Hewitt, Daniel Johnston, David Stuempfle, Chad Brown, Matt Jones, and Terry Zug in North Carolina; Chester Hewell, Matthew Hewell, C. J. Meaders, and John Burrison in Georgia; Winton and Rosa Eugéne in South Carolina; Johnnie and Winnie Brendel, Lou Sesher, Ola Belle Reed, Prince Twins Seven-Seven, Hagop Barın, and George Jevremović in Pennsylvania.

Back home, we are grateful to Indiana University for salaries that enable us to live comfortably in a pleasant small town and get away frequently for work in the field, and our university has provided funds that balance large expenses in the field through these generous programs: the College Arts and Humanities Institute, the Institute for Advanced Study, New Frontiers in the Arts and Humanities, the Provost Professor Research Award, and the Distinguished Faculty Emeritus Research Fund.

Along life's pathway we are blessed with the presence of dear friends: George and Samantha, Nazif and Maha, Bill and Mary Beth, Ray and Lorraine, Tom and Brooke, Greg and Jennifer, Brandon and Ellen, Vincent, Pat, Pat and Margot, Marius and Bobbie, Mark and Carol, Daniel and Kelsey, John and Pat, Steve and Denise, Jason and Amy, Eric and Solimar, Michael and Michiko, Scott and Jennifer, Judah and Rebecca, Dave and Jessica, Kendy and Rebecca, Elliott, Eduardo, Bob, Phil, Maggie, Gabi, Takashi, Jerry, Josh, Karen, and John.

For particular acts of kindness, during the long pandemic when the book was written, we remember Mark and Carol Hewitt, Rebecca Cohen, Ellen Barker, Brandon Barker, Marjorie Hunt, Emily Bryant, Micky Myers, Samantha Ann Matlock, Sara Kinne, Ray Cashman, Fionnán Mac Gabhann, and Ellen Adair.

Here at the end, we recall masters who have passed, Fred B. Kniffen, E. Estyn Evans, Paul Clayton Worthington, Jim Deetz, Doran Ross, Alan Dundes, and Kenny Goldstein. Then gathered again for talk, meals, and baseball games, we gain the affectionate support of the loved ones in a wide family: Neeru, Divya and Paul, Bobby and Chris, Judy and Mike, Polly, Harry and Tsering, Lydia, Ellen Adair and Eric, Katie, Carly, Maggie, Blake, Arjun, Layla, Mina, and Astor, and every day we are happily bound as a couple by the deep love that is enough.

Mestre Vitalino, by Manuel Eudócio, 2014

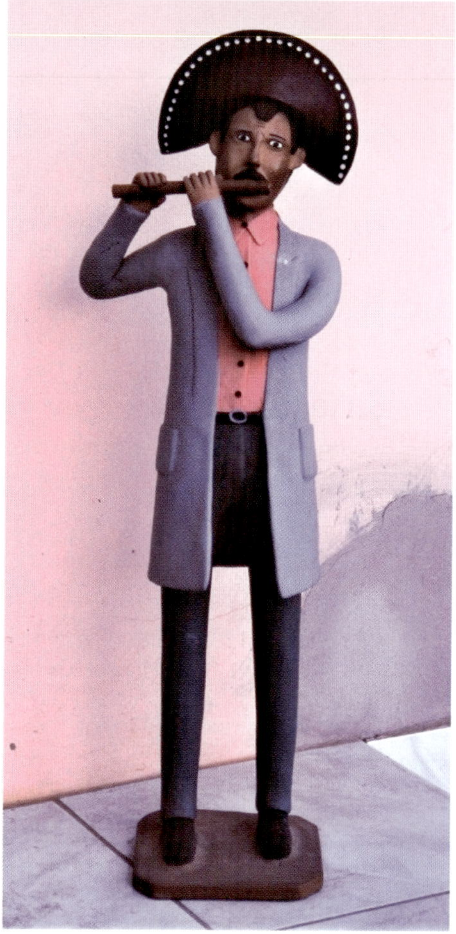

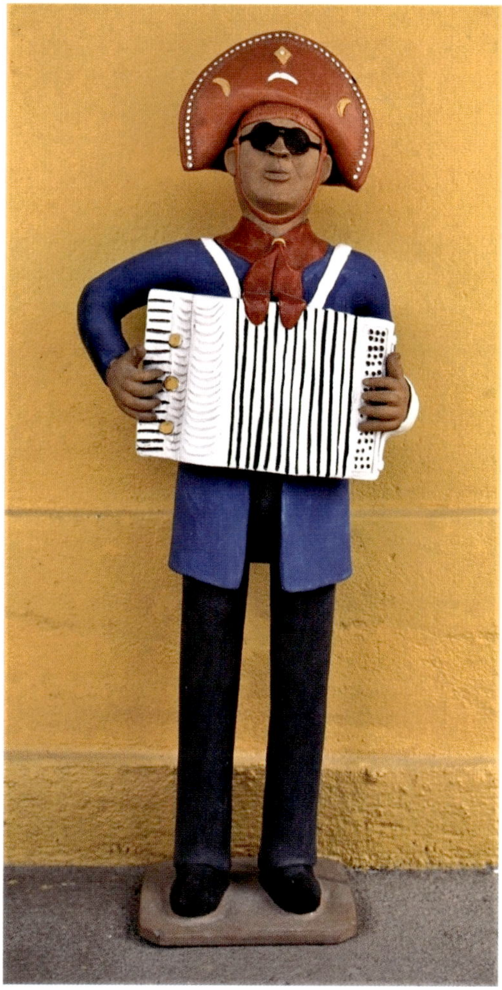

Luiz Gonzaga, by Manuel Eudócio, 2014

NOTES

CHAPTER ONE

P. 7. Argument over the definition of folk art. Two decades of thinking came to a satisfactory conclusion in a book-length essay: Glassie, *The Spirit of Folk Art*, in 1989. Steps along the way included Glassie, "Folk Art" in Dorson, ed., *Folklore and Folklife* (1972), pp. 253–80, and Glassie, "The Idea of Folk Art," in Vlach and Bronner, eds., *Folk Art and Art Worlds* (1986), pp. 269–74. Any reasonable definition will center on the conjunction of tradition and creation, but in practice definitions differ by orientation. Oriented by consumption, by collecting, they are apt to fix on the figurative and extend beyond tradition to the idiosyncratic. Orientated to creation, to the actions of the artist, they tend to hold to tradition and extend beyond the figurative to the abstract. Our orientation is to creation, to creative performances that are best understood through demonstration, through data drawn directly from long-term, intimate fieldwork: Shukla, *The Grace of Four Moons: Dress, Adornment, and the Art of the Body in Modern India*; Shukla, *Costume*; Glassie, *Turkish Traditional Art Today*; Glassie, *Art and Life in Bangladesh*; Glassie, *Prince Twins Seven-Seven*; Glassie, *Daniel Johnston*; Glassie and Shukla, *Sacred Art: Catholic Saints and Candomblé Gods in Modern Brazil*. This book, too, demonstrates what folk art is, relying on observations and interviews. The artists know what they are doing; we need only to be diligent and respectful, attending closely.

CHAPTER TWO

P. 17. Mestre Vitalino. There are two books about the master: Ribeiro's slim, early *Vitalino* and Cabral de Mello's later, more comprehensive *Vitalino*. Mestre Vitalino is treated and his works are pictured in several surveys: Coimbra, Martins, and Duarte, *O Reinado da Lua*, pp. 59–67; Amorim, *Pernambuco Feito à Mão*, p. 14; Lima and Lima, *Em Nome do Autor*, pp. 190–91; de Pontes, *Eu Me Ensinei*, pp. 21–22, 101; Mascelani, *O Mundo de Arte Popular Brasileira*, pp. 14–19, 63, 66–67, 70, 72–73, 78–79, 82, 188; Van de Beuque, *Brasilianische Volkskunst*, pp. 41, 46, 50–54, 56, 64, 67, 96; Lyra, *Brasil: Arte do Nordeste*, pp. 149–50. In addition: Vitalino is featured in "A Cerâmica Popular," an unpaginated section of *O Espírito Criador do Povo Brasileiro* by Alberto da Costa e Silva. Silvanildo Sill created a graphic book for children, *Vitalino: O Menino Que Virou Mestre*. José de Souza Martins contributed a postmodern essay on Vitalino to Tribe's *Heroes and Artists*. And Raul Lody edited the catalogue of an exhibition he curated of Pierre Verger's superb and historically valuable photographs of Mestre Vitalino's work and works, titled *Arte do Barro e O Olhar da Arte: Vitalino e Verger*.

P. 17. Vitalino's followers. Art is for everyone, they say in Brazil. Vitalino welcomed all into his art, which now provides the economic foundation for the small town of Alto do Moura. For the consumer, the prices remain affordable. A fine figure handmade by a famed master at the most usual size, around 28 centimeters tall, is priced between 150 and 200 *reais*, about 28 to 37 U.S. dollars in 2021. Fine, tiny miniatures are priced comparably. The grandest works, composed of six tall figures, peak at a thousand *reais*, about 184 dollars.

P. 17. Mestre Galdino. See chapter 17.

P. 19. Luiz Galdino. See chapter 18.

P. 21. Severino Vitalino. Interviews: January 23, 2007; September 18, 19, 2014; May 6, 2015. Severino in print: Martins, Luz, and Belchior, *Nova Fase da Lua*, pp. 108–111; Lima and Lima, *Em Nome do Autor*, p. 191.

P. 26. *Dom*, the gift, is generally acknowledged by the artists of the Northeast. A particularly rich explanation was provided by José Bezerra, a *santeiro*, a carver of saints, in Ibimirim; see Glassie and Shukla, *Sacred Art*, pp. 138–47.

P. 26. Inner necessity: Kandinsky, *Concerning the Spiritual in Art*, especially pp. 52–54. See too Kandinsky, "On the Question of Form," in Kandinsky and Marc, *The Blaue Reiter Almanac*, and Kandinsky's "Reminiscences," in Herbert, ed., *Modern Artists on Art*. Characterizing Kandinsky as sane, we direct you to Wole Soyinka's comments in *Art, Dialogue, and Outrage*, p. 168.

P. 33. Luiz Gonzaga and *Forró*: Sá, *O Sanfoneiro do Racho da Brígida: Vida e Andanças de Luiz Gonzaga – O Reio do Baião*; Marcelo and Rodrigues, *O Fole Roncou! Uma História do Forró*; de Oliveira Santos, *Forró: A Codificação de Luiz Gonzaga*. Recordings by Gonzaga are available in abundance; a good selection is heard on the CD, *O Melhor de Luiz Gonzaga* (São Paulo: BMG, 1989).

P. 33. Bill Monroe and Bluegrass: Cantwell, *Bluegrass Breakdown*; Rosenberg and Wolfe, *The Music of Bill Monroe*; Ewing, *Bill Monroe*.

P. 35. Maria Bonita's hat. Alto do Moura's artists sometimes give her the same sort of hat that Lampião wears, bent up, front and back, and decorated. Manuel Eudócio said that is wrong. She wore a common, round broad-brimmed hat, and all the evidence proves Manuel Eudócio to be right; see Élise Jasmin, *Cangaceiros*, p. 140.

P. 35. Lampião and Maria Bonita. Two books contain the history and end with extensive bibliographies on the topic of Lampião: Chandler's *The Bandit King* and *Apagando O Lampião: Vida e Morte do Rei do Cangaço* by Frederico Pernambuco de Mello. Recent books missing from those bibliographies include Jasmin's *Cangaceiros* (a full collection of handsomely reproduced photographs of Lampião and Maria Bonita, their small army, and their severed heads on display), Barreira's *Lampião e Maria Bonita* (which includes, pp. 82–83 analysis of the aesthetics of their attire), and de Souza's *Nas Pegadas de Lampião* (which argues, p. 17, that *artesanato* has created the touristic vision of Lampião). Eric Hobsbawm, in his excellent book *Bandits*, especially pp. 60–61, 92–93, treats Lampião as an instance of the social bandit. Such heroes of the people, with Robin Hood as the classic example, are celebrated in ballads and legends. Lampião is no exception, but the artists who represent Lampião in Pernambuco take a different route to creation. Despite all the information in print, they rely on a multitude of oral sources, from which they derive understandings that lead to personal opinions and to images, rather than poems or narratives. Lampião welcomed documentation, so there are many photographs — displayed in Jasmin's *Cangaceiros*, and other books as well — and even some footage on film, but the artists clearly derive their images mainly from other representations, rendered locally in clay or on woodblock prints.

P. 36. The owner of land: a foul colonel is profiled from within by Graciliano Ramos in *São Bernardo*.

P. 36. Elias Francisco dos Santos: Cabral de Mello, *Vitalino*, pp. 320–23.

P. 37. Padre Cícero. In *Bandits*, pp. 28, 93, Hobsbawm allies Padre Cícero with Lampião. From diverse sources, including her own fine fieldwork, Candace Slater produced a rich book on Padre Cícero, *Trail of Miracles*.

CHAPTER THREE

P. 43. Elias Vitalino. Interviews: May 29, June 3, 2019. Elias in print: Martins, Luz, and Belchior, *Nova Fase da Lua*, p. 112.

P. 47. In Cabral de Mello's *Vitalino*, p. 204, there is a photo of Vitalino and his band leaving the plane on arrival in Rio in 1960.

CHAPTER FOUR

P. 49. Emanuel Vitalino Neto. Interviews: May 30, 2019; November 19, 2021.

CHAPTER FIVE

P. 59. Vitalino Neto. Interview, May 24, 2019. Vitalino Neto in print: Martins, Luz, and Belchior, *Nova Fase da Lua*, pp. 113–15. In 2021, Vitalino Neto closed his store and declared that he would return to making clay figures in his grandfather's tradition.

CHAPTER SIX

P. 67. Manuel Eudócio. Interviews: January 23, 2007; September 18, 19, 2014; May 7, 2015. Manuel Eudócio in print: Montes, *Manuel Eudócio: Um Cronista do Seu Tempo*; Coimbra, Martins, and Duarte, *O Reinado da Lua*, pp. 77–80; Martins, Luz, and Belchior, *Nova Fase da Lua*, pp. 138–41; Amorim, *Pernambuco Feito à Mão*, pp. 36–39; Lima and Lima, *Em Nome do Autor*, pp. 194, 446; de Pontes, *Eu Me Ensinei*, pp. 102–107, 399–401; Mascelani, *O Mundo de Arte Popular Brasileira*, pp. 92, 135; Van de Beuque, *Brasilianische Volkskunst*, p. 65; Cabral de Mello, *Vitalino*, pp. 309–310; Glassie and Shukla, *Sacred Art*, p. 479.

P. 78. Droughts. The wide, dry interior of the Northeast was described by Euclides da Cunha in the Brazilian classic *Os Sertões*, translated as *Rebellion in the Backlands*; see especially pp. 14–63, 78–155. In *Waiting for Rain*, Arons catalogs the droughts and their dreadful consequences, pp. 29–32, 64–68, 95–107, 146–47, 171–77, and he surveys the literature inspired by the troubles, including da Cunha's *Os Sertões* and the touching novel by Graciliano Ramos *Vidas Sêcas*, translated as *Barren Lives*. In *Voices of Drought*, Michael Silvers traces the theme of the dry environment through musical performance in the Northeast.

P. 81. Mestre Manoel Cordeiro: Glassie and Shukla, *Sacred Art*, pp. 104–127.

P. 81. Politics. Aware of Rohter's critique in *The New York Review*, we still sympathetically followed Anderson's account, in *Brazil Apart*, of the Lula era in recent political history, which fits well enough with the mood on the streets of Bahia and Pernambuco.

P. 84. *Reisado*. As a parade on Epiphany, the *Reisado* is richly described in Jorge Amado's novel *Showdown*, pp. 330–35, 344–49. Silvers sketches the past of that sort of *Reisado* in *Voices of Drought*, pp. 51–52. Alto do Moura's *Reisado* absorbed *Bumba-Meu-Boi*, a folk drama known widely in Brazil. In *Folclore do Brasil*, the prolific, pioneering Brazilian folklorist Luis da Câmara Cascudo writes, pp. 33–40, that the play was known in northern and southern Brazil, and, welcoming fusion with other performances, it was called both *Bumba-Meu-Boi* and the *Reisado*. The Bull is a character from Portugal, he says, and the black couple, Mateus and Catarina, supplied the comic delight. In *Apresentação do Bumba-Meu-Boi*, Hermilo Borba Filho comments on the distribution of the play in Brazil, p. 11, and on pp. 29–126, he presents the complete text of a performance by a cast of 62 characters. In *An Interdisciplinary Study of the Ox and the Slave (Bumba-meu-Boi), A Satirical Music Drama in Brazil*, Kazadi wa Mukuna patiently surveys the literature and provides an admirable analysis of a particularly complex tradition of performance in Maranhão. Enactments of *Bumba-Meu-Boi* include hobby-horse actors of the kind once known in Europe as well as Brazil; see *Alford, The Hobby Horse*, pp. 112–13. *Bumba-Meu-Boi* is a drama of death and resurrection of a type once found widely in Europe that has been well documented as mumming: In England: Chambers, *The English Folk-Play*; Cawte, Helm, and Peacock, *English Ritual Drama*; Cass and Roud, *An Introduction to the English Mummers' Play*. In Ireland: Gailey, *Irish Folk Drama*; Glassie, *All Silver and No Brass*; Glassie, *The Stars of Ballymenone*, pp. 53–65; Cashman, "Mumming with the Neighbors in West Tyrone"; Cashman, "Mumming on the Irish Border." In Newfoundland: Halpert and Story, eds. *Christmas Mumming in Newfoundland*. In the West Indies: Abrahams, "'Pull Out Your Purse and Pay': A St. George Mumming from the West Indies." Comparable traditions in northern Europe are surveyed richly in Terry Gunnell's *Masks and Mumming in the Nordic Area*. For all their scattered differences, these events are consistent in the sociability of their rehearsal and visits in the community, consistent in their processions that provide opportunities for individual performances, and consistent in the drama's oppositional structure that prompts localization and inspires interpretation. As for interpretations of *Bumba-Meu-Boi*: In *Nordeste*, pp. 106–109, Gilberto Freyre, Pernambuco's historian, interprets the drama as a conflict between the rich, white land owner, represented by the Captain's horse, and the poor, black laborer, represented by the Bull whose revival is a triumph of reversal. In *Apresentação*, pp. 22–23, Borba Filho says that the Captain represents white people, Mateus represents black people, and when the play is performed by black people a victory is achieved in the Bull's revival. Kazadi wa Mukuna, in his paper in *Black Brazil*, argues that the sociability of the play, when performed by black actors, strengthens solidarity among people of African descent, and in his book, stressed on p.7, he asserts that the play functioned as a retaliatory expression by the slaves against the masters. In Alto do Moura, class, not race, was a unifying reality, social solidarity was the deep aim, and the pleasures of creative play rode on the surface.

P. 87. Icon and scene. The iconic option is exemplified by Manuel Eudócio's figures in this chapter, pp. 82–83. The scenic option is exemplified by figures by his son Luiz Carlos in the next chapter, pp. 106–113.

P. 88. Jaraguá: In *Apresentação do Bumba-Meu-Boi*, pp. 17–19, Borba Filho says the play has characters of three kinds: human, animal, and fantastic. The Jaraguá, one of the fantastic characters, is the ghost of a horse.

P. 90. Repertorial play. Jennifer Schacker elegantly describes a theatrical tradition in which characters are moved out of place and into new relations in *Staging Fairyland: Folklore, Children's Entertainment, and Nineteenth-Century Pantomime.*

CHAPTER SEVEN

P. 97. Luiz Carlos. Interviews: January 23, 2007; September 18, 19, 2014; May 6, 7, 11, 2015; May 16, 17, 20, 29, June 3, 2019; November 19, 20, 2021. Luiz Carlos in print: Martins, Luz, and Belchior, *Nova Fase da Lua*, pp. 148–50.

P. 115. Tracunhaém: Glassie and Shukla, *Sacred Art*, pp. 183–241.

P. 115. Edival Rosas: Glassie and Shukla, *Sacred Art*, pp. 27–82.

P. 124. Genilda. Interviews: September 18, 2014; May 6, 20, 2015; June 3, 2019; November 19, 2021.

CHAPTER EIGHT

P. 133. Ademilson. Interviews: May 20, 23, 2019; November 19, 20, 2021. Ademilson in print: Martins, Luz, and Belchior, *Nova Fase da Lua*, pp. 142–45; Amorim, *Pernambuco Feito* à *Mão*, p. 54; de Pontes, *Eu Me Ensinei*, pp. 108–111, 401.

P. 142. Caricature. Gilberto Freyre, *Brazil*, pp. 155–66. Also Freyre, *New World in the Tropics*, pp. 13–14, 210–19; and Freyre, *Order and Progress*, pp. 152–53.

P. 142. Aleijadinho. See Bretas, *O Aleijadinho: Antônio Francisco Lisboa*; Whitaker, *Antônio Francisco Lisboa: O Aleijadinho*; Sullivan, *Brazil*, pp. 238–53; Mann and Mann, *The 12 Prophets of Aleijadinho*. A traveler who wrote about Ireland under the name Robert Harbinson was thrilled in Minas Gerais, like travelers before and since, by the power and personality of Aleijadinho's sculpture: Robin Bryans, *Fanfare for Brazil*, pp. 182–202.

P. 142. Jorge Amado. The free and vigorous novels by Amado are also significant cultural documents. For their witness to Brazilian, and especially Bahian, culture, we have found these of his novels particularly useful and commend them to you: *The Violent Land*, *Showdown*, *Jubiabá*, *Tent of Miracles*, *The War of the Saints*, *Shepherds of the Night*, *Gabriela*, and *Tereza Batista*. All of those have been translated into English. Not in English, unfortunately, are his early, radical novel *Sour — Sweat* — and his valuable nonfictional guide to the place where he lived — and where two museums commemorate him and his work today — *Bahia de Todos-os-Santos*.

P. 142. Elisoneide. Interview, May 23, 2019.

CHAPTER NINE

P. 151. Helton. Interview: June 3, 2019.

P. 152. Silvano in print: Martins, Luz, and Belchior, *Nova Fase da Lua*, pp. 146–47.

CHAPTER TEN

P. 155. Zé Caboclo in print: Coimbra, Martins, and Duarte, *O Reinado da Lua*, pp. 68–76; Amorim, *Pernambuco Feita à Mão*, pp. 19, 26; Mascelani, *O Mundo de Arte Popular Brasileira*, pp. 12, 39, 62, 81, 87, 94–95, 140; Van de Beuque, *Brasilianische Volkskunst*, pp. 43–45, 47–49, 51, 56, 108–109, 111; Cabral de Mello, *Vitalino*, pp. 304–307.

P. 158. Marliete. Interviews: May 11, 2015; May 17, 25, 2019; November 20, 2021. Marliete in print: Martins, Luz, and Belchior, *Nova Fase da Lua*, pp. 117–19; Amorim, *Pernambuco Feito à Mão*, pp. 50–53; Lima and Lima, *Em Nome do Autor*, p. 195; de Pontes, *Eu Me Ensinei*, pp. 116–21, 402–404; Mascelani, *O Mundo de Arte Popular Brasileira*, pp. 69, 136; Cabral de Mello, *Vitalino*, pp. 307–309.

P. 163. Marliete refers to Ernestina, who is rarely mentioned today, but she appears in the older books: Coimbra, Martins, and Duarte, *O Reinado da Lua*, p. 84; Amorim, *Pernambuco Feito à Mão*, p. 19; Cabral de Mello, *Vitalino*, pp. 301–303.

P. 178. Marliete's prize-winning *A Noite de Núpencias* is pictured in de Pontes, *Eu Me Ensinei*, p. 121.

CHAPTER ELEVEN

P. 181. Socorro. Interviews: May 30, 31, June 1, 2019; November 20, 2021. Socorro in print: Martins, Luz, and Belchior, *Nova Fase da Lua*, pp. 120–22; Amorim, *Pernambuco Feito à Mão*, pp. 55; de Pontes, *Eu Me Ensinei*, pp. 124–25, 404–406; Real, *A Cultural Mosaic*, pp. 28, 41.

P. 181. Carmélia. Interviews: May 6, 2015; May 6, 23, June 3, 7, 2019; November 20, 2021. Carmélia in print: Martins, Luz, and Belchior, *Nova Fase da Lua*, pp. 123–25; Amorim, *Pernambuco Feito à Mão*, pp. 44–45.

CHAPTER TWELVE

P. 195. Paulo. Interviews: May 11, 2015; May 30, 2019. Paulo in print: Martins, Luz, and Belchior, *Nova Fase da Lua*, pp. 132–33.

P. 195. Antônio. Interviews: May 23, 30, 31, 2019. Antônio in print: Martins, Luz, and Belchior, *Nova Fase da Lua*, pp. 126–27; Amorim, *Pernambuco Feito à Mão*, pp. 40–43; de Pontes, *Eu Me Ensinei*, pp. 112–15, 401–402; Mascelani, *O Mundo de Arte Popular Brasileira*, pp. 48, 131; Van de Beuque, *Brasilianische Volkskunst*, p. 111.

P. 195. Emerson. Interviews: May 11, 2015; May 20, 24, 25, June 1, 3, 2019; November 19, 2021. Emerson in print: Martins, Luz, and Belchior, *Nova Fase da Lua*, pp. 124–25.

P. 196. *Massapê*. In *Nordeste*, pp. 47–49, Freyre argues that the pliable but firm *massapê* clay, which is used for ceramics, was perfect for growing sugar cane and was, as a result, foundational to Brazil's economic success.

P. 202. Quote on Northeastern misery, lifted from Anderson, *Brazil Apart*, p. 15.

P. 205. Emerson calls his image of a soccer team "modern," though his grandfather Zé Caboclo had shaped a soccer team out of clay decades earlier; see Van de Beuque, *Brasilianische Volkskunst*, pp. 108–109.

CHAPTER THIRTEEN

P. 213. Amanda. Interview, May 31, 2019. Amanda in print: Martins, Luz, and Belchior, *Nova Fase da Lua*, pp. 128–29; Amorim, *Pernambuco Feito à Mão*, p. 42.

CHAPTER FOURTEEN

P. 221. Luiz Antônio. Interviews: September 18, 2014; May 7, 11, 2015; May 17, 20, 24, 30, 2019; November 20, 2021. Luiz Antônio in print: Coimbra, Martins, and Duarte, *O Reinado da Lua*, pp. 86–88; Martins, Luz, and Belchior, *Nova Fase da Lua*, pp. 151–53; Amorim, *Pernambuco Feito à Mão*, pp. 46–49; Lima and Lima, *Em Nome do Autor*, p. 173; de Pontes, *Eu Me Ensinei*, pp. 126–29,

405–406; Mascelani, *O Mundo de Arte Popular Brasileira*, pp. 60–61, 67, 134–35; Van de Beuque, *Brasilianische Volkskunst*, pp. 43, 46, 48, 66, 114; Cabral de Mello, *Vitalino*, pp. 313–14.

P. 222. *Mestre*. In the United States the creator might wish to be an artist free of the need to teach, though in most of the world higher in estimation than the artist is the master — *mestre* in Portuguese, *maestro* in Italian, *usta* in Turkish, *sensei* in Japanese — a rank that can't be claimed, but must be granted, as Luiz Antônio says, by society, and that obliges the artist to create with exemplary excellence and to pass the tradition on, teaching freely. Mestre Vitalino created inventively and he welcomed others into his art, passing it on. Luiz Antônio sometimes stamps his work MESTRE in all caps, though he more consistently signs his name, freehand in cursive.

P. 227. Odete. Interview, May 7, 2015. Odete in print: Coimbra, Martins, and Duarte, *O Reinado da Lua*, pp. 86–88.

P. 228. Tradition. Amanda's comment that the tradition is always changing offers a key to general understanding, for most art is in some measure — in technique, say, or style or subject — traditional. The idea that tradition entails change is not new. William Morris, in a lecture from 1879, "Making the Best of It," printed in his collection *Hopes and Fears for Art*, said, on p. 158, "It is no longer tradition, if it is servilely copied, without change, the token of life." With that essay, along with the "The Lesser Arts" and "The Art of the People" in the same volume, and with "The Aims of Art" and "Useful Work versus Useless Toil" in *Signs of Change*, and with "The Lesser Arts of Life" in *Architecture, Industry and Wealth* — all dating between 1878 and 1892 — William Morris provided a firm foundation for the study of traditional art. All of those papers appear in volumes 22 and 23 of *The Collected Works of William Morris*, edited by his daughter May Morris. In 1994, almost a century after William Morris's death in 1896, a new national survey, *Swedish Folk Art*, edited by Barbro Klein and Mats Widbom, appeared with the subtitle *All Tradition is Change*. William Morris's influence is global in extent, deep in England, Scandinavia, and Japan, and his thought continues to provide a basis for democratizing arguments on art and society. There are many biographies; we recommend particularly E.P. Thompson's *William Morris* and Fiona MacCarthy's *William Morris: A Life for Our Time*.

P. 235. Luiz Antônio's *Máquina de Fazer Telha* is pictured in Coimbra, Martins, and Duarte, *O Reinado da Lua*, p. 88.

P. 236. Luiz Antônio's image of a procession with a statue of Christ appears in de Pontes, *Eu Me Ensinei*, p. 129.

P. 236. The *festa* for Yemanjá: Amado, *Bahia de Todos-os-Santos*, pp. 127–33; Carybé, *As Sete Portas da Bahia*, pp. 193–221; Drewal, *Mami Wata*, pp. 166–75; Shukla, *Costume*, pp. 28–31; Glassie and Shukla, *Sacred Art*, pp. 265–71; Otero and Falola, *Yemoja*, chapter 10.

P. 236. Key attributes are essential for identification of devotional images in Catholicism, Hinduism, and Buddhism, as they were in the religions of antiquity; see Hansen, *Classical Mythology*, pp. 123–26.

CHAPTER FIFTEEN

P. 243. Leonildo. Interviews: May 16, 17, 20, 24, 2019; November 20, 2021. Leonildo in print: Martins, Luz, and Belchior, *Nova Fase da Lua*, p. 155.

P. 244. Japan. In *The Unknown Craftsman*, Sōetsu Yanagi writes, pp. 148, 218–19, that Japan is the nation in which ceramic art is most widely and intensely appreciated, "a paradise for potters."

P. 247. Sacred imagery in Pernambuco, in Ibimirim and Tracunhaém: Glassie and Shukla, *Sacred Art*, pp. 103–47, 183–241.

P. 250. Repertory. Joining personal taste with memories of reception, the repertory runs a seam of connection between creation and consumption. Personal repertories appear in studies of individuals: of singers and composers of songs: Ives on Larry Gorman, Lawrence Doyle, and Joe Scott; Abrahams on Almeda Riddle in *A Singer and Her Songs*; Glassie on Ola Belle Reed in Glassie, Murphy, and Peach, *Ola Belle Reed and Southern Mountain Music on the Mason-Dixon Line*, pp. 20–165; Chowdhury on Abdul Halim Bayati (the most complete of such studies, available only in Bangla). Then the narrators and their repertories: Hyde on Thomas Casey; Ó Duilearga on Seán Ó Conaill; Cashman on Packy Jim McGrath in *Packy Jim*; Dégh on Zsuzsanna Palkó in *Hungarian Folktales*; Ferris on Ray Lum in *"You Live and Learn. Then You Die and Forget It All."* Then the makers and their repertories: Jones on Chester Cornett in *Craftsman of the Cumberlands*; Vlach on Philip Simmons in *Charleston Blacksmith*; Holm on Willie Seaweed in *Smoky-Top*; Cort and Nakamura on Hiroshima Kazuo in *A Basketmaker in Rural Japan*; Glassie on Prince Twins Seven-Seven (see especially pp. 355–417) and Daniel Johnston. When individual repertories combine toward a collective repertory, as they clearly do in the repertories we have sketched up to this point in Alto do Moura, a general cultural repertory becomes emergent. Such convergence is demonstrated in studies of contemporary Irish oral literature, by Glassie in *The Stars of Ballymenone* and by Cashman in *Storytelling on the Northern Irish Border*, and such coherence amid diversity also appears in Hansen's superb analysis of the genres of antiquity in *The Book of Greek and Roman Folktales, Legends, and Myths*, pp. 7–37. From the repertory as a whole, collectors of art can select pieces that please them or capture their values, and the collectors of folklore can select the bits that interest them, the most ancient songs, the most mysterious legends, the most whimsical works of art. The mature, ethnographic move, though, is to consider the repertory in its entirety, as a coherent interaction of parts, in order to reveal an artistically confected cultural worldview. So, having now sketched Alto do Moura's central repertory — dry land, daily work, musical and dramatic entertainment, heroes, and then saints towards the repertory's edge — we will welcome complications and elaborations from Alto do Moura, and then from Bezerros and other centers of production in the Northeast, working from within toward cultural understanding.

CHAPTER SIXTEEN

P. 251. Terezinha. Interviews: May 17, 20, June 1, 2019; November 19, 2021.

CHAPTER SEVENTEEN

P. 265. Tracunhaém: Glassie and Shukla, *Sacred Art*, pp. 183–241; Coimbra, Martins, and Duarte, *O Reinado da Lua*, pp. 25–55; Martins, Luz, and Belchior, *Nova Fase da Lua*, pp. 55–82; Lima and Lima, *Em Nome do Autor*, pp. 174–79.

P. 267. Lévi-Strauss, *The Way of the Masks* — an exemplary demonstration of the master's structural method.

P. 267. Mestre Galdino: Amorim, *Pernambuco Feito à Mão*, pp. 15, 18, 27; Mascelani, *O Mundo de Arte Popular Brasileira*, pp.

26–27, 46, 49, 51, 136–37; Cabral de Mello, *Vitalino*, p. 318.

P. 269. Joel Galdino. Interview, January 23, 2007. Joel in print: Martins, Luz, and Belchior, *Nova Fase da Lua*, pp. 156–57; Lima and Lima, *Em Nome do Autor*, pp. 196–97.

P. 270. Thiago Gonçalves Simões. Interview, May 23, 2019.

P. 273. *Carrancas*: Coimbra, Martins, and Duarte, *O Reinado da Lua*, pp. 112–25; Lima and Lima, *Em Nome do Autor*, pp. 115, 338–39; Sullivan, *Brazil*, pp. 484–87.

P. 273. Louco: Magalhães and Arestizábal, *7 Brasileiros e Seu Universo*, pp. 190–207; Rodman, *Genius in the Backlands*, pp. 74–84; Coimbra, Martins, and Duarte, *O Reinado da Lua*, pp. 129–36; Mascelani, *O Mundo de Arte Popular*, p. 134; Van de Beuque, *Brasilianische Volkskunst*, pp. 58, 70; Etchevarne, *Saberes e Fazeres: Artesanato Baiano*, p. 152.

P. 273. Celestino Gama da Silva (Louco Filho), his father, brother, and nephew: Glassie and Shukla, *Sacred Art*, pp. 277–301. In addition to the bibliographical references in *Sacred Art*: de Pontes, *Eu Me Ensinei*, pp. 224–27, 425–26.

CHAPTER EIGHTEEN

P. 281. George. Interviews: May 23, 2019; November 20, 2021.

P. 285. Luiz Galdino. Interview, May 29, 2019.

P. 288. The facts we were given don't align. Luiz says he saw Vitalino outside his uncle's shop just before the master's death in 1963. Thiago said that Mestre Galdino didn't come to Alto do Moura until 1974. It seems that Galdino had come earlier, managing a shop and learning about Vitalino. Then later he returned and began working with the clay in 1974.

P. 293. Leonildo's source for the *bonecas*. The art from the Vale do Jequitinhonha in Minas Gerais is treated in de Pontes, *Eu Me Ensinei*, pp. 254–303, 435–43, and it includes many standing figures of pretty women in clay. That certainly seems a source, and Leonildo is also right that the forms and colors elaborated in Alto do Moura.

CHAPTER NINETEEN

P. 301. J. Borges. Interviews: May 15, 2015; May 21, 2019. J. Borges in print: Borges, *J. Borges: Seu Perfil*; Borges and Coimbra, *Poesia e Gravura de J. Borges*; Penteado, Mills, and Tjabbes, *A Arte de J. Borges*; Monteiro, *Xilógrafos Nordestinos*, pp. 135–61; de Pontes and Magalhães, *A Xilogravura Popular*, pp. 19, 40–45, 48–56, 65–68, 76, 78–80, 94, 99–119, 127, 178, 187, 202, 208–213, 246–47, 250–51, 254, 259; Lima and Lima, *Em Nome do Autor*, pp. 170–71; de Pontes, *Eu Me Ensinei*, pp. 130–35, 406–407.

P. 308. In her excellent book on the *cordels*, *Stories on a String*, Candace Slater treats J. Borges on pp. 26, 49, 184, and 247, pictures him in the photos following p. 163, and comments on the future fate of the *cordels* on p.185.

CHAPTER TWENTY

P. 315. J. Miguel. Interviews: September 20, 2014; May 5, 2015; May 20, 2019; November 22, 2021. J. Miguel in print: Monte-Mór and Werneck, *Aproximações, Xilogravuras de Fabricio Lopez e J. Miguel*, especially pp. 15–27; Penteado, *A Arte de J. Borges*, pp. 24–25, 27; Amorim, *Pernambuco Feito á*

Mão, pp. 126–29; de Pontes, *Eu Me Ensinei*, pp. 136–39, 407–408; Jackson and Cervenka, *Bandits and Heroes, Poets and Saints*, pp. 22, 48 (where he is, unfortunately, given the wrong surname); Glassie and Shukla, *Sacred Art*, pp. 363–69.

P. 318. Giuseppe Baccaro describes Olinda's Children's Home on two unnumbered pages in *Woodcuts from Northeastern Brazil*, a booklet by Papi and Skirvsky, accompanying an exhibition at the Jamaica Center for Arts and Learning in New York.

P. 323. Implicit signature. The classic statement comes in *Finnegans Wake*, p. 115, when Joyce writes, "So why, pray, sign anything as long as every word, letter, penstroke, paperspace is a perfect signature of its own?"

P. 326. Baccaro on the colored prints: Borges and Coimbra, *Poesia e Gravura de J. Borges*, p. 160. In that book, pp. 157–62, and in Penteado's *A Arte de J. Borges*, pp. 34–39, Giuseppe Baccaro provides intimate commentary on the work of J. Borges.

P. 334. Salvador's painters of landscapes: Glassie and Shukla, *Sacred Art*, pp. 311–23.

P. 335. "Asa Branca." Climério de Oliveira Santos includes a full text of Luiz Gonzaga's song in his book *Forró*, p. 91. In 2021, J. Miguel brought it all together in a woodblock print showing the white-winged bird wearing Gonzaga's hat and playing his accordion.

P. 336. J. Miguel's *A Feira Nordestina* appears in de Pontes, *Eu Me Ensinei*, p. 139.

P. 338. For performances like the *Reisado*, see the notes to chapter 6, p. 84.

P. 340. Sacred painting in Olinda: Glassie and Shukla, *Sacred Art*, pp. 246–65.

P. 340. Aparecida: Alvarez, *Aparecida*.

P. 342. São Benedito. Glassie and Shukla, *Sacred Art*, pp. 93–97; Herstal, *Imagens Religiosas do Brasil*, no. 220; Maia, *O Museu de Arte Sacra*, p. 107; Nunes, *Museu de Arte Sacra de São Paulo — Sec. XVIII*, p. 38.

P. 342. Candomblé art in Salvador: Glassie and Shukla, *Sacred Art*, pp. 344–454. For Candomblé, see the notes to p. 532 in chapter 26.

P. 345. Padre Cícero: Slater, *Trail of Miracles*.

CHAPTER TWENTY-ONE

P. 349. Severino Borges. Interviews: September 28, 2014; June 10, 2019. Ana Maria. Interviews: September 16, 2014; May 14, 2019.

P. 352. Amaro and Nena in print: Penteado, *A Arte de J. Borges*, p. 26; de Pontes and Magalhães, *A Xilogravura Popular*, pp. 47, 63; Jackson and Cervenka, *Bandits and Heroes, Poets and Saints*, pp. 47, 61.

P. 359. Candomblé art: Glassie and Shukla, *Sacred Art*, pp. 261–71, 281–301, 333–63, 369–434.

P. 363. *Azulejos*: Pereira, *Portuguese Tiles*; Pinto de Matos, *Azulejos*.

CHAPTER TWENTY-TWO

P. 367. Pablo Borges. Interviews, June 4, 2019; November 22, 2021. Pablo in print: He appears as a little boy in the family photo in Penteado, *A Arte de J. Borges*, p. 24; and Pablo illustrated a colorful children's book, *Vlado* by Kuri (Maria Beatriz Farias de Souza), published by Caleidoscópio in Pernambuco in 2019.

P. 375. Preindustrial division and hierarchy in the atelier are well-documented for the artists of the Italian Renaissance. See Bruce Cole's *The Renaissance Artist at Work*, especially pp. 13–34. In the first chapter of *Raphael*, his energetic and deftly analytic biography of the artist, Antonio Forcellino describes in detail the workshop of Raphael's father in Urbino, where many worked together at different tasks and the great artist began to learn his art and develop the social skills that would make him the leader of a large team capable of the magnificent *Stanze* in the Vatican; see Antonio Paolucci, *Raphael's Rooms*.

CHAPTER TWENTY-THREE

P. 385. The poem by J. Borges: "J. Borges Recita Cordel Sobre Coronavírus e Isolamento Social." Globo.com, Pernambuco; accessed in April 2020.

P. 396. Repertorial contrast. Pernambucan statues and prints combine in their themes to exhibit a cultural worldview. An instructive contrast appears in the repertory of the nineteenth-century ceramic figures — different technically but comparable in style to those of Alto do Moura — made in Staffordshire, England. The Staffordshire repertory has been efficiently organized in a rich literature by and for collectors. In Staffordshire there was an outlaw (Dick Turpin), some saints (including Saint Sebastian, made for the Brazilian market), a variety of anonymous laborers, but the prime figures were royal, political, military, literary, and theatrical, joining into a national worldview derived from the mass medium of print, in contrast with the Pernambucan repertory, representing a regional worldview derived from local knowledge. Among the many useful books on Staffordshire are these: Read, *Staffordshire Pottery Figures*; Oliver, *The Victorian Staffordshire Figure*; Balston, *Staffordshire Portrait Figures of the Victorian Age*; Pugh, *Staffordshire Portrait Figures of the Victorian Era*.

P. 398. Folk art. Much of folk art does not differ in inherent principles from much of what is called fine art, but it is necessary to retain the category — whether it is named folk, vernacular, popular, regional, traditional, ethnographic, tribal, or even naive or primitive — to prevent much art of quality being neglected for reasons no better than that it was created by people who happened to be poor or rural or dark or female. Of the alternative names, the adjective "folk" is preferable. It immediately connects material and oral arts — folk art with folksongs and folktales — and it fits into the frame of a scholarly discipline, folklore, that has been developing for more than two hundred years. Over a century ago, in *The Celtic Twilight*, pp. 232–33, W. B. Yeats wrote, "Folk art is, indeed, the oldest of the aristocracies of thought, and because it refuses what is passing or trivial, the merely clever and pretty, as certainly as the vulgar and insincere, and because it has gathered into itself the simplest and most unforgettable thoughts of the generations, it is the soil where all great art is rooted."

CHAPTER TWENTY-FOUR

P. 405. Noam Chomsky. Language and art: Berwick and Chomsky, *Why Only Us*, pp.149–50. Also: Chomsky, *Problems of Knowledge and Freedom*, pp.12–15; Chomsky, *Language and Problems of Knowledge*, pp.4–6, 31–32, 152–53, 159–60, 171–72, 184; Chomsky, *What Kind of Creatures Are We?*, pp.vii––xxii, 5–9, 14, 25, 56–64, 127.

P. 405. Haripada Pal: Glassie, *Art and Life in Bangladesh*, pp.313–68.

P. 406. Muhittin Serin. A great *hattat*, a calligrapher of sacred texts, who works in the *talik* hand, Serin is also a leading scholar who has written a monumental historical survey, *Hat Sanatı ve Meşhur Hattatlar*, and excellent studies of the masters Şeyh Hamdullah, Aziz Efendi, and Kemal Batanay. Khalil Osman introduces Muhittin Serin's work and aesthetics in "A Discourse on Islamic Art," published in *Al-Qalam* in 1994.

P. 407. İbrahim Erdeyer: Glassie, *Turkish Traditional Art Today*, pp.497–562.

P. 408. Dell Hymes. The key text for performance theory is Hymes, *Foundations in Sociolinguistics: An Ethnographic Approach*. Published in 1974, it was preceded by a series of papers, beginning a decade earlier, that are listed in the book's bibliography, and followed by Hymes's *"In Vain I Tried to Tell You,"* in 1981, which refined the protocols of representation and analysis. Straight from Hymes, committed creative performance amid conditions in context is schematized for artifacts in the second chapter of Glassie, *Material Culture*.

P. 408. Others. These are among the works that have inspired our ethnographic action: Boas, *The Central Eskimo*; Boas, *Kwakiutl Ethnography*; Synge, *The Aran Islands*; Malinowski, *Argonauts of the Western Pacific*; Lowie, *The Crow Indians*; Reichard, *Spider Woman*; Ortiz, *The Tewa World*; Simmons, *Sun Chief*; Lewis, *Five Families*; Benedict, *The Chrysanthemum and the Sword*; Evans, *Mourne Country*; Roberts, *Up Cutshin and Down Greasy*; Murphy, *At Slieve Gullion's Foot*; Shahrani, *The Kirghiz and Wakhi of Afghanistan*; Anderson, *A Place on the Corner*; Labov, *The Social Stratification of English in New York City*; Kociejowski, *The Pigeon Wars of Damascus*; Goffman, *Behavior in Public Places*; Deetz, *In Small Things Forgotten*; Meinig, *The Interpretation of Ordinary Landscapes*; Lévi-Strauss, *Tristes Tropiques*; Agee and Evans, *Let Us Now Praise Famous Men*.

P. 409. Peter Flanagan: Glassie, *All Silver and No Brass*, pp.20–37; Glassie, *Passing the Time in Ballymenone*, pp.95–108, 669–711; Glassie, *The Stars of Ballymenone*, pp.155–87.

P. 410. Richard Bauman: Bauman, *Story, Performance, and Event*; Bauman, *A World of Others' Words*.

P. 411. Aysel Öztürk and carpet weaving in western Anatolia: Glassie, *Turkish Traditional Art Today*, pp.252–62, 571–776. See too: Brüggerman and Böhmer, *Rugs of the Peasants and Nomads of Anatolia*, pp.203–279.

CHAPTER TWENTY-FIVE

P. 416. North Carolina pottery. The great book is Zug's *Turners and Burners*. See too: Perry, *North Carolina Pottery*; Crawford, *Jugtown Pottery*; Brown, *The Remarkable Potters of Seagrove*; Wiedemann, *Controlled Burn*; Harpe and Dedmond, *Valley Ablaze*; Jones, *Endurance: Potting in the Twenty-first Century*; Hewitt, "The Poetry in North Carolina Pottery"; Hewitt, "A Few of My Favorite Things about North Carolina Pottery." Nancy Sweezy's *Raised in Clay*, from 1984, reports fine fieldwork from the South, including North Carolina.

P. 416. North Carolina's potters: Zug, *Burlon Craig*; Zug, "Entering Tradition: Kim Ellington, Catawba Valley Potter"; Millard, *Mark Hewitt: Potter*; Benfey, *At the Crossroads: Pottery by Mark Hewitt*; Hunter and Stuempfle, "A Study in Rhythm: The Stoneware of David Stuempfle";Brown, *Pamela and Vernon Owens: Potters of Jugtown*; Glasgow, *Rich History, Vibrant Present:*

Ceramics by Ben Owen III; Glassie, *Daniel Johnston*. In *The Potter's Eye* by Hewitt and Sweezy, pp.171–262, these Carolina potters are profiled: Kim Ellington, Mark Hewitt, Ben Owen III, Pam Owens, Vernon Owens, and David Stuempfle.

P. 419. Glazes. Zug, "The Salt Glaze," pp.147–49, and "The Alkaline Glaze," pp.99–101, in Hewitt, *Great Pots*; Barton, *Pottery in England*, pp.49, 119; Burrison, *Brothers in Clay* (the great book on the pottery of Georgia), pp.53–62; Burrison, "Alkaline-Glazed Stoneware." Landrum's source, the letters from 1712 and 1722 describing Chinese ash glaze, are presented in full by Tichane in *Ching-te-Chen*, pp.49–128.

P. 420. *Ebru*: Derman, *Türk Sanatında Ebru*; Eriş, *Mustafa Esat Düzgünman ve Ebru*; Türkmenoğlu, *Sudaki Nakış: Ebru*. For Mustafa Baydemir's slip-decorated earthenware: Glassie, *Turkish Traditional Art Today*, pp.411–24.

P. 421. Inspirational pots by artists from the Southern past: By Isaac Lefevers: Hewitt and Sweezy, *The Potter's Eye*, pp.152–59; Hewitt, *Great Pots*, pp.122–27. By Daniel Seagle: Hewitt and Sweezy, *The Potter's Eye*, pp.130–31, 136–49; Hewitt, *Great Pots*, pp.102–114. By Thomas Chandler: Hewitt and Sweezy, *The Potter's Eye*, pp.116–21; Hewitt, *Great Pots*, pp.31–51; Wingard, *Swag and Tassel: The Innovative Stoneware of Thomas Chandler*. By David Drake: Hewitt and Sweezy, *The Potter's Eye*, pp.122–27; Hewitt, *Great Pots*, pp.12–19; Todd, *Carolina Clay: The Life and Legend of the Slave Potter Dave*.

P. 423. Michael Cardew. The author of an important book on practice, *Pioneer Pottery*, Cardew also wrote an engaging autobiography, *A Pioneer Potter*. In her excellent biography of Cardew, *The Last Sane Man*, pp.379–81, Tanya Harrod describes Mark Hewitt at work with Cardew. Bernard Leach called Cardew his first and best student in *Beyond East and West*, pp.147–49. Leach moved to Japan in 1909, became a potter, and returned to England in 1920, with the great potter Shōji Hamada, to set up his pottery at St. Ives in Cornwall. Michael Cardew, in Ian Dobbie's *The Maker's Eye*, p.20, says that Leach's introduction of Asian influence to Britain was the most significant event in the history of twentieth-century pottery. Cardew, earlier trained at Braunton in Devon, arrived to learn more and replaced Hamada at Leach's shop in Cornwall. Later Bernard Leach's profoundly influential *A Potter's Book* had an impact on the young Mark Hewitt who arrived to learn at Cardew's shop at Wenford Bridge in Cornwall, where he replaced Svend Bayer as Cardew's leading apprentice. And so the noble line of English ceramic art runs from Leach to Cardew to Hewitt, then on to Mark's apprentices in North Carolina, notably Daniel Johnston. Mark and Daniel both discuss apprenticeship in Daniel Johnston's catalogue, *Pots from an Apprenticeship*, and see Glassie, *Daniel Johnston*, pp.17–39, for the apprenticeship experience.

P. 424. The tea ceremony. To understand *chanoyu* we relied on these sources: Sen'o Tanaka, *The Tea Ceremony*; Paul Varley and Kumakura Isao, eds., *Tea in Japan*; Okakura Kakuzo, *The Book of Tea*; Soshitsu Sen XV, *Tea Life, Tea Mind*; Ryoichi Fujioka, *Tea Ceremony Utensils*; and Sōetsu Yanagi, *The Unknown Craftsman*, pp.120–26, 147–57, 177–96, 212–14. Yanagi characterizes tea ware as irregular — neither intentionally distorted nor compelled to perfection, but irregular as natural things are. He prefers the adjective *shibui*, but says it indicates, like *wabi*, a peaceful, humble beauty. His vision is important for understanding the significance of tea, which, he contends, is not based on the drink but on the calm beauty of the ceramic utensils, and it is important in our context because, knowing that there was no word for folk art in Japanese, Yanagi coined the term *mingei*, which has become generally accepted. Yanagi's idea of *mingei*, folk art, was deeply influenced, by the *wabi* aesthetics of tea ware. Another influence was the historical pottery of China and Korea, created so deeply in the past that Yanagi could imagine it to be the yield of a surrender of ego into tradition during a repetitive process of modest "no-mind" anonymity, a Buddhist virtue. In his argument — spread through *The Unknown Craftsman* and compressed in *Folk-Crafts in Japan* — Yanagi was also influenced by William Morris (see the notes to Chapter 14, p. 228) — Morris's critique of capitalistic industrialization, his quest for a people's art, and his hope that the creators that Yanagi calls artist-craftsmen could inspire a revolutionary revival of general benefit. William Morris was such an artist, and Yanagi worked toward an understanding of *mingei* in collaboration with three such artists, the highly individualistic potters, Bernard Leach, Shōji Hamada, and Kanjiro Kawai. By and about them, we select a few key titles: Bernard Leach. By Leach: *A Potter's Book* (the influential text), *Beyond East and West* (the central text), *The Potter's Challenge*, and *A Potter in Japan*. About Leach: Whybrow, *The Leach Legacy*; De Waal, *Bernard Leach*. Shōji Hamada: Leach, *Hamada: Potter*; Peterson, *Shoji Hamada*; Wilcox, *Shoji Hamada: Master Potter*. Kanjiro Kawai: The National Museum of Modern Art in Kyoto has published a catalogue of Kawai's marvelous works, and Yoshiko Uchida gathered thoughts by Kawai in *We Do Not Work Alone*, published by Kawai's house museum in Kyoto, an elegant parallel with Vitalino's humble house museum in Alto do Moura. The results of Yanagi's thought and collaborative effort are museums of *mingei* and many books that credit Yanagi and picture — often old and generally anonymous — objects; for a few examples: Japan Folk Crafts Museum, *Mingei: Masterpieces of Japanese Folkcraft*; Munsterberg, *The Folk Arts of Japan*; and Moes, *Mingei: Japanese Folk Art*.

P. 426. Chōjiro: Raku Museum, *Chōjiro*.

P. 426. Hagi *yaki*. Historical and modern work: Kawano Ryōsuke and Enomoto Toru, *Hagi: 400 Ans de Ceramique*. Contemporary work by Agawa Norio and his colleagues: Glassie, *The Potter's Art*, pp.98–116. For general understanding, we refer you to a few of the many books in English on Japanese pottery: a model local study, Louise Allison Cort's *Shigaraki*, and these works of wider scope: Miller, *Japanese Ceramics*; Tsugio Mikami, *The Art of Japanese Ceramics*; Wilson, *Inside Japanese Ceramics*.

P. 433. Oribe: Murayama, *Oribe*; Kuroda and Murayama, *Classic Stoneware of Japan: Shino and Oribe*; Miyeko Murase, *Turning Point: Oribe and the Arts of Sixteenth-Century Japan*.

P. 433. Painted Japanese porcelain: Nagatake, *Kakiemon*; Kyushu Ceramic Museum, *Kakiemon: The Whole Aspect of Kakiemon Style*; Glassie, *The Potter's Art*, pp.91–98; Nakagawa, *Kutani Ware*; National Museum of Modern Art, *Japanese Painted Porcelain: Modern Masterpieces in Overglaze Enamel.*

P. 433. Pottery among the Native people in the Americas: Lévi-Strauss, *The Jealous Potter*, pp.9–10, 19–29, 32, 177–80.

P. 433. Nampeyo: Kramer, *Nampeyo and Her Pottery*; Elmore, *In Search of Nampeyo*; Blair and Blair, *The Legacy of a Master Potter: Nampeyo and Her Descendants*.

P. 435. Acoma: Nabokov, *Architecture of Acoma Pueblo*; Minge, *Ácoma* (the census of potters appears on pp.195–97); Hunt, *The Origin Myth of Acoma Pueblo*. The broad region is surveyed with characteristic clarity by D.W. Meinig in *Southwest.*

P. 435. Acoma pottery: Dillingham, *Acoma and Laguna Pottery*; Dillingham, *Fourteen Families in Pueblo Pottery*, pp.81–103; Peterson, *Lucy M. Lewis*; Duffy, "Carry It On for Me: Tradition and Familial Bonds in the Art of Acoma Pottery" (which includes, pp.8–78, an excellent illustrated description of Wanda Aragon making a pot); Duffy, "Bringing Them Back: Wanda Aragon and the Revival of Historic Designs at Acoma"; Glassie, *The Potter's Art*, pp.48–59; Nichols, *Voice of Mother Earth*, pp.75–88 (where pots by Frances Torivio, Lilly Salvador, and Wanda Aragon are pictured). Then here are a few of the general books on Pueblo pottery: Ruth Bunzel's early, superb *The Pueblo Potter*; Harlow, *Modern Pueblo Pottery* (Acoma, pp.74–80); Trimble, *Talking with the Clay* (Frances Torivio is quoted p.76); Hayes and Blom, *Southwestern Pottery* (Acoma, pp.46–55).

P. 441. Historical Turkish *çini*: Lane, *Later Islamic Pottery*, pp.57–67; Öney, *Türk Çini Sanatı*; Atasoy and Raby, *İznik Seramikleri*; Denny, *Iznik: The Artistry of Ottoman Ceramics*; Carswell, *Iznik Pottery*; Bilgi, *Dance of Fire*; Hitzel and Jacotin, *Iznik*; Ribeiro, *Iznik Pottery and Tiles in the Calouste Gulbenkian Collection*. An excellent account of the period during which *çini* was developed, and Sinan's architecture reached its peak, is provided by Halil Inalcik in *The Ottoman Empire: The Classical Age, 1300–1600.*

P. 441. Kütahya *çini*: Glassie, *Turkish Traditional Art Today*, pp.425–562; Glassie, *The Potter's Art*, pp.56–90; Akalın and Bilgi, *Yadigâr-i Kütahya*; Çini, *Ateşin Yarattığı Sanat: Kütahya Çiniliği*; Kolhan, *Çini: "Sır Altındaki Aşk"*; Şengel, *Mehmet Gürsoy: Yaşayan İznik Çinileri.*

P. 441. *Çini* in Jerusalem: Olenik, *The Armenian Pottery of Jerusalem*; Kenaan-Kedar, *The Armenian Ceramics of Jerusalem.*

P. 444. The atelier. The plan of Süsler Çini (since razed) appears on p.454 in Glassie, *Turkish Traditional Art Today*, and on p.459 there is a diagram of the Kütahya kiln, drawn by İbrahim Erdeyer.

P. 454. Zia: Harlow and Lanmon, *The Pottery of Zia Pueblo.*

P. 455. Face jugs. *The Meaders Family: North Georgia Potters*, an important book by Rinzler and Sayers — which was accompanied by a beautiful film of Cheever Meaders at work — catches the moment before face jugs became abundant. Then John Burrison documents the face jug era in Georgia: Burrison, *Brothers in Clay*, pp.74–76, 226–36, 269–75; Burrison, *From Mud to Jug*, pp.68–73, 105–151; Burrison, *Roots of a Region*, pp.128–33; Burrison, *Global Clay*, pp.99–105, 122–38. And for face jugs from throughout the South, from South Carolina, Georgia, North Carolina, and Alabama: Vlach, *The Afro-American Tradition in Decorative Arts*, pp.81–94; Baldwin, *Great and Noble Jar*, pp.79–88; Glassie, *The Potter's Art*, pp.36–47; Zug, *Turners and Burners*, pp.381–86; Huffman, *Catawba Clay*; Brackner, *Alabama Folk Pottery*, pp.206–211; Brown, *Of Mules and Mud*, pp. 43–49; Koverman, *Making Faces.*

P. 457. Stoneware statues in Japan. The exception to the general absence of statues in published stoneware surveys is Kawano and Enomoto, *Hagi: 400 Ans de Ceramique*, where, pp.100–123, historical images in clay of Hotei, Shōki, and pouncing lions are similar to those made in Hagi today.

P. 460. Lucky gods: Chiba, *The Seven Lucky Gods of Japan.*

P. 462. Ivan Lewis: Peterson, *Lucy M. Lewis*, pp.66–67, 70–73; Dillingham, *Fourteen Families in Pueblo Pottery*, pp.96–97. Cochiti's figurative work: Dillingham, *Fourteen Families*, pp.120–27; and Mittler's recent *Clay Mirror* presents a rich collection of Cochiti figures, divided by topic and artist. Works by Ivan and Rita Lewis appear on pp.156–59. Cochiti, the place and people: Lange, *Cochiti A New Mexico Pueblo, Past and Present.*

P. 462. Storytellers: Babcock and Monthan, *The Pueblo Storyteller*; Bahti, *Pueblo Stories and Storytellers.*

P. 464. Pertinent passages on idolatry from the Holy Koran: 5: 90–91; 6: 74–75; 7: 147–57; 19: 41–50; 21: 51–75; 26: 69–104; 30: 31; 37: 88–113; 41: 6–8.

P. 464. Islam's challenge to Byzantine art: Herrin, *Byzantium*, pp.95–96, 102–116, 322–24; Cameron, *Byzantine Matters*, pp.71–78, 83–84, 90–92. From among the fine books on Islamic art, we select these to recommend: Burckhardt, *Art of Islam*; Nasr, *Islamic Art and Spirituality*; Brend, *Islamic Art*; Grabar, *The Formation of Islamic Art.*

P. 466. Pottery in Bangladesh: Glassie, *Art and Life in Bangladesh*, pp.61–366; Glassie, *The Potter's Art*, pp.19–34; Shah Jalal, *Traditional Pottery in Bangladesh*; Mahmud, *Prospects of Material Folk Culture Studies and Folklife Museums in Bangladesh*, pp.80–96.

P. 470. The small book prepared to accompany the exhibition at the National Museum in Dhaka in 2000: Glassie and Mahmud, *Contemporary Traditional Art of Bangladesh*; relevant here are pp.4–14, 20–23.

P. 471. Haripada Pal: Glassie, *Art and Life in Bangladesh*, pp.313–66.

P. 471. Kumortuli: Dutta, *Image-Makers of Kumortuli and the Durga Puja Festival.*

P. 471. Shankharibazar: Shipra Sarkar, *Sankhasilpo*; Glassie, *Art and Life in Bangladesh*, pp.307–313.

P. 474. *Puja*: contact for benefit. In his book *Hinduism*, virtuous for being based on actual practice rather than ancient texts, Nirad C. Chaudhuri characterizes Hinduism, on p.14, as "a social contract between two acquisitive communities," one earthly, one divine (see pp.ix, 10–17).

P. 474. Saraswati Puja: Glassie, *Art and Life in Bangladesh*, pp.149–67, 190–95. Around the point set by the *murti* in *puja*, we can gather a few works to suggest something about the subcontinental context, beginning with Ananda K. Coomaraswamy who, like Yanagi, was influenced by William Morris: Coomaraswamy's early *The Indian Craftsman*; one of his general introductions, *The Arts and Crafts of India and Ceylon*; and his masterpiece, *The Transformation of Nature in Art*. Then books on ceramics: Cort and Mishra, *Temple Potters of Puri*; Haku Shah, *Form and Many Forms of Mother Clay*. Then books on clothing: Shukla, *The Grace of Four Moons*; Tarlo, *Clothing Matters*. Then a sampling from a vast, diverse literature featuring Hindu art: Blurton, *Hindu Art*; Michell, *Hindu Art and Architecture*; Saraswati, *A Survey of Indian Sculpture*; Sthpati, *Indian Sculpture and Iconography*; Mookerjiee, *Ritual Art of India*; Dutt, *Folk Arts and Crafts of Bengal*; Krishna, *Arts and Crafts of Tamilnadu.*

P. 474. *Darshan*: Eck, *Darśan: Seeing the Divine Image in India*; Shukla, *The Grace of Four Moons*, pp.26–56.

P. 478. Lost-wax casting of Hindu images: Glassie, *Art and Life in Bangladesh*, pp.441–

47. In general on Dhamrai: Mahmud, *Metalwork of Bangladesh*, pp.167–76.

P. 480. Ayyanar's earthenware horses: Kramrisch, *Unknown India*, pp.56–57, plates 1–8; Krishna, *Arts and Crafts of Tamilnadu*, pp.87–101.

P. 480. José Saramago. The key moments in the working life of the potter Cipriano Algor come in Saramago's *The Cave* on pp.11–13, 54–62, 176–77, 198–99, 251–58, 262 (the pottery is closed and he doesn't know how to do anything else), 306. Other novels by Saramago, casually referenced, are *Blindness*, *The Double*, and *Seeing*.

P. 481. Saramago on *azulejos* in Lisbon: *Journey to Portugal*, pp.342–43. Saramago comments on Amado's work in *The Notebook*, pp.32–34, and in his Foreword to Amado's *The Discovery of America by the Turks*, pp.v—viii.

P. 481. *Azulejos*: Pereira, *Portuguese Tiles from the National Museum of Azulejo*; Pinto de Matos, *Azulejos: Masterpieces of the National Museum in Lisbon*; Pinto de Matos, *Um Gosto Portugues: O Uso de Azulejo no Sécolo XVII*.

P. 482. Santo Antônio. One purpose in Saramago's delightful, late novel *The Elephant's Journey* was to establish that Saint Anthony of Padua was buried in Padua but born in Lisbon — see p.194 — where the saint's place of birth, under a church up on the hill, is a destination for pilgrims.

P. 482. Barcelos and Estremoz. José Saramago stopped at both of these centers for figurative ceramics during his *Journey to Portugal*. In Barcelos, pp.110–13, he repeated a legend that begat an endless series of roosters in clay. In Estremoz, pp.380–81, he visited the museum and found a "magical" gathering of figurines depicting quotidian rural life and work.

P. 484. Estremoz. The Irmãs Flores and figurative ceramics: Vermelho, *Sobre as Cerâmicas de Estremoz*; Vermelho, *Barros de Estremoz*, pp.68–94; de Matos, *Bonecos da Gastronomia* (painted clay figures by the Flores Sisters of people gathering, preparing, and consuming food); Calado, "O Figurado Conhecido por 'Bonecos de Estremoz'." Also in Estremoz, a variety of *maiolica*, called *faiança* and French in taste, has been produced; see Sven Stapf, *Faiança Portuguesa: Faiança de Estremoz*. And the Flores Sisters have also replicated *faiança* plates, similar to those in Stapf's book, pp.69–75.

P. 484. Historical images of Sant'Ana Mestra in Brazil: Herstal, *Imagens Religiosas*, nos.13, 25, 26, 38, 40, 41, 52, 64, 72, 96, 113, 114, 139, 140, 151, 154, 168, 199, 202, 205, 210, 222, 232, 238, 243, 249, 254; Guimarães, *Museu de Arte Sacra*, pp.71, 75, 78, 91; Nunes, *Museu de Arte Sacra de São Paulo, XVIII*, pp.41, 68–69; Whistler, *Opulence and Devotion*, p.85.

P. 486. Brazilian historical sacred art in clay: Herstal, *Imagens Religiosas*, pp.8, 48, 66; Flexor, "Imagery: Aspects of its Representation," p.64; Whistler, *Opulence and Devotion*, pp.38, 91; Talento and Hollanda, *Basílicas e Capelinhas*, p.200.

P. 486. Great Brazilian carvers. Francisco das Chagas: Amado, *Bahia de Todos-os-Santos*, pp.112–13; Talento and Hollanda, *Basílicas e Capelinhas*, pp.201–202; Pianzola, *Brasil Barroco*, pp.82–83. Aleijadinho: see the notes to chapter 8, p.142.

P. 487. The good old Brazilian mix of races: Amado, *Tent of Miracles*, p.322, and that is the deep theme of this excellent novel, which centers on a black Boasian writer. This positive attitude on racial mixture was shared by the Bahian novelist Jorge Amado and the Pernambucan historian Gilberto Freyre; see Freyre, *Brazil: An Interpretation* (from lectures at Indiana University in 1944), pp.22–23, 53, 119, 122, 128, 151; Freyre, *The Masters and the Slaves* (from 1946), pp.26, 83, 278–79, 311. But Freyre later retreated from his early integrative optimism in *New World in the Tropics* (1959), pp.145, 156–60, 167, 247.

P. 487. Rosalvo Santana: Glassie and Shukla, *Sacred Art*, pp.151–81. Lovely footage of Rosalvo at work begins the film by Pat Collins, *Henry Glassie: Field Work* (Harvest Films, 2019).

P. 487. Mexico. From conversations with Irene Aguilar in New Mexico, we presume a close comparability of the figurative work in Alto do Moura and Oaxaca, but having not been to Oaxaca, we refer you to Wasserpring, *Oaxacan Ceramics*, in which the Aguilar family is featured.

CHAPTER TWENTY-SIX

P. 489. The shotgun house: Kniffen, "Louisiana House Types"; Kniffen, "The Physiognomy of Rural Louisiana," pp.293–94; Vlach, "The Shotgun House: An African Architectural Legacy"; Glassie, "Architectural Vision in the Art of Winton and Rosa Eugéne," pp.44–47.

P. 489. Ibimirim: Glassie and Shukla, *Sacred Art*, pp.102–147; Gonçalves, *Santos e Santeiros de Ibimirim*; Martins, Luz, and Belchior, *Nova Fase da Lua*, pp.188–203.

P. 492. John Ruskin. Our particular reference is to the argument Ruskin made in a chapter of *The Stones of Venice*, in 1853. When William Morris reprinted it at the Kelmscott Press as *The Nature of Gothic: A Chapter of the Stones of Venice*, in 1892, he introduced it as "one of the very few necessary and inevitable utterances of the century." For the book: Peterson, *A Bibliography of The Kelmscott Press*, pp. xxvi, 12–14.

P. 493. Kınık: Glassie, *Turkish Traditional Art Today*, pp.411–23; Güner, *Anadolu'da Yaşmakta İlkel Çömlekçilik*, pp.74–77.

P. 495. Bangladeshi workshop plans. Rural planning appears in the map of a section of Kagajipara in Glassie, *Art and Life in Bangladesh*, p.69, and urban plans appear pp.240–303; Maran Chand Paul's shop (since razed) is on p.263.

P. 495. The plan of Daniel's shop: Glassie, *Daniel Johnston*, pp.52–59.

P. 497. Clive Bowen and Svend Bayer, the modern masters of Devonshire pottery, appear in McGara, *Country Pottery*, pp.114–15; Grant, *North Devon Pottery*, pp.174–76; Davies, *5 Devon Potters*, pp.7–23, 42–59; Glassie, *Daniel Johnston*, pp.26–34. Both artists, along with Leach and Cardew, have pots on display at the Victoria and Albert. For their work: Waterhouse, *Clive Bowen*; Bayer, *New Pots*. William Fishley Holland, another of the potters who worked in the Devon tradition, wrote a rich memoir, *Fifty Years a Potter*.

P. 498. Tracunhaém: Glassie and Shukla, *Sacred Art*, pp.182–241; Coimbra, Martins, and Duarte, *O Reinado da Lua*, pp.25–55; Martins, Luz, and Belchior, *Nova Fase da Lua*, pp.55–82; Lima and Lima, *Em Nome do Autor*, pp.174–79.

P. 499. Sonarpura: Shukla, *The Grace of Four Moons*, pp.92–112.

P. 499. Tahtakale: Glassie, *Turkish Traditional Art Today*, pp.41–78.

P. 499. Kütahya: Glassie, *Turkish Traditional Art Today*, pp.435–562.

P. 501. Weaving in the village: Glassie, *Turkish Traditional Art Today*, pp.631–746.

P. 504. Edival Rosas: Glassie and Shukla, *Sacred Art*, pp.27–82, especially pp.28–30.

P. 507. Wole Soyinka. On retrieval: Soyinka, *Myth, Literature, and the African World*, pp.120–25. On the context of retrieval: Soyinka, *Art, Dialogue, and Outrage*, pp.17–20, 27, 127–29, 226–30. Soyinka is a master of the energetic memoir. In the fifth of them, *You Must Set Forth at Dawn*, pp.188–221, he placed a coherent literary masterpiece that can be read as a warning against taking the idea of retrieval too literally. Told that a missing antique treasure of African art had been spotted in Brazil, he went to Brazil and snatched it from the studio of the famed painter Carybé, only to learn that he had stolen a reproduction made for sale by the British Museum. Retrieval is not a gathering of old objects but an extraction from objects of principles that can be employed in new creations.

P. 507. Mosques by Sinan in Istanbul with inspirational *çini* tiles: Günay, *Sinan*, pp.33, 94–97, 100–103, 235–37, 242, 246–47 (featuring photographs by Reha Günay, one of the worlds' best photographers); Aslanapa, *Mimar Sinan'in Hayatı ve Eserleri*, pp.54–57, 121–25; Necipoğlu, *The Age of Sinan*, pp.321–45; Kuran, *Sinan*, pp.114–20, 138–50; Goodwin, *A History of Ottoman Architecture*, pp.149–52, 272–76; Denny, *The Ceramics of the Mosque of Rüstem Pasha and the Environment of Change*; Cimok, *The Book of Rüstem Paşa Tiles*.

P. 508. New publications on old *çini*. They include the opulent books by Atasoy and Raby, Denny, Bilgi, Hitzel and Jacotin, and Ribeiro cited in the first note to p.441 in chapter 25.

P. 509. The original whirling floral favorite of antique *çini* plates: Atasoy and Raby, İznik *Seramikleri*, no.352; Atıl, *Turkish Art*, p.268; Atıl, *The Age of Sultan Süleyman the Magnificent*, p.259.

P. 510. Deruta: De Mauri, *Le Maioliche di Deruta: Una Pagina di Storia dell'Arte Umbra*, especially pp.35–49; De Mauri, *L'Amatore di Maioliche e Porcellane*, pp.67–76; Pagliacci, ed. *Antiche Maioliche di Deruta*; Busti and Cocchi, *Museo Regionale della Ceramica di Deruta*; Busti and Cocchi, *Museo della Fabrica di Maioliche Grazia di Deruta* (Antonio Margaritelli's work appears on p.285. The work of his master Spaccini appears on pp.246–66. Antonio, who began his apprenticeship at the Grazia shop at the age of fifteen, said the dates on Spaccini's works in this book are too early); Busti and Cocchi, *Fato in Deruta* (a book of fine reproductions; Gianni Marcucci appears on p.73); Perelli and Quintili, *Iridescenze* (which begins with an account of the revival and includes, p.33, a plate by Antonio Margaritelli); Minchilli, *Deruta: A Tradition of Italian Ceramics*.

P. 510. Historical Italian *maiolica*. Selections from a vast bibliography: Sani, *Italian Renaissance Maiolica*; Rackham, *Italian Maiolica*; Bellini and Conti, *Maioliche Italiane del Reinascimento*; Liverani, *Five Centuries of Italian Majolica*; Watson, *Italian Renaissance Maiolica from the William A. Clark Collection*; Hess, *Italian Maiolica: Catalogue of the Collections*; Berti, *Il Museo della Ceramica di Montelupo*; Mallet, *Xanto: Pottery-Painter, Poet, Man of the Italian Renaissance*.

P. 513. The original of Gianni Marcucci's historical grotesque plate: Sani, *Italian Renaissance Maiolica*, p.40; Fiocco and Gherardi, *Ceramiche Umbre dal Medioevo* *allo Storicismo*, p.101; Busti and Cocchi, *La Ceramica Umbra al Tempo di Perugino*, pp.130–31. A similar but different plate by Nicola Francioli was replicated in Deruta by Franco Busti: Busti and Cocchi, *Fatto in Deruta*, pp.62–63.

P. 518. *Tz'u-chou* stoneware: Yataka Mino, *Freedom of Clay and Brush through Seven Centuries in Northern China: Tz'u-chou Type Wares, 900–1600 A.D.* (of the 39 kiln sites listed on pp.250–51, most ceased production in the fourteenth century; only Pengcheng is noted as continuing into the twentieth century); Medley, *The Chinese Potter*, pp.123–35; Satō, *Chinese Ceramics*, pp.102–113; He Li, *Chinese Ceramics*, pp.139–40, 145, 167–69.

P. 522. Devon slipware, comparable in method to *Tz'u-chou* ware: Barker and Crompton, *Slipware in the Collection of the Potteries Museum and Art Gallery*, pp.60–63; Grant, *North Devon Pottery*, pp.33–34, 47–49, 69, 77, 118, 135, 145; Edgeler, *The Fishleys of Fremington*, pp.42–45, 111–18, 130–33; Kenny, McMillan, and Myrone, *British Folk Art*, pp.56–57.

P. 525. Tradition: Morris, *Hopes and Fears for Art*, pp.157–59; Eliot, "Tradition and the Individual Talent," in *Selected Essays*, pp.3–11; Cashman, Mould, and Shukla, *The Individual and Tradition*, pp.2–4; Glassie, "Tradition"; Glassie and Mahmud, *Living Traditions*, pp.25–108; Ben-Amos, "The Seven Strands of Tradition," reprinted in Ben-Amos, *Folklore Concepts*, pp.64–98.

P. 526. Prince Twins Seven-Seven: Glassie, *Prince Twins Seven-Seven: His Art, His Life in Nigeria, His Exile in America*; Glassie, "Prince Twins Seven-Seven, 1944–2011"; Beier, *A Dreaming Life: An Autobiography of Twins Seven-Seven*; Beier, *Contemporary Art in Africa*, especially pp.113–19, 169. That last book by Ulli Beier helps to document a revolutionary moment in the art — the painting and writing, the drama and music — in southern Nigeria that is also richly remembered by Wole Soyinka in his memoir *Ibadan*. It was in that environment of retrieval and creativity — a match for the Ireland of Yeats or the Italy of Michelangelo — that Prince's career took off.

P. 526. The Yoruba frame. Yoruba religion: Soyinka, *Myth, Literature, and the African World*, pp.1–36; Soyinka, *Of Africa*, pp.105–116, 135–70; Bascom, *The Yoruba of Southwestern Nigeria*, pp.70–97; Bascom, *Ifa Divination*; Abimbola, *Ifá: An Exposition of Ifá Literary Corpus*; Awolalu, *Yoruba Beliefs and Sacrificial Rites*; Drewal, *Yoruba Ritual*; Barnes, *Africa's Ogun: Old World and New*; Tishken, Fálọlá, and Akinyẹmi, *Ṣangó in Africa and the African Diaspora*; Murphy and Sanford, *Ọṣun across the Waters: A Yoruba Goddess in Africa and the Americas*. Yoruba art: Thompson, *Black Gods and Kings*; Thompson, "Aesthetics in Traditional Africa"; Thompson, "Yoruba Artistic Criticism"; Armstrong, *The Affecting Presence*; Armstrong, *Wellspring*; Armstrong, *The Powers of Presence*; Abiọdun, Drewal, and Pemberton, *The Yoruba Artist*; Drewal, Pemberton, and Abiọdun, *Yoruba: Nine Centuries of African Art and Thought*; Fagg and Pemberton, *Yoruba Sculpture of West Africa*; Walker, *Ọlọwẹ of Isẹ: A Yoruba Sculptor to Kings*; Bascom, *African Art in Cultural Perspective*, pp.85–92; Glassie, *Prince Twins Seven-Seven*, pp.263–302.

P. 530. The Ọṣun Festival: Falade, *The Comprehensive History of Osogbo*, pp.42, 44, 66, 174–90, and on pp.220, 224, Falade says that Oṣogbo is distinguished in art, being the home of Prince Twins Seven-Seven. In Murphy and Sanford, *Ọṣun across the Waters*, Olupona treats the Festival, pp.54–61, and it is described in Glassie, *Prince Twins Seven-Seven*, pp.227–34.

P. 532. Francisco Santos: Glassie and Shukla, *Sacred Art*, pp.423–54; Shukla, *Costume*, pp.51–59.

P. 532. Churches in Pelourinho: Bazin, *A Arquitetura Religiosa*, I, pp.299–311; II, pp.25–42; Talento and Hollanda, *Basílicas e Capelinhas*, pp.70–81, 92–97, 113–25, 163–65, 177–79; Amado, Damm, and Carybé, *Bahia*, pp.154–57.

P. 532. Painting in Pelourinho: Glassie and Shukla, *Sacred Art*, pp.305–344.

P. 532. Candomblé: Bastide, *The African Religions of Brazil*; Verger, *Orixás: Deuses Iorubas na África e no Novo Mundo*; Carybé, *Iconografia dos Deuses Africanos no Candomblé da Bahia*; Leal, *Os Orixás no Brasil*; Omari-Tunkara, *Manipulating the Sacred*; Johnson, *Secrets, Gossip, and Gods*; Wafer, *The Taste of Blood*; Glassie and Shukla, *Sacred Art*, pp.17–20, 261–301, 333–454.

P. 533. Connections between *orixás* and *santos*. The topic of syncretism is best treated in the best book on Candomblé, Bastide's *The African Religions of Brazil*. In chapter 12, he efficiently presents the regional variety of associations between the Yoruba gods and the Catholic saints, and the connections Bastide noted for Bahia in 1960 accord with those we found fifty years later in Salvador, the capital of Bahia.

P. 535. Photograph. We have attended many Candomblé services in Salvador, complying with the prohibition against photography, but since the publication of *Sacred Art*, so many of the participants began snapping shots with their cellphones that the prohibition relaxed in some *terreiros*, and at the edge of the city in 2018, while a member of the congregation was wandering through the ceremony with a big camera, we, a bit reluctantly took a couple of photos too.

P. 536. *Ferramentas*. The *ferramentas* of identification, carried by the dancers in the *terreiro*, are documented by Carybé in *Iconografia*, pp.49, 59, 79, 85, 101, 103, 117, 125, 145, 181, 191, 207, 213, 221, 229, 237, and by Leal in *Os Orixás*, pp.117, 124, 133–34, 142, 145, 159, 161. And see Thompson, *Flash of the Spirit*, pp.50–61.

P. 536. Brazilian makers of Exú in iron: Glassie and Shukla, *Sacred Art*, pp.381–421, 482–83; Thompson, *Face of the Gods*, pp.178, 300; Gandim, *Itaylé Ogun*, pp.70–95.

P. 537. Lavagem do Bonfim: Ickes, *African-Brazilian Culture and Regional Identity in Bahia*, pp.60–65, 71–73, 75–78, 105–107, 195–96; Bastide, *African Religions of Brazil*, pp.274–76; Amado, *Bahia de Todos-os-Santos*, pp.121–27; Carybé, *As Sete Portas da Bahia*, pp.163–91; Selka, *Religion and the Politics of Identity in Bahia*, pp.92–93; Glassie and Shukla, *Sacred Art*, pp.422–27.

P. 539. Pernambucan artists of the sacred in *Sacred Art*: Flávio Nogueira da Silva, pp.248–64; Mestre Manoel Cordeiro, pp.104–27; José Bezerra, pp.138– 46; Mestre Zuza, pp.232–41; Antonio Pimpo, pp.214–24.

P. 539. Bahian artists of the sacred in *Sacred Art*: Adilson de Jesus Santos, pp.333–44; Francisco Santos, pp.427–54; Celestino Gama da Silva and Wallace Araujo Silva, pp.277–301; Jorge Pacheco, Samuel Rodrigues, and Jose Adário dos Santos, pp.383–421; Maristela dos Anjos, pp.344–53; Nilo dos Santos, pp.355–79.

P. 539. What it is and is not: folk art is treated in relation to other categories of creation in Glassie, *The Spirit of Folk Art*. At last, it nearly reduces to something like this: folk art is the fine art of other people, and fine art is the folk art of the Western elite.

P. 539. Repertory. This note continues the line of thought from the notes to chapter 15, p.250. The basic idea is to read works in numbers from the specific to the general, from texts to culture, an idea exemplified, in 1948, by Tillyard's *The Elizabethan World Picture*, and continued, in 1999, by Pritchard's *Shakespeare's England*, which usefully arranges period texts toward a "shared world view." With our two books on Brazilian traditional art, we intend to demonstrate, with data from the field, an analytic procedure that moves from the individual repertory through the communal repertory and on to the regional repertory, aiming for a cultural worldview. What only takes time and dedication for the ethnographer becomes difficult, even impossible, as temporal distance increases, though historians supplied with adequate documents can recover repertorial depth and complexity; a fine, recent instance is Waiboer's *Vermeer and the Masters of Genre Painting*. If temporal distance — or social distance; see the excellent, disturbing *Phantom Africa* by Michel Leiris — prevents a recording or recovery of the basic personal repertory, it remains a fact that art begins with people who have names and goals, whose works assemble into repertories that build toward culture. The artist Luiz Antônio made that clear back in the fourteenth chapter of this book.

P. 540. Folk art, a sampling of books in English: Yanagi, *The Unknown Craftsman*; Moes, *Mingei: Japanese Folk Art*; Hauge, *Folk Traditions in Japanese Art*; Iannou, *Vernacular Visions: A Folklife History of Australia*; Glassie, *Art and Life in Bangladesh*; Coomaraswamy, *The Indian Craftsman*; Mode and Chandra, *Indian Folk Art*; Krishna, *Arts and Crafts of Tamilnadu*; Dutt, *Folk Arts and Crafts of Bengal*; Vequaud, *The Women Painters of Mithila*; Shukla, *The Grace of Four Moons*; Saksena, *Art of Rajasthan*; Kalter, *The Arts and Crafts of the Swat Valley*; Wulff, *The Traditional Crafts of Persia*; Glassie, *Turkish Traditional Art Today*; Griaule, *Folk Art in Black Africa*; Thompson, *Black Gods and Kings*; Armstrong, *The Affecting Presence*; Vogel, *Baule: African Art, Western Eyes*; Leiris and Delange, *African Art*; Hansen, *European Folk Art in Europe and the Americas*; Irmie and Focşa, *Romanian Icons Painted on Glass*; Hofer and Fél, *Hungarian Folk Art*; Schauss, *Contemporary Polish Folk Artists*; Schlee, *German Folk Art*; Wildhaber, *Swiss Folk Art*; Cuisenier, *French Folk Art*; Klein and Widbom, *Swedish Folk Art*; Kenny, McMillan, and Myrone, *British Folk Art*; Brears, *North Country Folk Art*; Glassie, *The Spirit of Folk Art*; Glassie and Shukla, *Sacred Art: Catholic Saints and Candomblé Gods in Modern Brazil*; Price and Price, *Maroon Arts*; Zarur and Lovell, *Art and Faith in Mexico: The Nineteenth-Century Retablo Tradition*; Oettinger, *Folk Treasures of Mexico*; Cahill, *American Folk Art: The Art of the Common Man in America, 1750–1900*; Lipman and Winchester, *The Flowering of American Folk Art, 1776–1876*; Ward, *American Folk: Folk Art from the Collection of the Museum of Fine Arts, Boston*; Burrison, *Shaping Traditions: Folk Arts in a Changing South*; Swank, *Arts of the Pennsylvania Germans*; Vlach, *The Afro-American Tradition in Decorative Arts*; Beardsley, *The Quilts of Gee's Bend*; Espinosa, *Saints in the Valleys: Christian Sacred Images in the History, Life and Folk Art of Spanish New Mexico*; Briggs, *The Wood Carvers of Córdova, New Mexico*; Hill, *Weaving New Worlds: Southeastern Cherokee Women and their Baskets*; Walsh, *The Great Tradition of Hopi Katsina Carvers*; Kent, *Pueblo Indian Textiles*; Bunzel, *The Pueblo Potter*; Holm, *Northwest Coast Indian Art*; Inverarity, *Art of the Northwest Coast Indians*; Wyatt, *Spirit Faces: Contemporary Native American Masks from the Northwest*; Ray, *Eskimo Masks: Art and Ceremony*.

BIBLIOGRAPHY

Abimbọla, Wande. *Ifá: An Exposition of Ifá Literary Corpus*. Ibadan: Oxford University Press, 1976.

Abiọdun, Rowland, Henry J. Drewal, and John Pemberton III, eds. *The Yoruba Artist: New Theoretical Perspectives on African Arts*. Washington: Smithsonian Institution Press, 1994.

Abrahams, Roger D. "'Pull Out Your Purse and Pay': A St. George Mumming from the British West Indies," *Folklore* 79 (1968): 176-201.

——. *A Singer and Her Songs: Almeda Riddle's Book of Ballads*. Baton Rouge: Louisiana State University Press, 1970.

——. *The Man-of-Words in the West Indies: Performance and the Emergence of Creole Culture*. Baltimore: Johns Hopkins University Press, 1983.

Achebe, Chinua. *Morning Yet on Creation Day: Essays*. Garden City: Anchor Press, 1975.

——. *Hopes and Impediments: Selected Essays*. New York: Doubleday, 1989.

Afsaruddin, Asma. *The First Muslims: History and Memory*. Oxford: Oneworld, 2008.

Agee, James, and Walker Evans. *Let Us Now Praise Famous Men*. Boston: Houghton Mifflin, 1960 [1941].

Akalın, Şebnem, and Hülya Yılmaz Bilgi. *Yadigâr-i Kütahya: Suna ve İnan Kıraç Kolesionunda Kütahya Seramikleri*. Istanbul: Vehbi Koç Vakfı, 1997.

Alford, Violet. *The Hobby Horse and Other Animal Masks*. London: Merlin Press, 1978.

Ali, Ahmed. *Al-Qur'ān: A Contemporary Translation*. Princeton: Princeton University Press, 1988.

Alloway, Lawrence, and Mary Davis MacNaughton. *Adolph Gottlieb: A Retrospective*. New York: The Arts Publisher, 1981.

Alvarez, Rodrigo. *Aparecida: A Biografia da Santa que Perdeu a Cabeça, Ficou Negra, Foi Roubada, Cobiçada Pelos Politicos e Conquistou o Brasil*. São Paulo: Editora Globo, 2014.

Alver, Bente Gullveig. *Creating the Source through Folkloristic Fieldwork: A Personal Narrative*. Helsinki: Suomalainen Tiedeakatemia, 1990.

Amado, Jorge. *Suor*. São Paulo: Companhia Das Letras, 2011 [1934].

——. *Jubiabá*. Margaret A. Neves, trans. New York: Avon Books, 1984 [1935].

——. *Sea of Death*. Gregory Rabassa, trans. Dartmouth: Tagus Press, 2013 [1936].

——. *The Violent Land*. Samuel Putnam, trans. New York: Alfred A. Knopf, 1977 [1943].

——. *Bahia de Todos-os-Santos: Guia de Ruas e Mistérios*. São Paulo: Companhia Das Letras, 2010 [1945].

——. *Gabriela, Clove and Cinnamon*. James L. Taylor and William L. Grossman, trans. New York: Alfred A. Knopf, 1962 [1958].

——. *Home is the Sailor: The Whole Truth Concerning the Redoubtful Adventures of*

Captain Vasco Moscoso de Arangão, Master Mariner. Harriet de Onís, trans. New York: Alfred A. Knopf, 1964 [1961].
——. *Shepherds of the Night*. Harriet de Onís, trans. New York: Alfred A. Knopf, 1967 [1964].
——. *Tent of Miracles*. Barbara Shelby, trans. New York: Alfred A. Knopf, 1971 [1969].
——. *Tereza Batista: Home from the Wars*. Barbara Shelby, trans. New York: Alfred A. Knopf, 1975 [1972].
——. *Showdown*. Gregory Rabassa, trans. Toronto: Bantam Books, 1988 [1984].
——. *The Discovery of America by the Turks*. Gregory Rabassa, trans. New York: Penguin Books, 2012 [1994].
Amado, Jorge, Flávio Damm, and Carybé. *Bahia, Boa Terra, Bahia*. São Paulo: Image, 1967.
Amado, Zélia Gattai, and James Amado. *Jorge Amado: Foto Biografia*. Rio de Janeiro: Alumbramento, 1986.
Amorim, Maria Alice. *Pernambuco Feito à Mão*. Recife: Sebrae, 2006.
Anagrius, Tomas. *Keramik från Kvidinge: Om Krukmakerierna i Kvidingebygden*. Kvidinge: Anagrius, 2007.
Anderson, Elijah. *A Place on the Corner*. Chicago: University of Chicago Press, 2003 [1976].
Anderson, Perry. *Brazil Apart: 1964-2010*. London, Verso, 2019.
Araujo, Emanoel, ed. *Carybé: O Universo Mitico de Hector Julio Paride Bernabó, O Baiano*. Salvador: Museu Afro Brasil, 2006.
Armstrong, Robert Plant. *The Affecting Presence: An Essay in Humanistic Anthropology*. Urbana: University of Illinois Press, 1971.
——. *Wellspring: On the Myth and Source of Culture*. Berkeley: University of California Press, 1975.
——. *The Powers of Presence: Consciousness, Myth, and Affecting Presence*. Philadelphia: University of Pennsylvania Press, 1981.
Arons, Nicholas Gabriel. *Waiting for Rain: The Politics and Poetry of Drought in Northeast Brazil*. Tucson: University of Arizona Press, 2004.
Arruda, Gustavo. *Dispara*. São Paulo: Antiqua, 2003.
——. *Gyro*. Salvador: Cispoesia, 2010.
Asfora, Alberto. *From Brazil with Love*. The Hague: Embassy of Brazil, 2005.
Ashton, Dore. *Picasso on Art: A Selection of Views*. Harmondsworth: Penguin Books, 1980.
Aslanapa, Oktay. *Mimar Sinan'in Hayatı ve Eserleri*. Ankara: Türk Kultürünü Araştırma Enstitüsü, 1988.
Atasoy, Nurhan, and Julian Raby. *İznik Seramikleri*. London: Alexandria Press, 1989.
Atıl, Esin. *Turkish Art*. Washington: Smithsonian Institution Press, 1980.
——. *The Age of Sultan Süleyman the Magnificent*. Washington: National Gallery of Art, 1987.
Awalt, Barbe, and Paul Rhetis. *Charlie Carrillo: Tradition and Soul/Tradición y Alma*. Albuquerque: LPD Press, 1995.
Awolalu, J. Omosade. *Yoruba Beliefs and Sacrificial Rites*. Brooklyn: Athelia Henrietta Press, 2001.
Ayres, James. *English Naive Painting: 1750-1900*. London: Thames and Hudson, 1980.
Babcock, Barbara A., and Doris Monthan. *The Pueblo Storyteller: Development of a Figurative Ceramic Tradition*. Tucson: University of Arizona Press, 1986.
Bacelar, Jeferson. "Blacks in Salvador: Racial Paths," in Crook and Johnson, eds. *Black Brazil* (1991): 85-104.
Bae, Young Dong. *Onggiwa Modumsal-i: Oegosan Onggimaeul*. Seoul: National Research Institute, 2011.
Bahti, Mark. *Pueblo Stories and Storytellers*. Tucson: Treasure Chest Publications, 1988.

Baldwin, Cinda K. *Great and Noble Jar: Traditional Stoneware of South Carolina*. Athens: University of Georgia Press, 1995.

Baldwin, James. *Notes of a Native Son*. Boston: Beacon Press, 1963 [1955].

——. *Nobody Knows My Name: More Notes of a Native Son*. New York: Dial Press, 1961.

Balston, Thomas. *Staffordshire Portrait Figures of the Victorian Age*. London: Faber and Faber, 1958.

Barker, David, and Steve Crompton. *Slipware in the Collection of the Potteries Museum and Art Gallery*. London: A&C Black, 2007.

Barker, K. Brandon, and Daniel J. Povinelli, eds. *The Aesop's Fable Paradox: An Unlikely Intersection of Folklore and Science*. Bloomington: Indiana University Press, 2021.

Barker, K. Brandon, and Claiborne Rice. *Folk Illusions: Children, Folklore, and Science of Perception*. Bloomington: Indiana University Press, 2019.

Barnes, Sandra T., ed. *Africa's Ogun: Old World and New*. Bloomington: Indiana University Press, 1989.

Barreira, Wagner G. *Lampião e Maria Bonita: Uma História de Amor e Balas*. São Paulo: Editora Planeta do Brasil, 2018.

Barton, K.J. *Pottery in England: From 3500 BC — AD 1750*. Newton Abbot: David & Charles, 1975.

Bascom, William. *Ifa Divination: Communication Between Gods and Men in West Africa*. Bloomington: Indiana University Press, 1969.

——. *The Yoruba of Southwestern Nigeria*. New York: Holt, Rinehart and Winston, 1969.

——. *African Art in Cultural Perspective: An Introduction*. New York: W.W. Norton, 1973.

——. "A Yoruba Master Carver: Duga of Meko," in d'Azevedo, ed. *The Traditional Artist in African Societies* (1974): 62-78.

——. *Sixteen Cowries: Yoruba Divination from Africa to the New World*. Bloomington: Indiana University Press, 1993 [1980].

——. *Contributions to Folkloristics*. Delhi: Archana, 1981.

——. *African Folktales in the New World*. Bloomington: Indiana University Press, 1992.

Başeğmez, Şinasi. *Icons*. Virginia Taylor Saçlıoğlu, trans. Istanbul: Yapı Kredi Yayınları, 1989.

Bastide, Roger. *The African Religions of Brazil: Toward a Sociology of the Interpenetration of Civilizations*. Helen Sabba, trans. Baltimore: The Johns Hopkins University Press, 2007 [1960].

Bauman, Richard. *Story, Performance, and Event: Contextual Studies of Oral Performance*. Cambridge: Cambridge University Press, 1986.

——. *A World of Others' Words: Cross-Cultural Perspectives on Intertextuality*. Oxford: Blackwell, 2004.

Baxandall, Michael. *Patterns of Intention: On the Historical Explanation of Pictures*. New Haven: Yale University Press, 1985.

Bayer, Svend. *New Pots*. Uppingham: Goldmark Gallery, 2007.

Bazin, Germain. *A Arquitetura Religiosa Barroca no Brasil*. 2 vols. Rio de Janeiro: Editora Record, 1983 [1956].

Beam, Bill, Jason Harpe, Scott Smith, and David Springs. *Two Centuries of Potters: A Catawba Valley Tradition*. Lincolnton: Lincoln County Historical Association, 1999.

Beardsley, John, William Arnett, Paul Arnett, and Jane Livingston. *The Quilts of Gee's Bend*. Atlanta: Tinwood Books, 2002.

Beck, Horace P., ed. *Folklore in Action: Essays for Discussion in Honor of MacEdward Leach*. Philadelphia: American Folklore Society, 1962.

Beckett, Samuel. *Waiting for Godot*. New York: Grove Press, 1954.

Beier, Ulli. *Contemporary Art in Africa*. London: Pall Mall Press, 1968.

——. *A Dreaming Life: An Autobiography of Twins Seven-Seven*. Bayreuth: Bayreuth University, 1999.

Bellini, Mario, and Giovanni Conti. *Maioliche Italiane del Rinascimento*. Milan: Antonio Vallardi, 1964.

Ben-Amos, Dan. "The Seven Strands of Tradition: Varieties in Its Meaning in American Folklore Studies," *Journal of Folklore Research* 21 (1984): 97-131.

——. *Folklore Concepts: Histories and Critiques*. Bloomington: Indiana University Press, 2020.

Benedict, Ruth. *The Chrysanthemum and the Sword: Patterns of Japanese Culture*. Boston: Houghton Mifflin, 1946.

Benfey, Christopher. *Red Brick, Black Mountain, White Clay: Reflections on Art, Family, and Survival*. New York: Penguin, 2013.

——. *At the Crossroads: Pottery by Mark Hewitt*. Boston: Pucker Gallery, 2015.

Bennett, Margaret. *Jerome: Just One More Song! Local, Social and Political History in the Repertoire of a Newfoundland-Irish Singer*. Grange of Locherlour: Grace Note, 2012.

Benson, Martha L., and Laura Lyon Redford. *Ozark Coverlets: The Shiloh Museum of Ozark History Collection*. Springdale: Shiloh Museum of Ozark History, 2015.

Berlinger, Gabrielle Anna. *Framing Sukkot: Tradition and Transformation in Jewish Vernacular Architecture*. Bloomington: Indiana University Press, 2017.

Berti, Fausto. *Il Museo della Ceramica di Montelupo: Storia, Tecnologia, Collezioni*. Firenze: Edizioni Polistampa, 2008.

Berwick, Robert C., and Noam Chomsky. *Why Only Us: Language and Evolution*. Cambridge: The MIT Press, 2016.

Biebuyck, Daniel P., ed. *Tradition and Creativity in Tribal Art*. Berkeley: University of California Press, 1969.

Bilgi, Hülya. *Dance of Fire: Iznik Tiles and Ceramics in the Sadberk Hanım Museum and Őmer M. Koç Collections*. Priscilla Mary Işın, trans. Istanbul: Vehbi Koç Foundation, 2009.

Birks, Tony, and Cornelia Wingfield Digby. *Bernard Leach, Hamada and Their Circle*. Oxford: Phaidon-Christie's, 1990.

Blair, Mary Ellen and Laurence. *The Legacy of a Master Potter: Nampeyo and Her Descendants*. Tucson: Treasure Chest Books, 1999.

Blurton, T. Richard. *Hindu Art*. Cambridge: Harvard University Press, 1993.

Boas, Franz. *The Central Eskimo*. Lincoln: University of Nebraska Press, 1964 [1888].

——. *Primitive Art*. New York: Dover, 1955 [1937].

——. *Kwakiutl Ethnography*. Helen Codere, ed. Chicago: University of Chicago Press, 1966.

Borba Filho, Hermilo. *Apresentação do Bumba-Meu-Boi*. Recife: Imprensa Universitária, 1966.

Borges, J. *J. Borges: Seu Perfil*. [Bezerros]: Author, n.d. [c. 2008].

——. *Como Se Faz uma Xilogravura e Como Se Escreve um Cordel*. [Bezerros]: Author, n.d. [c. 2010].

Borges, J., and Silvia Rodrigues Coimbra. *Poesia e Gravura de J. Borges*. Recife: Authors, 1996.

Bowman, Marion, and Ülo Valk, eds. *Vernacular Religion in Everyday Life: Expressions of Belief*. London: Routledge, 2015.

Boxer, C.R. *The Golden Age of Brazil, 1695-1750*. Berkeley: University of California Press, 1969.

Boyd, E. *Saints and Saint Makers of New Mexico*. Robin Farwell Gavin, ed. Santa Fe: Western Edge Press, 1998 [1946].

Brackner, Joey. *Alabama Folk Pottery*. Tuscaloosa: University of Alabama Press, 2006.

Brears, Peter C.D. *The English Country Pottery: Its History and Techniques*. Newton Abbot: David & Charles, 1971.

——. *North Country Folk Art*. Edinburgh: John Donald, 1989.

Brekke, Nils Georg, ed. *From Academic Art to Popular Pictures: Principles of Representation, Reproduction, and Transformation*. Bergen: Bergen Museum, University of Bergen, 2000.

Brend, Barbara. *Islamic Art*. Cambridge: Harvard University Press, 1991.

Brennan, Anne, and Phyllis Blair Clark. *Ben Owen III: A Natural Influence*. Wilmington: Louise Wells Cameron Art Museum, 2004.

Bretas, Rodrigo José Ferreira. *O Aleijadinho: Antônio Francisco Lisboa*. Belo Horizonte: Editora Itatiaia, 2002.

Briggs, Charles L. *The Wood Carvers of Córdova, New Mexico: Social Dimensions of an Artistic "Revival."* Knoxville: University of Tennessee Press, 1980.

Brisco, Bryce. *Bryce Brisco*. Raleigh: Lulu, 2011.

Brown, Charlotte Vestal. *The Remarkable Potters of Seagrove: The Folk Pottery of a Legendary North Carolina Community*. New York: Lark Books, 2006.

——. *Pamela and Vernon Owens: Potters of Jugtown*. Raleigh: Gregg Museum, North Carolina State University, 2008.

——. *The Family Business: 175 Years of Pottery by the Owen/Owens Families*. Seagrove: North Carolina Pottery Center, 2008.

Brown, Jerry. *Of Mules and Mud: The Story of Alabama Folk Potter Jerry Brown*. Joey Brackner, ed. Tuscaloosa: University of Alabama Press, 2022.

Brüggermann, W., and H. Böhmer. *Rugs of the Peasants and Nomads of Anatolia*. München: Kunst & Antiquitäten, 1983.

Bryans, Robin. *Fanfare for Brazil*. London: Faber and Faber, 1962.

Buckley, Anthony D., Criostóir Mac Cárthaigh, Seamas Ó Catháin, and Séamas Mac Mathuna, eds. *Border-Crossing: Mumming in Cross-Border and Cross-Community Contexts*. Dundalk: Dundalgan Press, 2007.

Bunzel, Ruth L. *The Pueblo Potter: A Study of Creative Imagination in Primitive Art*. New York: Dover, 1972 [1929].

Burckhardt, Titus. *Art of Islam: Language and Meaning*. Westerham: World of Islam Festival, 1976.

Burke, Kenneth. *A Grammar of Motives*. Berkeley: University of California Press, 1969 [1945].

——. *A Rhetoric of Motives*. Berkeley: University of California Press, 1969 [1950].

Burke, Peter. "Popular Poetry in the North-East: The Rise and Fall of the *Folhetos*," in Tribe, ed. *Heroes and Artists* (2001): 46-49.

Burrison, John A. "Alkaline-Glazed Stoneware: A Deep-South Tradition," *Southern Folklore Quarterly* 39:4 (1975): 377-404.

——. *The Meaders Family of Mossy Creek*. Atlanta: Georgia State University Art Gallery, 1976.

——. *Brothers in Clay: The Story of Georgia Folk Pottery*. Athens: University of Georgia Press, 1983.

——. *Shaping Traditions: Folk Arts in a Changing South*. Athens: University of Georgia Press, 2000.

——. *Roots of a Region: Southern Folk Culture*. Jackson: University Press of Mississippi, 2007.

——. *From Mud to Jug: The Folk Potters and Pottery of Northeast Georgia*. Athens: University of Georgia Press, 2010.

——. *Global Clay: Themes in World Ceramic Traditions*. Bloomington: Indiana University Press, 2017.

Busti, Giulio, and Franco Cocchi. *Fatto in Deruta: Ceramiche Tradizionale di Deruta*. Perugia: Futura, 2004.

Busti, Giulio, and Franco Cocchi. *La Ceramica Umbra al Tempo di Perugino*. Milano: Silvana, 2004.

Busti, Giulio, and Franco Cocchi. *Museo Regionale della Ceramica di Deruta: Ceramiche di Deruta dei Secoli XVII e XVIII.* Perugia: Editori Umbri Associati, 2008.

Busti, Giulio, and Franco Cocchi. *Museo della Fabbrica di Maioliche Grazia di Deruta.* Perugia: Electa Editori Umbri Associati, 2009.

Cabral de Mello, Paulino. *Vitalino, Sem Barro: O Homen: 80 Anos de Arte Popular.* Rio de Janeiro: Ministério da Cultura, 1995.

Cahill, Holger. *American Folk Art: The Art of the Common Man in America, 1750-1900.* New York: Museum of Modern Art, 1932.

Calado, Rafael Salinas. "O Figurado Conhecido por 'Bonecos de Estremoz'," in Fernandes, et al., *Figurado Português* (2005): 155-77.

Câmara Cascudo, Luís da. *Folclore do Brasil (Pesquisas e Notas).* Rio de Janeiro: Editôra Fundo de Cultura Brasil, 1967.

Cameron, Averil. *Byzantine Matters.* Princeton: Princeton University Press, 2014.

Campbell, John Lorne. *Stories from South Uist Told by Angus MacLellan.* London: Routledge & Kegan Paul, 1961.

Camus, Albert. *The Plague.* Stuart Gilbert, trans. New York: Vintage Books, 1991 [1948].

——. *The Rebel.* Anthony Bower, trans. London: Hamish Hamilton, 1953.

Cantwell, Robert. *Bluegrass Breakdown: The Making of the Old Southern Sound.* Urbana: University of Illinois Press, 1984.

Cardew, Michael. *Pioneer Pottery.* New York: St. Martin's Press, 1973 [1969].

——. *A Pioneer Potter: An Autobiography.* London: William Collins Sons, 1988.

Carswell, John. *Iznik Pottery.* London: British Museum Press, 1998.

Carybé. *As Sete Portas da Bahia.* Rio de Janeiro: Editora Record, 1976.

——. *Iconografia dos Deuses Africanos no Candomblé da Bahia.* São Paulo: Raízes, 1981.

Cashman, Ray. "Mumming with the Neighbors in West Tyrone," *Journal of Folklore Research* 37:1 (2000): 73-84.

——. "Mumming on the Irish Border: Social and Political Implications," in Buckley et al, eds., *Border-Crossing* (2007), pp. 39-56.

——. *Storytelling on the Northern Irish Border: Characters and Community.* Bloomington: Indiana University Press, 2008.

——. *Packy Jim: Folklore and Worldview on the Irish Border.* Madison: University of Wisconsin Press, 2016.

Cashman, Ray, Tom Mould, and Pravina Shukla, eds. *The Individual and Tradition: Folkloristic Perspectives.* Bloomington: Indiana University Press, 2011.

Cass, Eddie, and Steve Roud, *An Introduction to the English Mummers' Play: Room, Room, Ladies and Gentlemen.* London: The Folklore Society, 2002.

Castedo, Leopoldo. *The Baroque Prevalence in Brazilian Art.* New York: Charles Frank, 1964.

Cawte, E. C., Alex Helm, and N. Peacock. *English Ritual Drama: A Geographical Index.* London: The Folk-Lore Society, 1967.

Cellini, Benvenuto. *The Life of Benvenuto Cellini Written by Himself.* 2 vols. John Addington Symonds, trans. New York: Brentano's, 1906 [c. 1559].

Chambers, E. K., *The English Folk-Play.* New York: Russell and Russell, 1964.

Chandler, Billy Jaynes. *The Bandit King: Lampião of Brazil.* College Station: Texas A & M University Press, 1978.

Chaudhuri, Nirad C. *Hinduism: A Religion to Live By.* New York: Oxford University Press, 1979.

Chemeche, George. *Eshu: The Divine Trickster.* Woodbridge: Antique Collectors' Club, 2013.

Chiba, Reiko. *The Seven Lucky Gods of Japan.* Rutland: Charles E. Tuttle, 1996 [1966].

Chomsky, Noam. *Problems of Knowledge and Freedom: The Russell Lectures*. New York: Vintage Books, 1971.

——. *Language and Problems of Knowledge: The Managua Lectures*. Cambridge: The MIT Press, 1994 [1988].

——. *What Kind of Creatures Are We?* New York: Columbia University Press, 2016.

Chowdhury, Shafiqur Rahman. *Abdul Halim Bayati: Jiban o Sangit*. Dhaka: Bangla Academy, 2000.

Cimok, Fatih. *The Book of Rüstem Paşa Tiles*. Istanbul: A Turizm Yayınları, 2004.

Çini, Rıfat. *Ateşin Yarattığı Sanat: Kütahya Çiniliği*. Istanbul: Celsus Yayıncılık, 2002.

Cochran, Robert. *Singing in Zion: Music and Song in the Life of an Arkansas Family*. Fayetteville: University of Arkansas Press, 1999.

Coimbra, Silvia Rodrigues, Flávia Martins, and Maria Leticia Duarte. *O Reinado da Lua: Escultores Populares do Nordeste*. Recife: Banco do Nordeste, 2009 [1976].

Cole, Bruce. *The Renaissance Artist at Work: From Pisano to Titian*. New York: Harper and Row, 1983.

Collins, Pat. *Henry Glassie: Field Work*. Film. Baltimore, Co. Cork: Harvest Films, 2019.

Compton, Stephen C. *Seagrove Potteries Through Time*. Croydon: Arcadia, 2016.

——. *North Carolina Potteries Through Time*. Croydon: Arcadia, 2017.

Coomaraswamy, Ananda K. *The Indian Craftsman*. New Delhi: Munshiram Manoharlal, 1989 [1909].

——. *The Arts and Crafts of India and Ceylon*. New Delhi: Today and Tomorrow's Printers and Publishers, 1971 [1913].

——. *The Transformation of Nature in Art*. Cambridge: Harvard University Press, 1935.

Cort, Louise Allison. *Shigaraki: Potters' Valley*. Tokyo: Kodansha, 1981 [1979].

——. *Seto and Mino Ceramics: Japanese Collections in the Freer Gallery of Art*. Washington: Freer Gallery, Smithsonian Institution, 1992.

Cort, Louise Allison, and Nakamura Kenji. *A Basketmaker in Rural Japan*. New York: Weatherhill, 1994.

Cort, Louise Allison, and Purna Chandra Mishra. *Temple Potters of Puri*. Ahmedabad: Mapin, 2012.

Coulter, Catherine. *A Unique Likeness: Pottery Exhibition 2009*. Rocky Mount: The Arts Center, 2009.

Crafts Advisory Committee. *Michael Cardew: A Collection of Essays*. New York: Watson-Guptill, 1976.

Crawford, Jean. *Jugtown Pottery: History and Design*. Winston-Salem: John F. Blair, 1964.

Crook, Larry, and Randal Johnson, eds. *Black Brazil: Culture, Identity, and Social Mobilization*. Los Angeles: UCLA Latin American Center Publications, 1999.

Crowley, Daniel J., ed. *African Folklore in the New World*. Austin: University of Texas Press, 1977.

Cuisenier, Jean. *French Folk Art*. Tokyo: Kodansha, 1977.

Dalby, Liza. *Kimono: Fashioning Culture*. London: Vintage, 2001.

d'Azevedo, Warren L., ed. *The Traditional Artist in African Societies*. Bloomington: Indiana University Press, 1974.

da Costa e Silva, Alberto, ed. *O Espírito Criador do Povo Brasileiro, Atraves da Coleção de Abelardo Rodrigues do Recife*. Brasília: Palácio do Itamaraty, 1972.

da Cunha, Euclides. *Rebellion in the Backlands*. Samuel Putnam, trans. London: Picador, 1995 [1902].

DaMatta, Roberto. *Carnivals, Rogues, and Heroes: An Interpretation of the Brazilian Dilemma*. John Drury, trans. Notre Dame: Notre Dame University Press, 1991 [1979].

da Silva, Eduardo Pereira. *Sé de Évora: Um Guia Historico e Artístico*. Évora: Cabildo da Sé de Évora, 2009.

da Silva, Vagner Gonçalves. "Saints Noirs, Saints de Noirs: Coleur et Dévotion dans le Catholicisme Afro-Brésilien," in Falgayrettes-Leveau, ed. *Brésil* (2005): 171-89.

Davies, Peter. *5 Devon Potters*. Birmingham: Jones and Palmer, 2004.

Deetz, James. *In Small Things Forgotten: An Archaeology of Early American Life*. New York: Doubleday, 1996 [1977].

Dégh, Linda. *Hungarian Folktales: The Art of Zsuzsanna Palkó*. New York: Garland, 1995.

de Jesus, José Barreto. *Carybé e Verger: Gente da Bahia*. Salvador: Fundação Pierre Verger, 2013.

de Matos, Hernâni. *Bonecos da Gastronomia*. Estremoz: Gabinete de Informação da CME, 2010.

De Mauri, Luigi. *Le Maioliche di Deruta: Una Pagina di Storia dell'Arte Umbra*. Milano: Bottega di Poesia, 1924.

———. *L'Amatore di Maioliche e Porcellane*. Milano: Ulrico Hoepli, 2008.

de Mello, Frederico Pernambucano. *Apagando o Lampião: Vida e Morte do Rei do Cangaço*. São Paulo: Global, 2018.

Denny, Walter B. *The Ceramics of the Mosque of Rüstem Pasha and the Environment of Change*. New York: Garland, 1977.

———. *Iznik: The Artistry of Ottoman Ceramics*. London: Thames and Hudson, 2004.

de Oliveira Santos, Climério. *Forró: A Codificação de Luiz Gonzaga*. Recife: Cepe, 2013.

de Pontes, Edna Matosinho. *Eu Me Ensinei: Narrativas da Criatividade Popular Brasileira*. São Paulo: Via Impressa, 2017.

de Pontes, Edna Matosinho, and Fabio Magalhães. *A Xilogravura Popular: Xilógrafos e Poetas de Cordel*. Brasília: Museu Nacional da República, 2019.

Derman, M. Uğur. *Türk Sanatında Ebru*. Istanbul: Ak Yayınları, 1976.

———. *Letters in Gold: Ottoman Calligraphy from the Sakıp Sabancı Collection, Istanbul*. New York: Metropolitan Museum of Art, 1998.

de Sant'Ana, Alfonso Romano. *Baroque, the Soul of Brazil*. Diane Grosklaus, trans. Rio de Janeiro: Communicação Maxima, 1997.

de Souza, Anildomá Willians. *Nas Pegadas de Lampião*. Serra Talhada: Esdras Graphic, 2004.

de Voragine, Jacobus. *The Golden Legend*. Christopher Stace, trans. London: Penguin Books, 1998 [c. 1265].

De Waal, Edmund. *Bernard Leach*. London: Tate Gallery Publishing, 1997.

Dewhurst, C. Kurt, Betty MacDowell, and Marsha MacDowell. *Religious Folk Art in America: Reflections of Faith*. New York: E.P. Dutton, 1983.

Diateill, Erwan. "Les Religions Africaines au Brésil: Un Héritage Vivant," in Falgayrettes-Leveau, ed. *Brésil* (2005): 113-41.

Diaz, Josef, and Suzanne Stratton-Pruitt. *Painting the Divine: Images of Mary in the New World*. [Santa Fe]: New Mexico History Museum, n.d. [c. 2014].

Dillingham, Rick. *Acoma and Laguna Pottery*. Santa Fe: School of American Research Press, 1992.

———. *Fourteen Families in Pueblo Pottery*. Albuquerque: University of New Mexico Press, 1994.

Dobbie, Ian. *The Maker's Eye*. Rugby: Craft Council Exhibitions, 1981.

Dorson, Richard M., ed. *Folklore and Folklife: An Introduction*. Chicago: University of Chicago Press, 1972.

dos Santos, Ieda Machado Ribeiro. "Nesta Cidade Todo Mundo é d'Oxum: In This City Everyone is Oxum's," in Murphy and Sanford, eds. *Ọṣun across the Waters* (2001): 68-83.

Drewal, Henry John. "Art History, Agency, and Identity: Yorubá Transcultural Currents in the Making of Black Brazil," in Crook and Johnson, eds. *Black Brazil* (1999): 149-174.

——. *Mami Wata: Arts for Water Spirits in Africa and Its Diaspora*. Los Angeles: Fowler Museum at UCLA, 2008.

Drewal, Henry John, and John Mason, eds. *Beads, Body, and Soul: Art and Light in the Yorùbá Universe*. Los Angeles: Fowler Museum at UCLA, 1998.

Drewal, Henry John, John Pemberton III, and Rowland Abiọdun. *Yoruba: Nine Centuries of African Art and Thought*. Allen Wardwell, ed. New York: Harry N. Abrams, 1995.

Drewal, Margaret Thompson. *Yoruba Ritual: Performers, Play, Agency*. Bloomington: Indiana University Press, 1992.

Duffy, Karen M. "The Work of Virgil Boruff, Indiana Limestone Craftsman," *Midwestern Folklore* 22:2 (1996): 3-71.

——. "Carry It On for Me: Tradition and Familial Bonds in the Art of Acoma Pottery." Ph.D. Indiana University, 2002.

——. "Bringing Them Back: Wanda Aragon and the Revival of Historic Pottery Designs at Acoma," in Cashman, Mould, and Shukla, *The Individual and Tradition* (2011), pp. 195-218.

Dutt, Gurusaday. *Folk Arts and Crafts of Bengal: The Collected Papers*. Calcutta: Seagull, 1990.

Dutta, Krishna. *Image-Makers of Kumortuli and the Durga Puja Festival*. New Delhi: Niyogi Books, 2016.

Eck, Diana. *Darśan: Seeing the Divine Image in India*. Chambersburg: Anima, 1981.

Eco, Umberto. *Art and Beauty in the Middle Ages*. Hugh Bredin, trans. New Haven: Yale University Press, 1986.

Edgeler, John. *Michael Cardew and Stoneware*. Winchcombe: Cotswolds Living, 2008.

——. *The Fishleys of Fremington: A Devon Slipware Tradition*. Winchcombe: Cotswolds Living, 2008.

——. *Slipware and St. Ives: The Leach Pottery, 1920-1937*. Winchcombe: Cotswolds Living, 2010.

Edgü, Ferit. *Turkish Calligraphic Art (Karalama/Meşk).* [Istanbul]: Ada Press, n.d., [c. 1988].

Eliot, T.S. *Notes towards the Definition of Culture*. London: Faber and Faber, 1948.

——. *Selected Essays*. New York: Harcourt, Brace & World, 1964.

Ellison, Ralph. *Shadow and Act*. New York: Random House, 1964.

Elmore, Steve. *In Search of Nampeyo: The Early Years, 1875-1892*. Santa Fe: Spirit Bird Press, 2015.

Eriş, Muin Nursen. *Mustafa Esat Düzgünman ve Ebru*. Istanbul: Büyükşehir Belediyesi Kültür A.Ş. Yayınları, 2007.

Espinosa, José E. *Saints in the Valleys: Christian Sacred Images in the History, Life and Folk Art of Spanish New Mexico*. Albuquerque: University of New Mexico Press, 1967.

Espirito Santo, Diana, and Nico Tassi, eds. *Making Spirits: Materiality and Transcendence in Contemporary Religions*. London: I.B. Tauris, 2013.

Etchevarne, Carlos, et al. *Saberes e Fazeres: Artesanato Baiano*. Salvador: Instituto Mauá, 2010.

Etzel, Eduardo. *Arte Sacra Popular Brasileira: Conceito, Exemplo, Evolução*. São Paulo: Editora da Universidade de São Paulo, 1975.

Evans, E. Estyn. *Mourne County: Landscape and Life in South Down*. Dundalk: Dundalgan Press, 1967 [1951].

Evans, Timothy H. *King of the Western Saddle: The Sheridan Saddle and the Art of Don King*. Jackson: University Press of Mississippi, 1998.

Ewing, Tom. *Bill Monroe: The Life and Music of the Blue Grass Man*. Urbana: University of Illinois Press, 2018.

Fagg, William. *Tribes and Forms in African Art*. London: Methuen, 1965.

——. "The African Artist," in Biebuyck, ed. *Tradition and Creativity in Tribal Art* (1969): 42-57.

Fagg, William, and John Pemberton III. *Yoruba Sculpture of West Africa*. Bryce Holcombe, ed. New York: Alfred A Knopf, 1982.

Fakọyẹ, Lamidi, Bruce M. Haight, and David H. Curl. *Lamidi Ọlọnade Fakọyẹ: A Retrospective Exhibition and Autobiography*. Holland: De Pree Art Center, Hope College, 1996.

Falade, S. Ade. *The Comprehensive History of Osogbo*. Ibadan: Tunji Owolabi, 2000.

Falgayrettes-Levenau, Christine, ed. *Brésil: L'heritage Africain*. Paris: Musée Dapper, 2005.

Farmer, David. *The Oxford Dictionary of Saints*. Oxford: Oxford University Press, 2011.

Faulkner, William. *The Hamlet*. New York: Random House, 1940.

Fausto, Boris. *A Concise History of Brazil*. Arthur Brakel, trans. Cambridge: Cambridge University Press, 2006 [1999].

Feintuch, Burt, ed. *Eight Words for the Study of Expressive Culture*. Urbana: University of Illinois Press, 2003.

Félix, Anísio. *Filhos de Gandhi: A História de um Afoxé*. Salvador: Gráfica Central LTDA, 1987.

Fernandes, Isabel Maria, et al. *Figurado Português de Santos e Diabos Está o Mundo Cheio*. Porto: Livraria Civilização Editora, 2005.

Ferraz, Iara. *Margogipinho e a Tradição do Barro*. Sala do Artista Popular, 155. Rio de Janeiro: Centro Nacional de Folclore e Cultura Popular, 2009.

Ferris, William. *"You Live and Learn, Then You Die and Forget It All": Ray Lum's Tales of Horses, Mules, and Men*. New York: Anchor Books, 1992.

——. *James "Son Ford" Thomas: The Devil and His Blues*. New York: 8owse Gallery, 2015.

Fiocco, Carola, and Gabriella Gherardi. *Ceramiche Umbre dal Medioevo alla Storicismo: Orvieto e Deruta*. Faenza: Litografie Artistiche Faentine, 1988.

Flexor, Maria Helena Ochi. "Imagery: Aspects of its Representation," in Guimarães, ed. *Museu de Arte Sacra* (2008): 64-66.

Fontana, Bernard L., William J. Robinson, Charles W. Cormack, and Ernest E. Leavitt, Jr. *Papago Indian Pottery*. Seattle: University of Washington Press, 1962.

Forcellino, Antonio. *Michelangelo: A Tormented Life*. Allan Cameron, trans. Cambridge: Polity, 2009.

——. *Raphael: A Passionate Life*. Lucinda Byatt, trans. Cambridge: Polity, 2012.

Frank, Larry. *New Kingdom of the Saints: Religious Art of New Mexico, 1700-1907*. Santa Fe: Red Crane, 1992.

Freyre, Gilberto. *Nordeste: Aspetos da Influência da Cana sobre a Vida e a Paisagem do Nordeste do Brasil*. São Paulo: Global, 2010 [1937].

——. *Brazil: An Interpretation*. New York: Alfred A. Knopf, 1945.

——. *The Masters and the Slaves: A Study in the Development of Brazilian Civilization*. Samuel Putnam, trans. New York: Alfred A. Knopf, 1978 [1946].

——. *New World in the Tropics: The Culture of Modern Brazil*. New York: Alfred A. Knopf, 1959.

——. *Order and Progress: Brazil from Monarchy to Republic*. Rod W. Horton, trans. New York: Alfred A. Knopf, 1970.

Fry, Gladys-Marie. *Stitched from the Soul: Slave Quilts from the Ante-Bellum South*. New York: Dutton, 1990.

Fuentes, Carlos. *The Buried Mirror: Reflections on Spain and the New World*. New York: Houghton Mifflin, 1992.

Fujioka, Ryoichi. *Tea Ceremony Utensils*. Louise Allison Cort, trans. New York: Weatherhill, 1973.

Gailey, Alan. *Irish Folk Drama*. Cork: Mercier Press, 1969.

Gamwell, Lynn, and Simon J. Bronner. *Whirligigs: The Art of Peter Gelker*. Fullerton: California State University, 2014.

García Marquez, Gabriel. *One Hundred Years of Solitude*. Gregory Rabassa, trans. New York: Harper & Row, 1970 [1967].

———. *Chronicle of a Death Foretold*. Gregory Rabassa, trans. New York: Alfred A. Knopf, 1983.

———. *Living to Tell the Tale*. Edith Grossman, trans. New York: Alfred A. Knopf, 2003.

George, Kenneth M. *Picturing Islam: Art and Ethics in a Muslim Lifeworld*. Malden: Wiley-Blackwell, 2010.

Giffords, Gloria Kay. *Mexican Folk Retablos: Masterpieces on Tin*. Tucson: University of Arizona Press, 1974.

Girardot, Norman. *Envisioning Howard Finster: The Religion and Art of a Stranger from Another World*. Oakland: University of California Press, 2015.

Glasgow, Andrew. *Rich History, Vibrant Present: Ceramics by Ben Owen III*. Boston: Pucker Gallery, 2016.

Glassie, Henry. "William Houck, Maker of Pounded Ash Adirondack Pack-Baskets," *Keystone Folklore Quarterly* 12:1 (1967): 23-54.

———. *Pattern in the Material Folk Culture of the Eastern United States*. Philadelphia: University of Pennsylvania Press, 1968.

———. "Folk Art," in Dorson, ed., *Folklore and Folklife* (1972), pp. 253-80.

———. *Folk Housing in Middle Virginia: A Structural Analysis of Historic Artifacts*. Knoxville: University of Tennessee Press, 1975.

———. *All Silver and No Brass: An Irish Christmas Mumming*. Dublin: The Dolmen Press, 1976.

———. *Passing the Time in Ballymenone: Culture and History of an Ulster Community*. Philadelphia: University of Pennsylvania Press, 1982.

———. "The Idea of Folk Art," in Vlach and Bronner, eds., *Folk Art and Art Worlds* (1986), pp. 269-74.

———. *The Spirit of Folk Art*. New York: Harry N. Abrams, 1989.

———. "A Master of the Art of Carpet Repair: The Life of Hagop Barın," *Oriental Rug Review* 9:6 (1989): 32-38; 10:1 (1989): 16-22; 10:2 (1990): 38-43.

———. *Günümüzde Geleneksel Türk Sanatı*. Istanbul: Pan Yayıncılık, 1993.

———. *Turkish Traditional Art Today*. Bloomington: Indiana University Press, 1993.

———. *Art and Life in Bangladesh*. Bloomington: Indiana University Press, 1997.

———. *Material Culture*. Bloomington: Indiana University Press, 1999.

———. *The Potter's Art*. Bloomington: Indiana University Press, 1999.

———. "Style and Spirit in Representation," in Brekke, ed., *From Academic Art to Popular Pictures* (2000), pp. 9-20.

———. *Vernacular Architecture*. Bloomington: Indiana University Press, 2000.

———. *Mark Hewitt: Outside*. Wilmington: Louise Wells Cameron Art Museum, 2002.

———. "Mud and Mythic Vision: Hindu Sculpture in Modern Bangladesh," in Schrempp and Hansen, eds. *Myth* (2002): 203-222.

———. "Tradition," in Feintuch, *Eight Words for the Study of Expressive Culture* (2003), pp. 176-97.

———. *The Stars of Ballymenone*. Bloomington: Indiana University Press, 2006.

———. *Prince Twins Seven-Seven: His Art, His Life in Nigeria, His Exile in America*. Bloomington: Indiana University Press, 2010.

———. "Prince Twins Seven-Seven: 1944-2011," *African Arts* 45:1 (2012): 8-11.

———. "Architectural Vision in the Art of Winton and Rosa Eugéne," in Przybysz and Crosby, *Place It/Face It: Pottery by Eugéne* (2018), pp. 42-49.

———. *Daniel Johnston: A Portrait of the Artist as a Potter in North Carolina*. Bloomington: Indiana University Press, 2020.

Glassie, Henry, Clifford R. Murphy, and Douglas Dowling Peach. *Ola Belle Reed and Southern Mountain Music on the Mason-Dixon Line*. Atlanta: Dust-to-Digital, 2015.

Glassie, Henry, and Firoz Mahmud. *Contemporary Traditional Art of Bangladesh*. Dhaka: National Museum of Bangladesh, 2000.

Glassie, Henry, and Firoz Mahmud. *Living Traditions*. Dhaka: Asiatic Society of Bangladesh, 2007.

Glassie, Henry, and Pravina Shukla. *Sacred Art: Catholic Saints and Candomblé Gods in Modern Brazil*. Bloomington: Indiana University Press, 2018.

Goffman, Erving. *Behavior in Public Places: Notes on the Social Organization of Gatherings*. New York: Free Press, 1963.

Goldstein, Kenneth S. "William Robbie: Folk Artist of the Buchan District, Aberdeenshire," in Beck, *Folklore in Action* (1962), pp. 101-111.

——. *A Guide for Field Workers in Folklore*. Hatboro: Folklore Associates, 1964.

Gomes, Dias. *O Pagador de Promessas*. Rio de Janeiro: Editora Bertrand Brasil, 1987 [1960].

Gomes, Marco Aurélio A. de Filgueiras, ed. *Pelo Pelô: História, Cultura, e Cidade*. Salvador: Editora da Universidade Federal da Bahia, 1995.

Gonçalves, Fernando Augusto. *Santos e Santeiros de Ibimirim*. Sala do Artista Popular, 91. Rio de Janeiro: Centro Nacional de Folclore e Cultura Popular, 2000.

Gondim, Adenor. *Itaylê Ogun*. São Paulo: Pinacoteca do Estado, 2004.

Goodwin, Godfrey. *A History of Ottoman Architecture*. London: Thames and Hudson, 1971.

Grabar, Oleg. *The Formation of Islamic Art*. New Haven: Yale University Press, 1973.

Grant, Alison. *North Devon Pottery*. Appledore: Edward Gaskell, 2005.

Griaule, Marcel. *Folk Art in Black Africa*. Paris: Les Editions de Chéne, 1950.

——. *Conversations with Ogotemmêli: An Introduction to Dogon Religious Ideas*. London: Oxford University Press, 1970.

Guimarães, Francisco de Assis Portugal, ed. *Museu de Arte Sacra: Universidade Federal da Bahia*. Salvador: Impressão Bigraf, 2008.

Günay, Reha. *Sinan: The Architect and His Works*. Ali Ottoman, trans. Istanbul: YEM, 2009.

Güner, Güngör. *Anadolu'da Yaşmakta Olan İlkel Çömlekçilik*. Istanbul: Ak Yayınları, 1988.

Gunnell, Terry, ed. *Masks and Mumming in the Nordic Area*. Uppsala: Kungl. Gustav Adolfs Akademien för Svensk folkkultur, 2007.

Halloy, Arnaud. "Objects, Bodies and Gods: A Cognitive Ethnography of an Ontological Dynamic in the Xangô Cult (Recife, Brazil)," in Espirito Santo and Tassi, eds., *Making Spirits* (2013): 133-58.

Halpert, Herbert, and G. M. Story, eds. *Christmas Mumming in Newfoundland: Essays in Anthropology, Folklore, and History*. Toronto: University of Toronto Press, 1969.

Hansen, H. J. ed. *European Folk Art in Europe and the Americas*. New York: McGraw-Hill, 1967.

Hansen, William. *The Book of Greek and Roman Folktales, Legends, and Myths*. Princeton: Princeton University Press, 2017.

——. *Classical Mythology: A Guide to the Mythical World of the Greeks and Romans*. Oxford: Oxford University Press, 2020.

Haring, Lee. *Verbal Art in Madagascar: Performance in Historical Perspective*. Philadelphia: University of Pennsylvania Press, 1992.

Harlow, Francis H. *Modern Pueblo Pottery: 1880-1960*. Flagstaff: Northland Publishing, 1977.

Harlow, Francis H., and Dwight P. Lanmon. *The Pottery of Zia Pueblo*. Santa

Fe: School of American Research Press, 2003.
Harpe, Jason, and Brian Dedmond. *Valley Ablaze: Pottery Tradition in the Catawba Valley*. Conover: Lincoln County Historical Association, 2012.
Harris, Marvin. *Town and Country in Brazil: A Socio-Anthropological Study of a Small Brazilian Town*. New York: W.W. Norton, 1971 [1956].
Harrod, Tanya. *The Last Sane Man: Michael Cardew: Modern Pots, Colonialism and the Counterculture*. New Haven: Yale University Press, 2012.
Hauge, Victor and Takako. *Folk Traditions in Japanese Art*. New York: John Weatherhill, 1978.
Hayes, Allan, and John Blom. *Southwestern Pottery: Anasazi to Zuni*. Flagstaff: Northland Publishing, 1996.
Herbert, Robert L., ed. *Modern Artists on Art*. Mineola: Dover, 2000 [1964].
Herrera, Eduardo. *Elite Art Worlds: Philanthropy, Latin Americanism, and Avant-Garde Music*. New York: Oxford University Press, 2020.
Herrin, Judith. *Byzantium: The Surprising Life of a Medieval Empire*. Princeton: Princeton University Press, 2009.
Herstal, Stanislaw. *Imagens Religiosas do Brasil*. São Paulo: Grafitax, 1956.
Hertz, Carrie, ed. *Dressing with Purpose: Belonging and Resistance in Scandinavia*. Bloomington: Indiana University Press, 2021.
Hess, Catherine. *Italian Maiolica: Catalogue of the Collections*. Malibu: J. Paul Getty Museum, 1988.
Hewitt, Mark. "The Making of a Potter" *Ceramics Monthly* 39:1 (1991): 43-47.
——. "The Poetry in North Carolina Pottery," in Perry, *North Carolina Pottery* (2004), pp. 28-32.
——. *Falling Into Place*. Durham: Nasher Museum of Art at Duke University, 2010.
——. "A Few of My Favorite Things about North Carolina Pottery," in *Mark Hewitt's Big-Hearted Pots*. New Orleans: Ogden Museum of Southern Art, 2011, pp. 23-26.
——, ed. *Great Pots from the Traditions of North and South Carolina*. Seagrove: North Carolina Pottery Center, 2017.
Hewitt, Mark, and Nancy Sweezy. *The Potter's Eye: Art and Tradition in North Carolina Pottery*. Chapel Hill: University of North Carolina Press, 2005.
Hibbard, Howard. *Michelangelo*. New York: Harper and Row, 1974.
——. *Caravaggio*. New York: Harper and Row, 1983.
Hill, Sarah H. *Weaving New Worlds: Southeastern Cherokee Women and Their Basketry*. Chapel Hill: University of North Carolina Press, 1997.
Hitzel, Frédéric, and Mireille Jacotin. *Iznik: L'Adventure d'une Collection: Les Céramiques Ottomanes du Musée de la Renaissance Château d'Ecouen*. Paris: Éditions de la Réunion des Musées Nationaux, 2005.
Hobsbawm, Eric. *Bandits*. New York: Pantheon, 1981.
Hofer, Tamás, and Edit Fél. *Hungarian Folk Art*. Oxford: Oxford University Press, 1979.
Holbek, Bengt. *Interpretation of Fairy Tales: Danish Folklore in a European Perspective*. Helsinki: Suomalainen Tiedeakatemia, 1987.
Holland, W. Fishley. *Fifty Years a Potter*. Tring: Pottery Quarterly, 1958.
Holm, Bill. *Northwest Coast Indian Art: An Analysis of Form*. Seattle: University of Washington Press, 1965.
——. *Smoky-Top: The Art and Times of Willie Seaweed*. Seattle: University of Washington Press, 1983.
Holtzberg, Maggie. *Keepers of Tradition: Art and Folk Heritage in Massachusetts*. Lexington: Massachusetts Cultural Council, 2008.

Huffman, Barry G. *Catawba Clay: Contemporary Southern Face Jug Makers.* Hickory: A.W. Huffman, 1999.

Huffman, Barry Gurley, and Allen W. Huffman, Jr. *Hand-in-Hand: Visions and Voices of North Carolina Folk Artists.* Hickory: Authors, 2015.

Hunt, Edward Proctor. *The Origin Myth of Acoma Pueblo.* Peter Nabokov, ed. New York: Penguin, 2015.

Hunt, Marjorie. *The Stone Carvers: Master Craftsmen of Washington National Cathedral.* Washington: Smithsonian Institution Press, 1999.

Hunter, Robert, with David Stuempfle, "A Study in Rhythm: The Stoneware of David Stuempfle," in Robert Hunter and Ronald W. Fuchs, II, ed., *Ceramics in America* (2021/2022), pp. 159-205.

Hurston, Zora Neale. *Barracoon: The Story of the Last "Black Cargo."* Deborah G. Plant, ed. New York: Amistad, 2018 [c. 1931]

——. *Mules and Men.* Philadelphia: J.B. Lippincott, 1935.

Hyde, Douglas. *Beside the Fire: A Collection of Irish Gaelic Folk Stories.* London: David Nutt, 1910.

——. *Mayo Stories Told by Thomas Casey.* Dublin: Irish Texts Society, 1939.

Hymes, Dell, ed. *Reinventing Anthropology.* New York: Pantheon, 1972.

——. *Foundations in Sociolinguistics: An Ethnographic Approach.* Philadelphia: University of Pennsylvania Press, 1974.

——. *"In Vain I Tried to Tell You": Essays in Native American Ethnopoetics.* Philadelphia: University of Pennsylvania Press, 1981.

Ickes, Scott. *African-Brazilian Culture and Regional Identity in Bahia, Brazil.* Gainesville: University Press of Florida, 2013.

Impey, Oliver, ed. *Fourteenth Red: Sakaida Kakiemon XIV.* Fukuoka: Kataribe Bunko, 1993.

Inalcik, Halil. *The Ottoman Empire: The Classical Age, 1300-1600.* London: Phoenix Press, 2000 [1973].

Inverarity, Robert Bruce. *Art of the Northwest Coast Indians.* Berkeley: University of California Press, 1950.

Ioannou, Noris. *Ceramics in South Australia, 1836-1986: From Folk to Studio Pottery.* Netley: Wakefield Press, 1986.

——. *Vernacular Visions: A Folklife History of Australia: Art, Diversity, Storytelling.* Mile End: Wakefield Press, 2021.

Irimie, Cornel, and Marcela Focşa. *Romanian Icons Painted on Glass.* Bucharest: Meridiane, 1968.

Ives, Edward D. *Larry Gorman: The Man Who Made the Songs.* Bloomington: Indiana University Press, 1964.

——. *Lawrence Doyle: The Farmer-Poet of Prince Edward Island: A Study of Local Songmaking.* Orono: University of Maine Press, 1971.

——. *Joe Scott: The Woodsman-Songmaker.* Urbana: University of Illinois Press, 1978.

Jackson, Jason Baird. *Yuchi Ceremonial Life: Performance, Meaning, and Tradition in a Contemporary American Indian Community.* Lincoln: University of Nebraska Press, 2003.

——, ed. *Material Vernaculars: Objects, Images, and Their Social Worlds.* Bloomington: Indiana University Press, 2016.

Jackson, Marion E. and Barbara Cervenka. *Bandits and Heroes, Poets and Saints: Popular Art of the Northeast of Brazil.* Detroit: Con/Vida, 2013.

James, John. *The Master Masons of Chartres.* Sydney: West Grinstead Publishing, 1990 [1982].

Japan Folk Craft Museum. *Mingei: Masterpieces of Japanese Folkcraft.* Tokyo: Kodansha, 1991.

Jasmin, Élise. *Cangaceiros.* São Paulo: Terceiro Nome, 2006.

João do Rio. *Religions in Rio.* Ana Lessa-Schmidt, trans. New London: Librarium, 2015 [1904].

Johnson, Paul Christopher. *Secrets, Gossip, and Gods: The Transformation of Brazilian Candomblé*. Oxford: Oxford University Press, 2002.

Johnson, Samuel. *The History of the Yorubas: From the Earliest Times to the Beginning of the British Protectorate*. Lagos: C.M.S. Bookshops, 1960 [1921].

Johnston, Daniel. *Pots from an Apprenticeship*. Asheboro: Moring Arts Center, 2001.

Jones, Matt. *Endurance: Potting in the Twenty-first Century*. Asheville: Jones, 2014.

Jones, Michael Owen. *Craftsman of the Cumberlands: Tradition and Creativity*. Lexington: The University Press of Kentucky, 1989 [1975].

Jopling, Carol F., ed. *Art and Aesthetics in Primitive Societies: A Critical Anthology*. New York: E.P. Dutton, 1971.

Joyce, James. *A Portrait of the Artist as a Young Man*. New York: B.W. Huebsch, 1922 [1916].

———. *Ulysses*. Paris: Shakespeare and Company, 1922.

———. *Finnegans Wake*. New York: Viking Press, 1939.

———. *Stephen Hero: A Part of the First Draft of A Portrait of the Artist as a Young Man*. Theodore Spencer, ed. New York: New Directions, 1944.

Joyce, Rosemary O. *A Bearer of Tradition: Dwight Stump, Basketmaker*. Athens: University of Georgia Press, 1989.

Kalter, Johannes. *The Arts and Crafts of the Swat Valley: Living Traditions in the Hindu Kush*. London: Thames and Hudson, 1991.

Kandinsky, Wassily. *Concerning the Spiritual in Art and Painting in Particular*. New York: George Wittenborn, 1964 [1912].

———. "Reminiscences," in Herbert, ed. *Modern Artists on Art* (2000): 17-39.

Kandinsky, Wassily, and Franz Marc, eds. *The Blaue Reiter Almanac*. Klaus Lankheit, ed. New York: DaCapo Press, 1974 [1912].

Kawano Ryōsuke and Enomoto Toru. *Hagi: 400 Ans de Céramique*. Paris: Maison de la Culture du Japon à Paris, 2000.

Kay, Jon. *Folk Art and Aging: Life-Story Objects and Their Makers*. Bloomington: Indiana University Press, 2016.

Kay, Kathy L., ed. *Built upon Honor: The Ceramic Art of Ben Owen and Ben Owen III*. Charlotte: Mint Museum of Art, 1995.

Kelemen, Pál. *Baroque and Rococo in Latin America*. New York: Dover, 1967.

Kenaan-Kedar, Nurith. *The Armenian Ceramics of Jerusalem: Three Generations, 1919-2003*. Tel Aviv: Eretz Israel Museum, 2003.

Kenny, Ruth, Jeff McMillan, and Martin Myrone. *British Folk Art*. London: Tate Publishing, 2014.

Kent, Kate Peck. *Pueblo Indian Textiles: A Living Tradition*. Santa Fe: School of American Research Press, 1983.

Kikuchi, Yuko. "Hamada and the *Mingei* Movement," in Wilcox, *Shoji Hamada* (1998), pp. 21-25.

Kimmelman, Michael. *Portraits: Talking with Artists at the Met, the Modern, the Louvre and Elsewhere*. New York: Modern Library, 1999.

Kindig, Joe, Jr. *Thoughts on the Kentucky Rifle in its Golden Age*. New York: Bonanza Books, 1960.

Kirshenblatt, Mayer, and Barbara Kirshenblatt-Gimblett. *They Called Me Mayer July: Painted Memories of a Jewish Childhood in Poland before the Holocaust*. Berkeley: University of California Press, 2006.

Klassen, Teri. *Tennessee Delta Quiltmaking*. Knoxville: University of Tennessee Press, 2017.

Klee, Felix, ed. *The Diaries of Paul Klee, 1898-1918*. Berkeley: University of California Press, 1968 [1957].

Klein, Barbro, and Mats Widbom, eds. *Swedish Folk Art: All Tradition is Change*. New York: Harry. N. Abrams, 1994.

Kniffen, Fred B. "Louisiana House Types," in Wagner and Mikesell, eds., *Readings in Cultural Geography* (1962): 157-69.
——. "The Physiognomy of Rural Louisiana," *Louisiana History* 4:4 (1963): 291-99.
Kociejowski, Marius. *The Pigeon Wars of Damascus*. Emeryville: Biblioasis, 2010.
——. *God's Zoo: Artists, Exiles, Londoners*. Manchester: Carcanet, 2014.
Kolhan, Saim. *Çini: "Sır Altındaki Aşk."* Istanbul: Minval Yayınları, 2015.
Koverman, Jill Beute, ed. *I Made This Jar: The Life and Works of the Enslaved African-American Potter Dave*. Columbia: McKissick Museum, University of South Carolina, 1998.
——. *Making Faces: Southern Face Vessels from 1840-1990*. Columbia: McKissick Museum, 2001.
Kraay, Hendrik, ed. *Afro-Brazilian Culture and Politics: Bahia, 1790s to 1990s*. Armonk: M.E. Sharpe, 1998.
Kramer, Barbara. *Nampeyo and Her Pottery*. Albuquerque: University of New Mexico Press, 1996.
Kramrisch, Stella. *Unknown India: Ritual Art in Tribe and Village*. Philadelphia: Philadelphia Museum of Art, 1968.
Krishna, Nanditha. *Arts and Crafts of Tamilnadu*. Ahmedabad: Mapin, 1992.
Kubler, George. *The Shape of Time: Remarks on the History of Things*. New Haven: Yale University Press, 1978.
Kuran, Aptullah. *Sinan: The Grand Old Master of Ottoman Architecture*. Istanbul: Ada Press, 1987.
Kuri (Maria Beatriz Farias de Souza). *Vlado*. Lagoa dos Gatos: Caleidoscópio, 2019.
Kuroda, Ryōji, and Takeshi Murayama. *Classic Stoneware of Japan: Shino and Oribe*. Tokyo: Kodansha, 2002.
Kyushu Ceramic Museum. *Kakiemon: The Whole Aspect of Kakiemon Style*. Arita: Kyushu Ceramic Museum, 1999.
Labov, William. *The Social Stratification of English in New York City*. Washington: Center for Applied Linguistics, 1966.
——. *Language in the Inner City: Studies in the Black English Vernacular*. Philadelphia: University of Pennsylvania Press, 1972.
Lane, Arthur. *Later Islamic Pottery: Persia, Syria, Egypt, Turkey*. London: Faber and Faber, 1957.
Lange, Charles H. *Cochiti: A New Mexico Pueblo, Past and Present*. Austin: University of Texas Press, 1959.
Laude, Jean. *African Art of the Dogon: The Myths of the Cliff Dwellers*. New York: Viking Press, 1973.
Le Corbusier. *Journey to the East*. Ivan Zaknić, ed. and trans. Cambridge: The MIT Press, 1989 [1966].
Leach, Bernard. *A Potter's Book*. Levittown: Transatlantic Arts, 1973 [1940].
——. *The Potter's Challenge*. David Outerbridge, ed. New York: E. P. Dutton, 1975 [1951].
——. *A Potter in Japan, 1952-1954*. London: Faber and Faber, 1960.
——. *A Potter's Work*. London: Evelyn, Adams & Mackay, 1967.
——. *Hamada: Potter*. Tokyo: Kodansha, 1990 [1975].
——. *Beyond East and West: Memoirs, Portraits and Essays*. London: Faber and Faber, 1978.
Leal, Eneida. *Os Orixás no Brasil*. Rio de Janeiro: Spala, 1988.
Leiris, Michel. *Phantom Africa*. Brent Hayes Edwards, trans. Calcutta: Seagull Books, 2017.
Leiris, Michel, and Jacqueline Delange. *African Art*. Michael Ross, trans. New York: Golden Press, 1968.
Levi, Carlo. *Christ Stopped at Eboli: The Story of a Year*. Frances Frenaye, trans. New York: Noonday Press, 1991 [1947].
Lévi-Strauss, Claude. *Tristes Tropiques*. John and Doreen Weightman, trans. New York: Penguin Books, 1992 [1955].

——. *The Savage Mind*. Chicago: University of Chicago Press, 1966.
——. *The Way of the Masks*. Sylvia Modelski, trans. Seattle: University of Washington Press, 1982.
——. *The Jealous Potter*. Bénédicte Chorier, trans. Chicago: University of Chicago Press, 1989.
Lewis, J.M. *The Ewenny Potteries*. Cardiff: National Museum of Wales, 1982.
Lewis, Oscar. *Life in a Mexican Village: Tepoztlán Restudied*. Urbana: University of Illinois Press, 1963 [1951].
——. *Five Families: Mexican Case Studies in the Culture of Poverty*. New York: Basic Books, 1959.
——. *Pedro Martinez: A Mexican Peasant and His Family*. London: Secker & Warburg, 1964.
Li, He. *Chinese Ceramics: A New Comprehensive Survey*. New York: Rizzoli, 1996.
Lima, Beth, and Valfrido Lima. *Em Nome do Autor: Artistas Artesãos do Brasil*. São Paulo: Proposta, 2008.
Lima, Ricardo Gomes. *Louco Filho: Os Caminhos da Escultura no Recôncavo da Bahia*. Sala do Artista Popular, 44. Rio de Janeiro: Instituto Nacional do Folclore, 2004 [1988].
Lipman, Jean, and Alice Winchester. *The Flowering of American Folk Art: 1776-1876*. New York: Viking, 1974.
Liverani, Giuseppe. *Five Centuries of Italian Majolica*. New York: McGraw-Hill, 1960.
Lody, Raul. *A Roupa de Baiana*. Salvador: Associação das Baianas de Acarajé e Mingau do Estado da Bahia, 2003.
——. *Arte do Barro e o Olhar da Arte: Vitalino e Verger*. Recife: Instituto Cultural Banco Real, 2009.
Longfield, Ada K. *Some Irish Churchyard Sculpture*. Ballycotton: Gifford and Craven, 1976.
Lowie, Robert H. *The Crow Indians*. New York: Holt, Rinehart and Winston, 1956 [1935].
Ludwig, Allan I. *Graven Images: New England Stonecarving and its Symbols, 1650-1815*. Middletown: Wesleyan University Press, 1966.
Lyra, Paulo, ed. *Brasil: Arte do Nordeste*. Rio de Janeiro: Spala, 1986.
MacCarthy, Fiona. *William Morris: A Life for Our Time*. New York: Alfred A. Knopf, 1995.
Mack, Charles R. *Talking with the Turners: Conversations with Southern Folk Potters*. Columbia: University of South Carolina Press, 2006.
MacLachlan, Colin M. *A History of Modern Brazil: The Past against the Future*. Wilmington: SR Books, 2003.
Magalhães, Gisela, and Irma Arestizábal. *7 Brasileiros e Seu Universo*. Brasília: Departamento da Documentação e Divulgação, 1974.
Mahmud, Firoz. *Prospects of Material Folk Culture Studies and Folklife Museums in Bangladesh*. Dhaka: Bangla Academy, 1993.
——. *Metalwork of Bangladesh: A Study in Material Folk Culture*. Dhaka: Bangla Academy, 2009.
Maia, Pedro Moacir, ed. *O Museu de Arte Sacra da Universidade Federal da Bahia*. São Paulo: Banco Safra, 1987.
Malinowski, Bronislaw. *Argonauts of the Western Pacific: An Account of Native Enterprise and Adventure in the Archipelagoes of Melanesian New Guinea*. London: George Routledge and Sons, 1922.
Mallet, J.V.G. *Xanto: Pottery-Painter, Poet, Man of the Italian Renaissance*. London: Wallace Collection, 2007.
Mann, Graciela, and Hans Mann. *The 12 Prophets of Aleijadinho*. Austin: University of Texas Press, 1967.
Marcelo, Carlos, and Rosualdo Rodrigues. *O Fole Roncou! Uma História do Forró*. Rio de Janeiro: Zahar, 2012.
Margolis, Maxine L., and William E. Carter, eds. *Brazil: Anthropological Perspectives: Essays in Honor of Charles*

Wagley. New York: Columbia University Press, 1979.

Marinho, Justino. *Ubiraci Tibiriça: Pinturas*. Quebec: Maison Descultures Amerindiennes, 2003.

Marino, João. *Iconografia de Nossa Senhora e dos Santos*. São Paulo: Museu de Arte Sacra, 1996.

Marques, Lucas de Mendonça. "Forjando Orixás: Técnicas e Objetos na Ferramentaria de Santo da Bahia." M.A. thesis. Brasília: Universidade de Brasília, 2014.

Marriott, Alice. *María: The Potter of San Ildefonso*. Norman: University of Oklahoma Press, 1948.

Martins, Flávia, Rogerio Luz, and Pedro Belchior. *Nova Fase da Lua: Escultores Populares de Pernambuco*. Recife: Caleidoscópio, 2013.

Martins, José de Souza. "'Mestre' Vitalino, Popular Art in the Conformist Imaginary," in Tribe, ed. *Heroes and Artists* (2001): 50-53.

Mascelani, Angela. *O Mundo da Arte Popular Brasileira: Museu Casa do Pontal*. Rio de Janeiro: Casa do Pontal, 2002.

Matos, Matilde. *50 Anos de Arte na Bahia*. Salvador: EPP, 2010.

——. *Água: Reflexos na Arte da Bahia*. Salvador: Caramurê, 2012.

McCabe, Patrick. *Poguemahone*. London: Unbound, 2022.

McGara, Andrew. *Country Pottery: The Traditional Earthenware of Britain*. London: A&C Black, 2000.

McGriff, Meredith A. E. *The Michiana Potters: Art, Community, and Collaboration in the Midwest*. Bloomington: Indiana University Press, 2020.

Mecham, Denny Hubbard, Michelle Francis, and Charles Zug III. *The Living Tradition: North Carolina Potters Speak*. Conover: North Carolina Pottery Center, 2009.

Medley, Margaret. *The Chinese Potter: A Practical History of Chinese Ceramics*. Ithaca: Cornell University Press, 1976.

Meinig, D. W. *Southwest: Three Peoples in Geographical Change, 1600-1970*. New York: Oxford University Press, 1971.

——, ed. *The Interpretation of Ordinary Landscapes: Geographical Essays*. New York: Oxford University Press, 1979.

Merton, Robert K. *On Theoretical Sociology: Five Essays, Old and New*. New York: The Free Press, 1967.

Michell, George. *Hindu Art and Architecture*. London: Thames & Hudson, 2000.

Mikami, Tsugio. *The Art of Japanese Ceramics*. Ann Herring, trans. New York: Weatherhill, 1983 [1972].

Millard, Charles, ed. *Mark Hewitt: Potter*. Raleigh: Visual Arts Center, North Carolina State University, 1997.

Miller, Roy Andrew. *Japanese Ceramics*. Tokyo: Toto Shuppan, 1960.

Minchilli, Elizabeth Helman. *Deruta: A Tradition of Italian Ceramics*. San Francisco: Chronicle Books, 1998.

Minge, Ward Alan. *Ácoma: Pueblo in the Sky*. Albuquerque: University of New Mexico Press, 1991.

Mink, Janis. *Marcel Duchamp, 1887-1968: Art as Anti-Art*. Koln: Taschen, 2006.

Mino, Yutaka. *Freedom of Clay and Brush through Seven Centuries in Northern China: Tz'u-chou Type Wares, 960-1600 A.D.* Bloomington: Indiana University Press, 1980.

Mintz, Sidney W. *Sweetness and Power: The Place of Sugar in Modern History*. New York: Penguin Books, 1986.

Mintz, Sidney W., and Richard Price. *The Birth of African-American Culture: An Anthropological Perspective*. Boston: Beacon Press, 1992 [1976].

Mittler, Charlotte. *Clay Mirror: From Monos to Storytellers: Reflections from Cochiti Pueblo: The Tom and Charlotte Mittler Collection*. Bob Kepoun, ed. Santa Fe: Rainbow Man, 2020.

Mode, Heinz, and Subodh Chandra. *Indian Folk Art*. Peter and Betty Ross, trans.

New York: Alpine Fine Arts Collection, 1985.

Moeran, Brian. *Lost Innocence: Folk Craft Potters of Onta, Japan*. Berkeley: University of California Press, 1984.

Moes, Robert. *Mingei: Japanese Folk Art*. Alexandria: Art Services International, 1995.

Monteiro, Salvador. *Xilógrafos Nordestinos*. Rio de Janeiro: Fundação Casa de Rui Barbosa, 1977.

Montes, Maria Lucia. *Manuel Eudócio: Um Cronista do Seu Tempo*. Olinda: Centro de Convenções de Pernambuco, 2005.

Mookerjee, Ajit. *Ritual Art of India*. New York: Thames and Hudson, 1985.

Mór, Germana Monte, and Humberto Werneck. *Aproximações, Xilogravuras de Fabricio Lopez e J. Miguel.* São Paulo: Galeria Estação, 2010.

Morris, May, ed. *The Collected Works of William Morris*. 24 vols. London: Longmans, Green, 1910-1915.

Morris, William. *Hopes and Fears for Art: Five Lectures Delivered in Birmingham, London, and Nottingham*. London: Longmans, Green, 1898 [1882].

——. *Signs of Change: Seven Lectures*. London: Longmans, Green, 1903 [1888].

——. *News from Nowhere: Or, An Epoch of Rest, Being Some Chapters from a Utopian Romance*. Hammersmith: Kelmscott Press, 1892.

——. *Architecture, Industry and Wealth: Collected Papers*. London: Longmans, Green, 1902.

Morton, Elizabeth. "Lamidi Ọlọnade Fakẹyẹ, 1928-2009," *African Arts* 43: 3 (2010): 10-12.

Morton, Robin. *Come Day, Go Day, God Send Sunday: The Songs and Life Story, Told in His Own Words, of John Maguire, Traditional Singer and Farmer from Co. Fermanagh*. London: Routledge and Kegan Paul, 1973.

Mota, Urânia Texeira. *Louça de Deus: O Caxixi em Maragojipinho*. Salvador: Fast Design, 2011.

Mould, Tom. *Choctaw Tales*. Jackson: University Press of Mississippi, 2004.

——. *Gracious Fanatics: The Passion for Pottery in North Carolina*. Film. Burlington: PERCS, 2005.

Mount, Marshall Ward. *African Art: The Years Since 1920*. Bloomington: Indiana University Press, 1974.

Mukuna, Kazadi wa. "The Rise of Bumba-meu-Boi in Maranhão: Resilience of African-Brazilian Cultural Identity," in Crook and Johnson, eds., *Black Brazil* (1999): pp. 297-310.

——. *An Interdisciplinary Study of The Ox and the Slave (Bumba-meu-Boi), a Satirical Music Drama in Brazil.* Lewiston: Edwin Mellen Press, 2003.

Mundy-Castle, A.C., and Vicky Mundy-Castle. "Twins Seven Seven," *African Arts* 6:1 (1972): 8-13.

Munsterberg, Hugo. *The Folk Arts of Japan*. Rutland: Charles E. Tuttle, 1958.

——. *Mingei: Folk Arts of Old Japan*. New York: Asia Society, 1965.

Murase, Miyeko. *Turning Point: Oribe and the Arts of Sixteenth-Century Japan*. New Haven: Yale University Press, 2003.

Murayama, Takeshi. *Oribe*. Tokyo: Kodansha, 1982.

Murphy, Joseph M., and Mei Mei Sanford, eds. *Ọṣun across the Waters: A Yoruba Goddess in Africa and the Americas.* Bloomington: Indiana University Press, 2001.

Murphy, Michael J. *At Slieve Gullion's Foot.* Dundalk: Dundalgan Press, 1940.

——. *Tyrone Folk Quest*. Belfast: Blackstaff Press, 1973.

Nabokov, Peter. *Architecture of Acoma Pueblo: The 1934 Historic American Buildings Survey Project*. Santa Fe: Ancient City Press, 1986.

———. *A Forest of Time: American Indian Ways of History*. Cambridge: Cambridge University Press, 2002.

———. *How the World Moves: The Odyssey of an American Indian Family*. New York: Viking, 2015.

Nagatake, Takeshi. *Kakiemon*. Tokyo: Kodansha, 1981.

Naipaul, V.S. *The Middle Passage: Impressions of Five Societies — British, French and Dutch — in the West Indies and South America*. London: Picador, 1995 [1962].

Nakagawa, Sensaku. *Kutani Ware*. John Bester, trans. Tokyo: Kodansha, 1979.

Nasr, Seyyed Hossein. *Islamic Art and Spirituality*. Albany: State University of New York Press, 1987.

National Museum of Modern Art. *Japanese Painted Porcelain: Modern Masterpieces in Overglaze Enamel*. New York: Weatherhill, 1980.

National Museum of Modern Art. *Kanjiro Kawai: Catalogue of Kawatsu Collection*. Kyoto: National Museum of Modern Art, 1983.

Necipoğlu, Gülru. *The Age of Sinan: Architectural Culture in the Ottoman Empire*. Princeton: Princeton University Press, 2005.

Nelson, Marion, ed. *Norwegian Folk Art: The Migration of a Tradition*. New York: Abbeville Press, 1995.

Newman, Barnett. *Selected Writings and Interviews*. John P. O'Neill, ed. Berkeley: University of California Press, 1992.

Nichols, Linda Foss. *Voice of Mother Earth: Art of the Puebloan Peoples of the American Southwest*. Nagoya: Nagoya/Boston Museum of Fine Arts, 2000.

Notini, Anja. *Krukmakare: Möte med Tradition*. Stockholm: Streiffert, 1985.

Nunes, Luciana. *Museu de Arte Sacra de São Paulo: Imaginária — Séc. XVI, XVII*. São Paulo: Empório de Produções e Comunicação, 2002.

———. *Museu de Arte Sacra de São Paulo: Imaginária — Séc. XVIII*. São Paulo: Empório de Produções e Comunicação, 2002.

Oberlander, Fernando. *50 Anos de Arte na Bahia*. Salvador: Caixa Cultural, 2013.

Ó Duilearga, Séamus. *Seán Ó Conaill's Book: Stories and Traditions from Iveragh*. Dublin: Comhairle Bhéaloideas Éireann, 1981 [1948].

Oettinger, Marion. *Folk Treasures of Mexico: The Nelson A. Rockefeller Collection*. New York: Harry N. Abrams, 1990.

Okakura, Katuzo. *The Book of Tea*. Rutland: Charles E. Tuttle, 1956 [1906].

Ó Laoire, Lillis. *On a Rock in the Middle of the Ocean: Songs and Singers in Tory Island*. Dublin: Cló Iar-Chonnachta, 2002.

Olenik, Yael. *The Armenian Pottery of Jerusalem*. Tel Aviv: Haaretz Museum, 1986.

Oliver, Anthony. *The Victorian Staffordshire Figure: A Guide for Collectors*. London: Heinemann, 1971.

Olsen, Frederick L. *The Kiln Book: Materials, Specifications and Construction*. Iola: Krause, 2001.

Olupona, Jacob K. "Orișa Ọșun: Yoruba Sacred Kingship and Civil Religion in Ọșogbo, Nigeria," in Murphy and Sanford, eds. *Ọșun across the Waters* (2001): 46-67.

Omari-Tunkara, Mikelle Smith. *Manipulating the Sacred: Yoruba Art, Ritual, and Resistance in Brazilian Candomblé*. Detroit: Wayne State University Press, 2005.

Öney, Gönül. *Türk Çini Sanatı*. Istanbul: Yapı ve Kredi Bankası, 1976.

Ortiz, Alfonso. *The Tewa World: Space, Time, Being, and Becoming in a Pueblo Society*. Chicago: University of Chicago Press, 1969.

Osman, Khalil. "A Discourse on Islamic Art: Conversations with Dr. Muhittin Serin on the History, Characteristics and

Aesthetics of the Islamic Art of Calligraphy," *Al-Qalam* 1:1 (1994): 1-13.
Ó Súilleabháin, Seán. *Miraculous Plenty: Irish Religious Folktales and Legends.* William Caulfield, trans. Dublin: Comhairle Bhéaloideas Éireann, 2011 [1952].
Otero, Solimar, and Toyin Falola, eds. *Yemoja: Gender, Sexuality, and Creativity in the Latina/o and Afro-Atlantic Diasporas.* Albany: State University of New York Press, 2013.
Pagliacci, Umberto, ed. *Antiche Maioliche di Deruta: Per un Museo Regionale della Ceramica Umbra.* Rome: Amministrazione Provinciale di Perugia, 1980.
Palmer, Gabrielle. *Sculpture in the Kingdom of Quito.* Albuquerque: University of New Mexico Press, 1987.
Pamuk, Orhan. *The Naive and the Sentimental Novelist: The Charles Eliot Norton Lectures, 2009.* Nazım Dikbaş, trans. London: Faber and Faber, 2011.
Paolucci, Antonio. *Raphael's Rooms.* Catherine Burnett, trans. Milan: Edizioni Musei Vaticani, 2011.
Papi, Liza, and Karina Skirvsky. *Woodcuts from Northeastern Brazil.* Jamaica: Jamaica Center for Arts and Learning, 2000.
Passavant, G. *Verrocchio: Sculptures, Paintings and Drawings: Complete Edition.* Katherine Watson, trans. London: Phaidon, 1969.
Patterson, Daniel W. *The True Image: Gravestone Art and the Culture of Scotch Irish Settlers in the Pennsylvania and Carolina Backcountry.* Chapel Hill: University of North Carolina Press, 2012.
Patterson, Tom. *Reclamation and Transformation: Three Self-Taught Chicago Artists.* Chicago: Terra Museum, 1994.
Pearson, Barry Lee. *Virginia Piedmont Blues: The Lives and Art of Two Virginia Bluesmen.* Philadelphia: University of Pennsylvania Press, 1990.
Peek, Philip M. "The Isoko Ethos of Ivri," *African Arts* 20:1 (1986): 42-47, 98.
——. *African Divination Systems: Ways of Knowing.* Bloomington: Indiana University Press, 1991.
Penteado, José Octavio, Tânia Mills, and Pieter Tjabbes. *A Arte de J. Borges: Do Cordel á Xilogravura.* Recife: Livraria Progresso, n.d. [c. 2005].
Pereira, João Castel Branco. *Portuguese Tiles from the National Museum of Azulejo, Lisbon.* London: Scala, 1995.
Perelli, Antonio, and Attilio Quintili. *Iridescenze: Venti Lustri di Lusto: Deruta 1900-1999.* Deruta: Deruta Per…, 2009.
Perry, Barbara Stone, ed. *North Carolina Pottery: The Collection of the Mint Museums.* Chapel Hill: University of North Carolina Press, 2004.
Peterson, Susan. *Shoji Hamada: A Potter's Way and Work.* Tokyo: Kodansha, 1974.
——. *Lucy M. Lewis: American Indian Potter.* Tokyo: Kodansha, 1984.
Peterson, William S. *A Bibliography of the Kelmscott Press.* Oxford: Oxford University Press, 2002 [1984].
Pevsner, Nikolaus. *Pioneers of the Modern Movement: From William Morris to Walter Gropius.* London: Faber and Faber, 1936.
Pianzola, Maurice. *Brasil Barroco.* Rio de Janeiro: Distribuidora Record, 1983.
Piccolpasso, Cavaliere Cipriano. *The Three Books of the Potter's Art.* Bernard Rackham and Albert Van de Put, trans. London: Victoria and Albert Museum, 1934 [1548].
Pinto de Matos, Maria Antônia. *Azulejos: Masterpieces of the National Tile Museum in Lisbon.* Paris: Chandeigne, 2011.
——, ed. *Um Gosto Português: O Uso do Azulejo no Século XVII.* Lisbon: Atherna, 2012.
Pocius, Gerald L. *A Place to Belong: Community Order and Everyday Space in Calvert, Newfoundland.* Athens: University of Georgia Press, 1991.

Pope Francis. *Laudato Si': On Care for Our Common Home*. Encyclical Letter. Huntington: Our Sunday Visitor, 2015.

Price, Sally, and Richard Price. *Maroon Arts: Cultural Vitality in the African Diaspora*. Boston: Beacon Press, 1999.

Primiano, Leonard Norman. "Manifestations of the Religious Vernacular: Ambiguity, Power, and Creativity," in Bowman and Valk, eds. *Vernacular Religion in Everyday Life* (2015): 382-94.

Pritchard, R. E. *Shakespeare's England: Life in Elizabethan and Jacobean Times*. Glouchestershire: Sutton Publishing, 1999.

Prown, Jules David. *Art as Evidence: Writings on Art and Material Culture*. New Haven: Yale University Press, 2001.

Pryzbysz, Jane, and Katherine Crosby, eds. *Place It/Face It: Pottery by Eugéne*. Columbia: McKissick Museum, University of South Carolina, 2018.

Pugh, P. D. Gordon. *Staffordshire Portrait Figures of the Victorian Era*. Woodbridge: Antique Collectors' Circle, 1987.

Rackham, Bernard. *Early Staffordshire Pottery*. London: Faber and Faber, 1951.

——. *Italian Maiolica*. London: Faber and Faber, 1952.

Raku Museum. *Chōjiro: 400 Years Memorial Exhibition of Raku*. Kyoto: Raku Museum, 1988.

Ramos, Graciliano. *São Bernardo*. Padma Viswanathan, trans. New York: New York Review Books, 2019 [1934].

——. *Barren Lives*. Ralph Edward Dimmick, trans. Austin: University of Texas Press, 1997 [1966].

Ray, Dorothy Jean. *Eskimo Masks: Art and Ceremony*. Seattle: University of Washington Press, 1967.

Read, Herbert. *Staffordshire Pottery Figures*. London: Duckworth, 1929.

Real, Katarina. *A Cultural Mosaic: The Folk Art of Brazil*. San Diego: Mingei International Museum of World Folk Art, 1978.

Reichard, Gladys A. *Spider Woman: A Story of Navajo Weavers and Chanters*. New York: Macmillan, 1934.

Reina, Ruben E., and Robert M. Hill, II. *The Traditional Pottery of Guatemala*. Austin: University of Texas Press, 1978.

Rhead, G. Woolliscroft, and Frederick Alfred Rhead. *Staffordshire Pots and Potters*. New York: Dodd, Mead, 1907.

Ribeiro, Maria Queiroz. *Iznik Pottery and Tiles in the Calouste Gulbenkian Collection*. Jon Elliott, trans. Lisbon: Fundação Calouste Gulbenkian, 2009.

Ribeiro, René. *Vitalino: Um Ceramista Popular do Nordeste*. Recife: Ministério da Educação e Cultura, 1972.

Richardson, Robert H., ed. *Chesapeake Bay Decoys: The Men Who Made and Used Them*. Burtonsville: Decoy Magazine, 1991.

Rinzler, Ralph. *The Meaders Family: North Georgia Potters*. Film. Washington: Smithsonian Folkways Recordings, 1978 [1967].

Rinzler, Ralph, and Robert Sayers. *The Meaders Family: North Georgia Potters*. Washington: Smithsonian Institution Press, 1980.

Risério, Antonio. *Carnaval Ijexá*. Salvador: Corrupio, 1981.

——. "Carnival: The Colors of Change" in Crook and Johnson, eds. *Black Brazil* (1999): 249-59.

Roberts, Allen F., Tom Joyce, and Marla C. Burns, eds. *Striking Iron: The Art of African Blacksmiths*. Los Angeles: Fowler Museum at UCLA, 2018.

Roberts, Leonard W. *Up Cutshin and Down Greasy: Folkways of a Kentucky Mountain Family*. Lexington: University of Kentucky Press, 1959.

Rodman, Selden. *Genius in the Backlands: Popular Artists of Brazil*. Old Greenwich: Devin-Adair, 1977.

Rodrigues, Abelardo. "A Cerâmica Popular," in da Costa e Silva, ed. *O Espírito Criador do Povo Brasileiro* (1972): 43-44.

Rohter, Larry. "Brazil's Dead End," *The New York Review of Books* 67:7 (2020): 36-38.
Rosas, Edival. *Abaeté: O Predestinado*. Salvador: Omnira, 2014.
Rose, Muriel. *Artist-Potters in England*. London: Faber and Faber, 1955.
Rosenak, Chuck, and Jan Rosenak. *The Saint Makers: Contemporary Santeras y Santeros*. Flagstaff: Northland Publishing, 1998.
Rosenberg, Neil V., and Charles K. Wolfe. *The Music of Bill Monroe*. Urbana: University of Illinois Press, 2007.
Rothko, Mark. *The Artist's Reality: Philosophies of Art*. Christopher Rothko, ed. New Haven: Yale University Press, 2004.
——. *Writings on Art*. Miguel López-Remiro, ed. New Haven: Yale University Press, 2006.
Rousseau, Valérie. *Vestiges and Verse: Notes from the Newfangled Epic*. New York: American Folk Art Museum, 2018.
Rozelle, Robert V., Alvia Wardlaw, and Maureen A. McKenna, eds. *Black Art: Ancestral Legacy: The African Impulse in African-American Art*. New York: Harry N. Abrams, 1989.
Rugh, Andrea B. *Reveal and Conceal: Dress in Contemporary Egypt*. Syracuse: Syracuse University Press, 1986.
Rushdie, Salman. *Imaginary Homelands: Essays and Criticism, 1981-1991*. London: Granta Books, 1991.
Ruskin, John. *The Stones of Venice*. 3 vols. London: Smith, Elder, 1851-1853.
——. *The Nature of Gothic: A Chapter of the Stones of Venice*. Hammersmith: Kelmscott Press, 1892 [1853].
——. *Lectures on Architecture and Painting, Delivered at Edinburgh, in November, 1853*. New York: John Wiley, 1864.
Sá, Sinval. *O Sanfoneiro do Riacho da Brígida: Vida e Andanças de Luiz Gonzaga — O Rei do Baião*. Recife: Cepe, 2012.
Sabo, Rioletta, and Jorge Nuno Falcato. *Portuguese Decorative Tiles: Azulejos*. Russell Stockman, trans. New York: Abbeville, 1998.
Sadlier, Darlene J. *Brazil Imagined: 1500 to the Present*. Austin: University of Texas Press, 2008.
Safadi, Yasin Hamid. *Islamic Calligraphy*. London: Thames and Hudson, 1978.
Saksena, Jogendra. *Art of Rajasthan: Henna and Floor Decorations*. Delhi: Sundeep Prakashan, 1979.
Salvador, Mari Lyn C. *Cuando Hablan Los Santos: Contemporary Santero Traditions from Northern New Mexico*. Marta Weigle, ed. Albuquerque: Maxwell Museum of Anthropology, 1995.
Sanders, Herbert H. *The World of Japanese Ceramics*. Tokyo: Kodansha, 1967.
Sani, Elisa P. *Italian Renaissance Maiolica*. London: Victoria and Albert Museum, 2012.
Sansi, Roger. *Fetishes and Monuments: Afro-Brazilian Art and Culture in the Twentieth Century*. New York: Berghahn Books, 2010.
——. "'We Worship Nature': The Given and Made in Brazilian Candomblé," in Espirito Santo and Tassi, eds. *Making Spirits* (2013): 81-102.
Santos, Francisco. *África Bahia*. Salvador: Author, 2000.
——. *Os Deuses do Panteon Africano*. Salvador: EGBA, 2003.
Santos, Milton. *O Centro da Cidade do Salvador*. São Paulo: Editora da Universidade de São Paulo, 2012 [1959].
——. "Salvador: Centro e Centralidade na Cidade Contemporânea," in M. Gomes, ed. *Pelo Pelô* (1996): 11-29.
Saramago, José. *Journey to Portugal: In Pursuit of Portugal's History and Culture*. Amanda Hopkinson and Nick Caistor, trans. Orlando: Harcourt, 2000 [1990].
——. *Blindness*. Giovanni Pontiero, trans. New York: Harcourt Brace, 1997.
——. *The Cave*. Margaret Jull Costa, trans. New York: Harcourt, 2002.

——. *The Double*. Margaret Jull Costa, trans. New York: Harcourt, 2004.

——. *Seeing*. Margaret Jull Costa, trans. New York: Harcourt, 2006.

——. *The Notebook*. Amanda Hopkinson and Daniel Hahn, trans. London: Verso, 2010.

——. *Small Memories*. Margaret Jull Costa, trans. Boston: Houghton Mifflin Harcourt, 2011.

——. *The Elephant's Journey*. Margaret Jull Costa, trans. Boston: Houghton Mifflin, 2011.

Saraswati, S.K. *A Survey of Indian Sculpture*. Calcutta: K.L. Mukhopadhyay, 1957.

Sarkar, Shipra. *Sankhasilpo*. Dhaka: Bangla Academy, 1997.

Sartre, Jean-Paul. *Search for a Method*. Hazel E. Barnes, trans. New York: Alfred A. Knopf, 1963.

——. *Between Existentialism and Marxism*. John Matthews, trans. New York: William Morrow, 1976.

Satō, Masahiko. *Chinese Ceramics: A Short History*. New York: Weatherhill, 1981.

Savoy, Marc. *Made in Louisiana: The Story of the Acadian Accordion*. Lafayette: University of Louisiana at Lafayette Press, 2021.

Sawin, Patricia. *Listening for a Life: A Dialogic Ethnography of Bessie Eldreth through Her Songs and Stories*. Logan: Utah State University Press, 2004.

Sayers, Robert, and Ralph Rinzler. *The Korean Onggi Potter*. Washington: Smithsonian Institution Press, 1987.

Schacker, Jennifer. *Staging Fairyland: Folklore, Children's Entertainment, and Nineteenth-Century Pantomime*. Detroit: Wayne State University Press, 2018.

Schauss, Hans-Joachim. *Contemporary Polish Folk Artists*. New York: Hippocrene Books, 1987.

Schlee, Ernst. *German Folk Art*. Tokyo: Kodansha, 1980.

Schrempp, Gregory, and William Hansen, eds. *Myth: A New Symposium*. Bloomington: Indiana University Press, 2002.

Selka, Stephen. *Religion and the Politics of Ethnic Identity in Bahia, Brazil*. Gainesville: University Press of Florida, 2007.

Sen, Prabhas. *Crafts of West Bengal*. Ahmedabad: Mapin, 1994.

Sen, Soshitsu, XV. *Tea Life, Tea Mind*. New York: Weatherhill, 1979.

Şengel, Şirin. *Mehmet Gürsoy: Yaşayan İznik Çinileri*. Eskişehir: Osmangazi University, 2020.

Senna, Homero, ed. *Xilógrafos Nordestinos*. Rio de Janeiro: Fundação Casa de Rui Barbosa, 1977.

Serin, Muhittin. *Hattat Aziz Efendi*. Istanbul: Kubbealtı, 1988.

——. *Hattat Şeyh Hamdullah: Hayâtı, Talebeleri, Eserleri*. Istanbul: Kubbealtı, 1992.

——. *Hat Sanatı ve Meşhur Hattatlar*. Istanbul: Kubbealtı, 2003.

——. *Kemal Batanay: Bestekâr, Tambûrî, Hattat, Hâfiz*. Istanbul: Kubbealtı, 2006.

Sgarbi, Vittorio. *Caravaggio*. Milan: Skira, 2007.

Shah, Haku. *Form and Many Forms of Mother Clay*. New Delhi: National Crafts Museum, 1985.

——. *Votive Terracottas of Gujarat*. New York: Mapin, 1985.

Shah Jalal, Mohammad. *Traditional Pottery in Bangladesh*. Dhaka: International Voluntary Services, 1987.

Shahn, Ben. *The Shape of Content*. Cambridge: Harvard University Press, 1957.

Shahrani, M. Nazif. *The Kirghiz and Wakhi of Afghanistan: Adaptation to Closed Frontiers and War*. Seattle: University of Washington Press, 2002 [1979].

Shapiro, Mark. *500 Percent: Pottery by Mark Hewitt*. Boston: Pucker Gallery, 2017.

Shaw, Simeon. *History of the Staffordshire Potteries*. New York: Praeger, 1970 [1829].

Shirey, Heather. "Transforming the Orixás: Candomblé in Sacred and Secular Spaces in Salvador da Bahia, Brazil," *African Arts* 42:4 (2009): 62-79.

Shukla, Pravina. "Beads of Identity in Salvador da Bahia, Brazil," in Drewal and

Mason, eds. *Beads, Body, and Soul* (1998): 187-97.
——. "Afro-Brazilian Avataras: Gandhi's Sons Samba in South America," *Indian Folklore Research Journal* 1:1 (2001): 35-45.
——. *The Grace of Four Moons: Dress, Adornment, and the Art of the Body in Modern India*. Bloomington: Indiana University Press, 2008.
——. *Costume: Performing Identities through Dress*. Bloomington: Indiana University Press, 2015.
Sill, Sivanildo. *Vitalino: O Menino Que Virou Mestre: Biografia em Quadrinhos*. Caruaru: Author, 2012.
Silone, Ignazio. *Fontamara*. Michael Wharf, trans. New York: Harrison Smith and Robert Haas, 1934.
Silvers, Michael B. *Voices of Drought: The Politics of Music and Environment in Northeastern Brazil*. Urbana: University of Illinois Press, 2018.
Simmons, Leo W. *Sun Chief: The Autobiography of a Hopi Indian*. New Haven: Yale University Press, 1942.
Slater, Candace. *Stories on a String: The Brazilian Literatura de Cordel*. Berkeley: University of California Press, 1982.
——. *Trail of Miracles: Stories from a Pilgrimage in Northeast Brazil*. Berkeley: University of California Press, 1986.
Soyinka, Wole. *Death and the King's Horseman*. New York: Hill and Wang, 1987 [1975].
——. *Myth, Literature and the African World*. Cambridge: Cambridge University Press, 2005 [1976].
——. *Art, Dialogue, and Outrage: Essays on Literature and Culture*. New York: Pantheon, 1994.
——. *Ibadan: The Penkelemes Years: A Memoir, 1946-1965*. London: Methuen, 1994.
——. *You Must Set Forth at Dawn: A Memoir*. New York: Random House, 2006.
——. *Of Africa*. New Haven: Yale University Press, 2012.
Stapf, Sven. *Faiança Portuguesa: Faiança de Estremoz*. Regina Estácio Marques, trans. Toledo: Artes Gráfica, 1997.
Steele, Thomas J., S.J. *Santos and Saints: The Religious Folk Art of Hispanic New Mexico*. Santa Fe: Ancient City Press, 1994.
Stein, Gertrude. *Picasso*. Boston: Beacon Press, 1959 [1938].
Sthapati, V. Ganapati. *Indian Sculpture and Iconography: Forms and Measurements*. Sashikala Anath, trans. Pondicherry: Sri Aurobindo Society, 2002.
Strathern, Andrew and Marilyn. *Self-Decoration in Mount Hagen*. Toronto: University of Toronto Press, 1971.
Stratton-Pruitt, Suzanne. *The Virgin, Saints, and Angels: South American Paintings, 1600-1825, from the Thoma Collection*. Milan: Skira, 2006.
——, ed. *Journeys to New Worlds: Spanish and Portuguese Colonial Art in the Roberta and Richard Huber Collection*. Philadelphia: Philadelphia Museum of Art, 2013.
Strauss, Cindi, and Garth Clark. *Shifting Paradigms in Contemporary Ceramics: The Garth Clark and Mark Del Vecchio Collection*. New Haven: Yale University Press, 2012.
Sullivan, Edward J., ed. *Brazil: Body and Soul*. New York: Guggenheim Museum, 2002.
Suzuki, Daisetz T. *Zen and Japanese Culture*. Princeton: Princeton University Press, 1993 [1970].
Swank, Scott T. *Arts of the Pennsylvania Germans*. New York: W.W. Norton, 1983.
Sweezy, Nancy. *Raised in Clay: The Southern Pottery Tradition*. Washington: Smithsonian Institution Press, 1984.
Synge, J.M. *The Aran Islands*. Dublin: Maunsel, 1907.
——. *My Wallet of Photographs*. Lilo Stephens, ed. Dublin: Dolmen Press, 1971.
Szwed, John F., ed. *Black America*. New York: Basic Books, 1970.

——. *Space is the Place: The Lives and Times of Sun Ra*. New York: Pantheon Books, 1997.

——. *So What: The Life of Miles Davis*. New York: Simon and Schuster, 2002.

Tagore, Rabindranath. *Lectures and Addresses: Selected from the Speeches of the Poet.* Anthony X. Soares, ed. Delhi: Macmillan India, 1980.

Takahara, Takashi. "The World of Ogre-Tile Makers: The Onihyaku Line in Hekinan, Japan," in Cashman, Mould, and Shukla, *The Individual and Tradition* (2011), pp. 170-93.

——. *Onishi No Sekai*. Nagoya: Arm Inc., 2017.

Talento, Biaggio, and Helenita Hollanda. *Basílicas e Capelinhas: História, Arte e Arquitetura de 42 Igrejas de Salvador.* Salvador: Authors, 2006.

Tanaka, Sen'o. *The Tea Ceremony*. Tokyo: Kodansha, 1973.

Tarlo, Emma. *Clothing Matters: Dress and Identity in India*. London: Hurst & Company, 1996.

Thompson, E.P. *William Morris: Romantic to Revolutionary*. New York: Pantheon, 1977.

Thompson, Robert Farris. *Black Gods and Kings: Yoruba Art at UCLA*. Bloomington: Indiana University Press, 1976 [1971].

——. "Aesthetics in Traditional Africa," in Jopling, ed., *Art and Aesthetics in Primitive Societies* (1971): 374-81.

——. "Yoruba Artistic Criticism," in d'Azevedo, ed. *The Traditional Artist in African Societies* (1974): 18-61.

——. *African Art in Motion: Icon and Act*. Berkeley: University of California Press, 1974.

——. *Flash of the Spirit: African and Afro-American Art and Philosophy*. New York: Vintage Books, 1984.

——. *Face of the Gods: Art and Altars of Africa and the African Americas*. New York: Museum for African Art, 1993.

Tichane, Robert. *Ching-te-chen: Views of a Porcelain City*. Painted Post: New York State Institute for Glaze Research, 1983.

Tidmore, Stacy Anne. "The Art of Collection: Personal Creativity and Presentation in Everyday Life." Ph.D. Indiana University, 2003.

Tillyard, E.M.W. *The Elizabethan World Picture*. London: Chatto and Windus, 1948.

Tishken, Joel E., Tóyin Fálọlá, and Akíntúndé Akinyẹmi, eds. *Ṣangó in Africa and the African Diaspora*. Bloomington: Indiana University Press, 2009.

Todd, Leonard. *Carolina Clay: The Life and Legend of the Slave Potter Dave*. New York: W.W. Norton, 2008.

Toynton, Evelyn. *Jackson Pollock*. New Haven: Yale University Press, 2012.

Treib, Marc, and Ron Herman. *The Gardens of Kyoto*. Tokyo: Kodansha, 2003.

Tribe, Tania Costa, ed. *Heroes and Artists: Popular Art and the Brazilian Imagination.* Cambridge: Fitzwilliam Museum, 2001.

Trimble, Stephen. *Talking with the Clay: The Art of Pueblo Pottery*. Santa Fe: School of American Research Press, 1987.

Türkmenoğlu, Turan. *Sudaki Nakış: Ebru*. Istanbul: Milenyum Yayınları, 1999.

Uchida, Yoshiko, ed. *We Do Not Work Alone: The Thoughts of Kanjiro Kawai*. Kyoto: Kawai Kanjiro's House, 1973.

Upton, Dell, and John Michael Vlach, eds. *Common Places: Readings in American Vernacular Architecture.* Athens: University of Georgia Press, 1986.

van de Beuque, Jacques. *Brasilianische Volkskunst: Werke aus der Sammlung Casa do Pontal.* Frankfurt: Cámara Brasileira do Livro, 1994.

Varley, Paul, and Kumakura Isao, eds. *Tea in Japan: Essays on the History of Chanoyu*. Honolulu: University of Hawaii Press, 1989.

Vasari, Giorgio. *Lives of the Most Eminent Painters*. 2 vols. Marilyn Aronberg Lavin,

ed. Verona: Limited Editions Club, 1966 [1568].
Vequaud, Yves. *The Women Painters of Mithila*. London: Thames and Hudson, 1977.
Verger, Pierre Fatumbi. *Orixás: Deuses Iorubás na Africá e no Novo Mundo*. Salvador: Corrupio, 2002 [1981].
——. *Centro Histórico de Salvador: 1946 a 1952*. São Paulo: Editora Corrupio, 1989.
——. *Lendas Africanas dos Orixás*. Salvador: Corrupio, 1997.
Vermelho, Joaquim José. *Barros de Estremoz: Contributo Monográfico para o Estudo da Olaria e de Barrística.* [Estremoz]: Compta, 1989.
——. *Sobre as Cerámicas de Estremoz*. Lisbon: Edições Colibri, 2005.
Vlach, John Michael. *The Afro-American Tradition in Decorative Arts*. Cleveland: Cleveland Museum of Art, 1978.
——. *Charleston Blacksmith: The Work of Philip Simmons*. Columbia: University of South Carolina Press, 1992 [1981].
——. "The Shotgun House: An African Architectural Legacy," in Upton and Vlach, eds. *Common Places* (1986): 58-77.
Vlach, John Michael, and Simon J. Bronner, eds. *Folk Art and Art Worlds*. Ann Arbor: UMI Research Press, 1986.
Vogel, Susan Mullin. *Baule: African Art, Western Eyes*. New Haven: Yale University Press, 1997.
Vogt, Paul. *The Blue Rider.* Joachim Neugroschel, trans. Woodbury: Barron's, 1980.
Von Friesen, Otto. *Krukan från Raus*. Stockholm: Nordiska Museet, 1976.
Wafer, Jim. *The Taste of Blood: Spirit Possession in Brazilian Candomblé*. Philadelphia: University of Pennsylvania Press, 1991.
Wagner, Philip L., and Marvin W. Mikesell, eds. *Readings in Cultural Geography*. Chicago: University of Chicago Press, 1962.
Waiboer, Adriaan, ed. *Vermeer and the Masters of Genre Painting: Inspiration and Rivalry*. New Haven: Yale University Press, 2017.
Walker, Roslyn Adele. *Ọlọwẹ of Isẹ: A Yoruba Sculptor to Kings*. Washington: Smithsonian Institution, 1998.
Walsh, Barry. *The Great Tradition of Hopi Katsina Carvers: 1880 to Present*. Tucson: Rio Nuevo Publishers, 2019.
Ward, Gerald W.R., Abaigael Duda, Pamela A. Parmal, Sue Welsh Reed, Gilian Ford Shallcross, and Carol Troyen. *American Folk: Folk Art from the Collection of the Museum of Fine Arts, Boston*. Boston: MFA Publications, 2001.
Wardropper, Ian. *Bernini's Rome: Italian Baroque Terracottas from the State Hermitage Museum, St. Petersburg*. Chicago: Art Institute of Chicago, 1998.
Washburn, Dorothy K., ed. *Hopi Kachina: Spirit of Life*. Seattle: California Academy of Sciences, 1980.
Wasserspring, Lois. *Oaxacan Ceramics: Traditional Folk Art by Oaxacan Women*. San Francisco: Chronicle Books, 2000.
Waterhouse, Max. *Clive Bowen*. Uppingham: Goldmark Gallery, 2014.
Watson, Wendy M. *Italian Renaissance Maiolica from the William A. Clark Collection*. London: Scala, 1986.
Whistler, Catherine. *Opulence and Devotion: Brazilian Baroque Art*. Oxford: Ashmolean Museum, 2001.
Whitaker, Renato de Almeida. *Antônio Francisco Lisboa, O Aleijadinho*. Salvador: Museu de Arte Sacra da Universidade Federal da Bahia, 2002.
Whybrow, Marion. *The Leach Legacy: The St. Ives Pottery and Its Influence*. Bristol: Sansom, 1996.
Wiedemann, Barbara. *Controlled Burn: Wood-fired Pottery in Seagrove, North Carolina*. Seagrove: North Carolina Pottery Center, 2017.
Wilcox, Timothy, ed. *Shoji Hamada: Master Potter*. London: Lund Humphries, 1998.
Wildhaber, Robert. *Swiss Folk Art*. Zürich: Pro Helvetia, 1971.
Willett, Frank. "An African Sculptor at Work," *African Arts* 11:2 (1978): 28-33, 96.

——. *African Art*. New York: Thames and Hudson, 2006.
Williams, Sean, and Lillis Ó Laoire. *Bright Star of the West: Joe Heaney, Irish Song Man*. Oxford: Oxford University Press, 2011.
Wilson, Richard L. *Inside Japanese Ceramics: A Primer of Materials, Techniques, and Traditions*. New York: Weatherhill, 1995.
Wimberly, Fayette. "The Expansion of Afro-Bahian Religious Practices in Nineteenth-Century Cachoeira," in Kraay, ed. *Afro-Brazilian Culture and Politics* (1998): 74-89.
Wingard, Philip. *Swag and Tassel: The Innovative Stoneware of Thomas Chandler*. Columbia: McKissick Museum, 2018.
Wojcik, Daniel. *Outsider Art: Visionary Worlds and Trauma*. Jackson: University Press of Mississippi, 2016.
Wolfe, Tom. *The Painted Word*. New York: Bantam Books, 1976.
Woods, Vincent. *Lives and Miracles*. Galway: Arden House, 2002.
Woods, Vincent, and Henry Glassie. *Borderlines*. Carrick on Shannon: Leitrim County Council Arts Office, 2018.
Wright, Richard. *Black Boy: A Record of Childhood and Youth*. New York: Harper & Brothers, 1945.
Wroth, William. *Christian Images in Hispanic New Mexico: The Taylor Museum Collection of Santos*. Colorado Springs: Taylor Museum, 1982.
Wulff, Hans E. *The Traditional Crafts of Persia: Their Development, Technology, and Influence on Eastern and Western Civilizations*. Cambridge: The MIT Press, 1966.
Wyatt, Gary. *Spirit Faces: Contemporary Native American Masks from the Northwest*. San Francisco: Chronicle Books, 1995.
Yanagi, Sōetsu. *Folk-Crafts in Japan*. Tokyo: Kokusai Bunka Shinkokai, 1958.
——. *The Unknown Craftsman: A Japanese Insight into Beauty*. Bernard Leach, ed. Tokyo: Kodansha, 1978.
Yeats, W.B. *The Celtic Twilight*. Dublin: Maunsel; London: A.H. Bullen, 1902 [1893].
——. *The Cutting of an Agate*. London: Macmillan, 1919.
——. *Autobiographies: Reveries Over Childhood and Youth and The Trembling of the Veil*. New York: Macmillan, 1927.
Zarur, Elizabeth Netto Calil, and Charles Muir Lovell. *Art and Faith in Mexico: The Nineteenth-Century Retablo Tradition*. Albuquerque: University of New Mexico Press, 2001.
Zug, Charles G., III. "Pursuing Pots: On Writing a History of North Carolina Folk Pottery," *North Carolina Folklore Journal* 27:3 (1979): 34-55.
——. *The Traditional Pottery of North Carolina*. Chapel Hill: Ackland Art Museum, University of North Carolina, 1981.
——. *Turners and Burners: The Folk Potters of North Carolina*. Chapel Hill: University of North Carolina Press, 1986.
——. *Burlon Craig: An Open Window into the Past*. Raleigh: Foundations Gallery, Visual Arts Center, North Carolina State University, 1994.
——. "Consuming Pots: Listening to Mark Hewitt's Customers," in Millard, *Mark Hewitt* (1997), pp. 14-19.
——. "Entering Tradition: Kim Ellington, Catawba Valley Potter," in Cashman, Mould, and Shukla, *The Individual and Tradition* (2011), pp. 27-45.
——. *"Remember Me as You Pass By": North Carolina's Ceramic Grave Markers*. Seagrove: North Carolina Pottery Center, 2011.
——. "The Alkaline Glaze," in Hewitt, *Great Pots* (2017), pp. 99-101.
——. "The Salt Glaze," in Hewitt, *Great Pots* (2017), pp. 147-49.
Zug, Charles G., III, and Mark Hewitt. *Mark Hewitt: Stuck in the Mud*. Cullowhee: Belk Gallery, Western Carolina University, 1992.

INDEX

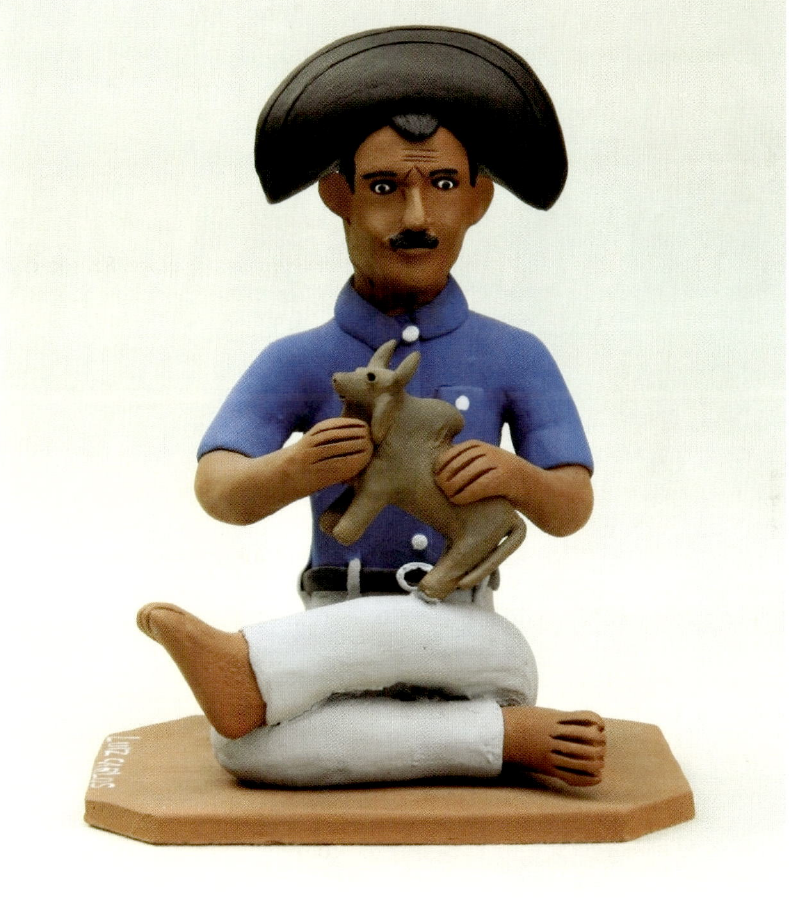

Mestre Vitalino by Luiz Carlos (18 cm tall), 2021